The DEFINITIVE
GUIDE *to*
PHILIP PULLMAN'S
HIS
DARK
MATERIALS

LAURIE FROST

■ SCHOLASTIC

To

Max and Iris

Scholastic Children's Books,
Euston House, 24 Eversholt Street,
London, NW1 1DB, UK

A division of Scholastic Ltd
London ~ New York ~ Toronto ~ Sydney ~ Auckland
Mexico City ~ New Delhi ~ Hong Kong

First published in the US by Fell Press, 2006
This edition published in the UK by Scholastic Ltd, 2008

ISBN 978 1407 10797 4

Printed in GGP Media GmbH, Pössneck

In-house illustrations by Colette Bezio, Michelle Heran, Monroe Tarver, M Rogers, G Waters (GW)
In-house photography by Philip Thistlethwaite, Ellen Levy-Finch
Original Book Layout Design by Dan Nolte
Original production coordinated by Buckley Books; Lydia Ondrusek, Ed.
Lisa Seed, Anne Ahlert, Project Mgrs, Nancy Davies, consultant

About the Author

Laurie Frost holds a PhD in English from Rice University in Houston, Texas, where she specialized in the contemporary novel. Her publications range from a popular culture article looking at companion animals in prose to a scholarly study of Anthony Powell's *A Dance to The Music of Time.* Born and raised in Miami, Florida, she lives in Alabama with her family. (When her dœmon settled as a sloth no one was surprised.)

FOREWORD

The author of any long story knows that at some point he or she is going to look back and check something. What was that character's surname? Could she see the tree from her bedroom window? Now that his brown eyes have become an important point in the story, did I at some point refer casually to his brilliant blue ones?

Most authors aren't lucky enough to have someone compile a list of the 'facts' they've invented. If the story is set in the real world, it isn't so bad; but when you're inventing cultures, peoples, places, religions, worlds, the presence of a careful observer who can calmly tell you that the currency of Cittàgazze is the corona and that dollars are used in Oxford (to take just one example from hundreds) is invaluable.

In fact it's amazing. I am astonished by Laurie Frost's diligence, and assiduity, and accuracy, and patience, and persistence, and the overall sheer intelligence and care that's been devoted to compiling this complete guide to the worlds I invented. It was easy for me: all I had to do was sit at my desk and if I didn't know something, I just made it up. Professor Frost had the far harder task of making sense of it and reducing it to order.

I can't recommend it too highly to the reader who's found anything interesting or enjoyable in this story of mine. I know I've returned to it frequently during the writing of the book I'm doing now, and I know I'll continue to do so. It's flattering, of course, to find one's work the object of such care and attention; but how much more satisfying when the work of reference that results is so accurate, and so interesting, and so full.

Philip Pullman
August 2006

TABLE OF CONTENTS

INTRODUCTION

Since the publication of *Northern Lights* in 1995, *His Dark Materials'* popular appeal, especially in the UK, has been matched by its critical success. Prizes honoring the books include the Carnegie Medal, the Guardian Children's Book Award (*Northern Lights*), and the Whitbread Book of the Year Award (*The Amber Spyglass*), and in 2005 Philip Pullman won the Astrid Lindgren Memorial Award, perhaps the most prestigious honor awarded to authors and illustrators of books for young people.

When I finished *The Amber Spyglass* in 2001, I was volunteering in a K-8 library. I was astonished that these three books had been classified as children's literature. In comparison to most of the novels in the school's library, this trilogy is far more sophisticated in its themes, vocabulary, assumption of its audience's range of knowledge, and complexity than any other three books on the shelves. A character's comments or actions work on one level in the immediate present of the book, but later, as the story progresses, their words or gestures take on a significance that couldn't be foreseen. Furthermore, in *His Dark Materials*, there is more going on than characters and conflicts. This is a novel of ideas—a novel of ideas over 1200 pages long.

So I started reading again, and it soon became obvious that if I wanted to appreciate *His Dark Materials* fully and be able comfortably to talk to students about, for example, Dust and dæmons, then what I needed was an index.

And so this book began. I started with three colors of highlighters: one for characters, one for places, and one for everything else. I would read a chapter, mark as I went, then stop and list all I had marked and the page numbers for each on one of three pages. And then I'd do the next chapter…

Now about this time, the fall of 2001, there were auroral displays that were visible over much of the continental US, down south as far as Tennessee and North Alabama, and one night I saw the faintest display, but a display nonetheless—a red glow above the horizon. I was looking for information and landed on a number of arctic studies websites, and along the way I learned that there *is* a Svalbard. I'd assumed such a place—the kingdom of the armoured bears—was a fiction, and of course it is—but not entirely. After that, I started having a look at a lot of other bits and pieces. I'd not heard of Skraelings, but they are real too. I'd once read of people having holes drilled in their heads as a desperate effort to cope with migraines, but the word trepanation wasn't one I'd had occasion to encounter, let alone use. And so on. So I started keeping track of these too.

But this was beginning to seem a huge project, and also one for which there was such a obvious need, that I didn't want to invest another year only to find out someone else had already completed and published such a book. I thought if something similar were already in the works, Philip Pullman was likely to know. I printed out a few pages, and sent them to him, and his response was generous and gracious. At this time, preparations for the theatrical adaptation of *His Dark Materials* were well underway. Pullman introduced my work to Lyn Haill, Head of Publications for the National Theatre, and a sampling of what would become this guide thus made its debut in the programme glossary for the 2003 production.

I stayed in touch intermittently with Philip Pullman, but I asked him few questions. It wasn't just that I didn't want to be a pest. The primary reason I didn't ask him to explain this or that is because my working premise—the premise of this book—is *everything there is to know* about *His Dark Materials* is in *Northern Lights/The Golden Compass*, *The Subtle Knife*, and *The Amber Spyglass*. We can enjoy speculating about what we don't know—like what kind of story Mary Malone and Will cooked up together to explain where they'd been, why they'd left behind smashed-up laboratory equipment (in Mary's case) and a dead man at the house in Will's—but those events would happen only in our imagination, beyond the finite worlds of His Dark Materials.

Five years ago my intention was for the index annotations to adhere strictly to what is in the three books themselves. I didn't want to foist my interpretation of His Dark Materials onto the users of my index. I started this project to clarify things in my own mind, and wished to make available such a tool to others. To a great extent, I've stuck with this plan.

But once I finished the easier elements, the ones about which relatively little is known, I had to face that each time I selected one detail to include and one not, I was favoring one interpretation over other competing, equally valid ones. Moreover, my editor encouraged me to add longer analyses, and so every now and then you'll find an essay of sorts. Their purpose isn't to tell you what to think, but to say, here are some things I've noticed and some connections that I've made: what do you think?

What I am assuming is that you've read these books carefully. This book may serve as a companion for you while you read the His Dark Materials trilogy—but if you've never read the trilogy please know this book does not replace it. If you have not already read His Dark Materials, you may as well be an extraterrestrial trying to understand what a human being is by reading an anatomy and physiology text. Philip Pullman created the universes of His Dark Materials. I am looking at its parts, its most basic building blocks, his materials, *his words—the elements* of his intelligent design.

This guide has its audience, a skull-cult (to invoke the spirit of Stanislaus Grumman) of initiated readers. There are many among us who like to keep their reading experiences private. There are others, the sraffies, for whom it was particularly fortunate that His Dark Materials' three volumes appeared during the same moment in history as did easy access to the internet and the emergence of fan websites. These sites are shared freely with strangers by their creators, typically anonymous, who have made a gift of their time and the money required to keep a site up and running. Readers of His Dark Materials have built a number of strong communities—republics all—on the web. Two that are as impressive for their quality as their scope are HisDarkMaterials.org and BridgetotheStars.net.

This book, then, is for the voracious readers, solitary and sociable, of His Dark Materials, those whose first impulse on finishing The Amber Spyglass was to reach for Northern Lights/The Golden Compass and begin again. I hope that all who, like me, know that the questions asked and issues raised in these books are ones that matter will put this guide to whatever use suits them best.

How to use
The Definitive Guide to His Dark Materials

Its Mechanics

This guide deals with the essential materials with which Pullman builds: words. It is organized as an index of alphabetized entries grouped into categories presented as a chapter. The role of each element is described or summarized to a lesser or greater extent depending on its prominence in the three books. Chapter numbers are listed for each entry so that users can refer to passages not covered in this book's summaries and see for themselves the contexts from which the entries' discussions are drawn.

While the primary emphasis is on what is found in *Northern Lights/The Golden Compass*, *The Subtle Knife*, and *The Amber Spyglass*, for many entries, extra-textual remarks provide an introduction to elements that our world shares in common with the novels'. There are four categories of this type of content:

Observations make connections between events in the stories that aren't explicitly stated in the novels; these comments are based on what we know, but are speculative, and thus need to be separated from the main entry.

Facts provide information about real world counterparts to the fictional elements of the books, and thus go well beyond what appears in *His Dark Materials*. Sources for this information are listed in Works Cited, and in some cases additional suggestions for further reading appear.

Updates In October 2005 Scholastic Children's Books in the UK released tenth anniversary editions of each volume of *His Dark Materials* with new material by Philip Pullman added to the books in the form of appendices of documents—notes, drawings, maps, letters, diaries—authored by Lord Asriel (*Northern Lights*), John Parry (*The Subtle Knife*), and Mary Malone (*The Amber Spyglass*). Random House issued a tenth anniversary edition of *The Golden Compass* in 2006 with the same appendix as is found in *Northern Lights*.

In spring 2007, Scholastic Children's Books published three new paperback editions of each volume of *His Dark Materials*. These do not include the tenth anniversary appendices but have what Philip Pullman calls Lantern Slides—short, impressionistic pieces, seldom more than a few sentences, providing a glimpse into an element of the trilogy, usually regarding a familiar character, setting, or idea but occasionally introducing someone or some place new. In the US, these Lantern Slides are included in the *His Dark Materials Omnibus* (2007), the trilogy published in one volume.

My Updates are based on these appendices and Lantern Slides.

Notes deal with text-level differences between the UK and US editions or between the three volumes of *His Dark Materials*.

Its Operation

Pullman resists the categorization of *His Dark Materials* as fantasy, and his argument is supported by the work's appeal to those readers who are not fans of the genre. The imaginary worlds Pullman creates, especially Lyra's, are at once much like ours and notably different.

What happens in the opening scene of the trilogy—a mischievous girl sneaks into a forbidden room and finds herself witnessing an inexplicable act—could happen in our own world, except that this possibility has been precluded by the first four words of 100,000: "Lyra and her dæmon."

We have entered a novel that is something new.

We don't expect—we don't want—the story to stop before it has even begun and a lecture on the nature of dæmons to commence. A discourse on dæmons is never provided, but we learn a lot about them nevertheless, from their primary attributes, like the differences between children's and adults', to less important but still intriguing aspects, like their ability to simultaneously translate and communicate in any language. Even the last scene of THE AMBER SPYGLASS provides new information about dæmons: they can keep secrets from their people. Occasionally an authorial voice will weigh in with a comment relevant to the action. For example, during Lyra's confrontation with her roommate at Bolvangar, Pan intimidates the other girl's dæmon, and we are told that children's conflicts are often settled in that manner. But typically what we come to know about a character or being, a place or idea is revealed in circumstances, that is, through what happens in the story. We find ourselves knowing things about these elements but aren't entirely sure why we believe them to be true.

The effect is cumulative and subtle, and thus it is hard to keep track of what we know— or think we know—about them, and a struggle to find where in the three books we learned what. The guide you are holding is a response to this. By making it easier to find all the passages in the three books relating to what interests you, this book can assist you to develop your own interpretation and evaluate what others have to say about this book.

The plausible unfamiliars of Lyra's world add another dimension to HIS DARK MATERIALS, and place it in the company of encyclopedic novels. The curious reader finds much delight in learning that what might seem invention, an element of fiction, is instead something of our own world, recalling Stanislaus Grumman correcting Lee Scoresby when the aëronaut calls Cittàgazze "a new world": "New to those not born in it…As old as yours or mine, otherwise" (SK chapter 14).

Those readers who have found Philip Pullman's worlds compelling and enriching, and do not want to leave them behind, will enjoy a casual browse through the sidebars, maps, and illustrations. In other words, this is at once a reference book and an invitation to escapism.

Editions, Abbreviations, Page Numbers, & Quotations

Editions cited

UK:
NORTHERN LIGHTS: Scholastic Point, 1998; Scholastic Children's Books, ©1995
THE SUBTLE KNIFE: Scholastic Point, 1998; Scholastic Children's Books, ©1997
THE AMBER SPYGLASS: Scholastic Point, 2001; Scholastic Children's Books, ©2000

US:
THE GOLDEN COMPASS: Knopf, 1996
THE SUBTLE KNIFE: Knopf, 1997

The Amber Spyglass: Knopf, 2000

References to the **appendices** of the *Northern Lights, The Subtle Knife,* and *The Amber Spyglass* are to these editions' **appendices:**

> *Northern Lights:* Scholastic Press, 2005
> *The Subtle Knife:* Scholastic Press, 2005
> *The Amber Spyglass:* Scholastic Press, 2005

References to **Lantern Slides** are to these editions:

> *Northern Lights:* Collector's Edition. Scholastic, 2007
> *The Subtle Knife:* Collector's Edition. Scholastic, 2007
> *The Amber Spyglass:* Collector's Edition. Scholastic, 2007

Note: The Lantern Slides are not numbered in these three books. The numbers that appear in the chapter lists are for the user's convenience and designate the order in which the Lantern Slides appear in their books.

Symbols	Abbreviations
❖ *Northern Lights/Golden Compass*	HDM: *His Dark Materials*
🗡 *The Subtle Knife*	NL: *Northern Lights*
🔪 *The Amber Spyglass*	GC: *The Golden Compass*
⑩ *10th Anniversary Editions*	SK: *The Subtle Knife*
LS *Lantern Slides*	AS: *The Amber Spyglass*

Editions, quotations, and usage

Quite often there are differences in spelling, punctuation or capitalization, and sometimes wording, in the UK and US editions. The quotations render what is found in the **UK editions.**

Since the quotations reflect what is found in the UK editions, I decided to extend this to matters of capitalization within the text, favoring, for example, the UK *republic (kingdom) of heaven* over the US *Republic (Kingdom) of Heaven,* and to the spelling of character names and types of creatures.

Each direct quotation in this guide is assigned a backnote numeral in the book's margins. Numbering restarts with each new chapter. The page numbers from the trilogy corresponding to these backnotes are collected in the **Works Cited and Informations Sources** section of the **Reference** chapter of the guide.

Listed Chapter Numbers

Great care has been taken to ensure that every chapter in which an element is found appears in the list for that element's entry. However, that does not mean that the exact word designating that element will always be found in the chapters listed. These are the exceptional cases:

When the term for an element is a descriptive substitute for what is not specifically named.
Examples: world of the mulefa, the tortured witch.

When an element is designated by multiple terms.
Example: the wheel trees, the seedpod trees, the wheel-pod trees, and other variants designating the same object.

When an element is described, but the term is not used.
Examples: silver guillotine, zombi.

Inferences.
Example: Juta Kamainen threatens to kill Stanislaus Grumman in the second chapter of THE SUBTLE KNIFE. The witch who kills Grumman at the end of the book is not named, but there are many reasons to infer it is Kamainen.

The purpose of allowing for inferences as a reason to include a chapter number is to enhance the usefulness of the lists. If an inference is possible but not useful, then the lists do not accommodate it. In other words, we can infer that every time Asriel appears, so does his dæmon Stelmaria, and so, arguably, their chapter number lists should match. But to do so would defeat the lists' purpose. In most chapters where Asriel appears, there is no mention of Stelmaria, and so it would be inefficient and misleading to include these. To find out about *Stelmaria,* you need to know what chapters make mention specifically of her.

Brief/brief mentions

This guide is intended to be thorough and inclusive, listing all the chapters in which any of the hundreds of elements categorized appears. However, elements differ in prominence within the trilogy and within chapters. Consider, for example, the silver guillotine. Here is the chapter list from its entry, which includes the terms *[brief]* and *brief mentions:*

Silver guillotine
NL/GC operation described 16; 18 *[brief]*
SK brief mentions: sound recalled in Mary's lab 4, blade's color compared to subtle knife's 8
AS Coulter on saving Lyra from 16 *[brief];* employed by Court in Alps 25.

Interpreting the list: The silver guillotine is a very important aspect of chapter 16 of NORTHERN LIGHTS/GOLDEN COMPASS, in which Lyra is nearly severed from Pan and chapter 25 of THE AMBER SPYGLASS, which finds Mrs. Coulter escaping intercision under its blade and Father MacPhail taking her place. But the device is also mentioned or alluded to elsewhere. Lyra alludes to it when she briefly mentions to Serafina that she was afraid she was going to die at Bolvangar. She is briefly reminded of it by the sound of the electronic devices in Mary's Cave, and when the subtle knife is first described, the colors visible in its blade are likened to those in the guillotine's. In these instances in THE SUBTLE KNIFE, the silver guillotine is the subject of a sentence only-- brief mentions. When Mrs. Coulter is his prisoner in the adamant tower, as Asriel mocks Mrs. Coulter for claiming to be concerned for Lyra, he briefly alludes to her role in the guillotine's invention, and a few pages later, as Coulter pleads her case before the high commandeers, she mentions saving Lyra from being its victim. Still, comparatively, the silver guillotine is not a prominent feature of chapter 16 of THE AMBER SPYGLASS, and this is indicated by the presence of *[brief].*

CHARACTERS

Characters

Alexandrovna, Lydia ✎

Genus: Human
Dæmon: Unnamed; form unknown
World: Lyra's
Physical Characteristics: Elderly; very quiet.
Background: The housekeeper for Otyets (Father) Semyon Borisovitch, the crude priest Will meets in Kholodnoye, Siberia, as he begins his travels through Lyra's world.
Role: Lydia Alexandrovna waits on the priest and Will, bringing first tea, then soup and bread.

Her sister is the source of the priest's news that armoured bears are traveling down the river close to Kholodnoye.

The priest's crude joke about the elderly woman and his vodka makes Will "hideously uneasy." [1]

AS 8

Alice [*See* Lyra] ✦

Role: Name Lyra gives as her own to the man in the top hat at the London street coffee stall.
NL/GC 6 [*brief*]

Allan ⚕

Genus: Human
World: Will's
Alliances: Sir Charles Latrom
Physical characteristics: Wears a "peaked cap" in his role as chauffeur of the dark blue Rolls Royce, but not in the house in his servant persona. [2]
Behavior: Doesn't do doors, although functioning as a chauffeur. Latrom, in the rear, opens the backseat door himself, but rather than sliding over, maintains his seat so that Lyra has to crawl past him both ways. This happens both when Lyra enters and exits the Rolls following her escape from the investigators at Mary Malone's.

Leaves Lyra and Will on the doorstep when he goes to tell his boss of their arrival and closes the door, perhaps even double-locking it, since Will hears both upper and lower bolts. Lingers in the background when Will and Lyra enter Latrom's house—more like a bodyguard than servant.
Role: Servant to Sir Charles Latrom. When they drive to the Summertown window, after Lyra and Will's visit, Sir Charles sits in the front of the Rolls with Allan and talks openly about the knife, the alethiometer, and his threats, which suggests a greater degree of intimacy than one would expect between a gentleman and the hired help.

SK 7, 8, 9 [*brief*]

AMA

Genus: Human
Dæmon: Kulang; form unsettled
World: Lyra's
Alliances: Any who are moral
Physical characteristics: Eight or nine years old.
Background: Himalayan peasant girl, daughter of a herdsman.
Behavior: Bold, brave, and compassionate; capable of acting courageously while feeling fear. Initially nervous in Mrs Coulter's presence when, like other villagers, she thinks Coulter may have a mysterious malevolent person hiding with her; less frightened after she is shown Lyra and told the girl is under a spell. Becomes enchanted by Coulter and her stories, and then thoroughly disillusioned.

Ama believes herself capable of rescuing Lyra on her own, even after witnessing Coulter's cruelty. Is very frightened of the windows, but still insists on accompanying Will.

Role: When Coulter claims that Lyra is under an enchanter's spell, the sympathetic child walks for three hours to seek a cure from a monastery's healer. Secures an antidote to the sleeping potion and administers it, thereby allowing Will and the Gallivespians to rescue Lyra.

The title of chapter 4 of *THE AMBER SPYGLASS* is "Ama and the Bats."

Observation: *Ama and the angel Balthamos have very different personalities, but faced with the most extreme and dire situations (Ama in the cave helping to rescue Lyra during the siege, and Balthamos in the mulefa's world, in arm-to-arm combat with Fr Gomez), both seemingly outmatched figures illustrate Iorek Byrnison's strategy for confronting danger: "I shall master the fear."*

AS   1, 2, visits monastery, sees Coulter strike Lyra 4; 10, meets Will 11, wakens Lyra 12; 13; 14 *[brief]*

AMA'S FATHER [*See* Dada]

ANDERSSON, ERIK

Genus: Human
Dæmon: Unnamed; form unknown
World: Lyra's
Background: Dancer
Role: As with everyone on her guest list for the cocktail party, Mrs Coulter's decision to invite him isn't based on pleasure in his company, but on her circle's perception of him as fashionable.

NL/GC 5 *[brief]*

ANFANG

Genus: Dæmon
Form: Pinscher
Human: Thorold
World: Lyra's
Physical characteristics: Described as "gaunt."
Observation: *Like many servants, Asriel's manservant Thorold's*

Doberman Pinscher

dæmon is a dog, but in keeping with someone who has handled Asriel for forty years, the breed of dog, Pinscher, is one known for its willpower and strength.

NL/GC on Svalbard 21 *[brief]*

SK Serafina's visit to Thorold 2 *[brief]*

ANGELICA ⚑✑

Genus: Human
World: Cittàgazze
Alliances: Her brothers, her society's prejudices
Physical characteristics: Red-haired girl about Lyra's age.
Background: Older sister to Paolo; younger to Tullio. Spectre-orphan.
Behavior: Verbally and physically aggressive; only cats intimidate her.
Role: The first Cittàgazzean Will and Lyra meet.

Tells Lyra and Will about Spectres, but silences Paolo when he mentions Tullio. Blames Lyra and Will when Tullio is lost to Spectres and vows revenge. Lyra surmises that Angelica knows Will has the knife. Leads armed gang of kids determined to kill Lyra and Will.

Tells Fr Gomez that a woman fitting Mary Malone's description has passed through Cittàgazze. She also tells him how Will and Lyra stole the knife and killed her brother. She thinks it would be a fine thing for Gomez to kill them both.

SK meets Lyra & Will 3; 5, 7; vows revenge 8; leads assault at belvedere 11; recalled by Lyra & Will 13

AS meets Gomez 10

ANNIE ✤

Genus: Human
Dæmon: Kyrillion; form unsettled
World: Lyra's
Physical characteristics: A tall redhead.
Background: Londoner; one of Lyra's fellow prisoners and roommates at the General Oblation Board's Experiment Station who is determined to be the authority on the Station's activities.
Behavior: Assertive
Role: Annie tells Lyra about the conference room where she and Kyrillion were tested in various ways in the presence of twenty or so scientists.

NL/GC 14, 16

ARCHAEOLOGIST, INSTITUTE OF ARCHAEOLOGY AT OXFORD UNIVERSITY ⚑ 4

Genus: Human
World: Will's
Physical characteristics: His diction ("big-to-do," "blokes," "you know, geologists or whatever," "the explorer type") suggests it is more likely he is a younger than an older man.
Behavior: Casual, informal—but Will has to ask a second time about another man who was

seeking information about the expedition; the archaeologist is apparently uneasy, and perhaps untrustworthy.

Role: Works for the Institute. In Oxford, Will learns that the sponsor for the ill-fated Alaskan expedition that employed his father was the Institute of Archaeology at Oxford University. He visits the Institute, where this archaeologist explains that the study was a preliminary dig to establish whether a full-scale expedition was justified, and only a small team of six or so men were involved, including a professional explorer, John Parry, recruited to provide practical support in outdoor survival.

The archaeologist also off-handedly mentions that whatever details are known about this expedition are fresh in his mind because another man had recently visited the Institute asking about one of the team members. Although he claimed to be a journalist, his description suggests he was one of the men who interrogated Elaine Parry and searched her home.

SK 4

5 | ARCHBISHOP ✤

Genus: Human
Dæmon: Unnamed; form unknown
World: Lyra's
Physical characteristics: Elderly.
Behavior: A "most hateful old snob," according to Mrs Coulter.
Role: The Archbishop's invitation to Mrs Coulter's cocktail party is based not on her desire to impress her friends (as it is with the fashionable dancer and the visiting princess) but because it would not be politically astute to exclude this bore.

NL/GC 5 *[brief]*

ASRIEL, LORD ✤⚷✐ ⑩ Ⓛ̲Ⓢ̲

Genus: Human
Dæmon: Stelmaria, a snow leopard
World: Lyra's, republic of heaven
Alliances: Jordan College, gyptians, supporters of his republic of heaven
Physical characteristics: Tall, with "powerful shoulders," a "fierce dark face," and dark "eyes that seemed to flash and glitter with savage laughter," his "movements were large and perfectly balanced, like those of a wild animal" and his voice "harsh."
Background: Lyra's father, whom she both "admired and feared greatly," was "involved in high politics, in secret exploration, in distant warfare."

Asriel made his fortune exploring Polar regions, but lost all his riches in a court judgment. This followed his killing (in self-defense) of Edward Coulter, the husband of Marisa Coulter, with whom Asriel had had an affair. The affair resulted in Lyra's birth and Mr Coulter's thwarted attempt on Asriel's life. How Asriel made rather than spent a fortune on distant travel to remote places is not explained.

Asriel's dispatch of Edward Coulter led to the courts removing Lyra from his custody and that of her gyptian nursemaid and putting the infant in care at a priory. Asriel in turn took her from the nuns, notwithstanding the court order. Gyptian John Faa tells

Lyra that her father's defiance stemmed from his "hatred of priors and monks and nuns." [9]

Asriel placed Lyra under the guardianship of the Master of Jordan College with the one condition that Mrs Coulter never be allowed near her. Lyra grew up believing that Lord Asriel was her paternal uncle and that both her parents were dead. During her childhood, Asriel would visit with Lyra briefly when his activities brought him to Jordan College.

Although he made a name for himself as a man of action and adventures, he was also an innovative chemist. Lord Asriel's accomplishments in this arena include his manipulation of the silver nitrate preparation used to develop photographs to yield one capable of showing Dust and what appears to be a city on the other side of the Aurora. He developed "an alloy of manganese and titanium" capable "of insulating body from dæmon," which, ironically, is put to use by the General Oblation Board to devise the silver guillotine. [10]

Lord Asriel was an aristocrat who balked at social conventions, taking witch Ruta Skadi as a lover, and forging close friendships with the East Anglia gyptians. He provided political and other support to gyptians, ranging from arguing in Parliament against measures detrimental to their well-being to risking his own life to save several gyptian children nearly lost in a flood.

Serafina Pekkala's dæmon Kaisa says that the witches' interest in Lyra stems from their respect for Asriel's "knowledge of the other worlds" and that "Dust-hunters" [11] (General Oblation Board) fear him.

Lord Asriel's fledgling republic of heaven, which has attracted beings from numerous worlds, seems to have been long planned. According to his manservant, Thorold, Asriel's long-term dislike of the church is both obvious and intense: "I've seen a spasm of disgust cross his face when they talk of the sacraments, and atonement, and redemption," but his [12] boss considers the church "too weak to be worth the fighting," choosing the Authority himself as a more worthy opponent. Even out of his world of birth and into his own, [13] Asriel remains a politician. For example, he convinces witch clan queen Ruta Skadi that her people can't stay out of the coming war between his republic and the Authority's kingdom, and, moreover, "to rebel was right and just, when you considered what the agents of the Authority did in his name" including in some worlds burning witches alive. [14] Ruta returns to her world eager to recruit other witch clans.

Behavior: John Faa considers Asriel a "high-spirited man, quick to anger, a passionate man." Witch-Consul Martin Lanselius believes neither scholarship nor statesmanship [15] matters most to him. In spite of his "ardent and powerful nature" Asriel doesn't give the impression of being despotic or wanting to rule. Although his master may seem "stark [16] mad," and his ambition "limitless," Thorold sees Asriel as one who "dares to do what men and women don't even dare to think." When Thorold tells Lyra that her father has left [17] with Roger, the servant claims his master has "a way special to himself of bringing about what he wants." [18]

The armoured bears "had never met anything quite like Lord Asriel's own haughty and imperious nature. He dominated even Iofur Raknison," the bear who sent Iorek Byrnison into exile and king of the island on which Asriel has been imprisoned by the [19] church. He had alternately "flattered and bullied Raknison," succeeding in having his [20] prison moved to higher ground and materials to fully equip a laboratory at his disposal. Asriel's power to get his own way seems to verge on the supernatural.

His cavalier attitude toward others' pain, glimpsed in his twisting Lyra's arm in the Retiring Room when she comes out of her hiding place to warn him about the poisoned

Tokay, is starkly displayed when Roger pleads for his life. Asriel takes "no notice except to knock him to the ground." Ma Costa told Lyra that the day Edward Coulter came after him, Coulter fired first, but Asriel grabbed the gun out of the man's hand, and "shot him right between the eyes and dashed his brains out." Then he took Lyra from her nurse, sat her atop his shoulders, and strolled "up and down in high good humour with the dead man at his feet."

While Lord Asriel wishes to establish a republic of heaven, with none of the usual authoritarians like kings and bishops, his behavior toward servants is far from democratic. He chastises Jordan College's butler, who seems on the verge of questioning an order, for not behaving in a suitably servile manner. After 40 years of devoted service, he still doesn't treat his manservant Thorold as his equal.

Surprisingly, on Svalbard, he doesn't seem to recognize Iorek Byrnison's name when Lyra explains how she arrived, but later, Asriel expresses pride in Lyra's manipulation of Iofur Raknison.

Lord Asriel's attitude toward Lyra changes from bemused tolerance of her childish antics at Jordan College, to mild contempt for her scruffiness and ill manners, and then to awe and admiration when she ventures into the world of the dead. But Lyra will never know that he took pride in her bravery.

His relationship with Coulter is more nuanced and complex. He forbids her contact with Lyra for twelve years and she is the agent responsible for his imprisonment in Svalbard, but when she reaches the summit as he blasts through the Aurora, their encounter is highly charged and passionate, and he invites her to come with him into a new world.

When she is his prisoner in the adamant tower, Asriel enjoys tormenting Coulter about her declaration of motherly concern for Lyra, but he allows her to hear his discussions with his commanders and to tour the armoury, and, when she disarms him once again, Lord Asriel is still convinced he can turn her theft of his intention craft to his own advantage.

When Lyra's parents finally realize that their only means to defeat Metatron is by dying along with the angel, the teasing is over and his farewell with Coulter is tender; he kisses her "gently."

Role: By establishing his republic in another world, Asriel incites an attack by the forces of the Authority. He sets into motion a rebellion by beings of all worlds who oppose the suppression of conscious beings wanting to know more about their own nature. His means of movement to this unpopulated world brings Lyra to Will, and Will in turn to the subtle knife.

According to Coulter, Asriel has been sentenced to death for heresy because he violated the conditions of his exile to Svalbard by continuing his philosophical investigations. Lyra finds his prison to be more impressive than Raknison's palace.

When Lyra learns of his departure for a mountaintop with his various scientific devices and Roger in tow, she makes the connection between this development and Asriel's description the night before of the energy released during intercision. Roger dies when Asriel severs his dæmon.

Asriel comes to the conclusion that "the future of every conscious being" depends on Lyra and Will—and their dæmons—staying out of Metatron's clutches, and considers whether saving them might be the "sole purpose" of his republic. As he makes his plans to go after Metatron, he initially asks his commanders not to worry Mrs Coulter but to protect her if possible during the coming battle. But instead Coulter and Asriel work as partners to lure Metatron to the edge of the abyss. He battles through extreme pain to succeed with Coulter in defeating Metatron.

Chapter 21 of NORTHERN LIGHTS/THE GOLDEN COMPASS is titled "Lord Asriel's Welcome."

Observation: *Asriel is probably in his early sixties.* THE SUBTLE KNIFE *begins in 1997 (1985 [year Parry vanished] + 12 [Will's age]). The year of the floods in East Anglia was 1953, or 44 years ago. When Asriel rescued two children during the floods, he was likely at least 16, so he is at the very least 60 years old (16+44=60). This would make him a contemporary of Lord Boreal's. Mrs Coulter, age 35 at her death, is easily young enough to be Asriel's daughter.*

Although his plans are discussed by a number of characters, Lord Asriel himself does not make an appearance in THE SUBTLE KNIFE. *Neither does Iorek Byrnison.*

Update: A somewhat different perspective on Lord Asriel is offered in Dr Stanislaus Grumman/Col. John Parry's notes in the appendix to the **10**TH anniversary edition of THE SUBTLE KNIFE. In their brief acquaintance, Grumman learned that Asriel had a daughter "of whom he was very proud." Asriel carries a picture of Lyra with him on his travels, which he showed to the shaman, and Lantern Slide 7 in NORTHERN LIGHTS notes that Asriel had arranged with the Domestic Bursar at Jordan College that photograms be taken of Lyra annually and sent to him. (This revelation must not have been reciprocated, since Asriel is surprised to hear from the angel Baruch that Grumman has a son.)

Grumman characterizes Asriel as "a remarkable man, both proud and generous" and believes that "If anyone could lead a rebellion against the church in this world, or even further, it would be Asriel." When Grumman meets Giacomo Paradisi and sees what the subtle knife can do, he decides his mission is to enlist the knife and bearer in Asriel's campaign.

NL/GC Retiring Room presentation 1, 2; visit with Lyra 3, Faa tells Lyra of her parentage 7, discussed at Roping 8, Kaisa on 11; Lyra compares to Iorek, discusses with Scoresby 13; Coulter discusses with Bolvangar staff 16, discussed on way to Svalbard 18, Santelia on 19, interview with Lyra on Svalbard 21, Lyra pursues 22; Roger's intercision, his discussion with Coulter, departure 23; [LS] Lantern Slides 4, 7
  brief mentions: and Master's gift of alethiometer 4, cocktail party rumors 5, Lyra tells Tony Costa about 6, 10, 12, 15, 17, 20

SK Discussed by Serafina, Thorold, Lanselius, Skadi, Scoresby 2; Lyra tells Will about his bridge 3, Skadi joins angels flying to his fortress 6, Boreal and Coulter discuss his plans 9, Grumman addresses Scoresby on his cause 10, Skadi on 13, Grumman addresses Will about 15
  brief mentions: 4, 5; 7 [by Lyra of "her father" to investigators]

AS Balthamos and Baruch on 2, receives Baruch 5, troops on way to Coulter's cave 9, spies try to persuade Will to join 13; meeting with high commanders (and Coulter), his armoury described 16; rescues Coulter in Alps 25; makes decision regarding Metatron, tells Coulter he lied when he said in Svalbard he'd destroy Dust 28; sees Dust falling into abyss 30; battles Metatron, dies 31
  brief mentions: 3, 6, 8, 11; troops' arrival 12; 14, 15, 17; Lyra discusses with Tialys 18; 19, 23; discussed in Geneva 24; Parry's ghost on his republic's prospects 26; 29, 36, 37, Master on 38

ATAL ✐

Genus: Mulefa

World: Mulefa's

Physical characteristics: Atal's distinguishing characteristics are left unstated but Mary can recognize her among mulefa, the peaceful individuals that resemble antelope she meets in another world.

Background: Of an age when she is expected to marry, which in her case will mean leaving her village to find a suitable mate.

Behavior: Expresses affection by nuzzling Mary's neck with her trunk and displays great anxiety about Mary's safety when the woman climbs trees.

Role: In response to Mary Malone's explanation of Shadow-particles, Atal describes sraf, which inspires Mary to create the amber spyglass. Through Mary and Atal's dialogues, the philosophy by which the mulefa live is revealed.

Atal discusses the sraf and Shadows with Mary, the history of the mulefa, and the mutual reliance of the seedpod trees and her species on one another. She and Mary engage in mutual grooming, and it is following one of these sessions that Mary discovers that applying seed oil to the lacquer plates allows her to see sraf. Once Mary can see sraf, Atal brings her friend to Sattamax, mulefa elder, who asks Mary's help in diagnosing the cause of the seedpod trees' sickening. Her parting gift to Mary is wheel tree oil and seeds.

AS   explains sraf, takes Mary to Sattamax 17; 32, 33; alerts Mary to sraf's return
      brief mentions: raises alarm as *tualapi* approach 10; anxiety at Mary's climbing 20; 27, 37; parting with Mary 38

AUTHORITY, THE ⚑✎

Genus: Angel

World: Kingdom of heaven, Clouded Mountain

Alliances: Metatron (Regent), Father MacPhail, "Holy Church," Consistorial Court of Discipline, Oblation Board, College of Bishops

Physical characteristics: Mrs Coulter sees the crystal litter carrying the Authority transported out of the Clouded Mountain where he dwells. Secured in the litter is "an angel...indescribably aged" who "cackled and muttered" and "uttered a howl of such anguish" that it pains Coulter. When Lyra and Will stumble upon the abandoned crystal litter under attack by cliff-ghasts, they pity its passenger, who "was terrified, crying like a baby." Lyra sees a "demented and powerless" being whose "groaning whimper that went on and on" ends only when Lyra reaches in to help him out. He then "tried to smile, and to bow," looking on her with "innocent wonder"; she feels he is "as light as paper, and he would have followed them anywhere, having no will of his own, and responding to simple kindness like a flower to the sun."

Tradition holds that the Authority can be killed by Æsahættr, the god-destroyer, a name by which the subtle knife is known.

Background: King Ogunwe, one of Asriel's high commanders, says this being "has been known by that name since the Authority first set himself above the rest of the angels." Also known as "God, the Creator, the Lord, Yahweh, El, Adonai, the King, the Father, the Almighty...all names he gave himself," according to Balthamos.

Balthamos maintains that the Authority was "the first angel" but "never the creator" and like other angels is "formed of Dust," but the Authority told "those who came after him that he had created them." When some angels discovered that this was not true, they rebelled, and he banished them from his kingdom. At the start of his reign he set up "a world of the dead," which Balthamos describes as "a prison camp." According to No-Name the harpy, when the Authority set up this world, he gave the harpies their "power to see the worst in every one." Metatron says the Authority was relentless in his condemnation when "the sons of heaven fell in love with the daughters of earth."

Behavior: Much is known about the behavior of those claiming to be acting as his agents, but little is known of the Authority's own present-day actions or attitudes.

The angel Baruch says that the Authority has put the running of his kingdom into Metatron's hands and plans to move out of the Clouded Mountain, which Metatron then will turn into "an engine of war." The Authority and his Regent, having decided that "conscious beings of every kind have become dangerously independent," wants to set up a "permanent inquisition in every world." Baruch warns that they intend to start their campaign by destroying Asriel's republic.

Role: While many of HIS DARK MATERIALS' characters identify their actions and beliefs as in accordance or in opposition to his commands, the Authority himself appears only briefly and is obviously incapable of controlling himself, let alone others. That notwithstanding, the characters' ideas of the Authority are a primary force fueling the action and conflicts of the novels.

The title of Chapter 31 of THE AMBER SPYGLASS is "Authority's End."

Observation: *The church and Magisterium may consider itself in alliance with the Authority, but there is no indication that this is reciprocal or that at this time in its history the Authority is much interested in human affairs.*

SK   Thorold on 2, described by Ruta Skadi 13, Grumman on 15

AS   Balthamos on 2; Ogunwe on 16, harpies on 23, crystal litter departs Clouded Mountain 30, released by Will and Lyra
    brief mentions: Baruch tells Asriel about 5; 6, 8, 24, 28, 36

> ## Philip Pullman on the Authority:
> *From an interview on Readerville*
>
> "The God who dies is the God of the burners of heretics, the hangers of witches, the persecutors of Jews, the officials who recently flogged that poor girl in Nigeria who had the misfortune to become pregnant after having been forced to have sex—all these people claim to know with absolute certainty that their God wants them to do these things. Well, I take them at their word, and I say in response…that God deserves to die."
>
> "The Authority…is an ancient IDEA of God, kept alive artificially by those who benefit from his continued existence."

BALTHAMOS ⚔ ✐ [LS]

Genus: Angel

World: all, except world of the dead

Alliances: Baruch, unnamed female angel "banished" by the Authority (when she found out he was not her creator).

Physical characteristics: Slender, with narrow wings, and "his face bore an expression that mingled haughty disdain with a tender, ardent sympathy, as if he would love all things if only his nature could let him forget their defects." Eats, but very lightly. When he has to pretend to be Will's dæmon, the animal form he most often chooses is that of a blackbird.

Background: "…not of a high order among angels."

Behavior: Devoted to Baruch, who was once a man but through Balthamos' intervention is now an angel rather than a ghost. Says he and Baruch "feel as one, though we are two" and, although they can read each other's minds, "talking is best": the two "loved each other with a passion."

Neither Balthamos nor Baruch seems to consider how Will might feel when they say that they had been following Stanislaus Grumman/John Parry but did not intervene when the witch was poised to assassinate the man.

When Will tells him to take the shape of an animal and pretend to be Will's dæmon, Balthamos balks at the "unspeakably humiliating" notion but agrees. After Baruch chides him for being impatient with Will who cannot be expected to understand angelic issues, Balthamos apologizes to Will and promises to be kinder.

Balthamos knows when it happens that Baruch has died; he grieves deeply and violently, "reckless and wild and stricken, cursing the very air, the clouds, the stars," feeling that "half his heart had been extinguished." Will asks him to try to be strong, like Baruch was—"Be like him for me," and after a day's brooding, Balthamos tells Will that he'll do all he can for him, "cheerfully and willingly for the sake of Baruch."

Balthamos is too frightened to act during the confrontation in the Himalayan cave with Coulter. But when grief and shame have so weakened him that he can no longer fly, he summons his last strength to capture the dæmon of the priest, Fr Gomez, who intends to assassinate Lyra.

Role: The angels follow Grumman/Parry, knowing he was seeking the knife bearer—their task being to take Will and the knife to Asriel. Balthamos later clarifies this, saying that he and Baruch want to use the knife to get Asriel's attention so they can tell him what they've "discovered in the Clouded Mountain," and, secondly, they want to keep the knife away from the Authority's Regent Metatron. Along with Baruch, he is waiting for Will when the boy discovers that Lyra is gone. Assists Will after Lyra is abducted and explains to him the nature of the battle in which the boy has a central role.

Balthamos proves helpful in the guise of Will's dæmon as the boy travels through Lyra's world; it is by way of the angels that Will knows where to find her.

Balthamos and Iorek Byrnison have little in common, but they agree that Will is foolishly fascinated by Coulter. The angel puts himself between the Authority's soldiers and the children, as Will, Lyra, and Ama, the village girl, flee Coulter's cave but abruptly vanishes when threatened by the troops' dæmons.

Next seen pursuing Fr Gomez in the mulefa's world where he succeeds in thwarting the assassin. Weakened and in pain, he calls on Baruch for help and finally manages to drown Gomez. He then dissipates.

The title of the second chapter of THE AMBER SPYGLASS is "Balthamos and Baruch."

Observation: *Balthamos' companion Baruch is unusual among angels; he was once a man and was saved from the world of the dead when Balthamos transfigured him as an angel. So too was Metatron, who as a man was known as Enoch before being made an angel by the Authority. On earth, Enoch and Baruch were brothers. If the Authority, who claimed to create the angels, can make a man an angel, and if Balthamos, a much lower order of angel can do so as well, then this power which initially may seem to confer special status to the Authority (i.e. making of a man an angel) is not evidence that the Authority is unique or unlike (other) angels.*

SK   first encounter with Will 15 (unnamed)

AS   explanations to Will 2, Baruch on at Asriel's 5; anguish at Baruch's death, acts as Will's dæmon 8; in Himalayas 11, 12; flees cave during battle 13; battles Gomez, dies 35; [LS] Lantern Slide 2
     brief mentions: 9, 14, 15, 16, 33, 36, 37

BARUCH ⚔️✏️

Genus: Angel

World: All, except world of the dead.

Alliances: Balthamos, unnamed female angel "banished" by the Authority (when she found out he was not her creator). ⎪48

Physical characteristics: Younger than his partner Balthamos and "more powerfully built, his wings snow-white and massive." Can fly extraordinarily fast. ⎪49

Background: A rare case of a human who became an angel after death. Balthamos saved his ghost from consignment to the world of the dead, but details of his transfiguration are not provided. In his earthly existence 4,000 years ago in Will's world, he was one of Metatron's brothers. This connection allows him to gain access to the Clouded Mountain.

Behavior: Baruch is kinder and more tolerant than Balthamos. Will asks how he will find them again in Lyra's world after leaving to visit Asriel, and Baruch replies, "I shall never lose Balthamos." Before he leaves on this journey, he kisses Will goodbye. ⎪50

Baruch wants to help Asriel, but his primary allegiance seems to be with his friend: "he looked up to Balthamos as to the fount of all knowledge and joy." ⎪51

Role: Attains and provides key information regarding Metatron, the subtle knife, and Lyra to Asriel, and locates Lyra for Will.

Along with Balthamos, he is waiting for Will when the boy discovers that Lyra is gone. Baruch reconnoiters Lyra's whereabouts, reports to Will and Balthamos, and then heads to Asriel's fortress, where he is mortally wounded on approach. But he is carried into the basalt fortress and able to deliver vital information to Asriel before dying.

Dies with the name of Balthamos on his lips.

The title of the second chapter of *The Amber Spyglass* is "Balthamos and Baruch."

SK first encounter with Will 15 (unnamed)

AS explanations to Will 2; at Asriel's, dies 5; mourned by Balthamos 8
brief mentions: 9, 13, 14, 15, 16, 28, 33, 35, 37

BASILIDES, TEUKROS ✏️

Genus: Human

Dæmon: Unnamed; nightingale

World: Lyra's

Alliances: Asriel

Physical characteristics: Middle-aged; thin, pale.

Behavior: Respectful and dedicated; works to the point of exhaustion during the Church's attacks on Lyra.

Role: Asriel's alethiometer reader.

Asriel uses Basilides' skills to find Coulter's cave. It is also Basilides who reports to Asriel and his commanders that although Lyra is still in the world of the dead, the bomb did not find her. He gives Asriel the bad news about Metatron's plans for gaining control of Will and Lyra by capturing their dæmons, and the implications of this for all conscious beings.

Common Nightingale
Luscinia megarhynchos hafizi

© A. Audevard – Oman 2004

Observation: *In Will's world, Basilides was one of the leading Gnostic philosophers of 2nd century Egypt. The Greek name* Teukros *means the builder.*

AS determines Coulter's location 5; reveals Metatron's plan 26

BEAR-SERGEANT ❖

Genus: Armoured bear
World: Lyra's
Alliances: Iofur Raknison
Physical characteristics: This bear wears polished armour and a plumed helmet when he patrols the coast of Svalbard, in keeping with Raknison's sense of fashion style for his subjects.
Behavior: Like his peers, he is indifferent to the stench of the refuse-filled palace grounds and halls. He seems to be unaware of his own strength compared to that of his captive.
Role: This Bear-Sergeant summons troops to takes Lyra prisoner after she falls from Lee Scoresby's balloon near Raknison's palace. Inside the palace, he narrates the story of the bears' triumph depicted in the murals carved on the walls, and then knocks Lyra into a dungeon cell.
NL/GC 18, 19

BECK, IAN ⑩

Genus: Human
World: Will's
Role: The collection of Lord Asriel's papers housed in the Jordan College Library, which appears in the **10ᴛʜ** anniversary edition of NORTHERN LIGHTS, was bought at auction by Beck, "a celebrated artist." It is a mystery how these writings, apparently from another world, came to be among the contents of the auction lot of a deceased Oxford scholar's effects.
Facts: *Artist Ian Beck illustrated the appendices of the* **10ᴛʜ** *anniversary editions of* HIS DARK MATERIALS *and the program notes for the National Theatre's production of Pullman's novels, as well as Pullman's retelling of* Puss in Boots *(1999), one of many children's books to Beck's credit. In 2006, he published his first novel for young readers,* Tom Trueheart, Boy Adventurer.
10ᴛʜ: *SK appendix*

BELACQUA, COUNT ❖

Genus: None
Role: The imaginary identity of Lyra's father. For all her life, Lyra's father, Lord Asriel, has been claiming to be her paternal uncle. According to him, the Count and his wife (Lyra's father and mother) were both killed in an aëronautical accident.
NL/GC 5 *[brief]*

BELACQUA, LYRA ❖ ⚱

Note: This entry refers only to those occasions when Lyra's full name is employed.
Role: Lyra's full name, Lyra Belacqua, is only occasionally used. John Faa gives her full name at the gyptians' Roping. Farder Coram introduces her by full name to Iorek Byrnison, and Lyra herself uses the name around Iorek. Serafina Pekkala uses it at her witch-council and when seeking the girl in Cittàgazze. Shaman Stanislaus Grumman,

assuring Lee Scoresby he understands the conditions under which the aëronaut will make the trip to Cittàgazze, refers to Lyra Belacqua—although Scoresby does not.

[*See* **Lyra; Silvertongue, Lyra**]

NL/GC brief mentions: by Faa 7, Coram 10; Lyra 11, 19; Lyra renamed 20

SK   brief mentions: by Serafina 2, 6; Grumman 10

BELISARIA ❖

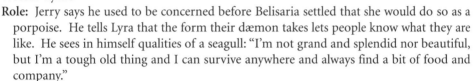

Glaucous Gull

Genus: Dæmon
Form: Seagull
Human: Jerry, an able seaman and Lyra's friend on her journey north
World: Lyra's
Role: Jerry says he used to be concerned before Belisaria settled that she would do so as a porpoise. He tells Lyra that the form their dæmon takes lets people know what they are like. He sees in himself qualities of a seagull: "I'm not grand and splendid nor beautiful, but I'm a tough old thing and I can survive anywhere and always find a bit of food and company."

NL/GC 10 *[brief]*

BELLA ❖

Genus: Human
Dæmon: Unnamed; form unsettled
World: Lyra's
Physical characteristics: "the dark plump one."
Behavior: Friendly, compliant.
Role: One of Lyra's fellow prisoners and roommates at the General Oblation Board's Bolvangar Experiment Station, along with Martha and Annie. Rarely gets to complete a sentence before Annie, another child, interrupts her.

NL/GC brief mentions: 14, 16

BERNIE THE PASTRY COOK [*See* **Johansen, Bernie**]

BISHOP ❖

Genus: Human
Dæmon: Unnamed; form unknown
World: Lyra's
Physical characteristics: Dressed "in a bishop's purple".
Role: Presumably a bishop, or possibly the Archbishop that Mrs Coulter invited so he wouldn't take offense at being excluded from the festivities. This party guest is overheard by Lyra boasting that Asriel won't "be troubling us for quite some time" since he is imprisoned on Svalbard.

NL/GC 5 *[brief]*

BOATMAN ✐

Genus: Indeterminate

World: World of the Dead

Physical characteristics: "Aged beyond age," "crippled and bent" with sunken eyes and grey skin. Incapable of being physically hurt by any of his passengers, dead or alive.

Background: Long experienced in dealing with the anger and denial of those he ferries.

Behavior: Unperturbed by the journey he makes. Firm regarding Pantalaimon, but not cruel. Disinterested in Lyra's claim that she will return from the land of the dead, noting only that no one has ever done so; refuses to debate it.

Role: Rows Lyra, Will, and the Gallivespian spies to the land of dead. Assures Lyra when she disembarks that if Pan is still at the dock, he'll tell him Lyra swears she'll find him again.

Observations: *His nature is a mystery. On the one hand, physicality is suggested by his handling of the boat, but his invulnerability to physical assault and the incompatibility of his decrepit appearance and his bodily strength suggest an inhuman essence in spite of his form.*

Facts: *In Greek mythology, the dead must cross an underground lake or river to their last resting place in Hades. Charon, the ferryman, with few exceptions, demands as payment for passage a coin that the deceased's family placed in their mouths. Charon refuses to ferry those who can not pay, and their souls are doomed to wander in an in-between realm, neither of life nor of death. (The boatman Will and Lyra encounter does not expect to be paid.)*

AS 21

BOREAL, LORD (AKA CARLO; LATROM, SIR CHARLES) ❖ ⚕ ✐

[*See* **Latrom, Sir Charles** *for Boreal's activities in Will's world*]

Genus: Human

Dæmon: Unnamed; Mailed-headed, emerald-eyed serpent

World: Lyra's; enters Will's using alias Sir Charles Latrom; dies in Cittàgazze

Alliances: The Church's General Oblation Board and the Consistorial Court of Discipline

Physical characteristics: [*See* **Latrom, Sir Charles**]

Background: His work at the Ministry of Theology appears to require a high degree of protection from inquiry. When gyptian spies seeking information about children abducted by the General Oblation Board discover that Boreal and the Ministry of Theology are involved, Frans Broekman and Tom Mendham try to uncover more about Boreal's role. According to another on their team, "Frans and Tom were swallowed alive as soon as they got near Lord Boreal."

Atlantic Salt Marsh Snake

Behavior: Powerful and sly—but susceptible to Coulter's charms, a weakness that proves his undoing. When Coulter gets what she wants from him, she poisons the man.

Role: Claims the Master of Jordan College is his friend when introduced to Lyra. Lyra in turn tries to impress him by speaking of Dust and the Oblation Board, to which he responds that Mrs Coulter is adept at procuring children and Lyra will probably aid her in this. Several gyptians go missing trying to learn about his work for the Oblation

Board. Asriel tells Coulter he knows she had an affair with Boreal.

Lyra's feelings that she has met Latrom before are clarified when she realizes that Sir Charles Latrom and Boreal are the same man. Boreal/Latrom is the only character besides John Parry/Stanislaus Grumman to have established lives and identities in both Lyra's and Will's worlds. Unlike Parry/Grumman, he has been able to travel from one to the other at will, thus retaining his physical health. [*See also* **Latrom, Sir Charles** and **Carlo**]

Facts: *Boreas is the Greek god of the north wind. The Northern Lights are also called the aurora borealis (but never in* His Dark Materials, *where they are simply the Aurora).*

NL/GC first encounter with Lyra 5
> *brief mentions:* 7, involvement with Ministry of Theology 9, Asriel tells Coulter he knows Boreal was one of her lovers 23

SK *brief mentions:* 2, Lyra realizes he's Latrom 9; Lyra thinks that for all his cleverness, Coulter can manipulate him 11

AS *brief mentions:* 2, ability to maintain his health by returning to own world recalled 35

Borisovitch, Otyets (Father) Semyon 🖉

Genus: Human
Dæmon: Unnamed; crow
World: Lyra's
Alliances: Presumably the church
Physical characteristics: "Immense, grey-bearded" priest with "fat dirty fingers," he smells of "tobacco and alcohol and sweat." |57 58 59|
Background: Village priest in Kholodnoye, Siberia.
Behavior: Interests are playing cards, smoking, and drinking large quantities of vodka while sharing his views with young teenaged boys, if his day with Will is a typical one. Makes Will very uneasy, especially when he holds Will's hands to test how cold they are, and then lets his own rest on Will's knees, all the time encouraging the boy to spend the night in his home. Repeatedly and "with a threatening heartiness" encourages Will to drink shots of straight vodka. When he is finally resigned to Will's departure, the priest hugs "him tightly...kissing his cheeks, right, left, right again." |60|
Role: Although Borisovitch considers armoured bears "children of the devil" and that all witches "should be put to death, every one," his hateful warning about the bears stopping for fuel in a neighboring village proves useful to Will, directing him to Iorek Byrnison. |61 62|
AS 8

Boy in striped tee shirt ⚜

Genus: Human
World: Cittàgazze
Alliances: Other Spectre orphans
Physical characteristics: About Will's age
Behavior: Violent and aggressive. First seen leading an attack against a cat in the town of Cittàgazze until stopped by Will, this unnamed boy seems bound for mortal combat with Will.
Role: The boy, armed with a pistol, along with Angelica (sister of the teen with whom Will fought for the subtle knife) lead a gang that attacks Lyra and Will. The boy and Will are

about to fight when Kaisa, the snow goose dæmon of the witch Serafina Pekkala, arrives and so shocks the child that he falls from the building.

SK   attacks cat 5; attacks Will and Lyra at belvedere 10

BRAKS, ADRIAAN ✤

Genus: Human
Dæmon: Unnamed; form unknown
World: Lyra's
Background: Gyptian
Role: Wants gyptian leader John Faa's assurance (which he readily gives) that their journey North to rescue children abducted by the Gobblers won't become an expedition to rescue Lord Asriel.

NL/GC 8 *[brief]*

BROEKMAN, FRANS ✤

Genus: Human
Dæmon: Unnamed; form unknown
World: Lyra's
Background: Gyptian
Role: Captured or killed in London during a gyptian spy mission with partner Tom Mendham, while attempting to discover the significance of the involvement of Lord Boreal in the General Oblation Board's abduction of children. Fate unknown.

NL/GC 9 *[brief]*

BROEKMAN, SAM ✤

Genus: Human
Dæmon: Unnamed; form unknown
World: Lyra's
Background: Gyptian
Role: His rescue some years past by Lord Asriel from a hostile Turk is an incident cited by gyptian leader John Faa as an example of Asriel's good will, and a reason that the gyptians should shelter the runaway Lyra from Mrs Coulter or other pursuers.

NL/GC 8 *[brief]*

BROKEN ARROW, DR ✤

Genus: Human
Dæmon: Unnamed; form unknown
World: Lyra's
Background: Skraeling
Role: Arctic explorer pointed out by Mrs Coulter to Lyra as they lunch together at the Royal Arctic Institute.
Observation: *On the back of the map in* LYRA'S OXFORD, *Smith and Strange, Ltd, lists among its publications* The Proto-Fisher People of L'Anse aux Meadows *by Leonard Broken Arrow.*

NL/GC 4 *[brief]*

BROOGS, LISSIE [*See* Lyra] ✤
Role: How Samoyeds pronounce "Lizzie Brooks."
NL/GC 14 *[brief]*

BROOKS, LIZZIE [*See* Lyra] ✤
Role: Name Lyra uses with Samoyeds and Bolvangar staff.
NL/GC 14, 15

BROTHER J. ⑩
Genus: Human
Dæmon: Unnamed; form unknown
World: Lyra's
Role: Brother J. suggests that a "holy war" is the proper response to the things detailed in the pages from Mary Malone's journal, which have landed in the archive of the Magisterium. Her descriptions of the mulefa's world are deemed "wicked imaginings" and yet another of the "blasphemous accounts" by heretics of "supposed 'other worlds.'"
AS appendix.

BROTHER LOUIS [*See* Louis, Brother]

BUTLER AT JORDAN COLLEGE [*See* Wren]

BYRNISON, IOREK ✤ ⚖ ✎
Genus: Armoured bear
World: Lyra's
Alliances: **Fellow** armoured bears, Lyra, Scoresby, Serafina Pekkala, John Faa's gyptians
Physical characteristics: Over 10 feet tall and four times the size of a brown bear, with claws as long as a hand or the "length of daggers," "small black eyes," a black nose, and ivory fur. 63 64 Weighs nearly 2 tons when wearing his armour.
Background: Once the "wealthy and high-ranking" king of Svalbard's *panserbjørne* or armoured bears, he was sent into exile because, "out of [his] own control," he killed a bear 65 in an angry fight over a female.
    Longtime friend of Lee Scoresby, with whom he fought in the Tunguska campaign.
    When Dr Lanselius, the Witch-Consul in the port city of Trollesund, Norroway, brings Iorek to the gyptians' attention, he is working at a sledge depot for "meat and spirits." Stripped of his armour when exiled, he had made himself another set out of sky 66 iron in Nova Zembla, but the Trollesund authorities confiscated it as Iorek lay in a drunken stupor. He is considered a "dangerous rogue" by the townsmen of Trollesund, 67 who claim that when he realized his armour had been confiscated, Byrnison rampaged and killed two men. But he is tolerated in Trollesund for his "wondrous skill with metals." 68
Behavior: Iorek Byrnison's sense of self is "pure and certain and absolute." He can show 69 "brutal power, but a power controlled by intelligence." On seeing hundreds of witches 70 flying as to war, Lyra asks if he is frightened. His response stays with her: "Not yet. When

I am, I shall master the fear."

When he argues Lyra shouldn't go to find Roger's ghost because her "business is with life," she counters that "our business is to keep promises, no matter how difficult they are," and Iorek accepts this.

When the gyptians fearfully retreat from Lyra on her return with Tony, the severed child, Iorek admonishes all of them—leaders, employers, and friends alike, including king John Faa, Farder Coram, and Lee Scoresby: "Shame on you! Think what this child has done! You might not have more courage, but you should be ashamed to show less!"

His intuitive morality is further revealed in his hesitancy about repairing the subtle knife. Until he had to decide about mending the knife, he had "never been troubled before, never in doubt," and he worries that in fixing the knife he has "stepped outside bear nature" by interfering in human affairs.

Iorek shows great tenderness toward Lyra.

Role: A loyal warrior, he comes to Lyra's aid in battle or provides transport at several critical points. By repairing the subtle knife, he provides Lyra and Will the means to go to the world of the dead and to release the ghosts, and makes it possible for Will to return to his world.

Iorek Byrnison gives Lyra, whose prior relationships, especially with adults, have been superficial and determined by expediency, the experience of loving and being loved.

Iorek takes Lyra on the search that the alethiometer has prompted, leading to Gobbler victim Tony Makarios. After the Samoyed hunters kidnap Lyra, Iorek remains with the gyptians and arrives at Bolvangar to conduct a one-bear campaign against the numerous Tartar guards.

Lyra tells usurper-king Iofur Raknison that she is Iorek Byrnison's dæmon but will, instead, be his if he vanquishes Iorek. This clever scheme so pleases Iorek that he renames her (Lyra Belacqua) *Lyra Silvertongue*. Raknison challenges him to mortal combat, and Iorek wins. He eats the heart of his vanquished enemy, reclaims his kingdom, and rids it of the trappings of Raknison's obsession with all things human.

Iorek brings Roger and Lyra to Asriel, and the following morning takes a frantic Lyra in search of her father and his captive, Roger. Leaving his troops to fight attacking hostile witches and then Coulter's Tartars, Iorek parts from Lyra only when he is too heavy to risk crossing a snow bridge spanning a chasm.

Lyra's experiences with Iorek allow her to see that when Will turns from conflict, it isn't out of cowardice. Will is "the bravest fighter she ever saw, as brave as Iorek Byrnison," and like the bear, Will doesn't fight impulsively but only when situations require it—and then they both fight long and hard.

When Iorek learns of Scoresby's death from Serafina Pekkala, he swims into a new world (Cittàgazze) to find his friend's body. Because Serafina has put a spell on Lee's corpse to keep it from decaying, Iorek can do his friend the honor of eating his "flesh and blood" as he vows to avenge Lee's death.

The climatic changes brought on by Asriel's blast threaten the bears' survival on Svalbard, and Iorek charters a boat to take several dozen bears to the snow-covered Himalayas. On this journey, Iorek meets Will, who challenges the bear to a duel, under the pretense of solving a conflict between villagers and bears, in a remote area of Siberia where the boat has stopped for fuel. Iorek knows who Will is; and that the duel, during which Will shreds Iorek's helmet with the knife, is a sham, but is effective in defusing the situation. When he has a chance to examine the knife, Iorek responds intuitively: "I can think of it [what the knife does] but not understand what I am thinking." 77

Reunited with Lyra in the Himalayas, Iorek tells her about Lee's death. He reluctantly agrees to repair the knife, and warns Will that if the boy wishes to return from the land of the dead, he must not think of his mother when cutting windows. Reconciled to Lyra's determination to make this journey, Iorek tells Lyra if they both survive, she—and Will— will always be welcomed in his kingdom.

Iorek next appears with his subjects on the plains below the basalt fortress, heading one of many legions of warriors from various worlds fighting for Asriel's republic. He navigates through the chaos of the battlefield and safely delivers Lyra and Will to the grove where their dæmons are hiding and under attack by Spectres. There he meets Lee Scoresby's ghost. Iorek cuts short Will and Lyra's farewell to him, bumping them onward toward their dæmons.

Chapter 10 of *Northern Lights / The Golden Compass* is titled "The Consul and the Bear," which refers to witch-consul Dr Martin Lanselius's recommendation that the gyptians employ armoured bear Iorek Byrnison.

Observation: *Like Asriel, Iorek Byrnison does not make an appearance in* The Subtle Knife.

NL/GC Lanselius on, Coram and Lyra meet 10; sets the return of his armour as his price for aiding gyptians, retrieves with Lyra's help 11; takes Lyra alone to village 12; shames gyptians and Lee when they shun Tony, tells his story to Lyra 13; battle with Tartars at Bolvangar 17; Lyra and Serafina discuss 18; returns to Svalbard 19; mortal combat with Raknison, eats heart of vanquished enemy, reclaims kingdom 20; takes Lyra in pursuit of Asriel, battles witches and Coulter's Tartar soldiers 22
     brief mentions: 14, 15, 16; arrives at Asriel's 21; 23

SK *brief mentions:* 1, 2, 5; compared to Will 7; 10, 11, 13

AS discussion with Serafina, goes to Scoresby's body 3; meets Will 8, journey to Himalayas 9, warns Will against Coulter 11; reunited with Lyra, discusses repairing knife 14; repairs knife, warns Will not to think of his mother when cutting, parts from Lyra and Will 15; caught in nets, rescued by Will, meets Lee Scoresby's ghost 31
     brief mentions: 4, 12, 13, 16, 18; approaches Asriel's fortress 28; 29, 32, 37, 38

Cansino, Sam ⚡

Genus: Human

Dæmon: Unnamed; form unknown

World: Lyra's

Physical characteristics: Has a black beard.

Background: Fur trader and a Texan acquaintance of Lee Scoresby.

Behavior: Enjoys his vodka. His anecdotes about Grumman suggest a fair storytelling ability, and an interest in others.

Role: Contributes to aëronaut Scoresby's store of knowledge regarding Stanislaus Grumman. Cansino talks about when Grumman stepped into a trap and seriously cut open his leg. He tells how Grumman treated himself with bloodmoss, making notes on the progress of his recovery while continuing to shout orders regarding star-sightings to his crew. Cansino also says Grumman once rejected a witch who wanted him for her lover, and he believes Grumman is dead.

SK 6

CANZONA, MICHAEL ✤

Genus: Human
Dæmon: Unnamed; form unknown
World: Lyra's
Background: Gyptian. Head of one of the six families of Faa's group.
Role: Second in command for voyage north.
NL/GC brief mentions: 8, 10

CAPTAIN (ARMOURED BEARS') ✑

Genus: Human
Dæmon: Unnamed; form unknown
World: Lyra's
Background: Hired in Siberia, speaks little English, and smokes a pipe.
Behavior: Incurious, the captain minds his own business, which is keeping his boat safe while fulfilling his contracted obligations. He is not intimidated by the hostile villagers who do not want the bears' boat to stop at their town for fuel, even when one of his sailors is shot.
Role: Hired by Iorek Byrnison and some of his subjects to take them from the melting icecaps of Arctic Siberia as far downriver to the Himalayas as possible.
AS   outside Kholodnoye 8; journey to Himalayas 9

CAPTAIN (GYPTIANS' VOYAGE TO MULEFA'S WORLD) ✑

Genus: Human
Dæmon: Unnamed; form unknown
World: Lyra's
Role: Guided by witch Serafina Pekkala to the mulefa's world to pick up Mary Malone, Lyra, and Will.
AS   38 *[brief]*

CARBORN, COLONEL ✤

Genus: Human
Dæmon: Unnamed; form unknown
World: Lyra's
Background: Arctic explorer who crossed the North Pole in a balloon.
Role: The elderly colonel's casual acquaintance with Mrs Coulter impresses Lyra when they lunch at the Royal Arctic Institute.
Observation: *On the back of the map in* LYRA'S OXFORD, *Smith and Strange, Ltd, lists among its publications* By Zeppelin to the Pole *by Lt Col. J. C. B. Carborn.*
NL/GC 4 *[brief]*

CARLO [*See* Boreal, Lord *and* Latrom, Sir Charles]

CASSINGTON SCHOLAR ❖

Genus: Human
Dæmon: Unnamed; form unknown
World: Lyra's
Background: One of the Jordan College Scholars present in the Retiring Room during Asriel's lecture that opens *HIS DARK MATERIALS*.

    The Cassington Scholar is chosen on the basis of his suitability to "challenge the faith of the Scholars," according to Asriel.
Role: Claims the Barnard-Stokes hypothesis about the existence of other worlds is mathematically sound. Believes the armoured bears would never scalp their enemies.

    On Svalbard, Asriel and Lyra discuss his calling the story of Adam and Eve a fairy tale.
NL/GC brief mentions: 2; ideas on Adam and Eve 21

CASTOR ✐

Genus: Dæmon
World: World of the dead
Background: Unidentified ghost-child's late dæmon.
Role: When Lyra, Will, and the Gallivespians journey through the world of the dead, they encounter many ghost-children still longing for their lost dæmons, including a child who regrets never having a chance to say goodbye to "my Castor."
AS   21 [brief]

CAT WHO LEADS WILL TO WINDOW ⚔✐

Genus: Feline
World: Will's, Cittàgazze
Alliances: Will and Lyra
Physical characteristics: Tabby; reminds Will of his cat Moxie, back home in Winchester.
Behavior: Friendly and curious. Recognizes that Pantalaimon poses no threat even in his cat form. Remarkably trusting of Will, knowing he will protect her, although he is the same age and size as her Cittàgazze attackers. To Lyra, her attitude seems not unlike a dæmon's.
Role: When Will pauses in Oxford to watch this cat, he discovers the window to Cittàgazze.

    When she is viciously attacked by a mob of kids in Cittàgazze, who believe that all cats are of the devil and should die, Will comes to her rescue. The cat later returns the favor in Sir Charles Latrom's yard. After Will retrieves the alethiometer, Latrom and Coulter have caught up with Will who is nearly through a window, but the cat attacks the golden monkey, and Lyra and Will escape.

    "The Cat and the Hornbeam Trees" is the title of the first chapter of *THE SUBTLE KNIFE*, and she is the subject for the woodcuts accompanying this chapter and chapter 5, "Airmail Paper."
Observation: *Will has a special affinity for cats even before he discovers that the true form of his dæmon is a cat: there is Moxie, his only childhood friend, and the cat at the hornbeam trees. And when he meets Lyra for the first time, she hurls herself snarling at his chest and then retreats to "crouch in the corner of the dark landing like a cat at bay." He*

Tabby Cat
Lydia Ondrusek

finds the best way to handle her is to stay "calm and quiet as if she were a strange cat he was *making friends with."*

SK   1; attacked by mob, rescued by Will 5; Lyra asks Cittàgazze kids why they attacked it 7; at Latrom's 9; Will's chance encounter with cat recalled in rural Cittàgazze 13 *[brief]*

AS   Will's chance encounter with cat recalled in world of mulefa 31 *[brief]*

CAWSON ❖

Ellen Levy Finch

Irish Setter

Genus: Human

Dæmon: Unnamed; red setter

World: Lyra's

Physical characteristics: Either sickly, elderly or overweight; his footsteps are heavy and his breathing punctuated by wheezes.

Background: Steward at Jordan College. Rings the bells to mark the half-hour point before a meal and supervises the waiters. Superior to the Butler, who resents his status.

Behavior: Lyra wants to avoid Cawson's wrath, which she knows would be his response to her entering the Retiring Room. He has hit her on two previous occasions.

Role: Lyra hides in a closet instead of leaving the room when the Steward comes to make certain all is in order. She is thus later present and able to stop Asriel from drinking the poisoned Tokay.

NL/GC 1
   brief mentions: 3, 9

CEREBATON ❖

Genus: Dæmon

Form: Unknown

Human: Simon Le Clerc

World: Lyra's

Role: Her name is inscribed in the crypt of Jordan College, where her human served as Master from 1765-1789.

NL/GC 3 *[brief]*

CHAPLAIN ❖

Genus: Human

Dæmon: Unnamed; form unknown

World: Lyra's

Physical characteristics: The Chaplain's fingernails are dirtier than her own, Lyra states in response to a criticism by Lord Asriel.

Background: Jordan College Scholar.

Role: Among the Chaplain's duties is contributing to the education of Lyra. Interested in investigations of Dust; fascinated by the photograms Lord Asriel shows the Scholars in the Retiring Room. The Librarian tells the Master of Jordan College during Asriel's presentation that he thinks the Chaplain is already on Asriel's side, as they consider the best way to deny Asriel future funding for his expeditions North.

NL/GC 2

brief mentions: Lyra discusses his fingernails with Asriel, and later his lessons with Pan 3; Lyra pretends to Coulter that what she knows of Dust comes from a conversation of his she overheard 4

CHARLES [*See* Librarian, Jordan College]

CHARLIE ✦
Genus: Human
Dæmon: Unnamed; form unsettled
World: Lyra's
Background: Gyptian.
Role: This boy claims that in Banbury, a town not far from Oxford, he saw one of the Gobblers take a little boy out of his garden and put him in a white truck before quickly speeding off. He is questioned during the conversations following the disappearance of Billy Costa.
NL/GC 3 *[brief]*

CLERIC ⚲
Genus: Human
Dæmon: Unnamed; form unknown
World: Lyra's
Physical characteristics: Wears dark clothing.
Role: Among those present when a witch is tortured under the supervision of Cardinal Sturrock on board a boat near Svalbard. Comes out to greet Coulter when she arrives on the boat; is surprised Lord Boreal is not with her.
SK 2 *[brief]*

CLIFFORD, SERGEANT ⚲
Genus: Human
World: Will's
Physical characteristics: Well-dressed young woman.
Behavior: Lyra, seeing hardness and distrust in the sergeant's eyes, is not taken in by the woman's initial attempt at friendliness.
Role: Accompanies Inspector Walters to Dr Mary Malone's lab, where Walters questions Lyra. When Lyra runs away from the lab, Malone gets in her visitors' way, and Clifford falls, blocking Walters' exit and giving Lyra a few minutes' advantage.
SK 7

COLE, IGNATIUS ✦
Genus: Human
Dæmon: Musca; form unknown
World: Lyra's
Background: Jordan College Master, 1745-1748.
Role: Buried in crypt where Roger and Lyra play.
NL/GC 3 *[brief]*

COMMISSIONAIRE ❖

Genus: Human
Dæmon: Unnamed; form unknown
World: Lyra's
Role: Lyra's impression is that he is the equivalent at Coulter's apartment building of a college's porter, only he wears a uniform decorated with medals.
Observation: *At the cocktail party, he doubles as a servant.*

NL/GC brief mentions: 4; servant and bouncer for Coulter's party 5

COOPER, DR ❖ ✎

Genus: Human
Dæmon: Unnamed; rabbit
World: Lyra's
Alliances: General Oblation Board and the Consistorial Court of Discipline
Physical characteristics: Although his appearance is not specified, the many references to his nervous personality suggest a man lacking a formidable physical presence.
Background: Experimental theologian.
Behavior: Nervous at Bolvangar; extremely agitated in Geneva. Compliant and submissive to authority, as indicated by his behavior toward Mrs Coulter at Bolvangar and Father MacPhail in Geneva.
Role: Formerly involved in severing children from their dæmons at Bolvangar. Later, in Geneva, he develops a bomb powerful enough to penetrate other worlds.

Quizzed by Coulter at Bolvangar regarding security failings allowing for the liberation of the severed dæmons. Interrogated in Geneva by MacPhail, president of the Consistorial Court of Discipline, about the energy release produced by severing. A prisoner rather than a guest of MacPhail, he is beltless, secured in a white tile room with only a chair, bunk and a bucket, wondering "what new discomfort was coming." He is able to escape further torment (and, according to MacPhail, secure the Authority's forgiveness for not informing the Court about the Oblation Board's activities) by reconstructing experiments in harnessing and using the energy released by severing.

Last seen semi-conscious at the bottom of a flight of stairs. He had been taking a packet containing a lock of Lyra's hair to his lab when Gallivespian Lord Roke stung him. Roke retrieved the packet, but strands were missing.

NL/GC 16

AS given orders by MacPhail 6; explains workings of bomb 24

COOPER, MRS ⚜ ✎

Genus: Human
World: Will's
Physical characteristics: Her advanced age is revealed in her posture. She smells of lavender.
Background: Mrs Cooper taught Will piano when he was younger. She lives alone, but has a daughter in Australia.

Did Dr Cooper Nearly Sever Lyra and Pan?

Cooper is arguably the doctor who directed that Lyra be severed when she was discovered eavesdropping at Bolvangar. Three men are present during the discussion about the missing dæmons. Mrs Coulter addresses only one by name: Dr Cooper, and she seems to give her orders for review of the alarm system directly to him. While he replies to her criticisms "wearily," when she asks about new separation technologies, the one who answers is said to be "relieved" at the change in topic, suggesting that Cooper, although not named, is the lead doctor (the other two men offer only simple interjections). 82 83

When Lyra and Pan are caught, the two men holding them turn to a third, who gives the order that she be severed immediately, and this man's nervous gestures ("The man who seemed to be in charge...tapped his teeth with a thumbnail. His eyes were never still; they flicked and slid and darted this way and that") are similar to those attributed to Cooper in Geneva. 84

However, Dr Cooper's dæmon is identified as a rabbit in THE AMBER SPYGLASS. But when Lyra and Pan are struggling to escape the silver guillotine, the battle is described as being two against six: Lyra and her dæmon, and the three men and theirs: "A badger, an owl, and a baboon." 85 86

Behavior: When Will and his mother arrive unannounced on her doorstep, Mrs Cooper is hesitant to agree to let his mother stay at her home for a few days. However, she is so touched by Will's and his mother's love for each other (and his desperation) that she consents.

Will's intuition that she will be capable and compassionate is confirmed by two alethiometer readings several days apart. Lyra tells Will that the lady taking caring of his mother is "ever so kind. No one knows where your mother is, and the friend won't give her away." 87

Role: Although she is hardly more than an acquaintance, Mrs Cooper is the only person Will knows with whom he can leave his mother while he goes to Oxford. Her acceptance of his odd and awkward request allows Will's journey to begin.

SK 1

> *brief mentions:* Will considers calling 4; alethiometer reports she is treating Elaine kindly 5, 11; 13

AS *brief mentions:* Will considers returning to his world and calling 18; 35; Will recalls day he left his mother with her 38

CORAM, FARDER ❖ ✐

Genus: Human

Dæmon: Sophonax, a large "autumn-colored cat" 88

World: Lyra's, visits mulefa's

Alliances: Asriel, Lyra, and Serafina Pekkala

Physical characteristics: Crippled; needs crutches or "sticks" to walk. His face is "skull-like" and he is beset by "continual trembling." But his voice is "rich and musical" with a range of tones rivaling the colors of his cat dæmon's gorgeous coat, and when Farder Coram laughs, his tremors stop, and his face looks "bright and young." 89 90 91

Background: Gyptian "see-er" (or seer). Saved Serafina Pekkala's life when he was a young man. Serafina bore him a son who died in childhood, leaving Coram heartbroken, but 92 93 only Serafina speaks of this. Their relationship didn't survive the loss of the child, and she had to return to Lake Enara and assume the position of clan-queen when her mother died. However, after their break-up, she helped him when he was wounded by a poisoned arrow in a war with the Skraelings. After this serious injury, Coram devoted himself to study, and has recently kept up with developments regarding the discovery of Rusakov Particles, or Dust, the General Oblation Board's rise to power, Lord Asriel's explorations, and Lyra's upbringing.

> ## Great epidemic
>
> Possibly the epidemic that killed Coram's son was the Asian influenza pandemic of 1957. In England and Wales, this flu killed 6,716, and over 30,000 deaths were attributed to complications such as pneumonia, resulting from the epidemic.

Behavior: Kind and compassionate toward Lyra. He likely was a force to be reckoned with as a young man, but now his physical weakness, coupled with good humor, renders him far more accessible than the commanding John Faa, for example.

Reunited with Lyra in the mulefa's world ("If I had the tongue of an angel, I couldn't tell you how glad I am to set eyes on you again"), he is troubled by the hurt he sees in her eyes. But he is heartened by seeing the window out of the world of the dead, and tells Faa that he wants to talk to Lyra about it, "and learn how it came about, and what it means."

Role: The kindness, support, and sustained attention he shows Lyra is a new experience for this 12-year old girl. His relationship with Serafina Pekkala brings Lyra to the witch's attention, and he works with Lyra as she learns to read the alethiometer.

Proves knowledgeable about mechanics of alethiometer, the meaning of many of its symbols, and state of mind essential for reading it, although he'd seen it used only once before. Familiar with spy-flies from African journeys and with witches' ways. Receptive to help from Witch-Consul Martin Lanselius, armoured bear Iorek Byrnison, and Kaisa, Serafina's dæmon.

Note: *In* Northern Lights *(but not in* The Golden Compass*), Farder Coram enters the fray when the gyptians and witches attack Bolvangar, searching for Lyra, "casting around anxiously, leaning on his stick, his autumn-coloured dæmon leaping through the snow and looking this way and that." Lyra is already in Scoresby's balloon. She calls down to him, and he cries back, "You're safe, gal? You're safe?". She reassures him, and he calls up until the balloon is too far away for her to hear, "Go well, my child—go well—go well, my dear—."*

NL/GC 7, 8; and alethiometer, spy flies 9; history with Serafina Pekkala, visits Lanselius, meets Iorek 10; with Kaisa 11; 13, 17; Serafina on 18
> *brief mentions:* 12, 14, 21, 23

AS 38
> *brief mentions:* 23, 37

Costa, Billy ✥

Genus: Human
Dæmon: Unnamed; form unsettled
World: Lyra's
Physical characteristics: Likely the same age as Lyra and Roger because they all get along well together; his dæmon is still changing. Sharp-eyed with good night vision, he leads the children away from Bolvangar the night of the break-out.
Background: Gyptian Gobbler victim abducted during a Jericho Horse Fair; son of Ma

Costa, brother of Tony, and an Oxford playmate of Lyra's and Roger's.

Behavior: Readily accepts orders from Lyra at Bolvangar but likely was less compliant in Jericho as a member of the prominent gyptian family from whom Lyra once captured a narrow boat.

Role: The discussion about his abduction is the first time Lyra hears about the Gobblers' arrival in Oxford and is one of the events mobilizing John Faa's group of gyptians to action.

At Bolvangar when Lyra arrives. Stands guard with Roger while Lyra and Kaisa take advantage of a fire drill to release the separated dæmons who have been stored in cages stacked in a shed.

Reunited with his brother Tony when the gyptians liberate the Station's prisoners.

NL/GC 3, 6; 7 *[brief]*; Lyra sees at Bolvangar, stands guard while Lyra and Kaisa release caged dæmons 15; reunited with gyptians 17

Costa family ❖ ✐ *LS*

Genus: Human

World: Lyra's

Alliances: extended family, Eastern Anglia gyptians, Asriel, Lyra

Background: Gyptians. Part of the Stefanski family, one of the six families under Faa's leadership, they keep an eye on Lyra during their visits to Oxford. Lyra could have been raised as a Costa. Ma Costa and Asriel wished the Costas to assume guardianship following Asriel's trial for the death of Edward Coulter, after which Lyra was removed from his custody.

The Costa family offered Lyra refuge aboard their narrow-boat

Their prosperity is evident in the quality of their boat. In happier times, Lyra and her gang enjoyed an ongoing feud with them, culminating in Lyra briefly capturing their boat, an incident that will initially worry her when she meets John Faa—she expects to be chastised, but finds him amused.

Role: By chance, they rescue Lyra in London; by choice and with considerable risk to themselves, they hide her aboard their boat.

Costa family members are among those who undertake the rescue mission to Bolvangar.

[*See also* **Costa, Billy; Costa, Ma;** *and* **Costa, Tony**]

NL/GC boat incident described, Billy goes missing 3; in Fens 7; *LS* Lantern Slide 8
brief mentions: 6, 8

Costa, Ma ❖ ✐

Genus: Human

Dæmon: Unnamed; hawk

World: Lyra's

Alliances: extended family, Eastern Anglia gyptians, Asriel, Lyra

Physical characteristics: Grey-haired woman with "lungs of brass and leather" and "hands

Red-Tailed Hawk

98

99 like bludgeons"; strong enough to deliver a "mighty blow" to a horse trader.

Background: Gyptian. Matriarch of the Costa family. Nursed Lyra as infant but never talked with her about it until after Faa told Lyra about Coulter and Asriel. After Asriel lost all his possessions and Coulter abandoned Lyra, Ma asked the Court to let her adopt or foster Lyra but was refused.

Behavior: Tough but kind. Fiercely protective of her children. Seeing her angry, Lyra warns her friends to stay out of the way or risk a smack. However, for all her strength, she leaves the room when Tony's talk turns to speculations on what happens to kids taken by the Gobblers.

Role: Among her children is Billy, who was stolen by Gobblers. Her anxiety over his whereabouts when he had been missing for just a few hours causes Lyra to recognize that something unusual was happening in Oxford.

100
101 **Note:** *In* Northern Lights, *Ma's dæmon is a hawk—and a large dog. In* The Golden Compass, *he is always a hawk, but a curious passage recalls his spell as a dog: "her dæmon,*
102 *a hawk, bent gently to lick Pantalaimon's wildcat head." In the* **10**th *anniversary edition of* Northern Lights *Ma's dæmon is a hawk both times he is mentioned, who "crooned a quick*
103 *welcome to Pantalaimon."*

NL/GC reacts to Billy's disappearance 3; on narrowboat in London 6; cares for Lyra in Fens 7; tells Lyra about being her nursemaid 8
    brief mentions: 9, 20

AS   23 *[brief]*

Costa, Tony ✣ *LS*

Genus: Human

Dæmon: Unnamed; hawk

World: Lyra's

Alliances: extended family, Eastern Anglia gyptians, Lyra

Physical Characteristics: Favors leather jackets and multiple silver rings; slicks back his hair before going out drinking for the evening.

Background: Gyptian. Billy's older brother.

Behavior: Less gloomy and more at ease the further he gets from London and the more deeply into the Fens. Fond of telling tall tales about creatures of Northern forests, Tartars, and armoured bears.

Role: Rescues Lyra from net-throwing Turk traders (who Tony assumed were Gobblers) the night Lyra flees Coulter's party. Shoots an arrow into one Turk's neck. He and several other gyptians were in London hoping to capture Gobblers in the act of abducting children so that they could force them to tell where they have taken the children they steal, including Tony's brother, Billy. Takes Lyra to hide on his family's boat when he learns that she is on the run from Mrs Coulter, who is deeply involved with the Gobblers, or General Oblation Board.

    Active in liberation of Bolvangar, the General Oblation Board's Experiment Station.

Observation: *There is no mention of Ma Costa's husband or Billy's and Tony's father. While Ma is a formidable figure, Tony seems to fill the role of head of the family on those occasions when a man is required.*

NL/GC rescues Lyra in London 6; in Fens 7; *LS* Lantern Slide 8
    brief mentions: 8, 9, 11, 12, 17, 21

COULTER, EDWARD ❖

Genus: Human

Dæmon: Unnamed; form unknown

World: Lyra's

Background: Politician, adviser to king; husband of Mrs Coulter. Stormed Asriel's home in search of Lyra, the infant child of his wife and Asriel. Killed, in self-defense, by Asriel.

Role: The results of his death included Asriel's loss of all money and property, and the infant Lyra's placement first in a priory and then at Jordan College.

NL/GC Faa on 7; Ma Costa on 8

COULTER, MRS MARISA ❖ ⚕ ✎ LS

Genus: Human

Dæmon: Golden monkey; Unnamed

World: Lyra's, Will's, Cittàgazze, Asriel's republic, Authority's kingdom (Clouded Mountain), the abyss

Alliances: The church, General Oblation Board, her self-interests

Physical characteristics: Thirty-five years old when she dies. A "beautiful young lady" with "sleek black hair" likely cut shoulder-length since it "framed her cheeks" and a "gentle musical voice" (to Will it is "intoxicating: soothing, sweet, musical, and young, too"), she is first seen wearing a "yellow-red fox-fur" and holding a "jewelled breviary." When Will sees her at Sir Charles Latrom's, he is shocked by how beautiful she is, "lovely in the moonlight, her brilliant dark eyes wide with enchantment, her slender shape light and graceful." [104] [105] [106] [107] [108] [109]

Seems to possess a strong sexual magnetism, and fully exploits the power this confers, using it to attempt, usually successfully, to get her way with everyone from Lord Boreal/Latrom to King Ogunwe to a Swiss Guard to Will, culminating with the Authority's Regent, Metatron.

Lyra noticed the "metallic" smell of Coulter's skin when angered, detectable under a veil of perfume. Coulter seems "charged with some kind of anbaric force" and smells of "heated metal." [110] [111]

Background: Generally referred to as Mrs Coulter, the first use of her given name, "Marisa," is by Asriel as they stand before the bridge to the world beyond the Aurora.

Widow of Edward Coulter, adulterous lover of Asriel, and mother of Lyra. Member of St Sophia's College, Oxford, but works in London where she lives in a "pretty" and "charming" apartment in an exclusive area and seems to know only powerful or fashionable people, whose conversation is limited to discussing others like themselves. [112]

Not as highly born as Asriel but "ambitious for power," which Asriel says she first tried to gain through marriage and then through the Church. A member of the Royal Arctic Institute, a rare distinction for a woman. Claims to have spent three months in Greenland studying the Aurora. Visited Svalbard, where she promised the new bear king Iofur Raknison (whose position she may have helped him secure) that she would gain his baptism if he kept Asriel prisoner on the island and allowed her to set up another Bolvangar-type station. Has also traveled in Africa. There, she was intrigued by *zombis* and came up with the idea of intercision, and likely attained the spy flies that she sends after Lyra when the girl runs away from London. Able to be further separated than [113] normal from her dæmon, an ability she shares with witches and shamans.

The Master of Jordan College tells Lyra the woman was widowed when her husband, Edward Coulter, a rising politician, died an accidental death. Gyptian king John Faa, revealing to Lyra the truth of her parentage, tells a different story. According to Faa, she planned to disown Lyra and tell her husband their baby had died because she feared she'd be unable to convince Mr Coulter that Asriel's child was his, and then "turned her back" on Lyra when Mr Coulter was killed and Asriel disgraced. This was a relief to Lyra's gyptian nursemaid Ma Costa, who had feared Mrs Coulter would mistreat the baby.

When Asriel left Lyra in the care of the Jordan College Master, her father's one condition was that the Master never allow Coulter near Lyra. Faa speculates that she must have something on the Master for him to break his word to Asriel. He not only lets her see the child, but allows her to take Lyra away. Although Lyra seemed to think, before he killed Roger, that one day she would be able to accept Asriel as her father, she could never imagine coming to terms with Coulter as her mother. Similarly, Coulter tells Asriel that Lyra is "more yours than mine." Asriel doesn't neglect using this remark later to provoke Coulter, reminding the woman that twice she tried to take hold of her daughter, and twice she ran away, and if he were Lyra, if caught by Coulter again, he too would flee once more.

Behavior: On first meeting Mrs Coulter, the children who become her abductees perceive her as "angelic," "gracious and sweet and kind" when she asks them for their "help"; as one of her party guests asks, "what child could resist her?" But once in Bolvangar, the General Oblation Board's Experiment Station, her young victims speculate in her absence that she likes watching children being killed; and at just the sight of her in the complex, "a little shiver ran almost instantaneously through the whole canteen, and every child was still and silent."

Like these children, Lyra initially considered her "the most wonderful person" she had "ever met," and is enticed by the "kind and wise" lady's enchanting stories about the North and her travels. Later, Lyra finds it "nowhere near so easy" to believe Coulter is her mother as she does Asriel her father, especially given Pan's hatred of Coulter's dæmon.

Even the Bolvangar Experiment Station scientists consider Mrs Coulter's attitude toward intercisions—she seems to enjoy watching them—to be "ghoulish."

Trying to learn of the witches' prophecy regarding Lyra, Coulter personally continues the torture of a captured witch, breaking her prisoner's fingers, one by one.

In Cittàgazze, the witch Lena Feldt feels (as she spies on Coulter) that the woman "had more force in her soul than anyone she had ever seen," and is not surprised that Coulter can manipulate even the Spectres. As Lyra tells Will, "*she* wouldn't be afraid of Spectres… she's so ruthless and cruel, she could boss them… She could command them like she does people and they'd have to obey her, I bet. Lord Boreal is strong and clever, but she'll have him doing what she wants in no time." And Lyra is right on both counts. Most people are intimidated by Coulter. She alone understands the psychology of Spectres—namely, that if she can show them 20 witches to destroy, they will leave her alive and functioning.

Of a dozen clerics on board a boat off the coast of Svalbard, only the Cardinal will stand up to her. She treats servants and those of lesser social standing with undisguised contempt. One measure of the change Coulter begins to undergo following her near-intercision in the Alps is her courtesy to the orderly who serves her coffee in Asriel's adamant tower.

Danger excites her. With a battle raging all around the cave in the Himalayas and the subtle knife broken, Coulter exalts in the power she feels she has gained over Will, and is "full of joy and life and energy." She steals Asriel's intention craft from his armoury, knowing fully well that he could easily shoot her down. In her interview with Fr MacPhail in Geneva, she knows it is dangerous to call the Authority senile and decrepit, and obsolete, but she can't stop herself, so "intoxicating" does she find tormenting the priest. [126]

When THE AMBER SPYGLASS opens, Mrs Coulter is keeping Lyra in a drugged sleep. She slaps the wakening Lyra viciously when the girl resists drinking the sleeping potion. But once the girl is again immobilized, Coulter engages in a bizarre imitation of mothering, "crooning baby-songs." She cuts a bit of Lyra's hair to place in a locket necklace as a keepsake, a rare act of sentimentality on her part and one that nearly results in Coulter's intercision, Will and Lyra's death, and (by extension) Metatron's victory.

In the Himalayas, when the village child Ama asks if there is someone else with her in the cave Coulter is occupying, "A novel answer occurred to Mrs Coulter… She could tell the truth. Not all of it, naturally, but some. She felt a little quiver of laughter at the idea." Asriel feels "she lied in the very marrow of her bones." Her expertise as a liar is [127] [128] proven when she passes the ultimate test—she succeeds in lying to an angel, convincing Metatron that Asriel has Lyra's dæmon.

Will has to struggle with his knowledge of her cruelty and Coulter's appeal as "a more complicated and richer and deeper Lyra." She homes in on Will's greatest vulnerability [129] when she suggests that his mother would act as she has and do anything to protect her child. Will is uncertain whether Coulter was "monstrously clever" to make such a comparison or just lucky. What exactly she was intending to do when she went to the Himalayas—to save Lyra or to bide her time to deliver her as a prize to the church—is unclear.

When Coulter addresses Asriel's three commanders, she aims most of her emotional display at the only human among the three, King Ogunwe, knowing the effect she has on men. The Gallivespian spy Captain Lord Roke "sensed in her a nature as close to that of a scorpion as he had ever encountered." [130]

Metatron's analysis of Coulter as "a cess-pit of moral filth" lists as evidence her "corruption and envy and lust for power," along with a "pure, poisonous, toxic malice" [131] and a total lack of mercy or empathy or even shame; "what he saw in her would be insufficient" to convince him that she would not betray her own child. However, when [132] she has a few last moments alone with Asriel, Coulter claims to have surprised herself by finding that she loves Lyra "so much my heart is bursting with it." [133]

Role: Lyra's mother. By creating the General Oblation Board (and directing its abduction of children to the Bolvangar Experiment Station where they are subjected to intercision), and by exiling Asriel to Svalbard (the ideal site for his scheme to break a passage through the Aurora to a new world), Mrs Coulter sets in motion the conflicts fueling HIS DARK MATERIALS. She also helps settle them when, with Asriel, she wrestles the Authority's Regent, Metatron, into the abyss.

Chapter 24 of THE AMBER SPYGLASS is titled "Mrs Coulter in Geneva."

Update: The fifth Lantern Slide in NORTHERN LIGHTS notes that Mrs. Coulter chose her lovers for their "power and influence" and felt no affection toward any of them.

Observation: *An advertisement of their publications by Smith and Strange, Ltd., found on the back of the map in* LYRA'S OXFORD, *reveals another dimension to Marisa Coulter: she is the author of* The Bronze Clocks of Benin.

NL/GC abducts Tony in Limehouse, meets Lyra in Oxford 3; Lyra falls under her spell, agrees to live in London 4; Lyra's attraction to Coulter wanes, culminating at cocktail party 5; Lyra tells gyptians of Coulter's link to Gobblers 6; revealed by Faa as Lyra's mother 7; her spy flies attack Lyra 9; meets with Bolvangar doctors 16; at Bolvangar with Lyra after thwarting intercision, attacked by own spy flies 17; Santelia on, Lyra and Raknison discuss 19; bear counselors on her schemes 20; Asriel on 21; her troops attack bears 22; with Asriel at his bridge, first use of Marisa 23; $\boxed{LS}$ Lantern Slide 5

> *brief mentions:* 8, 10, 13; Lyra's roommates on 14; 15, 18

SK   tortures witch 2; converses with Latrom 9; kills Latrom, sets Spectres on Feldt and zombis on witches guarding Lyra 15

> *brief mentions:* 4, 5, 7, 11, 13

AS   in Himalayan hide-out 1; Baruch searches for, finds where she is hiding Lyra 2; Ama witnesses her cruelty 4; discussed by Consistorial Court 6; Will is enchanted, tormented by 11; battle at cave, stand off with spies 12; stung by Tialys, loses Lyra 13; prisoner in Asriel's tower, pleads case before his commanders, tours armoury, steals intention craft 16; MacPhail's prisoner in Geneva 24; faces intercision at bomb launch site, rescued by Asriel 25; at rest in Asriel's tower, considers future, her age revealed as thirty-five 28; pilots intention craft to Clouded Mountain, gets Metatron to follow her to edge of abyss 30; farewell with Asriel, descends into the abyss taking Metatron with her 31; $\boxed{LS}$ Lantern Slide 8

> *brief mentions:* Roger speaks of in Lyra's dream [between 3 & 4]; 5, 9; Will lets Lyra believe her mother kindly took care of her in cave 14; 15, 18, 23, 35; Serafina breaks arrow reserved for her 36; 37, 38

COUSINS ✦ ✏

Genus: Human

Dæmon: Unnamed; form unknown

World: Lyra's

Role: Jordan College's Master's manservant, and "an old enemy of Lyra's."

When, upon her return to Jordan, he greets her "warmly" with "affection in his voice," Lyra, surprised, thinks, "Well, he *had* changed."

Observation: *Or is it Lyra who has changed? If the tone is ironic, perhaps the sentence should appear as "Well,* he *had changed."*

NL/GC brief mentions: 3, 4

AS 38 [brief]

CRAFTSMAN (MULEFA) ✏

Genus: Mulefa

World: Mulefa's

Behavior: Intrigued by Mary Malone's interest in making a solid sheet of the lacquer the mulefa use to strengthen and polish wood. A good teacher, suggesting alternative approaches to problems, for example, using an acid, rather than a knife, to peel off the wood backing that Mary needed when she began painting the layers of lacquer.

Role: Teaches Mary how to handle the sap-lacquer the mulefa use as a varnish, and that she will fashion into lenses for the amber spyglass.

AS 17 [brief]

CUSTOMS OFFICERS, SUBURBS OF THE WORLD OF THE DEAD ✏

Genus: Human form; status between living and dead is unspecified (but Lyra and Will, who have by this time seen many ghosts, know that they are not ghosts)

World: Suburbs of the world of the dead

Physical characteristics: The first official the travelers meet is described as a thin, nondescript man, age not readily apparent, in "a drab and tattered business suit" 136 clutching papers; the second is similarly dressed and bland.

Behavior: While the first of these men seems simply weary and reticent, the second speaks to Lyra and Will in a manner described as "not unkindly."

Role: Directs Will and Lyra away from the ghosts with whom they've arrived, telling them they have to go to a holding area where those who reach these suburbs by mistake must stay until they die. Gives them papers (written on which are meaningless words) for the official at the gate, who offers no new information.

AS 19 *[brief]*

"Dada" 🖊

Genus: Human

Dæmon: Unnamed; crow

World: Lyra's

Background: Herdsman father of Ama, the little girl who brings food to Mrs Coulter when she hides with Lyra in the cave in the Himalayas.

Role: Waits patiently some distance back from her cave (out of respect for Mrs Coulter's claim that she is a holy woman who has vowed to speak with no men) while Ama visits with the woman and her sleeping daughter.

AS brief mentions: 1, 4

Dean, Jordan College ✦

Genus: Human

Dæmon: Unnamed; form unknown

World: Lyra's

Background: Jordan College scholar.

Behavior: Offended by Asriel's display of what he claims is Stanislaus Grumman's head. The Dean derides his fellow Jordan College Scholar when Trelawney, the Palmerian Professor, says that the new king of the armoured bears, Iofur Raknison, wants a dæmon. Contemptuous when Asriel claims to have a photogram showing a city in another world behind the Aurora.

Role: Present during Asriel's Retiring Room presentation about his journey North.

NL/GC 2

Deputy Director, Imperial Muscovite Academy Observatory ⚷

Genus: Human

Dæmon: Unnamed; form unknown

World: Lyra's

Role: When aëronaut Lee Scoresby visits the observatory on Nova Zembla seeking information about the shaman Stanislaus Grumman, this Deputy Director recalls meeting Grumman at the Imperial German Academy in Berlin. He counters the

Observatory Director's claim that Grumman is an Englishman with his own opinion that Grumman is German.

SK 6 *[brief]*

De Ruyter, Benjamin ❖

Genus: Human
Dæmon: Unnamed; form unknown, but has to be some type of bird or perhaps a flying insect
World: Lyra's
Background: Gyptian. Head of one of the six families of Faa's group. In charge of spying and intelligence for voyage North.
Role: Subject of one of Lyra's first alethiometer readings, which, although she didn't realize it at the time, announced de Ruyter's death before the news was delivered by one of the man's companions that he had been killed in the headquarters of the General Oblation Board, Ministry of Theology, London.

NL/GC 8 *[brief]*, death 9

Dick ❖ Ⓛⓢ

Genus: Human
Dæmon: Unnamed; form unknown
World: Lyra's
Role: Sixteen-year-old acquaintance of Lyra's in Oxford, possibly connected to the college next to Jordan, St Michael's College. Hangs out near its gates.
Update: The sixth Lantern Slide in *Northern Lights* provides this boy, whose expertise in spitting so impressed Lyra, a last name: Orchard, as well as the distinction of being Lyra's first crush.

NL/GC 3 *[brief]*, Ⓛⓢ Lantern Slide 6

Director, Imperial Muscovite Academy Observatory ⚕

Genus: Human
Dæmon: Unnamed; form unknown
World: Lyra's
Role: Contributes to aëronaut Lee Scoresby's store of knowledge regarding Stanislaus Grumman. When Scoresby explains he is seeking information about the shaman scientist Grumman, the director says he met Grumman seven years previously, and believes he is an English geologist; on these two points, his colleagues object, one claiming Grumman to be German, and one, a paleo-archaeologist.

SK 6; his claim that Grumman is English confirmed 10 *[brief]*

Docker, Professor ❖

Genus: Human
Dæmon: Unnamed; cat
World: Lyra's

Physical characteristics: Middle-aged, looks like a scholar to Lyra.

Behavior: Indiscreet; tells a journalist during a party at Mrs Coulter's of Coulter's involvement with the General Oblation Board. Tries to get Lyra (who thinks he might be drunk) out of his way by suggesting the girl go chat with Lord Boreal so that he can continue his pursuit of the journalist Adele Starminster.

Role: Trying to impress a young woman journalist at Mrs Coulter's cocktail party, he tells her about Rusakov Particles or Dust, the General Oblation Board, why it's commonly known as the Gobblers, and Mrs Coulter's involvement with the Board. He speculates that Lyra knows all about the Board, but is "safe" from it herself.

Last seen being discreetly but decisively removed from Coulter's party by two men.

NL/GC 5

137

DOCTOR AT BOLVANGAR (FIRST) ❖

Genus: Human
Dæmon: Unnamed; marmot
World: Lyra's
Physical characteristics: His voice reminds Lyra of a Jordan College Scholar's. She notes that in his coal-silk coat, he is not as well equipped for the cold as she is in her furs.

Marmot

Bill Hickey, U.S. Fish and Wildlife Service, Jan 2002

Behavior: Asks Lyra what she was doing in the area. After she tells a story claiming to have been with her father until they were attacked, he begins to try to convince her not to trust her own memory. The story he wants Lyra to believe is that she had been separated accidentally from her father, and kindly Samoyeds brought her to the Station, where any day now her father will come looking for her. He tells her she witnessed no fighting, and that what she thinks she remembers is just a bad dream, an effect of the cold.

Role: This doctor is the one who buys Lyra off the Samoyeds once he is sure her dæmon is still changing.

NL/GC 14

DOCTOR AT BOLVANGAR (SECOND) ❖

Genus: Human
Dæmon: Unnamed; moth
World: Lyra's
Role: Becomes "agitated" when, during a physical examination routinely performed at the Experiment Station, Lyra asks why he cuts away children's dæmons. He denies he has any idea what she is talking about.

Polyphemus Moth

James Leupold, U.S. Fish and Wildlife Service, Nov 2001

NL/GC 15

DOCTORS AT BOLVANGAR (THREE WHO NEARLY SEVER LYRA) ❖

Genus: Human
Dæmon: Unnamed; baboon, badger, owl
World: Lyra's
Role: Mrs Coulter reviews with three doctors the security breach of the shed housing

severed dæmons, the performance of the silver guillotine, and Lord Asriel's death sentence, a conversation that makes clear the purpose of the Station, as Lyra eavesdrops from a ceiling's crawlspace. After Coulter leaves, the doctors discuss her eagerness to watch intercisions, and Lyra is so distressed that she can't stifle a gasp. One of these doctors, a mustached and freckled man, exposes Lyra hiding in the ceiling panels and holds onto her even when she bites his arm hard enough to draw blood. A second grabs Pantalaimon, violating a strict taboo. All are uneasy about what Lyra has heard, and the third gives the order that she be immediately intercised.

Olive Baboon

Gary M. Stolz, U.S. Fish and Wildlife Service, Dec 2001

Note: *One of these three is very likely Dr Cooper* [see].

NL/GC 16

Eisarson, Søren ✦

Genus: Armoured bear
World: Lyra's
Alliances: Counselor to Iorek Byrnison
Physical characteristics: Elderly
Background: Out of favor during Raknison's reign because he was unsympathetic to Raknison's plan to let Coulter build an experiment station on Svalbard. He foresaw a time when the armoured bears would be reduced to being Coulter's lackeys.
Behavior: Stayed loyal to Byrnison during the true king's exile.
Role: He updates newly restored King Iorek Byrnison about the reign of the vanquished Iofur Raknison, particularly the dead usurper's susceptibility to Coulter, who planned to build on Svalbard another Bolvangar—"only worse." Also relates his own involvement in "negotiating with Lord Asriel about the terms of his [Asriel's] imprisonment."

NL/GC brief mentions: 20, 21

Enoch ✑

Genus: Human
World: Will's
Alliances: Authority
Physical characteristics: Lived sixty-five years.
Background: Before Metatron was an angel, he was a man, Enoch, and his brother was Baruch, whom he later disowned. When Asriel relates his history, which he says is found in the "apocryphal scriptures," he says little more than that Enoch was six generations from Adam. The Authority made him into the angel Metatron when he died, and he later served the Authority as Regent.
Behavior: Was "lover of flesh."
Role: During Metatron's earthly existence as Enoch one of his siblings was Baruch, who, at death, was also made an angel; this fraternal connection is used by Baruch to learn of Metatron's plans. [*See also* **Metatron**]

AS   brief mentions: Baruch on 5, Asriel on 28, Metatron on 30

Enoch becomes Metatron

In Will's world, there are several passages in the Bible forming the basis for the belief that Enoch became an angel at death: "And he walked with God, and was seen no more: because God took him" (Genesis 5:24) and "By faith Enoch was translated, that he should not see death" (Hebrews 11:5).

When Asriel mentions the "apocryphal scripture," he is referring to materials that also exist in Will's world, the three Books of Enoch. These were fairly well known until about the 4th century AD, when they fell out of favor and just fragments were assumed to have survived, until the 18th century when several scrolls were found, and over the past two centuries others have surfaced.

One of the curious things that Metatron says to Mrs Coulter about his time as Enoch is "I understood it when the sons of heaven fell in love with the daughters of earth, and I pleaded their cause with the Authority."

In Will's world, the Biblical basis for this is likely Genesis 6:2: "The sons of God seeing the daughters of men, that they were fair, took to themselves wives of all they chose." The *Books of Enoch* expand on this story about angels who descended to earth and married human women. Their children were giants. In some versions of the story, the giants' appetites could not be controlled and violence and cannibalism were the outcome. In another, these angels, whom Enoch called "Watchers," shared angelic knowledge and secrets with humans, thus enraging God. The giants' (or the Watchers') and women's children were eliminated by The Flood, along with the rest of humanity irredeemably corrupted, having failed to heed the warnings God passed to them through his prophet Enoch.

Another apocryphal text, the *Book of Jubilees*, says that Enoch was the first man to learn the art of writing. He was instructed by angels and recorded their secrets of astronomy, time, and history.

142

ENQUIRER ✧

Genus: Human
Dæmon: Unnamed; form unknown, but may be a snake
World: Lyra's
Background: Jordan College Scholar
Role: One of the quieter Scholars present during Asriel's Retiring Room seminar, he is an "enquirer" who asks no questions.
Observation: *A curious description of the Enquirer: "His dæmon was at the time coiled around his neck in the form of a snake" (NL 21/GC 22) suggests that Pullman initially considered allowing adults' dæmons to be capable of changing forms.*

NL/GC 2 [brief]

FAA, LORD JOHN ✧ ⚲ ✎

Genus: Human
Dæmon: Unnamed; crow
World: Lyra's; visits Mulefa's and Cittàgazze
Alliances: Gyptians, Asriel, Lyra
Physical characteristics: In his seventies, "tall and bull-necked and powerful."
Background: King of Eastern Anglia gyptians.

Crow

U.S. Fish and Wildlife Service, Feb 2002

143

Behavior: The power of his presence reminds Lyra of Asriel and the Master of Jordan. Although
144 he treats her "very gently," at their first meeting Lyra "was afraid of John Faa, and what she was
145 most afraid of was his kindness." He is firm in his opinions as he leads his people toward a decision, but their willingness to raise questions or offer contrary opinions suggests a history of tolerance for others' views. No stranger to battle, he advises the gyptians who want vengeance against the Gobblers that they need to take care not to let their emotions rule their actions, and to keep the goal of rescuing the children clearly in mind. He is all for punishing those who have harmed his people, but stresses delaying satisfaction of that impulse until the children are safe. His consideration of alternative explanations for the recent unusual behavior of the Jordan College Master also suggests an open and analytical mind. Will is impressed by Faa's "power tempered by courtesy, and he thought that it would be a good way
146 to behave when he himself was old; John Faa was a shelter and a strong refuge."

Role: Ensures Lyra's safety from Coulter and others on her trail, tells her of her parentage, and organizes the gyptians' rescue mission to Bolvangar.

When shown the window out of the world of the dead, Lord Faa says, "To know that after a spell in the dark we'll come out again to a sweet land like this, to be free of the sky
147 like the birds, well, that's the greatest promise anyone could wish for."

The title of chapter 10 of NORTHERN LIGHTS/THE GOLDEN COMPASS is "John Faa."

Facts: *Johnnie Faa was the name of a gypsy king during the reign of James V in the 1540s. A century later, Sir John Faa of Dunbar found his way into folk legends when he tried to elope with a Countess. Their romantic adventure ended with Faa hanged and the Earl imprisoning his wife for the rest of her life.*

NL/GC at Roping, with Lyra 7; at second Roping 8; relents, lets Lyra join rescuers under Coram's care 9; employs Scoresby 10, Kaisa addresses 11; leads gyptians inland 12, 13; injured by Samoyeds 14; at Bolvangar 17
brief mentions: 6, 15, 18, 21

SK 10 *[brief]*

AS in world of mulefa 36
brief mentions: 3, 15, 35

FELDT, LENA

Genus: Witch
Dæmon: Unnamed; snow bunting
World: Lyra's
Alliances: Serafina Pekkala's Lake Enara witch clan
Background: Among Pekkala's group at Bolvangar rescue.
Role: Betrays Lyra's and Will's location and confesses the witches' name for Lyra. Her attempt to exchange information for her dæmon's release from Spectres under Coulter's control is futile.

She is eager to kill Coulter in Cittàgazze, but curious too about what Coulter is telling the man with her. Mistakenly believes herself safe from Coulter's notice by means of a spell of invisibility. Coulter makes it clear she was never fooled, and instigates the witch's dæmon's torture by a Spectre. As soon as she has the information from Feldt that she wants, Coulter directs the Spectres to attack.

SK killed by Spectres 15

AS *brief mentions:* corpse seen 2; Coulter recalls 16

FIORELLI, JOHNNY ◈

Genus: Human
Dæmon: Unnamed; form unknown
World: Lyra's
Background: Attends gyptian horse fairs.
Role: Possibly the same man as the horse trader Ma Costa walloped that day, when her inquiries into Billy's whereabouts brought a complaint about the boy running off when he should have been working. A number of children last saw Billy Costa tending Fiorelli's horse during the Jericho Horse Fair.

NL/GC 3 *[brief]*

FRA PAVEL RAŠEK [*See* Pavel, Fra (Rašek)]

GHOST BOY FROM WILL'S WORLD ✐

Genus: Ghost
World: World of the dead
Physical characteristics: Thin, around 12 years old.
Role: Will asks if any ghosts from his world (where people don't have dæmons) are in the crowd, and the answers from this boy recalls what Will has learned earlier that day. The ghost had lived with no knowledge of his dæmon, but after his death knew fully well what it felt like not to have one.

AS   22 *[brief]*

GHOST GIRL ✐

Genus: Ghost
World: World of the dead
Physical characteristics: About 9 or 10 years old. Like all ghosts, she can't speak above a whisper.
Role: The ghost of a little girl, a few years younger than Lyra and Will, is the first to speak to the travelers. She is concerned about the scratch on Lyra's head, and tells Lyra that the harpies do worse things than physically assault the ghosts, but she won't elaborate. She is curious about why Lyra and Will are looking for Roger. Satisfied with the explanations, she then leads the way further into the masses of ghosts.

AS   22

GHOST GIRL 2 ✐

Genus: Ghost
World: World of the dead
Role: When the ghost children's talk turns to dæmons, this child says that when she was alive she knew her death but not her dæmon. She once thought that her "death" was the same thing as the dæmons the other ghosts were missing and wonders what will happen to her without her death.

AS   22 *[brief]*

148 **GHOST OF OLD WOMAN** ✎

Genus: Ghost

World: Mulefa's world, world of the dead

Role: On emerging from the world of the dead, but before dissipating, this ghost stops to tell Mary Malone, "Tell them stories. They need the truth. You must tell them true stories and everything will be well." While the ghost means for Mary to tell true stories to the harpies when she enters the world of the dead, Mary interprets her words to mean that it is time to tell Will and Lyra the truth about why she left the Church.

AS   32 [brief]

Gary M. Stolz, U.S. Fish and Wildlife Service, Dec 2001

Vervet Monkey

GOLDEN MONKEY ✦ ⚘ ✎

Genus: Dæmon

Form: Monkey

Human: Mrs Coulter

World: Lyra's

Physical characteristics: He has the "form of a monkey, but no ordinary monkey: his fur is
149
150
151 long and silky and of the most deep and lustrous gold," "each hair seeming to be made of
152 pure gold"; with a "gold-fringed black face." His hands are variously described as black,
153
154 "black horny hands," or "a small furry golden hand with black fingernails" and "his nails
155
156 perfect horny claws" on "hard black fingers."

Behavior: Cruel, even sadistic.   When Lyra defies Coulter, the monkey tortures
157 Pantalaimon with "a cold curious force that was horrifying to see and even worse to feel."
And even at first glance his meanness is obvious to Will: "The golden monkey's teeth were bared, his eyes glaring, and such a concentrated malevolence blazed from him that Will
158 felt it almost like a spear."

In Svalbard, Coulter and Asriel's passion, which seemed to Lyra "more like cruelty than love" is reflected in their dæmons' behavior, "the snow leopard tense, crouching with her claws just pressing in the golden monkey's flesh, and the monkey relaxed, blissful,
159 swooning on the snow."   At the Cittàgazze campsite, the monkey behaves seductively toward Boreal/Latrom's serpent dæmon as Coulter works on the human; when the dæmon dies as her victim succumbs to Coulter's poison, the monkey disdainfully shakes off the fainting serpent he was stroking moments earlier.

Contemptuous of Coulter's decision to hide with Lyra in the Himalayan cave, he passes the time by tearing the wings off live bats. When he tries the same with the Gallivespian Salmakia's arms, he is thwarted due to her associate Tialys poised and ready to spur Coulter's neck with a debilitating poison.

Like a witch's dæmon, physically he can be much further than normal from his human.

Role: In spite of her apparent grace, beauty, and charm, the depths of ugliness and deceit in Coulter's character are made manifest in the monkey's actions and responses he evokes.

The golden monkey is first seen snatching Tony Makarios' dæmon as Coulter lures the boy to the Gobblers. His ability to be separate from Coulter allows him to sneak about, seeking out people's secrets for his person. In London, Lyra worried that he knew about the alethiometer, and later at Bolvangar, even as Lyra is recovering from nearly being severed from Pan, he violates the taboo about a dæmon never touching a person

Philip Pullman on the golden monkey:

"The golden monkey doesn't have a name because every time I tried to think of one, he snarled and frightened me. What's more he hardly speaks either."

not his own as he searches Lyra's body for the alethiometer.

At Saint-Jean-Les-Eaux, where President MacPhail plans to separate the golden monkey from Coulter for the energy their intercision would release, the monkey and Coulter manage to escape. He goes to the aid of Lord Roke when the Gallivespian breaks a leg but has to leave him when a witch attacks Coulter. The golden monkey enters the resonating chamber and seizes the lock of Lyra's hair destined to guide the bomb—but one strand eludes him.

In the battle with Metatron on the edge of the abyss, the golden monkey first tears at one of the angel's wings, then bites his hand as Metatron hoists a rock to deliver a fatal blow to Asriel. The monkey holds tight "with teeth, claws, and tail" as Coulter tries unsuccessfully to block Metatron from raising a wing. Finally, the golden monkey, still pulling Metatron's hair, meets his end when Coulter throws herself against their enemy, joining her lover and her dæmon, plunging all into the abyss together. 160

The golden monkey is the subject of the woodcut for chapter 9 of *The Subtle Knife*, "Theft."

Observation: *While many very minor, single-appearance dæmons are named, Mrs Coulter's never is, and is referred to simply as "the golden monkey" or "the monkey," in lowercase in both UK and US editions.*

NL/GC working with Coulter to abduct Limehouse kids 3; tortures Pan, sneaks away during party 5; after Lyra and Pan are nearly intercised 17; with Stelmaria 23
  brief mentions: 4, 7, 11, 14; arrives at Bolvangar 15; 16

SK on boat for witch's torture 2, at Latrom's 9, with Boreal's dæmon 15

AS 1, tortures bat 4, Will's contempt for 11, abuses Salmakia 12; at Asriel's, theft of intention craft 16; in Geneva 24; nearly severed, attempts rescue of Roke 25; tentative play with Stelmaria 28; co-pilots intention craft to Clouded Mountain 30; farewells with Stelmaria, battles Metatron, dies 31
  brief mentions: 13, 18

Gomez, Father Luis

Genus: Human

Dæmon: Unnamed; green-backed beetle

World: Lyra's; passes through Will's (not described) and Cittàgazze; dies in mulefa's world

Alliances: The Consistorial Court of Discipline

Physical characteristics: Young. His eyes blaze, face pales, and body trembles when he considers the honor of serving as the Court's assassin.

Salt Creek Tiger Beetle

Background: The youngest member of the Consistorial Court of Discipline and a regular practitioner of preemptive penance.

Behavior: Zealot; unperturbed that his assignment means he can expect no help if he encounters trouble during his mission, as the Court intends to maintain deniability about its involvement.

He is initially impressed by the beauty of the *tualapi*, the huge birds of the mulefa's world, but when one approaches him, he does not hesitate to shoot its head off. When he realizes that the *tualapi* know he caused the death of one of their own, he sees in this "the basis of a fruitful understanding," and is satisfied knowing their fear will place them in his control.

Believing his mission is about to come to a successful conclusion, he considers whether to return to his world or stay in the mulefa's "to convince the four-legged creatures, who seemed to have the rudiments of reason, that their habit of riding on wheels was abominable and Satanic, and contrary to the will of God."

Role: Father Luis Gomez volunteers to assassinate Lyra when the Court decides that killing her is their best hope of eliminating the threat she poses as the new Eve: "the crucifix around his neck and the rifle at his back were twin tokens of his absolute determination to complete the task."

In Cittàgazze, he believes it is his "sacred task" that prevents his being harmed by Spectres. Encounters Angelica, the vicious sister of the boy Will fought, and from whom he learns about Will and Lyra's connection to the subtle knife and the direction Mary Malone was seen taking.

His assassination plans are prevented just as he approaches shooting range by the angel Balthamos. Gomez tries to trick Balthamos; but he slips on a wet stone. The angel takes advantage of Gomez's mistake, and, using the last of his strength, drowns him.

Lizards devour his corpse.

AS　volunteers to be assassin, receives instructions 6; meets Angelica 10, kills *tualapi* 27, Mary sees him in mulefa's world 34; hunts Lyra, battles Balthamos, dies 35
　　brief mentions: 7, 17, finds window to mulefa's world 20, corpse devoured 36

GRACIOUS WINGS [*See* No-Name]

GRANDFATHER CLIFF-GHAST ⚱

Genus: Cliff-ghast
World: Lyra's
Physical characteristics: Blind, weak-voiced, "the oldest of all cliff-ghasts."
Background: Remembers times even before the appearance of humans in his world. The young bring him carrion and ask his opinions.
Behavior: His physical weakness doesn't diminish his chortling delight as he considers Asriel's inevitable failure—and the feasting that will follow on the accumulation of corpses Asriel's war against heaven will surely bring.
Role: Introduces, via a report from the witch Ruta Skadi, the idea that without Æsahættr, Asriel's failure in his war against the Authority is certain.

SK　13

GRUMMAN, STANISLAUS (AKA PARRY, JOHN; JOPARI) ❖ ⚱ ✐ ⑩ *LS*

Note: The following is limited only to those passages in which John Parry is acting under the Grumman assumed identity.
Genus: Human
Dæmon: Sayan Kötör, an osprey
World: Lyra's, born John Parry in Will's, becomes Stanislaus Grumman in Lyra's, dies in Cittàgazze

Alliances: Asriel's campaign

Physical characteristics: Once a strong man in superior condition, the 11 or 12 years he has spent away from the world of his birth have left him physically ruined. Those the aëronaut Lee Scoresby interviews on his search for Grumman recall a "lean man, tough, powerful, curious about everything," but when Scoresby meets him, he appears "gaunt, blazing-eyed" with "black hair…streaked with grey" and is suffering from advanced heart disease. [166] [167]

Will Parry, before he realizes that the stranger he has met in Cittàgazze is his father who disappeared in an Alaskan blizzard, is struck by his "blazing blue eyes in a haggard face," "stubborn jaw," and "thin body hunched in a heavy cloak trimmed with feathers," whose voice is at once "resonant, harsh, but breathless." The Siberian Tartar tribe who adopted him probably conducted a trepanning on him (drilled a hole in his head), if being initiated into a "skull-cult" involves this operation, a question left open to speculation. [168] [169] [170]

Background: Dr Stanislaus Grumman is a legend in his own time, the subject of colorful stories and speculation among everyone from arctic trappers to the European academic community.

Variously thought to be English or German, a geologist or archaeologist, and, among those who think he is dead, killed in Skraeling wars, beheaded, or buried in an avalanche. According to the legends, Grumman came rapidly onto the scientific scene seven or nine years previously following the publication of his theory on magnetic polarities. He was reportedly looking for evidence of civilizations 30,000 years old buried under ice and had once rejected the advances of a witch who wanted him for her lover. He was at one time a member of Jordan College.

Aëronaut Lee Scoresby had heard that this shaman knows the location of a magical object that gives extraordinarily powerful protection to the one who has it, so wants to get Lyra under its protection, and thus decides to track down Grumman. But Umaq, Scoresby's Tartar sledge driver on the island, says the man sought may be "neither dead nor alive" but in the "spirit world." Scoresby learns Grumman is considered a shaman by the Yenisei Pakhtars, the Siberian Tartar tribe who adopted him. To them he is "Jopari" (a corruption of "John Parry"). Scoresby finds the shaman in a Siberian village, disproving the various reports of his demise. [171]

Grumman tells Scoresby that while looking for a legendary "rent in the fabric of the world," he and two others accidentally left their world during a blizzard. They were unable to find the passage back again; and before finding an entry to Lyra's world, the other two men were killed by Spectres.

Grumman worked his way from the Arctic to Berlin, where he received his academic credentials before being initiated into a skull-cult, and later becoming a shaman. He made "useful discoveries," ranging from how to prepare a bloodmoss ointment to the history of the subtle knife. His only regret was being "sundered forever" from his wife and son. [172] [173]

Behavior: The trappers and seal hunters who knew Grumman years previously remember a man with a "tongue like barbed wire," but the man Scoresby meets is mannerly, calm, and respectful, repeatedly assuring the aëronaut throughout their difficult balloon journey into Cittàgazze that he trusts his judgment. Highly respected by the headman of his Tartar village, and, when Grumman and Scoresby depart for their journey, the villagers come to seek the shaman's blessings. [174]

Grumman is at once still a practical man retaining the discipline and attitude of the soldier John Parry, and a shaman, a man who has trained his mind to accomplish extraordinary feats. When Scoresby comments that he thought shamans could fly, the practical Grumman counters with the observation that indeed he does have the gift of flight; after all, here he is in a balloon, flying, after using his powers to summon a pilot and his craft. And when Scoresby wonders if he used magic to get a fire going in a storm, Grumman says credit should go instead to dry matches and the Boy Scouts' motto, "Be prepared." But if Scoresby and Grumman are both practical adventurers, their conversation entering Cittàgazze reveals a contrast in perspective. Scoresby wants to rescue a boy who is attracting Spectres, but Grumman feels that betrays an ignorance of "the way this world works," and urges them onward: "if you want to put an end to cruelty and injustice you must take me further on, I have a job to do."

Dr Grumman swears he'll respect the price Scoresby sets for the journey into Cittàgazze, which is that Grumman tell the bearer of the knife that Lyra must be under its protection, and he reiterates this promise when he and Scoresby part in Cittàgazze. But when Grumman finds the bearer, he breaks his oath to Scoresby, telling Will to get the knife to Asriel, rather than instructing him to use it to protect Lyra (and even though he knows that Asriel's republic is doomed).

Role: As *His Dark Materials* opens, Grumman's expedition, sponsored by the German Academy in Berlin, is eighteen months overdue, and he is presumed to have died accidentally. Asriel speculates that Grumman had been investigating the other world visible beyond the Aurora and contends he has evidence that Grumman is dead—but not by accidental means, displaying what he claims to be Grumman's scalped and trepanned head.

In Cittàgazze, Scoresby single-handedly takes on the battalion that has pursued the two so that Grumman can escape and find the bearer. He shows unexpected strength when he struggles with Will. After subduing his opponent and finding the boy has lost two fingers, Grumman declares that Will is the knife bearer. Grumman dresses Will's wound with bloodmoss, staunching his bleeding, and tells the boy that the coming war will be between "those who want us to know more and be wiser and stronger, and those who want us to obey and be humble and submit." When Will says he wants no part of it, the man replies, "You haven't any choice: you're the bearer: it's picked you out."

John Parry's identity as Grumman drops away as he recognizes Will as his son. At the same moment Will sees he has found his father, but the elder Parry is immediately killed by a well-aimed arrow launched by Juta Kamainen, the witch whose love he once rejected. Will promises his dead father that he will go to Asriel, but this is before he discovers that Lyra has been abducted.

[*See also* **Parry, John; Jopari**]

Update: Dr Stanislaus Grumman/Col. John Parry's notes, contained in the appendix to the **10th** anniversary edition of *The Subtle Knife*, chart his progress from the Alaska window through Siberia to England and, finding it harder to adapt to a different world's Europe than to live in its remotest regions, back to Siberia. The appendix reveals that Grumman/Parry had extensive knowledge of the witch clans.

Asriel's first impression of Grumman apparently was that the stranger was nothing special, but he soon learned Grumman was "no fool." Grumman, in contrast, admired Lord Asriel, with whom he shared the story of his passage through a doorway in Alaska, in another world.

When Grumman met Giacomo Paradisi and saw what it could do, he knew the subtle knife was the tool Asriel needed most.

NL/GC Asriel's evidence of his demise 2
> *brief mentions:* 5, 7, Scoresby's skepticism of Asriel's report 13

SK Scoresby talks about at witch council 2, recalled in Nova Zembla 6, meets Scoresby 10; enters Cittàgazze, brings down zeppelins in trance, parts from Scoresby 14; meets Will 15; **LS** Lantern Slide 1
> *brief mentions:* 3, 4, 5, 13

AS *brief mentions:* 3, Baruch surprises Asriel 5; 14

10TH: *NL* appendix

10TH: *SK* appendix

HARTMANN, SIMON ✤

Genus: Human
Dæmon: Unnamed; form unknown
World: Lyra's
Background: Gyptian. Head of one of the six families of John Faa's group.
Role: In charge of finances for the voyage North to rescue the gyptian and any other children imprisoned by the General Oblation Board (Gobblers).

NL/GC 8 *[brief]*

HAWKER, PETER ✤

Genus: Human
Dæmon: Unnamed; form unknown
World: Lyra's
Background: Gyptian
Role: Likely waited in his boat during the gyptian spy mission to the Ministry of Theology in London. Brings home to the Fens the dying gyptian Jacob Huismans, who was injured breaking into the Ministry, and sends for Farder Coram to hear the wounded man's report.

NL/GC 9 *[brief]*

HEADMISTRESS ✎

Genus: Human
Dæmon: Unnamed; form unknown
World: Lyra's
Role: When Lyra returns to her world, the Master of Jordan College and Dame Hannah Relf (head of St Sophia's College) encourage her to consider meeting with the Headmistress of the boarding school associated with St Sophia's. Relf describes the Headmistress as "energetic, imaginative, kindly."

AS 38 *[brief]*

178

HESTER ✤⚔✎

Genus: Dæmon
Form: Hare
Human: Lee Scoresby
World: Lyra's

Jackrabbit / Hare

W.L. Miller,
National Park Service/
Yellowstone National Park

Physical characteristics: Although as "plain and scrawny as a hare could be," she has remarkable eyes of "gold-hazel, flecked with rays of deepest peat-brown and forest-green." Good at maintaining a neutral expression by half closing her eyes and laying her ears flat. Has sharp claws. Fur color is grey-brown.

Behavior: Like her human, she is taciturn, "tough and brave." But while Scoresby is inclined toward speculation, his dæmon deals with the situation immediately at hand. When Scoresby, seeking cover in the Cittàgazze world, wonders if they have "discharged [their] duty" by getting Grumman to his destination, Hester reminds him that, with one Imperial Guard zeppelin still on their trail, they need to focus on "survival first, morals later." She accepts that Scoresby would rather not have to keep shooting at the approaching Imperial Guard troops as they crouch behind a boulder in Alamo Gulch. Killing, Hester says, "Makes no sense. Do it anyway." Her practicality is balanced by Scoresby's tenderness.

Role: When Lyra first meets Scoresby in Trollesund, Scoresby keeps the gyptians she's with occupied by playing cards while Hester discreetly delivers a warning to Pan.

Leaving the observatory on Nova Zembla, she is attacked by the owl dæmon of the Magisterium's censor (known only as the Skraeling), who just misses Scoresby with an arrow. Scoresby shoots back, and it is Hester who encourages Lee to take the dead Skraeling's ring that identifies him as an agent of the Magisterium, reasoning that as soon as the Skraeling's report, already sent by messenger bird, reaches the church authorities, "we're done for anyway. Take every advantage we can in the meantime."

The ring does prove useful, allowing Scoresby to retrieve his requisitioned balloon, but also alerts the Magisterium to his whereabouts. During the gun battle at Alamo Gulch, Hester blames herself for their predicament, since it was her idea to take the ring. But Lee will listen to no such nonsense. Hester reminds Lee to use the flower Serafina Pekkala gave him to call for help, but it is too late. Her final act is to remark that there's no point in dying with an unused bullet, so Scoresby shoots the zeppelin itself, and it explodes, eliminating the last of the remaining troops.

The ghost of Scoresby is grateful that the passage Will opens out of the world of the dead means his atoms will be reunited with Hester's and together once again they'll float with the breeze.

Hester is the subject of the woodcut for chapter 14 of THE SUBTLE KNIFE, "Alamo Gulch."

NL/GC in Trollesund (unnamed) 11

SK conflict with Skraeling 6; in Siberia 10; in Cittàgazze, dies 14

AS *brief mentions:* remembered by Scoresby's ghost 29; reunited with Scoresby 31

HEYST, FATHER ❖

Genus: Human
Dæmon: Lizard; Unnamed
World: Lyra's
Physical characteristics: Elderly but far from emaciated.
Background: Intercessor at Jordan College. As such, he leads services, prays, hears confessions, and preaches.

Dave Geoke, U.S. Fish and Wildlife Service, Jan 2002

Pygmy Horned Lizard

Behavior: Seems as if he would like to reach out to Lyra; is worried about her lack of female companions, but can't figure out how to talk to her.

Role: His interactions with Lyra provide an example of her life among the Scholars. Considers Lyra to be "not spiritually promising," but also seems "genuinely interested" in her activities. Believes her attraction to the crypts shows an interest in history.

NL/GC 3 *[brief]*

184

HJALMURSON, HJALMUR ✧

Genus: Armoured bear

World: Lyra's

Physical characteristics: Weaker and younger than his King, Iorek Byrnison, to whom he should have adopted a submissive stance.

Background: This is the bear Iorek Byrnison killed, causing his exile. Hjalmur Hjalmurson had inexplicably and uncharacteristically provoked Iorek. Søren Eisarson, counselor under both Byrnison and his successor, Iofur Raknison, thinks it likely Hjalmurson had been acting under the influence of a drug, slipped to him by Raknison, who would have received it for that purpose as a gift from Coulter.

Role: The consequences of his death include the availability of the exiled Iorek Byrnison for hire to the gyptians and Iorek's subsequent involvement with Lyra.

NL/GC brief mentions: 2

HOPKINS, MRS ⑩

Genus: Human

World: Will's

Role: Mary Malone's landlord, she is likely the "nice old lady" who owns the property Mary leases close to the lab and University Parks.

10TH: *AS* appendix

HOOK, GERARD ✧

Genus: Human

Dæmon: Unnamed; form unknown

World: Lyra's

Background: Gyptian

Role: Captured or killed during the gyptian spy mission to the General Oblation Board's Ministry of Theology, London, headquarters. Efforts to rescue him failed, and his fate remains unknown.

NL/GC 9 *[brief]*

HORSEWOMAN ⚔

Genus: Human

World: Cittàgazze

Physical characteristics: Rides and dresses like a man.

Behavior: Alternately comforting and serious with the children she is taking into the countryside. Does not speak to the witches who camp with her party.

Role: Joachim Lorenz's unnamed partner; she accompanies a group of Cittàgazzean Spectre-orphans and some adults out of the Spectre-infested cities and to remote areas.

SK   6 *[brief]*

HUISMANS, JACOB ✣

Genus: Human
Dæmon: Unnamed; ferret
World: Lyra's
Background: Gyptian
Role: Mortally wounded while spying at the Ministry of Theology, London. He is carried back to the Fens on Peter Hawker's boat with an arrow still deeply embedded in his shoulder. Lives just long enough for his dæmon to tell what happened.

Black-footed Male Ferret

NL/GC 9

HUISMANS, MISTRESS ✣

Delmarva Fox Squirrel

Genus: Human
Dæmon: Squirrel; Unnamed
World: Lyra's
Physical characteristics: Wears a red flannel apron.
Background: Gyptian aboard Jacob Huismans' boat addressed by Farder Coram simply as Mistress. She could be Jacob's mother, wife, or sister; she clearly has every right to be with the dying man.
Behavior: Not pleased to see that Lyra is accompanying Farder Coram, but doesn't argue when he asks that she be allowed to stay. She is distraught and shaking, and very disturbed by Jacob's pain.
Role: When Jacob Huismans returns mortally wounded while spying at the Ministry of Theology in London, Farder Coram is summoned to hear what has happened. He is let on board by this very distressed woman.

NL/GC 9 *[brief]*

INQUIRER, CONSISTORIAL COURT OF DISCIPLINE ✐

Genus: Human
Dæmon: Unnamed; form unknown
World: Lyra's
Alliances: Consistorial Court of Discipline
Background: One of the twelve members of the Consistorial Court of Discipline, he takes the lead in questioning witnesses testifying before the Court at the College of St Jerome, Geneva.
Role: Interrogates Fra Pavel, the alethiometrist, both about what he heard the witch (tortured aboard the boat off Svalbard) confess about the prophecy regarding Lyra and about what he has learned since through his readings.

NL/GC 4

Intercessor, Gabriel College ❖

Genus: Human

Dæmon: Unnamed; form unknown

World: Lyra's

Background: Keeps a photo-mill on the high altar of Gabriel College's Oratory in Lyra's Oxford. He uses the black and white sails of its spinner to illustrate how ignorance, the black side of the sails, flees the light, while the white sails, or wisdom, moves toward it. The Jordan College Librarian simply says that photons move the sails.

Role: Their memories of his photo-mill suggest to Lyra and Pan the idea that elementary particles may influence the movement of the needles on the alethiometer.

NL/GC brief mentions: discussed by Lyra and Pan 9; remembered by Lyra during talk about Dust with Serafina 18

Intercessor, Jordan College [*See* Heyst, Father]

Ivanovitch, Will

Role: What the Russian priest Otyets (Father) Semyon Borisovitch insists on calling Will,— *Ivan* being the Russian equivalent of *John*, Will's father's name, and *vitch* meaning *son of*.

AS 8 [brief]

Jackson ⑩

World: Lyra's

Role: Was present when Asriel took photograms of the city beyond the Aurora. An associate or employee of Lord Asriel's, Asriel placed him in charge of compiling lists of pieces of equipment needed and investigating their costs for another expedition.

10ᴛʜ: *NL appendix*

Jansen, Dirk ✎

Genus: Human/Ghost

World: Holland-like world, world of the dead

Physical characteristics: Middle-aged, outdoorsy, trim

Background: Died from having his throat cut during wartime; his corpse was left in the bushes.

Behavior: Knows but can't quite believe that he is dead; scared of hell. Doesn't know where he is going or how to get there, but knows that he must move on toward a destination.

Role: Man Will first sees dead in one world, then as a ghost in the next world he cuts through to, indicating to Will that he has found the world of the dead.

AS 18

Jaxer ❖

Genus: Human

Dæmon: Unnamed; form unknown

World: Lyra's

Physical characteristics: Young man

Background: Gyptian. Possibly a member of the Costa family.

Role: With Tony Costa hunting Gobblers in London the night Lyra runs away from Coulter's. Participates in rescuing the girl from the net-throwing Turk traders trying to kidnap her.

NL/GC 6 *[brief]*

JERRY ✤

Genus: Human

Dæmon: Belisaria, a seagull

World: Lyra's

Physical characteristics: Large man

Background: Able seaman. Possibly a gyptian but more likely in their employ since he seems to meet Lyra only after the gyptians set sail. He works aboard the boat that carries the gyptians from the Fens of Eastern Anglia to Norroway during the first phase of their mission to rescue their children. First went to sea before his dæmon had settled.

Behavior: Easy-going; patient with Lyra, but not condescending. Considers himself not particularly special in any enviable way, but hardy and practical like his seagull dæmon, and always able to find work and friends.

Role: Lyra's seaman friend on the journey North teaches her to sew, encourages staying busy to avoid seasickness, gets her to do chores by showing her how sailors swab decks and make their beds, and assures the girl she'll learn much about herself when Pan's form is fixed. Jerry makes a waterproof case from oilskins for Lyra's alethiometer.

NL/GC 10

JOHANSEN, BERNIE ✤ *LS*

Genus: Human

Dæmon: Unnamed; form unknown

World: Lyra's

Physical characteristics: Unusual in that his dæmon is the same sex as himself.

Background: Half-gyptian pastry cook at Jordan College.

Role: Kept John Faa, gyptian leader, informed about Lyra during her childhood, stressing the concern of the Master of Jordan College for the child.

Update: In a Lantern Slide in *NORTHERN LIGHTS*, "Benny" offers an anecdote regarding Lyra's escapades at Jordan College to lighten the tone when the Costa family are complaining about Lyra taking their boat. He tells them of the time Lyra tried to save a starling from the Kitchen cat, but decided when the bird died to roast it instead. When Lyra was thrown out of his Kitchen by the Chef, she left the bird behind. It ended up on the Master's plate. Lyra was unrepentant when she learned that he had passed a very unpleasant night following the Feast

NL/GC brief mentions: at Jordan day Roger disappears 3; discussed by Faa 7; *LS* Lantern Slide 8

JOPARI (AKA GRUMMAN, STANISLAUS; PARRY, JOHN)

Role: Reportedly Stanislaus Grumman's Tartar name and how he is known as a shaman.

Grumman tells Lee Scoresby that it is a corruption of "John Parry," his given name from the world of his birth. [*See also* **Grumman, Stanislaus; Parry, John**]

SK brief mentions: 6; Grumman explains origin 10; 15

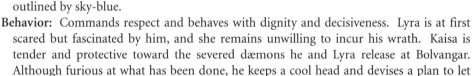

Snow Goose

Mathew Perry, U.S. Fish and
Wildlife Service, Aug 2003

Kaisa ✦↓✐

Genus: Dæmon
Form: Goose
Human: Serafina Pekkala
World: Lyra's
Physical characteristics: Grey or white in color; "elegant and wild simultaneously," with a cry described as a "piercing whoop." Has black eyes narrowly outlined by sky-blue.

185
186

Behavior: Commands respect and behaves with dignity and decisiveness. Lyra is at first scared but fascinated by him, and she remains unwilling to incur his wrath. Kaisa is tender and protective toward the severed dæmons he and Lyra release at Bolvangar. Although furious at what has been done, he keeps a cool head and devises a plan to let them out so that a break-in isn't suspected.

Role: Like his human, Kaisa provides critical information and help to the gyptians, Lyra and those protecting her. As a witch's dæmon, he is able to do this independently, entering situations alone where Serafina Pekkala's appearance would attract the wrong kind of attention. He is the first to assert definitely that there are innumerable worlds.

In response to Farder Coram's request to their consul for the witches' help in rescuing their missing children, Kaisa visits the gyptians' boat docked in Trollesund. He seems to assume that the gyptians' purpose in coming North is to "make war," but isn't surprised to hear that their mission is to rescue their children. Kaisa provides directions to the General Oblation Board's Experiment Station at Bolvangar, along with additional information about its fortification and suspected activities.

187

He also acknowledges to Lyra that the witches are very interested in her, in part, because they respect her father's knowledge of the other worlds of which they've long been aware.

When Lyra is captured in an ambush by Samoyeds and sold to the Experiment Station, Kaisa, as a witch's dæmon, is able to come on his own to Lyra during a fire drill. He lets her know that the gyptians and Iorek Byrnison are only a day's march away, and then together he and Lyra break into a storage shed where they discover severed dæmons warehoused in cages, and Kaisa liberates them. Once again in Cittàgazze, Kaisa appears unexpectedly in the nick of time to save Will and Lyra by scaring away an attacking mob of children.

Observations: *Described on first appearance as "a beautiful grey goose whose head was crowned with a flash of pure white" and again as a "grey goose"; however, in* The Subtle Knife, *he is called a "snow-goose" and his color is "white."*

188
189
190
191

NL/GC visits gyptians' boat 11, at Bolvangar 15
   brief mentions: 10, 12, 17

SK at boat off Svalbard, Thorold's, Lake Enara 2; 3 [brief]; at belvedere in Cittàgazze 11

AS 36 [brief]

KAMAINEN, JUTA ⚓✎ ⑩

Genus: Witch
Dæmon: Robin; Unnamed
World: Lyra's, dies in Cittàgazze
Alliances: Serafina Pekkala's witch clan.
Physical characteristics: Just a bit older than 100 years—young
for a witch—Juta is full-faced with a ruddy complexion and
"rich black hair."

Robin

Background: Witch who once wanted Stanislaus Grumman for her lover; he turned her
down.

Behavior: Strong-willed but seemingly capable of submitting to authority. Loves intensely;
thwarted, hates passionately.

Role: Grumman's assassin. Kamainen is likely the sentry on duty at the Cittàgazze campsite
the night Serafina Pekkala has gone to Scoresby's aid. When she sees Will head up the
mountain for a walk, she "silently took to the air, not to disturb him but to see he came
to no harm." Coming upon Stanislaus Grumman (the former John Parry), she kills him
because, she tells the distraught Will, she loved the man—a statement the boy finds
utterly incomprehensible. The witch then kills herself. During her absence from the
camp, Coulter abducts Lyra and Juta's sister witches are lost to the Spectres.

Update: The key to Stanislaus Grumman's map of the witch-lands in the appendix to the **10**TH
anniversary edition of *THE SUBTLE KNIFE* identifies Juta as the clan-queen for the Lake Visha
witches.

Note: *Juta Kamainen is not mentioned by name as the sentry witch who follows Will when he
leaves the campsite. However, this witch has a robin dæmon, as does Kamainen, and there
seems no other explanation for her appearance on the mountaintop where
Grumman/Parry dies.*

SK   sentry witch with robin dæmon follows Will, kills Grumman/Parry 15
    brief mentions: at Lake Enara 2, witch rejected by Grumman mentioned 6, referred to by
        Grumman and Scoresby but not by name 10; 13

AS   *brief mentions:* not named but described as Parry's killer 3; 13, 33

10TH: *SK* appendix

KAROSSA ✦

Genus: Dæmon
Form: Unsettled
Human: Unnamed child at Bolvangar.
World: Lyra's
Role: Bolvangar child's dæmon who was once tormented by the golden monkey.

NL/GC 16 *[brief]*

KASKU, IEVA ⚓

Genus: Witch
Dæmon: Unnamed; form unknown
World: Lyra's
Alliances: Unallied

Background: Witch queen
Role: One of the witch-queens Ruta Skadi plans to persuade to join Asriel's campaign.
SK 13 *[brief]*

KERIM ❖

Genus: Human
Dæmon: Unnamed; form unknown
World: Lyra's
Physical characteristics: Young man
Background: Gyptian. Probably a Costa: when Ma Costa enters the Roping, her son Tony is on one side of her, Kerim the other.
Role: With Tony Costa hunting Gobblers in London the night Lyra runs away from Coulter's; aids in rescuing her from the net-throwing, kidnapping Turk traders.
NL/GC brief mentions: in London 6; in Fens 7

KIGALIK, MATT ⚲

Genus: Human
World: Will's
Background: Eskimo friend of Jake Petersen. Lives in the vicinity of Colville, Alaska.
Behavior: Can track a man for several days unseen. Careful about what he says.
Role: Describes Alaskan window to John Parry.

     In a letter home to his wife, Parry describes meeting Kigalik. Not only does the Eskimo provide Parry an idea of what the window looks like, he also corrects Jake Petersen's coordinates and provides the detail that Parry needs to go about fifty steps west of a rock shaped like a bear on the north side of a creek to see the window.

     Parry also hears from Kigalik about the recent visit of a Soviet spy also assumed to be looking for the window, and writes that he got the impression that Kigalik "bumped him off."
Facts: *There is a Kigalik River in the vicinity of Parry's Alaskan window.* 195
SK 5

KIRJAVA ⚲✎

Genus: Dæmon
Form: Initially invisible or internal; then unsettled. Settles as a cat.
Human: Will Parry
World: Her existence is revealed when separated from Will in the world of the dead, a time when she visits many other worlds with Pan. Begins her relationship with Will in the mulefa's world. Returns with him to their own world.
Physical Characteristics: Settled form proves to be "a cat of no ordinary size, and her fur was lustrous and rich, with a thousand different glints and shades of ink-black, shadow-grey, the blue of a deep lake under a noon sky, mist-lavender-moonlight-fog...To see the meaning of the word *subtlety*, you had only to look at her fur."
Role: Even before Kirjava is visible, Lyra is certain of her existence, and imagines that the 196 dæmon of the boy she's just met would "express a nature that was savage, and courteous,

and unhappy." When the cat who Will followed through the Sunderland Avenue window into Cittàgazze jumps into the boy's arms after he takes on the kids abusing it in that world, Lyra is convinced his dæmon has finally appeared. The behavior of this same cat in helping them flee from Latrom/Boreal in Oxford again brings to her mind how his dæmon would behave, if it were not internalized within him.

Will becomes aware that what Lyra has been arguing all along—that he has a dæmon, whether he knows it or can see it or not—is true when the boatman maneuvers the children and spies into the world of the dead, where dæmons can not go. He feels tremendous psychic and physical pain. Later, Kirjava will recall, "I didn't know I was born until I was torn away from his heart." While their humans were in the world of the dead, Kirjava visited other worlds with Pantalaimon.

Will feels agony again when Metatron's forces are trying to seize Kirjava and Pantalaimon. Lyra is the first to hold her, seizing her as Will does Pan when they are escaping Metatron into the mulefa's world. While Kirjava and Pan are still playing hard to get in the mulefa's world, Kirjava is named by Serafina Pekkala.

When Will sees his dæmon for the first time, Kirjava is in the form of a bird; for the rest of his life he'll remember the feeling of "sweet rightfulness of her coming back to him." During one of their last times alone together in the world of the mulefa, Will reaches for Pan, and Lyra responds by stroking Kirjava. At that point, she knew "neither dæmon would change now, having felt a lover's hands on them."

As Will and Lyra say good-bye in the Botanic Garden, Kirjava shares one last kiss with Pan. Will must break the subtle knife, and first thinks of his mother, but when this fails to shatter the knife, Kirjava tells Will to think instead of Lyra.

Observation: *It is not surprising that Will's dæmon's settled form is that of a cat, considering the roles his pet cat Moxie and the Sunderland Avenue stray played in setting in motion the events that lead Will to Cittàgazze, the knife, his father, Lyra, and all that followed. [See also* **Sophonax**]

Note: *Kirjava is not named until near the end of* THE AMBER SPYGLASS. *Most of these chapters do not contain the word* Kirjava, *but do include references to her.*

SK   *brief mentions:* 1, 4, 5, 8, 9

AS   Will pained at their separation 21; under threat by Metatron, sighted near Asriel's fortress; grabbed by Lyra, rescued from battle 31; hides with Pan from Will in world of mulefa 35; discussion with, named by Serafina 36; seen by Will, with Pan delivers sad news 37; farewells with Pan, tells Will how to break the knife 38
        brief mentions: 8, 14, 18, 23, 26; sought by Will on battlefield 29; 32

Koopman, Ruud and Nellie ✦

Genus: Human
Dæmon: Unnamed
World: Lyra's
Background: Gyptian children rescued by Lord Asriel during the floods of '53.
Role: John Faa cites Asriel's involvement in aiding the

Floods of '53

On January 31 to February 1 1953, coastal England experienced severe flooding. The Fens suffered significant damage. Over 300 people on England's coasts died, and 20,000 were evacuated; industry, farmlands, and infrastructures in these areas were devastated as well. Following the floods, measures were taken to prevent a recurrence, but the low-lying Fens remains especially vulnerable.

gyptians during this time of need as one of the reasons the gyptians owe him a debt they can repay by helping to keep Lyra safely hidden among them.

NL/GC 8 [brief]

Kulang 🖉

Genus: Dæmon
Form: Unsettled
Human: Ama, the Himalayan child
World: Lyra's
Behavior: Kulang displays fearful concern when he senses the sleeping Pantalaimon's distress, despite Ama being deceived by the tender treatment her dæmon receives at the cave from the golden monkey.
Role: Encourages Ama in her decision not to tell her father about what she has seen Coulter do to Lyra, but to wake the girl themselves. Balthamos in his guise of Will's dæmon is able to put Ama at ease by playing and communicating with Kulang.

AS   brief mentions: 1, 4, 11

Kyrillion ✦

Genus: Dæmon
Form: Unsettled
Human: Annie, a prisoner at Bolvangar Experiment Station
World: Lyra's
Role: In a conference room, Annie and Kyrillion were tested in various ways in the presence of twenty or so scientists. When Lyra announces her plan to go in the space above the ceiling tiles and spy on the meetings, Annie wants to come too. She backs down when Pantalaimon challenges Kyrillion, a confrontation of dæmons being a common way for children to resolve conflicts.

NL/GC 16 [brief]

Lanselius, Dr Martin ✦ ⚕ 🖉

Mike Boylan, U.S. Fish and Wildlife Service, Jan 2002

Royal Green Snake

Genus: Human
Dæmon: Unnamed; green serpent
World: Lyra's
Alliances: Witch clans he serves, claims neutrality when with Coram, clearly against the Magisterium when with Serafina Pekkala
Physical characteristics: Described as "a fat man with a florid face and a sober black suit," his eyes are as green as his serpent dæmon's.
Background: Witch-Consul at Trollesund, Norroway, he is a human who mediates between the witch clans and the human communities of Lapland. Possibly the son of a witch and a man.
Behavior: Lanselius is cautious with Farder Coram regarding the General Oblation Board's activities, as if he intends to maintain deniability about any aspect of their conversation. He is more expansive when discussing the history of the alethiometer, but not forthcoming about how he knows that Lyra has the instrument (or how his dæmon

201

knows—she seems to tell him) or that Lyra can read it.

When Serafina Pekkala comes to visit the witch-consul, he acts as if he is scared to be seen talking to her. He admits that he too, like Serafina, fears Mrs Coulter.

Role: Brings Iorek Byrnison to the gyptians' attention and introduces the idea of Lyra fulfilling a witches' prophecy. Gets Coram's message asking for help to witch Serafina Pekkala, who sends her goose dæmon Kaisa that night to visit the gyptians.

Farder Coram and Lyra visit Lanselius for information about Serafina Pekkala and local activities that could indicate the location of the Gobblers; he suggests the gyptians seek out Iorek Byrnison. After asking to see Lyra's alethiometer, he provides some history of the device and tests Lyra's ability to read it, including a test to see if Lyra can pick from forty bundles the one cloud-pine used by Pekkala. Dr Lanselius tells Coram he believes Lyra to be the child witches have long prophesized about who has a "great destiny" that can only be fulfilled "far beyond" her own world.

Much later, Serafina Pekkala visits Lanselius for news about the Magisterium, other witch clans, the church, and Asriel.

Lanselius is the man referred to in the title of chapter 10 of Northern Lights/The Golden Compass, "The Consul and the Bear."

Note: *The US edition of* The Amber Spyglass *departs from the other two volumes' use of* witch consul *(or* consul*) and uses instead* Witches' Consul *(or* Consul*) to refer to Lanselius; the* UK Amber Spyglass *also replaces* witch *with* witches'.

NL/GC 10
     brief mentions: 11, 18

SK 2

AS 23 *[brief]*

Latrom, Sir Charles (aka Boreal, Lord; Carlo) 🗡🖊 LS

Genus: Human

Dæmon: Snake with emerald mailed head and "gold-rimmed black eyes"; Unnamed

World: Will's (world of origin is Lyra's)

Alliances: His own interests, claims to be working for the British intelligence or security forces

Physical characteristics: Variously described as "in his sixties," "late sixties," "late middle age," or "elderly"; "fleshy and smooth-skinned," silvery-haired, with eyes "large, dark and long-lashed and intense"; and a "sharp, dark-pointed tongue." Favors a cologne that gives him the scent of "hot-house flowers so rich you can smell the decay at their roots," a Panama hat, and linen suit. Latrom has dry lips and sweats excessively.

Background: Calling card identifies him as a CBE and a knight. Lives in a well-secured home, Limefield House, in Old Headington, Oxford. Collects antiques, including telescopes and compasses. Unlike John Parry/Stanislaus Grumman, Latrom has maintained his health by returning periodically to the world of his birth (Lyra's), where he is Lord Boreal. Likely the man Paradisi left the Oxford window open for, hoping to lure him to Cittàgazze and its Spectres. Knows that the national security forces are interested in finding John Parry; he is "in touch with those who run the spies."

Behavior: An obviously wealthy man with expensive tastes, he is "smooth, dishonest and powerful." Although he initially appears "kind and friendly and very clean and smartly dressed," he makes Pan uneasy and reminds Lyra of the smell at usurper bear-king Iofur [215] Raknison's "where the air was perfumed but the floor was thick with filth." The former [216] bearer of the subtle knife, Giacomo Paradisi, stresses to Will and Lyra that they must not [217] trust him and that Latrom has no intention of returning the alethiometer if they give him the knife.

Role: When Latrom pays a visit to Dr Mary Malone and Oliver Payne, claiming to be a retired civil servant formerly involved in scientific policy, he is aware of their desperate need for immediate funding to keep their Dark Matter Unit operating, and he knows that Lyra has made contact with Malone. He insinuates that their future funding would depend on informing him personally of any contact they have with Lyra and allowing his interests to dictate the direction of their research.

His theft of the alethiometer in order to acquire the subtle knife brings Will to the knife and reveals Will to be its bearer; his introduction of Coulter to Cittàgazze leads to Lyra's abduction.

After coming upon a doorway opening directly to their world without Cittàgazze intervening, he brings Mrs Coulter to Will's world. He tells her he knows the location of "a dozen or so" windows, and is curious about whether Coulter's *zombis* would be affected by Spectres, figuring that if he doesn't get the knife from Will, entering Cittàgazze [218] under their protection could be another way to get to the knife.

When Will and Lyra return to Limefield House, Will cuts a window, enters, retrieves the alethiometer, and after a struggle, escapes. Lyra, seeing him with her mother, realizes Latrom is Lord Boreal.

At their Cittàgazze campsite, Latrom yields to Coulter's seduction and tells her about the subtle knife. Having got from him all she wanted, Coulter poisons Latrom. Coulter puts some of his belongings to use in her Himalayan hideout; Will takes others for use on his journey.

Latrom's hand and serpent dæmon are the subjects of the woodcut for chapter 7 of *THE SUBTLE KNIFE*, "The Rolls Royce."

[*See also* **Boreal, Lord** and **Carlo**]

Facts: *CBE stands for Commander of the British Empire, one of five levels of the Order of the British Empire, an honor established in 1917 by King George V to recognize primarily non-combatant service. Two of the levels confer knighthood, but Commander does not.*

In recognition of his contributions to British literature, Philip Pullman was awarded the CBE in the 2004 New Years Honours List.

Medlar [see update] is a type of fruit that has to begin to decompose before it can be eaten. Until it begins to rot, medlar is too hard to bite and its flesh too astringent to eat.

Update: The seventh Lantern Slide in *THE SUBTLE KNIFE* mentions the peculiar cologne favored by Latrom. It is described as a floral oil with a "flesh-like scent" comparable to that of medlar. Latrom shoplifted the oil from a bazaar stall in an unspecified world's Damascus.

SK notices Lyra at museum 4; gives her a ride, steals alethiometer, Lyra shows Will his calling card (first appearance of Latrom), sets alethiometer's ransom 7; explains where to find subtle knife 8; Coulter's visit and Will's reclaiming of alethiometer 9; visits Malone and Payne 12, seduced and poisoned by Coulter 15; [LS] Lantern Slide 7

AS his corpse, Will takes his supplies 2
 brief mentions: 1, 11, 26, 37

LE CLERC, SIMON ❖

Genus: Human
Dæmon: Cerebaton; form unknown
World: Lyra's
Background: Jordan College Master, 1765-1789
Role: Buried in the crypt where Roger and Lyra played during their childhoods at Jordan College.

NL/GC 3 *[brief]*

LENTARA, TANJA ⑩

Genus: Witch
Dæmon: Unnamed; form unknown
World: Lyra's
Role: This witch is the clan-queen for the witches of the Lake Umolese region and was at one time Lord Asriel's lover. From her he learned that the witches are aware of the city beyond the aurora, and that they claim that it is most easily seen when the aurora is very active, which they associate with increases in sunspot activity.

NL/GC appendix

10TH: *NL* appendix

10TH: *SK* appendix

LIBRARIAN, JORDAN COLLEGE ❖ ✐

Genus: Human
Dæmon: Unnamed; form unknown
World: Lyra's
Alliances: Anti-Asriel; Anti-General Oblation Board
Physical characteristics: An old man; if his age is roughly the same as his longtime friend the Master of Jordan College's, he'd be in his seventies.
Background: Jordan College Scholar and an old friend of the Master of Jordan College. First name is Charles.
Behavior: Aware of the Master's plot to poison Asriel; he is relieved by its failure, but did nothing to stop it. When the Master muses on whether to talk with Lyra about what the alethiometer says about her having an important role to play in coming events, the librarian counters, "She wouldn't listen...I know her ways only too well. Try to tell her anything serious and she'll half-listen for five minutes and then start fidgeting." He finds even more absurd the Master's notion of discussing Dust with Lyra: "Why should a distant theological riddle interest a healthy thoughtless child?"
Role: His discussion with the Master after Lord Asriel's Retiring Room presentation allows insight into the Master's motives for poisoning Asriel's wine and provides background on the issues involved in the matters Asriel has raised.

NL/GC 2
    brief mentions: 3, 4, 9
AS 21 *[brief]*

LISTER, DR ⚶

Genus: Human

World: Will's

Role: Having spotted this name on a pigeonhole, Lyra convinces the porter in Mary Malone's building that she is expected in Dr Lister's office as a ruse to get past his desk.

SK 4 *[brief]*

LIZZIE ✧ ⚶

Role: Lyra's alias in Bolvangar and in Will's Oxford.

NL/GC 14, 15

SK 3, 7

LONSDALE, MRS ✧ ⚶ ✐ 𝘓𝘚

Golden Retriever

Genus: Human

Dæmon: Unnamed; retriever

World: Lyra's

Physical characteristics: Has enough physical strength to bathe and dress an uncooperative and surly Lyra.

Background: Second cousin to the father of Roger Parslow, the playmate of Lyra's captured by the Gobblers.

Behavior: Claims to care for Lyra, though the child gives her "little enough reason and no thanks." Displays exasperation and impatience with Lyra's scruffiness and sloppiness, berating her and punctuating these complaints with the occasional smack. Performs her duties efficiently, but never behaves in a motherly fashion toward the girl.

Role: Jordan College housekeeper, she is responsible for making the half-wild Lyra minimally presentable and mannerly, especially when guests visit the College.

NL/GC 3, 4; 10 *[brief]*; 𝘓𝘚 Lantern Slide 2

SK 3 *[brief]*

AS brief mentions: 14, 19

LORD FAA [*See* Faa, Lord John]

LORENZ, JOACHIM ⚶

Genus: Human

World: Cittàgazze

Physical characteristics: Firm with his horse and comfortable with his rifle. Serafina Pekkala "saw sorrow in his face...and strength" and a "calm wariness."

Background: Horseman accompanying a group of Cittàgazzean refugees, with the duty to flee if the travelers encounter Spectres so that at least he and his partner, a woman, will survive and be able to care for any children in the party whose parents are lost to Spectres. "Not a learned man," but well versed in Cittàgazzean legends.

Behavior: Pragmatic and survival-oriented. If another war in heaven is coming, he could

224 bear the losses it would entail, if at its end, the Spectres were swept "back into the pit they come from."

Role: He tells the witches Ruta Skadi and Serafina Pekkala much about Cittàgazze's history, Spectres, and armies of angels flying toward the North Pole, while the witch-queens camp with the travelers he and his partner are escorting.

SK 6

Louis, Brother ✎

Genus: Human
Dæmon: Unnamed; rabbit
World: Lyra's
Alliances: Consistorial Court of Discipline
225 **Physical characteristics:** "fresh-faced" and young
Background: Convenor of the Secretariat of the Consistorial Court of Discipline, College of St Jerome, Geneva

Cottontail Rabbit

Behavior: Obedient but resentful of many slights by Father MacPhail, the Court's president, including the expectation that he perform awkward tasks without understanding why. Tries to be friendly to Coulter, in spite of her haughty rudeness toward him. In fact, his submissive attitude makes her treat him in ever more insulting ways.

Role: Has the awkward assignment of removing from the sleeping Mrs Coulter's neck her locket to obtain the key ingredient for the bomb. And then, once MacPhail has removed half the lock of Lyra's hair kept within its charm, of reclasping it around the woman's neck. This he fails to do, leaving it on her pillow (which would have alerted her to the theft, had not the Gallivespian spy Lord Roke done so already).

Observation: *He is very nervous about taking the necklace, more so, it seems, by his proximity to a beautiful sleeping woman's flesh than by the dubious nature of the enterprise.*

AS 24

Lovat, Hugh ❋ ✎

Genus: Human
Dæmon: Unnamed; form unsettled
World: Lyra's
Background: Kitchen boy at St Michael's College, Oxford
Role: Friend of Lyra and Roger; involved the previous year in briefly hijacking the boat belonging to the Costas, a gyptian family, as a prank in the ongoing battle of Oxford versus gyptian kids.

Notes: *Hugh is mentioned by name earlier in* THE GOLDEN COMPASS *than he is in* NORTHERN LIGHTS.

NL/GC 3 *[brief]*
AS 23 *[brief]*

Lyall, Francis ❋

Genus: Human
Dæmon: Zohariel; form unknown

World: Lyra's
Background: Jordan College Master, 1748-1765.
Role: Buried in the College crypt that Roger and Lyra liked to explore.
NL/GC 3 [brief]

Lyra ✦ ⚲ ⚗ ⑩ [LS]

Genus: Human
Dæmon: Pantalaimon, a pine marten (when settled)
World: Lyra's
Alliances: Those she loves: Roger, Iorek Byrnison, and Will
Physical characteristics: A "small and slight, but wiry" girl with "darkish blond" or lion-like tawny hair, "pale blue" eyes and an expression characterized as a "mixture of the very young...and a kind of deep, sad wariness." Twelve or so years old and pre-adolescent 226 when *His Dark Materials* begins, small enough to easily pass as eleven at Bolvangar, she is thirteen at the series' end. When she returns to Oxford, the Master of Jordan College sees Lyra has lost the "child's unconscious grace" but also that she is growing into a 227 beautiful woman.
Background: Her legal name is Lyra Belacqua, but she uses the one bestowed upon her by armoured bear Iorek Byrnison: Lyra Silvertongue.

The child of an affair between Mrs Edward (Marisa) Coulter and Lord Asriel. Lyra was left with Asriel and cared for by gyptian Ma Costa. But when Edward Coulter learned the truth, he charged into Asriel's estate, where Asriel killed him in self-defense. However, while the killing was justifiable, Coulter also by law had a right to avenge his wife's and Asriel's adultery, so Lyra was removed from Asriel's custody and the court rejected the appeal by Ma Costa for Lyra to continue in her care. Lyra was placed by court order in a priory of the Sisters of Obedience. Asriel then withdrew her from there and left Lyra under the care of the Master of Jordan College with the one condition—that Coulter never be allowed near her. Lyra grew up believing that both her parents died in an aëronautical accident in the North. Asriel visited his daughter with some degree of regularity, but told her he was her paternal uncle.

When Will and Lyra discuss going to the world of the dead, Lyra reflects that she never realized it at the time, but she and Pan were left to bring up themselves; that while Mrs Lonsdale saw to her clothes and so forth, she never showed Lyra any affection. Lyra adds that in spite of all the awful things her mother has done, Coulter looked after her in the cave, she thinks, because she remembers vaguely being held up in her arms. Will doesn't tell her that this would have been when Lyra was being forced to drink more sleeping potion.

Left largely on her own at Jordan College, "in many ways Lyra was a barbarian," a 228 "coarse and greedy little savage," "half-wild cat" like the "urchins and ragamuffins" with 229 230 whom she played. But while she is content to play with the children of the College servants, especially her best friend Roger, Lyra senses that she belongs in part to Asriel's world of glamour and power. Lyra has never owned a doll or played organized ball games but quickly excels at games at Bolvangar, being a natural athlete and leader. Before she lived with Mrs Coulter, she had never shopped for her own clothes or washed her own hair. Most of her clothes are hand-me-downs, and most of her care was handled by servants. She does gain some, albeit marginal, practical experience during her stay on the

Costas' boat in peeling potatoes and making tea.

Dr Martin Lanselius tells gyptian Farder Coram that witches have long prophesized about a child who has a "great destiny" that can only be fulfilled "far beyond" her own world. He believes Lyra to be that child. Witch Serafina Pekkala tells aëronaut Lee Scoresby that the child of the witches' prophecy "is destined to bring about the end of destiny." Scoresby contends that Lyra has "more free will than anyone I've ever met" and is impressed by her bravery in coming North to rescue Roger, while Serafina wonders if the fates brought Roger North so Lyra would follow and bring Asriel what he needs. According to Ma Costa, Lyra is a fire person. She tells the girl: "you got-witch oil in your soul. Deceptive, that's what you are."

Behavior: Generally, Lyra is a "sanguine and practical" child. The Master of Jordan College tells her that although she rarely "found it easy to obey," she's "never been a bad child," but rather has "a lot of goodness and sweetness...and a lot of determination." But while her disobedience at Jordan College is routine, in a serious situation she behaves much differently. On the journey to Bolvangar with the gyptians, she does not test leader John Faa's patience or the limits he sets her. She respects him, and behaves with a maturity that would stun the Jordan College scholars.

The Librarian assures the Master that if he were to try to discuss Dust with Lyra, she wouldn't be interested, but her behavior when the Retiring Room is cleared of all but Lyra and Asriel suggests otherwise: she questions Asriel about Dust even before she asks to see Grumman's head.

Lyra's behavior is adaptable; she is adept at figuring out what is needed to prevail in situations ranging from manipulating the ego of the usurper armoured bear king, Iofur Raknison, to hiding out in the open of Will's Oxford. At Bolvangar, it is apparent to Lyra that she can put the adults' inexperience at handling large groups of children to her use. In Will's world at Mary Malone's building, she adopts a "bland and vacuous docility" to convince the porter she isn't worth his bother. Seeing police approaching the bench where she and Will have been sitting, rather than fleeing, she initiates a conversation, asking for directions to the museum where she and her brother were to meet their parents, an act that enrages Will until he sees the reasoning she's employed.

While she trusts her feelings about people, she revises them when faced with contrary evidence. She immediately trusts Lee Scoresby, as he does her. But while Lyra tells Mrs Coulter at Bolvangar that Lord Asriel wouldn't have allowed intercisions to take place if he knew what was going on there, when she witnesses his murder of Roger through intercision, she realizes how wrong she has been, and henceforth never considers him worthy of trust.

At Jordan College, Lyra won't cry out in pain or weep, even when Asriel twists her arm. She is ashamed to cry in front of her own mother in Bolvangar. In Cittàgazze, after she startles him at their first meeting, Will hits her face hard enough to raise a bruise, and still she won't cry. But as she matures, she ceases to need to appear so tough, crying freely when parting from Iorek Byrnison in the Himalayas. And as she and Will flee the cave, leaving Mrs Coulter on the ground grasping her ankle poisoned by the Gallivespian's spur, Lyra leaves with a "great and furious sob" since, "after all, Mrs Coulter was the only mother she would ever have."

When they discuss going to the world of the dead, Lyra admits she is frightened, and Will realizes he is the only person to whom she would confess her fear.

Lyra takes very much to heart armoured bear Iorek Byrnison's reply when she asks if he is frightened in thinking about the coming war. He tells her he isn't, but "when I am, I shall master the fear." On finding severed child Tony Makarios, she feels fear and revulsion, but her compassion and courage prevail. When Iorek is preparing to fight Iofur Raknison, Lyra fears Iorek will lose. But "she would not do him the treachery of looking away, for if he looked at her he must see her shining eyes and their love and belief, not a face hidden in cowardice." When she has to leave Pan behind to go to the world of the dead, as with Iorek, she forces herself not to look away from his agony.

Lyra is a good liar, but not imaginative, which proves advantageous in her scheming since those who are very imaginative can find their own fears of probable outcomes limiting their ability to act. When Coulter stops her intercision at Bolvangar, Lyra has to invent a tale to tell about where she's been in the months since she vanished from London, and this story-telling helps Lyra recover from the terror of the silver guillotine: "now that she was doing something difficult and familiar and never quite predictable, namely lying, she felt a sort of mastery again, the same sense of complexity and control that the alethiometer gave her." She knows intuitively that what makes a good story is the balance between vagueness and possibility. Later in the Himalayas, when they learn that the Gallivespian spies intend to stick with them, Lyra considers that while Will is very brave, she is far better at "lying and betraying and cheating," and this leaves her feeling "warm and virtuous, because she did it for Will, never for herself."

On the trip North, Lyra for the first time begins to reflect on her own feelings, and finds the "experience interesting but uncomfortable." After she becomes involved with Will, not only does she find she has become more perceptive about others' feelings, she feels that when it comes to Will "she was developing a new kind of sense, as if he were simply more in focus than anyone she'd known before." As Mary Malone talks about falling in love, Lyra senses that she is discovering new parts of herself that she never knew existed. She then tells Will, "I love you, Will, I love you—."

She learns much from Will, ranging from her assertion to Tialys, the Gallivespian spy, that one should pay for things one takes as Will had told her back in Cittàgazze, to resisting showing off to her friends how far she and Pan can be apart when she returns to Oxford, having learned from Will "the value of silence and discretion."

Role: *Northern Lights/The Golden Compass*

As the trilogy begins, Lyra leaves behind her childhood in the relative safety of Jordan College, her own small world she believes herself to have mastered. In vastly contrasting situations, she learns much about false appearances and assumptions.

Roger's abduction, even more than the sinister behavior of the College Master and the topics discussed during Asriel's last visit to Oxford, showed Lyra that her world "was changing around her," but she is soon distracted by the captivating Mrs Coulter: "nothing and no one else existed now for Lyra." The Master gives Lyra the alethiometer before she leaves, telling her to "keep it private." In London Lyra soon feels "confined and cramped"; when she hears that Coulter "is the Oblation Board," all of what she thought she knew changes. Lyra flees, beginning a journey that will end with Roger's intercision, and Asriel's establishing the republic of heaven.

Eastern Anglia gyptians hide Lyra in the Fens, where she discovers that not only was her understanding of her present life flawed but the story of her past was a lie. Lyra's ability to read the alethiometer gains her a place on the gyptians' search for their children, leading her to meet armoured bear Iorek Byrnison, aëronaut Lee Scoresby, and witch Serafina Pekkala, who all become her devoted friends. Kidnapped in a raid, Lyra is sold to the Oblation Board's Experiment Station, no longer rescuing but in the same wretched situation as the Gobblers' victims. She is nearly severed from Pan the night the Station is stormed by Iorek, the gyptians, and Serafina's witches, and Scoresby flies Lyra and Roger to Svalbard. But cliff-ghasts attack, and Lyra is captured by armoured bears serving the usurper king Iofur Raknison. She tells Raknison that she is Iorek's dæmon but will be his if Raknison vanquishes Iorek, a scheme devised to give Iorek a chance for a fair fight when he returns to Svalbard. When she sees how weary Iorek looks, Lyra fears she has done him a terrible wrong, but he wins back his throne.

On Svalbard, when Lyra learns Asriel has left with Roger and various scientific devices, she makes the connection between this development and Asriel's description that night of the energy released during intercision. Roger is severed, and Asriel walks into a new world. Lyra blames herself for bringing the boy she thought she had saved to his death. She believes Asriel when he tells Coulter he'll find the source of Dust and destroy it, and decides to get to it before he does.

THE SUBTLE KNIFE

Lyra doesn't find Asriel or Dust but she does find Will Parry in Cittàgazze, and when she extends her quest into his world, she sets in motion those incidents that lead Will to the subtle knife, and Coulter, Lord Boreal, Grumman/Parry, Scoresby, the angels Baruch and Balthamos, and Mary Malone to Cittàgazze.

250   Lyra thought Will "appeared out of nowhere in order to help her" and is shocked by the alethiometer telling her to help him instead. Her guilt at the trouble she feels she has caused Will makes Lyra refrain from using the alethiometer to ask questions about his father during the journey through the world of Cittàgazze. When Serafina Pekkala leaves to answer a call for help from Scoresby, and Will goes off alone on the walk that leads him to his father, Lyra is kidnapped by Mrs. Coulter.

THE AMBER SPYGLASS

Lyra learns that no lie has the power of a vividly told story informed by the truth of deeply felt experiences in the world. Now a young woman, Lyra learns to forgive her own and others' mistakes and comes to know almost more than can be borne about love and loss.

251   In the drugged sleep in which Mrs Coulter keeps her hostage, Lyra dreams of Roger's
251   ghost in the world of the dead. When he asks why he's imprisoned in such a place, Lyra vows in her dreams to rescue him. Awakened but still feeling "sad and wicked and sorry" Lyra believes she must honor that promise to end her "torment and sorrow," even though it means separating from Pan and risking her own life. And so Lyra and Will begin their perilous journey. In the suburbs of the world of the dead, "suffering for Pan and with Pan
252   and because of Pan," she leaves her dæmon behind. The Master of Jordan College's prophecy that Lyra will be forced to commit a painful betrayal is fulfilled.

In the world of the dead, Lyra's role as storyteller, her initial failure and the subsequent success that insures her survival gains a new dimension in the world of the mulefa, where she becomes, perhaps for the first time, a listener more attentive to another's story than her own. As Mary describes her first kiss, Lyra realizes the nature of her feelings for Will. When Lyra returns to her world, she makes learning to read the alethiometer again her goal, beginning with formal study at St Sophia's College (she is
253   promised by the Master that Jordan "is your home for as long as you need it"). At the end of *HIS DARK MATERIALS* Pan and Lyra recall Will's father's words, that there is no afterlife that matters more than this life, and that they must live thoughtfully and help others to

build on this earth in their own world the republic of heaven.

Update: The last Lantern Slide in The Amber Spyglass describes eighteen-year-old Lyra working her way through reference books until she sees patterns in the sequence of symbols of an alethiometer reading. Her report of this breakthrough is tantalizingly noted as "the second thing she said to Will next day in the Botanic Garden."

NL/GC hides in Retiring Room, saves Asriel, wants to know about Dust 1, 2; childhood days at Jordan, learns Billy Costa is missing, panics when she can't find Roger 3; meets Coulter, receives alethiometer, moves to London with Coulter 4; defies Coulter, runs away 5; rescued from net-throwers by Tony Costa, given shelter on his family's boat 6; lives in Fens with gyptians, meets Faa and Coram, learns truth about her past 7; finds she can read alethiometer, overcomes Faa's resistance to taking her on rescue mission 8; attacked by Coulter's spy flies as gyptians are nearly out of England 9; interview with Lanselius, meets Iorek 10; learns from Kaisa of witches' interest in her, meets Scoresby, tells Iorek where to find his armour 11; with help of Iorek finds Gobbler victim Tony Makarios 12; mourns Tony, further develops friendship with Iorek 13; captured by Samoyed traders, sold to Bolvangar 14; finds Roger and Billy at Bolvangar, with Kaisa liberates caged dæmons 15; taken to silver guillotine 16; flees Coulter, sets fire, rescued, flies with Roger and Iorek out of Bolvangar in Scoresby's balloon 17; meets Serafina, falls out of balloon 18; taken prisoner in Svalbard, meets Raknison, convinces him she is Iorek's dæmon 19; witnesses fight to death between Iorek and Raknison 20; rides Iorek to Asriel's, last conversation with her father 21; goes with Iorek and bears in pursuit of Asriel, crosses snow bridge alone 22; fails to save Roger from intercision, Roger dies, witnesses her mother and father's debate and his departure, leaves her world 23; LS Lantern Slides 2, 4, 6, 7, 8

SK meets Will in Cittàgazze 1; topic of tortured witch's interrogation and at witch council 2; learns about Spectres, gets to know Will, enters his world 3; realizes Will's Oxford isn't hers, visits museum, meets Latrom, seeks answers from Malone 4; reveals to Will she knows about him from asking alethiometer, evening out in Oxford with Will, sees Will rescue cat from gang 5; attracted to but scared of Tower, second visit to Malone, runs from investigators, accepts ride from Latrom, realizes her alethiometer has been stolen, confesses to Will, first visit to Latrom's 7; attempts to help Will in duel at Tower of Angels, supports him as he learns to use knife 8; tends to Will's injuries, keeps guard as he retrieves alethiometer 9; Scoresby sets her safety as his price for flying Grumman into world of Cittàgazze 10; attack at belvedere 11; topic of discussion between Malone and Payne, warning from Latrom, instructions from Shadows 12; with witches and Will in Cittàgazze 13; Lena Feldt reveals witches' prophecy regarding her to Coulter, Will finds her gone and witches guarding her dead 15; LS Lantern Slides 5, 8
 brief mentions: 6, 14

AS dreams between chapters beginning with 1 & 2 through 7 & 8; drugged sleep 1; Will refuses to go to Ariel 'til Lyra is safe 2; Ama secures potion for, sees Coulter striking 4; subject of discussions between Asriel and Roke, Baruch 5; Consistorial Court hears testimony that she is Eve, makes plans to assassinate 6; Will and Ama make plans to rescue, Coulter talks about with Will 11; awakened by Ama 12; Will gives back her alethiometer, tells him of her dreams, confrontation with spies 13; reunited with Iorek, consults alethiometer about fixing knife and going to world of dead 14; helps with forge, tries to get Iorek to understand about wanting to see Roger's ghost, parts from Iorek 15; discussed at Asriel's fortress, Coulter claims to be acting for her good 16; joins ghosts moving toward suburbs of world of dead 18; tells outlandish story to family in suburbs, argues with Tialys about summoning her Death 19; leaves Pan behind, attacked by No-Name 21; conversations with ghosts, suggests to Will they free them 22; reunited with Roger, tells true story about life at Jordan College 23; Coulter discusses with MacPhail, bomb to kill her readied 24; meets Scoresby's ghost, falls into abyss, sees Roger and other ghosts freed 26; topic at adamant tower, Asriel expresses pride in, is determined to keep Metatron from getting hold of her through Pan 28; hunts for Pan on battlefield 29; with Will releases Authority, sees Iorek, grabs Kirjava 31; meets mulefa, reunited with Mary 32; feelings stirred by Mary's story 33; in love with Will 35; Serafina discusses with Pan and Kirjava, and Mary 36; reunited with Pan, learns her future can't be with Will, loses ability to read alethiometer 37; leaves world of mulefa with gyptians, enters Cittàgazze and his Oxford with Will, Serafina, and Mary, visits bench at Botanic Garden, says goodbye to Will, discusses future her with Relf and Master 38; LS Lantern Slides 6, 9
 brief mentions: 3, 7, 8, 9, 10, 17, 20, 25, 30, 34

10TH: *SK* appendix (Asriel's daughter)

10TH: *AS* appendix

MacPhail, Father Hugh

Genus: Human
Dæmon: Unnamed; lizard
World: Lyra's
Alliances: Consistorial Court of Discipline
Physical characteristics: Harsh-voiced, grey-haired, very thin, high-strung, tall man in his forties.

Collared Lizard

U.S. Fish and Wildlife Service, Jan 2002

Background: Scottish. Youngest president in its history of the Consistorial Court of Discipline, College of St. Jerome, Geneva, a position that the holder keeps for life. He subsists on bread, fruit, and water only, and exercises with the intensity of a world-class athlete.

Behavior: The extent of MacPhail's fanatical dread of Dust is clearly seen when he proclaims, "…if in order to destroy Dust we also have to destroy the Oblation Board, the College of Bishops, every single agency by which the Holy Church does the work of the Authority—then so be it … better a world with no Church and no Dust than a world where every day we have to struggle under the hideous burden of sin."

He impatiently assures Fra Pravel that he will not be accused of heresy for reporting what he has learned, but as the alethiometrist delivers testimony before the Court, he is obviously frightened and intimidated by MacPhail's conduct. Condescending toward Brother Louis, but sweet to Father Gomez. Retains a civil tone toward Mrs Coulter even as she baits him, but keeps her a prisoner.

The more apparently accommodating MacPhail is, the more agitated and terrified the former Bolvangar staff member, Dr Cooper, becomes as the Court's President gives him the task of reconstructing all that was discovered at the General Oblation Board's Experiment Station about the energy released during intercision.

When he decides to sacrifice his own life to see the bomb launched, "he looked like some gloomy Spanish painting of a saint in the ecstasy of martyrdom."

Role: Proposes Lyra's assassination and sends another member of the Court, Father Gomez, to find the child and to kill her. Directs one of the younger priests to steal Coulter's locket to get a strand of Lyra's hair for the guidance mechanism of a bomb that he has threatened, bullied, and perhaps tortured a scientist formerly employed by the General Oblation Board into developing for the purpose of tracking down and killing Lyra.

Decides to punish Mrs Coulter for not bringing him Lyra when she abducted the girl from Cittàgazze by severing Coulter from her dæmon, thereby releasing the energy needed to launch into another world the bomb intended to kill Lyra. When Coulter escapes the silver guillotine, he chooses what he considers to be martyrdom, conducting his own intercision, and dies.

AS   6, 9 [brief], 24, 25

Magda/Magda's death

Genus: Human/death
World: Suburbs of the world of the dead
Physical characteristics: Very, very old woman with wrinkled face and "glittering eyes"; her death's face seems "so ancient it was almost a skeleton."
Background: Near her death in a literal way. Called Granny by her family—Martha and

Peter, their two children and baby, and an older man—with whom she lives in a suburb of the world of the dead, along with her death. Apparently confined to bed.

Behavior: Appears interested in what's going on. Her death's conduct is mildly flirtatious, pinching her cheek to illustrate to the travelers how he and Magda live "together in kindness and friendship," unlike most people and their deaths.

Role: Magda's death, whom Lyra, Will, and the spies meet when they seek shelter for the night with her family, provides the most useful information on what they must do to cross over from the suburbs to the world of the dead. He tells them that they've got to "call up" their own deaths, "make friends, be kind, invite your deaths to come close to you, and see what you can get them to agree to."

Observation: *Magda's death is described as looking not so much human as like the figure in a picture prominently displayed in Magda's family's shanty: a "jaunty skeleton with a top hat and dark glasses"—which itself sounds quite a bit like an image associated with the rock group The Grateful Dead.*

AS 19

MAGNUSSON, CAPTAIN ✦

Genus: Human
Dæmon: Unnamed; form unknown
World: Lyra's
Role: Employed by Mrs Coulter to sail the children kidnapped by the General Oblation Board north to Lapland.

NL/GC 3 *[brief]*

MAKARIOS, TONY ✦ ✐

Genus: Human
Dæmon: Ratter; usually a sparrow or a mouse (unsettled)
World: Lyra's
Physical characteristics: Somewhere between eight and ten years old. Father could have been Chinese or Greek; mother's ancestry includes Irish, Skraeling, and Lascar.
Background: His alcoholic mother, although not unkind, is neglectful. He fends for himself in London's Limehouse slums, eating what he can steal from street stalls. His summoning by a nurse (and subsequent disappearance) has happened recently enough at Bolvangar that when Lyra arrives, the kids she meets remember the boy. Dies during the night in the gyptian camp after being found by Iorek and Lyra. The gyptians cremate his remains before they move on, but first Lyra places between his teeth a dæmon coin she has devised to honor the memory of his lost Ratter.
Behavior: Considered dull-witted, but he is tender toward his mother. According to Bridget McGinn, Tony asked not what was going to happen to him, but to his dæmon, Ratter. She says he was quite direct and told the nurse he knew that the doctors were going to kill his dæmon.

When Lyra and Iorek Byrnison find him, Tony, who is referred to as a "half-boy" or "half-child," is not surprised to see a little girl and an armoured bear appear looking for him in the middle of nowhere, nor is he scared. All he wants is for someone to find his dæmon.

Role: Exemplifies the plight of the Gobblers' victims and the horror of intercision. His entrapment by Coulter marks the entry of the Gobblers and their founder into the story.

NL/GC abducted 3; alethiometer alerts Lyra to a lost being, maybe a child 12; Lyra meets Tony, his death, cremation 13; recalled at Bolvangar, his dæmon's empty jar 15
    brief mentions: 14, 17, 21, 23

AS   19 *[brief]*

263 MAKEPWE, FATHER

Genus: Human
Dæmon: Unnamed; form unknown
World: Lyra's
Alliances: Consistorial Court of Discipline
Physical characteristics: "ancient and rheumy-eyed."
Role: Oldest of the twelve members of the Consistorial Court of Discipline, he is present when Fra Pavel, the alethiometrist, gives testimony to the Court, and with his peers follows the Court's President Hugh MacPhail into council chambers for further private discussions.

AS   6 *[brief]*

MALONE, DR MARY

Genus: Human
Dæmon: Unnamed; Alpine chough
World: Will's, Cittàgazze, mulefa's
Alliances: Lyra, the mulefa, Will and his mother
Physical characteristics: Perhaps in her late thirties, she

Alpine Chough

© Tim Farr

264
265
has "short black hair and red cheeks," dresses simply. Build is "stocky," but she is physically fit.
Background: As a child she was "a good little girl" who as she grew up came to believe she had a spiritual vocation. Claims she was "pleased with myself. Too much. I was holy *and* I was
266
clever." Became a nun, but left the Church shortly after finishing her doctorate. The turning point in her life is described at length in chapter 33 of *THE AMBER SPYGLASS*, "Marzipan."

After she left the Church, she lived with a man for several years and took up camping and rock-climbing. When Lyra meets her, Mary is principal investigator at the Dark Matter Research Unit, Oxford University. Mary doesn't seem attached to her possessions or professional status, nor does she appear to be in any serious relationship at the time of Lyra's appearance. However, as her letters make clear in the appendix to the **10**ᴛʜ anniversary edition of *THE AMBER SPYGLASS*, she is passionate about particle physics.
267
Behavior: The "exhaustion and despair" she feels when Lyra first enters her lab disappears as she becomes excited by Lyra's ability to communicate with the Shadow-particles. She is willing to listen to the child; even when Lyra is challenging and correcting her, she treats her with respect. She finds discussing good and evil in a scientific unit "*embarrassing*"; she tells Lyra, "One of the reasons I became a scientist was not to have to think about that
268
kind of thing." But she can accept Lyra's criticism that investigating the Shadows can't be done without considering questions of good and evil.

She is trusting of the communications she receives from the Shadows, going as far as destroying University property, faking identification, and lying to the police before walking away from her life and into a new world. In contrast, she immediately distrusts Sir Charles Latrom. She is altogether opposed to the concept of the Ministry of Defense becoming involved with research into the manipulation of consciousness. She objects to compromising her integrity as a scientist in the interest of gaining funding.

Adept at achieving the state of mind described by the Romantic poet John Keats as "capable of being in uncertainties, mysteries, doubts, without any irritable reaching after fact and reason." Her experience in reading the I Ching is an indication of a broad search 269 for wisdom extending beyond the confines of her own cultural tradition; her open-mindedness allows her to assimilate with surprising ease into a different world and form relationships with conscious beings quite unlike any even imagined in her world of origin.

When mulefa elder Sattamax tells Mary that compared to the mulefa, she appears to "think and act with the speed of a bird." Mary's reaction is to feel "a strange flattery: the 270 idea of herself as swift and darting and bird-like was new and pleasant, because she had always thought of herself as dogged and plodding." 271

In the mulefa's world, she achieves a "deep slow ecstasy at being one with her body and the earth and everything that was matter." Mary tells Will and Lyra she is "solitary 272 but happy," and when Serafina Pekkala asks about her plans, Mary realizes that she hasn't 273 given a return to her world any thought, telling the witch, "I've been very happy here. The happiest I've ever been in my life, I think." 274

Role: According to the Shadow-particles (or Dust, or angels), the task of this ex-nun physicist is to play the tempter or serpent in a drama in which Lyra is Eve. By doing so, she inadvertently accomplishes what the mulefa asked of her: find a way to return sraf to their world. As their host in the mulefa's world, she provides the children comfort and rest while they find their dæmons, fall in love, and learn they must be forever parted.

Mary resists the impulse to hug Will at first meeting. They shake hands instead, and "a current of understanding and respect passed between them," the beginning of a "life-long" friendship. Mary says that only the two of them can ever really understand what 275 they've experienced, and notes that both will need to learn to live with their dæmons in a world of people who have no idea that they have them. Her position of being in trouble with the authorities for destroying University property also makes her seem compatible to Will, and he is grateful for her promise to help him help his mother.

In her journal entries included in the appendix to the 10ᴛʜ anniversary edition of THE AMBER SPYGLASS, Mary notes that Will possesses the same "fierce direct quality" that impressed her in Lyra. Part of her "can't believe there are no relatives" who will help him with his mother, but another part objects, "Actually if he says it, I believe it. I'd believe anything from him." She plans to look into becoming his legal guardian, and acknowledges too that not all the benefit will be Will's: "And I'll need him. I could help. I could do that." Chapter 7 of THE AMBER SPYGLASS is titled "Mary, Alone." 276

Observation: *A postcard from Mary Malone to a friend marking Mary's arrival in Oxford after leaving the convent is among the miscellaneous documents in* LYRA'S OXFORD.

Update: The 10ᴛʜ anniversary edition of THE AMBER SPYGLASS features an appendix from the "strictly confidential" archives of the Magisterium. It includes a curious collection of fragmentary writings by Mary Malone, from letters to colleagues to a scrap asking her landlady to let the plumber in. Her personal notes, in letters to friends or journal entries, deal with the strange, even sanity-challenging, experience of twice finding herself in another world, the very bearable lightness of being she felt on leaving the convent, the impact of witnessing Lyra and Will's love, and her regret that she didn't bring a camera along.

SK meets Lyra 4; warns Lyra about police 7; interview with Latrom, talks to Shadows 13
  brief mentions: 5, 8

AS in Cittàgazze 7, enters world of mulefa 10; sees sraf, given task 17; figures out trees' problem 20; 27; meets Will, reunited with Lyra 32, 33, 34, 35, 36; sees her dæmon, begins helping Will 38; **LS** Lantern Slides 1, 5
  brief mentions: 16, 23, 37

10TH: *AS* appendix

MAN IN TOP HAT ❂

Genus: Human
Dæmon: Unnamed; lemur
World: Lyra's
Role: Lyra accepts his offer to pay for her coffee and sandwich when she stops at a refreshment stall after running away from

Ring Tailed Lemurs

Adrian Pingstone, August 2003, Wikimedia Commons

Coulter's London residence. But she declines his attempt to add a little brandy to her coffee and tries to dissuade him from paying her more attention with one of her tall tales.

NL/GC 6 *[brief]*

MARGARET ❖

Genus: Human
Dæmon: Unnamed; form unknown
World: Lyra's
Background: Gyptian
Role: Mother at Roping who tells leader John Faa that she hopes he will show no mercy to the Gobblers. Although he understands her position, Faa emphasizes that the immediate top priority is the safety of the children, but he will be ruthless in their pursuit and punishment.

Note: *Margaret's question prompts a more vivid reply by John Faa in* NORTHERN LIGHTS *than the one he makes in* THE GOLDEN COMPASS. *He tells the angry woman, "My own hammer is thirsty for blood… she's been a-hanging in my boat and dreaming; but she can smell blood in the wind from the North. She spoke to me last night and I said soon, gal, soon."*

277

NL/GC 8 *[brief]*

MARK ⚑

Role: Will's alias (Mark Ransom) when he visits Oxford with Lyra.
SK   brief mentions: 3, 7

MARTHA ❖

Genus: Human
Dæmon: Unnamed; form unsettled
World: Lyra's
278
Physical characteristics: Thin, "subdued-looking child"

Role: Another Gobbler victim. One of Lyra's three "roommates" at Bolvangar, the General Oblation Board's Experiment Station.

NL/GC 3 *[brief]*

Martha, wife of Peter ✒

Genus: Human

World: Suburbs of the world of the dead

Physical characteristics: Of child-bearing age

Background: Presumably the same as her husband Peter's; she arrived in the suburbs of the world of the dead by accident and can't move on until her death tells her it is time to die.

Behavior: Lets her husband Peter do most of the talking, but is attentive to her guests, inviting them to sit down, encouraging Peter to give the spies a before-dinner drink, and adding potatoes to stretch the stew so that there will be enough for all.

Role: Lyra, Will and the Gallivespian spies stay with her family—two children, a baby, her husband, an older man, and a grandmother—in their shanty in a suburb of the world of the dead the night before they cross over to the world of the dead.

AS 19; 21 *[brief]*

Martins, Semyon Karlovich ⑩

Genus: Human

Dæmon: Unnamed; form unknown

World: Lyra's

Role: Father Martins is the witch consul for Queen Ruta Skadi's clan. He operates out of Novgorod.

SK appendix

10ᴛʜ: *SK* appendix

Martyr ✒

Genus: Ghost

World: World of the dead

Physical characteristics: Young woman

Background: Died a martyr hundreds of years previously. Had believed that those who died for their faith or denied the world's pleasures, choosing years of solitary prayer and sacrifice instead, would be rewarded after death by a blissful eternity in heaven.

Behavior: First to come forward after Lyra tells the ghosts that, according to her alethiometer, those ghosts who leave through the window Will cuts will drift apart, as their dæmons did when their people died.

Role: Encourages her fellow ghosts to leave the world of the dead since their present existence in "a place of nothing" is one with "no hope of freedom, or joy, or sleep or rest or peace," and although drifting apart may mean "oblivion," "it won't be nothing" because they will be part of "the physical world which is our true home and always was." 279

The ghost of a monk strongly objects to her arguments.

AS 23

MASTER OF JORDAN COLLEGE ✤ ⚡ ✎ LS

Genus: Human
Dæmon: Unnamed; raven
World: Lyra's
Alliances: Jordan College, the Magisterium, Lyra
Physical characteristics: Although he is in his mid-to-late seventies, his bearing reminds Lyra of the strength she sees in John Faa and Lord Asriel. Dresses in black, down to his well-worn shoes: "In his black suit and black tie he looked

Raven

as much like his dæmon as anyone could." Even his "hooded, clouded eyes" are like his raven dæmon's. Rarely smiles; when he tries to, what crosses his face is indistinguishable from a "grimace of sadness."

Background: Jordan College Master and a Member of the Prime Minister's Cabinet Council. Never referred to otherwise than as "Master."

When he placed his illegitimate daughter under the Master's guardianship, Asriel had gained from the Scholar an assurance that Coulter would never be allowed near Lyra.

Behavior: Collects "heavy pictures" and "glum silver." Particularly friendly with the College Librarian, in whom he even confided his plan to poison Asriel.

Faa sees him as a man "having terrible choices to make; whatever he chooses will do harm."

Role: Gives Lyra her alethiometer, and it is his prophecy of Lyra's painful betrayal that is fulfilled when she leaves Pan behind to cross to the land of dead.

In the opening scene of the trilogy, the Master poisons Lord Asriel's wine. His reasons are not personal and he stands to gain nothing. The Master's plan is thwarted by Lyra, although the Master never knows how Asriel knew the wine was poisoned.

When Lyra returns to her world, the Master, who "loved the girl dearly," assures her, "You will never be lost while this college is standing, Lyra. This is your home for as long as you need it," and tells her that her father left money with him for her use, although this is not true and her support will come from him.

NL/GC poisons Tokay 1, talks with Librarian 2, summons Lyra to his Lodgings for dinner 3, gives Lyra alethiometer 4, Faa discusses with Lyra 7, Coulter discusses with Lyra 17, LS Lantern Slide 8
    brief mentions: 5, 10, 18, 21

SK   *brief mentions:* 2, 3, 4, 8, 9, 13

AS   his prophecy regarding Lyra fulfilled 21 *[brief]*, 38

MATAPAN ✎

Genus: Dæmon
World: World of the dead
Role: Unidentified ghost-child's dæmon.
AS   22 *[brief]*

McGINN, BRIDGET ✤

Genus: Human
Dæmon: Unnamed; form unsettled

280
281
282
283
284
285

World: Lyra's

Physical characteristics: Blond

Behavior: Talkative and observant, but when she is called to leave the lunchroom, her voice becomes "hardly audible" and her "face vivid with fear." | 286

Role: Child at the General Oblation Board's Experiment Station. At lunch she recalls the last time anyone saw Tony Makarios, the boy who had attracted notice because his dæmon rarely changed. He was told by a nurse to come along with her for "a little operation. Just a little cut." But while Bridget is discussing what this operation must | 287 involve, she is interrupted and summoned to go along with one of the Station's nurses.

NL/GC 15

McKay ✧

Genus: Human

Dæmon: Unnamed; form unknown

World: Lyra's

Alliances: General Oblation Board

Background: Research student in charge of the storage area for severed dæmons that Kaisa and Lyra break into at the General Oblation Board's Experiment Station.

Role: His assurances that the shed was secured and alarms set are relayed to Coulter as she questions the senior staff about how the severed dæmons could have been released.

NL/GC 16 *[brief]*

"The men" ⚱ ✎

Genus: Human

World: Will's

Physical characteristics: Both are strong; the surviving one is described as being very large with very light blond hair.

Background: If Sir Charles Latrom/Lord Boreal is to be believed, they are from the government's security services and began hunting John Parry in earnest after Asriel broke through to other worlds. Their credentials are unknown.

Behavior: They harangue the confused and anxious Elaine Parry, refuse to speak about their business with Will, but leave when the enraged boy orders them out of his home.

Role: The unwarranted searches of John Parry's home, and harassment of his wife Elaine by two men, are the catalyst for Will's decision that he must learn the truth behind his father's mysterious disappearance twelve years ago.

The two men break into the Parry home for the second time the night after Will has taken his mother to stay with another woman. Will is awakened by the intruders, and one man dies when, rammed by Will and tripped by Moxie, the family's cat, he falls down the stairs.

When Lyra wonders what Will will do if, when he returns to his own world, the men are still after him, he replies that he isn't worried: "We've seen worse than them, after all." | 288

[*See also* **Walters, Inspector**]

SK in Winchester 1, in Oxford 4, Will tells Lyra about 13
      brief mentions: 3, 5, 8, 9

AS *brief mentions:* 9, 13, 19, 35

MENDHAM, TOM ✦

Genus: Human
Dæmon: Unnamed; form unknown
World: Lyra's
Background: Gyptian
Role: Captured or killed during a gyptian spy mission to London with partner Frans Broekman. Fate unknown.

NL/GC 9 *[brief]*

METATRON ✦

Genus: Angel
World: All
Alliances: the Authority (initially), kingdom of heaven, his own ambition
Physical characteristics: To Coulter, but for his blinding light, he looked "exactly like a man in early middle age, tall, powerful, and commanding," but she can't tell if he is clothed or winged "because of the force of his eyes. She could look at nothing else." Proves in the battle at the abyss to be formidably strong. When Coulter grabs the angel's hair, she finds "his strength was enormous: it was like holding the mane of a bolting horse." In spite of the two humans' and their dæmons' fierce efforts, when Asriel is about to lose consciousness, Metatron "still wasn't hurt."
Background: Presumably rules on behalf of the Authority, whom the angel claims has retired to contemplate "deeper mysteries." However, when Metatron has the crystal litter moved out of the Clouded Mountain and away from the battlefield, it is because he wants the Authority "kept alive for a while yet," which suggests that Metatron has other plans than to continue indefinitely as the Authority's Regent. Already he is using those angels "who had fallen in love with human women, with the daughters of men, so long ago" as guards at the Clouded Mountain—in spite of their banishment by the Authority when Metatron was still Enoch the man.

The angel Baruch knew Metatron 4,000 years ago when he was the man Enoch. They were brothers, but Enoch "cast [him] out." During Enoch's sixty-five years as a man, he had many wives, and, loving "their flesh," he understood when angels consorted with human women. However the Authority, despite Enoch's pleas, directed his future Regent to "prophesy their doom." When Enoch died, he was elevated to the status of an angel by the Authority and renamed Metatron.
Behavior: Brutal, cruel, cunning, powerful, and vain.

In the several thousand years since he ceased to be a man, Metatron has not lost his desire for beautiful women. Coulter uses this to her advantage. In spite of his "profound intellect [which] had had thousands of years to deepen and strengthen itself," Metatron, "blinded by his twin obsessions: to destroy Lyra and to possess her mother," will bring about his own downfall.
Role: Officially the Authority's Regent, but seems to have surpassed his king. According to the angel Baruch, Metatron is becoming more involved in human affairs because the Authority "considers that conscious beings of every kind have become dangerously independent." The condition of the Authority when Lyra and Will release him from the crystal litter suggests that Metatron has been pursuing his own agenda for some time.

Metatron's transformation of the dwelling of the Authority, the Clouded Mountain, into an "an engine of war" supports Baruch's claim that he plans to attack Asriel's republic. Asriel fears Metatron far more so than he does the Authority; he thinks Metatron capable of setting up interventions "worse than anything the Consistorial Court of Discipline could dream up." | 300 | 301

Metatron's plan is exposed to Asriel by his alethiometrist. Asriel believes that if Metatron succeeds in seizing the children's dæmons, "the future of every conscious being" will be increasingly compromised by the forces of repression. Knowing Metatron to have once been a man, Asriel figures that the Regent could be tempted into one-on-one combat. Metatron nearly manages to ascend out of the abyss with Asriel and the golden monkey holding onto him, but with the help of Coulter and Stelmaria, together they all fall into the abyss.

[*See also* **Enoch**]

AS attempts attack on Will and angels 2, Baruch tells Asriel about 5, his plan to capture Will's and Lyra's dæmons 28, Coulter approaches in Clouded Mountain 30; Coulter and Asriel drag into abyss 31
   brief mentions: 8, 36

Miti, Reina 🗡 ✏ ⑩

Genus: Witch
Dæmon: Unnamed; form unknown
World: Lyra's
Background: Witch-queen of the Tikshozero and arch-enemy of Queen Katja Sirkka's Miekojärvi witch clan. | 302
Role: Miti's was one of the clans Ruta Skadi intended to persuade to join her in fighting for Asriel, and Skadi succeeded. Miti's clan and six or so others enter battle alongside Skadi's, attacking angels emerging from the Authority's base of operations, the Clouded Mountain.

SK 13 *[brief]*, appendix

AS 29 *[brief]*

10ᴛʜ: *SK* appendix

Monk (perhaps) ✏

Genus: Ghost
World: World of the dead
Physical characteristics: Looks "like a monk: thin, and pale even in his death, with dark zealous eyes." | 303
Background: Considers the world in which he dwelt before dying to be "a vale of corruption and tears." | 304
Behavior: Rudely pushes away the martyr's ghost, crossing himself and praying.
Role: Tries to dissuade fellow ghosts from leaving the world of the dead through the window Will cuts, claiming Lyra to be an "agent of the Evil One himself" who will lead | 305 the ghosts to hell. Claims where the ghosts are now is a "blessed place...which the eyes of faith see as it is, overflowing with milk and honey and resounding with the sweet hymns of the angels." | 306

AS 23

MONTALE, ALFREDO ✐

Genus: Human
World: Will's
Physical characteristics: While Mary Malone says he isn't particularly good-looking, she
does mention his "soft black hair and beautiful olive-coloured skin and dark, dark eyes."
Background: Italian scientist who Mary Malone met at a conference in Lisbon.
Behavior: Puts people at their ease; "nice and clever and funny."
Role: Montale was the first man the adult Mary Malone had ever felt a strong attraction to;
her desire for him prompted her to recognize that she was not satisfied with her life in the
Church.

AS   33   *[brief]*

MOXIE ⚲✐

Genus: Feline
World: Will's
Physical characteristics: Tabby
Background: Will Parry's cat.
Behavior: Silent and friendly, apparently inclined to rub against the legs of strangers.
Role: Accidentally causes the fatal fall of one of the men searching Will's house for any
documents relating to his father, lending urgency to Will's quest for information.

SK   1
      brief mentions: 5, 9, 13
AS   2   *[brief]*

MUSCA ✻

Genus: Dæmon
Form: Unknown
Human: Ignatius Cole
World: Lyra's
Role: Lyra and Roger see his name on the tomb of his human, who was briefly the Jordan
College Master from 1745-1748.

NL/GC 3 *[brief]*

NEAR-ADOLESCENT CITTÀGAZZE BOY ⚲

Genus: Human
World: Cittàgazze
Physical characteristics: Has black hair and is tall and thin; nearly adolescent. The Spectres
are so thick around him he appears to "shimmer."
Background: Spotted by Lee Scoresby through his telescope as he and Stanislaus Grumman
fly over the city of Cittàgazze.
Behavior: Although he cannot yet see Spectres, they cluster about him "like flies around
meat" to the extent that he seems to feel their presence, and acts occasionally as if
bothered by some type of nuisance insect.
Role: Their reactions to this boy's plight show the difference in Grumman's and Scoresby's

understanding of right action. Scoresby wants to rescue the boy, who almost certainly will otherwise soon be lost to the Spectres. But stopping to do so would jeopardize Grumman's chances to find the bearer of the subtle knife, and they too would be attacked by Spectres.

Grumman says that if Scoresby wants an "end to cruelty and injustice, then the better thing to do is to take his passenger where he needs to go. But Scoresby retorts that "the place you fight cruelty is where you find it, and the place you give help is where you see it needed." 311

312

SK 14 *[brief]*

Nell ❈

Genus: Human
Dæmon: Unnamed; form unknown
World: Lyra's
Background: Gyptian.
Role: Questions John Faa at the second Roping about sending women on the voyage North to take care of rescued children.

NL/GC 8 *[brief]*

Nelson ⚚

Genus: Human
World: Will's
Alliances: British Ministry of Defense
Background: Physicist with academic credentials and Ministry of Defense secret funding.
Behavior: John Parry's first impression is that he is "a genial dimwit" whose ineptness, 313 demonstrated by failing to arrange transport for his equipment, has stalled the trip into the Brooks Mountain Range of Alaska. Later, Parry learns that the delay was a ruse while Nelson gathered information about what the scientist, like Parry, is really interested in: the "anomaly" or opening to another world.

Parry hints to Nelson that he knows that he too is looking for the window. Nelson neither acknowledges nor denies Parry's suspicions.
Role: Like John Parry, Nelson is a member of what is supposed to be an archaeological expedition to Alaska. In his last letters home, Parry described Nelson's unusual preparations for the Nuniatak dig, for example, taking radiation suits into the mountains.

Even after Parry happens to discover that Nelson too is looking for the window, Parry's plans remain the same; he writes to his wife Elaine that he intends to go off alone to look for the legendary window, but "If I bump into Nelson wandering about on Lookout Ridge I'll play it by ear." 314
Observation: *In Lyra's world, where John Parry has assumed the name Stanislaus Grumman, the former explorer tells aëronaut Lee Scoresby that when he left his world through the Beringland (Alaska) window, he was accompanied by two other men, both of whom were victims of Cittàgazze's Spectres. While one of these could have been Nelson, there is no textual evidence confirming such a conjecture, but the interest in Parry's personal papers suggests that the Ministry of Defense may not be convinced that their man Nelson was simply lost in a blizzard.*

SK 5

No-Name

Genus: Harpy

World: World of the dead

Alliances: Authority (originally), ghosts who sustain her with true stories

Physical characteristics: Vulture-sized, jagged-clawed, smelling of death, she has tangled black shoulder-length hair that stands on end like massed snakes when she's angered. No-Name has a woman's face and breasts, slime-clotted eyes, bloody vomit-crusted lips, and a hateful expression on a face that though unwrinkled appears ancient, having witnessed thousands of years of suffering. Cannot be killed or hurt.

Background: When he created the world of the dead, the Authority gave the harpies the "power to see the worst in every one" and that is what they have fed on for thousands of years.

Behavior: Screeches, jeers, and cackles with tremendous force and volume. Although she does claw Lyra, Will believes that No-Name ran into her by mistake, and that she and the other harpies do not want to make physical contact, but prefer to attack by screaming torments. Knows her victims' greatest vulnerabilities; for instance, she needles Will about his mother being alone.

Prideful; feels she would lose honor and status if the task given her by the Authority is undermined. The ability of the ghosts to leave the world of the dead, she predicts, would cause them to cease to fear and respect her.

Keeps her promise of showing Will the best place to cut a window out of the world of the dead. Heroic in her rescue of Lyra.

Role: Leads Lyra, Will, and their party to a spot in the world of dead where Will can cut through to another world. No-Name fears the loss of a sense of purpose, until Salmakia suggests that as the "guardians and keepers of this place," they can guide the ghosts from the river launch to the window Will cuts and receive the ghosts' stories as earned payment. Xaphania will later remind Lyra and Will of this condition, and encourage them to help the people of their worlds understand the necessity of living lives full enough so that when they die they can pay the harpies with true stories.

When Lyra slips off the ledges and begins the endless fall into the abyss, No-Name flies down, and, even though Lyra's weight threatens to drag the harpy into the abyss as well, pulls the girl to safety.

Leaving the world of the dead for the last time, Lyra tells the harpy that she deserves to be called something more fitting than "No-Name," and gives her the name, "Gracious Wings."

AS   attacks Lyra 21; 22 *[brief]*; harpies' history and spies' proposal 23; saves Lyra from abyss 26; renamed 29

Ogunwe, King

Genus: Human

Dæmon: Unnamed; cheetah

World: Lyra's

Alliances: Asriel's republic

Physical characteristics: Described as "powerful and deep-voiced."

Background: African king; however, he says his "proudest task" is working with Asriel to set "up a world where there are no kingdoms at all."

Behavior: Speaks his mind. He objects to Coulter remaining in their company while Asriel

Cheetah

and his commanders make their plans. He isn't soothed when Asriel says he will "guarantee Mrs Coulter's behavior," objecting that Asriel might be "tempted" by her. Relents following Coulter's pleadings. Although he remains somewhat suspicious of her, she rightly judged that her feminine charms were best directed at him. When Coulter steals the intention craft, Ogunwe's immediate response, stopped by Asriel, is to have his troops fire on the craft. Asriel admits to the king that his concern about Coulter's presence was justified. He is surprised by Coulter's shocked reaction at hearing that the Authority is not the Creator, but just another angel.

Role: One of Asriel's three high commanders.

Ogunwe leads the forces sent to rescue Lyra from Mrs Coulter's Himalayan hideout, suffering a minor head wound in the ensuing conflict. While Lyra gets away, he does capture Coulter and transports her to the basalt fortress. Later, after he is resigned to Coulter accompanying his commanders on Asriel's tour of the fortress armoury, he complies with Coulter's request to tell her what he knows about Gallivespians, angels, and the Authority. Discusses the Clouded Mountain with Asriel.

When Asriel makes his decision to lure Metatron into hand-to-hand combat on the ledges of the abyss, he leaves Ogunwe in charge of the armies defending the fortress.

AS in gyropter en route to Himalayas 9; described, objects to Coulter's presence in tower and then converses with her in armoury 16; talks with Asriel about Metatron 28
  brief mentions: 5, 11, 12, 13, 14

Old farmers of Cittàgazze

Genus: Human
World: Cittàgazze
Background: Childless married couple living well away from their nearest neighbors. Farm olives, make cheese.
Behavior: Very generous and welcoming to Mary Malone because Spectres flee from her.
Role: They replenish abundantly Mary Malone's dwindling food supplies as she hikes through Cittàgazze.

Later, Father Gomez questions what seems to be same couple on whether Mary has passed their way.

AS brief mentions: 7, 17, 20

Old lady with lorgnette

Genus: Human
Dæmon: Unnamed, scarlet macaw
World: Lyra's
Behavior: Curious, perhaps haughty; not pleased with being told what she can't believe.
Role: This guest at Mrs Coulter's cocktail party assumes that Lyra is Coulter's daughter and wonders to the girl why she isn't attending the school where her mother studied. Corrected by Lyra, who tells her she is Coulter's assistant, the woman asks who Lyra's parents are. When Lyra explains that they were the Count and Countess Belacqua, who died in an accident, her dæmon becomes impatient, but Lyra simply moves on.
Facts: *A lorgnette is a pair of eyeglasses or opera glasses that aren't worn but instead have a*

Scarlet Macaw

E. Sandra Keller

short handle by which the user brings them to her face.
NL/GC 5 *[brief]*

ORDERLY, ADAMANT TOWER ✐

Genus: Human
Dæmon: Unnamed, terrier
World: Lyra's

Soft-Coated Wheaten Terrier

Behavior: Apologetic and somewhat unnerved by the consequences of his intrusion on the angel Baruch, although Asriel assures him that he was simply following the set procedure of knocking and entering without waiting for a reply.

Nervous when near Coulter, who, having been captured by Ogunwe in the Himalayas, is angry and tied to a chair in Asriel's chambers.

Role: Fetches food and drink, announces visitors, conveys messages.

Interrupts Asriel's unplanned visit with Baruch; the draught of air from his opening the door causes the injured angel's dissipation. Luckily the angel has already delivered his most critical information.

Much later brings Asriel and Coulter the news that Will and Lyra's dæmons are at the gate.

Observation: *Arguably, the orderly mentioned in these chapters may not always be the same individual, but the familiarity with Asriel's personal quarters suggests a position like that of a personal manservant, as Thorold was to Asriel in Lyra's world. There is also mention of a call being put out for a medical orderly when Baruch is carried in to the adamant tower.*

AS   *brief mentions:* with Baruch 5; unnerved by Coulter 16; treated politely by Coulter 28

320

OXENTIEL, MADAME ✐

Genus: Gallivespian
World: Gallivespians' (origin), Asriel's republic
Alliances: Asriel's republic
Physical characteristics: Grey-haired; alert expression.
Background: Second-in-command under Lord Roke of the Gallivespians allied with Asriel. Takes over after the death of Lord Roke, who was killed at the launch site of the Consistorial Court of Discipline's bomb. Inherits Roke's blue hawk.
Behavior: Assertive and firm.
Role: Leads Gallivespians into battle, rescues Will and Lyra from the Authority's troops, and takes the children to find their dæmons, following Asriel's orders.

AS   28, 31

PAGDZIN *TULKU* ✐

Genus: Human
Dæmon: Unnamed, bat
World: Lyra's
Physical characteristics: Has long grey beard, bright eyes.
Background: Greatly respected healer, having recently cured villagers

Mexican Long-Nosed Bat

of an outbreak of white fever in the Himalayan region where Coulter is hiding Lyra.

Behavior: Blunt but not mean in addressing Ama, the little girl who comes to him for a potion.
Role: Renowned healer at Cho-Lung-Se monastery whom Ama (the herdsman's daughter) seeks out. She feels the monk can provide a potion to counter the sleeping sickness spell that Coulter claims is the reason her daughter can't awaken.

Pagdzin *tulku* gives in to Ama's pleas and provides an antidote for Coulter's sleeping potion, which he prepares by mixing ingredients indicated by his bat dæmon. He then tells the girl that next time she visits he expects the whole truth from her, not just part of the story.
Facts: *A tulku is a reincarnated lama; the Dalai Lama is a tulku.*
AS 4; 14 *[brief]*

PALMERIAN PROFESSOR [*See* Trelawney]

PANTALAIMON / PAN ✦ ⚵ ✐ LS

Pine Marten

Genus: Dæmon
Form: Pine marten (initially unsettled)
Human: Lyra
World: Lyra's (origin), all others Lyra visits except the world of the dead, and during their separation many others, including the Gallivespians'.
Physical characteristics: In his settled form as a pine marten, he is "like a large and powerful ferret, red-gold in colour, lithe and sinuous and full of grace." Martens are closely related to ermine, one of Pan's favorite forms when changing. | 321
Behavior: Provides a counterpoint to Lyra: more cautious, to some extent a better judge of people. When they are alone, he freely criticizes her, but when Lyra is challenged, he always stands with her, and when she is distraught, criticism is withheld and support freely given.

In the opening scene of *HIS DARK MATERIALS*, Pan urges Lyra to be more cautious. He is uneasy about hiding in the Retiring Room and warns Lyra, "Behave yourself." When she asks | 322
him if he thinks the Tokay has been poisoned, Pan replies, "I think it is, like you do," and | 323
when in turn he asks Lyra what she plans to do about it, she replies, "I didn't have anything in mind, and well you know it." Their relationship at this stage has some semblance to that | 324
of siblings; for example, when Pan was too agitated to sleep the night before they left for London, Lyra "snapped at him" and he in turn "became a hedgehog out of pique." | 325

As she gains maturity, Lyra becomes more attuned to Pan's warnings. For example, when she first considers exploring the Tower of Angels in Cittàgazze, he "was fluttering anxiously on her shoulder, just as he had… in the crypt at Jordan College, and she was a little wiser now" and so they make a quick retreat. | 326

He is an astute judge of character; Lyra sometimes lets her own agenda obscure her perceptions of those in whom she places trust. Because she is determined to go to the North and thinks Coulter will take her, Lyra is reluctant to face her unhappiness in London. But Pan sees more clearly what her status is with Coulter; he tells Lyra she is turning into Coulter's pet. His torment by the golden monkey when Lyra angers Coulter leads to a permanent, "powerful loathing" of Coulter's dæmon. In Will's Oxford, Pan | 327
senses that the man Lyra meets in the museum (who introduces himself as Sir Charles Latrom) is a danger to Lyra, and tries to warn her. After the alethiometer is stolen, Lyra and Will are compelled to go to the Tower of Angels to seek the subtle knife. Pan tries to

cooperate as fully as he can with Will, realizing their situation is Lyra's fault.

Pan is just as adept at spotting the good in people. He forces Lyra to overcome her initial fear at the appearance of armoured bear Iorek Byrnison. He senses that Dr Mary Malone is on their side and not the police's when detectives corner Lyra in Malone's office in Will's Oxford.

Most notably, Pan seems to know how important Will is to Lyra even before she does. In the Tower of Angels, Will is hurting and bleeding and unable to cope with what Paradisi is trying to teach him about the knife. Pan, without consulting Lyra, breaks the biggest taboo governing dæmons. In the form of a wolfhound, he goes to Will and licks his wounded hand, restoring Will's calm and focus. Will trusts Pan as well. As Lyra, Will, and the witches journey through Cittàgazze, the reticent boy can confide in Pan alone his fear of dying. Pan tries to reassure Will, telling him that Lyra considers him her best friend and thinks he is as brave as Iorek Byrnison.

While he may privately be critical of Lyra, he doesn't stand for others threatening his person and most often his actions and reactions parallel hers. When Lyra scrambles to the rooftops of Jordan College to scream her frustration at the lack of interest in Roger's absence the day Billy Costa disappears, Pan shrieks along with her. He is bossy to Mrs Lonsdale's dæmon when the housekeeper bosses Lyra around; his "eyes flash red" when he thinks the Master of Jordan College intends to send Lyra to a girls' boarding school. In Cittàgazze, he takes the form of a leopard to surprise the Spectre-orphan mob threatening Lyra, Will, and the Oxford cat.

Pan's behavior at the most critical times shows unconditional love for Lyra. An early example is when the two are nearly severed at the General Oblation Board's Bolvangar Experiment Station. After their ordeal, Pan "lay against [Lyra's] bare skin…loving her back to herself" but stayed wary and "thought to her: We're only safe as long as we pretend." He even shows jealously when Lyra lets the Gallivespians perch on her shoulder to rest during their journey into the suburbs of the world of dead. When they are stranded on the mountaintop in Svalbard and decide to venture into the world to which Asriel has opened a passage, Pan reminds Lyra, as together they leave behind their world, that she is never alone.

But most touching is Pan's behavior in the world of the dead. He urges Lyra to turn back as they approach Peter's house in the suburbs of this world. He is fearful and does not want Lyra to go with her death, but the boatman refuses to ferry Lyra, Will, and the spies across to the entrance of the world of the dead if they take Pan. Their parting is excruciating. Will sees Pan become like "a creature so sunk in misery that it was more misery than creature." But when finally he is left behind on the banks of the river, her dæmon shows his love for Lyra by not asking why or trying to make her feel guilty, but instead holding "himself quiet so as not to distress the human who was abandoning him."

Role: As Lyra moves from her carefree days of play in Oxford through an increasingly dangerous and complicated world, Pan helps her clarify her thoughts about her experiences and provides practical assistance. Lyra's and Pan's relationship provides the richest illustration of the depth and complexity of the human-dæmon bond.

He shares Lyra's thrill when she occasionally achieves a "glimpse of meaning" as she learns to read the alethiometer. On their way to Bolvangar, Pantalaimon is more frightened than Lyra is about approaching the severed child Tony Makarios. Even so, he would have reached out for him, were it not for the taboo against touching other dæmons' people. When angels surround Will and Lyra as they sleep, her dæmon "gazed

328
329
330
331
332

around unafraid. Pantalaimon seemed to accept the attention as Lyra's due."

On the mountaintop in Svalbard where Asriel has taken Roger, Pan battles Asriel's snow leopard dæmon Stelmaria for Roger's dæmon Salcilia. After Asriel kills the boy while severing his dæmon, Pan and Lyra discuss their options. Pan reasons that if Coulter and Asriel both believe Dust is bad, it must be good, and he encourages Lyra to seek its source.

During his separation from Lyra, Pan and Will's dæmon Kirjava visit many worlds. They end up in Asriel's republic, unaware of the threat posed by Metatron, who intends to capture them as a way of getting hold of Will and Lyra.

Still mad with their people, Pan and Kirjava play hard to get in the mulefa's world, until the witch Serafina Pekkala confronts them. They learn from Serafina that because of their separation in the world of the dead, he and Lyra, and Kirjava and Will, will be able to be physically far apart from one another, like witches and their dæmons. Serafina also admonishes Pan and Kirjava to help their people cope with the wrenching pain of the separation that will soon be required. Before they leave the mulefa's world, Pantalaimon assumes his final form, that of a pine marten.

As Will and Lyra part and Will prepares to close the window between his world and Cittàgazze, from which Lyra will voyage home to her world, Pan shares a last kiss with Kirjava.

His Dark Materials closes with Pan and Lyra in the Botanic Garden. When she asks if he'll ever reveal what he and Kirjava did during the time she was in the world of the dead, Pan says he'll tell her one day, as Kirjava will tell Will.

NL/GC in Retiring Room 1, 2; at Jordan, in Jericho 3; thoughts on alethiometer, Master 4; growing hostility toward, abused by golden monkey 5; attacked by dæmons of throwing net villains 6; in Fens 7, 8; comments on alethiometer, attacked by spy flies 9; plays with dolphins 10; meets Hester, forces Lyra to go to Iorek 11; frightened at what they might find when searching for lost boy 12; feels pity for Tony 13; captured, taken to Bolvangar 14; communicates with Roger's dæmon to keep Lyra and Roger's relationship unnoticed, examined by doctors, comforts dæmons released from cages 15; fights with Lyra to keep from being severed 16; suggests fire alarm, creating explosion after escape from Coulter, rallies other dæmons to assume forms that would keep their people warm 17; provides light as firefly in dungeon, encourages Lyra as she faces Raknison 19; becomes owl to help track where Asriel has taken Roger, flies to other side of ice bridge to encourage Lyra forward 22; battles Stelmaria as Lyra attempts to save Roger, encourages her to cross over to other world 23

   brief mentions: in balloon, crash on Svalbard 18; stays hidden while Lyra pretends to be Iorek's dæmon 20; comforts Lyra after her father's hostile reception 21

SK meets Will 1; Will astounded when he speaks 3; mistrustful of Latrom, determined Lyra should be polite with Malone 4; anxious at Tower, becomes bird to help see way to escape Walters, realizes Malone is a friend and Latrom a danger, talks to Will when Lyra is too ashamed to 7; flies up to windows in Tower to tell Lyra and Will what to expect, takes on bear's and wildcat's form trying to intimidate Tullio, breaks taboo to comfort Will 8; discusses Will with Lyra, reassures frightened Will as Lyra pretends to sleep 13; [LS] Lantern Slide 5

   brief mentions: becomes a leopard to intimidate Spectre-orphans abusing cat 5, acts as lookout at Latrom's 9, tries to intimidate mob at belvedere 11, on hike through world of Cittàgazze countryside 15

AS Ama sees him become a porcupine to escape golden monkey's clutches and Coulter in turn striking Lyra 4; awakens 12; nearly spurred by Salmakia 13; as bird flapping wings, helps at Iorek's forge 15; takes forms chosen to intimidate spies, scared of ghost 18; jealous of spies and Lyra's death, scared of her death 19; tries to dissuade Lyra from crossing with boatman, left behind, deals with abandonment with concern not to distress Lyra further 21; Lyra's agony at his absence 22, 23; under threat by Metatron, spotted near basalt fortress 28; 29; rescued by Will on battlefield 31; hides from Lyra 33, 35; talks with Serafina, then returns to Lyra 36; assumes settled form of pine marten 37; last kiss with Kirjava, hints of secrets he shared with Kirjava alone, discusses republic of heaven with Lyra 38; [LS] Lantern Slide 9

   brief mentions: 1, 11, 14, 26, 30, 32

PAOLO ♀🖋

Genus: Human

World: Cittàgazze

Alliances: His brother and sister

Physical characteristics: Redheaded. Young enough to be dominated by his 12-year-old sister and ignorant about why he should keep his older brother Tullio's plans secret.

Background: Younger brother of Tullio and Angelica.

Behavior: More talkative than his sister thinks he should be. Participates in stoning the cat Will had followed through the Oxford window; later among those children incited by his sister's accusations who lead the attack on Lyra and Will.

Role: Alerts Lyra and Will to the presence of Tullio in the Tower of Angels.

      Nearly reveals Tullio's plan to steal the subtle knife to Lyra and Will but is silenced by a smack from his sister. Claims "I ain afraid of Spectres, all right…Kill the buggers." Blames Will and Lyra for Tullio being caught by Spectres; vows revenge. Meets Father Gomez who is on the trail of Mary Malone and Lyra, and proves a useful informant to the assassin.

SK   3

      brief mentions: 5, 7, 8, 11

AS   9 *[brief]*

PARADISI, GIACOMO ♀🖋 ⑩

Genus: Human

World: Cittàgazze

Alliances: Torre de Angeli's Guild. Against Latrom/Boreal.

Physical characteristics: White-haired old man. Missing his little and ring fingers.

Background: Will's predecessor as the bearer of the subtle knife, he held it on behalf of the Torre de Angeli's Guild. Paradisi has visited other worlds, including Lyra's, and is familiar with dæmons.

Behavior: Authoritative, in spite of the injuries Tullio has inflicted, insisting on Will's attention as he teaches him to use the knife.

Role: Paradisi recognizes Will's loss of two fingers as signaling that Will is to be the next bearer of the subtle knife, and that it is time for the knife to leave his possession. He instructs Will on cutting and closing windows, and tells him the rules for its use.

      Paradisi plans to poison himself rather than be a victim of the Spectres, his inevitable fate once he has surrendered the knife to Will.

      Will later sees carrion crows flocking to the Tower.

Update: Dr Stanislaus Grumman/Col John Parry's notes in the appendix to the **10**ᴛʜ anniversary edition of *THE SUBTLE KNIFE* characterize Giacomo Paradisi as "a good man, but limited" for whom "the burden of bearing the knife was becoming too great."

SK   7, 8; corpse alluded to 11 *[brief]*

AS   *brief mentions:* 2, 34, 37

10ᴛʜ: *SK appendix*

Parry, Elaine ⚓✒ ⑩ LS

Genus: Human

World: Will's

Physical characteristics: Like her son Will, Elaine Parry has "broad cheekbones," "wide eyes," and "straight black brows." When he takes her to stay with Mrs Cooper, she has make-up on one eye only, untidy hair, a musty smell, and a "distracted half-smile." She also has a bruised cheek, the cause of which is unstated. | 335 | 336

Background: Much loved by but "sundered forever" from her husband, John Parry; her "most precious possession" is her collection of his letters home. She often told Will that one day he would "take up [his] father's mantle." | 337 | 338 | 339

Since he was seven, Will has known he must protect her from her anxieties and the "enemies" in her mind. Will fears that she'd be taken away if anyone found out about her illness. | 340

Still misses and loves her husband, who disappeared in Alaska some eleven years previously. Her financial needs are met through a trust set up by John Parry before he left for Alaska, but she appears to have no friends or family. When she is well, both she and her son are content with the company of one another, but when she is not, all the responsibility for both is Will's.

Behavior: Although she had "times when she was calmer and clearer than others" and some when "she laughed at her fears" and was "full of love and sweetness," at other times she'd be in "such a state of fear and madness that she could barely speak." Her condition has included symptoms of paranoia (believing she is being spied on at the grocery) and obsessive compulsions (touching each slat in every park bench). The repetitive questions she can't answer during the repeated visits by mysterious men seeking information about her long-absent husband make Will fear that this time his mother will break down completely. | 341 | 342

Coulter compares her desire to protect Lyra with what she imagines Will's mother would have done, had she found herself and her son in similar circumstances, which shocks Will. Although he will come to recognize that Coulter knew she was using the knowledge she had somehow attained of Elaine Parry's fragile state to break his concentration, his initial reaction is to think that "his mother, after all, had not protected him; he had had to protect her." Later, remembering her sitting up all night with him when he was ill, he knows their reversal of roles wasn't what she would have chosen. | 343

Role: The wife of John Parry and the mother of Will, her appearance in the trilogy is brief, but the love Will feels for her guides the boy's decisions. He seeks the truth about his father in hope that with the answers, he and his mother can live unmenaced by threats and intrusions from the world beyond their tiny family. When his hand pains him, Will misses her care.

Will is cutting a window to escape from the cave with Lyra when a trick of the light causes the boy to see, not Coulter's, but his mother's face "reproaching him" instead. The knife breaks. His desire that Elaine Parry not feel abandoned by his failure to return is Will's "most pressing reason" for wanting the knife repaired and his fear of not getting home, just as his father failed to return from Alaska, is what worries him most about visiting the world of the dead. Gradually, and with help from Iorek Byrnison, Will realizes that when he is cutting a window, only by acknowledging his worry about what is happening back in his world to his mother—and putting it temporarily aside, which is different from denying it—can he keep the knife from shattering. | 344 | 345

The pain Will feels, entering the world of the dead and being separated from the dæmon he has never seen, is compared to how he would feel if his mother knew that he had denied her love but still offered herself up as a sacrifice to spare him suffering. Parting from his father's ghost, Will wishes that he, his mother, and his father could have been together again as a family, but finds some solace in knowing he can tell his mother that his father was faithful to her always.

Will is committed to returning to his world to take care of his mother, but fears she has since been institutionalized and thus he probably will be, too; however, Mary Malone assures him that she will help them both in every way she can.

Update: All of Colonel John Parry's handwritten notes in the appendix to the **10th** anniversary edition of *The Subtle Knife* are straightforward and informative until he tries to record his feelings about never seeing his wife and son again. Multiple false starts follow the introductory phrase "As for Elaine" until they are abandoned with the simple confession: "I cannot speak."

SK 	1, 5, Will discusses her with Lyra 13, 15, appendix, [LS] Lantern Slide 4
	brief mentions: 3, 4, 7, 8, recalled by Grumman 10, 11

AS 	2, 8, 9; Coulter makes Will feel unmothered 11; knife breaks when Will thinks of her 12; Will's fear of not getting back to her when knife is broken 14; Will discusses her with Iorek Byrnison 15; Mary Malone promises to help 38
	brief mentions: 2, 8, 9, 13, 18 and Will's agony entering world of dead 21, harpies torment Will with 23; 29, 33, 35, 37

10th: *SK* appendix

10th: *AS* appendix

Parry, John ⚔️ ✐ ⑩ [LS]

[*See also* **Grumman, Stanislaus** *for his life under that name*]

Genus: Human

Dæmon: Sayan Kötör, an osprey

World: Will's, Lyra's, Cittàgazze (dies), world of the dead (his ghost)

Alliances: Asriel's republic

Physical characteristics: Described by Will's mother as 'handsome…brave and clever." Has blue eyes and a "jutting jaw." Was once in top physical condition, but his stay in a world not his own has reduced him to a lean, prematurely aged, old man, with an abnormally rapid pulse. Still, when he and Will struggle on the mountaintop, Parry's grip is so strong that even when Will bites the man, he doesn't let go.

Background: One-time Boy Scout, former officer in the Royal Marines turned professional explorer, he led or assisted expeditions to remote areas. Disappeared in 1985 during an Oxford University Institute of Archaeology survey in Alaska, when he left his world and couldn't find his way back. His letters home during this trip reveal that Parry has been in this region of Alaska at least once before and is actively seeking the "anomaly," "a doorway into the spirit world." There are, however, no pictures in their household of Parry on expeditions in remote locales or objects brought back from his travels, a fact that troubles Will as he grows older.

Parry made arrangements before going to Alaska for quarterly payments of funds from a family trust to be paid into his wife's account. Possibly his parents or relations were well-to-do but cold toward his wife Elaine and their child: approaching Sir Charles

Latrom's grand home, Will has a sudden brief memory of a visit when he was very young to an old man and woman in a similarly fine house who had made his mother cry and left her upset for a long time afterwards.

Behavior: In Alaska, he wrote home every few days, updating his wife on his experiences. What will prove his last words home are "I'll bring you back a trophy from the spirit world—I love you forever—kiss the boy for me—." 349

Although he never had a chance to get to know his son during his lifetime, John Parry's ghost is impressed with Will's actions in the world of the dead. Parting from his father's ghost, Will tells him that while Parry had said in Cittàgazze that Will is a warrior, he always had fought only because he had to, and even if he can't choose his nature, he can still decide what he will and won't do.

Personable and adaptable, Parry gets on agreeably in Alaska with everyone from Eskimo Matt Kigalik and miner Jake Petersen to the physicist team member Nelson. Petersen apparently sees him as trustworthy enough to suggest he talk to Kigalik. The Eskimo, too, seems to view Parry as sincere since he provides Parry a description of the window and landmarks near it, as well as exact coordinates for its location.

However, with Nelson he deliberately casts himself in a different light, preferring instead to "pretend to be bluff Major Parry, stout fellow in a crisis but not too much between the ears," the stereotypical explorer on the Alaskan survey more for his muscle 350 and guts than for his brains, and someone who will pose no threat to the scientist. Parry knows Nelson is looking for the anomaly, a window to another world, and not on the expedition to launch weather balloons, but doesn't confront the man.

Role: Will Parry's search for information about his lost father, John Parry, brings Will to Lyra. In the world of the dead, Parry's ghost saves Will and Lyra by quickly giving orders to Will that deflect the bomb on its way straight to Lyra. With Lee Scoresby's ghost and others, he battles Spectres while Lyra and Will find their dæmons.

John Parry's appearances in *HIS DARK MATERIALS* are, for the most part, in his letters home and in his identity as Stanislaus Grumman; his ghost, however, provides significant help to Will and Lyra in the world of the dead.

According to what Will pieces together (from newspaper archives and his father's letters) the account of his last days in communication with his team, was 19-24 June 1985, when he was accompanying an expedition by Oxford University's Institute of Archaeology to Noatak, Alaska.

Lyra tells Will that the alethiometer had told her: she should help him find his father. Lyra and Pan speculate about Will's father but she promises Will she won't use it to find out personal things about him.

John Parry's ghost suggests to Lee Scoresby's that they enter the battle between the republic and kingdom of heaven for Asriel's side and take advantage of their dæmon-less state to fight the Spectres, which will allow Lyra and Will a chance to find their dæmons and escape. With Lee's ghost, he keeps the children's dæmons from the Spectres while Will cuts a window. Once knowing the children and their dæmons are safe, Parry and Scoresby "allowed their atoms to relax and drift apart, at long long last." 351

[*See also* **Grumman, Stanislaus**]

Update: When Stanislaus Grumman met Giacomo Paradisi and saw what the knife could do, he had the option of asking that Paradisi cut a window to his world of origin so he could return home and resume his life as John Parry. Not doing so, although leaving Parry with the

352   "deepest guilt," was, he feels, the only honorable response to his circumstances: "I could have gone back to them; but then I would not have been the man my son would wish me to be."

SK   1; Will consults his lawyer, newspaper reports, Institute of Archaeology staff 4; Lyra tells Will she knows about him, his letters home from Alaska 5; Will realizes why his father is being hunted 9; Grumman on 10; Pan and Lyra, Will and Lyra discuss 13; finds his son, dies 15; ⟦*LS*⟧ Lantern Slides 1, 4
        brief mentions: alethiometer on 7; 11, 14

AS   mourned by Will 2; Will wants to go to world of dead to see 14; Will find his ghost, tells Will what to do about bomb, plans to fight Spectres, tells where dæmons are and of his life in Lyra's world, warns of inevitable failure of Asriel's republic 26; leads ghosts into battle with Spectres 29; says goodbye to Will, dissipates 31; Will realizes that what his father said about republic applies to himself and Lyra as well 37
        brief mentions: 8, 9, 11, 13, 15, 18, 19, 22, 33, 35, 38

10TH: *SK* appendix

PARRY, WILL [*See* Will]

PARSLOW FAMILY ✥

Genus: Human

World: Lyra's

Role: For five generations, male members of this family have worked at Jordan College, maintaining its walls and roofs. Until he is old enough to labor alongside his father, young Roger Parslow works in the College kitchen. Mrs Lonsdale, a housekeeper at the College, is also a Parslow.

NL/GC 3 *[brief]*

PARSLOW, ROGER [*See* Roger]

PARSLOW, SIMON ✥ ⚲ ✎

Genus: Human

Dæmon: Unnamed; form unsettled

World: Lyra's

Background: Member of the Oxford family of Parslows

Role: Friend of Lyra in her Oxford; involved in briefly hijacking the boat belonging to their gyptian playmate Billy Costa's family as a prank.

   Seeing the initials *SP* on what she believes is the identical stone in Will's Oxford to the one her friend marked in her world makes Lyra think both Oxfords must be home to a Simon Parslow.

Observation: *The relationship of Simon Parslow and Roger Parslow is unclear. Presumably, they are not brothers and may not even be cousins; in* THE GOLDEN COMPASS, *Simon is described as one of Lyra's and Roger's "friends."*

353   *Simon is mentioned by name earlier in* THE GOLDEN COMPASS *than he is in* NORTHERN LIGHTS.

NL/GC 3 *[brief]*

SK   4 *[brief]*

AS   23 *[brief]*

Pavel, Fra (Rašek)

Genus: Human

Dæmon: Unnamed; frog

World: Lyra's

Alliances: Magisterium; Consistorial Court of Discipline

Physical characteristics: "Thin-faced man"; looks like a scholar.

Green Tree Frog — 354

Jane M. Rohling, U.S. Fish and Wildlife Service, Jan 2002

Background: Coulter considers his readings of the alethiometer to be "thorough" but slow. | 355
He is generally unfavorably compared to his counterpart in the Society of the Work of the Holy Spirit.

Behavior: Tells the Consistorial Court of Discipline he has difficulty remembering what the witch tortured by Coulter had said of the prophecy regarding Lyra, since witnessing her torment left him feeling "faint and sick." | 356

Very anxious and nervous during his testimony. Scared that he will be punished as a heretic for what he must testify the alethiometer says about the subtle knife and Lyra's position as a new Eve. Even more terrified to report that although he has discovered Coulter is in the Himalayas with Lyra, he hasn't yet been able to determine her exact location. If that were not bad enough, he must admit that the alethiometrist working for the Society of the Work of the Holy Spirit may be closer to an answer than he is.

Role: Alethiometrist, who, after years of study, can only interpret by consulting many reference volumes. Is amazed when his instrument tells him that Lyra can interpret hers "without the books of readings. If it were possible to disbelieve the alethiometer, I would do so." | 357

On board the Cardinal's ship off Svalbard's coast, he tells the Cardinal and Coulter that Lyra is in another world, but is unable immediately to determine what is prophesized about Lyra; Coulter decides to torture the answer out of the captured witch instead of waiting for his reading.

Last seen in Geneva, nervously testifying before by the Consistorial Court of Discipline, his latest assignment in the Church or Magisterium.

Observation: *The unknown alethiometrist—although mentioned several times, Fra Pavel's counterpart in the Society of the Work of the Holy Spirit is never identified.* | 358

Facts: Fra, *short for the Italian* frate, *is a title for an Italian monk or friar; the English equivalent would be* Brother.

SK 2

AS 6, Coulter's critique 24
    brief mentions: 10; last name stated 16

Payne, Oliver LS

Genus: Human

World: Will's

Alliances: Whoever is paying his salary

Physical characteristics: Likely around the same age as Malone—mid-thirties—since they seem to be on a comfortable first name basis. His professional future doesn't seem as certain or his reputation as established as he'd like.

Background: Mary Malone's junior colleague in the Dark Matter Research Unit, Oxford University, and an amateur archaeologist. On job interviews in Geneva when Lyra meets

Malone, and Malone has the impression he may have found a position there. If Mary were to leave, and Payne were to accept Latrom's conditions, he would become the Unit Director.

359 **Behavior:** Payne is characterized as "impatient…skeptical, and preoccupied" when Mary tries to explain what has been happening in their lab during his absence. He is not eager to be associated with the direction Mary seems inclined to take toward investigating the possibility that their new elementary particle could be conscious. Not, it seems, because he believes it to be bad science, but because he doesn't want his career derailed by becoming associated with ideas so out of the ordinary.

    More politically savvy than Mary, perhaps, since he realizes that of course Latrom's offer of funding will come with some strings attached. Unswayed by Malone's discomfort at what might follow by coupling investigations into manipulating consciousness with defense work.

Role: While Mary views Latrom's "offer" as an ultimatum—comply with his terms or be shut down—Payne thinks interest in their project is great enough that the Ministry of Defense simply will take the project over, with or without them.

    His "fooling about" with various objects, some of which had been handled by people, others not, led to Mary Malone's conclusion that Shadow-particles are conscious.

SK   4 *[brief]*; impatience with Mary, receptiveness to Latrom 12

AS   *brief mentions:* 16, 32; *LS* Lantern Slide 5

PEARSON AND SOAR ⑩

Genus: Humans
Dæmons: Unnamed; forms unknown
World: Lyra's
Roles: During the period represented by his notes in the **10**ᵀᴴ anniversary edition of *NORTHERN LIGHTS/GOLDEN COMPASS*, Lord Asriel, pleased with their help in securing materials from Smith and Strange, was planning to consult them again as he prepared for another expedition.

    [*See also* **Smith and Strange, Ltd.** *in* **Social Structures: Financial/Commerce**]

10ᵀᴴ: *NL* appendix

PEKKALA, SERAFINA ❖ ⚶ ✎ ⑩ *LS*

Genus: Witch
Dæmon: Kaisa, a snow goose
World: Lyra's, Cittàgazze, mulefa's, Will's
Alliances: Her clan of witches, Lyra, the gyptians; also Iorek Byrnison, Lee Scoresby
Physical characteristics: Over 300 years old, she has a fair complexion, green eyes and a voice like the sound the Aurora makes. Will is immediately impressed by her "astounding gracefulness, the fierce cold lovely clarity of her gaze, and by the pale bare limbs, so
360   youthful, and yet so far from being young." Serafina has fair hair, in which she wears a wreath of scarlet flowers, and as long as she is wearing them, these flowers do not wither.
Background: Queen of a witch clan based near Lake Enara. Gyptian Farder Coram saved her life forty years ago, thus placing her under an "obligation" to help the gyptians.

Although she would have "forsaken the star-tingle and the music of the Aurora...to be a gyptian boat-wife" to Farder Coram, she tells Lyra, "you cannot change what you are, only what you do. I am a witch. He is a human." The depth of her grief at their son's death was such that when Farder Coram was wounded in a battle with Skraelings, she sent spells and potions, but felt she didn't have the strength to come to him. She hoped he would one day find a human wife. _{361 362}

Her clan was unaligned until Coram calls in his favor. She will help the gyptians find their lost children, but isn't committed to deeper involvement, until her dæmon Kaisa reports what he has seen at the Bolvangar Experiment Station. Serafina is outraged and puts her full support behind those opposing the Dust-hunters.

Behavior: Compassionate and brave, Serafina is a skilled and fearless warrior. When she kills the tortured witch who has no chance for survival, Serafina, with no back-up support, has to enter the circle of torturers and is defenseless, with her back to them, when she slits the bound witch's throat. Still, she acts quickly and deliberately enough to escape the tight quarters of the small boat unharmed. Leaving the boat, she kills a Cardinal and possibly a second man, and evades gunfire from three rifles. At Bolvangar, she shoots from a distance of only three feet an arrow directly into the eye slit of a Tartar guard's helmet with such force it comes halfway out of the back of his head.

She is loyal, with a strong sense of duty and responsibility. Serafina is under no obligation to Iorek Byrnison, but she goes to Svalbard to tell him of his friend Lee Scoresby's death, even apologizing for not being able to come to Lee's aid in time. When her mother dies and she becomes clan-queen, she shifts her attention from her own desires to serve the clan. In Cittàgazze, she isn't swayed by Ruta Skadi to join Asriel's army. Although she supports his republic, Serafina sticks with her decision to help Lyra and Will.

Serafina is empathetic; she can imagine how an old and disabled Farder Coram might feel to see her again as beautiful as when they were lovers, and so sends her dæmon to the gyptians' boat rather than coming herself. Remembering Kaisa's behavior many years back, she understands how Will and Lyra's dæmons feel about having been left behind in the world of the dead. She demonstrates tolerance and good will—unless there is cause not to, and then she is a firm opponent. Serafina forms friendships with humans of two worlds, as well as armoured bear Iorek Byrnison.

Role: Sends her dæmon to the gyptians with the information they need to find the General Oblation Board's Bolvangar Experiment Station. Twice appears to save Lyra, first from Coulter during the liberation of Bolvangar, and later in Cittàgazze when Lyra and Will are under attack. Serafina comes to the mulefa's world and convinces Kirjava and Pantalaimon to give their full support to their humans. Finally, she guides the gyptians to the mulefa's world to bring Lyra, Will, and Mary Malone home to their worlds.

Observation: *The insight Serafina shares with Lyra, "you cannot change what you are, only what you do," is recalled when Stanislaus Grumman/John Parry tells Will, who has said he* _{363 364} *doesn't want to be the knife's bearer, but has to admit that he fought for and won the subtle knife: "Then you're a warrior. That's what you are. Argue with anything else, but don't argue with your own nature." But while Scoresby argued that Serafina's world view doesn't* ₃₆₅ *allow for free will, notice that Serafina's formulation provides for choice, and, interestingly, Will comes to the same conclusion as Serafina had expressed. When he parts from his father's ghost, Will recalls his father's words on the mountain in Cittàgazze, and says, "Father, you were wrong. I fought because I had to. I can't choose my nature, but I can choose what I do.*

366   *And I will choose, because now I'm free."*

NL/GC Lanselius, Kaisa on 10; shoots Tartar, saves Lyra and Roger 17; conversations with Scoresby, Lyra on way to Svalbard 18; [LS] Lantern Slide 9
brief mentions: 11, 13, 15, 20, 22, 23

SK intervenes in witch's torture, visits Lanselius and Thorold, leads witch-council 2; enters world of Cittàgazze, learns about Spectres 6; rescues Will and Lyra at belvedere 11; casts spell to stop Will's bleeding, discussions with Skadi 13
brief mentions: 3, 4, 10, 14, 15

AS visits Iorek 3; talks with Pan and Kirjava, and Mary 36; brings gyptians to mulefa's world 37; goes with Lyra into Will's world for their farewell 38
brief mentions: Lyra's dream between 2 & 3; 4, 6, 9, 14, 15, 23

10TH: *SK* appendix

PERKINS, ALAN 🗡

Genus: Human

World: Will's

Background: Office is on the High Street, Oxford. Last contact with John Parry was when the explorer set up a trust from which Perkins was to send money to Elaine Parry every three months until receipt of instructions to stop.

Behavior: Not unfriendly, but cautious, refusing to give out any personal information over the phone.

Role: Parry family's lawyer or solicitor.

Suggests to Will that he check out the information pertaining to his father's disappearance that is a matter of public record, perhaps by beginning with news articles published at the time his father vanished.

Will is on the verge of visiting Perkins' office when he sees one of the men who used to demand information from his mother enter the same building; he will not make contact with Perkins again.

Observation: *In the Knopf (US) edition, the term* lawyer *is used both when Will makes his call and when he goes to Perkins' High Street office; however, in the Scholastic Point (UK) edition,* solicitor *appears in place of* lawyer *at the end of chapter 4.*

SK 4 *[brief]*

PETER ✏

Genus: Human

World: Suburbs of the world of the dead

367   **Physical characteristics:** Has a face described as "stolid, harmless, and mild."

Background: Lives in a crowded shack with his family, who came to the suburbs of the world of the dead some indeterminate time in the past.

Behavior: Initially scared of Lyra, Will, and the Gallivespians, but relaxes and proves a good host and source of information.

Role: Kind to Lyra and Will in the suburbs of the world of the dead, allowing the children and Gallivespian spies to spend the night in his home and share his family's meager food. Explains how people's deaths are always with them, but not visible to the living. Will and Lyra are the first people he's seen without their deaths since he found himself in this world.

AS 19; 21 *[brief]*

PETERSEN, JAKE ⚑

Genus: Human

World: Will's

Alliances: Friend of the Eskimo Matt Kigalik. Trusts John Parry.

Physical characteristics: Older than John Parry.

Background: A gold miner whom Parry met on a previous Alaskan expedition. Seems to be based in Fairbanks, where Parry finds him in a seedy bar. While he hasn't seen the window to the other world, he knows an Eskimo who has.

Behavior: Enjoys drinking Jack Daniel's and discussing Arctic and Eskimo myths and legends. Generally comfortable in noisy bars, but prefers his own apartment for discussing the window with Parry.

Role: Provides John Parry a nearly correct set of coordinates for the Brooks Range window Parry seeks, and, more importantly, tells Parry of his friend in Colville Bar, Matt Kigalik, who seems to trust Petersen's judgment of Parry's character enough to share what he knows with the explorer.

SK   5

POLICEMAN ⚑

Genus: Human

World: Will's

Alliances: Oxford police, presumably

Physical characteristics: Appears to be very young.

Background: On watch inside an unmarked van parked adjacent to the tented window on Sunderland Avenue in Oxford. Unaware of the nature of what he is guarding.

Behavior: Readily emerges from his van at Malone's approach; examines her identification. Seems embarrassed to admit that seeing a woman claiming to be a physicist, he assumed it had to be Mary Malone, when in fact before him stands Dr Olive Payne, also a physicist, also a woman.

Role: Stops Mary Malone outside tented window, but Malone's fake ID gets her in as she obeys the Cave's injunction to "Deceive the guardian."

SK   12 *[brief]*

PORTER AT JORDAN COLLEGE [*See* Shuter]

PORTER AT OXFORD UNIVERSITY PHYSICS BUILDING ⚑

Genus: Human

World: Will's

Background: Sits behind a long desk, which Lyra sees as indicative of his inferior status compared to the Jordan College porter, who commands his own lodge.

Behavior: Performs his duties in a cursory fashion, quizzing Lyra on her business in the building, but happy to resume reading the paper when she simply mentions the name of someone on staff. Glances with disinterest when she departs the building. More cautious the second time Lyra visits, phoning Malone to confirm Lyra's claim she's expected. Too slow to get round his desk to chase Lyra when she flees the investigators in Malone's lab.

Role: His greater attention to his job the second time Lyra visits and his later replacement by a security guard suggest the growing notice Lyra's visits to Dr Mary Malone's Dark Matter Research Unit has attracted.

SK   brief mentions: 4, 7, 11

POSTNIKOVA, PRINCESS ✦

Genus: Human
Dæmon: Unnamed; form unknown
World: Lyra's
Role: On Mrs Coulter's party list, which means she must be considered fashionable, since social standing rather than friendship appears to be Coulter's key determinant for issuing invitations to her home.

NL/GC 5 *[brief]*

PRECENTOR ✦

Genus: Human
Dæmon: Unnamed; form unknown
World: Lyra's
Physical characteristics: His advanced age is indicated by his "shaky voice."
Background: Jordan College scholar.
Role: Present at Lord Asriel's Retiring Room seminar; asks Asriel to clarify whether what the younger man has called the Aurora is also known as the Northern Lights.
Facts: *In Will's world's Church of England, the Precentor directs the choir.*
Note: *In* THE GOLDEN COMPASS, *Lyra and her cronies sneak through his garden; this passage does not appear in* NORTHERN LIGHTS.

NL/GC 5 *[brief]*

PRIEST, TROLLESUND ✦

White Pelican

John Foster, U.S. Fish and Wildlife Service, Jul 2003

Genus: Human
Dæmon: Unnamed; pelican
World: Lyra's
Background: Apparently does well for himself, since his is one of only a few brick residences in the village.
Role: Iorek Byrnison's armour, stolen by the town's authorities, is hidden in the cellar of the priest's home. The priest has unsuccessfully attempted to exorcise it of evil spirits.

    When Iorek comes to reclaim his armour, the priest finds himself hurled from his house, but, except for his pride, escapes uninjured.

NL/GC 11 *[brief]*

PRESIDENT, CONSISTORIAL COURT OF DISCIPLINE [*See* MacPhail, Father Hugh]

RAKNISON, IOFUR ✦ ⚑ ✎ [LS]

Genus: Armoured bear
Dæmon: A doll with human form that he dresses like Mrs Coulter
World: Lyra's

Alliances: Mrs Coulter

Physical characteristics: Both taller and larger than Iorek Byrnison, and seems to Lyra more human-like than she expected. Though draped with the type of finery that on any other bear would have seemed absurd and tacky, Lyra is struck by the impression he gives of possessing "enormous strength and energy and craft"; he looks "barbaric and magnificent." His six-inch claws are sheathed in gold leaf. Unperturbed by flies buzzing about his face or by his throne room's stench of waste. |368

    Unlike Iorek's, his armour is highly polished, and he wears chain-mail to protect his underbelly. But in the tournament between Iofur and Iorek, Raknison's chain-mail sark hinders his movement, and his denial of his bear nature makes him vulnerable to trickery.

Background: Born a prince among Svalbard's armoured bears. He has kept it a secret that as a young bear he unknowingly killed his own father, as Lyra discovers during an alethiometer reading prompted by Raknison's desire for proof that she is a dæmon. According to Jordan College Scholar Trelawney, who claims the bear king displays "ludicrous affectations" for all things human, what Raknison wants most is a dæmon. |369

    Involved with both Coulter and Asriel. As Jotham Santelia, an academic once in Raknison's favor and now in his dungeon, sees it: "He's done what they both want. He's kept Lord Asriel isolated, to please Mrs Coulter; and he's let Lord Asriel have all the equipment he wants, to please *him*." |370

    Coulter may have helped him secure his position by supplying a drug that Raknison slipped to Hjalmur Hjalmurson, causing the younger bear inexplicably and uncharacteristically to provoke former King Iorek Byrnison. Iorek lost control and killed his subject. He was dethroned and exiled in consequence. Coulter also promised King Raknison that she would gain his baptism if he kept Asriel prisoner on the island and allowed her to set up another experiment station like that at Bolvangar in his kingdom. But only those with dæmons can ever be baptized.

Behavior: Considered "clever in a human way...skillful and subtle," his demeanor reflects "triumph, slyness, apprehension, and greed." Determined to increase the Svalbard bears' contacts with humans and to influence his subjects to live more like humans do and less as armoured bears always have. He and Byrnison represent opposing "kinds of beardom." And because Iofur Raknison does not want to be a bear, unlike bears, he can be tricked—which is how Iorek Byrnison finally defeats his adversary in a one-on-one battle to the death. |371 |372

Role: Iofur Raknison's scheming for the throne of Svalbard and his banishment of Iorek Byrnison put Iorek in the circumstances where Iorek was able to meet the gyptians and Lyra.

    The bond of trust between Lyra and Iorek Byrnison is further deepened when she helps him regain his kingdom. Imprisoned in the usurper-king's palace dungeon, Lyra talks herself out of the cells by telling Raknison that she herself is a dæmon (she argues since humans' dæmons have animal forms, naturally, animals' dæmons would have human forms). He agrees to a formal and public duel to the death with Iorek Byrnison where he is killed by the former king who rips from Raknison's chest the dead bear's heart, and eats it to seal his victory.

Update: The fourth Lantern Slide in Northern Lights says that Lord Asriel figured he could get away with lying to Raknison once he saw the bear-king's doll-dæmon. Asriel knew that unlike other armoured bears who couldn't be tricked, Raknison would be easily deceived.

Note: *The chapter in which Raknison is defeated by Byrnison is titled "À Outrance" in* NORTHERN LIGHTS *and "Mortal Combat" in* THE GOLDEN COMPASS. *À outrance is a French phrase meaning with utmost hostility, a fight to the death—mortal combat.*

NL/GC discussed in Retiring Room 2; 11, 13; Serafina and Lyra discuss 18; Lyra discusses Iorek in his throne room 19; duel with Iorek, dies 20; counselors describe his reign 21; ⟦LS⟧ Lantern Slide 4
brief mentions: 11, 13

SK   brief mentions: 2, 4

AS   brief mentions: 15, 28, 30

RANSOM, LISA/LIZZIE ⚷

Role: Alias Lyra uses in Will's Oxford.

SK   brief mentions: 3, 4, 7

RANSOM, MARK ⚷

Role: Alias Will uses in Will's Oxford.

SK   brief mentions: 3, 7

RAŠEK, FRA PAVEL [See Pavel, Fra]

RATTER ✧

Genus: Dæmon
Form: Unsettled
Human: Tony Makarios
World: Lyra's
Physical characteristics: Usually a sparrow or a mouse.
Behavior: Her infrequent changes of form were perplexing to the General Oblation Board's doctors at the Bolvangar Experiment Station, since Tony at age nine or so is obviously pre-pubescent. Seems "slow-witted."
Role: When Lyra finds Gobbler victim Tony Makarios hiding in a remote village somewhere between Trollesund and the Bolvangar Experiment Station, the little boy's only concern is for his severed dæmon.

When his person dies, Lyra etches "Ratter" on a coin she places between the teeth of Tony's corpse, remembering similar tributes to dæmons she'd seen with skulls in the crypt of Jordan College.

During her own imprisonment at Bolvangar, Lyra learns of the day Ratter was severed from Tony, and in the Station warehouse storing severed dæmons, Lyra sees her cage labeled with his name, now empty, since Tony is dead.

NL/GC in Limehouse 3; Tony asks for 9; dæmon-coin 10; remembered at Bolvangar, her empty cage 15

REGENT [*See* Metatron]

REGIUS PROFESSOR OF COSMOLOGY [*See* Santelia, Jotham]

RELF, DAME HANNAH ✧ ✎

Genus: Human
Dæmon: Unnamed; marmoset
World: Lyra's

Alliances: A friend of the Master of Jordan College

Physical characteristics: Grey-haired older woman with a face revealing a keen intelligence and wisdom.

Background: Head of St Sophia's College and an expert on the alethiometer.

Behavior: The night Lyra first meets Dame Hannah—also when she meets Coulter for the first time—the young girl's impression is of a serious and boring old lady, an object for scorn or pity, like all female scholars.

> However, when Lyra returns to Oxford, older and wiser, she "found that her memory was at fault: for this Dame Hannah was much cleverer, and more interesting, and kindlier by far than the dim and frumpy person she remembered." 374

> Seems to feel an affectionate admiration for Lyra. Wisely offers Lyra suggestions rather than presuming to tell her what to do.

Role: Encourages Lyra to consider studying at St Sophia's when she is old enough to do so, and invites her to consider a boarding school associated with the College as a place where she could study and develop some friendships until then. Concurs with the Master's recommendation that Lyra make re-learning to read the alethiometer her life's work, and offers to work with her privately whenever the young woman is ready to begin.

NL/GC brief mentions: first seen as Master's Lodging 3; 4

AS 38

Reynolds, Jessie ✤

Genus: Human

Dæmon: Unnamed; form unsettled

World: Lyra's

Alliances: Like the other children whose parents work in the Covered Market, she is a friend of Lyra's, Simon Parslow's, and their circle.

Background: Daughter of an Oxford saddler who has a stall in the Covered Market near Jordan College.

Role: When Simon Parslow tells Lyra about Jessie's disappearance, Lyra uses the tale to impress some of her teenaged College acquaintances by telling them all about the Gobblers.

NL/GC 3 *[brief]*

Roger [Parslow] ✤ ⚔ ✎

Genus: Human

Dæmon: Salcilia; unsettled

World: Lyra's, world of the dead (his ghost)

Alliances: Lyra

Physical characteristics: Twelve years old, more or less, very likely the same age as Lyra.

Background: Introduced as the Jordan College "kitchen boy" and Lyra's "particular friend" with whom she engaged in the "endless permutations of alliance and betrayal" that dominated the lives of children in Oxford colleges. Their adventures included commandeering the boat belonging to the Costas, a gyptian family. 375 376

Behavior: A fitting co-conspirator for Lyra, although somewhat more circumspect than she; for example, he's reluctant to drink the excessive quantity of wine she claims to enjoy, or to tamper with the dæmon-coins in the crypts. In the world of the dead, he warns her to be careful when she gets cocky on the edge of the abyss.

Role: Lyra's guilt over the role she inadvertently played in Roger's death, and the dreams she had during her drugged sleep in Coulter's cave of rescuing him as she did at Bolvangar, culminate in her decision to go to the world of the dead to find her friend.

When Will cuts the window, Roger's is the first ghost to leave the world of the dead. He "turned to look back at Lyra, and laughed in surprise as he found himself turning into the night, the starlight, the air…and then he was gone, leaving behind such a vivid little burst of happiness that Will was reminded of the bubbles in a glass of champagne."

Note: *There's a passage at the end of* THE GOLDEN COMPASS *about Roger that doesn't appear in* NORTHERN LIGHTS:

"'We got it wrong, though, Pan. We got it all wrong about Roger. We thought we were helping him…' She choked, and kissed Roger's still face clumsily, several times. 'We got it wrong,' she said.

'Next time we'll check everything and ask all the questions we can think of, then. We'll do better next time.'"

> NL/GC at play with Lyra at Jordan, discovered missing 3; at Bolvangar, stands guard for Lyra and Kaisa 15; rescued by Serafina and Scoresby 17; balloon trip to Svalbard 18; reunited with Lyra on Svalbard 20; at Asriel's 21; Lyra learns Asriel has taken him 22; Lyra and Pan fail to save him, intercised, dies 23
> *brief mentions: 4, 5, 6, 7, 8, 9, 12, 14, 16, 19*

> SK   *brief mentions: 4, 5, 13*

> AS   Lyra dreams of 1, between 1& 2, 2 & 3, 3 & 4, 4 & 5, 5 & 6, 6 & 7; Lyra talks about her dreams to Will 13; Will, Lyra discuss with Iorek 15; Lyra talks about to Tialys and her death 19; Lyra and Roger reunited 22; Lyra recalls their Oxford days 23; at abyss, released from world of dead 26
> *brief mentions: 14, 18, 21, 35, 37*

ROKE, LORD ✎

Genus: Gallivespian

World: Gallivespians' (origin), Asriel's, Lyra's

Alliances: Asriel's republic

Physical characteristics: The Gallivespian spy captain for Asriel is "no taller than Lord Asriel's hand-span, and as slender as a dragonfly"; he is "armed with a poisonous sting in the spurs on his heels."

Background: Rides on a blue hawk and communicates with his associates via a lodestone resonator.

Behavior: Typically Gallivespian: "proud and touchy" with a "haughty and malevolent tongue" that can put even Coulter in her place.

Studies human behavior. For example, although he is "impervious to her charm" and considers Coulter's nature "as close to that of a scorpion as he had ever encountered," he is "interested in its effect on others."

Role: One of Asriel's three high commanders, he issues orders to his subordinates Salmakia and Tialys to stay with Lyra and Will. Roke instructs them to placate Will since he has the knife and can get Lyra to safety in another world—her safety being their top priority.

Asriel directs Roke to sneak aboard the intention craft when it becomes obvious Coulter means to steal it.

Lord Roke reveals himself to Coulter, who is a prisoner of Father MacPhail's, and tells her that he is in Geneva to both help and spy on her. Attempts to retrieve the lock of Lyra's hair after it is stolen and alerts Coulter to the theft.

At the bomb launch site in the Alps, Lord Roke attacks a guard and steals his keys, allowing Coulter to get away from MacPhail before he can effect her intercision. His plan to retrieve the strands of Lyra's hair from the bomb's resonating chamber is unsuccessful and he dies in the attempt.

AS   Updates Asriel 5, issues orders to Salmakia and Tialys 11; in meeting with Asriel's high commanders, brusque with Coulter—who backs off, sneaks aboard intention craft 16; in Geneva 24; at bomb launch, dies 25
  brief mentions: 6, 9, 12, 13, 14, 28

Rokeby, Nicholas ✦

Genus: Human
Dæmon: Unnamed; form unknown
World: Lyra's
Physical characteristics: Heavy-set; has black beard.
Background: Gyptian. Head of one of the six families of John Faa's group of Eastern Anglia gyptians.
Role: In charge of securing a ship for the voyage North to rescue their children abducted by the Gobblers.

NL/GC brief mentions: 8, 9, 10

Salcilia ✦ ✎

Genus: Dæmon
Form: Unsettled
Human: Roger
World: Lyra's
Role: Her intercision from Roger yields the energy Asriel uses to break through to new worlds.
  In spite of the best efforts of Pantalaimon, and Salcilia's own struggle, she is not able to get away from Lord Asriel's dæmon, the snow leopard Stelmaria.

NL/GC at Jordan 3; at Bolvangar (only use of name) 15; attempts to flee Asriel, thwarted by Stelmaria 23
  brief mentions: 17, 18, 21

AS   23 *[brief]*

Salmakia, Lady ✎

Genus: Gallivespian
World: Gallivespians' (origin), Lyra's, desert world, Holland-like world, world of the dead and its suburbs, Asriel's republic, mulefa's
Alliances: Asriel's republic, officially; Lyra and Will
Physical characteristics: The general impression she and her partner make is that they are "strong, capable, ruthless, and proud," although "her face was calm and kindly," not beautiful but comforting. Her voice, tiny but clear, "would lap you in safety and warm you with love." The Lady wears a full silver skirt with a green blouse; her feet are spurred and she wears no shoes. 385 386 387

  At eight years, she is old; the life expectancy of Gallivespians is nine to ten years.
Background: Gallivespian spy. Partner is the Chevalier Tialys. Lady Salmakia had been Lord Roke's spy at the Society of the Work of the Holy Spirit. Reports that the Society

believes Lyra will soon play a critical role in a coming crisis.

Behavior: Initially her relationship with Will and Lyra is one of mutual distrust and antipathy (right after she and her partner have introduced themselves, she seizes Pan when Lyra laughs at her). She defuses the tension between Will and Tialys when the spies learn the truth about the knife, by going out of her way to be gracious toward Iorek Byrnison, treating him in a manner befitting a king.

388
Tialys sees in the world of the dead that her "face is drawn" and her "hands are pale and tight," and guesses that like himself she has been quietly suffering since leaving the suburbs of the world of the dead. When she and Tialys know they are dying, they do not tell the children but are resolved to stay with them as long as they can. Stays alive through sheer will power until Madame Oxentiel, her spy captain, can reach the children.

Role: While her relationship with Lyra and Will is initially stormy, the alethiometer warns
389
Lyra that the children not try to lose the spies "because your lives depend on them." Salmakia and her partner, Tialys, will fulfill this prediction by negotiating with No-Name the harpy, leading to the harpy guiding the spies and the children on a perilous journey to the spot where Will can safely cut a window out of the world of the dead. Tialys' plan that they require true stories of the ghosts in exchange for not escalating their tormenting gibes is partially satisfactory. Still, No-Name fears the loss of a sense of purpose, until
390
Salmakia suggests that as the "guardians and keepers of this place" they can guide the ghosts from the river launch to the window Will cuts and receive the ghosts' stories as earned payment.

When the ghosts are discouraged by the long trek to the spot where Will can cut the window, Lady Salmakia encourages them. Terribly weakened, she stays alive long enough after leaving the world of the dead to turn her responsibility for the children over to the spy commander Madame Oxentiel.

Buried by Will and Lyra in the mulefa's world.

The title of chapter 13 of *THE AMBER SPYGLASS* is "Tialys and Salmakia."

AS   tricks priest 6, leaves Geneva for Himalayas 9; at Coulter's cave, caught by golden monkey 12; kills Swiss guards, confrontations with Lyra and Pan, described, seizes Pan 13; confrontation with Will regarding Iorek, eavesdropping 14; fails to convince Will to go with repaired knife to Asriel 15; activities reported at Asriel's 16; follows Will and Lyra to suburbs of world of dead 18; Lyra reconciled to her and Tialys' following them to world of dead 19; begins searching ghosts for Roger, considers attacking harpies 21; discusses dæmons with Tialys, finds Roger 22; bargains with harpies 23; weakening, feeds dragonfly her blood 26; enters Asriel's world's battlefield on Lyra's shoulder 29; holds on until Oxentiel arrives, dies 31
brief mentions: 5, 28; buried in mulefa's world 32

SANDLING

Genus: Dæmon
World: World of the dead
Role: Ghost-child's lost dæmon.

AS   22 [brief]

SANTELIA, JOTHAM

Genus: Human
Dæmon: Unnamed; snake
World: Lyra's
Alliances: Was once in Iofur Raknison's favor but is now his prisoner.

Physical characteristics: Has unkempt shoulder-length hair and a grey beard. Chained to the wall in Raknison's dungeons.

Background: Regius Professor of Cosmology at University of Gloucester. Came to Svalbard to set up a university planned by Raknison, but "was betrayed by lesser men." Claims to have "discovered the final proof of the Barnard-Stokes hypothesis." | 391

Behavior: Rants against Trelawney, the Palmerian Professor at Jordan College, whom he accuses of plagiarism (as well as being responsible for his current bleak prospects) and the Royal Arctic Institute, which apparently has not taken his work seriously. While appearing mad, he is still susceptible to Lyra's flattery and sensibly argues that Raknison's attempts to please both Asriel and Coulter are bound to fail. Seems disinterested in whether or not he has been regularly fed. Believes his dæmon's tongue can discern the likelihood that something will happen.

Role: Lyra's cellmate at Raknison's castle fort, he gives Lyra useful information about Byrnison's status among the Svalbard armoured bears and Raknison's relationships with Coulter and Asriel.

Observation: *Santelia apparently survives his ordeal: on the back of the map in* LYRA'S OXFORD, *Smith and Strange, Ltd lists among its publications,* A Prisoner of the Bears *by Professor Jotham D. Santelia. Perhaps he was inspired by Lyra's admonishment that his "knowledge ought not to just vanish… It ought to be passed on so people remember you."* | 392

NL/GC 19; 20 *[brief]*

SATTAMAX ✎

Genus: Mulefa

World: Mulefa's

Physical characteristics: Elderly; "at the base of his trunk was a scatter of white hairs, and he moved stiffly, as if he had arthritis." | 393

Background: Leader of the mulefa. Apparently had some foreknowledge that Mary Malone would come to see the sraf and has told Atal to bring her to him when that day came.

Behavior: Commands much respect; Mary's amber spyglass shows her that his is an especially "rich and complex" "Shadow-cloud." | 394

Role: Before assembled mulefa, he asks Mary Malone's assistance in restoring to health the seedpod trees on which the mulefa's civilization depends and in defeating the *tualapi*, the huge birds that terrorize mulefa villages.

When the gyptians arrive to carry Will and Lyra back to their worlds, he greets them graciously and shows his human counterparts, John Faa and Farder Coram, the window out of the world of the dead through which emerge the ghosts seeking at once dissipation and reunion with the living world.

Observation: *Sattamax seems to have special insight into Mary Malone's inner self, telling her that compared to the mulefa, she appears to "think and act with the speed of a bird." Mary later learns her dæmon is a bird.* | 395

AS described, asks Mary for help 17; 20; takes Coram and Faa to see window out of world of the dead 38

SAYAN KÖTÖR ⚥ ⑩

Genus: Dæmon

Form: Osprey

Human: Stanislaus Grumman (*aka* John Parry, Jopari)

World: Will's (internal), Lyra's, Cittàgazze (dies)

Physical characteristics: White headed and breasted; otherwise black. Considered by Grumman to be part of his "own nature…and bird-formed, and beautiful."

Behavior: Shares Grumman's shamanistic powers. She summons flocks of birds to obstruct an enemy zeppelin, and, like a witch's dæmon, she can travel farther from her person than people's dæmons normally can. Aboard Scoresby's balloon, even as the winds grow treacherously strong, the osprey remains perched and watchful on the rim of the basket.

John Good, Yellowstone National Park, 1966

Osprey

Role: Forever separated from his wife and son, Grumman seems to have found solace in her companionship as he wandered in the Arctic of his new world.

When the aëronaut Lee Scoresby flies her human to the world of Cittàgazze in search of the subtle knife and its bearer, the osprey flies ahead and above the trees of the thickly wooded forests of Cittàgazze to determine their best route.

Camped in the forest, Scoresby dreams of flying at her side as she calls for the aid of every bird for miles around to obstruct and destroy the pursuing forces of the Magisterium. Awake, he realizes that together Grumman and his dæmon have brought down all but one of the Imperial Guard of Muscovy's troop transport zeppelins.

Vanishes when Grumman dies.

Update: Included in the appendix to the **10**ᴛʜ anniversary edition of *The Subtle Knife* is a drawing by Grumman of Sayan Kötör.

SK   described 6 *[brief]*; observes Scoresby 10; leads attack on zeppelins 14; vanishes 15; Parry's drawing of her, 10th appendix

10ᴛʜ: *SK* appendix

Scoresby, Lee ❖ ⚑ ✎ LS

Genus: Human

Dæmon: Hester, a hare

World: Lyra's, Cittàgazze (dies), world of the dead, Asriel's (as ghost)

Alliances: Lyra, Lyra's allies

Physical characteristics: Rugged, "whiplash-lean," "with a thin black moustache and narrow blue eyes, and a perpetual expression of distant and sardonic amusement," Scoresby is likely at least in his mid-fifties (he is thinking about retiring and tells Grumman he hasn't seen his mother's ring in well over 40 years).

Background: Balloon aëronaut. A New Dane, he was raised in the country of Texas where he played in the Alamo's ruins. A longtime friend of Iorek Byrnison, with whom he fought in the Tunguska wars, Lee speaks bits of at least six languages. Childless and unmarried, he would like to make up to Lyra for how her parents failed her.

Looks forward to retiring to a small cattle farm where he can enjoy "the evening wind over the sage, and a ceegar, and a glass of bourbon whiskey." However, sailing away with Grumman, he reflects that he hadn't meant what he told Serafina: "Soaring upwards, with a fair wind behind and a new world in front: what could be better in this life?"

Behavior: Scoresby can navigate a small boat down the Yenisei River using for guidance "only his memory of having flown over the country some years before, but that memory was good." He is a romantic—while others speculate how foolish Grumman has to have been 401 to turn down the love of a witch, Lee muses that perhaps he was simply being faithful to the woman he loved. He finds Serafina Pekkala attractive, but doesn't let these feelings show.

A polite man of few words, fond of his cigars, he was "too cool by nature to rage at fate; his manner was to raise an eyebrow and greet it laconically." Lee counters Serafina's 402 observations on destiny with a defense of free will and choice. Allegiance to abstractions doesn't interest him as much as treating kindly those who most need help, and he is disgusted by the Magisterium's spy's passion for martyrdom. When he wants to stop and help the Spectre-orphans but Grumman urges him on, Lee argues, "seems to me the place you fight cruelty is where you find it, and the place you give help is where you see it needed." 403

Scoresby dislikes violence, despises being forced to kill, even in self-defense, but before the ambush at Alamo Gulch, he has killed four times previously, including the Skraeling on Nova Zembla. In his last battle, fighting for or against a particular side's force isn't of

One Name Explained: Lee Scoresby

Photo by Roger Viollet Collection/Getty Images

Lee Van Cleef starred as Marshal Chris Adams in The Magnificent Seven Ride! (1972)

Philip Pullman has identified two sources for the name of Lee Scoresby, one of his own favorite characters in the trilogy: Lee Van Cleef and William Scoresby.

Actor Lee Van Cleef appeared in a number of Westerns, including *High Noon; The Good, The Bad, and the Ugly; The Magnificent Seven; For A Few Dollars More,* and other tales of bounty hunters, desperadoes, and treasure hunters—all variations on the theme of outlaws and lawmen in the wild west.

William Scoresby, Sr (1760-1829) of Whitby, North Yorkshire, captained whaling ships in arctic waters. In 1806, when Scoresby, Sr, navigating through the ice off Spitzbergen, the largest of Svalbard's islands (Svalbard ranges from 81° N to 74° N), made it to 81° N, he had gone further toward the North Pole than had any Caucasian before him. His record was broken in 1828 by Sir William Parry, who traveled to 82° N.

William Scoresby, Jr (1789-1857) began his arctic explorations aboard his father's whalers and made yearly expeditions off the coast of Greenland from 1803-1822, and gained renown as a scientist. In 1820 he published *An Account of the Arctic Regions,* which laid the foundation for future arctic studies in geography, natural history and physical sciences.

Scoresby, Jr was the first to show that the temperature of arctic waters is warmer below than on the surface. Terrestrial magnetism was one of his particular interests, which he continued to study even after ceasing his arctic explorations in 1823 and becoming ordained in 1825 as an Anglican clergyman. He devised improvements in compass needles at the request of the British Admiralty, lectured in America, and in 1856 journeyed to Australia to make observations on magnetism in the southern hemisphere. His accomplishments as a mapmaker led to a large area off Greenland's east coast being named Scoresby Sound in his honor, and there is a Scoresby, Victoria, Australia commemorating his southern travels.

interest as long as what he does helps Lyra. He doesn't shoot until he is shot at, and then, with 30 bullets and 25 soldiers coming at him, he defends his position, killing 18 men and using his last bullet to blow up the rest of the troops' zeppelin. During the course of the battle, he sustains multiple wounds. Hit in the shoulder, Lee felt there was "a great deal of pain waiting to spring on him, but it hadn't raised the courage yet, and that thought gave him the strength to focus his mind." Lee takes a few more bullets, and the pain closes in like a "pack of jackals, circling, sniffing, treading closer." He dies at high noon.

404
405

Dreaming of flying with Grumman's dæmon, he "felt the strangest of pleasures: that of offering eager obedience to a stronger power that was wholly right."

406

Role: Although the time they spend together is only a matter of days, Scoresby is a faithful friend to Lyra and is willing to die if there is a chance his death will keep her from harm. With the gyptians, Iorek Byrnison, and Serafina Pekkala's witch-clan, Lee Scoresby rescues Lyra and Roger from Mrs Coulter during the evacuation of Bolvangar, and flies them to Svalbard. He locates Stanislaus Grumman, flies him into Cittàgazze, and deflects the shaman's enemies, an act of self-sacrifice without which Will would never have been reunited, however briefly, with his father. Scoresby's ghost is re-united with Lyra in the world of the dead. and later, on a battleground, with Iorek. There, with John Parry's and others' ghosts, he fights the Spectres until the children manage to grab their dæmons and escape to a safe world.

Update: The third Lantern Slide in *NORTHERN LIGHTS* provides a glimpse into Scoresby's past. He became a balloon aëronaut by chance when he came to the North during a gold rush. He found no gold, but won the balloon in a card game.

Scoresby had many lovers, but none could compare to a witch from the Karelia region who was killed in battle.

NL/GC introduces himself to Lyra, suggests she go to Iorek while he distracts gyptians, guards Iorek's armour from townspeople while the bear hunts seal 11; vouches for Iorek's trustworthiness 12; talks with Lyra about flying to Svalbard, Iorek 13; flies Lyra, Roger, and Iorek away from Bolvangar 17; exchanges philosophies with Serafina, balloon damaged when cliff-ghasts attack 18; Roger reports balloon crashed into a mountain, alethiometer says it's still aloft 20; **LS** Lantern Slide 3
brief mentions: of unnamed balloonist for hire 10; 14, 15, 21, 22, 23

SK addresses witch council about his goal of finding Grumman and special instrument to keep Lyra safe 2; gathers information at bar and observatory on Nova Zembla, shot at and in turn kills Magisterium's censor 6; goes to Tartar village, meets Grumman, agrees to take him to Cittàgazze, pursued out of his world by Magisterium's soldiers 10; descends into forest cover when pursued by zeppelins, dreams or has visionary experiences as Grumman uses shamanic powers to bring down zeppelins, takes on remaining regiment of soldiers to give Grumman a chance to fulfill his mission, eliminates all troops, dies of injuries suffered in battle 14; **LS** Lantern Slide 1
brief mentions: balloon sighted by witches 13; Serafina receives his call for help 15

AS Iorek honors his friend by eating his corpse 3; his ghost re-united with Lyra 26; with Parry's and other warriors' ghosts enters battlefield to fight Spectres 29; meets Iorek during battle, says farewell to Lyra, dissipates once he knows she and Pan are safe 31
brief mentions: 9; mourned by Lyra 14, 15; 32

Argus fin, Wikimedia Commons

SEAL HUNTER 🗡

Genus: Human
Dæmon: Unnamed; lemming
World: Lyra's
Physical characteristics: Old
Role: An otherwise unidentified man at Nova Zembla's

Lemming

Samirsky Hotel's bar, who contributes to aëronaut Lee Scoresby's store of knowledge regarding Stanislaus Grumman. Reports that he saw the man being trepanned during a two-night long ritual by a tribe of Tartars who call him "Jopari." Believes the shaman knew the location of a magical object, but had been killed in Skraeling wars in Beringland.

Recommends the Imperial Muscovite Academy's Observatory as Scoresby's next stop.

SK   6; his information proves correct 10 *[brief]*

SECURITY MAN, MALONE'S LAB 🗡

Genus: Human
World: Will's
Physical characteristics: Bulky. In uniform and armed—either with a pistol or a mobile phone.
Role: Being forced to show him identification on entering her building (when always before an indifferent porter was the only person at its entrance) alerts Mary Malone that she has little time in which to get on her computer and attempt to communicate with the Shadows.

SK   12 *[brief]*

Soft-Coated Norwich Terrier

Ellen Levy Finch

SENTRY, ASRIEL'S ✎

Genus: Human
Dæmon: Unnamed; terrier
World: Asriel's republic
Role: Challenges those who approach Asriel's fortress. On duty when the angel Baruch is found wounded; has him brought into the guardroom out of the cold while he phones the officer on duty.

Much later catches sight of Pantalaimon and Kirjava as cats outside the gates of the fortress, but can't coax them in. Has word sent to Asriel.

AS   brief mentions: 5, 28

SENTRY, TROLLESUND ❖

Genus: Human
Dæmon: Unnamed; husky
World: Lyra's
Background: Guards Sysselman's residence.
Behavior: Somewhat indecisive and clumsy.
Role: Pursues Iorek Byrnison to the priest's house. When the bear emerges in his armour, the man tries to flee, but is caught. Nearly has his head crushed in Iorek's jaws before Lyra comes to his rescue.

NL/GC 11 *[brief]*

SERGEANT IN SERVICE OF CONSISTORIAL COURT OF DISCIPLINE ✎

Genus: Human
Dæmon: Unnamed; form unknown
World: Lyra's

Physical characteristics: Large man.

Background: Holds the keys to Coulter's handcuffs.

Role: At the Saint-Jean-les-Eaux launch site for the Consistorial Court of Discipline's bomb, he is spurred by the Gallivespian spy Lord Roke in a successful maneuver to take from him the key for Coulter's manacles, thus allowing her to escape intercision.

AS   25 *[brief]*

SERGI ⚑

Genus: Dæmon

Form: Bluethroat

Human: Ruta Skadi

World: Lyra's

Role: Like his human's, Sergi's is a daring personality, but even he is intimidated and seeks the warmth of Ruta Skadi in the presence of angels.

Bluethroat Male

SK   6

       brief mentions: 2, 13

SHAMAN TURUKHANSK, THE ⑩

Genus: Human

Dæmon: Unnamed; form unknown

World: Lyra's

Role: Taught Stanislaus Grumman/Colonel John Parry how to make an ointment from bloodmoss and harp-flower root.

SK   appendix

10TH: *SK* appendix

SHUTER ✵ ✑

Genus: Human

Dæmon: Unnamed; form unknown

World: Lyra's

Physical characteristics: An old man.

Background: Porter at Jordan College.

Behavior: Pleased when he imagines Lyra in trouble with the Master.

Role: Blamed for spilling the Tokay, the rare wine Asriel has requested and the Master of Jordan College has poisoned (Asriel himself had knocked it over).

Note: THE AMBER SPYGLASS *passage simply mentions a porter locking up for the night at Jordan College, so this may—or may not—refer to the same elderly Mr Shuter who was blamed for spilling of the Tokay.*

NL/GC 1; 3 *[brief]*

AS   38

SILVERTONGUE, LYRA

Role: Given to Lyra by Iorek Byrnison in recognition of her deceit of Iofur Raknison. Lyra uses it—and never again Belacqua—as her true name.

NL/GC named by Iorek 20; 22 *[brief]*

SK   brief mentions: Lyra uses with Will 1; Serafina uses 2; Lyra uses with Mary 4; 6

AS   brief mentions: Iorek remembers 3; used by Will with Iorek 8, 9; used by Iorek 15; adopted by Gallivespians 22; its origin recalled when Lyra renames No-Name 29

SIMON ✠

Genus: Human

Dæmon: Unnamed; form unsettled

World: Lyra's

Role: Child at Bolvangar. His theories that Coulter likes to watch children being killed and that Tartars drill holes in their heads to let Dust in, are discussed by Lyra and her "roommates" Bella, Annie, and Martha.

NL/GC 14 *[brief]*

SIRKKA, KATJA ⑩

Genus: Witch

Dæmon: Unnamed; form unknown

World: Lyra's

Role: Queen Katja Sirkka's Miekojärvi witch clan is entangled in an age-old feud with Queen Reina Miti's Tikshozero clan that is so bitter, the queens have "sworn to kill each other on sight."

10ᴛʜ: *SK* appendix

SISTER AGNES ✎
SISTER MONICA

Genus: Human

Dæmons: Unnamed; forms unknown

World: Lyra's

Alliances: Consistorial Court of Discipline, College of St Jerome, Geneva

Background: Nuns in the Order of St Philomel.

Roles: Serve as stenographers during the interrogation of Fra Pavel at the College of St Jerome, Geneva. Although neither says a word during the alethiometrist's testimony, one of the two nuns gasps, and both hasten to make the sign of the cross, when Pavel hesitantly confesses that his instrument says that Lyra is "in the position of Eve…. the cause of all sin."

AS   6 [brief]

SISTER BETTY ✠

Genus: Human

Dæmon: Unnamed; pretty bird

World: Lyra's

Behavior: Both woman and dæmon show no curiosity. They

Yellow Warbler (a pretty bird)

407

have been severed.

Role: Nurse at Bolvangar.

NL/GC 15 *[brief]*

Sister Clara ✧

Genus: Human

Dæmon: Unnamed; white dog

World: Lyra's

Physical characteristics: In her mid-thirties.

Behavior: Has a "brisk, blank, sensible air." Shows no curiosity. Behavior of her dæmon chills Lyra; woman, too, is like an automaton.

Role: Nurse at Bolvangar and an example of a human severed from her dæmon who has been able to keep the dæmon near her as a peculiar type of pet.

Suggests Lyra exchange the alethiometer for a cute little doll baby with a face as blank as the nurse's own, but doesn't find the girl's refusal interesting enough to argue about.

Indifferently summons the lively little girl Bridget McGinn to her doom.

NL/GC 14; 15 *[brief]*

Sister Clare ⑩

Genus: Human

World: Will's

Role: Cited by Mary Malone (in a fragment of a letter included in the appendix to the **10**ᴛʜ anniversary edition of *The Amber Spyglass*) as an example of a nun who left the convent. Sister Clare couldn't cope with the outside world, and so returned, in spite of her lack of faith. Mary's point is that her experience has been entirely different.

10ᴛʜ: *AS* appendix

Skadi, Ruta 🗡✎ ⑩

Genus: Witch

Dæmon: Sergi, a bluethroat

World: Lyra's, Cittàgazze, Asriel's republic

Alliances: Her witch-clan; Asriel's republic

Physical characteristics: Black-haired, black-eyed 416-year-old witch. Wears a crown adorned with the fangs of snow tigers she herself killed to get back at a Tartar tribe who worshipped the beasts.

Background: Queen of the Latvian Lake Lubana witch clan. Their consul, Semyon Karlovich Martins, is in Novgorod. Ruta had once been Asriel's lover, and she uses a spell of invisibility to get into his bedchamber when she visits the basalt fortress. She has also traveled in the southern hemisphere of her world.

Behavior: Described as "beautiful, proud, and pitiless"; said to live "so brilliantly in her nerves that she set up a responding thrill in the nerves of anyone close by." She feels a surge of gratitude for the physical life she and her dæmon enjoy when she compares herself to the incorporeal angels.

When the Tartar tribe that snubbed her suffered a psychic breakdown after she killed the tigers they worshipped, they fearfully wanted to worship her instead, but Skadi refused, asking "what good would worship do her?...It had done nothing for the tigers." 412

Role: Campaigns among the different witch-clans for recruits to fight for Asriel's republic. She supports it because it opposes the Magisterium, which in every region of the world has worked to destroy happiness.

Last seen leading her clan with those she has recruited into battle against angels emerging from the Clouded Mountain.

Remarks: *Skadi is the Norse goddess of winter; Scandinavia is named for her.*

SK speech at witches' council 2; visits world of Cittàgazze with Serafina, leaves with angels for Asriel's 6; reports on Asriel's fortress, cliffghasts' conversation 13

AS *brief mentions:* 3, 16, leads clan into battle 29; 36

10TH: *SK appendix*

SKRAELING, THE 🗡

Snowy Owl

Genus: Human

Dæmon: Unnamed; snowy owl with orange eyes

World: Lyra's

Physical characteristics: Identifiable as not one of the Observatory's scientists but as the Magisterium's censor by his ring (which bears the Church's symbol).

Background: Censor for the Magisterium assigned to the Imperial Muscovite Academy's Observatory on Nova Zembla. His charge is to repress any findings considered heretical.

Behavior: Hester directs Scoresby's attention to the hostility and suspicions reflected in the Skraeling's dæmon's stare. The censor is quiet during the scientists' conversation with Scoresby until Lee mentions Dust—and then all are quiet.

Role: Lee Scoresby kills the Skraeling in self-defense, and takes the man's official ring identifying him as an agent of the Magisterium (at Hester's suggestion).

SK 6

brief mentions: Scoresby uses his ring 10; recalled by Hester 14

Mr. Ardo X. Meyer, NOAA's Ark - Animals Collection, 1959

SOCIETY OF THE WORK OF THE HOLY SPIRIT PRIEST ✎

413

Prebles Meadow Jumping Mouse

Genus: Human

Dæmon: Unnamed; mouse

World: Lyra's

Background: Lives at the Society's headquarters in Geneva.

Behavior: Gullible and likely power hungry; he breaks his vows in order to acquire a personal advantage over his brothers in the priesthood.

Role: Lady Salmakia gained her knowledge of the Society of the Holy Spirit's plans by approaching this priest's dæmon as they slept, so they would think it a dream, and planting the idea in their minds "that the man perform a forbidden ritual designed to invoke the presence of Wisdom." The priest succumbed. During the ritual, Lady Salmakia made her presence known, and "the priest now thinks he can communicate with Wisdom"—the Lady Salmakia, who lives in his bookcase.

From the priest they learn the Society believes that Lyra will soon have to make a critical choice affecting the fate of everyone, and that the Society is close to discovering

U.S. Fish and Wildlife Service, Jan 2006

her whereabouts.

Facts: *In the Gnostic tradition, Wisdom, or Sophia, is the supreme force of creation, preceding and exceeding the God of the Old Testament.*

AS   5 *[brief]*

SOLDIER IN SERVICE OF CONSISTORIAL COURT OF DISCIPLINE ✐

Genus: Human

Dæmon: Unnamed; dog

World: Lyra's

Physical characteristics: Young man.

Background: Charged with task of escorting Coulter off the zeppelin at the Saint-Jean-les-Eaux launch site for the Consistorial Court of Discipline's bomb.

Behavior: Nearly proves susceptible to his prisoner Mrs Coulter's charms.

Role: Although Coulter's first ploy fails, given this soldier does not have the key to uncuff her, her complaints about her handcuffs—all the time underscoring her difficulties walking in the wind without the use of her hands by falling against him—do succeed in extracting from this soldier the information about who is holding the keys.

Stung by Lord Roke when he comes to the aid of his sergeant, whom the Gallivespian spy had spurred so he could get the key to Coulter's cuffs.

AS   25 *[brief]*

SOPHONAX ✸

Genus: Dæmon

Form: An "autumn-colored cat"

Human: Farder Coram

World: Lyra's

Physical characteristics: Huge but sleek, double the size of an ordinary cat, golden-eyed, and elegant, Lyra has never seen a more beautiful dæmon. In sunlight her fur is seen to be "tawny-brown-leaf-hazel-corn-gold-autumn-mahogany." Lyra would love to stroke her, but knows she can't.

Behavior: Queenly and sensuous.

Role: Her grace and health, the comfort she obviously feels in her body, provide a marked contrast to the crippled and deteriorating appearance of her human perhaps suggesting what Farder Coram was like when a young man and the witch Serafina Pekkala's lover.

Notes: *Compare the description of Sophonax to the settled form of Kirjava, Will Parry's dæmon, who is described "a cat of no ordinary size, and her fur was lustrous and rich, with a thousand different glints and shades of ink-black, shadow-grey, the blue of a deep lake under a noon sky, mist-lavender-moonlight-fog… To see the meaning of the word* subtlety, *you had only to look at her fur."*

The last reference to Sophonax in NORTHERN LIGHTS *is not found in* THE GOLDEN COMPASS. *In* NORTHERN LIGHTS, *before Scoresby's balloon lifts off from Bolvangar, Lyra sees John Faa forcing the Tartar guards to retreat toward the Station's burning buildings and "Farder Coram, casting around anxiously, leaning on his stick, his autumn-colored dæmon leaping through the snow and looking this way and that." Lyra yells to him from the balloon, and a relieved Coram shouts back his farewell.*

NL/GC brief mentions: 7, 9, 17

STARMINSTER, ADÈLE ✤

Genus: Human
Dæmon: Unnamed; butterfly
World: Lyra's
Physical characteristics: Young enough that Lyra thinks she's a student.
Background: Journalist. Uninvited guest at Coulter's party.
Behavior: Flirts with Professor Docker. Naively makes her interest in Lyra obvious when she suggests they separate from the crowd and find a quiet place to talk.
Role: Her treatment, by a very quiet but very vindictively enraged Mrs Coulter, is an early example of Coulter's force of personality and cruelty. The force of Coulter's rage sends Adèle's butterfly dæmon into a faint as the young woman is removed from the party.

NL/GC 5

Swallowtail Butterfly

Ron Singer, U.S. Fish and Wildlife Service, Oct 2002

STEERSMAN ⚔

Genus: Human
Dæmon: Unnamed; seagull
World: Lyra's
Background: Thinks Serafina Pekkala is one of the witches working with the Magisterium and that she has come to guide him to the launch.
Role: Inadvertently allows Serafina Pekkala onto Cardinal Sturrock's boat off the coast of Svalbard, where a witch is being tortured into revealing what the witches know about Lyra.

SK 2 [brief]

STEFANSKI, ADAM ✤

Genus: Human
Dæmon: Unnamed; form unknown
World: Lyra's
Background: Gyptian
Role: Head of one of the six families (the one the Costa family belongs to) of Eastern Anglia gyptians under the leadership of John Faa. In charge of weapons and troops.

NL/GC brief mentions: 8, 9, 10

STELMARIA ✤ ✎

Genus: Dæmon
Form: Snow leopard
Human: Asriel
World: Lyra's, Asriel's, the abyss of the world of the dead
Physical characteristics: Stelmaria's eyes are green, tawny or golden; her coat is spotted. Her demeanor is "proud and beautiful and deadly."
Behavior: Her roar when Lyra argues with Asriel is enough to stifle the quarrelsome child. Her embrace of the golden monkey seems permeated with tension, a contrast to the languorous attitude of the golden monkey when Lyra watches Asriel and Coulter's

Snow Leopard

Ron Singer, U.S. Fish and Wildlife Service, Feb 2002

416

encounter following Roger's death.

Role: Lord Asriel's dæmon. Her dominance of Roger's dæmon is critical to Asriel's success in breaking through the Aurora; later, her strength is fully engaged in the battle with Metatron.

Stelmaria is the subject of the woodcut for "Lord Asriel's Welcome," chapter 21 of *Northern Lights*.

NL/GC 1, eyes described as green 2; 21, battles Pan and Lyra at Roger's intercision, flirts with golden monkey 23
   brief mentions: intimidates misbehaving Lyra 3; 13

AS eyes described as golden 5; and golden monkey 28; sees Dust falling into abyss 30; battles Metatron, dies 31
   brief mentions: 16, 23, 25

Steward at Jordan College [*See* Cawson]

Sturrock, Cardinal ⚱

Genus: Human
Dæmon: Unnamed; macaw
World: Lyra's
Alliances: Church
Physical characteristics: Old
Behavior: Unlike other clerics present, he is not intimidated by Coulter's sarcasm or display of temper.
Role: Presides over the torture of a witch of the Taymyr clan. Disbelieves Coulter's claim of not knowing witches' prophecy concerning Lyra. Killed by Serafina Pekkala as she flees after delivering the tortured witch from further suffering.

SK 2

Sub-Rector ✸

Genus: Human
Dæmon: Unnamed; form unknown
World: Lyra's
Physical characteristics: Elderly
Background: Jordan College scholar
Role: His familiarity with trepanning and scalping is used by Asriel to focus attention on these subjects when introducing the head that supposedly was Grumman's.

NL/GC 2

Sultan, Sunda Straits ⑩

Genus: Human
Dæmon: Unnamed; form unknown
World: Lyra's
Role: When the Sultan tells Lord Asriel that his collection of manganese modules is for "ritual purposes," Asriel refrains from telling him what he thinks of his host's response, namely, that he is a "barefaced liar."

10th: *NL* appendix

Swiss Guardsman

Genus: Human
Dæmon: Unnamed; wolf-dog
World: Lyra's
Alliances: Magisterium
Physical characteristics: Armed with a crossbow.
Role: With two of his comrades, he is blocking Will and Lyra's path from Coulter's cave to the window to safety Will had cut previously. He takes aim at Will, but the boy shoots him first.

Dog resembling [perhaps] a Swiss guard wolfdog, Australian Shepherd ancestry

Ellen Levy Finch

AS 13 *[brief]*

Sysselman

Genus: Human
Dæmon: Unnamed; form unknown
World: Lyra's
Physical characteristics: Bulky with a high-pitched voice and "fussy" demeanor.
Background: Governor of Trollesund
Role: Warns armoured bear Iorek Byrnison that the consequences will be dreadful should the bear ever return to Trollesund. Iorek totally ignores him.

417

NL/GC 11

Thorold

Genus: Human
Dæmon: Anfang, a pinscher
World: Lyra's
Alliances: Asriel
Physical characteristics: Old, "long-jawed and grizzled and steady-eyed" but still "healthy and vigorous."
Background: Lord Asriel's manservant for 40 years, which he claims gives him more understanding of the man than a mother or wife could have. His tenure allows him, he tells Serafina Pekkala, to see "where he's a-heading even if I can't go after him." Placed in charge of securing supplies for at least one of Lord Asriel's expeditions.
Behavior: Kind to Lyra. Enjoys Serafina's attention, but doesn't deceive himself about her reason for giving it. Forthright, loyal, modest, and honest, but his devotion to Asriel doesn't extend to being passive when Asriel takes Roger out into the cold. Staying on at Svalbard until he hears from Asriel he's to do otherwise, or he dies.
Role: Wakes Lyra when a frenzied Asriel leaves with Roger, telling her Asriel needed a child to complete his experiment. This gives her a chance to try to stop him, or, failing that, to follow him out of her world.

418
419

420
421

His conversation with Serafina Pekkala provides insight into his boss's behavior.

NL/GC 1 *[brief]*; greets Lyra and Roger on Svalbard 21; awakens and warns Lyra 22
SK 2
10TH: *NL* appendix

TIALYS, CHEVALIER

Genus: Gallivespian

World: Gallivespians' (origin), Lyra's, desert world, Holland-like world, world of the dead and its suburbs, Asriel's republic, mulefa's

Alliances: Asriel's republic, officially; Lyra and Will

Physical characteristics: Dark-haired Tialys is "strong, capable, ruthless, and proud." Wears full, capri-length silver pants and a green shirt. No shoes cover his spurred feet. At eight years old, he is a late middle-aged Gallivespian.

Background: Gallivespian spy whose partner is the Lady Salmakia. Expert at communicating by way of a lodestone resonator. Has recently been Lord Roke's spy at the Consistorial Court of Discipline.

Behavior: Initially his relationship with Will and Lyra is one of mutual distrust and antipathy. Calls Lyra "a thoughtless insolent child," which she seems to accept as her due. But before he can launch into Will, the boy reminds the spy that respect is a two-way affair. The pragmatic Tialys, not knowing that the knife is broken, backs down. When he confronts Will about not being forthcoming about the state of the knife, Will counters that the spies would have taken advantage of the situation, and that Tialys only knows of it now because he has been eavesdropping. Furious, the Chevalier backs down and apologizes.

Although afterward he will tell Salmakia that when they left the suburbs of the dead and crossed the river, he "felt as if my heart had been torn out and thrown still beating on the shore," he never revealed his pain to the others or complained. When he and Salmakia know they are dying, they do not tell the children, but are resolved to stay with them as long as they can.

Lyra is amazed by his bravery in addressing the harpies: "How did he dare to speak to these creatures as if he had the power to give them rights? Any one of them could have snapped him up in a moment, wrenched him apart in her claws …yet there he stood, proud and fearless."

Role: The alethiometer warns Lyra that she and Will need the spies. Tialys and his partner will fulfill this prediction by their negotiations with No-Name the harpy. Leaving the world of the dead, he encourages those ghosts who intend to fight to bear in mind that the top priority is helping Will and Lyra find their dæmons. Tialys uses the last of his strength to spur one of the cliff-ghasts threatening the children. When he dies, Will is deeply grieved.

The title of chapter 13 of *THE AMBER SPYGLASS* is "Tialys and Salmakia."

AS   6; leaves Geneva for Himalayas 9; stings Coulter at cave 12; kills Swiss guards, confrontation with Will when Salmakia seizes Pan 13; confrontation with Will regarding Iorek, eavesdropping 14; fails to convince Will to go with repaired knife to Asriel 15; activities reported at Asriel's 16; argues with Lyra in suburbs of world of dead 18; reconciled to entering world of dead 19; 21, 22; addresses harpies 23; discusses battle plan with ghosts, expresses pride in Will and Lyra's achievement 26; rallies ghost troops, enters Asriel's world's battlefield 29; dies fighting cliff-ghasts 31
brief mentions: 5, 28; buried in mulefa's world 32

Margin numbers: 422, 423, 424, 425

TILLERMAN

Genus: Human

Dæmon: Unnamed; cormorant

World: Lyra's

Physical characteristics: Elderly, remote

Background: Gyptian

Double-Crested Cormorant

Lee Karney, U.S. Fish and Wildlife Service, Apr 2004

Role: His dæmon saves Pantalaimon from Coulter's mechanical spy-flies, which attack when Lyra briefly goes on deck before the gyptians leave England.

NL/GC 9 *[brief]*

Tim ✎

Genus: Human
World: Will's
Physical characteristics: All Mary remembers now is that he looked "nice." | 426
Background: Was at a birthday party with Mary Malone years ago when she was twelve, and Mary "fell in love with him." Spent time with Mary on six or so occasions before his | 427 family moved out of town.
Role: When Mary Malone describes remembering how she felt when Tim, the first boy she ever kissed, ever so gently fed her a bit of marzipan, the effect on Lyra is to bring to the surface her feelings for Will.

AS 33 *[brief]*

Tortured witch ⚶ ✎

Genus: Witch
Dæmon: Unnamed; tern
World: Lyra's
Background: From the Taymyr clan. Taken prisoner during the battle at Bolvangar.

Least Tern

S. Maslowski, U.S. Fish and Wildlife Service, Mar 2003

Role: Tortured by Cardinal Sturrock and Mrs Coulter because they believe she can tell of the prophecy regarding Lyra. Her legs already "twisted and broken," her fingers are | 428 broken one by one by Coulter. Desperate, beginning to give her torturers what they want, the brutalized witch pleads for release by Yambe-Akka, the goddess who comes to a witch as she dies. Serafina Pekkala responds to the woman's longing for death, and stabs her quickly and efficiently through the heart.

SK 2
    brief mentions: recalled by Coulter 9, and by Serafina 13; Coulter to Feldt 15
AS Fra Pavel's testimony 6; Serafina mentions to Mary 36 *[brief]*

Trelawney, Professor ✤ ⑩

Genus: Human
Dæmon: Unnamed; form unknown
World: Lyra's
Background: Palmerian Professor, Jordan College. Visited Svalbard during the reign of Iofur Raknison. Area of study is gamma-ray photons. Lord Asriel does not expect to be able to count on his support for funding his future expeditions. Accused of plagiarism by | 429 Jotham Santelia, Lyra's cellmate on Svalbard, who blames Trelawney for his present predicament in Svalbard. | 430
Behavior: Talkative, enjoys revealing the breadth of his knowledge whenever possible. Undeterred by the laughter of his colleagues and by the unconcealed disdain of his Dean.
Role: Trelawney's comments on Asriel's presentation introduce several topics that will

prove of great interest to Lyra. He asks Asriel if the photogram of a city behind the Aurora relates to the Barnard-Stokes hypothesis. Trelawney counters the Cassington Scholar's declaration that the *panserbjørne* couldn't be involved in Grumman's presumed scalping and trepanation, and when he claims that what Iofur Raknison wants most is a dæmon, he is laughed at by his fellow Jordan College Scholars. But Lyra, hiding in the closet, is intrigued. His remarks will provide the inspiration for her scheme by which she tricks Raknison, gives Iorek Byrnison the chance he needs to regain his kingdom, and saves herself from a Svalbard dungeon.

Update: On the back of the map in *LYRA'S OXFORD,* Smith and Strange, Ltd. lists among its publications, *Fraud: an Exposure of a Scientific Imposture* by Professor P. Trelawney, an intriguing title in light of Santelia's accusations.

NL/GC 2; Santelia on 19
   brief mentions: Lyra recalls his opinion of Raknison 13, 18

10ᴛʜ: *NL* appendix

TULLIO ⚔️ ✏️

Genus: Human
World: Cittàgazze
Physical characteristics: Teenager; has curly red hair.
Background: Brother of Paolo and Angelica. Stole the subtle knife from its bearer, Giacomo Paradisi, and assaulted him. Likely been in the Tower for several days, based on his siblings' uneasiness.
Behavior: Violent. When Lyra and Will approach the Tower of Angels, Pantalaimon sees Tullio engaged in a solitary dance, moving "as if he was fighting something invisible," and Will and Lyra hear him talking to himself with the "voice of a madman." Attacks Will as soon as he sees him.
Role: Tullio is the teenager Will is compelled to fight before Will is revealed to be the next bearer of the subtle knife. Defeated in a violent, no-holds-barred fight by Will, who has seen what Tullio has done to Paradisi.

   Angelica and Paolo, consumed by a thirst for vengeance for the loss of their brother, lead a gang of kids to attack Will and Lyra, whom they declare to be Tullio's "murderers."

SK encounters, fights Will 8; 11
   brief mentions: 3, 5, 7, 13

AS *brief mentions:* 9, 12

TUNGUSK HUNTER ⑩

Genus: Human
Dæmon: Unnamed; form unknown
World: Lyra's
Role: Subject of a photogram by Lord Asriel, possibly the one shown in the retiring room of Jordan College.

10ᴛʜ: *NL* appendix

TURK, THE ✢

Genus: Human

Dæmon: Unnamed; form unknown

World: Lyra's

Role: Asriel negotiated with the Turk to save the life of gyptian Sam Broekman, an incident cited by John Faa as a reason for the gyptians to aid Asriel's daughter, Lyra.

NL/GC 8 *[brief]*

TYLTSHIN, IVAN KASYMOVICH ⑩

Genus: Human

Dæmon: Unnamed; form unknown

World: Lyra's

Role: This shaman, who lived to the east of the Yenisei River not far from Norisk, was a "great and good man," who, Dr Stanislaus Grumman/Col. John Parry, writes, "taught me everything I know about the spirit world."

10TH: *SK* appendix

UMAQ ⚔

Genus: Human

Dæmon: Unnamed; arctic fox

World: Lyra's

Physical characteristics: An old man from the region of the Ob River in Siberia.

Arctic Fox

Sowls, Art / Flint Paul, U.S. Fish and Wildlife Service, Apr 2006

Background: Aëronaut Lee Scoresby's Tartar dog sledge chauffeur on the island of Nova Zembla, where Scoresby has gone seeking information that will lead him to Stanislaus Grumman. Hired to take Scoresby north from the settlement frequented by prospectors and fur traders to as near as he can get to the Imperial Muscovite Academy's Observatory.

Behavior: Bargains for a good price for his service, which Scoresby pays, there not being many others willing to take the job. Navigates by landmarks and the nose of his dæmon, which is fortunate since compass readings are no longer reliable.

Role: Directs Scoresby to Yenisei Tartars for news of Grumman. Says a similar "sky opening" causing climatic changes had happened "many thousand generation" ago: "Sky fall open, and spirits move between this world and that world...The spirits close up the hole after a while. Seal it up. But witches say the sky is thin there, behind the northern lights." Predicts that things will return to normal this time as well "but only after big trouble, big war. Spirit war."

SK 6

434
435

VAN GERRIT, RAYMOND ✢

Genus: Human

Dæmon: Unnamed; form unknown

World: Lyra's

Background: Gyptian

Behavior: Begins with a display of obstinacy, challenging Faa's leadership at both ropings. After his second complaint that the gyptians are being asked to put too much at risk for Lyra, Faa so thoroughly shames him that he is booed and hissed by his peers, and slips down into his chair rather than standing to defend his position.

Role: Challenges Faa about the rescue of landlopers' children and the gyptians' obligation to Lyra.

NL/GC 7, 8

van Poppel, Piet ✤ LS

Genus: Human

Dæmon: Unnamed; form unknown

World: Lyra's

Background: Gyptian.

Role: Lyra so admired the pattern of lilies and roses he painted on his narrow-boat that she tried to duplicate the design on her best dress, first with paint and then with thread, before finally giving up and working instead on a story to appease Mrs. Lonsdale.

NL/GC LS Lantern Slide 2

van Poppel, Roger ✤

Genus: Human

Dæmon: Unnamed; form unknown

World: Lyra's

Background: Gyptian. Head of one of the six families of John Faa's group of Eastern Anglia gyptians.

Role: In charge of supplies, except for arms and ammunition, for voyage North

NL/GC brief mentions: 8, 9

Verhoeven, Jack ✤

Genus: Human

Dæmon: Unnamed; form unknown

World: Lyra's

Background: Head of a Fens gyptian family under the leadership of John Faa.

Role: His sons are placed under arrest, the family's boat is sunk, and he is killed before the gyptians leave England.

NL/GC 9 *[brief]*

Village headman ⚓

Genus: Human

Dæmon: Unnamed; wolverine

World: Lyra's

Physical characteristics: Old, very wrinkled.

Background: Head of the village of Yenisei Pakhtars (a tribe

Wolverine

of Siberian Tartars) where the shaman known to these people as both Dr Grumman and Jopari has been living. Has several wives and a wooden house.

Behavior: Seems at once distressed and relieved to think of Jopari's departure. Knows that Grumman has summoned Scoresby for a flight to another world. Receives Scoresby's gift of smokeleaf with graciousness. Tells him to speak with respect when addressing Grumman, both because the man Scoresby seeks is a shaman and because he is unwell.

Role: Chief of the village where the aëronaut Lee Scoresby finds the shaman Stanislaus Grumman/John Parry/Jopari.

SK 10

VILLAGER WITH LANTERN (BETWEEN TROLLESUND AND BOLVANGAR) ✦

Genus: Human
Dæmon: Unnamed; Arctic fox
World: Lyra's
Physical characteristics: Old man with very wrinkled, broad face.
Behavior: As Iorek, Lyra, and Tony leave, the man says he wants to be paid for the fish Tony clutches in place of his dæmon.
Role: This old man brings out a lantern for Lyra's use in looking for the severed Tony Makarios. Tells Lyra and Iorek that there are other children like the one in the fish house wandering in the woods.

NL/GC brief mentions: 12, 13

VILLAGER WITH RIFLE (BETWEEN TROLLESUND AND BOLVANGAR) ✦

Genus: Human
Dæmon: Unnamed, wolverine
World: Lyra's
Behavior: This man is so nervous and fearful Lyra fears he will accidentally shoot off his rifle.
Role: Opens his door just long enough to point to the fish house where Tony Makarios shelters.

NL/GC 12 *[brief]*

VRIES, DIRK ✦

Genus: Human
Dæmon: Unnamed; form unknown
World: Lyra's
Background: Gyptian.
Role: Asks John Faa at the Roping if the gyptian leader knows why children are being abducted.

NL/GC 8 *[brief]*

WALTERS, INSPECTOR ⚱

Genus: Human
World: Will's

Alliances: Presumably the British government

436 **Physical characteristics:** Described as "tall powerful man with white eyebrows."

Background: May be one of men who searched Will's house; the description fits. Claims to be from the British government's Special Branch. Latrom claims to be working with him.

Behavior: Begins his examination of Lyra casually, even blandly, asking, for example, if she wants to be a scientist when she's grown up, and then tricks her by asking out of the blue if Will is staying at the same place in Oxford she is.

Role: Questions Lyra in Mary Malone's lab about her background and interest in the scientist's work.

SK described 7, 12

WILL (PARRY, WILL) 🔪 ✒ ⑩ *LS*

Genus: Human

Dæmon: Kirjava; cat

World: Will's, Cittàgazze, Lyra's, beach world, desert world, Holland-like world, world of the dead and its suburbs, Asriel's republic, mulefa's

Alliances: His mother and Lyra

Physical characteristics: Twelve years old when THE SUBTLE KNIFE opens. He was born the year his father disappeared, which was in June 1985, and since his father described his son

437 as "not yet one," he must have been born very early in the year. Has "broad cheekbones,"

438 "wide eyes," and "straight black brows." Will is described as stocky, being too heavy for Serafina Pekkala to carry on her cloud-pine branch. To his father, the boy seems slim,

439 "and his expression exhausted and savage and wary, but alight with a wild curiosity." To

440 gyptians Farder Coram and John Faa, Will appears "young, but very strong, and deeply stricken." He will live at least until his mid-seventies ("Sixty years and more would go

441 by") and his memories of Lyra and of meeting Kirjava will be as vivid then as the moments themselves once were.

Background: Hometown is Winchester, England. The son of Elaine and John Parry, Will has no recollection of his father, who vanished during Will's infancy. Will's childhood has been defined by two needs that far exceed the capacity of any child to fulfill: his need to protect his mother (who suffers from intermittent bouts of undiagnosed emotional problems, including paranoia) and his need, his sense of obligation, to find his father.

Since he was seven, Will has felt that he must protect his mother from her anxieties

442 and the "enemies" in her mind. This he does willingly: "He loved her so much he would

443 have died to protect her." Will fears that she'd be taken away and he would end up in foster care if anyone found out about her illness. Asking for help is thus not an option, and he is torn between beating up kids who torment her and not attracting anyone's attention.

His mother still misses and loves her husband, who disappeared in Alaska some eleven years previously. She encourages her son Will to think of his father as a man worthy of respect and emulation.

Will seems to know of no friends or family on whom he can call, and when Elaine Parry is well, both she and her son are content with the company of one another. But when she is not, all the responsibility for both of them is Will's. He has taken it upon himself, in her times of calm, to get his mother to teach him how to keep house and cook. Will can't tell Lyra about how other people think in his world, claiming it is something he doesn't "know much about…All I know is keeping secret and quiet and hidden." | 444

After years of taking care of his mother, Will "longed for his father as a lost child longs for home." Will has been sustained (and also intrigued) by his mother's assurance | 445 that he will "take up" his father's "mantle." In a sense, he literally does take up his father's | 446 mantle when he removes the shaman's cloak from his father's body and puts it on. Will promises the father he found alive then lost to death in the same moment, "whatever you wanted me to do, I promise, I swear I'll do it." But as is usually the case for Will, he finds | 447 he is again beset by conflicting obligations: what his father wanted, what the angels want, what is best for his mother, and what he wants—which is what is best for Lyra.

When, in THE SUBTLE KNIFE's opening pages, Will Parry walks through Oxford's Sunderland Avenue window into a new world, and looks back, it is his own world from which he "turned away with a shudder: whatever this new world was, it had to be better than what he'd just left." | 448

Behavior: Will is an exceptionally complex person. He can challenge an armoured bear to a public duel, shred the bear's helmet with an unusual knife—and moments later disappear into the crowd of onlookers. He tries not to draw attention to himself, but once he has made up his mind, he refuses to be swayed from his agenda and will not be treated with disrespect—not by an angel, or a Gallivespian with poisonous spurs, or a harpy. He is proficient at physical combat, willing to hurt rather than be hurt—and hates violence.

Because of the teasing and insults he suffered about his mother's unusual behavior, Will learned to fight schoolyard bullies. As is usual with Will, he has reflected on his own behavior and the nature of these fights, concluding that they aren't about skill, but about being able to hurt your adversary more than you are hurt: "you had to be willing to hurt someone else, too, and he'd found out that not many people were, when it came to it; but he knew that he was." His adversaries back off, convinced that Will would not hesitate to | 449 kill to protect Elaine Parry from further torment.

But fighting has no intrinsic appeal to him. He understands, for example, Lyra's feeling bad about Tullio after the battle for the knife, yet he reminds her that they had no choice. Had there been another way to get the knife, they would have done things differently. When he has to kill a Swiss Guard to get away with Lyra from Coulter's cave, he is physically sick afterwards: "Will *did not want* this." The day after the Special Services | 450 man died falling down the Parry's stairs, the reality of the man's death hits Will. He dazedly wanders into a museum, where he spends nearly an hour in physical agony at the thought of what has happened. What allows him to master his own self-loathing is recalling his mother's neediness and the dead man's cruel badgering of her and intrusion into their home.

He is compassionate and risks harm to himself to protect a cat, but also threatens—giving every indication of meaning it—to kill Lyra if she brings the authorities to him, and he is frightening even to a witch when enraged. Brave and loyal, an exceptionally loving person, with exceptional inner resources, he is very much like Lyra.

Thoughtful, reflective, honest, and practical, he is perceptive in ways unusual in a boy his age, or most people for that matter. He has considered the ethics of fairness, and discriminates between the not fair of having a mother who needs help (putting that in the category of earthquakes and storms for which no one is to blame) vs. the not fair of abandoning her, which is a matter of right and wrong. He checks the impulse to ask the angel Xaphania what he should do with his life, deciding he'd rather not know what his future work is because he wants to believe he has choices: "Whatever I do, I will choose it, no one else." Xaphania responds, "Then you have already taken the first steps toward wisdom."

Not unlike Serafina Pekkala's ability to make herself invisible, Will can make himself "intensely inconspicuous": "he performed the magic that had deflected all kinds of curiosity away from his mother and kept them safe for years. Of course, it wasn't magic, but simply a way of behaving. He made himself quiet and dull-eyed and slow." Because Will has deceived adults all his life, he thinks he can handle Mrs Coulter in the Himalayas. Mrs Coulter proves his most formidable opponent; she knows that making veiled insinuations about his mother's love for her boy will cause him the deepest pain.

When the witch who kills his father responds to Will's claim to be the shaman's son that that it is "impossible," Will replies, "You think things have to be _possible_? Things have to be _true_!" Even through her own fear and emotional turmoil she sees that "this young wounded figure held more force and danger than she'd ever met in a human before" so great is his "immense and shattering despair." Witch Ruta Skadi says Will reminds her of Lord Asriel; Serafina Pekkala admits to her sister-witch that she hasn't "dared" to look into the boy's eyes.

Any appearance of complacency on Will's part is deceptive. He is a strong-willed, commanding leader, starting as he means to go on. The night they meet, he tells Lyra that he cooked, so she'll clean. When she objects, he says he won't take her with him into Oxford. He doesn't whine or threaten, just delivers a simple statement of fact: no work, no window—and goes to bed. When Lyra wants to go upstairs first in the Tower of Angels, she argues that she should because it is her fault they are there in the first place. But Will counters that since it is her fault, she has to do as he says. With adults he is no less commanding. When he takes his mother to stay with Mrs Cooper, the boy is the one clearly "in charge of this business" bending two women to his "implacable" will.

His desire that Elaine Parry not feel abandoned by his failure to return, and his fear

Promises

Will's dilemma about whether to fulfill his promise to his father to go to Asriel or to hunt for Lyra is repeated in the Himalayas. He tells Iorek, "I'm pulled apart." He wants to go home to his mother "because _I could_," but thinks perhaps the angels and his father were right and he should take the knife to Asriel, but he also wants to talk to his father's ghost in the world of the dead and to help Lyra find the forgiveness she needs from Roger.

In the Himalayas, Iorek tries to dissuade Lyra from going to the world of the dead by telling her that "while you are alive, your business is with life." But she quietly replies that "our business is to keep promises, no matter how difficult they are."

In Cittàgazze, Will chose the living over promises to the dead. Interesting too is that Grumman/Parry consciously broke his promise to Lee Scoresby that he'd tell the bearer of the knife to keep Lyra under its protection. When Will breaks his promise to his father, the promise Grumman broke is effectively fulfilled, and Will chooses what Scoresby wanted. And, moreover, by breaking his promise to his dad, Will achieves what Parry wanted. By helping Lyra instead of going to Asriel, Will ventures into the world of the dead and scores the greatest victory in the battle with the Authority when he opens the window out of that world.

of not getting home (just as his father failed to return from Alaska), is Will's "most pressing reason" for wanting the knife repaired—and what worries him most about visiting the world of the dead. But not even his despair at his father's murder compares to what he feels when he learns that he will not be able to share his life with Lyra: "All his life he'd been alone, and now he must be alone again, and this infinitely precious blessing that had come to him must be taken away almost at once... And he found himself gasping and shaking and crying aloud with more anger and pain than he had ever felt in his life." With his mother, Will felt like he

> ## Philip Pullman on what becomes of Will: 460
>
> Asked during a readerville.com forum what's next for Will, Pullman replied, "I think he will go home and find that his mother is already in hospital, being looked after. I think that Mary will help him make everything straight about the man he killed...Later I think he'll go to medical school and become a doctor." 461

always had to hide from her any fears about her health or their future that he felt, but his love for Lyra is strong enough that he knows it will withstand the exhibition of honest and intense despair. When he kisses Lyra for the last time, he tries to hold onto the thought, "Being cheerful starts *now*." 462

Growing up, Will Parry's "heart craved to hear the words, 'Well done, well done, my child.'" In the world of the dead, John Parry's ghost with "pride and tenderness" replies 463 to his son with the words the boy has longed to hear: "Well done, my boy. Well done 464 indeed."

Role: With the subtle knife, Will makes the most effective stand in human history against the Authority's gratuitous cruelty when he releases the ghosts from the world of the dead. Moreover, by teaching the angel Xaphania how to close windows and breaking the knife so that no more will ever be cut, he stops the flow of Spectres into uncountable worlds. This he does at considerable cost to himself.

Meeting Lyra begins the series of events through which Will becomes the bearer of the subtle knife, finds his father, meets his dæmon, and gains the friendship of Mary Malone. As Lyra's friend, he retrieves the alethiometer when it is stolen, and he later rescues her from Coulter's cave. Under the protection of the knife, and with the help of the ghosts he has liberated, he and Lyra regain their dæmons, and he finds a world of sanctuary for them both.

He brings to Lyra a capacity for love developed at home in his first 12 years. This gives Will the strength and tenacity he needs to prevail over the hardships and uncertainties of his journey through five worlds and home again, undertaken to learn the truth about his father. As they journey through these worlds, Will and Lyra learn to love and trust and make sacrifices for each other, and for the general well-being of all conscious beings.

Update: The fourth Lantern Slide in THE SUBTLE KNIFE reveals that the source of Will's vague memory of once having been to a home resembling Sir Charles Latrom's is a visit Will and his mother made to his paternal grandparents when Will was six. Will did not recognize the Parrys as his relations, but sensed that they viewed his mother with disdain. From that point on, "his savage resolution never to let her be exposed to that brutality again" made Will his mother's protector.

In contrast, the fourth Lantern Slide in THE AMBER SPYGLASS looks forward to Will's future. As the bearer of the subtle knife, Will gained a "sense of feeling without touching, of knowing without spoiling, of apprehending without calculating," which is reawakened when Will studies medicine. He proves to be such a gifted diagnostician that he finds himself engaged in a "lifelong process of learning to explain" his rare talent.

SK   his childhood recalled, leaves home, finds window, enters Cittàgazze, meets Lyra 1; goes into Oxford seeking answers about his father 3, 4; hears Lyra's story, confrontation with Spectre-orphans abusing cat, reads father's letters 5; realizes that best chance of finding father is by retrieving alethiometer, visits Latrom 7; battles Tullio, loses fingers, becomes bearer of the subtle knife 8; reclaims alethiometer 9; weakening from blood loss, gets Lyra to ask alethiometer about his mother but hasn't chance of asking of his father, battle with Spectre-orphans at belvedere 11; Latrom warns Malone and Payne about, Shadows tell Mary to help 12; witches attempt to halt bleeding with potion and spell, tells Lyra about his childhood, talks with Pan about dying, Serafina and Skadi discuss 13; recognizes Grumman as his father, sees father die and witch kill herself, takes father's cloak 15; [LS] Lantern Slides 4, 5

AS   discussions with Baruch and Balthamos, practices with knife, kills attacking angel as Metatron approaches, refuses to go to Asriel until Lyra is safe 2; Asriel hears about from Baruch 5; Consistorial Court on 6; in Lyra's dream [between 6 & 7, 7 & 8]; unwilling guest of Siberian priest, learns of boatload of armoured bears, stages duel as means of meeting Iorek, boards bears' boat 8; journey to Himalayas 9; meets Ama, conversation with Coulter 11; enters cave with Ama, knife breaks, becomes Coulter's hostage, reunited with wakened Lyra, gets Coulter's gun when she's stung by spies 12; kills Swiss Guard, hears of Lyra's dreams, tells Tialys off 13; asks Iorek's help in fixing the knife, decides to go to world of dead to see his father's ghost 14; works with Iorek as he mends the knife, confrontation and reconciliation with Iorek 15; final decision to go to world of dead, truce with spies, cuts into world at war and then into one of ghosts 18; spends night in suburbs of world of dead 19; crosses over to world of dead, feels anguish at being apart from dæmon, tormented by harpies 21; with ghosts, embraces Lyra's wish to liberate ghosts 22; searches for place to cut window, comforts Lyra when she's berated by hostile ghosts 23; meets his father's ghost, cuts remaining strand of Lyra's lock guiding bomb and places in uninhabited world, watches with horror as Lyra slips into abyss, cuts window releasing ghosts to world of mulefa 26; discussed at adamant tower 28; battles Spectres in Asriel's world as he and Lyra seek dæmons 29; among cliff-ghasts 30; battles cliff-ghasts, releases Authority from crystal litter, saves Iorek from net-throwers, grabs Pan, parts with father 31; meets mulefa and Mary 32; discussions with Mary 34; on fairness and his future, tells Lyra he loves her, their first kiss 35; discussed by Serafina, Kirjava, and Pan, and Serafina and Mary 36; meets Kirjava, his anguish, shows Xaphania how to close windows 37; meets John Faa, parts with Lyra, breaks knife, goes home with Mary, missed by Lyra 38; [LS] Lantern Slides 2, 4, 8, 9
       brief mentions: 4; Roke reports on to Asriel 16; MacPhail and Coulter discuss 24

10ᴛʜ: *SK* appendix

10ᴛʜ: *AS* appendix

Witch at Saint-Jean-Les-Eaux ✎

Genus: Witch

Dæmon: Unnamed; seagull

World: Lyra's

Alliances: Consistorial Court of Discipline

Role: This witch takes her orders from Father MacPhail, President of the Consistorial Court of Discipline. She shoots at Coulter, just missing her, then engages in hand-to-hand combat. When her dæmon sees a chance to snatch the Gallivespian Lord Roke, she takes off on her cloudpine to come to her dæmon's aid, but Roke spurs the witch in flight. With her last breath the witch warns MacPhail of an incoming craft; he disinterestedly steps over her body, making his way to the silver guillotine.

AS   25

WITCH EATEN BY SPECTRE [*See* Feldt, Lena]

WITCH WHO FLIES WIRE TO AURORA ❖

Genus: Witch
Dæmon: Unnamed; raven
World: Lyra's
Role: Aids Asriel by carrying a power line into the clouds as he tries to break through to the world behind the Aurora. With this power supply, he effects Roger's intercision. That yields a tremendous burst of energy, which, combined with the Aurora's, blasts open a passage between worlds.
NL/GC 3 *[brief]*

WREN ❖

Genus: Human
Dæmon: Unnamed; dog
World: Lyra's
Physical characteristics: Overweight
Background: Jealous of Cawson, who as the Steward is his superior. Eager to please Scholars, especially if by so doing he learns things before the Steward does.
Behavior: Nearly objects when Asriel asks him to do something out of the ordinary, but catches himself.
Role: Butler at Jordan College.
NL/GC 1

XAPHANIA ✐

Genus: Angel
World: All but the world of the dead
Alliances: Asriel
Physical characteristics: Described as "not shining, but shone on, though there was no source of light." She is "tall, naked, winged" and inconceivably old. Unaffected by heat and noise. [465]
Background: Of a far higher rank of angel than Baruch or Balthamos. One of Asriel's three high commanders; in charge of his angelic forces. Has been wandering since renegade angels' first rebellion failed. Siding now with Asriel as the best hope for ending the Authority's tyranny.
Behavior: Lyra and Will see her as both "austere and compassionate." Expresses regret for Lyra and Will's situation, but explains why the windows must be closed, adding that "every single being who knows of your dilemma wishes things could be otherwise: but there are fates that even the most powerful have to submit to. There is nothing I can do to help you change the way things are." [466] ... [467]
Role: Xaphania takes action at the end of Asriel's war and Lyra and Will's journey. She provides essential aid to Asriel by locating and facilitating his access to the edge of the abyss into which Coulter and Asriel will lure Metatron. She explains to Will and Lyra why

all windows but one must be closed and what must be done to keep that one open.

AS   16; on Metatron 28; in mulefa's world 37
   brief mentions: 30, 36, 38

YAKOVLEV ⚔

Genus: Human
Dæmon: Unnamed; form unknown
World: Lyra's
Background: Fur trader in whose trap Grumman stepped.
Behavior: Considered a fool by his fellow trappers
Role: One of the stories Lee Scoresby hears in a Nova Zembla   describes the wound Grumman suffered by stumbling into a trap set by Yakovlev.

SK   6 *[brief]*

ZOHARIEL ✦

Genus: Dæmon
Form: Unknown
Human: Francis Lyall
World: Lyra's
Role: Dæmon of the Jordan College Master who served from 1748-1765.

NL/GC 3 *[brief]*

Is Xaphania the angel Baruch and Balthamos serve?

Maybe. In their account of themselves to Will, Balthamos says that he and his companion serve the one who was "banished" by the Authority when she found out that he was not, in spite of his claims, her creator. And Xaphania identifies herself as one who rebelled against the Authority. Also, it seems that there are fewer female than male angels. She is the angel that Asriel has chosen as one of his three high commandeers. So she may be the one.

But maybe not. The sampling of angels is small, so that may account for why she is the only female angel seen. And if Balthamos and Baruch claim her as their leader, why would they need Will and the subtle knife in order to gain an audience with Asriel about what they learned in the Clouded Mountain? Wouldn't they pass that information to Xaphania and count on their leader to relay it to Asriel? So maybe she is not the renegade angel that Balthamos and Baruch claim to follow, but one of many renegades with her own followers, whom perhaps she has brought to Asriel's fortress.

Cross-Reference of Characters:
Characters by World of Origin

World: Lyra's

Adam Stefanski
Adele Starminster
Adriaan Braks
African rifleman
Ama
Annie
Archbishop
Armoured bears' boat's captain
Bear-Sergeant
Bella
Benjamin de Ruyter
Bernie Johansen
Billy Costa
Bishop
Bridget McGinn
Broken Arrow
Brother J.
Brother Louis (CCD)
Buchner (Jordan College scholar)
Bull (Jordan College scholar)
Bursar (Jordan College)
Bursar's clerks (Jordan College)
Cairncross (Jordan College scholar)
Capt Magnusson
Cassington Scholar
Cawson
Cesar (Jordan College scholar)
Chaplain (Jordan College)
Charlie
Chef (Jordan College)
Cleric
Clerics (Magisterium's boat)
Close (Jordan College scholar)
Col. Carborn
Commissionaire
Costa family

Costas-Dimitriades (Jordan College
    scholar)
Cousins (Jordan College)
Crew members, Consistorial Court of
    Discipline's zeppelin
Dada
Davids (Jordan College scholar)
Dean, Jordan College
Deputy Director, Observatory
Dick
Director, Observatory
Dirk Vries
Doctor who buys Lyra
Doctor who examines Lyra
Doctors in conference room
Dr Cooper
Dr Martin Lanselius
Edward Coulter
Enquirer, Jordan College
Erik Andersson
Evans (Jordan College scholar)
Farder Coram
Father Heyst
Flight engineers, Consistorial Court of
    Discipline's zeppelin
Fr Gomez (CCD)
Fr Heyst (Jordan College)
Fr MacPhail (CCD)
Fr Makepwe (CCD)
Fra Pavel (CCD)
Francis Lyall
Frans Broekman
Gerard Hook
Guard, College of St Jerome
Guards at dungeon (armoured bears)
Guarnieri (Jordan College scholar)
Gyptians' boat captain
Gyrocopter navigator

Hannah Relf
Headmistress
Hesketh (Jordan College scholar)
Hjalmur Hjalmurson
Hugh Lovat
Hydro-anbaric station engineers and
    technicians
Ieva Kasku
Ignatius Cole
Inquirer (CCD)
Intercessor (Gabriel College)
Iofur Raknison
Iorek Byrnison
Jack Verhoeven
Jacob Huismans
Jaxer
Jerry, Able Seaman
Jessie Reynolds
Johnny Fiorelli
Julia Ojaland (witch queen)
Junior Scholars
Juta Kamainen
Katja Sirkka
Kerim
Kholodnoye villagers
King Ogunwe
Kirkham (Jordan College scholar)
Laboratory technicians, Consistorial
    Court of Discipline
Langdale (Jordan College scholar)
Lee Scoresby
Lena Feldt
Librarian, Jordan College
Lord Asriel
Lord Boreal
Lord John Faa
Lydia Alexandrovna
Lyra
Ma Costa
Maidservant for Trollesund priest
Margaret
Marshall (Jordan College scholar)
Martha
Master of Jordan College
McKay
Michael Canzona

Miller (Jordan College scholar)
Mistress Huismans
Mortensen (Jordan College scholar)
Mrs Coulter
Mrs Lonsdale (Jordan College)
Nell
Nellie Koopman
Nicholas Rokeby
Old lady with lorgnette
Orderly, Adamant Tower
Otyets (Father) Semyon Borisovitch
Pagdzin *tulku*
Parslow family
Paula Pyhäjäron(witch queen)
Peter Hawker
Piet van Poppel
Pilot, Consistorial Court of Discipline's
    zeppelin
Polk (Jordan College scholar)
Precentor
Priest (Trollesund)
Priest, Society of the Work of the Holy
    Spirit
Princess Postnikova
Prof Docker
Raymond van Gerrit
Reina Miti
Rental boat clerk
Roger
Roger van Poppel
Ruta Skadi
Ruud Koopman
Søren Eisarson
Saddler in the Covered Market
Sailor whose dæmon settled as dolphin
Sailors (Byrnison's boat)
Sailors (Magisterium's boat)
Sam Broekman
Sam Cansino
Sara Leiro (witch queen)
Seal Hunter
Semyon Karlovich Martins
Sentry
Serafina Pekkala
Sergeant serving MacPhail
Shawcross (Jordan College scholar)
Shuter (Jordan College)
Simon

Simon Hartmann
Simon Le Clerc
Simon Parslow
Sister Agnes (stenographer)
Sister Betty (nurse, Bolvangar)
Sister Clara (nurse, Bolvangar)
Sister Monica (stenographer)
Skraeling censor
Soldiers pursuing Grumman and Scoresby
Soldiers serving MacPhail
Steersman
Stourbridge (Jordan College scholar)
Sub-Rector
Swiss Guards
Tanja Lentara
Tartar guards
Technicians, Consistorial Court of
    Discipline's zeppelin
Teukros Basilides
Third woman at dinner in the Master's
    Lodge
Tillerman
Tom Mendham
Tony Costa
Tony Makarios
Top hat man
Tortured witch
Trelawney (Palmerian professor)
Trickett (Jordan College scholar)
Umaq
Village headman
Villagers hostile to armoured bears
Warehouse clerk
Wilmington (Jordan College scholar)
Witch who aids Asriel on Svalbard
Witch who aids MacPhail at bomb launch
Wren
Yakovlev
Young bear who helps Lyra and Roger
Young bears whom Lyra and Roger ride
Visitors:
  Balthamos
  Baruch
  Chevalier Tialys
  Giacomo Paradisi (10th anniv)
  John Parry/Stanislaus Grumman

Lady Salmakia
Lord Roke
Sayan Kötör
Will

World: Will's

Alan Perkins
Alfredo Montale
Allan
Archaeologist
Dr Lister
Elaine Parry
Gallery attendant, Ashmolean Museum
Ian Beck
Inspector Walters
Inspector Walters' deceased partner
Jake Petersen
John Parry
Librarian
Mary Malone
Matt Kigalick
Milkman (Winchester)
Motorists
Mrs Cooper
Mrs Hopkins
Nelson
Nuniatak dig team
Oliver Payne
Police, Radcliffe Square
Police, Sunderland Ave.
Porter, Physics Building
Reference librarian
Security Guard, Physics Building
Sgt Clifford
Shopkeeper, Covered Market
Tim
Two men, physics building
Will Parry
Visitors:
  Father Luis Gomez
  Lord Boreal/Charles Latrom
  Lyra
  Mrs Coulter
  Pantalaimon
  Serafina Pekkala

World: Cittàgazze

Angelica
Boy in striped tee-shirt
Evacuee children
Father (Spectre victim)
Giacomo Paradisi
Horsewoman
Joachim Lorenz
Near adolescent boy
Old farmers
Old woman on a cart (Spectre victim)
Paolo
Spectre orphans gang
Tullio
Young woman (Spectre victim)
Visitors:
Balthamos
Baruch
Farder Coram
Father Luis Gomez
Gyptian boat captain
John Parry/Stanislaus Grumman
Hester
Iorek Byrnison
John Faa
Juta Kaimainen
Kirjava
Lena Feldt
Lee Scoresby
Lord Boreal/Charles Latrom
Lyra
Mary Malone
Mrs Coulter
Pantalaimon
Ruta Skadi
Sayan Kötör
Serafina Pekkala
Will

World: Suburbs of the world of the dead

Boatman
Customs officers

Dirk Jansen
Magda
Magda's death
Martha, Peter, their children and baby
Mother and child ghost
Visitors:
Lyra
Lyra's death
Pantalaimon
Lady Salmakia
Chevalier Tialys
Will

World: World of the dead

Ghost-boy
Ghost boy from Will's world
Ghost girl
Ghost girl 2
Ghost of old woman
Gracious Wings/No-Name
Ghost of Martyr
Ghost of Monk
John Parry
Roger
Lee Scoresby
Thin, angry ghost
Visitors:
Lyra
Lady Salmakia
Chevalier Tialys
Will

World: Holland-like world

Dirk Jansen
Visitors:
Lyra
Pantalaimon
Lady Salmakia
Chevalier Tialys
Will

World: Mulefa's

Atal
Craftsman
Sattamax

Visitors:

Balthamos
Captain, Gyptians' ship to mulefa's world
Farder Coram
John Faa
Ghost of old woman
Father Luis Gomez
Kirjava
Lyra
Mary Malone
Pantalaimon
Serafina Pekkala
Roger [his ghost]
Lady Salmakia [her corpse]
Lee Scoresby [his ghost]
Chevalier Tialys [his corpse]
Will
Xaphania

World: Gallivespians'

Chevalier Tialys
Lady Salmakia
Lord Roke
Madame Oxentiel

Visitors:

Pantalaimon
Kirjava

World: Asriel's republic

*All are immigrants; it is no
conscious being's world of origin.*

Armoury:

Locomotive attendant
Locomotive engineer
Mechanics and artificers
Miners
Technicians

Adamant Tower:

Lord Asriel
Teukros Basilides
King Ogunwe
Orderly, Adamant Tower
Madame Oxentiel
Lord Roke
Sentry, Adamant Tower
Xaphania

Guests:

Baruch
Mrs Coulter
Ruta Skadi

Battlefield:

African rifleman
Angels bearing crystal litter
Authority
Iorek Byrnison
Kirjava
Lyra
Reina Miti
Madame Oxentiel
Pantalaimon
John Parry [his ghost]
Lady Salmakia
Lee Scoresby [his ghost]
Ruta Skadi
Chevalier Tialys
Will

Characters by Type

Angels
- Authority
- Balthamos
- Baruch
- Metatron
- Xaphania

Armoured Bears
- Bear-Sergeant
- Iorek Byrnison
- Søren Eisarson
- Hjalmur Hjalmurson
- Iofur Raknison

At Basalt Fortress (Asriel's Side)
- Teukros Basilides
- Orderly
- King Ogunwe
- Lord Roke
- Sentry
- Xaphania

Bolvangar Adults
- Dr Cooper
- Doctor who buys Lyra
- Doctor who examines Lyra
- Doctors in conference room
- McKay
- Sister Betty
- Sister Clara
- Tartar guards

Bolvangar Kids
- Annie
- Bella
- Billy Costa
- Lyra
- Tony Makarios
- Martha
- Bridget McGinn
- Roger
- Simon

Cittàgazze Adults
- Horsewoman
- Joachim Lorenz
- Giacomo Paradisi
- Old farmers

Cittàgazze Kids
- Angelica
- Boy in striped tee-shirt
- Near adolescent boy
- Paolo
- Tullio

Clergy
- Archbishop
- Bishop
- Brother J.
- Brother Louis (CCD)
- Chaplain (Jordan College)
- Cleric
- Fr Gomez (CCD)
- Fr Heyst (Jordan College)
- Fr MacPhail (CCD)
- Fr Makepwe (CCD)
- Fra Pavel (CCD)
- Inquirer (CCD)
- Intercessor (Gabriel College)
- Priest (Trollesund)
- Priest, Society of the Work of the Holy Spirit
- Semyon Karlovich Martins (witch consul)
- Otyets (Father) Semyon Borisovitch

Dæmons (by Name)

Name	Form	Person
Anfang	pinscher	Thorold
Belisaria	seagull	Jerry
Castor	unsettled	ghost child
Cerebaton	unknown	Simon LeClerc
Hester	hare	Lee Scoresby
Kaisa	goose	Serafina Pekkala
Karossa	unsettled	unnamed Bolvangar child
Kirjava	cat	Will
Kulang	unsettled	Ama
Kyrillion	unsettled	Annie
Matapan	unsettled	ghost child
Musca	unknown	Ignatius Cole
Pan	pine marten	Lyra
Ratter	unsettled	Tony Makarios
Salcilia	unsettled	Roger
Sandling	unsettled	ghost child
Sayan Kötör	osprey	Stanislaus Grumman
Sergi	blue throat	Ruta Skadi
Sophonax	cat	Farder Coram
Stelmaria	snow leopard	Lord Asriel
Zohariel	unknown	Francis Lyall

Gallivespians

Mme Oxentiel
Lord Roke
Lady Salmakia
Chevalier Tialys

Gyptians

Adriaan Braks
Frans Broekman
Sam Broekman
Michael Canzona
Charlie
Farder Coram
Billy Costa
Costa family
Ma Costa
Tony Costa
Lord John Faa
Raymond van Gerrit
Simon Hartmann

Peter Hawker
Gerard Hook
Jacob Huismans
Mistress Huismans
Jaxer
Jerry
Bernie Johansen
Kerim
Nellie Koopman
Ruud Koopman
Margaret
Tom Mendham
Nell
Piet van Poppel
Roger van Poppel
Nicholas Rokeby
Benjamin de Ruyter
Adam Stefanski
Tillerman
Dirk Vries
Jack Verhoeven

Himalayans

Ama
Dada
Pagdzin *tulku*

Jordan College Scholars & Employees

Cassington Scholar
Cawson
Chaplain
Ignatius Cole
Cousins
Dean, Jordan College
Enquirer, Jordan College
Father Heyst
Bernie Johansen
Simon Le Clerc
Librarian, Jordan College
Mrs Lonsdale
Francis Lyall
Master of Jordan College
Parslow family
Roger Parslow
Simon Parslow
Precentor
Shuter
Sub-Rector
Trelawney (Palmerian professor)
Wren

Londoners

Lord Boreal
Broken Arrow
Col. Carborn
Commissionaire
Edward Coulter
Mrs Coulter
Prof Docker
Capt Magnusson
Tony Makarios
Old lady with lorgnette
Princess Postinaka
Top hat man

Mrs Coulter's Cocktail Party Guests

Erik Andersson
Archbishop
Bishop
Prof Docker
Princess Postnikova
Adele Starminster

Mulefa

Atal
Craftsman
Sattamax

Nova Zembla/Siberia

Otyets (Father) Semyon Borisovitch
Sam Cansino
Deputy Director, Observatory
Director, Observatory
Stanislaus Grumman
Seal Hunter
Umaq
Village headman
Yakovlev

Oxford Adults (excluding Jordan College's)

Johnny Fiorelli
Headmistress
Intercessor, Gabriel College
Hannah Relf

Oxford Kids

Dick
Hugh Lovat
Lyra
Roger Parslow
Simon Parslow
Jessie Reynolds

Oxford Adults, Will's World

Allan
Archaeologist
Ian Beck
Sgt. Clifford
Mrs Hopkins
Sir Charles Latrom
Librarian
Dr Lister
Mary Malone
Motorists
Oliver Payne
Alan Perkins
Police, Radcliffe Square
Police, Sunderland Avenue
Porter, Physics Building
Security Guard, Physics Building
Shopkeeper, Covered Market
Inspector Walters

Servants and Other Employees

Lydia Alexandrovna
Allan
Armoured bears' boat's captain
Gyptians' boat captain
Cawson (Jordan College)
Commissionaire
Cousins (Jordan College)
Jerry, Able Seaman
Bernie Johansen (Jordan College)
Mrs Lonsdale (Jordan College)
Capt Magnusson
Orderly, Adamant Tower
Parslow family (Jordan College)
Porter, Physics Building
Sergeant serving MacPhail
Soldiers serving MacPhail
Shuter (Jordan College)
Steersman
Sister Agnes (stenographer)
Sister Betty (nurse, Bolvangar)
Sister Clara (nurse, Bolvangar)
Sister Monica (stenographer)

World of the Dead and Its Suburbs

Boatman
Customs officers
Ghost boy
Ghost girl 1
Ghost girl 2
Ghost of martyr
Ghost of monk
Ghost of old woman
No-Name/Gracious Wings
Dirk Jansen
Magda
Magda's death
Martha, wife of Peter
Peter
Martha & Peter's two children and baby

Witches

Lena Feldt
Juta Kamainen
Ieva Kasku
Dr Martin Lanselius (witch consul)
Tanja Lentara
Semyon Karlovich Martins (witch consul)
Reina Miti
Serafina Pekkala
Katja Sirkka
Ruta Skadi
Tortured witch
Witch who aids Asriel on Svalbard
Witch who aids MacPhail at bomb launch

PLACES AND PEOPLES

Places and Peoples:
Words of the Worlds

LYRA'S WORLD SPELLING	WILL'S WORLD EQUIVALENT
Afric	African
Beringland	Alaska
Bodley's Library	Bodleian Library
Brytain	Britain
Brasil	Brazil
Cathay	China
Corea	Korea
Eastern Anglia	East Anglia
Eireland	Ireland
Falkeshall	Vauxhall
Falkeshall Gardens	Vauxhall Gardens
German Ocean	North Sea
Grand Junction Canal	Grand Union Canal
Gyptians	gypsies
Hollanders, Hollands	Dutch
Muscovy	Russia
New Denmark	North America
New France	Canada
Nippon	Japan
Norroway	Norway
Sibirsk	Siberian
Sheldon Building	Sheldonian Theatre
St Barnabas the Chymist	St Barnabas
Sveden	Sweden

Places and Peoples:

The Worlds

This section indexes passages relating in general to the worlds of HIS DARK MATERIALS. *For information about a particular place or people, see the sections on:* **Cities, Countries, Regions, Continents, and Elements of Topography; Structure and Streets; The Oxfords;** *or* **Peoples.** *If from context it is obvious that a world is being discussed or described, and different or new information defining that world is provided, that chapter is included in the list.*

Many of the names for these worlds are not ones that appear in HIS DARK MATERIALS *(Beach world, Desert world). They are simply descriptive terms to identify an unnamed world.*

ASRIEL'S WORLD [*See* **Republic of heaven**]

BEACH WORLD ✐

Physical characteristics: This is a very quiet world of sloping sand dunes and a nearly motionless sea. Beyond the beach, most notable among the dense vegetation are fern-like trees. It offers very little besides refuge; there is no food or fresh water.

Role: Will first escapes to this world with the angels Baruch and Balthamos, when the three are ambushed by Metatron and his scout. It provides temporary refuge for him and Lyra (along with the Gallivespian spies) the night after Iorek Byrnison repairs the subtle knife.

AS Will and angels in 2; Will, Lyra and spies in 15; mentioned by Roke 16 [*brief*]; group departs 18

CHAINED SLAVE WORLD ✐

Physical characteristics: One world Will cuts through to, as he tests his perception of resonance gives him a glimpse of a dirty industrial factory in which chained slaves toil.

Role: Will discovers that windows to different worlds feel different.

AS 2 [*brief*]

CITTÀGAZZE WORLD ✧ ⚱ ✐ ⑩ [LS]

Physical characteristics: This world is in a heavy fog when Lyra arrives. Once the fog lifts, she is able to see she is on one of a series of rising cliffs. In the distance, there is a town with a harbor and lighthouse. When Stanislaus Grumman and Lee Scoresby fly into this world by balloon, they too see an ocean on their left, as well as a curving coastline, a headland, and then the city. Beyond the lighthouse is a stone breakwater. They fly over the city and toward the high green hills or mountains in the distance.

Along its coastal regions, this world seems to have a mild, temperate climate hospitable to lush vegetation. Lemon and olive groves give way to thick conifer forests. The interior of the regions of the world is more forbidding; steep, jagged, barren, parched and rocky mountains are blisteringly hot during the day, but temperatures drop quickly at night. Vegetation is scarce, riverbeds dry, and the topography is distinguished by limestone crags and boulders; ravines, passes, and gulches. On its highest mountain peak is a barren region that looks colorless but for flashes of white stone when the moonlight breaks through the clouds. There is a small, cold lake three hours down the mountain from where Lyra is abducted.

What Mary Malone finds when she enters Cittàgazze through the Oxford window is "devastation…Spectre-eaten adults and wild scavenging children." The influx of Spectres [1] hit the cities harder than the surrounding countryside, but the rural areas are by no means safe.

Role: The first mention of this world is when Lord Asriel shows his photograms of the Aurora to the Jordan College scholars in the opening scene of *Northern Lights/The Golden Compass*; he points out the outline of a city just visible beyond the curtains of the Aurora. In spite of the image, the College Dean is highly skeptical.

While it is the town in which the Tower of the Angels is located that is named Cittàgazze, the world is unnamed and known only as "Cittàgazze world" or the "world of [2] Cittàgazze." [3]

This is the world of origin of the Guild of the Torre degli Angeli, the inventors of the subtle knife. And it is in this world where:

- Will meets Lyra
- Serafina Pekkala rescues Will and Lyra
- Mrs Coulter kills Charles Latrom/Lord Boreal and abducts Lyra
- Will regains and loses his father
- Lee Scoresby and Stanislaus Grumman/John Parry die
- The angels Baruch and Balthamos come to Will, and
- Mary Malone and Father Gomez find the window to the mulefa's world

"…Lee saw first a lighthouse, then the curve of a stone breakwater, then the towers and domes and red-brown roofs of a beautiful city around a harbour…"
SK chapter 14

Library of Congress, LC-DIG-ppmsc-09394, 1890–1900

Ragusa, Dalmatia (now Dubrovnik, Croatia) is the model for the setting of Brian Aldiss's The Malacia Tapestry, a novel Pullman cites as influencing his description of Cittàgazze.

Before Asriel broke open the huge hole in the sky above Svalbard, the only way to pass from one world to another was through Cittàgazze. Since then, direct passage from world to world (*e.g.* Will's to Lyra's) has become possible but exceedingly risky because of the influx of Spectres.

People's dæmons in this world are internalized (not visible). Its children are violently hostile toward cats, believing them to be Satanic. While witches are known of abstractly and assumed to "treat with the devil," actual witches [4] flying on cloud-pine branches are not among the beings of this world. Angels, however, are sometimes glimpsed passing through the world of Cittàgazze.

Returning with the gyptians from the world of the mulefa, Lyra and Will spend part of their last hour together in this world's city of Cittàgazze.

Note: *Other than a very few references to the* world of Cittàgazze *or the* Cittàgazze world, *this place is unnamed. Therefore, context has been used to decide whether a reference to* this world *or* different world *or* other world *and so on is to the Cittàgazze world and so belongs here.*

NL/GC glimpse of in Asriel's photogram 2; alluded to by Kaisa 11, and briefly by Serafina 18; Asriel tells Lyra he is going there 21; bridge to 23

SK Will enters, finds Lyra 1, and Will and Lyra discuss 3; witches enter, its history 6; Spectre-orphans tell Lyra about, Latrom's plan 7; Paradisi on 8; Latrom and Coulter discuss 9; Grumman tells Scoresby about 10; Serafina finds Lyra in 11; journey through its rural areas 13; Scoresby delivers Grumman to, dies in 14; Coulter and Latrom visit, Latrom and Feldt eliminated in, Grumman finds bearer of subtle knife and Will finds father, John Parry killed, Will discovers witches dead, Lyra gone, and angels waiting in 15; [LS] Lantern Slides 3, 5
  setting: 1, 3, 5, 6, 7, 8, 9, 11, 13-15

AS Will and angels in 2; Iorek visits 3; Malone travels through 7; Gomez enters 17; gyptians enter 38
  brief mentions: in Will's remembrances of golden monkey 11, of entering 18; Gomez finds window in 20; by Parry's ghost 26; in Mary's thoughts of 300 years ago 27; its Spectres 37
  setting: 2, 3, 7, 38

10ᴛʜ: *AS* appendix

Dead, World/Land of the ✎

Physical characteristics: At the start of his reign, the Authority created the world of the dead, which Balthamos describes as "a prison camp," and populated it with harpies. To the harpies he gave the "power to see the worst in every one, and they have fed on the worst ever since."

When Will attempts to cut a window into the world of the dead, the surface seems smooth and the knife initially moves easily, but it then meets great resistance and the air itself tries to keep Lyra, Will and the Gallivespian spies from passing through the window. The world itself cannot be entered directly, but the window Will cuts leads to its suburbs. In these suburbs, the dead board a boat, and a ferryman rows to the island on which is found the gate to the world of the dead. [*See* **Suburbs of the world of the dead**]

The gate at this landing stage is a wooden door in a stone wall protected by harpies. Beyond the gate Will and Lyra find countless ghosts on a vast plain with scattered dead trees mysteriously and dully lit by a source-less light.

Role: In the drugged sleep in which Mrs Coulter keeps her hostage Lyra, the girl is beset by dreams of Roger in the world of the dead. Lyra's best friend, whom she saw die on Svalbard, is now a ghost, asking what he had done so wrong to have been imprisoned in such a place. Lyra believes only by asking Roger's forgiveness will she ever lay to rest what has become "a torment and a sorrow." She proposes using the knife to go to the world of the dead, and Will (who wants to speak to his father's ghost) agrees. The alethiometer verifies Lyra's feeling she should make this journey, but warns that it will be very dangerous.

At the gate to the world of the dead, the harpies refuse entrance to the living children and spies, and Lyra's offer of a story as payment for passage backfires when she lies and the harpies attack. Will has to use the knife to defend Lyra and gain access. The ghosts cluster around the living children, drawn to the feeling of being alive, and Lyra and Will resolve to release the ghosts from their endless gloom. Tialys is of the opinion that by doing so it will "undo everything. It's the greatest blow you could strike. The Authority will be powerless after this."

Will's efforts to cut a window out of the world of the dead fail because every place he tries opens into the underground of another world, but the harpy, No-Name, agrees to take Will to a place where cutting a window is possible. A long march through darkness, tunnels and caves is made even worse when the Consistorial Court of Discipline's bomb opens an abyss and Lyra is nearly lost when she slips. Their agony of being separated from their dæmons in a place of such hopelessness is alleviated only when Will finds his father's ghost and Lyra sees Roger's and Lee Scoresby's.

Will is able to cut a window through to the mulefa's world and Roger's is the first ghost to leave the world of the dead. They leave this window open.

[*See also* **Abyss** in **Alethiometer, Subtle Knife, Amber Spyglass.**]

AS   Lyra dreams of [between 1 & 2, 2 & 3, 3 & 4]; Balthamos on 2; Lyra's need to visit 13; alethiometer on 14; discussed with Iorek 15; Will cuts through to ghosts' road to 18; its suburbs 19; entrance to, harpies of 21; ghosts of 22; Roger in, harpies on 23; Grumman and Scoresby in, its abyss 26; Basilides on 28; Lyra, Will re-enter, leave with warrior ghosts 29; Asriel sees ghosts of 30; Will and Lyra choose to keep window out of open 37; window visited by Faa and Coram 38

   brief mentions: ghosts from seen near abyss 31, separation from dæmons in world of mulefa feels different than when in 32; by Will to Mary 33; by Serafina to dæmons 36

DESERT WORLD ✐

Physical characteristics: A barren world with white rocks and sand.

Role: The only world Will can find that allows him to access the interior of Mrs Coulter's Himalayan cave. Will worries that, in the moonlight, this world's whiteness will be apparent when he cuts into the deep darkness of the cave. The gleaming light proves useful, however, to Will and Lyra as they run from soldiers and find the refuge of the window Will had left opened.

AS   Will enters with Ama 12; Will, Lyra, spies spend night in 13; group leaves in morning 14

GALLIVESPIANS' WORLD ✐

Physical characteristics: The world of origin of the Chevalier Tialys and the Lady Salmakia (the diminutive but fierce spies who accompany Lyra and Will to the world of the dead) is populated by two varieties of conscious beings. In his explanation to Mrs Coulter, the African King Ogunwe refers to the types as Gallivespians and "humans," whom he implies are the same size as he and his listener.

Role: Most of this world's humans submit to the Authority. They have accepted an age-old contention that the Gallivespians are "diabolic" and should be eliminated. This campaign by the "big people" to exterminate the "little people" is confirmed by Pantalaimon who with Kirjava visited this world while their people, Lyra and Will, were in the world of the dead. The hatred directed toward them by the Authority's followers has prompted the Gallivespians' participation in Lord Asriel's rebellion.

The science of this world—or of its Gallivespian population, at least—is far enough advanced that the theory of quantum entanglement has practical applications. Their communication device, the lodestone resonator, is an example of such a technology. [*See also* **Gallivespians** *in* **Other Beings**]

AS   Tialys explains lodestone resonator 14; Ogunwe on 16
   brief mentions: by Tialys 13, by Lyra and Tialys 18, 19 and Pan 36

HOLLAND-LIKE WORLD 🖉

Physical characteristics: Will's first impression of this world is that it looks like he imagines his world's country of Holland would. He is attracted by its apparent tidiness, but is soon disillusioned. This is a world at war.

Role: Here the travelers are able to find food to take on the next stage of the journey before they leave the worlds of the living. After he cuts his next window, Will recognizes what appears to be the same man he had just seen lying in the bushes with his throat cut now up and moving about. Will and Lyra have met their first ghost. The trip to the world of the dead has begun.

AS 18

KINGDOM OF HEAVEN 🖉

Physical characteristics: Like the Clouded Mountain, this phrase is used as a synonym for the Authority's world. However, while the Clouded Mountain is used to describe a physical place, the "kingdom of heaven" refers to the concept of the Authority's power base.

Role: Lyra remembers John Parry's ghost as saying that "the kingdom was over, the kingdom of heaven, it was all finished. We shouldn't live as if it mattered more than this life in this world, because where we are is always the most important place." What he actually said was "we have to build the republic of heaven where we are, because for us there is no elsewhere," warning Will and Lyra that their dæmons can live only in their worlds of origin.

Witch Serafina Pekkala tells Mary Malone that according to the rebel angel Xaphania, who sees human history as "a struggle between wisdom and stupidity," "the forces of the kingdom have met a setback," but "they'll regroup under a new commander and come back strongly, and we must be ready to resist."

> # Philip Pullman on the kingdom of heaven and the republic of heaven:
>
> *"The kingdom of heaven promised us certain things... But now that, for me anyway, the King is dead, I find that I still need these things that heaven promised, and ... I don't think I will continue to live after I'm dead, so if I am to achieve these things I must try to bring them about—and encourage other people to bring them about—on earth, in a republic in which we are all free and equal—and responsible—citizens."*
>
> —*Third Way: Heat and Dust, an interview with Philip Pullman, by Huw Spanne*

[*See also* **Clouded Mountain** *in* **Applied Sciences: Transportation**]

Observation: *In the UK Scholastic Point editions,* kingdom of heaven *is always lower-cased, as is* republic of heaven. *In the US Random House editions, both are always capitalized.*

AS Ogunwe and Asriel discuss 28; battle with Asriel's republic 29; Coulter, Metatron meet at Clouded Mountain 30; Xaphania on 36; Lyra and Pan on 38
   brief mentions: by angels 2, 5, and Ogunwe 16; 31, 35

LYRA'S WORLD ❄ ⚷ 🖉 ⑩ 🄻🅂

Physical characteristics: While the idea of other worlds is introduced in *HIS DARK MATERIALS* in *NORTHERN LIGHTS'/THE GOLDEN COMPASS'S* opening scene, this is the only world we visit in the first book. It is only when the concept is no longer theoretical that comparing Lyra's world to others is an option. Thus its first mention is when Asriel's experiment succeeds.

There are many differences between Lyra's and Will's worlds, subtle and not so subtle. The geography is generally the same, but the political boundaries are fascinatingly different, and there are a number of beings in Lyra's world not found in Will's: talking scavenger foxes, cliff-ghasts, armoured bears, and witches, to name a few. Additionally, Lyra's world's cities are smaller, with more open spaces and less traffic, and fewer hordes of people blocking her way. Most importantly, though, is that in Lyra's world people's dæmons are externalized and take the form of animals, initially changing at will, then settling in one form in adolescence.

Her brief glimpse of Will's world leaves Lyra certain that her own is superior, but for its lack of hamburgers, popcorn, and movies.

Role: In *THE SUBTLE KNIFE*, Lyra's world becomes more thematically complex than it was in the first volume where it served as the novel's setting, as intriguing and surprising as it was there. It is now no longer *the* world but *a* world.

When John Parry made it through the Alaskan window, and into Lyra's world, he was deeply gratified to meet his dæmon for the first time, *seeing* what in his own world is just a "silent voice in the mind and no more." Will knows his trip in this world to find Lyra after she has been abducted by Mrs Coulter will be complicated by his lack of a visible dæmon, and so he directs the angel Balthamos to serve as such. The Siberia of Lyra's world where Will's trek begins is in a state of upheaval from the climatic changes brought on by Asriel's tearing of the sky. Svalbard's armoured bears are threatened by changes to their environment to the extent that their king Iorek Byrnison is taking a contingent to the Himalayas.

During Lyra's absence, the turbulence which caused such ecological mayhem in the Arctic manifested in political uncertainty in England. After relatively minor troubles in Oxford, life in the colleges resumed its ordered pace.

HIS DARK MATERIALS ends in Lyra's world, with Lyra and Pan promising one another that they too will someday build a republic of heaven—in their own world.

Observation: *Perhaps it is Will's assumption that he won't be able to see his dæmon, or his belief that his is internalized, that makes it impossible for Will to see Kirjava until after his trip to the world of the dead. His father, in contrast, had no knowledge of dæmons, and so saw his immediately.*

Note: *Very seldom is the phrase* Lyra's world *found, and of course all of the first volume of* HIS DARK MATERIALS *is set in Lyra's world. The purpose here is to show how Lyra's world compares to the other worlds, especially Will's. Again, context is key.*

NL/GC 23
setting: all

SK Lyra on 1; Lyra recounts her departure from, lack of traffic, use of gold 3; Lyra prefers to Will's, describes to Malone 4; Lyra reconsiders its superiority in all things after seeing movies 5; and witches 6; Lyra longs for after Latrom's theft 7; Will realizes Latrom is from 8; Latrom and Coulter discuss 9; Parry on 10; Skadi on 13
  brief mentions: of Scoresby's childhood in 14, *zombi* from 15
    setting: Svalbard, Lapland 2; Nova Zembla 6; Siberia 10

AS Will enters 2; climate changes 3; Will's first view of people in, Balthamos acts as dæmon in 8; Tialys on 22; Lyra's true tale of 23; Parry's ghost describes entering 26; Lyra asks Will if he'll visit her there 35; Xaphania on 36; Lyra offers to leave forever 37; Lyra returns to, changes in 38; [LS] Lantern Slide 3
  brief mentions: by Baruch to Asriel on Grumman, Lyra's location 5; of Ama in 10; by Roke about Iorek 16; Lyra recognizes world of suburbs of dead as not her own 18; in Lyra's tall tale 19; Mary considers 300 years ago in 27; Asriel and Coulter discuss night he left his 28;

Parallel Worlds & Divergent Histories

When the angels have closed all but one window, Xaphania says, the worlds will be restored to their former positions, and Lyra's and Will's (our own) Oxfords will be in parallel alignment. But although the geographies of their worlds will again correspond, the worlds' histories never can.

At times it seems as if Lyra's world is like Will's, but stuck in a previous historical era. Lord Asriel, hunting on horseback at his vast estate, seems to belong to a feudal society, but Mrs Coulter, dining at the Royal Arctic Institute and hosting cocktail parties, doesn't. Their world's astronomers claim Earth is one of six planets, but they do know that the planets revolve around the sun. There are cars and trucks, but these are not numerous. Photography seems to be a new invention, and information technologies are primitive. However, it is in Lyra's world that a bomb equipped with a tracking device capable of locating its intended victim based on a sample of her DNA is launched.

Inexplicably, in Lyra's world there are witches who live hundreds of years longer than ordinary humans, bears who talk and work with metals, and people's souls are visible to themselves and others, taking the forms of animals. The people of the mulefa's world do not physically resemble those of either Will's or Lyra's worlds. Each world follows a different path of evolution.

But if the worlds shared the same origin before some chance divergence, then they are all based on the same laws of physics. Visitors to other worlds do not immediately suffer any physical distress, so the basic elements needed to support life must be not only present but in the same proportions in these worlds. The worlds seem to revolve on their axes and around the same star, our Sun, at the same rates, so time has not stalled in any world.

Lyra's world feels more familiar to us than does the mulefa's, not only because its conscious beings look like us, but because its history seems so familiar and plausible,

except that through chance or choice, things have turned out differently there.

For example, in Lyra's world, Tartar forces have overpowered Muscovy. In our world, too, St. Petersburg and Moscow have repeatedly come under siege, so while the source of the threat is different, the target is unsurprising. More subtle difference between the Russias of the two worlds gradually emerge; ethnicities like the Samoyeds, who have all but disappeared from Will's world, are well enough known in her world that Lyra isn't surprised to hear that her captors in Lapland are Samoyed hunters.

In Will's world, Moscow was conquered by the Tartars in 1382, and for several hundred years, from the 13th to 15th century, the Tartars, nomadic tribes originally from the area of Mongolia, dominated a vast region from Eastern Europe, through southern Russia, to Manchuria in the Far East. Best known among the rulers of the Mongol Empire was Genghis Khan. But in Will's world, the rise of fortified cities and the difficulty for nomadic warriors of managing a vast empire eliminated the Tartar threat.

About the time the Tartars were being pushed back in Will's world, another historical event of immeasurable importance in his world didn't seem to have happened in Lyra's: the Protestant Reformation. The church of Lyra's world is a peculiar institution. Its trappings—crucifixes, churches, priests—seem familiarly Catholic, but its last pope (the papacy was eliminated) was John Calvin, who shared the same name as a rabid anti-Catholic Protestant of Will's world. Its Magisterium's seat of power is Geneva, Switzerland, again in Will's world associated with Protestantism. Moreover, *Christian* is not a word ever used by any clergy of Lyra's world (it is spoken once in this world, when Lyra addresses Iofur Raknison).

In one of their few peaceful moments in the Cittàgazze world, Will and Lyra both speculate

rifleman from 29; by Mary of evolution in 33
      setting: Himalayas 1, Siberia 2, Arctic 3, Himalayas 4, Geneva 6, Siberia 8, 9; Himalayas 11-15, Geneva 24, Alps 25, Oxford 38

10TH: *NL* appendix

10TH: *SK* appendix

on what might have been—what if Asriel had been poisoned or Will hadn't followed a cat through the Oxford/Cittàgazze window. Perhaps HIS DARK MATERIALS also plays with the "what might have been's" on a larger scale in the contrasts between Lyra's and Will's worlds.

What if, for example, the Norse colonies in Vinland had flourished, and, when Denmark claimed Greenland in the 1600s, it had further colonized the North American continent? Could what we call "America" and "Canada" (words not used in Lyra's world) have been "New Denmark" or "New France" instead?

In Will's world, the Vikings reached L'Anse aux Meadows, Newfoundland, Canada and established colonies in Greenland, but these settlements disappeared, and Norway and Denmark claimed no lands in North America when the French and English began their campaigns to dominate the continent. One theory is that the Vikings were thrashed by the native peoples of these lands, whom they called Skraelings. In Lyra's world, Skraelings are among the ethnic groups represented in the Magisterium's forces.

Missing from Lyra's world is the sense that England or Britain ever had the empire it once possessed in Will's world. Its role in Lyra's world is instead played by Denmark, which is competing with France, once a powerful presence in North America in Will's world, for domination of the continent.

Lee Scoresby remembers his friends pretending to be Danes and French when they played in the ruins of the Alamo. In Will's world, the Texans lost the Alamo to the Mexicans, but shortly thereafter US troops vanquished the Mexicans, and a few years later the Republic of Texas joined the United States.

The **10**TH anniversary editions of HIS DARK

MATERIALS expand our sense of Lyra's world. Lord Asriel has traveled to Sunda Straits (in Will's world's Indonesia) and is familiar with Javanese or Balinese devil-masks, and Stanislaus Grumman met Giacomo Paradisi in Baku, Azerbaijan, on the Caspian Sea in the Mideast.

A glance at the *Globetrotters* guides by Smith and Strange, publishers of the map in LYRA'S OXFORD, as well as at the locales featured in other stray bits that found their way into that book (such as the *Zenobia's* ports of call) further underscores the historical divergences of Will's and Lyra's worlds. Maps of Mesopotamia are available alongside those for the Ottoman Empire, the Levant, and Patagonia, just a few examples of kingdoms or nations that once were a part of Will's world but are no longer. The reason for the absence of Spain and Italy as players in whatever would have been Lyra's world's equivalent to an Age of Exploration and the subsequent colonization of the New World is also suggested by the map list—they don't even exist as nations in Lyra's world. In their place, respectively, are the regions of Catalonia, Castile, and Portugal, and of Sicily, Sardinia, and Naples. Lyra's world's Africa still has its kingdoms in the Sahara, Benin has an empire, and Zimbabwe is another center of power on the continent.

Social structures, economic systems, and technologies arise from the cumulative effects of uncountable events of chance and choices. It is not surprising that in spite of parallel positions in space, Lyra's and Will's worlds differ in many particulars. The evolution of witches and armoured bears, and the visibility of dæmons, and their role in the history of Lyra's world, is a more intriguing question.

MULEFA'S WORLD ✎ ⑩ LS

Physical characteristics: Before she meets the mulefa, Mary is most intrigued by the geology and plant life in this new world, and soon notices that through its savannahs of many-shaded grasses and wild flowers run what appear to be "rivers of rock." It appears to her that there are no flatlands in this world. Reeds grow along the rivers and in marshes and mudflats; the beaches and sea are unspoiled.

Mary is amazed by the size of the trees growing in clusters on the plains, which she estimates to be fifty percent taller than California's majestic redwoods. These trees, with their "dense and dark green" foliage and golden red trunks, are essential to the lives of the conscious beings of this world.

Flocks of hummingbirds attract her attention, but more intriguing is the anatomy of the deer-sized grazing animals she sees: their legs are arranged in a diamond rather than rectangular configuration. Most astonishing, of course, are the mulefa. Like the grazers, they are also deer-sized with a diamond pattern describing the arrangement of their limbs, but they have used the seedpods from the enormous trees to fashion wheels, which they hook onto their fore and aft legs, allowing them to roll along the rock-river paths. Mary soon realizes that these are not animals like the grazers, but people, like herself.

As she becomes more familiar with the mulefa and their world, Mary Malone is impressed by the way in which these beings live in harmony with their environment: "everything was linked together, and all of it, seemingly, managed by the mulefa." Moreover, their environment has provided what they need; she notes that the mulefa could only have evolved in a world that provided the equivalent of smooth roads.

The window Will cuts releasing the ghosts from the world of the dead opens here on a coastal ridge, about an hour's mulefa-gallop north of the village where Mary has lived as a cherished guest.

Role: In this world, Will and Lyra yield to the temptation to love and come to know fully what the experience of loving can entail; Mary Malone learns the way of life of a different people, the mulefa; and through the window Will opens, the ghosts from the world of the dead enter, dissolve and become part of a universe again.

Mary first sees nothing but beauty in this world and in the lives of the mulefa. But their world is threatened. The mulefa tell Mary that for most of their existence they lived in a state of "perpetual joy." Then 300 years ago it seemed as if "some virtue had gone out of the world"; the seedpod trees began to fail, and if they cease, the mulefa will not survive. Making a bad situation worse are the malevolent birds known as *tualapi* that destroy the mulefa's food stores and damage the decreasing reserves of seedpods.

After they find their dæmons during the battle between the republic and kingdom of heaven, Will and Lyra seek sanctuary in the mulefa's world. Here they recognize their love

Pillsbury Picture Co., Library of Congress, LC-USZ62-132177, 1907

Man Standing Next to California Redwood

for one another, and their love reverses the pattern of loss in this world. Sraf again falls naturally into the flowers of the seedpod trees, so there is every reason to believe that the way of life of the conscious beings of this world will be preserved. [*See also* **Mulefa** *in* **Other Beings**]

Note: *In the US Random House edition of* THE AMBER SPYGLASS, *mulefa is always in italics. It usually is plain text in the UK Scholastic Point edition.*

AS   Mary enters, first views of trees, topography, grazers, mulefa 7; history, social structures, balance between mulefa and environment, tualapi of 10; Sattamax on failure of sraf 17; Gomez finds window 20; Mary climbs seedpod tree in, diagnoses problem with seedpods, Gomez enters and kills tualapi 27; Lyra and Will find sanctuary in, look for dæmons, meet mulefa, and find Mary, Mary sees ghosts enter 32; shellfish harvesting and story-telling in 33; Mary sees increasing outflow of Dust and Gomez riding tualapi in 34; Will and Lyra find love in groves of, Balthamos and Gomez die in, Dust returns to 35; Serafina visits 36, dæmons return to Will and Lyra in 37; gyptians arrive in, view ghosts entering, humans depart 38; LS Lantern Slides 3, 6, 7
    brief mentions: of ghosts' entrance 26; Lyra and Will return to world of dead after spending night in 29
      setting: 7, 10, 17, 20, 27, 32-38

10TH: *AS* appendix

RAINSTORM WORLD

Physical characteristics: A world in which heavy rain is pouring down.

Role: After parting from Lyra at the Botanic Garden, Will knows he must break the subtle knife. He tries to replicate his mental state in Mrs Coulter's cave when he first accidentally broke the knife while thinking suddenly of his mother as he cut a window. It doesn't work; instead, he opens his last window into this world.

AS   38 *[brief]*

REPUBLIC OF HEAVEN/LORD ASRIEL'S WORLD

Physical characteristics: This world of Asriel's is a two-day flight from the Siberian tundra of Lyra's world for the angel Baruch, who is a particularly strong flier. The first sighting of Lord Asriel's world is in THE SUBTLE KNIFE, in witch Ruta Skadi approaches it with a troop of angels coming to join the republic. Through an "invisible gateway," the fliers have left the world of Cittàgazze for Asriel's. On the eastern horizon Skadi sees a mountain range of "jagged spears of black rock, mighty broken slabs and sawtooth ridges piled in confusion like the wreckage of a universal catastrophe." A stinking sulphur lake fills a canyon below the mountain range. On the highest peak is a basalt fortress. Beneath the fortress is the armoury; on its highest rampart is the adamant tower, Lord Asriel's command post.

    The plains' groves of wild ivy, briars, brambles and nettles give the dæmons a place to hide from the Spectres but also complicate Will and Lyra's efforts to grab them.

Role: The *republic of heaven* and *Lord Asriel's world* are used to refer to the same place; however, *republic of heaven* more specifically denotes Asriel's concept of a world without kingdoms. *Asriel's world* is the physical locale in which his basalt fortress and adamant tower are to be found, and his scheme executed. Here, Asriel has gathered into a previously unpeopled world those wishing to build a world without kingdoms and rulers.

    According to King Ogunwe, one of Asriel's high commanders, Asriel did not devise his republic for the purpose of invading the kingdom of heaven, but has made certain that it will be ready to defend itself should the Authority attack. Certainly the most, perhaps only, developed facilities in this world are the munitions factories, and the only type of work being done, it seems, is related to the republic's defense.

The battle between the forces of Lord Asriel's republic and the Authority's kingdom of heaven is complicated by the influx of opportunist, unaligned cliff-ghasts. It takes place on the plains below the republic's fortress. The ghosts, led by those of John Parry and Lee Scoresby, battle Spectres; Iorek Byrnison and the armoured bears, as well as troops of Gallivespians, fight the kingdom of heaven's forces on the ground, as witches fight angels in the sky above. It is while Will and Lyra are searching for their dæmons in this world's chaos that they chance upon the crystal litter in which the Authority is trapped and abandoned.

Asriel's republic attracted beings from many different worlds who shared Asriel's vision of a world without political or ecclesiastical authorities, and with no allegiance to the Authority; but it was doomed to failure, according to the ghost of John Parry. Before they leave the world of the dead for Asriel's, he warns Will and Lyra that dæmons cannot thrive in any but their own worlds and so "we have to build the republic of heaven where we are, because for us there is no elsewhere."

As *His Dark Materials* ends, the last words of the trilogy conclude the thought of what Lyra and Will hope to do with their life—and that is to build "...the republic of heaven."

[*See also* **Structures and Streets: Adamant tower, Basalt fortress**]

Note: *In the UK Scholastic Point editions,* republic of heaven *is always lower-cased, as is*

Other worlds

Traveling to the North with the gyptians, Lyra sees the Aurora firsthand and glimpses the city beyond. She soon learns from the witch Serafina Pekkala's dæmon, Kaisa, that "Witches have known of the other worlds for thousands of years...They aren't part of this universe at all; even the furthest stars are part of this universe, but the lights show us a different universe entirely. Not further away, but interpenetrating with this one," and, although they are "as close as a heartbeat... we can never touch or see or hear these other worlds except in the Northern Lights." There, the Aurora's "charged particles" make "the matter of this world thin."

The possibility that there are other worlds and the seductive, intriguing idea that they might be visited, a central premise upon which *His Dark Materials* is based, is raised in the opening scene of *Northern Lights/The Golden Compass*.

Kaisa says that the witches' interest in Lyra stems from their respect for Asriel's "knowledge of the other worlds" and that "Dust-hunters," *i.e.* the General Oblation Board, fear him because they "think he

intends to use Dust ... to make a bridge between this world and the world beyond the Aurora." The church of Lyra's world considers the belief in other worlds a heresy. Barnard and Stokes, the two experimental theologians who offered mathematical proof of these worlds' existence, were eliminated. Pursuing the topic was made grounds for excommunication. Even those who dared to think about these worlds, Lord Asriel says, assumed that fundamental physical laws would prohibit citizens of one world visiting any other. However, he reports, they "were wrong; we learned to see the world up there. If light can cross, so can we. And we had to learn to see it."

Traditional cultures in the North did not require mathematical arguments to develop hypotheses about what lies behind the Aurora. In Will's world, the Eskimos of Alaska believe that there are doorways to a "spirit world." However, unlike the spiritual worlds of heaven and hell the church of Lyra's world proclaims, this one possesses physicality. The Eskimos' initiation of a shaman requires the candidate to bring back a "trophy" from the other world he kingdom of heaven. *In the US Random House editions, both are always capitalized.*   26

SK   first view of as Skadi approaches 6; Skadi's reports of her visit, gathering armies 13; Grumman, angels try to persuade Will to take knife to Asriel in 15 *[brief]*

AS   basalt fortress and adamant tower described, Baruch visits 5; troops fight kingdom's in Himalayas 12, 13; Coulter as Asriel's captive in, high commanders meet, Ogunwe on its purpose and defensive posture toward kingdom 16; Parry's ghost on 26; meeting of commanders, Clouded Mountain and kingdoms' troops approach, dæmons sighted near 28; ghost warriors, Lyra, Will enter battle in 29; Authority abandoned in 30; Lyra and Will release Authority, find dæmons, depart 31

> *brief mentions:* by angels 2; Tialys communicates with 11, 14 and tries to persuade Lyra, Will to wait for gyropters coming from 15; by Coulter to MacPhail 24; of finding dæmons in 35; Parry's warning recalled 37; Lyra and Pan discuss 38
> *setting:* 5, 16, 28-31

Shaggy blue beast world

Physical characteristics: Bison-sized grazing animals with blue shaggy fur live here.

Role: When his hand is feeling better, Will tests the feel of the windows. In his experiments, he cuts briefly through to this world. [*See* **Windows** *in* **The Subtle Knife**]

AS   2 *[brief]*

visits. In Lyra's world, the Siberian Tartars also believe in a spirit world behind the Northern Lights, and that the recent climatic changes the North is experiencing happened once before when a large breach opened between this world and that one.

According to the angel Balthamos, there are "myriads of worlds." Those angels with whom witch Ruta Skadi flies to Asriel's republic tell her that there are gateways invisible to her that the angels use to move through worlds. Skadi is fascinated, when she visits Asriel's fortress, by the variety of beings representing many different worlds who have gathered: male, female, "fighting spirits" and "lizards and apes, great birds with poison spurs, creatures too outlandish to have a name I could guess at." Kaisa's claims that there are "millions of other universes" and Asriel's belief in "uncountable billions of parallel worlds" seem plausible.

The prospect of other worlds is of interest psychologically and imaginatively. Each world seems to feel different. Even light has a different feel to it when its source is another world. Lyra, disoriented by the similarities and differences she sees co-existing when she compares Will's Oxford to what she knows as Oxford, begins to doubt what is real. When she sees Simon Parslow's initials just where he'd carved them in her Oxford, Lyra thinks, "There might be a Simon Parslow in this world. Perhaps there was a Lyra." In a photograph   27
of Samoyed hunters in the Pitt-Rivers Museum, she recognizes from her world the   28
men, the sledge, and its rope, and wonders, "Was there only one world after all, which   29
spent its time dreaming of others?"

But a more reflective Lyra is willing to consider with Will whether there might be other worlds where their lives would be different had they made different choices, recalling Asriel's explanation on Svalbard of   30
"possibility-collapses," where possibilities   31
are eliminated on a micro level – "Except   32
that other worlds have sprung into being, on   33
which they *did* happen."   34

However, both Lyra and Will must learn a painful lesson about other worlds. First the ghost of John Parry and then the angel Xaphania tell them that they can only live full lives in the worlds of their birth because dæmons cannot survive in any but their own worlds.   35

SUBURBS OF THE WORLD OF THE DEAD (TOWN) ✏

Physical characteristics: Before they can reach the ghosts they seek, Will, Lyra, and the spies have to pass through the suburbs of the world of the dead, which combines the worst aspects of a garbage dump and squalid refuge camp. As they follow the ghosts farther in, they notice that the world is being drained of color and the landscape seems to fade away. The Gallivespians attribute this to the ghosts progressively forgetting the worlds of their lives. They head toward a ruined dump heap of a settlement, stinking of thick smoke and rot, where they are stopped by some kind of humans acting the part of customs officers, who can tell them no more than that they have to wait since they are not dead.

36   The place where they spend the night is a one-room plywood home that is "clean but shabby." Pictures cut from magazines posted on the living room wall and a pattern made of repeated sooty thumbprints mark attempts at decoration. The kitchen is defined by its iron stove, the dining area by a table and bench, and the bedrooms by a crib, the granny's bed, and one other. On a dresser is a shrine of sorts with a picture of a top-hatted skeleton as its centerpiece. Collected beneath it are bits of colored glass, fake flowers, shells and so on.

When it is time to cross into the world of the dead, Lyra's death leads the travelers through deepening mist to the jetty jutting into the scummy, slimy waters where the boat
37   will be ... a "foul and dismal shore, so bleak and blasted with disease and poison."

Role: In this last stop before crossing over to the world of the dead, Lyra learns she must convince her death, who, like her dæmon, has always been with her, to let her go on to that world. When her pleas are successful, this is where she commits the betrayal the Master of Jordan College predicted, leaving Pantalaimon behind as she, Will and the spies board the boat that will ferry them to the gates of the world of the dead.

Will and Lyra think they have cut through to the world of the dead when they see a man's corpse in one world and then the same man seemingly animate, moving and talking, but physically unsubstantial, in a second world. However, they come to realize that there are stages in the world of the dead. Until they board a boat and are ferried to the other side, the location of ghosts they seek (Roger's and John Parry's) is inaccessible. The spot from which they must make the crossing is variously referred to as a "suburb" or "town" of the dead.

Lyra must abandon Pan in its suburbs to enter the world of the dead.

Observation: *The picture of the jaunty skeleton with top hat and shades may well be a replica of a poster by Rick Griffin for the Grateful Dead.*

AS   chapter title, first views 18; description, stay 19; departure from 21
         setting: 18-19, 21

TROPICAL RAINFOREST WORLD ✏

Physical characteristics: Will and Iorek hear the sounds of monkeys, insects, birds, and frogs through the window to this world.

Role: When Will and Iorek Byrnison disembark the boat they have taken to the Himalayas of Lyra's world, Will is able to show the bear what the subtle knife can do. He cuts a window into this obviously different world.

AS   9 *[brief]*

UNINHABITED WORLD ✏

Physical characteristics: Uninhabited and undescribed

Role: When the ghost of John Parry alerts Will that a bomb is coming at Lyra, he quickly cuts a window into this uninhabited world, shoves the rest of the strand of Lyra's hair that is guiding the bomb through, and immediately closes it. The bomb is then diverted to that world.

AS 26 *[brief]*

WILL'S WORLD ⚕ ✏ ⑩ LS

Physical characteristics: While teaching Xaphania to close windows, Will cuts one into his own world, where "machines were turning, chemicals were combining, people were producing goods and earning their living." 38

Role: Will's world is the home of Will Parry and physicist Mary Malone. It is the world that his father, John Parry, left and could never find again, living instead in Lyra's world as Stanislaus Grumman. This is the second-home world of Lord Boreal, in his assumed identity of Sir Charles Latrom. For Will, it is where he parts from Lyra forever.

While Lyra feels at home in the world of her birth—even when she is danger—Will's relationship to his own world is uneasy. His childhood of uncertainty, with a missing father and a mentally ill mother, has culminated in his blaming himself for the accidental death of a man who broke into his home in the middle of the night. He can't explain to Lyra how other people think in his world, claiming his world is something he doesn't "know much about… All I know is keeping secret and quiet and hidden." 39

When he walks through the window into a new world, and looks back, it is his own world from which he "turned away with a shudder: whatever this new world was, it had to be better than what he'd just left." 40

The second world Lyra visits after leaving her own is Will's. For her, Will's Oxford and Will's world are the same. As would be expected, Lyra does not feel at home in his world. She finds it much harder to tell a lie there, and lying has always been her favorite way out of awkward situations. And, without dæmons, she is curious about how people in Will's world are able to discover their true natures.

Sir Charles Latrom finds he has been able to use his experience as Lord Boreal in the Council of State of their world to worm his way deeply into the power structure of Will's. Father MacPhail warns Father Gomez that he will be appalled by the decadence of Malone's [Will's] world. The rebel angel Xaphania says there were many instances in Lyra's world of struggles between humans who sought wisdom and the agents of the Authority who resisted original thinking. Mary's response is that Xaphania could have been talking about Will's/her world.

When Serafina Pekkala asks about her plans, Mary realizes that she hasn't given a return to her own world any thought because her weeks in the mulefa's world have been "The happiest I've ever been in my life, I think." Lyra and Will spend their final moments 41 together in the Botanic Garden here in his Oxford before she steps back into Cittàgazze with Serafina Pekkala to complete the journey to their world. Mary Malone and Will must prepare to re-enter their world fully, each knowing that they face battles with the authorities, but also that they have the support of one another.

SK   Will leaves, discovers his is one of several or many 1; Will and Lyra compare departures from their, Lyra enters 3; Lyra's reaction to dæmonless humans of, tells Malone she comes from another 4; Lyra impressed with its movies and street food, Parry's letters describe doorway out of 5; Lyra finds self unprepared for dangers of 7; Will realizes isn't Latrom's 8; Latrom explains to Coulter 9; Grumman explains to Scoresby 10; Mary consults with Shadow-particles in, receives instructions, leaves 12; Will on its children's cruelty 13; 🅛🅢 Lantern Slide 6
         brief mentions: by Will of Spectres and 11, by Grumman of Boy Scouts in 14, by Will of climate change in 15
               setting: 1, 3-5, 7, 8, 9, 12

AS   Will's thoughts of father, angels on 2; Parry's ghost on 26; Mary on her life in 33; Will on not feeling he knows much about 35; Serafina and Mary discuss 36; Will and Lyra discuss 37; Lyra's last visit, Mary and Will's return 38; 🅛🅢 Lantern Slide 3
         brief mentions: by Baruch to Asriel 5; by Court regarding Will, Mary 6; in Mary's thoughts of her recent past 7; in Will's remembrances of golden monkey 11; by Will to Lyra 13; in Mary's thoughts 17; Will recognizes world of suburbs of dead as not his own 18 and ghosts from 22; Mary considers 300 years ago 27; by Lyra introducing Mary and Will 32; in Mary's thoughts 34
               setting: 38

10TH: *NL* appendix

10TH: *SK* appendix

10TH: *AS* appendix

Gyptian Canal Routes in England

The Fens of Lyra's world seem much wilder and wetter than those of Will's. However, even though the Fens of Will's world have been drained for agricultural development for the past several hundred years, there are still a number of navigable canals in East Anglia and throughout England. These are some routes in Will's world that might have counterparts in Lyra's.

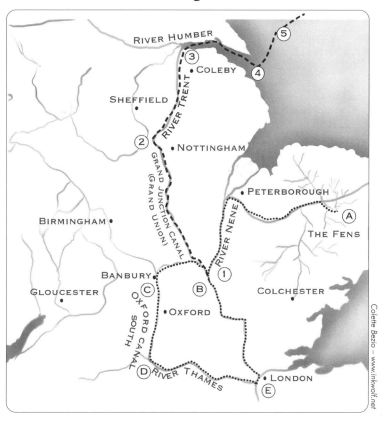

Colette Bezio – www.inkwolf.net

Fens to Oxford and London:

A. A number of smaller canals join the River Nene, which would take the gyptians to...
B. the Grand Junction Canal (now called the Grand Union, in Will's world). A short trip northerly would take them to...
C. the Oxford Canal. They'd then sail south through Banbury to reach Jericho or Port Meadow in Oxford. Continuing further south on the Oxford Canal, they'd reach...
D. the Thames, and that would bring them into...
E. London, where they could turn into the Grand Junction Canal (as they did the night they rescued Lyra) before heading home to the Fens.

Fens to German Ocean:

While it is possible that the gyptians could have begun their sea journey to Norroway from the mouth of the Thames east of London, or from the mouth of the Nene, for example, the description of Lyra's time in hiding aboard first the Costas' and then Farder Coram's boat seems like the gyptians' route out of England took a number of days. Moreover, hiring a ship in London would have been risky, given the hunt on for Lyra, and their chance of finding a sea-going vessel in the Fens less likely than at a large port city.

One possible point of departure could have been the River Humber. In Will's world, ferries run between the port city of Hull on the Humber and ports in southern Norway. The last town where the gyptians stop is called Colby, and while there isn't a Colby on the east coast of England in Will's world, there is a Coleby not far from the River Humber. The gyptians, then, could have left the Fens on

1. the Nene...
2. headed north on the Grand Junction...
3. continued through Lincolnshire on the River Trent, leaving their narrowboats for the ship at Colby [Coleby]...
4. and set sail out of England on the River Humber...
5. which would take them to the German Ocean [North Sea].

Scoresby's Journeys in Lyra's World

1. Lee Scoresby is hired by the gyptians in Trollesund, and is proceeding with them by sledge to Bolvangar when the group is attacked by Samoyed traders.
2. He appears in Bolvangar in his balloon during the gyptians' battle with the Station's Tartar guards, and collects Lyra, Roger, and Iorek Byrnison.
3. With an escort from Serafina

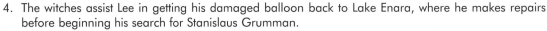

Pekkala's witch clan, he heads toward Svalbard, but off the coast is attacked by cliff-ghasts.
4. The witches assist Lee in getting his damaged balloon back to Lake Enara, where he makes repairs before beginning his search for Stanislaus Grumman.
5. He first stops at Nova Zembla for news of Grumman.
6. He then flies to the mouth of the Yenesei River, stores his balloon, and rents a boat.
7. He uses this to reach the Tartar village where the shaman has been living. The two sail upriver, retrieve the balloon, and fly out of Lyra's world and into Cittàgazze.

Gyptians' Route to Bolvangar

1. The gyptians hire a boat suitable for crossing the German Ocean.
2. They arrive in the Norroway port town of Trollesund.
3. From there, they travel by sledge to Bolvangar.

Colette Bezio – www.inkwolf.net

Where the Witchlands are in Will's World

The **10TH** anniversary edition of *THE SUBTLE KNIFE* includes Stanislaus Grumman's hand-drawn map of the witchlands of Lyra's world, with a key identifying each clan-queen. Some of the areas he labels have easily discernable equivalencies in Will's world. Often, however, his spelling is close to, but not quite the same, as a geographically comparable region in Will's world. Thus, the places on this map are simply places in Will's world that possibly correspond to places in Lyra's.

Will's world

1. Vizhas, Russia
2. Narva, Ida-Virumaa, Estonia
3. Tikshozero, Russia
4. Lubana, Madonas Rajons, Latvia
5. Inari, Lapplands Lan, Finland
6. Lodja, Parnumaa, Estonia
7. Mielojarvi, Ita-Suomen Laani, Finland
8. Keitele, Ostra Finlands Lan, Finland
9. Ozero Umbozero, Murmanskaya Oblast'

Lyra's world (queen / place)

1. Juta Kamainen / Lake Visha
2. Julia Ojaland / Navia
3. Reina Miti / Tikshozero
4. Rutà Skadi / Lubana
5. Serafina Pekkala / Lake Enara
6. Paula Pyhäjäron / Lake Ladoga
7. Katya Sirkka / Miekojärvi
8. Sara Leiro / Keitele
9. Tanja Lentara / Lake Umalese

Gobbler Sightings in England

The Gobblers avoid detection by never staying in one place for long. Before they hit Oxford and snatch Billy Costa and Roger, they have already struck the Oxfordshire villages of Banbury and Cowley, the industrial cities of Manchester and Sheffield, the remote Fens town Norwich, London's Limehouse slums, and other towns across central England.

Colette Bezio – www.inkwolf.net

England: Both Sides of the Window

The Englands of Lyra's world and Will's world have a number of towns in common, including their capital city, London, and Oxford. Some are mentioned only in the context of Lyra's world, but are in Will's as well, for example, Bristol and Abingdon. A few places appear only in connection with Will's world, but that, of course, doesn't mean they aren't part of Lyra's.

Colette Bezio – www.inkwolf.net

○ *those mentioned in context of Lyra's world*
▲ *mentioned only in context of Will's world*   △ *mentioned in context of both worlds*

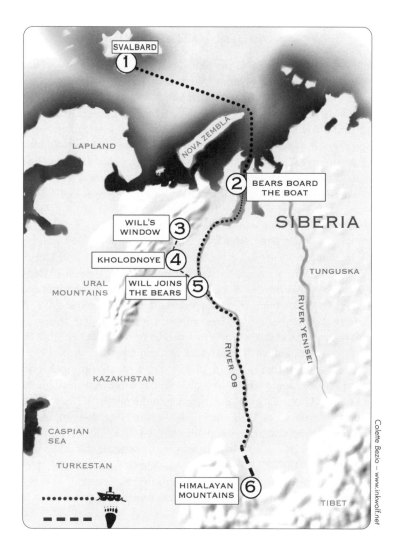

Colette Bezio – www.inkwolf.net

Will and the Bears' Journey to the Himalayas

1. Iorek Byrnison and his armoured bears swam from Svalbard to the mouth of the River Ob in Siberia.
2. There, they hired a steamer and crew.
3. Meanwhile, Will and Balthamos have been traveling on foot in the tundra, having entered Lyra's world through a window Will cut in Cittàgazze.
4. At Kholodnoye, Will is waylaid by a priest and learns that a ship of armoured bears is trying to buy fuel at a village not far away.
5. Will heads there, bargains a peace with the villagers who had been refusing to deal with the bears, and asks Iorek to join the bears on their journey downriver...
6. to the Himalayas where Mrs Coulter has taken Lyra.

Sailing to the Himalayas

Would it be possible to get to the Himalayas by boat from the Arctic Ocean?

Maybe. Although a look at maps in ordinary atlases might suggest otherwise, if you use a map program (or a specialized atlas) that allows you to zoom into an area for greater detail (I used Microsoft's Encarta), you will find that, in the region between where the Ob River ends and the Himalayas begin, there are numerous intermittent streams and lakes. Their appearance is dependent on season, snow melt, and precipitation levels.

If we assume Lyra's world shares the same topographical features as ours, it is likely the ice melts and flooding that Will witnesses in Siberia would mean these intermittent streams and lakes would be present—and quite possible even more would develop, providing links where none have been recorded in Will's world.

With these assumptions in mind, here is a possible route:

Although unnamed, based on the location of Kholodnoye, it seems highly probable that Will and the armoured bears sail down the Ob River, the first major river the bears would reach if Iorek Byrnison journeyed to Siberia from Svalbard past Nova Zembla.

The River Ob flows north. One of Semyon Borisovitch's examples of cataclysmic events in the tale he tells Will is that for at least a week, the river near his village flowed south (this would increase the likelihood of all intermittent streams filling in the south). The river's source is in the Altai Mountains (roughly latitude 49" 10' N, longitude 87" 33' E) where the nations of Russia, Mongolia, China, and Kazakhstan meet.

It is from this point that the bears' boat's route depends on much smaller rivers and streams (and the occasional lake) as it makes its way southwest through the Chinese province Xinjiang Uygur Zizhiqu, the province to the north of Tibet. This province is dominated by a desert called Tarim Pendi. If the bears can, they might just get through this stretch by staying at its northern perimeter. At roughly 47" 12' N, 87" 11' E, these small streams empty into a lake from which flows the Ulungur He River.

By about 46" 2' N, 90" 9' E, conditions will worsen for a boat going to the Himalayas, because it is now dependent on seasonal streams to cross a desert. If they make it this far, they will find a large intermittent lake near the village of Lükqün (42" 36' N, 89" 47' E) and another at 42" 1' N, 88" 39' E.

They could then head toward another lake, Lop Nur (40" 9'N, 90" 29'E). More intermittent streams and lakes will take them to a permanent lake at 37" 52'N, 90" 43' E, Gas Hure Hu. They are now approaching the foothills of the Himalayas in the Arijin and Kunlun Mountains in the Tibetan Plateau. By 33"11'N, 90"13'E, they are in Tibet among permanent glaciers and valleys where they would likely find monasteries and prayer flags.

Places and Peoples:

Cities, Countries, Regions, Continents, and Elements of Topography

Alamo to Zaire

ABINGDON [*See* The Oxfords]

AFRICA [*See* Afric, Africa, African *in* Peoples]

ALAMO / ALAMO GULCH (THE GULCH) 🗡

The Alamo. About 180 soldiers of the Republic of Texas managed for 11 days to hold off several thousand Mexican troops at the Alamo, San Antonio, Texas—odds nearly as bad as Scoresby alone vs. 25 troops of the Imperial Guard.

World: Lyra's and Cittàgazze

Role: Texan Lee Scoresby, recollecting childhood play at the Alamo monument, names the position he defends to his death in the Cittàgazze countryside *Alamo Gulch*. In "a narrow defile… where a dry river bed emerged from a fold in the cliffs," Scoresby fires down on the approaching troops, giving Grumman the opportunity to continue his quest for the bearer of the subtle knife.

The title of Chapter 14 of THE SUBTLE KNIFE is "Alamo Gulch."

Facts: *A gulch is a deep ravine. In Will's world, the Alamo still stands in the city of San Antonio in south central Texas.*

SK 14 *[brief]*

42

ALASKA 🗡 ⑩ LS

World: Will's

Role: John Parry was presumed lost when he and two other team members disappeared in the Brooks Mountain Range in a remote region of this US state, during a survey expedition sponsored by Oxford University's Institute of Archaeology to Nuniatak. Their journey began in the city of Fairbanks and continued into remote regions. When the team failed to make contact with the North American Arctic Survey Station in Noatak, a search was initiated that extended from the Brooks Range to the Bering Sea.

One of Parry's letters was written at a campsite near Umiat. Parry's last letter was posted from Colville Bar, and tells of his meeting with the Eskimo Matt Kigalik, who

Brooks Range

provided Parry map coordinates for the Brooks Range anomaly, the window to another world. Eskimo legends claim a mile or so north of Colville River, on a spur of Lookout Ridge, is a "doorway." As part of his initiation, an apprentice shaman would enter the spirit world through it, and return bearing a trophy.

Alaska is known as Beringland in Lyra's world.

Update: Included in the appendix to the **10TH** anniversary edition of THE SUBTLE KNIFE is a sketch of what Col. John Parry names "Bear Rock," the large bear-shaped rock he mentions in his last letter home to Elaine Parry as a landmark in the vicinity of the Alaska window.

As Stanislaus Grumman in Lyra's world, Parry told Lord Asriel and Giacomo Paradisi about this window.

Facts: *Umiat, a settlement on the Colville River, is one of the coldest places in Alaska. With a permanent population of approximately five people, phone, radio, and TV service is available, but there is no public provision of water or electricity.*

NL/GC appendix

SK   news reports 4; letters from 5; Lantern Slide 6

10TH: *NL* appendix

10TH: *SK* appendix

Brooks Mountain Range, Alaska

U.S. Fish and Wildlife Service, Apr 2005

ALPS ⚷✎

World: Lyra's, Will's

Role: Camping and climbing in the Alps (a mountain range in her world's Europe), taught Dr Mary Malone much that she would put to use in her travels to the mulefa's world.

The Alps in Lyra's world are the location of the cataract of Saint-Jean-les-Eaux, site of the hydro-anbaric generating station near the launch site of the Consistorial Court of Discipline's bomb.

SK   12 *[brief]*

AS   25

AMSTERDAM ✤

World: Lyra's

Role: Base for the expedition that aëronaut Lee Scoresby had intended to join—but which fortuitously never materialized, leaving him in Trollesund, and thus available for hire by gyptians.

NL/GC 10 *[brief]*

ARCTIC, ARCTIC ✤⚷✎ ⑩

World: Lyra's, Will's

Role: In Lyra's world, it is where explorers, trappers, traders, and drifters gravitate; shamanism and skull cults thrive; children are taken to be severed by the General Oblation Board; witch clans and armoured bears peacefully co-exist; scavenging foxes talk; cliff-ghasts (detested by all) shriek with mirth at others' misfortunes; and sunny warm worlds are glimpsed behind the flickering lights of the Aurora.

Climatic changes follow Asriel's breaking open the sky above Svalbard, affecting the Arctic region at large in serious and far-reaching ways. Melting ice fields lead to widespread flooding. There are changes in sea currents and the direction rivers flow.

In Will's world, the Arctic attracts arch-aeologists and physicists, and is prime real estate for military radar installations.

In both worlds, its Aurora fascinates observers.

Frozen Tundra

U.S. Fish and Wildlife Service, Feb 2003

Observation: *In* THE GOLDEN COMPASS, *Arctic is uppercased as a proper noun (e.g. "a child up in the Arctic" [Chapter 3] and "food in the Arctic" [4]) and lowercased as an adjective (e.g. "arctic regions" [1], "arctic relics" [4], "arctic cold" [12], "arctic fox" [13], and "arctic night" [17]). However, in* NORTHERN LIGHTS *and in US and UK editions both of* THE SUBTLE KNIFE *and* THE AMBER SPYGLASS *Arctic is always uppercased.*

NL/GC explorers 4
> *brief mentions:* in Retiring Room 2, by Pan 3, cold 12, night 17

SK Americans' and Russians' interest in 4; drifters and trappers in 5
> *brief mentions:* sledges 1, fog and magnetic variations in 2, journey to Headington and trip to 7, by Scoresby, Grumman 10

AS ice melt in 3, 8, 9
> *brief mentions:* silence of 18, of gyptians and Lyra in 38

10TH: *NL* appendix

10TH: *SK* appendix

ARCTIC OCEAN

43

World: Lyra's

Role: When Will searches for Lyra, he travels through her world's Siberia. The region is still feeling the effects of Asriel's blast over Svalbard. Otyets Semyon Borisovitch tells the boy that one of the effects of the recent "great convulsion" was that the river near his village of Kholodnoye (likely the Ob) that had always flowed north into the Arctic Ocean changed direction, and for a few weeks flowed south into Central Asia before reverting to its northward flow.

AS 8 *[brief]*

ASIA, ASIAN, ASIATIC

World: Lyra's

Role: Associated with Samoyeds and Tartars in Lyra's world.

NL/GC brief mentions: represented on alethiometer by camel 10, Samoyed's appearance described as "Asiatic" 14

SK and alethiometer 4 *[brief]*

AS and approach to Himalayas 9 *[brief]*

ATLANTIC OCEAN

World: Will's

Role: Mary Malone, having been reawakened to the richness of life in the material world at a conference in the port city of Lisbon, Portugal, symbolically ends her life as a nun by throwing her crucifix into this ocean.

AS   33 *[brief]*

Australia ✦ ⚕ ✐ ⑩

World: Will's

Role: Since her daughter is now living in Australia, Mrs Cooper, Will's former piano teacher, has a spare bedroom where Elaine Parry can stay.

SK   1 *[brief]*

10ᴛʜ: *AS* appendix

Baku *[See* Caspian Sea*]*

Baltic Sea ✦

World: Lyra's

Role: The trilogy opens with information that the Tartars are rumored to have invaded Muscovy, with their next target being St. Petersburg, and then the Baltic Sea. With those sites under their control, they would be in the position to dominate Western Europe.

NL/GC 1 *[brief]*

Banbury *[See* The Oxfords*]*

Bear Rock   *[See* Alaska*]*

Benin ⚕ ⑩

World: Lyra's, unspecified

Role: According to Joachim Lorenz, three hundred years ago (during its glory days), Benin sent ambassadors to Cittàgazze before the invasion of the Spectres.

Lord Asriel wonders if there is a common origin to *sepikwu* or s*empekwu,* words he likely heard in Java and Madagascar, denoting something similar to the zombi of Benin in Africa.

Facts: *There is a West African nation of the same name in our world, located between Nigeria and Togo on a bay of the Atlantic Ocean.*

SK   6 *[brief]*

10ᴛʜ: *NL* appendix

Bergamo ⚕

World: Unspecified

Role: Like Benin, Bergamo once traded with Cittàgazze world; its "commedia players" were popular guest performers.

Facts: *There is a northern Italian province of the same name in our world.*

SK   6 [brief]

BERINGLAND ⚲

World: Lyra's

Role: Site of Skraeling wars in which Stanislaus Grumman may have been involved. According to a trapper in Nova Zembla, the shaman was killed in these battles.

Later, Lee Scoresby learns from (a very much) alive Stanislaus Grumman that Beringland, first known to Parry/Grumman as Alaska, is where John Parry left his world of origin.

Facts: *In Will's world, the Bering Strait is named for Vitus Jonassen Bering (1680-1741), a Danish explorer who led a Russian expedition to see if the continents of Asia and North America were joined in the Arctic.*

SK   brief mentions: in report about Grumman 6, and by Grumman 10

BERING SEA [*See* Alaska]

BERLIN ❖ ⚲ ⑩

World: Lyra's

Role: Location of the institution that sponsored Stanislaus Grumman's last expedition.

When Lee Scoresby is trying to track Grumman's movements, the Imperial Muscovite Academy's Observatory's Deputy Director reports having once met Grumman in Berlin.

NL/GC 2 [brief]

SK   brief mentions: Lee hears about at observatory 6, and from Grumman 10

10TH: *SK appendix*

BRASIL ⚲

World: Lyra's

Role: Coulter used to wonder if Lord Boreal was visiting this country when he would be inexplicably absent for long stretches, not knowing that then he was in a different world, living under the name Sir Charles Latrom. It once traded with the Cittàgazze world.

SK   brief mentions: and Cittàgazze 6, and Boreal 9

BRISTOL ❖

World: Lyra's

Role: The extent of Jordan College's wealth is suggested by the claim that it would be possible to walk from Oxford to this seaport town without ever leaving the College's properties.

NL/GC 3 [brief]

BROOKS RANGE [*See* Alaska]

BRYTAIN ❖

World: Lyra's

Role: Nation of which Jordan College, Oxford is a part.

Observation: *Found only in* Northern Lights; *changed to* England *in* The Golden Compass, *but found as well in the list of maps published by Smith and Strange, Ltd. in* Lyra's Oxford.

NL 3 [brief]

Cader Idris, North Wales ⚔ *LS*

World: Will's

Role: Location of a window to another world.

Facts: *Cader Idris, a mountain in the Snowdonia range in northern Wales, is associated with a number of legends; most often cited is the notion that those who sleep on the mountain's slopes will awaken as either madmen or poets.*

Before leaving home to attend Exeter College, Philip Pullman lived for ten years in Harlech, Gwynedd county on the coast of Wales, not far from Cader Idris.

SK LS Lantern Slide 6

California ✎

World: Will's

Role: The mulefa's world's trees are far taller than this US state's famed redwoods. On her visits to California, Mary Malone learned about tree-climbing techniques (a skill she employs in the mulefa's world), and drank Margaritas—but presumably not at the same time.

AS   brief mentions: of redwoods 7, tree-climbing 20, and margaritas in 27

Caspian Sea ⑩

World: Lyra's

Role: Dr Stanislaus Grumman/Col. John Parry had met the former bearer of the subtle knife, Giacomo Paradisi, at the port city of Baku on the Caspian Sea.

Facts: *It is a matter of debate whether the Caspian Sea is in fact a sea or a lake since it has been landlocked for 5.5 million of its 30 million-year history. Its bordering nations are Azerbaijan, Iran, Kazakhstan, Turkmenistan, Uzbekistan, and Russia. In the late nineteenth and early twentieth centuries, much of the world's oil came from drilling in the Caspian Sea.*

Baku is the capital of Azerbaijan, a small nation that was formerly part of the Soviet Union. It borders Iran to the south, Russia to the north, and Georgia and Armenia to the west. To the east is the Caspian Sea.

10ᴛʜ: *SK appendix*

Cathay ✎

World: Lyra's

Role: The city of Hang Chow in Cathay figures in the outlandish story Lyra tells her hosts in the suburbs of the world of the dead. She identifies it as the spot where she, Will, and Roger were headed in the clipper ship that rescued them when pirates from Wapping sank the boat they had stolen from the gyptians.

Facts: *Obsolete term for China in Will's world.*
AS   19 *[brief]*

CATTE STREET [*See* The Oxfords]

CAVE, COULTER'S ✐ *LS*
World: Lyra's
Role: When Mrs Coulter abducts Lyra from Cittàgazze, she takes her back to the Himalayas
of their world, where she hides out with the girl in a cave.

Once the dwelling of a holy man and now used only by bats, the cave is in a heavily
wooded area a three-hour walk from Cho-Lung-Se. It is about thirty feet deep and is
situated halfway up a cliffside, which poses logistical complications for both Lord Asriel's
forces, which arrive by gyropter, and the forces of the Consistorial Court of Discipline's
zeppelins. Its entrance is obscured by a large rock, where Ama, the herdsman's daughter,
leaves food for the mysterious woman and her sleeping child.

The angel Baruch locates it for his companion Balthamos and Will. He draws a series
of maps, showing it with greater specificity each time, from the general area's three
mountains and the glacier that winds through them, to the prayer flags surrounding a
shrine near the cave.

When the river becomes too shallow for the boat Iorek and Will share, they
disembark; a three-day walk brings them to the valley of mist, waterfalls, rainbows, and
Coulter's cave.

AS   Ama visits, Coulter shows her Lyra, golden monkey shows impatience 1; Baruch's report to
Balthamos, Will 2; Ama enters while Coulter is out, hides when she returns, and sees Lyra slapped
4; in Baruch's report to Asriel 5; troops from Consistorial Court, Asriel' republic approach 9; Ama
shows Will, Will visits 11; Will cuts window into, Ama wakens Lyra, Will breaks knife in 12; Will,
Lyra, Ama, Balthamos, spies flee 13; Coulter explains why she was hiding in to Asriel's
commanders 16, and MacPhail 24; *LS* Lantern Slide 8
brief mentions: Remembered by Lyra 14, Will 38

CAVE, IOREK'S ✐
World: Lyra's
Role: Iorek Byrnison sets up a forge to mend the subtle knife at the entrance to the cave
where he has been staying in the Himalayas.

AS   Will and Lyra discuss knife with Iorek 14; Iorek sets up forge at entrance to 15; Iorek's uneasiness
about knife recalled 37

CENTRAL ASIA ✐
World: Lyra's
Role: Following climatic changes in the Arctic so dramatic they threaten the Svalbard bears'
survival, Iorek Byrnison's armoured bears hope to find refuge in Central Asia's coldest
mountain ranges.

AS   3 *[brief]*

CHÂTEAU-VERT [*See* The Oxfords]

CHERWELL [*See* The Oxfords]

CHICAGO [*See* Particle Physics *in* Natural Sciences: Scientific Studies]

CHINA/CHINESE ✵ ⚱ ✎ ⑩
World: Lyra's, Will's
Role: Origin of the I Ching.
   Mary Malone uses the experience of visiting this land of exotic pleasures as a metaphor for experiencing physical love when she explains to Lyra and Will how she came to realize how much of life she'd never know if she remained a nun.
Update: In her journal, Mary Malone compares the tonal inflections in Chinese to the motions the mulefa make with their trunks when speaking some words.

NL/GC and Tony Makarios' looks 3 *[brief]*

SK   and I Ching 4

AS   *brief mentions:* and I Ching 7, 10; in metaphor 33, appendix

CHO-LUNG-SE ✎
World: Lyra's
Role: Location of the monastery from which Ama secures a potion to awaken Lyra.
AS   4 *[brief]*

CITTÀGAZZE (CITY) ✵ ⚱ ✎ ⑩ LS
World: Cittàgazze
Role: It is in this city that Lyra meets Will and he becomes the bearer of the subtle knife.
   Since Lyra ends up in its world by using Lord Asriel's bridge, Cittàgazze is likely the city of palm trees, "honey-coloured temples and colonnades, broad boulevards and sunlit parkland" beyond the Aurora that Lord Asriel photographed.
   Situated on a bay some thirty or forty miles wide, the atmosphere of the city is reminiscent of the Mediterranean or Caribbean, with its palms and oleanders, hot air "laden with the scent of flowers and with the salt smell of the sea," flowering trees, balconies, courtyards and squares, and hilly parklands. A broad boulevard runs along a white-sanded bayshore and at the harbor front are a

"Will found himself facing a harbor enclosed from the left by a stone breakwater and from the right by a headland on which a large building ... stood floodlit among flowering trees and bushes ... and beyond the breakwater the starlight glittered on a calm sea."

SK chapter 1

The harbor of Ragusa, a source for Pullman's description of Cittàgazze, is protected by a headland, a promontory surrounded on three sides by water, and a breakwater, the rectangular barrier separating the docks from the open sea.

Library of Congress, LC-DIG-ppmsc-09395, 1890-1900

> *"At one point they came to a tower standing on its own in a little square ... a simple battlemented tower four stories high."*
>
> SK chapter 3

Ragusa, Dalmatia (now Dubrovnik, Croatia) influenced Brian Aldiss's creation of the city of Malacia, and his novel The Malacia Tapestry inspired Pullman's depiction of Cittàgazze

Library of Congress, LC-DIG-ppmsc-09403, 1890-1900

casino, an opera house and spacious gardens. A beach area features paddleboats and a diving platform. Leading inland from the boulevard are narrow streets with sidewalk cafes. Larger structures include a white temple, grand hotels, a red-and-white-striped lighthouse, and "a simple battlemented tower four stories high"—the Torre degli Angeli, or Tower of the Angels. But the charm of the city is compromised. Many of its buildings are nearly ruined, repeatedly and poorly patched. Peeling plaster, broken windows, loose doorframes, and potholed roads are evidence of neglect.

Once a prosperous trade center, Cittàgazze's fortunes changed 300 years ago when the Guild of the Torre degli Angeli—"alchemists, philosophers, men of learning"— "became curious about the bonds that held the smallest particles of matter together." One product of their investigations was the subtle knife, and one consequence was the windows it cut into other worlds let in the Spectres that invaded the city and devastated its economy. The name Cittàgazze means "city of magpies." Magpies are thieves, and since the Spectres' arrival, the only industry has been thieving by the Guild's philosophers, who "pass into other worlds and steal from them and bring back what they find. Gold and jewels, of course, but other things too, like ideas, or sacks of corn, or pencils."

When Asriel broke open a passage between his world and Cittàgazze's, a "great storm" and fog followed, bringing in "hundreds and thousands" of lethal Spectres, and ending the "rough balance" in which Cittàgazzeans and Spectres had co-existed. A mass evacuation of the city's adults followed, and Spectres-orphans, those children left behind when their parents were lost to Spectres, roam about in gangs.

When Will Parry enters the window he has chanced upon in Oxford, he finds a town that is "utterly silent and empty," showing signs of sudden evacuation. Will and Lyra meet when Will chooses the rooms above a cafe as a place to stay where he'd feel comfortable. He soon realizes that in an empty city, he has chosen the only structure with another person in it. Their first encounter with the citizens of this world is when they meet the girl, Angelica, and her younger brother, Paolo. This pair will become their brutal enemies, blaming Will and Lyra for the loss of their brother, Tullio, to Spectres when Will becomes the bearer of the subtle knife that Tullio had stolen.

Aspects of the city's history are recounted to witches Serafina Pekkala and Ruta Skadi by: Joachim Lorenz, whom they meet escorting evacuees through the countryside; by Giacomo Paradisi, former bearer of the subtle knife, to Lyra and Will after he shows Will how to use the knife; and in Oxford by Sir Charles Latrom/Lord Boreal to his guest Mrs Coulter.

Lyra and Will spend their last hours together in this city, before he cuts through to his Oxford. When they part, she is in this city with Serafina and the gyptians.

Note: *Although not named in the first volume of* HIS DARK MATERIALS, *it is likely that*

Cittàgazze is the city behind the Aurora, and those mentions are listed here, as are descriptions that come before we learn the city's name.

NL/GC *[not named]* in Asriel's photograms 2; Kaisa on, "city in the lights" 11; Asriel on his plan to go to 21; Asriel, later Lyra and Pan leave their world for 23
   brief mentions: by Lyra of photograms to Faa 7; in Lyra's thoughts 13, 20, 22

SK   Will enters, description of 1; children, Spectres, ruined buildings of 3; Will considers place of safety, Lyra and Will return to find cat under attack 5; Lorenz on history of 6; Spectre-orphans on Tower's Guild 7; Latrom, Paradisi on 8; window near villa to Latrom's in Headington 9; villa and belvedere in suburban parkland area 11; Lyra, Will and witches leave city, Lyra and Will discuss kids of 13; Scoresby and Grumman view from balloon 14; **LS** Lantern Slides 3, 8
   brief mentions: Will's letters in 4, Mary's first sight of 12, by Latrom of subtle knife of 15

AS   Gomez meets kids of 10, Lyra, Will, Mary, Serafina walk through on way to his Oxford 38
   brief mentions: by Will 2, of Mary's entrance through Sunderland Avenue window 7, in Will's thoughts 33, by Will to Lyra 35, Lyra to Will on first meeting in 37

10TH: *NL* appendix (implied)

10TH: *AS* appendix (implied)

CITTÀGAZZE (WORLD) [*See* The Worlds]

CLERKENWELL [*See* London]

COLBY, RIVER COLE ❄

World: Lyra's

Role: The River Cole estuary is the last stretch of inland water on which the gyptians travel to Colby, the port town where they will begin the sea voyage across the German Ocean to Lapland. Outside of town, the spy flies sent after Lyra by Mrs Coulter attack Pantalaimon.
   [*See map* **Gyptian Canal Routes in England**]

NL/GC 9 *[brief]*

COLE [*See* Colby, River Cole]

COLVILLE BAR, COLVILLE RIVER [*See* Alaska]

COREA ⚑✎

World: Lyra's

Role: One of the countries that used to send ambassadors to Cittàgazze before the influx of the Spectres. A source of the enamel dishes the gyptians present as gifts to the mulefa.

Observation: *Likely Will's world's Korea.*

SK   6 *[brief]*

AS   38 *[brief]*

COWLEY [*See* The Oxfords]

DAMASCUS ⚑ **LS**

World: unspecified

Role: City visited by Latrom/Boreal, who stole a vial of floral oil from a stall in one of its

East Anglia and the Fens

Lyra's world's Eastern Anglia is likely the East Anglia of Will's world, which was one of the seven kingdoms of Anglo-Saxon Britain that emerged as the Kingdom of England in the early tenth century. Today, broadly defined, East Anglia designates the region including the counties of Cambridgeshire, Lincolnshire, Suffolk, Norfolk, and northern Essex. Philip Pullman was born in Norwich in East Anglia, and lived with his grandparents near there in the village of Drayton, Norfolk for a time during his childhood. Largely rural, the region is noteworthy for its coastal areas, rivers, and nature preserves, as well as Norman and medieval cathedrals, churches, and other architectural sites.

When Britain was conquered by the Romans in AD 43, Colchester, Essex, was arguably the most important city in Britain. The Romans withdrew from England in the early fifth century. Invasions by Germanic peoples followed, including the Saxons and the Angles, from whom East Anglia takes its name. Originally known as the Kingdom of the East Angles, it united the south folk and the north folk (Suffolk and Norfolk), but by 918 had come under the rule of the most powerful of the seven kingdoms, Wessex.

The Fens, East Anglia are a wetland area in Cambridgeshire, Lincolnshire, and Norfolk. In the 17th century land speculators, in spite of local resistance, began draining its bogs and marshes for farm land. The peaty soil proved quite fertile; however, as it dried and contracted, the land began to sink, and so more drainage was needed. Windmills could not keep up with the cycle of drainage, shrinkage, and flooding. Steam powered, and, later, electrical pumps were more successful at keeping the water away.

It would seem that by the mid-sixteenth century, the histories of Lyra's and Will's worlds' Englands had diverged. Just as the Reformation seems never to have taken hold in Lyra's England, the Fens appear to have remained in their natural state.

[*See* map Gyptian Canal Routes in England]

bazaars.

Facts: *In Will's world, Damascus is the capital of the nation of Syria and may be the oldest continuously inhabited city in the world.*

SK ⬛ *LS* Lantern Slide 7

DEAD, WORLD/LAND OF THE

[*See* **The Worlds**]

DENMARK 🗡

World: Will's

Role: As he looks for the world of the dead, Will cuts a window into a world that initially reminds him of what he's heard about the Denmark of his world.

[*See* **Worlds: Holland-like worlds**]

AS   18 [*brief*]

EAST, THE ✤

World: Lyra's

Role: The illness that killed the son of witch Serafina Pekkala and gyptian Farder Coram originated in the East of their world.

NL/GC 18 [*brief*]

EASTERN ANGLIA ✤

World: Lyra's

Role: The gyptians who protect Lyra consider its fens their home.

NL/GC brief mentions: Fens of 7, gyptians of 10

EGYPT ⚱

World: Will's

Role: When a furious Lyra learns that Sir Charles Latrom is holding her alethiometer hostage until she and Will bring him the subtle knife of Cittàgazze, she tries to insult the old man by saying if he had a dæmon it would be a dung beetle. Amused, Latrom informs Lyra that Egyptian pharaohs took as their treasured symbol the scarab, which is a fancy name for a dung beetle.

SK   8 *[brief]*

Scarab Beetle

EIRELAND ⚶

World: Unspecified

Role: One of the countries that three hundred years ago sent ambassadors to Cittàgazze.

Facts: *In our world,* Eire *is the Irish spelling of the English* Ireland.

SK   6 *[brief]*

ENGLAND/ENGLISH/ENGLISHMAN ✧⚶✎

World: Lyra's, Will's

Role: Nation in which Lyra and Will live in their separate worlds.

In THE GOLDEN COMPASS, Jordan College is said to have investments all across England; in NORTHERN LIGHTS Brytain is the land cited in this passage. But in both books, Part One ends with the gyptians setting sail on the German Ocean and Lyra running up on deck "only to find that most of England had vanished in the mist."

England has been terrorized by "Gobblers," who have struck in Manchester, an industrial city where Jordan College has financial interest; Stratford, Northampton, the Fens town of Norwich, Oxford, and London.

NL/GC Gobbler strikes in 3
       brief mentions: gyptians depart 9, Bolvangar doctor recognizes Lyra as 14

SK   *brief mentions:* compared to Cittàgazze 1, and speculation about Grumman's background 6, Latrom as representative of upper class in 7, Grumman revealed as 10

AS   *brief mentions:* Will's 8, and Lyra's nationality 16; Mary's first trip out of 33, changes in 38

EUROPE/EUROPEAN ✧⚶⑩

World: Lyra's

Role: Europe is compared to New France; neither can boast of a center for experimental theology superior to Oxford's Jordan College.

Lee Scoresby describes Stanislaus Grumman as a European when questioning the headman of the Tartar village. In the appendix to the **10TH** anniversary edition of THE SUBTLE KNIFE, Col. John Parry/Stanislaus Grumman notes that he considered his arrival from Siberia to Moscow the point where he temporarily re-assumed his identity as a European in Lyra's world.

NL/GC brief mentions: Tartars threatening 1, experimental theology in 3

SK   10 *[brief]*

10TH: *SK* appendix

FAIRBANKS [*See* Alaska]

Philip Pullman on the Fens:

Philip Pullman in an interview by Jennie Renton for Textualities, an on-line magazine, noted that the Fens of Lyra's world is more extensive than in Will's:

"In Lyra's parallel world the area of the Fens hasn't been drained—as it has in our world—it's still a complicated maze of rivers. Somehow, I had a feeling that the Gyptians would have a lot of Dutch in them—perhaps because there has always been a lot of commerce between the Fens and the Low Countries. And so their language contains Dutch words and speech rhythms."

FEN/FENS/FEN COUNTRY

World: Lyra's

Role: Where "gyptians ruled," a "wide and never fully mapped wilderness of huge skies and endless marshland in eastern Anglia… where eels slithered and… eerie marsh-fires flickered." The dialect of its dwellers shows a strong Dutch influence.   56

The few non-gyptians, or landlopers, in gyptian parlance, offer little interference or help in gyptian matters, probably because the Fens' bogs and swamps seem to them good for little other than getting lost. This affords the gyptians some sovereignty. The search for Lyra seems to be conducted with more official scrutiny on its borders than along its canals, and airships cannot fly lower than a defined distance over Fen country. Permanent structures, in addition to wharves and jetties, include the gyptians' zaal, or meeting hall, and eelmarkets. The streets are cobblestoned.

Note: Fen *or* Fens *is always capitalized in the UK volumes. In the US editions, they are always lowercased in* THE GOLDEN COMPASS *and always uppercased in* THE AMBER SPYGLASS.

NL/GC described, gyptians of 7; Lyra's stay, search for Lyra in, jetties and cobbles of 8; gyptians prepare for departure from 9

    brief mentions: Costas leave London for 6; Coram recalls as where he met Serafina 10, Lyra recalls a conversation with Pan in 18

AS *brief mentions:* Lyra regrets she'll never be able to take Will to 35, gyptians of arrive in world of mulefa 38

The Fens as illustrated by Frank Southgate. Punt-Gunners' Houseboats on Breydon-Watching For Fowl.

Frank Southgate, The Norfolk Broads by William Alfred Dutt

GENEVA

World: Lyra's, Will's

Role: In Lyra's world, this is the city where Pope John Calvin moved the Papacy and the Magisterium is headquartered; the Consistorial Court of Discipline meets in the city's College of St Jerome.

In Will's world, Geneva is where Dr Mary Malone's colleague Oliver Payne interviews for and is offered a job.

"Mrs Coulter in Geneva" is the title of chapter 24 of THE AMBER SPYGLASS.

NL/GC brief mentions: location of Magisterium 2, 19, 21

SK *brief mentions:* Payne and 4, 12

AS Court meets 6, Coulter visits 24; Gomez recalls 35 *[brief]*

GENEVA, LAKE OF

World: Lyra's

Role: Its zeppelin docking area, used by the Swiss Guards in the service of the Consistorial Court of Discipline, is the departure point for the troops headed to the Himalayas to seize or destroy Lyra and Mrs Coulter.

AS 9 *[brief]*

GERMAN OCEAN ✧

World: Lyra's

Role: Its tide reaches as far as Teddington, a district west of the center of London, by way of the River Isis (Thames River).

    The gyptians cross this ocean on their voyage north to Lapland to find those of their children who've been abducted by the Gobblers.

NL/GC tides 3*[brief]*, gyptians set sail on 9; ocean journey 10 [unnamed]

GLASGOW ✧ [LS]

World: Will's

Role: A hotel room in this city is noted as the location of an unacknowledged window to another world.

Facts: *Glasgow is the largest city in Scotland.*

NL/GC [LS] Lantern Slide 6

GODSTOW [See The Oxfords]

GRAND JUNCTION CANAL ✧

World: Lyra's

Role: The Costa family's narrow boat is on this London canal the night Lyra flees Coulter's apartment and is rescued from the net throwers by her gyptian friends.

Facts: *In Will's world, the Grand Junction Canal, which extends from London north to Birmingham, joined the Grand Union Canal system in 1929.*

    [*See map* **Gyptian Canal Routes in England**]

NL/GC 6

GREAT NORTHERN OCEAN ✧

World: Lyra's

The German Ocean

For centuries, what is now known as the North Sea was also called the German (sometimes spelled Germain) Ocean or Sea, and it was not until 1914 that England officially adopted the name North Sea. Interestingly, however, the 1927 English language travel book *Baedeker's Great Britain*, one of the widely known *Baedeker's Guide Books* series, uses German Ocean on its main fold-out map of the British Isles.

The history of the naming of the sea provides insight into the impact of cartographers' choices, the influence of political power on naming, and the way point of view is reflected in place names. Maps from the 16th and 17th centuries use the Latin terms *Mare Germanicum*, *Oceanus Germanicus*, and *Oceanus Britannicus*, as well as *North Sea*. Cartographer Gerard Mercator, whose late 16th century atlases became authoritative references for subsequent mapmakers, favored *Mare Germanicum* (German Sea) and *Oceanus Germanicus* (German Ocean). As the Netherlands became a leading world naval power in the 17th and 18th centuries, North Sea found favor. From the Dutch perspective, living in a land south of this body of water, *North Sea* makes sense.

Today, North Sea is almost universally used, with some exceptions. On maps published in Denmark for the Danish market, the name *Vesterhavet (Western Sea)* is still used, reflecting that nation's relative point of view. Where the North Sea touches the German coast, *German Bay* appears on some German maps.

Role: Its currents were mapped by Dr Broken Arrow, a Skraeling explorer with extensive experience in arctic regions.

NL/GC 4 *[brief]*

GREENLAND ✧

World: Lyra's

Role: Coulter told Lyra she once visited Greenland to study the Aurora.

NL/GC 4 *[brief]*

HAMPSHIRE ⚑

World: Will's

Role: Will Parry claims the county of Hampshire as the location of his school when questioned about his travel to Oxford on a weekday. He says he was granted permission to miss classes in order to conduct research in Oxford.

Facts: *Will's hometown, Winchester, is in Hampshire county.*

SK 4 *[brief]*

HANG CHOW [*See* Cathay]

HEADINGTON/OLD HEADINGTON [*See* The Oxfords]

HEIDELBERG [*See* Abbey of St Johann *in* Structures and Streets]

HIGH BRAZIL ✧

World: Lyra's

Role: Lyra considers stowing away on the boat the gyptians plan to hire for the expedition north to rescue their children, but she worries about making a mistake and ending up in the wrong country, some strange place like High Brazil.

Observation: *The relationship between the* High Brazil *of Lyra's fears and the* Brasil *Coulter once suspected Lord Boreal of disappearing to is unknown.*

NL/GC 9 *[brief]*

HIMALAYA, HIMALAYAS, HIMALAYAN VALLEY ✐ ⑩

World: Lyra's

Role: Location of the cave where Mrs Coulter hid Lyra after abducting her from Cittàgazze. The cave is located in a lush, windy, misty valley with a river running through it near the snow line, among rhododendrons and pine trees. The high altitude sunlight, ice and mist combined "enveloped the head of the valley in perpetual rainbows." The only settlement

---

Himalayan Prayer Flags

When the Himalayas are described, two images are often used: rainbows and flags. The latter, "faded silken flags," "red silk banners half-torn by the winds," "tattered flags on the shrine," could refer to the prayer-flags of Tibetan Buddhism if that faith and its practices are something Lyra's and Will's worlds share. Woodcuts are used to block-print simple images and prayers on these flags. The winds are meant to carry the prayers to the heavens, and the flags are left out in the rain and strong mountain winds until they are scraps. Traditional colors and what they might represent are blue, wind; white, water; red, fire; green, wood or vegetation; and yellow, earth. These prayer flags are the subject of the woodcut for chapter 1, "The Enchanted Sleeper" in **10**TH anniversary edition of *THE AMBER SPYGLASS*.

57
58
59
60

is some herdsmen's houses. Prayer flags mark a shrine near a glacier at the valley's head.

AS   described 1; first use of name in Baruch's report to Will, Balthamos 2; Iorek remembers Scoresby's description of place where snow never melts 3, Ama visits monastery in [not named] 4; Baruch tells Asriel of Lyra's location 5; Pavel reports as Coulter's location to Court 6; Will views in atlas 8 *[brief]*; Iorek and Will arrive in as armies head toward 9, Will meets Ama and Coulter 11, war in 12, escape from 13, visit with Iorek 14, 15

The Himalayas, from the International Space Station

NASA (www.nasa.gov), Earth Observatory (www.earthobservatory.nasa.gov/Observator)

10TH: *AS* appendix

HOLLAND, HOLLANDERS, HOLLANDS

World: Lyra's, Will's

Role: The people of this nation are among the settlers of the Eastern Anglia fens in Lyra's world.

NL/GC brief mentions: and Fens 7, freighter from 10

AS   appearance of 18 *[brief]*

INDIES

World: Lyra's, Will's

Role: Region in Lyra's world as well as Will's. When Lyra isn't understood by a clerk in Will's Oxford, she assumes it is because the man appears to be from the Indies and so doesn't understand English well.

SK   4 *[brief]*

ISIS [*See* River Isis *in* The Oxfords]

JAVA

World: Lyra's

Role: The Sunda Straits separate the islands of Java and Sumatra in the South Pacific Ocean. A sketch of what may be a Javanese devil mask accompanies Lord Asriel's notes on possible variations of the African zombi in the region.

10TH: *NL* appendix

JERICHO [*See* The Oxfords]

KAMCHATKA

World: Lyra's

Role: As a test question to measure whether Lyra can read her alethiometer, Dr Lanselius asks if she can tell him why the Tartars are interested in Kamchatka. While it might be guessed that the Tartars are after the gold found in the region, Lyra's reading is that the Tartars' interest in it is a ruse, and that although they would like to appear to be planning an attack, they don't see it as prudent to do so.

NL/GC 10 *[brief]*

KARELIA ✸ LS

World: Lyra's

Role: Homeland of one of Lee Scoresby's lovers, a witch who was killed in battle.

Facts: *In our world, Karelia is a region now shared by northwestern Russia and western Finland, bordered on the north by the White Sea and the south by the Gulf of Finland. John Parry's map of the witchlands in* THE SUBTLE KNIFE **10TH** *anniversary edition places several witch clans in what we would call Karelia.*

NL/GC LS Lantern Slide 3

KAZAKHSTAN ✸

World: Lyra's

Role: Leader John Faa assures his gyptian followers that while the top priority is the rescue of the abducted children, he'll see to it that the Gobblers are "broken and shattered." He adds that his "hammer is thirsty for blood, having seen no action since he "slew the Tartar champion on the steppes of Kazakhstan."

Facts: *In Will's world, Kazakhstan, populated historically by Turkic and Mongol nomadic tribes, was conquered by Russia in the 18th century. It became part of the Soviet Union in the 1930s, and emerged as the second largest independent state after Russia with the collapse of the Soviet state. It is bordered by Russia on the north, China to the east, other republics formerly part of the Soviet Union to the south, and the Caspian Sea to the west.*

Note: *Faa's description of his weapon's bloodthirstiness is not found in* THE GOLDEN COMPASS.

NL 8 *[brief]*

KHOLODNOYE ✎

World: Lyra's

Role: Will passes through this grubby Central Siberian village, home of a domed church, during the initial days of his search for Lyra. Its wooden, tin-roofed buildings are askew because of tremors and floods accompanying the climatic changes wrought by Asriel's blasting through the Aurora. Here he is waylaid by the talkative, crude, and more than likely lecherous priest, Semyon Borisovitch.

AS 8

KINGDOM OF HEAVEN [*See* The Worlds]

LAKE ENARA ✸ ⚔ ✎ ⑩

World: Lyra's

Role: Serafina Pekkala's witch clan's home is near the lakeshore in this heavily forested area. There the witches meet at a gathering cave to discuss their course of action in regards to

Lyra and the coming confrontation between Lord Asriel and the Authority.

Observation: *In Cittàgazze, the witches find a cave in which to camp, which suggests that rather than building houses, witches may prefer to dwell in caves.*

NL/GC Lanselius tells Coram Serafina is now that witch clan's queen 10 *[brief]*

SK   gathering of witch clans at 2
        brief mentions: Serafina uses when introducing herself 6, Scoresby tells of witch council meeting at 10

AS   Serafina queen of 3 *[brief]*

10TH: *SK* appendix

LAPLAND ✤

World: Lyra's

Role: Asriel pretended to be on a diplomatic mission to Lapland's king while actually searching for the explorer Stanislaus Grumman, rumored to be on an expedition to the magnetic north pole. Captured Gobblers reveal this is the general area to which children abducted by the General Oblation Board are taken.

    Lapland is home to witch clans, including Serafina Pekkala's. Her clan's consulate can be found in Lapland's main seaport of Trollesund, Norroway.

Observation: *Superstition and legends of Will's world have claimed Lapland as a home to witches; Milton alludes to this tradition in Book II, lines 663-665 of* Paradise Lost *when Sin, personified as a woman above the waist and a serpent below, is compared to Hecate, a mythological goddess: "when called/In secret, riding through the air she comes/Lured with the smell of infant blood, to dance/With Lapland witches." Witches were rumored to kill infants and use their blood in potions, but in Lyra's Lapland, the killing of children's souls and spirits—and not by witches—is the issue.*

NL/GC brief mentions: Asriel's expeditions and 1, 2; Coulter on 4, Gobblers and 9, gyptians' arrival in 10
      [Unnamed location through which gyptians journey 11-13 and where Bolvangar is located 14-17]

LATVIA/LATVIAN ⚑

World: Lyra's

Role: Witch-Queen Ruta Skadi's homeland.

SK   *brief mentions:* 3, 6, 13

LENA ⑩

World: Lyra's

Role: Stanislaus Grumman/Col. John Parry's first encounter with Lord Asriel was at the mouth of this Siberian river.

Facts: *The world's 10th longest river, the Lena begins just west of Lake Baikal in Central Siberia and 2,800 miles later empties into the Laptev Sea in the Arctic Ocean. The region considered the mouth of the Lena River is a 250 mile-wide delta. When it thaws in May, the frozen tundra emerges as a wetland which for several months provides a nesting and breeding area for a variety of migrating bird species.*

10TH: *SK* appendix

LIMEHOUSE ❖

World: Lyra's

Role: Clarice Walk resident Tony Makarios is abducted by the Gobblers' founder, Mrs Coulter, from the cluttered streets of this poor, rough industrial district of London. It is dominated by the Shot Tower where the boy spends his days wandering through the slum's fortune-paper stalls, fruit mongers, and fried-fish carts. Coulter leads Tony down Denmark Street to Hangman's Wharf and King George's Steps where the Gobblers' prey are warehoused before sailing to Trollesund, Norroway.

NL/GC 3

LISBON ✐

World: Will's

Role: Conference site in Portugal where the nun and physicist Mary Malone fell in love with Alfredo Montale, and decided to leave the Church.

AS 33 [brief]

LONDON ❖ ⚕ ✐ ⑩

World: Lyra's, Will's

Role: Cultural and political capital of the England of Lyra's world's (as well as that of Will's). Where Mrs Coulter lives, and takes an eager Lyra "intoxicated" by tales of "restaurants and ballrooms, the soirées at Embassies or Ministries, the intrigues between White Hall and Westminster." They seem to Lyra "accompanied by a scent of grown-upness, something disturbing but enticing at the same time: it was the smell of glamour." 62 Along with glamour, London also has "murky" air, "laden with fumes and soot and clangorous with noise." When Lyra runs away from Coulter's, she finds herself leaving the 63 London of theatres and wealth behind for long stretches along the river of ugly little houses, factories, warehouses, and "occasionally a dismal oratory." 64

In Will's world, London is a sprawling metropolis encompassing distinct districts and neighborhoods, and it appears the same is true of Lyra's. There are Clerkenwell, where the Ministry of Theology is located; the towns along the River Isis (or Thames), for example, the villages of Henley, Maidenhead, and Teddington; the fashionable district, Falkeshall, known for its gardens and fountains by day and its fireworks displays at night; and the slums of Limehouse.

Facts: *In Will's world's London, the Vauxhall Pleasure Gardens, in one of the oldest sections of London, opened in 1661. By the early 19th century, it was famous for illuminated fountains, fireworks and even balloon launches.*

The earliest property owner was the Fitzgerold family, whose youngest daughter married the soldier Fulk le Breant who served King John (1166-1216); in subsequent years, the area dominated by their estates was known as Fulk's Hall, Fawkes Hall, and Foxhall before settling as Vauxhall.

Update: Notes in the appendix to the **10TH** anniversary edition of *THE SUBTLE KNIFE* reveal that it was when he reached the London of Lyra's world that the former Col. John Parry realized "how truly different this world was from mine." Just as Lyra would later reflect that it was harder to survive in Will's mock-Oxford than in the frozen arctic of her own world, Parry found

65   it "harder to live in the streets I thought I knew than in the wilds of Siberia."

NL/GC Lyra moves to 4; social scene 5; theatre district, docks and warehouses 6; Clerkenwell, government district 9
> *brief mentions:* politics and 2; suburbs of Falkeshall, Henley, Maidenhead, Teddington, Limehouse 3; Northern Progress Exploration Company of 10, hometown of several Gobbler victims in Bolvangar 14, by Coulter 17

10TH: *SK* appendix

10TH: *AS* appendix

LOOKOUT RIDGE   [*See* Alaska]

LORD ASRIEL'S WORLD   [*See* The Worlds]

MADAGASCAR ⑩

World: Lyra's

Role: Lord Asriel speculates that the Javanese or Balinese *sepikwu* or *sempekwu* may be like the African zombi of Benin; or that these words, or what they denote, may have a common origin in the languages of Java, Madagascar, and Benin.

Facts: *Madagascar is an island nation in the Indian Ocean, which is located between Africa and India.*

10TH: *NL* appendix

MAIDENHEAD   [*See* London]

MANCHESTER   [*See* England]

MIDLANDS ⚔

World: Will's

Role: Region to which Will was headed when he found the Oxford window into Cittàgazze. He was headed there not for any purpose, but because he simply felt he had to keep moving after the crisis in the pre-dawn hours that morning.

SK   13 *[brief]*

MINNESOTA   [*See* Particle Physics (Natural Sciences: Scientific Studies)]

MISSISSIPPI RIVER, THE ✎

World: Will's

Role: Mary Malone compares the movement of Dust leaving the mulefa's world that she sees with her amber spyglass to the flow of the Mississippi.

AS   *brief mentions:* 34, 36

MOROCCO ✤

World: Lyra's

Role: Farder Coram examines one of the spy flies Lyra manages to catch when they attack Pantalaimon on the deck of a gyptian boat, and says he has seen such a thing before in this African nation. He adds that their most likely source, Mrs Coulter, has also traveled in the southern hemisphere.

NL/GC 9 *[brief]*

MORTLAKE ✥

World: Lyra's

Role: Town on the River Isis where the legendary magician Dr Dee lives.

NL/GC 3 *[brief]*

MOSCOW ⑩

World: Lyra's

Role: Emerging from Siberia, the erstwhile Col. John Parry became the European Stanislaus Grumman in this city.

10TH: *SK* appendix

MULTIPLE WORLDS [*See discussion* Other Worlds *in* The Worlds]

MUSCOVY, MUSCOVITE(S) ✥ ⚑ ✐

World: Lyra's

Role: City or principality claiming as its own the man who discovered Rusakov particles (commonly known as Dust), Boris Mikhailovitch Rusakov.

Under siege by Tartars in Lyra's world. Sir Charles Latrom, or as she knows him, Lord Boreal, tells Mrs Coulter that their world's Muscovy is known in the one she is visiting as the Soviet Union.

Its Imperial Academy maintains an observatory on Nova Zembla. Soldiers from the Imperial Guard of Muscovy pursue Lee Scoresby and Stanislaus Grumman into Cittàgazze, where Scoresby dies in a gun battle while Grumman escapes.

Observation: *The* Muscovy *of Lyra's world likely refers to more than the present day City of Moscow of Will's world. A more appropriate comparison might be to the East Slavic state, Muscovy, which grew out of the founding in 1147 of a small village that took its name from the Moskva or Moscow River.*

Note: *There is one more reference to Muscovites in the Random House (US)* THE SUBTLE KNIFE *than in the Scholastic Point (UK) edition. An Observatory scientist asks a question during their discussion with Scoresby about Grumman. In the US edition, the questioner is a Muscovite; in the UK, a Yoruba.*

NL/GC brief mentions: Tartars and 1; and Rusakov 5, 21

SK   brief mentions: observatory 6; and Soviet Union 9 *[brief]*; its Imperial Guard in Siberia 10, and

Dr Dee of Mortlake

In Will's world, Dr John Dee (1527-1608), magician, astrologer and spy for Queen Elizabeth I, is credited as the developer of Enochian Magick—based on his communications with many angels, in particular, Uriel. His Mortlake residence housed a library of over 4,000 manuscripts, an extraordinary collection for its day; unfortunately, it was lost to fire. Enochian Magick hearkens back to tales of the same Enoch who causes so much trouble in *HIS DARK MATERIALS*. Enoch, in the Jewish mystical tradition, was taught by the angels, including Uriel, and at death joined their forces as Metatron.

in pursuit of Scoresby, Grumman 14

AS   *brief mentions:* Scoresby's death and troops from 3, 14

NEW DENMARK   [*See* New Dane/New Danish/New Denmark *in* Peoples]

NEW FRANCE ✥

World: Lyra's

Role: Like Europe, it lacks a center for experimental theology superior to Oxford's Jordan College.

Observation: *Most likely the equivalent of part of North America in Will's world, which it shares uneasily with New Denmark.*

NL/GC 3 *[brief]*

NEW WORLDS   [*See* Other worlds]

NEW ZEALAND   [*See* Particle Physics *in* Natural Sciences: Scientific Studies]

NIPPON, NIPPONESE ⚔

World: Lyra's

Role: Aëronaut Lee Scoresby thinks this language might be the source for the name by which the Tartars know the shaman Stanislaus Grumman, "Jopari."

The Nippons' adversaries include Muscovites, who used a naphtha-based weapon against them. Grumman tells Scoresby he fears they too are facing a fire attack from the Imperial Muscovite Navy, in spite of the wet conditions of the forest in Cittàgazze in which they've taken cover.

Facts: *The source of the word* Nippon, *which is the actual name for* Japan, *is the Chinese pictograph for "Land of the Rising Sun."*

SK   *brief mentions:* source for Jopari 6; enemy of Muscovites 14

NOATAK   [*See* Alaska]

NORHAM GARDENS   [*See* The Oxfords]

66 NORROWAY ✥

World: Lyra's

Role: The General Oblation Board's Bolvangar Experiment Station is a four days' march northeast of Trollesund, a port city of Norroway. Dr Martin Lanselius says that the Norroway government is not "officially aware" of the true purpose of the establishment calling itself the Northern Progress Exploration Company, claiming to be searching for minerals in Norroway's interior.

Observation: *Likely Norway of Will's world.*

NL/GC 10 *[brief]*

North/north ❖ ⚓ ✐ LS

World: Lyra's

Role: The words *North* and *north* are used in several ways in HIS DARK MATERIALS, and to complicate matters, the word is not consistently upper- and lowercased in US and UK editions, either when compared to each other or when looked at singly.

Moreover, the meanings of the word often overlap. One could argue that in the first book a reference to going north means just going in the direction opposite south, while going North denotes this but has additional connotative meanings as well. But in the second and third volume of the trilogy, such a distinction can't be made because only *north* is used.

Whether it is upper- or lowercased, North/north seems to be more than just a synonym for the Arctic; it does, of course, denote a place, and all that is applicable to the Arctic is true for the word. But the way it differs from *Arctic* is that North/north can also signify an idea—and, in fact, the second chapter of NORTHERN LIGHTS/THE GOLDEN COMPASS is titled "The Idea of North." The conceptual significance is underscored again at the end of Part One of NORTHERN LIGHTS/THE GOLDEN COMPASS as seasick Lyra leaves England with the gyptians: "And so began her journey to the North." When she and 67 Roger leave with Iorek Byrnison for Lord Asriel's prison house on Svalbard, this is designated as "the final part of their journey north." 68

The Master of Jordan College tells the Librarian that he tried to poison Lord Asriel to keep Lyra "safe for a little longer. I would have liked to spare her a journey to the 69 North." Lord Asriel says the "darkness and obscurity" of the Far North suited the General Oblation Board for its intercision experiments. Gyptian John Faa calls the North a "land of dark." 70 71

For Lyra, North is a place that is exciting, mysterious, and dangerous—but enticing. She has been told that both her parents died in an aëronautical accident in the North. The man she's been led to believe is her uncle, Lord Asriel, returns from the North with a scalped and trepanned head he displays to Jordan College scholars. Lyra's response is to beg Asriel to take her along when he returns to the North. Even though she is unhappy living with Mrs Coulter, Lyra plays along with the charade of training to be Coulter's assistant: such was "that tantalizing hope of going North." She hears that somewhere in the North is where the 72 Gobblers take the children they kidnap to do unknown but surely awful things, perhaps using them as slaves in uranium mines. She hears Asriel is the prisoner of the armoured bears on the far north island of Svalbard, and she begs gyptian John Faa to let her go on the rescue expedition to the remote North.

Lyra finds in the North what she likely never expected such a journey to provide, the life-long friendship of three adults who would sacrifice their lives for her (including one who does): the witch Serafina Pekkala, armoured bear Iorek Byrnison, and aëronaut Lee Scoresby.

But what she most often feels in the North is not an invigorating thrill of excitement but instead nauseating terror and heartbreaking sorrow. It is

John Parry, professional explorer, accompanied a team of archaeologists to the far North because they wanted an experienced person on the team to deal with "survival stuff," like polar bears. (SK 4)

where she finds the pathetic severed child Tony Makarios and is nearly severed from her own daemon Pantalaimon. It is where she realizes just how little feeling her father has for her. Worst of all, North is where she watches her best friend Roger die—a death for which she blames herself.

She also finds a bridge to another world, where she finds another type of very real love with Will.

Note: *Upper and lower case spellings are both used to denote Arctic regions. In* THE GOLDEN COMPASS *and* NORTHERN LIGHTS north *is used as an adjective, e.g.* "*move north,*" "*up north,*" *while* North *is used as a noun always preceded by* the, *with a few exceptions, e.g. Lyra thrilled… hearing the word* North;" *however, in* NORTHERN LIGHTS North *is used much more frequently, including in these instances.*

But this changes in THE SUBTLE KNIFE *and* THE AMBER SPYGLASS *where north is used exclusively, both as a noun preceded by* the *(e.g. SK 9 [Latrom to Coulter], 13 [Skadi to Serafina], AS 8 [Borisovitch to Will]) as well as to denote a general direction (e.g. SK 13, AS 3).*

The Ideas of North

In Siberia, the lecherous priest Semyon Borisovitch tells Will that "All things from the north are devilish." Interestingly, there are precedents for this statement, which Borisovitch slips in among a catalogue of things Will would be wise to hate. The Arctic has been both demonized—the vast and uncharted stretches, unpopulated and inhospitable (and, in winter, always dark) evoke a reaction of fearful distrust. But it also has been idealized—for its purity, the unspoiled glistening ice, over which the sun never sets in summer, and its freedom from the spoilage of human civilization. For more on this topic, see *The Idea of North* by Peter Davidson.

There are Biblical passages favoring the negative view of the North; for example, Jeremiah 6:1: "Evil threatens from the north and mighty destruction" (see also Jeremiah 1:14, 4:6), and Lucifer is linked to the North in Isaiah 14:12-19:

> "How have you fallen from the heavens
> O morning star, son of the dawn
> …You said in your heart;
> 'I will scale the heavens
> Above the stars of God
> I will set up my throne;
> I will take my seat on the Mount of Assembly,
> in the recesses of the North
> I will ascend above the tops of the clouds.
> I will be like the Most High.'
> Yet down to the nether world you go
> to the recesses of the pit."

Milton picks up on this in *Paradise Lost*. In Book V, lines 686-89 Satan rallies his troops:

> "I am to haste,
> And all who under me their banners wave,
> Homeward with flying march where we possess
> The quarters of the north, there to prepare."

The North—of some world—is where Satan and the other reprobate angels plot against the kingdom of heaven in *Paradise Lost*, and in *HIS DARK MATERIALS*, Lord Asriel leaves his world from one of its farthest habitable northern points to establish his republic.

(There are two instances of North in The Subtle Knife *in both the UK and US—but these are at the start of sentences.)*

In The Amber Spyglass *in instances where perhaps in the US and certainly in the UK North would be expected, north is used instead, e.g. Fr MacPhail's reference to the "cliffghasts of the north" (24).*

NL/GC chapter title, Asriel's report from, Lyra asks that he take her there 2; Coulter to Lyra about going to 4; Pan's doubts about Coulter's plans 5; where Gobbler victims are thought to be taken, Tony Costa on creatures of 6; Faa proposes rescue party going to 7, 8; Lyra's eagerness to go, beginning of journey to 9; smell of, Northlanders, Coram's proposal to Iorek and 10; [LS] Lantern Slide 3

> *brief mentions:* Asriel's recent travels in 1; as Gobbler destination 3; silence of 12; Svalbard in 13; Coram in 17; by Serafina, Lyra 18; Asriel on Oblation Board and 21

SK *brief mentions:* Alaska in 4, Latrom to Coulter about explorer's disappearance 9, gestures of friendship in 10, Skadi on witches of 13

AS Borisovitch on evil things of 8

> *brief mentions:* Svalbard in 3, stars of 14, Iorek on 15, Roke on armoured bears of 16, cliffghasts of north 24; witches' north-land 36, Coram recalls taking Lyra to north-lands 38

Northampton [*See* England]

North Pole/Pole/Polar [*See* Pole]

Norwich [*See* England]

Nottingham ⚲

World: Will's

Role: Will tells his father's lawyer, Mr Perkins, that he is headed to this town, apparently chosen out of the blue. His decision to give the false impression that he is just passing through Oxford is motivated by Will's fear that the police may be looking for him.

SK 4 *[brief]*

Nova Zembla ✦⚲✑

World: Lyra's

Role: A bear's armour is made of sky-metal, which is among Nova Zembla's natural resources. When he was exiled, the dethroned armoured bear king Iorek Byrnison was also required to surrender his armour. Byrnison, needing his armour like Lyra needs her dæmon, came to this island and made himself another.

Aëronaut Lee Scoresby visits the island during his quest for information about shaman Stanislaus Grumman. He checked first at the Samirsky Hotel's bar where trappers, traders, and drifters gravitate, and later the Imperial Muscovite Academy's Observatory. The largest local industry appears to be a fish-packing station.

Facts: *In Will's world, the preferred English alphabet spelling for this Arctic archipelago has shifted from* Nova Zembla *to* Novaya Zemlya. *Either way, the phrase translates as* new land. *While both of its two major islands are mountainous, the northernmost features many glaciers; the southern of the two, tundra.*

NL/GC brief mentions: source of sky iron 13; winds blow Scoresby away from Svalbard towards 18, 20

SK   Scoresby visits for news of Grumman, kills Skraeling censor in self-defense, learns from Tartar sledge driver of Grumman's village 6
> *brief mentions:* Scoresby's plans 2; Scoresby recalls death of Skraeling on 10, 14

NOVGOROD ⑩

World: Lyra's

Role: Location of Semyon Karlovich Martins, the witch consul for Ruta Skadi's clan.

Facts: *The Russian city of Novgorod is located between Moscow and Saint Petersburg.*

10TH: *SK* appendix

NUNIATAK   [*See* Alaska]

OB [RIVER, REGION] ⚱

World: Lyra's

Role: Arctic region, inhabited by Tartars. Homeland of Umaq, aëronaut Lee Scoresby's sledge driver on Nova Zembla.

Observation: *The Ob River, although not mentioned by name, is likely the one near Kholodnoye that Borisovitch discusses with Will, and the one Iorek uses on his journeys south with his bear subjects and Will.*

SK   6 *[brief]*

OLD HEADINGTON   [*See* The Oxfords]

OPHIUCUS, CONSTELLATION OF ⚱

Role: Location in the sky above Cittàgazze world where witch Ruta Skadi approaches the angels to take her to Lord Asriel's basalt fortress.

Facts: *In mythology, Ophiuchus, or the Serpent Holder, was once the physician Aesclepius. Aesclepius was trying to revive Orion the Hunter when Zeus hurled a thunderbolt at him to appease Hades, who complained that Aesclepius' healing skills were reducing new arrivals to the underworld.*

> *Ophiuchus is seen in the northern hemisphere in summer. It contains the second closest star to earth, Barnard's Star.*

Note: *The US editions use a different spelling for the constellation:* Ophiuchus.

SK   6 *[brief]*

OTHER WORLDS   [*See discussion* Other Worlds *in* The Worlds]

POLE, MAGNETIC; POLE, NORTH; POLE (POLAR) ✦ ⚱

World: Lyra's

Role: Pole or Polar refers to the North Pole in *HIS DARK MATERIALS*.

> Addressing the assembled Jordan College scholars, Lord Asriel claims that Stanislaus Grumman's last expedition was headed to the magnetic pole to make celestial measurements. Grumman first made a name for himself nine or so years back with a study on magnetic variations in the magnetic pole.

When Mrs Coulter visits Sir Charles Latrom (Lord Boreal) in Will's world, he confirms her speculation that extreme disturbances to the magnetic fields in her world following Lord Asriel's opening of a passage to Cittàgazze must have caused changes in other worlds. This has led to renewed interest in the disappearance a decade back of three men in a remote region of Alaska, where a doorway to another world is rumored to exist.

Witches navigate by the Polar Star.

NL/GC brief mentions: Grumman and magnetic pole 2, Carborn's flight over 4, long nights 15, in metaphor 16, Polar Star 17, direction of balloon flight 18, sky above Svalbard 20, frozen sea 23

SK brief mentions: Grumman and magnetic pole, angels and 6; Asriel and magnetic pole 9

PORT GALVESTON ✢

World: Lyra's

Role: Where aëronaut Lee Scoresby will book passage when he's ready to retire. He tells witch Serafina Pekkala that he plans to buy a small cattle farm and "never leave the ground again."

Facts: *In Will's world, Galveston, Texas, is south of Houston, on the Gulf of Mexico.*

NL/GC 18 *[brief]*

PORT MEADOW [*See* The Oxfords]

PORTUGAL [*See* Lisbon]

PRAGUE ✢

World: Lyra's

Role: City where, in the seventeenth century, alethiometers were first devised by a scholar trying to adapt a compass for use in astrology.

NL/GC 10 *[brief]*

REPUBLIC OF HEAVEN/LORD ASRIEL'S WORLD [*See* The Worlds]

RIVER ISIS [*See* The Oxfords]

SAINT-JEAN-LES-EAUX ✑

World: Lyra's

Role: Remote wilderness location, on a spur of the Alps, of a cataract or high, large waterfall. The only development in the area, accessible to some extent by zeppelin, is a hydro-anbaric generating station, which the Consistorial Court of Discipline uses when it launches a bomb intended to kill Lyra.

The title of Chapter 25 of THE AMBER SPYGLASS is "Saint-Jean-Les-Eaux."

AS discussed in Geneva 24 *[brief]*; bomb launch 25

SAKHALIN ⚲

World: Lyra's

Role: According to the Samirsky Hotel's barman's informant, an Inuit, Stanislaus

Grumman was buried alive under an avalanche in the Sakhalin region.

Observation: *There is a town of this name east of the Urals and north of the Volga in Russia, but given that an Inuit is the source of information about Grumman's doings, the island of Sakhalin in extreme eastern Russia, north of Japan and just west of the Bering Sea, is the more likely choice. Also, its high snow accumulations make Sakhalin Island vulnerable to avalanches.*

SK 6 *[brief]*

Sant'Elia ⚲

World: Cittàgazze

Role: Close to the city of Cittàgazze, it is the redhead Angelica's first guess for where Will and Lyra belong when she learns that they are not from her hometown.

Cittàgazzean Joachim Lorenz tells witches Serafina Pekkala and Ruta Skadi that he was caught in the hills near this town when the strange fog that brought with it so many Spectres blew into his world.

SK *brief mentions:* by Angelica 3, Lorenz 6

Scotland/Scot ⚲

World: Will's

Role: When she left the Church, Dr Mary Malone took up hiking and rock-climbing, skills that prove useful in her quest through two worlds for Lyra and Will. Scotland had been one of her favorite destinations during what proved to be a time of preparation for her most important journey.

Father Hugh MacPhail, president of the Consistorial Court of Discipline, is a Scot.

SK Mary and 12

AS MacPhail as 6

Semyonov Range ⚲

World: Lyra's

Role: The Yenisei Pakhtars (a Tartar tribe) and their honored guest shaman Stanislaus Grumman, also known by them as Jopari, live near these mountains in central Siberia.

SK 6 *[brief]*

Sheffield ✦ ⑩

World: Lyra's

Role: Lord Asriel visited a smelting plant in this city once targeted by the Gobblers to see a test of the Hadfield process.

NL/GC 3 *[brief]*

10ᴛʜ: *NL* appendix

Siberia/Siberian/Sibirsk ✦ ⚲ ✐ ⑩

World: Lyra's

Role: Sibirsk regiments of Tartar troops, in the employ of the General Oblation Board, patrol the Bolvangar Experiment Station.

Aëronaut Lee Scoresby visits the island of Nova Zembla in Siberia during his quest for information about shaman Stanislaus Grumman.

Will enters Lyra's world in an unpopulated area of tundra and marshland (which proves to be Siberia), and soon meets Iorek Byrnison. He, with a few dozen of his subjects, is headed downriver through Siberia to the Himalayas in search of a climate still hospitable to bears.

NL/GC brief mentions: aboriginals of discussed in Retiring Room 2, by Tony Costa 6, and Bolvangar's Tartar guards 12

SK 10; Asriel asks if his republic is known of in 13 *[brief]*

AS Will enters 2 [unnamed], travels through on foot 8, and in bears' boat 9

10TH: *SK* appendix

SKY-CITY [*See* Cittàgazze *in* The Worlds]

SOUTH LANDS, SOUTH-LANDS, SOUTHERN ✣ ⚶

World: Lyra's

Role: Farder Coram identifies the spy flies that Mrs Coulter sends after Lyra as being from the southern land of Morocco in Africa, where he and Coulter have visited.

Witch Ruta Skadi says agents of the Authority commit crimes against children in the south, just as they do in the North.

NL/GC and Africa 9 (southern) *[brief]*

SK brief mentions: Skadi on mutilation of children in 2 (south lands), 13 (south-lands UK, southlands US)

SOVIET UNION [*See* Soviets/Soviet Union *in* Peoples]

ST PETERSBURG ✣

World: Lyra's

Role: If the Tartars take control of Muscovy, their next targets are St Petersburg and the Baltic Sea.

NL/GC 1 *[brief]*

STRATFORD [*See* England]

SUBURBS OF THE WORLD OF THE DEAD [*See* The Worlds]

SUMATRA / SUNDA STRAITS ⑩

World: Lyra's

Role: The islands of Sumatra and Java in the South Pacific Ocean are separated by the Sunda Straits.

10TH: *NL* appendix

SUMMERTOWN [*See* The Oxfords]

SUNGCHEN ✏

World: Lyra's

Role: Sungchen Pass is on Iorek Byrnison and Will's route to the Himalayan cave where Coulter has hidden Lyra. Byrnison bids farewell to his subjects here, telling them that this is where they'll gather when it is time to return to their homeland of Svalbard.

AS 9 [brief]

SVALBARD

World: Lyra's

Role: Island nation of the *panserbjørne* (or armoured bears) and site of Asriel's exile, where he plans a bridge to another world, which entails creating a "breach in the sky above Svalbard."

Svalbard's interior is "mountainous, with jumbled peaks and sharp ridges deeply cut by ravines and steep-sided valleys" and extremely cold. When Lyra arrives, the snow is thigh-deep. The bears live on the "iron-bound coast" where they hunt seals and walruses. Svalbard's perimeter's 1000-foot high cliffs are plagued by cliff-ghasts. There is no wood on the island, but coal pits are numerous. The area where Asriel spent his exile and where he breaks open the sky, is south of the frozen sea that reaches to the Pole.

> ## Iorek Byrnison describes Svalbard
>
> Lyra "asked Iorek Byrnison about Svalbard, and listened eagerly as he told her of the slow-crawling glaciers; of the rocks and ice-floes where the bright-tusked walruses lay in groups of a hundred or more, of the seas teeming with seals, of narwhals clashing their long white tusks above the icy water; of the great grim iron-bound coast, the cliffs a thousand feet and more high."

To the east and west are "great jagged peaks thrusting sharply upwards, their scarps piled high with snow and raked by the wind into blade-like edges as sharp as scimitars."

Although they have visited and been imprisoned there, no people have ever otherwise lived and worked on the island. Traditionally, the bears live in ice forts, and forge iron into armour in fire mines.

As HIS DARK MATERIALS opens, Iofur Raknison, the prince who succeeded former king Iorek Byrnison following his exile, has rejected this culture. Raknison has built a palace and has imposed on his subjects ways of life suitable for humans but not for bears. Mrs Coulter plans to manipulate him into allowing other experimental stations on the island like the General Oblation Board's at Bolvangar: "There are human laws that prevent certain things that she was planning to do, but human laws don't apply on Svalbard."

Lord Asriel claims the preserved body of explorer Stanislaus Grumman was found in the ice off Svalbard's coast. The night Lyra learns of Mrs Coulter's involvement with the General Oblation Board or Gobblers, she also learns that the man she thinks of as her uncle is being held on Svalbard as a prisoner. Lyra declares her intention of finding her friend Roger, but secretly determines to rescue Asriel as well.

With the restoration of King Iorek Byrnison, Svalbard's future is less uncertain. He commands an immediate clearance of all that reflects Raknison's human influence on Svalbard. However, the hole Asriel makes in the sky over Svalbard radically changes its climate: "the mountains lay bare and black, and only a few hidden valleys facing away from the sun had retained a little snow in their shaded corners." Iorek moves his bears to the Himalayas, hoping that the snows in those mountains will not have melted as

Ny Alesund, Svalbard, Norway

Svalbard's have, and that his subjects will find a hospitable environment. But he discovers that even a warm sea is better for them than no sea at all.

Parting from her in the Himalayas after repairing the subtle knife, Iorek tells Lyra she "will always be a welcome and honoured visitor to Svalbard; and the same is true of Will." 85

The title of Part Three of NORTHERN LIGHTS/THE GOLDEN COMPASS is "Svalbard."

NL/GC Asriel claims to have found Grumman's head near, discussion of its *panserbørne's* new king 2; Kaisa's report on bears' new king, their prisoner Asriel's plan for bridge 11; Iorek describes, Lyra questions Scoresby about 13; departure from Bolvangar for 17; flight to, attack by cliff-ghasts, Lyra's arrival and arrest by Raknison's guards 18; Lyra's imprisonment, Santelia on politics of, Lyra's interview with Raknison 19; Lyra reunited with Iorek on, combat, Iorek reclaims throne, Roger and Lyra reunited, its recent history 20; journey to and night at Ariel's 21; Iorek and Lyra chase Asriel and Roger, attack by witches, attack by Coulter's Tartars 22; death of Roger on, breach opened in sky above, departure from of Asriel, and Lyra and Pan 23

    brief mentions: of Asriel's imprisonment on 5, 8; of Lyra's plans 15; by Coulter on Asriel's possible execution on 16

SK Serafina approaches and is alerted to torture of witch on ship near, Serafina visits Thorold on, Scoresby recalls flight from 2

    brief mentions: by Lyra of her father's house 1; Lyra tells Will about 5; by Serafina, Skadi 13

AS Serafina visits, Iorek's decision, cliff-ghasts and arctic foxes 3; Iorek tells Lyra he will return to and invites her, as well as Will to visit 15

    brief mentions: Asriel recalls Lyra's visit to 5; MacPhail asks Cooper about Asriel's blast 6; by Will to Borisovitch 8; lack of mountains, breach above 9; Lyra remembers taking Roger to 13; by Lyra to Iorek 14; Coulter to Asriel 28; Lyra to Master 38

SVEDEN

World: Lyra's

Role: Gyptians trade for products of its silver mines. Silver cups are among the gifts they present their unusual hosts when they come to mulefa's world to collect Mary Malone, Will, and Lyra.

Observation: *Likely Sweden of Will's world.*

AS 38 *[brief]*

TAYMYR

World: Lyra's

Role: Homeland of the clan of the unfortunate witch captured at Bolvangar, whose torture by Coulter and clerics ends only when Serafina Pekkala intervenes to save her sister witch further agony with a knife thrust to the broken woman's heart.

SK 2 *[brief]*

TEDDINGTON [*See* England]

TEXAS, COUNTRY OF; TEXAN ✤ ⚔ ✎

World: Lyra's

Role: Aëronaut Lee Scoresby's homeland. He is a New Dane as well as a Texan. Scoresby grew up near enough to the Alamo to use it as a playground, and remembers vast stretches of sagelands and prairies not unlike those in mulefa's world.

Facts: *Texas, now part of the United States, was briefly a sovereign republic from 1836 to 1846. No mention of the United States or America (or Canada) appears in* NORTHERN LIGHTS/THE GOLDEN COMPASS; *the landmass equivalent seems to be called New Denmark. So it seems Scoresby may be both a Texan and a New Dane in the same sense that Will is both English (from England) and European (England is part of Europe). If Lee were of Will's world, he'd be a Texan (from Texas) and an American/North American (Texas is a state in America, and The United States of America is on the continent of North America.)*

[*See also* **Alamo** and **New Denmark**]

NL/GC brief mentions: Scoresby's background 10, 11, 17

SK   brief mentions: Scoresby's 2, and Cansino's backgrounds 6; by Scoresby to Grumman 10

AS   brief mentions: Scoresby's background 3, 26; sagelands of 29, world of mulefa and prairies of Scoresby's homeland 31 [implied]

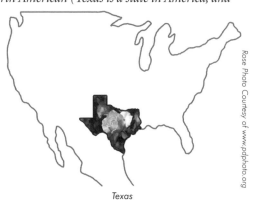

Texas

Rose Photo Courtesy of www.pdphoto.org

THAMES ✎

World: Lyra's

Role: River featuring in the tall tale Lyra tells her hosts in the suburbs of the world of the dead.

Observation: *In Oxford, the Thames River and the River Isis are one and the same.* Isis *is used twice in* NORTHERN LIGHTS/THE GOLDEN COMPASS, *but* Thames *does not appear at all. It seems unlikely that Lyra would adopt the name used in Will's world for the river in her yarn, a fantasy based on many of her favorite Oxford escapades, e.g. playing in the claybeds or on gyptian narrow boats. The description of the route that the River Isis, not Thames, takes through London suggests in fact that there may be no Thames in Lyra's world, or that* Thames *and* Isis *are interchangeable for the whole course of the river.* [*See also* **River Isis** *in* **The Oxfords**]

AS   19 [brief]

TIBET ✎

World: Lyra's

Role: Source of the river Will and Iorek Byrnison take from Siberia toward the Himalayan mountain cave where Mrs Coulter has hidden Lyra.

AS   8 [brief]

TROLLESUND ✤ ⚔ ✎ ⑩

World: Lyra's

Role: Largest seaport in Lapland and home to witch consul, Dr Martin Lanselius.

Behind the little town are snow-capped mountains. The town's structures, many of which are grouped closely together around the harbor, are generally wooden with steep roofs; the priest's house, however, is brick, a scarce and expensive building material in these parts. The spire of the town's oratory is its highest structure. Its depot area is little more than a few concrete warehouses in muddy ground, a smoke-filled cafe, and the dump of a tavern servicing men off the boats, Einarsson's Bar.

The town is the point at which the gyptian expedition to find their children moves inland, and where Iorek Byrnison and aëronaut Lee Scoresby join the rescue effort. When the gyptians arrive, the mountains are snow-capped but green grass is still visible below the summits. By the time they leave, it has snowed enough that once they are away from the town's roads, the sledges run smoothly.

When witch Serafina Pekkala visits Lanselius after Asriel breaks through the Aurora, she sees more ships in its harbor than ever before. The Magisterium is assembling a huge army that includes *zombi*, soldiers without dæmons. The townspeople have not been able to disregard the *zombis*' frightful presence, although the authorities try to keep these special warriors hidden from view.

Update: On Col. John Parry's map in the appendix to the **10TH** anniversary edition of *THE SUBTLE KNIFE*, Trollesund is located on the coast of Norway, roughly parallel to but a bit north of Lake Enara.

NL/GC Lapland's main port, described, visit to witch consul and Iorek 10; Aurora above harbor, visit by Kaisa, Lyra meets Scoresby waiting with gyptians for final arrangements, Iorek reclaims armor from priest's house, Sysselman warns Iorek not to return, gyptian party departs 11; Serafina and Lyra discuss her visit to witch consul at 18
 brief mentions: by Iorek to Lyra 13, by Lyra to Coulter 17, Lyra to Asriel 21

SK Serafina visits consul in 2; Scoresby mentions as he tells Grumman his reason for visit 10 *[brief]*

AS Lyra tells Roger's ghost about visit to Lanselius 23 *[brief]*

Strange Doings in the Tunguska

On June 30, 1908, over 2,150 (830 sq mile) square kilometers of forest in a remote and sparsely populated region of Siberia called Tunguska were incinerated or knocked flat by an explosion estimated variously as equivalent to 15-40 megatons of TNT. As far as some 900 kilometers southeast (550 miles) of the presumed point of impact, disturbances in the earth's magnetic field were detected. An influx of cosmic dust colored sunsets throughout Europe and Asia for many days.

The consensus is that the area was devastated by a meteor exploding 6 to 10 kilometers (4 to 6 miles) above earth. A crater would be expected if the earth's surface experienced a direct hit; none was found. Speculation continues, and theories proposing UFO involvement behind the event are many, varied, and persistent.

Investigations of the site were hampered by its remoteness, two world wars, and the political upheavals of the 20th century; moreover, following the event, according to one astronomer, "The shaman-chief of the Tungus people, or Evenks, had for years virtually sealed off the region, proclaiming it 'enchanted.' The Evenk people had long been fearful of further enraging the gods whose wrath they believed had been responsible for 1908 explosion." One eyewitness reportedly said, "The sky split apart and a great fire appeared."

Readers of *HIS DARK MATERIALS* may find themselves reminded of another Tartar's claim that long ago "the sky fell apart"—Umaq, commenting to Lee Scoresby on the recent, but not unique, upheavals caused by the hole in the sky Asriel created.

TUNGUSK/TUNGUSKA ❖ ⚜

World: Lyra's

Role: The Sub-rector of Jordan College claims that Tungusk aboriginals scalp their victims. Lee Scoresby once rescued Iorek Byrnison from the Tartars during what he calls the Tunguska campaign.

Much later, when he addresses Serafina Pekkala's witch-clan, Scoresby says that a Tungusk hunter once told him of Stanislaus Grumman's interest in a special "object that gives protection to whoever holds it."

NL/GC brief mentions: aboriginals of discussed in Retiring Room 2; Scoresby on fighting in 11, 13

SK   Scoresby on hunter from 2 *[brief]*

TURKESTAN ✑

World: Lyra's

Role: Gyptians admire this country's "silken tapestries," selecting several to give as gifts to their unusual hosts when they come to mulefa's world to collect Mary Malone, Will, and Lyra.

Facts: *In Will's world, the region of Turkestan is a huge area covering much of what was known as the Silk Road, the trading routes from the Mediterranean to China. Once dominated by nomadic Mongol, or Tartar, tribes, Turkestan was conquered by Russia in the 19th century, and in the 20th was part of the Soviet Union. Following the collapse of that nation, several autonomous countries emerged from the former Turkestan, including Kazakhstan.*

AS   38 *[brief]*

TURUKHANSK ⑩

World: Lyra's

Role: A shaman from this Siberian region taught Stanislaus Grumman/Col. John Parry how to make an ointment from bloodmoss and harp-flower root.

Facts: *Turukhansk is a town at the mouth of the Turukhan River, which is a tributary of the Yenisei River.*

10TH: *SK appendix*

UMIAT [*See* Alaska]

UPPSALA ❖

World: Lyra's

Role: Gyptian Farder Coram tells Lyra that this is the only place he had ever before seen an alethiometer read.

Facts: *Uppsala is located north of Stockholm, Sweden, and is the site of the first university in Scandinavia, Uppsala University, which was founded in 1477.*

NL/GC 7 [brief]

URALS ⚜ ✑

World: Lyra's

Role: Mountain range where fur-trader Sam Cansino first met Stanislaus Grumman. When Will asks Father Semyon Borisovitch, the priest of the Central Siberian village Kholodnoye, to show him the village's location in an atlas, Will, discovers that he is east of the Urals.

SK 6 *[brief]*

AS 8 *[brief]*

Van Tieren's Land ✦

World: Lyra's

Role: Captain Hudson, Arctic explorer, visited this land. Relics from his expedition are among those displayed at the Royal Arctic Institute in London, where Lyra dines with Mrs Coulter.

NL/GC 4 [brief]

Volgorsk ⚷

World: Lyra's

Role: Some renegade witches from this region still worked for the General Oblation Board, even after the horrors of Bolvangar were exposed.

SK 2 *[brief]*

Wapping [*See* Cathay]

Warsaw ⑩

World: Lyra's

Role: Col. John Parry became the scientist Stanislaus Grumman in this European city.

10ᴛʜ: *SK* appendix

Watlington [*See* The Oxfords]

White Ham [*See* The Oxfords]

Winchester ⚷ ✎

World: Will's

Role: Will Parry's hometown. Will and his mother live in a late 20th century housing development of dozens of identical modest homes. Theirs is distinguished only by having a poorly kept yard. On the second floor of the two-story house are two bedrooms and a spare room that he mother uses for sewing. The house's configuration is closely matched by the apartment where Will meets Lyra in Cittàgazze.

Facts: *Will's hometown is roughly 48 miles (73 km) south of Oxford.*

SK 1; Will tells Lyra of childhood [implied] 13
    brief mentions: Will answers Angelica 3, Lyra claims as her hometown when interrogated 7

AS Will tells Lyra about ghost-like man in his hometown 18 [implied] *[brief]*

WITCH-CLAN LANDS ⑩

World: Lyra's

Role: The appendix to the **10TH** anniversary edition of *THE SUBTLE KNIFE* includes a map by Dr Stanislaus Grumman/Col. John Parry of the witch-clan lands, roughly corresponding to Will's world's Lapland.

While the borders between these lands are "definite" they aren't fixed, but instead "vary from season to season with the flowering of plants and the migration of animals."

10TH: *SK* appendix

YARNTON [*See* The Oxfords]

YENISEI RIVER ✤ ⚕ *LS*

World: Lyra's

Role: River running near the Tartar village which is hosting shaman Stanislaus Grumman. When Lee Scoresby rents a boat to take him to Grumman's village, he finds that melting Arctic ice has caused the river to flood. The unseasonably warm temperatures have turned its banks into a foul, insect-infested swamp.

The Yenisei is the subject of the woodcut for chapter 10 of *THE SUBTLE KNIFE*, "The Shaman."

NL/GC by Scoresby to Lyra regarding Grumman 13

SK   seal hunter, Umaq on Grumman's whereabouts and 6; Scoresby's journey on 10; Scoresby and Grumman enter Cittàgazze a day and a half after leaving 14 *[brief]*; *LS* Lantern Slide 1

ZAIRE ⚕

World: Will's

Role: This African nation figures in an adventure story involving a leopard that John Parry tells the physicist Nelson in Alaska, after discovering that the scientist is also looking for the entrance to another world. Parry's aim is to disarm Nelson by making himself appear to be the stereotypical explorer—hired more for his muscle and guts than for his brains.

SK   5 *[brief]*

Places and Peoples:
Structures & Streets

ABBEY OF ST JOHANN ❖
World: Lyra's
Role: Farder Coram mentions this as being the nearest location to Lapland he knows of where reference books used for making alethiometer readings can be found.
Facts: *In Will's world there is an Abbey of St Johann in Müstair, Switzerland, which has been designated a UNESCO human culture site of international importance because of its frescoes, created at the time of Charlemagne's reign and the abbey's founding around 800.*
NL/GC 10 *[brief]*

ABINGDON LOCK [*See* The Oxfords]

ABYSS [*See* The Alethiometer, the Subtle Knife, and the Amber Spyglass: The Alethiometer]

ADAMANT TOWER ✎
World: Asriel's republic
Role: Situated on the highest rampart of Asriel's basalt fortress, its rooms, which provide views in all directions, serve as Asriel's command post and living quarters. The rooms are furnished with a table, chairs, map chest, camp bed, and coal brazier. The flag flying on the pole atop the tower is not described.
    The title of chapter 5 of THE AMBER SPYGLASS is "The Adamant Tower."
Facts: *Adamant comes from the Greek word for diamond and means indestructible.*
    In Milton's Paradise Lost, *Satan and the other fallen angels are confined in hell by "gates of burning adamant" (Book II, line 436).*
AS   described, Baruch visits 5; Roke receives message 12 [brief]; Coulter Asriel's prisoner in, meeting of high commanders 16; Coulter rests as Ogunwe and Asriel watch approach of Clouded Mountain, conference with high commanders and Basilides, Asriel and Coulter review their past 28

ALAMO [*See* Alamo, Alamo Gulch (the gulch) in **Cities, Countries, Regions, Continents & Elements of Topography**]

ANBARIC PARK [*See* The Oxfords]

ARMOURY ✎
World: Asriel's republic
Role: Located beneath the basalt fortress, this is where the arms for Asriel's republic are devised, manufactured, and stored.

Pandemonium

Chapter 16 of THE AMBER SPYGLASS is named "The Intention Craft"; the presentation of this machine is the climax of the tour of Asriel's armoury. The epigraph for this chapter is taken from *Paradise Lost* [See **Epigraphs**].

Hurled into hell, Satan and the other rebel angels contemplate their next move and decide to check out the prophesized creation of a new world and new type of being (earth and man). Whether they will re-wage the war on heaven or move the battle to this new world, the rebels prepare for war, and Pandemonium arises "… in an hour/ What in an age they [human nations] with incessant toil / And hands innumerable scarce perform." (I, 697-99)

Asriel and his followers in remarkably little time constructed a massive munitions factory, which, like Satan's, was built within the center of a hill or mountain ("opened into the hill a spacious wound" [I, 689]), through which flowed "a river of sulphurous molten metal" ("veins of liquid fire" [I, 701]) into "row upon row of moulds" ("a various mould" [I, 704]).

But while the lamps of Satan's arena are suspended from the roof and "yielded light / As from a sky" (I, 729-30), Asriel's factory foregoes lighting from torches, pillars, or sconces and uses instead "crystals… scattered loosely on the floor" that provide light but no heat.

Access from the adamant tower begins with a long flight of stairs lit by flaring sconces. The stairs descend from the battlements into a great hall, where "glowing crystals" are set into massive pillars. An electric train provides transport into the very noisy, very hot armoury. The air is foul with the stench of sulphur. All machines seem to be of a monstrous scale: there are hammers "the size of houses," rivers of molten metal, and "gigantic slicing machines" that cut, then "pressed sheets of inch-thick iron as if it were tissue-paper."

Further down, manufacturing is replaced by mining in a cool, quieter cavern "where stalactites hung gleaming with strange colors." From here, a large section of the mountain has been removed. Enormous iron doors open onto a launching pad and runway.

Lord Asriel takes his three high commanders—Xaphania, King Ogunwe, and Lord Roke, along with his captive, Mrs Coulter, on a tour of the armoury, which ends with his unveiling of an intention craft and Mrs Coulter's hijacking of it.

AS first use of term, tour of 16
  brief mentions: description of fortress's "arsenals and magazines" 5, compared to Byrnison's forge 15 [unnamed]

ASHMOLEAN MUSEUM [*See* The Oxfords]

BALLIOL COLLEGE [*See* The Oxfords]

BANBURY ROAD [*See* The Oxfords]

BASALT FORTRESS 🔖 ✐ ⑩

World: Asriel's republic

Role: Asriel's command center. So named because its "battlements were formed of single slabs of basalt half a hill in height," it is situated at the "end of a range of saw-toothed mountains." Outside the fortress, it is cold and windy, but beneath it are arsenals and forges powered by volcanic fires.

The basalt fortress is the subject of the woodcuts for "Æsahættr," chapter 13 of THE SUBTLE KNIFE and chapter 5, "The Adamant Tower" in the **10TH** anniversary edition of THE AMBER SPYGLASS [*See also* **Adamant Tower, Armoury**].

Facts: *Basalt is an igneous rock formed of volcanic lava. The natural highways in the mulefa's world are formed of basalt.*

Lydia Ondrusek

Basalt Columns

Note: *Also included are references to* the fortress, *if the fortress considered is Asriel's basalt fortress.*

SK Skadi and angels approach 6, Skadi tells Serafina and witches of her visit to 13

AS described, Baruch attacked outside, guards bring inside 5; underground halls connected by anbaric locomotive railway, factories, armoury, hangar for intention craft 16 [unnamed]; Coulter tells MacPhail about 24; Coulter and Asriel return to, kingdom's forces approach, Lyra and Will's dæmons sighted near, Asriel puts Ogunwe in charge of defending 28; kingdom and republic battle on plains below 29; Xaphania's troops find fissure beneath, Lyra and Will encounter cliff ghasts below 30; Will breaks open crystal litter, Iorek enters battle, Will and Lyra find dæmons, ghosts of Parry and Scoresby dissipate below 31 [unnamed]
brief mentions: spies' communications with 9, factories of compared to Iorek's forge 15, by Tialys 13, 19

Basalt

Basalt is the most common rock in the earth's crust. The Moon's basins are basaltic, and basalt is one of the constituents of some meteors. Its origin is volcanic, that is, it is an igneous rock, raised from the earth's mantle by the tremendous heat of an eruption. Although basalt deposits are generally unremarkable, one natural characteristic in particular of basalt is of interest in imagining Lord Asriel's fortress.

In some cases, following volcanic eruptions, basalt or densely pooled lava cooled slowly into even, long, symmetrical columns that look as if they are manmade. The columns appear jointed together; the joints are caused by cracks that occur as the basalt cooled. Usually the columns are hexagonal.

Examples of basalt columns are found in such widely separated spots as the Giant's Causeway in County Antrim, Northern Ireland; and the Devil's Postpile in east-central California, near Yosemite National Park.

BELVEDERE

World: Cittàgazze
Role: Described as a small, circular, temple-like building with a portico, its top floor is an observation area defined not by walls, but by open arches. An iron circular staircase in the room's center dominates the interior; the building is unfurnished except for sculptures of goddesses set within niches in the walls. Will and Lyra, besieged by a violent mob of Spectre-orphans, hoped to find refuge within the building, but instead were trapped when the staircase collapsed. They are rescued from there by the arrival of a troop of Serafina Pekkala's witches.

"The Belvedere" is the title of chapter 11 of *THE SUBTLE KNIFE* and the subject of that chapter's woodcut.
Facts: *A belvedere is a building designed to provide good views of pleasing surroundings. A pantiled roof is made of*

> **Philip Pullman on the belvedere woodcut for Chapter 11 of *THE SUBTLE KNIFE* (UK editions):**
>
> "This building was actually designed by Andrea Palladio in the sixteenth century, but I don't know if it was ever built. I copied it from his design."

clay S-shaped tiles. The top curve of one fits into the bottom curve of the next tile and so on. Since no overlapping is involved, a sloped, pantiled roof would be hard to climb up, because there would be no edges to rest the foot against or to grip. This is fortunate for Will and Lyra, as the Spectre-orphans are reduced to crawling slowly up the tiles on their hands and knees. Roof edge gutters insure that Will and Lyra don't simply slide off when they make their way over broken tiles to get off the building.

Note: *Other than on the page that begins chapter 11, the word* belvedere *is not used in* THE SUBTLE KNIFE. *It does appear at the end of* THE AMBER SPYGLASS; *Will uses it when he thanks Serafina Pekkala for coming to the rescue in Cittàgazze.*

SK   described but not named, attack by Spectre-orphans, arrival of witches 11

AS   first use of term in by Will in farewell to Serafina 38 *[brief]*

BERLIN ACADEMY ❖ ⚲ ⑩

World: Lyra's

Role: The sponsor of Stanislaus Grumman's last trip North, the Berlin Academy is very likely the same as the Imperial German Academy, the "Academy in Berlin" and "German Academy."

NL/GC Asriel mentions Academy in Berlin, German Academy in presentation at Jordan 2 *[brief]*

SK   fur-trader and scientists at observatory on Nova Zembla discuss Grumman and 6; Grumman tells Scoresby about 10

10TH: *SK* appendix

BOATYARD, PORT MEADOW [*See* Port Meadow *in* The Oxfords]

BODLEY'S LIBRARY [*See* The Oxfords]

BOLVANGAR ❖ ⚲ ✎

World: Lyra's

Role: The title of Part Two of *NORTHERN LIGHTS/ THE GOLDEN COMPASS* is "Bolvangar"; the title of chapter 14 in these books is "Bolvangar Lights."

The word *Bolvangar* is used throughout *HIS DARK MATERIALS* to refer to the General Oblation Board's Experimental Station, where the Board tests experimental techniques for severing children from their dæmons. The term originated with the witches, who translate "Bolvangar" as meaning "fields of evil."

Lyra first hears the word used by witch Serafina Pekkala's dæmon Kaisa, who comes to gives the gyptians directions on how to reach the site and some information about its security forces. He adds, "There is an air of hatred and fear over the place… Animals keep away."

Founded ten years ago by Mrs Coulter and paid for by the church, it is a four days' march northeast of Trollesund (a port city of Norroway), into an uninhabited, remote inland area. The Station is supposedly an outpost of the Northern Progress Exploration Company, which is in Norroway under the pretense of searching for minerals, according to Witch-Consul Martin Lanselius. Lanselius is aware that this company "imports children" but says that this is not generally known by the townspeople of Trollesund, nor is the Norroway government "officially aware" of the company's true purpose. However, according to Iorek Byrnison, the people of the town know what is going on but "they pretend not to see, because the child-cutters bring money and business." | 104 | 105

When Iorek Byrnison is restored as the rightful king of the armoured bears, the former counselors of the usurper Iofur Raknison reveal that Coulter had planned another experiment station for Svalbard like that at Bolvangar.

The Bolvangar complex, surrounded by an electrified fence and guarded by Northern Tartars, is constructed of metal and concrete with tunnels linking most of its buildings. Its power needs are supplied by imported coal spirit.

The Station's "brilliantly lit" interior has a "faint perpetual hospital-medical smell" and "coming from the walls all around was a slight humming sound, almost too low to hear, the sort of sound you had to get used to or go mad." The ceiling is made of | 106 translucent, moveable panels. The foyer is designed as an airlock to provide a transition from the bitter cold outdoors to the overheated interior. Corridors extend in either direction from the foyer. These lead to a cafeteria with twelve round tables, steel trolleys, and a hatch where children receive their food and return their dishes; a nurses' lounge; the kitchen, and store rooms.

Thirty to forty boys and girls are housed in dormitory rooms with moveable lockers, and there is a co-ed recreation room. Examination rooms range from those for conducting in-take evaluations that have couch beds, filing cabinets, cupboards, first aid materials, and showers; to those housing specialized laboratory equipment. Behind the front office is the conference room, designed to hold roughly twenty adults and used for demonstrations and lectures. Mrs Coulter has her own private room at the Station, pleasantly scented and softly lit.

Other structures include a zeppelin mooring mast and, unconnected to any other, a "squat, square" locked shed about seven feet high for storing severed dæmons in stacked | 107 glass cases.

The most closely guarded secret of Bolvangar is the device for severing person and dæmon: the silver guillotine. This device is kept in a "chamber with dazzling white tiles and stainless steel" protected by a heavy door that "opened by means of a large wheel," | 108 like a bank vault's lock.

On her way to Svalbard, Lyra, now safely in Lee Scoresby's balloon, hears from Serafina Pekkala that the gyptians "have laid waste to Bolvangar... killed twenty-two guards and nine of the staff, and they've set light to every part of the buildings that still stood. They are going to destroy it completely." | 109

Note: *Also known as* the Station; *chapter references include those to* the Station *as well as Bolvangar, and those describing its rooms.*

SK   torture of witch captured at, discussed in witches' council 2; Skadi on 13
　　　brief mentions: sounds in Mary's Cave and 4; Lyra thinks of on her way to Headington 7, when
　　　she sees Coulter at Latrom's 9, and talks to Will about Serafina 11; Grumman and
　　　Scoresby on 14; Lena Feldt and 15

AS   MacPhail on 6; Lyra recalls to Iorek to persuade him to fix knife 14
　　　brief mentions: Roke on Court's interrogations and 5, Lyra remembers going to find Roger at
　　　13, Coulter on saving Lyra at 16, Lyra thinks of when leaving Pan 21, by Roger's ghost to
　　　Lyra 23, Dr. Cooper and 24, by Serafina to dæmons 36

Botanic Garden, The (the garden) [*See* The Oxfords]

Bridge, Asriel's ✦ ⚑

World: Lyra's to Cittàgazze

Role: Lord Asriel tells Lyra on the night she arrives at his "prison" in Svalbard that if light can cross from one world to another (and seeing the city beyond the aurora means it can), then, given enough energy, it must be possible to build a bridge to that world. That same night he achieves his aim.

But there are costs, beginning with Lyra's friend's Roger's life. Severing the child from his dæmon is Asriel's source of the extraordinary energy surge needed to break through the aurora. Other costs of his bridge include extreme climactic changes in his own world, and, in Cittàgazze world, a massive influx of Spectres.

What Asriel gains for himself is freedom from the threat of execution as a heretic and the chance to establish his republic of heaven. The creation of the bridge begins a series of events culminating in one great blow against the Authority.

When Lyra and Pan walk over Asriel's bridge into Cittàgazze world, what is set in motion is the journey leading her to Will, and Will to the subtle knife, and both to the world of the dead, where Will cuts a window allowing the ghosts of the dead to escape their consignment to a world of endless emptiness and hopelessness.

The first mention of Asriel's bridge is when the witch Serafina Pekkala's dæmon Kaisa visits the gyptians searching for their children. He says "Dust-hunters," the witches' term for the Oblation Board, think Asriel will somehow use Dust "to make a bridge between this world and the world beyond the Aurora."

"The Bridge to the Stars" is the title of the last chapter of *Northern Lights/The Golden Compass*. Lyra's and Pan's decision to walk away from their world is not followed by a description of the bridge they (and Asriel) traverse, and the word "bridge" is not used again until *The Subtle Knife*. Lyra tells Will that she got to the Cittàgazze world by walking across a bridge her father had built.

Interestingly, before she reaches Asriel's bridge, Lyra must cross a fragile bridge of packed snow, leaving behind Iorek Byrnison since the bridge cannot bear his weight. When it falls away completely into what appears to be a great chasm or abyss after she reaches the other side, Lyra can no longer turn back.

NL/GC Kaisa on 11; Serafina on 18 [brief]; Asriel tells Lyra his plan 21; in title of last chapter, Asriel
　　　then Lyra cross 23

SK   *brief mentions:* by Lyra to Will 1, 3

BURGER KING [*See* The Oxfords]

CAFÉ 1, CITTÀGAZZE ⚑

World: Cittàgazze

Role: Will is attracted to this café on a broad boulevard located near the Oxford/Cittàgazze Sunderland Avenue window. It has green tables for outdoor seating on the sidewalk it fronts, and a zinc-topped bar inside. A cooler is stocked with bottled lemonade.

SK *brief mentions:* described, Will buys lemonade 1; reference point for finding window to Oxford 3, 5

CAFÉ 2, CITTÀGAZZE ⚑✎

World: Cittàgazze

Role: Will decides he needs to find a place to spend the night in this strangely deserted world. He can't see himself in the city's grand hotels, but is instead drawn to a café with living quarters above it. On the café walls are photos of boxers and accordion players. The kitchen is fairly well stocked with food, although some has spoiled. On the second floor is an apartment with a layout similar to Will's home in Winchester. A narrow flight of stairs leads to a front room opening onto the landing, a bath, and two bedrooms. This is where Lyra bursts into his life.

SK public areas and private rooms above described, Will and Lyra meet, Will cooks dinner in 1; Lyra cooks, breakfast at sidewalk tables and discussions with city's children 3; Will tends to hurt cat, reads father's letters in 5; Lyra arrives with news of theft 7 [unnamed]; Lyra tends Will's wounds, Will takes letters, he and Lyra depart for last time 9

AS *brief mentions:* Lyra and Will remember first meeting at 37, Will, Lyra, Mary, and Serafina walk by 38

BROAD, THE [*See* The Oxfords]

CHAPEL (JORDAN COLLEGE) [*See* Jordan College *in* The Oxfords]

CHAPEL OF THE HOLY PENITENCE ✎

World: Lyra's

Role: Near the College of St Jerome in Geneva, the headquarters for the Consistorial Court of Discipline.

AS 24 [*brief*]

CLARICE WALK [*See* Limehouse *in* Cities, Countries, Regions]

CLAYBEDS [*See* The Oxfords]

COLLEGE OF IZMIR ✤

World: Lyra's

Role: In a tall tale Lyra tells when she is living on the Costa family's narrow boat in the Fens, the Sultan of Turkey directs his Ambassador, a member of the College of Izmir, to poison Lord Asriel during a visit to Jordan College. The Ambassador sprinkles a powder in Asriel's glass, but Asriel sees what the man has done. Lord Asriel then proposes a toast, and suggests that he drink from the Turk's glass and the Turk from his, to symbolize the friendship between Jordan College and the College of Izmir. The Turk is caught; he can't refuse, so he drinks and dies an agonizing death.

Observation: *Lyra's story merges two actual events she has witnessed: the Master of Jordan College's attempt to poison Lord Asriel, and John Faa's account of Lord Asriel negotiating with "the Turk" to save a gyptian's life.*

Facts: *There is an Izmir. Located on the Aegean Sea, this ancient city, founded around 3000 BC, is the third largest in Turkey today. The Greek form of its name is* Smyrna, *which readers of* LYRA'S OXFORD *may recall as the destination stop circled on a brochure for the S.S.* Zenobia *cruise to the Levant, an area very roughly corresponding to ancient and contemporary nations of the Holy Land, e.g. Palestine, Israel, Lebanon, Syria, Jordan, etc.*

NL/GC 8 [brief]

COLLEGE OF ST JEROME ✎

World: Lyra's

Role: Located near Lake Geneva, the College serves as the headquarters of the Consistorial Court of Discipline. The College features tall spires, cloisters, and gables. The Court's president, Fr MacPhail has rooms in a square tower; they are austere and unpleasant.

Dr Cooper, formerly employed at the General Oblation Board's Bolvangar Experiment Station is a "guest" in the stark chambers of the College's cellars, where he has been "invited" to reconstruct all that was learned at his former job site about the energy released through intercision.

Mrs Coulter parks the stolen intention craft on a rooftop of the college, removes several roof tiles, drops into an attic, and picks a lock to the kitchen to gain access to the street. Thus, she is able to enter through the main gate. She ends up locked in a guest room, which like the rest of the facility, is shabbily furnished and ineptly bugged, and then chained in its cellars awaiting intercision.

AS   Court conducts interrogation of Pavel, MacPhail announces plans, visit to its cellars, MacPhail and Gomez conspire, Tialys in residence at 6; Coulter arrives and meets with MacPhail, her locked room, MacPhail's conference with Cooper, Roke's attack on Louis, Coulter's removal to cellars of 24

CORNMARKET STREET [*See* The Oxfords]

COVERED MARKET [*See* The Oxfords]

CRYPT [*See* Jordan College *in* The Oxfords]

Coulter's apartment ❖

World: Lyra's

Role: Frills, flounces, flowers, and pretty things abound in Mrs Coulter's London apartment and seem grand and elegant to Lyra, who has lived her life in a shabby room with mismatched furniture. Coulter's rooms are brightly lit, wallpapered in gold and white, and carpeted in leaf green. Gilt-framed pictures hang on its walls, and tabletops hold Coulter's collection of "pretty little china boxes and shepherdesses and harlequins of porcelain." The bathroom is pretty in pink, and the curtains of Lyra's charming carpeted bedroom are decorated with suns, stars, and moons.

NL/GC Lyra's arrival, described, compared to Jordan 4; cocktail party at, Lyra flees 5; mentioned by Coulter to Lyra at Bolvangar 17 *[brief]*

Dark Matter Research group/Unit (Mary's lab) [*See* The Oxfords]

Denmark Street [*See* Limehouse *in* Cities, Countries, Regions]

Department of Physical Sciences [*See* The Oxfords]

Eelmarket ❖

World: Lyra's

Role: One of the few permanent structures in the gyptians' Fens homeland, it is located near their zaal, or meeting hall. Eels are a staple in gyptian cuisine.

NL/GC 7 *[brief]*

Einarsson's Bar ❖

World: Lyra's

Role: Iorek Byrnison lived behind this dump on Langlokur Street under "a crude concrete shed with a red neon sign flashing irregularly over the door" during his exile from Svalbard. At Bolvangar, Lyra, trying to account to her mother for the months since she ran away from Coulter's apartment, claims to have been employed as a barmaid at this establishment.

NL/GC Lyra visits Iorek at with Coram 10 and alone 11; Lyra tells Coulter she worked as a maid at 17 *[brief]*

Embankment, the ❖

World: Lyra's

Role: Mrs Coulter lives on the north side of the Embankment in an upscale London neighborhood. Although her street is a main thoroughfare, many small, less-frequented streets connect to it, and Lyra takes to these when she runs away.

NL/GC brief mentions: Lyra's arrival at Coulter's 4, and departure 6

EXPERIMENTAL STATION [*See* Bolvangar]

FALKESHALL GARDENS ❖

World: Lyra's

Role: This is where the zeppelin from Oxford carrying Coulter and Lyra lands, at which point a boat takes them to the Embankment's exclusive "mansion-blocks" and Coulter's home.

NL/GC 4

FISH-HOUSE ❖ ⚷

World: Lyra's

Role: As the gyptians are traveling from Trollesund to Bolvangar, the alethiometer tells Lyra that in a village a few hours off their route is a strange boy. Lyra can't interpret in what way this boy is unusual, but fearing it could be Roger, she convinces John Faa to let Iorek Byrnison take her there.

In a small settlement by a lake, they are directed to a "narrow wooden shack" on a jetty. There among the racks for drying gutted fish they find Gobbler victim Tony Makarios. The severed child clutches a frozen fish, and pleads for the return of his dæmon.

NL/GC Iorek and Lyra arrive at 12, and remove Tony from 13

GABRIEL COLLEGE [*See* The Oxfords]

GERMAN ACADEMY [*See* Berlin Academy]

HALL, THE (DINING) [*See* The Oxfords]

HANGMAN'S WHARF [*See* Limehouse *in* Cities, Countries, Regions]

HIGH STREET [*See* The Oxfords]

IMPERIAL GERMAN ACADEMY [*See* Berlin Academy]

IMPERIAL MUSCOVITE ACADEMY ⚷

World: Lyra's

Role: Its facilities include an observatory on Nova Zembla, which aëronaut Lee Scoresby visits in his quest for information about shaman and scientist Stanislaus Grumman.

SK 6 *[brief]*

INSTITUTE OF ARCHAEOLOGY [*See* The Oxfords]

JORDAN COLLEGE (THE COLLEGE) [*See* The Oxfords]

KING GEORGE'S STEPS [*See* Limehouse *in* Cities, Countries, Regions]

LANGLOKUR STREET [*See* Einarsson's Bar]

LIBRARY, JORDAN COLLEGE [*See* Jordan College *in* The Oxfords]

LIBRARY GARDEN, JORDAN COLLEGE [*See* The Oxfords]

LIMEFIELD HOUSE [*See* The Oxfords]

LODGE [*See* Jordan College *in* The Oxfords]

MAGDALEN BRIDGE [*See* The Oxfords]

MAGDALEN COLLEGE [*See* The Oxfords]

MASTER'S LODGING [*See* Jordan College *in* The Oxfords]

MELROSE QUADRANGLE [*See* Jordan College *in* The Oxfords]

MINISTRY OF DEFENSE ⚲

World: Will's

Role: Provides funding for the physicist Nelson's participation in the Oxford University Institute of Archaeology survey in Alaska, from which three men, including John Parry, disappeared in 1985.

Parry's suspicions of the true nature of Nelson's presence among the archaeologists is aroused when he finds that the crate supposedly holding Nelson's weather balloons is instead packed with radiation suits. Moreover, Parry knows what financial codes the Ministry of Defense uses on its paperwork, and, he writes home to his wife, he has seen those on Nelson's forms.

SK 5 *[brief]*

MINISTRY OF THEOLOGY ✦

World: Lyra's

Role: Gobblers captured by gyptian Benjamin de Ruyter confessed that the headquarters of the General Oblation Board was located in the Ministry of Theology. Along with several others, de Ruyter is killed in the Ministry's building in White Hall while trying to discover the whereabouts of the children abducted by the Gobblers.

NL/GC 9

NORTH AMERICAN ARCTIC SURVEY STATION ⇟

World: Will's

Role: Will's search for information about his father's disappearance uncovers several articles about the expedition in Alaska sponsored by Oxford University's Institute of Archaeology from which John Parry and two other team members disappeared. One reported that the team had reached the North American Arctic Survey Station at Noatak, Alaska; the next, two months later, announced that Parry and two other men were presumed missing since they had not replied to any communication signals sent into the mountains from this station.

SK   4 [brief]

OBSERVATORY (IMPERIAL MUSCOVITE ACADEMY'S) ⇟

World: Lyra's

Role: Owned by the Imperial Muscovite Academy and located on Nova Zembla, the Observatory is staffed by a multi-national team. Aëronaut Lee Scoresby hires a Tartar sledge driver to take him there on his quest for information about Stanislaus Grumman. The Observatory complex includes the main domed observatory, a smaller one, office buildings, and a residence hall. Its windows are blackened.

The astronomers are free with their impressions of Grumman, offering conflicting tales of his interests, but when asked about Dust, they defer to the Skraeling Censor for the Magisterium.

SK   6

ORATORY, JORDAN COLLEGE [*See* Jordan College *in* The Oxfords]

PALACE OF IOFUR RAKNISON ❈⇟

World: Lyra's

Role: Iofur Raknison, the prince who succeeded exiled Iorek Byrnison, longs to be a human, and has imposed on his subjects many human ways, whether remotely adaptable to bears or not. Rather than living in the traditional ice fort of the Svalbard bears, Raknison has built himself a palace, more massive than Jordan College and with a soaring watchtower.

Into its massive stone walls have been carved fantasy tableaux of vanquished Skraelings and Tartars toiling as slaves in the bears' mines; others feature conveyances from all parts of the world voyaging to Svalbard with presents for its king. Ironically, for the most part, the carvings can't be seen because the walls are streaked with bird droppings.

In the relative warmth of the castle's interior, bird droppings form only a small part of the stench emanating from the filth of blood, rancid blubber, animal waste and wasted parts of devoured beasts, all of which have fallen to the ground, seemingly never to be removed, and none of which fazes the bears.

Lyra and Pantalaimon find themselves in the dungeon of this castle after falling from Lee Scoresby's balloon. The armoured bears she meets there seem ill at ease in their surroundings, clothing, and responsibilities.

The stench of Raknison's inner sanctum is the worst yet: heavy perfume is added to the already odiferous mixture. The ante-chambers boast a "preposterous decoration: the walls were rich with gilt plasterwork… and the florid carpets were trodden with filth." Seabirds nesting on cornices and in chandeliers continue to add to the filth through which Lyra must trudge toward Raknison's throne of granite. This monstrosity could have seemed imposing were it not "decorated with over-elaborate swags and festoons of gilt that looked like tinsel on a mountainside." ₁₁₈

The palace grounds include a combat arena for dueling, with stands for spectators, including a special area for she-bears. Here, Iorek Byrnison wins back his throne as his subjects watch. And as soon as the restored King Byrnison finished eating the heart of the defeated, his subjects "swarmed to the Palace and began to hurl great blocks of marble from the top-most towers… over the cliffs to crash on the jetty hundreds of feet below." ₁₁₉

NL/GC mentioned in Retiring Room 2; Lyra taken to 18; Raknison's chambers 19; tournament at, destruction of 20; Lyra discusses with Asriel 21

SK Latrom's odor reminds Lyra of 4 *[brief]*

PALMER'S TOWER [*See* Jordan College *in* The Oxfords]

PARLEY ROOM ✦

World: Lyra's

Role: Located in the gyptians' Zaal or meeting hall, the parley room is a parlor, a place for conversation, not unlike Jordan College's Retiring Room. It has a fireplace, sideboards for silver and porcelain serving pieces, and a large table with seating for twelve. It is here that Lyra meets with gyptian leaders John Faa and Farder Coram, and learns about her own past.

Facts: *Parler is French for "to talk"; in English,* parley *commonly means to converse casually, as in Mrs Coulter's comment to the Consistorial Court of Discipline's Brother Louis that he had better take her to its president Fr MacPhail because she didn't make her way to Geneva just "to parley with a scrivener."* ₁₂₀

NL/GC Lyra's visit with Faa and Coram 7; Lyra intrudes during Faa's and council's meeting 8

PHYSICS (SCIENCE) BUILDING, OXFORD UNIVERSITY [*See* The Oxfords]

PIE STREET, LONDON [*See* Limehouse *in* Cities, Countries, Regions]

PILGRIM'S TOWER [*See* Limehouse *in* Cities, Countries, Regions]

PITT-RIVERS MUSEUM [*See* The Oxfords]

PRIEST'S HOUSE, TROLLESUND ✦ ₁₂₁

World: Lyra's

Role: The officials of Trollesund hid Iorek Byrnison's armour in the cellar of this older house, which is "made of costly bricks." The front door and windows of the house are the worse for wear after Byrnison's unauthorized reclamation of his stolen property.

Observation: *The home of Otyets (Father) Semyon Borisovitch, the village priest in Kholodnoye, Siberia, is the biggest on its road. Homes that are larger or made of finer materials than their parishioners' is something the priests of Trollesund and Kholodnoye*

share in common.
NL/GC 11

Retiring Room [*See* Jordan College *in* The Oxfords]

Ring road [*See* The Oxfords]

Royal Arctic Institute/Royal Arctic Society ✧

World: Lyra's

Role: This was one of Lyra's favorite places to visit in London when she lived with Mrs Coulter, one of the Institute's few female members. Coulter had impressed Lyra by pointing out in its dining room a number of well known explorers, including Dr Broken Arrow and Colonel Carborn. She showed Lyra the exhibits in the Institute's library of the original items used on famous polar expeditions and took her to meetings and lectures for its members.

It is a twenty-minute walk through narrow streets from Coulter's Embankment residence, and the only location in London Lyra feels confident she can find when she runs away.

If the Royal Arctic Institute and the Royal Arctic Society are the same, Lyra hears of it again from Jotham Santelia, Lyra's cellmate at Iofur Raknison's palace on Svalbard. Santelia has ambitions of becoming the Vice-Chancellor of the university the bear-king plans to establish on Svalbard—presumably for armoured bears.

NL/GC Lyra and Coulter's lunch at 4; Santelia rages against 19
brief mentions: events at 5, location of 6

Royal Geological Museum ⚑

World: Lyra's

Role: When Lyra visits the Pitt-Rivers museum in Will's world's Oxford, she compares it to the Royal Geological Museum which she once visited with Mrs Coulter in their own London.

Observation: *No such visit is recorded in* Northern Lights/The Golden Compass. *Perhaps Lyra is thinking about the Royal Arctic Institute's display areas.*

Facts: *In Will's world's London, the neighboring Natural History Museum absorbed the Geological Museum of the British Geological Survey in 1986.*

SK   4 [*brief*]

Rutherford Appleton ⑩

World: Will's

Role: A stray page from a letter included in the appendix to the **10th** anniversary edition of *The Amber Spyglass* records Mary Malone's request of a friend or colleague for help in reserving a block of time at a facility where 100 terrawatts of power, a laser and cooling system would be available for an experiment. She notes that while Rutherford Appleton could accommodate her needs, she wouldn't be able to get on their schedule for months, and she feels she is on the verge of a discovery.

Observation: *Philip Pullman's April 2005 newsletter (www.philip-pullman.com) describes a visit to the Rutherford Appleton Laboratory in Oxfordshire, where studies of dark matter and dark energy are devised, and the lab's plans for an underground facility in Yorkshire to shield their search for specific particles from interference by ground-level radiation.*

10TH: *AS appendix*

SAMIRSKY HOTEL ⚑

World: Lyra's

Role: Lee Scoresby, in his quest for information about Stanislaus Grumman, visits the Samirsky's bar and buys rounds of drinks to keep its patrons—trappers, traders, and others looking for work in the Arctic—talking about the mysterious shaman.

SK 6

SENIOR COMMON ROOM (OR SCHOLARS' COMMON ROOM) [*See* Jordan College *in* The Oxfords]

SHELDON BUILDING [*See* The Oxfords]

SMOKEMARKET [*See* Colby *in* Cities, Countries, Regions]

SOUTH PARADE [*See* The Oxfords]

SPEAKING GROUND (GATHERING-GROUND) ✎

World: Mulefa's

Role: This is a meeting place where mulefa from different villages gather to address issues of common concern, the mulefa equivalent of the Eastern Anglia gyptians' zaal. A low, carefully shaped mound with access ramps serves as a platform. Here, the elder zalif Sattamax asks Mary Malone's help in diagnosing the cause of the failure of the seedpod trees.

AS described, Sattamax's speech 17; Mary's report 20; gyptians welcomed at ("gathering ground") 38

ST BARNABAS THE CHYMIST [*See* The Oxfords]

ST CATHERINE'S ORATORY ✦

World: Lyra's

Role: Site of Mrs Coulter's first appearance in *HIS DARK MATERIALS*. The premier Gobbler, she emerges, jewel-embellished prayer book in hand, to lure Limehouse street urchin Tony Makarios with the promise of hot chocolatl to the warehouse through which the General Oblation Board processes its victims.

NL/GC 3 *[brief]*

ST JOHN'S COLLEGE [*See* The Oxfords]

St Michael's Chapel [*See* The Oxfords]

St Michael's College [*See* The Oxfords]

St Peter's ⚜

World: Will's

Role: Will guesses England must have a number of St Peter's schools, and so offers this name when answering questions about why he is alone in Oxford on a school day. He says he has its approval to visit Oxford to conduct research into the Institute of Archaeology survey in Alaska from which three men disappeared in 1985.

SK   4 [brief]

St Sophia's College [*See* The Oxfords]

Staircase Twelve [*See* Jordan College *in* The Oxfords]

Station [*See* Bolvangar]

Sunderland Avenue [*See* The Oxfords]

Torre degli Angeli/Tower of Angels, tower ⚜ ✎

World: Cittàgazze

Role: The Torre degli Angeli, or Tower of Angels, was once the center for Cittàgazze's Philosophers' Guild, the creators of the subtle knife. With the recent huge plague of Spectres, any remaining Guild members have fled the Tower and the town like the rest of the city's adults. The only remaining inhabitant of the Tower is the bearer of the subtle knife, Giacomo Paradisi.

The Tower of Angels stands at one end of a small square plaza. On two sides are narrow alleys paved with cobblestones. At its rear is a wall topped with broken glass to repel intruders to the formal herb garden and the fountain it encloses. The structure is a four-story "square stone tower;" it has flagstone floors and a blackened oak staircase. Carved angels with folded wings flank its doorway, and the interior is reminiscent of a museum, with swords, shields, and spears on the walls. But it is dark, with the only light coming from small, deeply recessed windows.

One floor is devoted to a poorly preserved library. On the roof are a battlemented parapet, square gutters, and a greenhouse-type structure.

When she heads off to Will's Oxford alone and passes the Tower, Lyra is inexplicably scared to enter the building and, although she doesn't know its significance, feels compelled to get away. Pantalaimon's reaction to her initial plan to explore the Tower reminds Lyra of his behavior when she switched dæmon-coins in the skulls back in the Jordan College crypt.

After defeating Tullio (the would-be-bearer who has terrorized Paradisi) in a bloody struggle on its rooftop, Will is trained in the Tower's chambers to serve as the bearer of the subtle knife.

When Mary Malone and Serafina Pekkala walk through Cittàgazze a little ways behind Will and Lyra, who are getting ready to enter his Oxford and say goodbye, they casually pass "a square tower with a doorway opening into darkness," which recalls Will and Lyra's first sighting of the "simple battlemented tower" with the "half-open door," an "intriguing" structure they pass "a bit reluctantly." But to the women the tower is just another building sharing a palm-shaded boulevard with sidewalk cafes.

When Will cuts a window on the roof of the Tower into his world, he finds himself looking over a graveyard in North Oxford, close enough to Sunderland Avenue that he can see the hornbeam trees in the distance.

"The Tower of Angels" is the title of the eighth chapter of THE SUBTLE KNIFE.

Note: *The word* Torre *never appears alone.* Tower/tower *does, and the lowercase* tower *appears in both British and American editions. After the first use of the phrase* Tower of Angels, *the word* Tower *used alone is sometimes uppercased in the UK edition.*

SK   Lorenz on Guild of, first uses of "Torre degli Angeli" and "Tower of Angels" 6; Lyra and Pan apprehensive at doors of, Latrom on 7; Pan looks in windows, interior described, battle on rooftop, Will's wound treated inside, Will becomes bearer, Paradisi on Guild of 8
   brief mentions: Will and Lyra first view of described 3, cat abused by children cornered at 5 [unnamed]; Lyra on seeing Tullio through window, Will sees carrion crows circling 11, by Will of cat and kids at 13, Scoresby and Grumman fly past 14

AS   *brief mentions:* by Angelica to Gomez 10, Will remembers Tullio 13, by John Parry's ghost of Guild of 26, Mary thinks of Guild of 34, Mary and Serafina pass by, Will and Lyra share last look at 38

TOWER OF ANGELS   [*See* Torre degli Angeli]

TURL STREET   [*See* The Oxfords]

UNIVERSITY LIBRARY   [*See* Bodley's Library *and* Jordan College *in* The Oxfords]

UNIVERSITY OF GLOUCESTER ✧
World: Lyra's
Role: Jotham Santelia, Lyra's cellmate on Svalbard, was once the Regius Professor of Cosmology at this university.
Facts: *There is not a University of Gloucester in Will's world, but there is a University of Gloucestershire.*
NL/GC 19 *[brief]*

VILLA, CITTÀGAZZE ⚑
World: Cittàgazze
Role: Not far from the city of Cittàgazze is a parkland featuring a white stucco two-story villa, with both a kitchen garden and a formal garden, adorned with statues and a fountain. Behind the columned villa the land slopes upwards to a forest, and between the house and the forest is the belvedere.

The night after he retrieves the alethiometer, Lyra and Will sleep in the servants' quarters of the villa, but they must make a hasty departure in the morning when a gang of belligerent Spectre-orphans arrive.

SK   briefly described as reference point for window to Latrom's house 9; Lyra and Will stay at 11

WINE CELLARS   [*See* Jordan College *in* The Oxfords]

YAXLEY QUAD   [*See* Jordan College *in* The Oxfords]

ZAAL ✦

World: Lyra's

Role: Built of wood on the scarce high ground (or Byanflats) in the Fens, the Zaal is the meeting hall where the gyptians gather for Byanropings (or Ropings). Seating is on benches except for the heads of the six families, elder Farder Coram, and Faa, who sit on carved chairs on a raised platform. A loud bell is used to open and close the meetings. A few other permanent buildings share the raised ground with the Zaal, and there are jetties and mooring areas for the narrowboats that converge in the area. The council's conference room, the parley room, connects to the Zaal.

NL/GC described, first Roping at 7; second Roping at 8; 9 *[brief]*

ABINGDON ✤ ✐

World: Lyra's

Role: This town on the River Isis, within walking distance of Jordan College, figures in Lyra's schemes to capture a gyptian narrow boat, and its lock provides one of the details of the story Lyra tells the family in the suburbs of the world of the dead.

NL/GC brief mentions: in Lyra's plans for capturing boat 3, 4

AS brief mentions: in Lyra's tale in suburbs of world of dead 19, by Lyra in lie to harpies 21, in Lyra's true story 23

ABINGDON LOCK [*See* Abingdon]

ANBARIC PARK ✤

World: Lyra's

Role: Lyra is reminded of the antennas and transformers at the Anbaric Park outside Oxford when she sees one of Asriel's photograms of an Arctic scientific outpost.

NL/GC 2 [brief]

The Ashmolean Museun of Art and Archaeology, Beaumont Street, Oxford

Ian Giles

ASHMOLEAN MUSEUM ⚲

World: Will's

Role: In order to distract the police from looking at her and Will as anyone more interesting than the average lost tourists, Lyra feigns interest in, and asks directions to, this museum.

View of Oxford from Tom Tower, Christ Church College—domed building is the Radcliffe Camera, a reading room of the Bodleian Library

Penrose and Palmer

Will objects to her strategy of hiding in plain sight.

125   **Observation:** *Likely the "large museum" Will visits after leaving the Institute of Archaeology; both are on Beaumont Street.*

SK brief mentions: Will wanders into [unnamed] 4; when Lyra asks directions 5 *[brief]*

Balliol College

BALLIOL COLLEGE ⚑

World: Lyra's, Will's

Role: College in both Lyra's and Will's Oxfords. Lyra immediately recognizes it, along with Broad and Cornmarket Streets and the Bodleian Library, when she and Will enter the center of his Oxford. She is distressed to find that Jordan College, which is near these places in her Oxford, is missing.

SK 3 [brief]

Balliol College

BANBURY ROAD ⚑

World: Will's

Role: Banbury Road intersects Sunderland Avenue, the location of the Oxford window to Cittàgazze. When Lyra and Will enter his Oxford, they walk along the Banbury Road to Summertown, a neighborhood north of Central Oxford, where they board a bus. Along their way, they pass near Dr Mary Malone's lab in the cluster of science buildings of Oxford University and its adjacent parks before the Banbury Road merges with Woodstock Road near the city center.

"That en't the Cornmarket? And this is the Broad. There's Balliol. And Bodley's Library, down there. But where's Jordan?"—Lyra

126

SK Will and Lyra walk then ride a bus down to city centre on 3
      brief mentions: Lyra and Will walk up to window on 5, Latrom offers Lyra a ride near 7, Mary leaves her car on 12

BODLEY'S LIBRARY ❖⚑✎ LS

World: Lyra's, Will's

Role: Dame Hannah Relf of Sophia College in Lyra's world confirms what Lyra has long suspected: Bodley's Library houses references books for reading the alethiometer.

[*See also* **University Library**]

Inside the Bodleian Library

Update: The last Lantern Slide in THE AMBER SPYGLASS describes Lyra and Pan studying the reference books for the alethiometer in Duke Humfrey's Library.

Facts: *In Will's world, Duke Humfrey's Library, located above the Divinity School, was completed in 1488, thus predating by over a hundred years the founding by Thomas Bodley of the library that would bear his name and absorb this earlier collection. Today, Duke Humfrey's Library is the main reading room for books and manuscripts dated before 1641, including those donated by Humfrey, Duke of Gloucester (1390-1447), King Henry V's* *youngest brother.*

Observation: *Likely equivalent to the Bodleian Library of Will's Oxford. Dame Hannah Relf uses "Bodley's Library" as does Lyra, which suggests this may be its real name in Lyra's world, and not a shortened form of Bodleian.*

NL/GC alethiometer reference books and 9 *[brief]*

SK brief mentions: Lyra sees in Will's Oxford 3; Will heads to 4, Will and Lyra meet near 5 *[Note: not named as Bodley's or Bodleian in chapters 4 and 5, but area descriptions suggest "university library" mentioned at the end of Chapter 4 is Bodleian/Bodley's Library.]*

AS Relf on 38 *[brief]*, **LS** Lantern Slide 9

BOTANIC GARDEN, THE (THE GARDEN) 🖉 **LS**

World: Lyra's, Will's

Role: The title of last chapter of THE AMBER SPYGLASS is "The Botanic Garden," and the garden is the setting for Lyra and Will's last moment together and for the last scene of HIS DARK MATERIALS.

Because the Garden, located along the High Street just beyond Magdalen Bridge, exists in both Lyra's and Will's Oxfords, Lyra chooses it as the site where she and Will part. She takes Will to a bench "under a spreading low-branched tree," almost at the end of the

The Bodleian

In Will's world, Oxford University's collection of books and manuscripts dates back to at least 1490, but its library was loosely organized until Thomas Bodley in effect refounded it in 1602.

The Bodleian is now a multi-building complex, but the Old Bodleian Library and Divinity School may be what, in our Oxford, Lyra recognizes, and in her own world calls, "Bodley's Library." The main library buildings face Catte Street.

On their first visit to Will's Oxford, Lyra and Will apparently plan to meet up at the "university library." Once Lyra arrives at the bench where Will has been waiting, they 127 "walked along towards a round building with a great leaden dome, set in a square

Penrose and Palmer

Radcliffe Camera

bounded by honey-colored stone college buildings and a church." The Bodleian would be what any visitor to Oxford 128 would consider the university library, and the round building would thus be the Radcliffe Camera, an early-mid 18th century building now housing reading rooms. Leaving Radcliffe Square, they would see the University Church of St Mary the Virgin. The church structures mainly date from the 16th century, but its tower is one of the oldest still standing in Oxford, dating from the 13th century.

The Bodleian is not the library that Will would have visited earlier that day to read the newspaper accounts of his father's disappearance; he wouldn't have been allowed easy access. The most likely would have been a branch of the Oxfordshire public library system, Central Library Westgate, at the Westgate shopping complex—a short walk from the High Street offices of the Parry family lawyer and the Institute of Archaeology on Beaumont Street.

129 garden, and is pleased to see that in Will's world, the tree and seat are the same as in hers. Will and Lyra vow to one another that they will return in their own worlds each Midsummer's Day at noon, and sit for an hour, knowing that the other is doing the same.

At the Garden's gate, Will cuts his last window. Lyra and Will part in Cittàgazze before Will steps back through to the Garden in his world. When Lyra returns to her world, she finds solace in her knowledge that "in that other Oxford where she and Will had kissed good-bye, the bells would be chiming too, and a nightingale would be singing, 130 and a little breeze would be stirring the leaves in the Botanic Garden."

Facts: *Although most are open to the public, a botanic (or botanical) garden differs from a park or commerical garden attraction. Its primary purpose is educational, and emphasis is on including species of interest to plant research scientists associated with its sponsoring institution. The Botanic Garden Will and Lyra visit is part of Oxford University.*

AS 38, ⟦*LS*⟧ Lantern Slides 5, 9

Ian Giles

Behind the bicycles and iron fence, at the intersection of Broad and Cornmarket Streets, the St Mary Magdalen churchyard can be seen. This could be the "old stone church" Lyra recognizes as also belonging to her world's Oxford.

BRIDGE [*See* **Magdalen Bridge**]

BROAD, THE ⚑

World: Lyra's, Will's

Role: Street in Lyra's and Will's Oxford where they disembark the bus that they boarded on Banbury Road.

Facts: *Broad Street (which like many Oxonians in Will's world Lyra calls "the Broad") is in close proximity to Balliol College, the Bodleian Library, a particular stone church, and Cornmarket Street.*

SK 3 *[brief]*

BURGER KING ⚑

World: Will's

Role: Where a weary Will eats in Oxford. He has spent the day on the road from Winchester, hitchhiking and catching buses, trying to figure out how to cope with the crisis from that morning.

Facts: *There are today two Burger Kings in Oxford. If Will took the most direct route from Winchester to Oxford (and if it was open in 1997), Will likely ate at the Burger King on Cornmarket Street.*

SK 1 *[brief]*

CASTLE MILL BOATYARD [*See* **Port Meadow, Facts**]

CATTE STREET ⚑

World: Lyra's, Will's

Role: Lyra discovers that there is a Catte Street in Will's Oxford, just like in her own. She finds that someone has etched into a stone at the end of the street the initials SP, just as Simon Parslow had done on a rock in the same position in her Oxford.

SK 　4 *[brief]*

Château-Vert ✥

World: Lyra's
Role: Wooded area to the east of Oxford that Lyra can see when she climbs out of her bedroom window and up to the roof of the building housing Staircase Twelve.

NL/GC 3 *[brief]*

Cherwell ✥ ✐

World: Lyra's
Role: Lyra thinks back on bathing in Oxford's Cherwell River, where very young children swim naked, while (older and more modest) she and Roger have separate baths in Svalbard. She is again reminded of swimming in the Cherwell when she leaves a sleeping Will and goes alone to bathe in the mulefa's world.

The Cherwell

Penrose and Palmer

Facts: *Pronounced "Charwell" in Will's Oxford, the Cherwell is popular for punting (maneuvering a narrow low boat with a long pole) and famous for Parson's Pleasure, a stretch where grown men (not small children) forego swimming attire.*

NL/GC 21 *[brief]*
AS 　33 *[brief]*

Claybeds ✥ ✐

World: Lyra's
Role: Play place for Lyra during simpler times. The battles with the brick-burners' children in its mud once seemed to her some of her greatest escapades; they are among the first anecdotes about her life at Jordan College that she tells Mrs Coulter the night they meet.

Hurling mud clumps at the brick-burners' children when playing in the Claybeds was also Lyra's inspiration for prompting all the Bolvangar escapees to throw snow in the eyes of their Tartar guards.

Even more importantly, Lyra's adventures there prove the perfect material for the true story she tells in the world of the dead. The details she recalls are so vividly rendered, even the harpies stop to listen. Lyra tells the ghosts how it felt to squish her fingers in the mud and how the mud would try to suck her down as she waded and how when the weather was warm and sunny for several days, the mud would dry and then she would carefully try to lift up large flat slices of it, and it would be dry on top and still moist underneath. She recalls the various smells of the Claybeds: smoke from kilns and the clay-burners' cooking fires, those emanating from the river, and those blown in with the wind through the willows. She replayed in her tales the battles between the Oxford townies and the clay-burners that ended with all combatants covered from head to toe in mud.

NL/GC Lyra and 3; recalled at Bolvangar 17
      brief mentions: by Lyra to Coulter 4, Lyra misses 5

AS   Lyra remembers playing with Roger 13 [*brief*]; in Lyra's true story 23

CORNMARKET STREET ⚔

World: Lyra's, Will's

Role: From the landmarks that are similar between their two worlds, Lyra is immediately able to recognize this street when she and Will arrive in his Oxford's city center.

SK   3 [*brief*]

Waterstone's Bookshop has occupied the building on the south corner of Cornmarket and Broad since 1998

COVERED MARKET ✦ ⚔ LS

World: Lyra's, Will's

Role: When Billy Costa and Roger are snatched by the Gobblers, Lyra learns that Jessie Reynolds, the daughter of the saddler in the Covered Market, disappeared the previous day.

    Lyra feels more comfortable in Will's Oxford's Covered Market than she does most places in the strange but familiar city.

Facts: *While there have been shops on or near the same site since the Middle Ages, today's Covered Market dates from 1772, and is bordered by Cornmarket, Market, Turl and the High Streets.*

Note: Covered Market *is capitalized in* NORTHERN LIGHTS *but not in* THE GOLDEN COMPASS. *It is capitalized in both the UK and US editions of* THE SUBTLE KNIFE.

NL/GC brief mentions: Jessie Reynolds and 3, in Lyra's account of Gobbler snatchings to Faa 7, LS Lantern Slide 6

SK   4

COWLEY ✦

World: Lyra's

Role: Gobblers are suspected of stealing a child from this town near Oxford.

NL/GC 3 [*brief*]

CRYPT [*See* Jordan College]

DARK MATTER RESEARCH GROUP/UNIT (MARY'S LAB) ⚔ ✏

World: Will's

Role: Mary Malone tells Lyra that her laboratory, located in two small rooms on the second floor of the Department of Physical Sciences, Oxford University is the only place in the world looking into what Lyra calls Dust.

    The office is a "small room, crowded with tottering piles of papers and books". In an adjoining room is what Lyra considers "some kind of complicated anbaric machinery"— the specially configured computer Mary refers to as the Cave, that Lyra (and, later, Mary

Malone) uses to communicate with Shadow-particles.

When Lyra arrives in Will's Oxford, the Research Unit is on the verge of collapse; Malone has little hope of future funding, and her co-investigator Dr Oliver Payne has a job offer elsewhere. Sir Charles Latrom implies that he could finagle a bailout, but only if the research proceeds along the terms he dictates.

The question of its future is determined when the Shadow-particles tell Mary to destroy the Unit's equipment and to follow Lyra into other worlds. She follows their instructions.

Note: *Both* Dark Matter Research group *and* Dark Matter Research Unit *appear only once in* HIS DARK MATERIALS. *Also listed here are more casual references to Mary Malone's laboratory.* ₁₃₂ ₁₃₃

SK   described 4; Lyra's second visit 7; Latrom's visit, Mary's last visit 12

DEPARTMENT OF PHYSICAL SCIENCES 🗡

World: Will's

Role: Dr Mary Malone is attached to this department, which means it must be the administrative unit of her Oxford University overseeing the Dark Matter Research Unit.

SK   12 *[brief]*

GABRIEL COLLEGE ✴

World: Lyra's

Role: College next to Jordan College. When Pan and Lyra discuss what force moves the alethiometer's needle, they are reminded of Gabriel College's photo-mill.

NL/GC brief mentions: next to Jordan 3, searched after Lyra disappears 8; Lyra and Pan recall its Oratory's photo-mill 9, 18

GODSTOW ✴

World: Lyra's

Role: Site of an old nunnery near Oxford rumored to harbor a werewolf and ghosts. Pantalaimon claims he saw a ghost there, but Lyra missed it.

NL/GC werewolf of 5, and Pan's ghost 9

HALL, THE [DINING]   [*See* Jordan College]

HEADINGTON/OLD HEADINGTON 🗡 🖋

World: Lyra's, Will's

Role: Affluent neighborhood of Oxford in which Sir Charles Latrom lives. Will and Lyra must venture there to retrieve her stolen alethiometer.

Note: *Headington is in both Lyra's and Will's Oxfords; Latrom's neighborhood of Old Headington may just be in Will's.* ₁₃₄

THE AMBER SPYGLASS reference to Headington appears only in the Scholastic Point (**UK**) *edition. In the Random House edition* (**US**)*, when Will is thinking he could cut a window into Mrs Coulter's cave just as he did at Latrom's house,* Oxford *appears rather than* ₁₃₅

Cold War Star Wars

The man Will talks with at the Institute of Archaeology in Oxford tries to put the era of the Nuniatak dig in Alaska into a historical context by linking the mid-1980s to "the height of the cold war," "Star Wars," and Russians and Americans "building enormous radar installations all over the Arctic."

The term *cold war*, lowercased in both the US and UK *HIS DARK MATERIALS* but typically uppercased in US histories, refers to the period following World War II (or late 1940's) and ending with the collapse of the Soviet Union in 1991. While the US and Soviet Union never engaged in a full scale war, this period was dominated by mutual distrust and the proliferation of nuclear arms, which only heightened the tension between the two superpowers. In 1983 the US President Ronald Reagan proposed a Strategic Defense Initiative (SDI). It used space-based systems to protect the US from nuclear missile attacks by creating an X-ray laser barrier launched from satellites to stop enemy missiles from reaching their target. Failing that, SDI used satellites to launch missiles that would intercept the enemy's. The name Star Wars was first applied derisively by those who thought the plans more appropriate to science fiction than national policy, but its supporters adopted the phrase as capturing the visionary nature of the scheme. SDI as key to US national defense ended with the 1992 election of President Clinton.

Headington.

SK   Latrom's calling card specifying "Old Headington," Lyra and Will visit to ask for return of alethiometer 7; Will retrieves alethiometer while Latrom entertains Coulter 9

AS   Will recalls 11 *[brief]*

HIGH STREET ⚜✎

World: Will's

Role: The spot where Will and Lyra part is located just off this main street in central Oxford. Lyra's request to go to the Botanic Garden leads them down the High Street to its gate just opposite Magdalen College. Will had been on it previously when looking for the offices of Alan Perkins, the Parry family's lawyer.

SK   4 *[brief]*

AS   38 *[brief]*

INSTITUTE OF ARCHAEOLOGY ⚜

World: Will's

The Institute of Archaeology, Beaumont Street, Oxford

Role: Oxford University division that sponsored the expedition to Alaska during which John Parry and others were lost in 1985. Will Parry visits the Institute during his search for answers about his father's disappearance, but receives little information he didn't already know—except that another man, claiming to be a journalist, has recently visited the Institute asking about the same incident.

Facts: *The Institute of Archaeology at Oxford was founded in 1961. It is located on Beaumont Street, as is the Ashmolean Museum.*

SK   4

ISIS [*See* River Isis]

JERICHO
World: Lyra's
Role: Area of Oxford where the gyptians docked their boats during their visits to the town, and Lyra and Roger played—until the day Billy Costa was abducted, and Lyra first heard that the Gobblers had arrived in Oxford. The most notable structure in the warren of narrow streets and "little brick terraced houses" is the square-towered oratory of St Barnabas the Chymist.
Remarks: *Pages from a guidebook to Jericho are included as one of the fragments in* LYRA'S OXFORD. *Jericho is the site of much of the novella's action. The home and laboratory of Sebastian Makepeace, alchemist, is in the district's Juxon Street, not far from the Eagle Ironworks and Fell Press.*

Ian Giles

St. Barnabas Church dominates our world's Jericho, Oxford, just as "the great square-towered oratory of St Barnabas the Chymist" could be seen above its neighborhood's "narrow streets" of "little brick terraced houses."

136

NL/GC Horse Fair and, search for Billy Costa in 3; Tony Costa mentions to Lyra 6 *[brief]*
AS Lyra mentions to Roger's ghost 23 *[brief]*

JORDAN COLLEGE (THE COLLEGE) 🔟 *LS*
World: Lyra's
Physical characteristics: Jordan College faces Turl Street, backs up to the University library, and is bordered by St Michael's and Gabriel Colleges on its sides. From his Lodge on Turl Street, the porter monitors Lyra's comings and goings in an attempt to keep her within the College boundaries. The College began to spread underground in the Middle Ages: "Tunnels, shafts, vaults, cellars, staircases had so hollowed out the earth below Jordan… that there was almost as much air below ground as above." Among these underground places are the crypts and extensive wine cellars, both play places for Lyra and her best friend Roger, the College's kitchen boy. Another of her favorite pastimes is leaping from roof to roof of the closely spaced buildings.

137

Penrose and Palmer

An example of a Dining Hall, Christ Church

Of the colleges in Lyra's Oxford, it "was the grandest and richest," and its "buildings, which were grouped around three irregular quadrangles, dated from every period from the early Middle Ages to the mid-eighteenth century."

138

Jordan College's buildings are built around the perimeters of three quadrangles. The oldest buildings of the College border Yaxley Quadrangle, including Staircase Twelve, where Lyra lives on the top floor; the chapel adorned with "stone pinnacles;" and the Master's Lodgings. The rear of the Master's Lodge overlooks the Library garden, which is bordered on its westerly side by the Library and Palmer's Tower. On one side of Palmer's Tower is the Chapel, and these two structures separate the Quadrangle and the Yaxley Quad. On the garden's other side is the Library, which borders Melrose Quadrangle. The afternoon sun shining in the passage between the Library and

139

Palmer's Tower illuminates the Library Garden and the Master's Drawing Room. Other places include the Scholars' Common Room, Kitchen and Buttery.

The Crypt

Located below the College Oratory, and also referred to as the catacombs, it is the burial site of Jordan College's past masters and scholars, and a play place for Lyra and Roger. Each master is buried in an oak coffin resting in a wall niche, accompanied by a stone tablet inscribed with the master's name, and a brass plaque with the name and an image of his dæmon. For lesser Collegians, the Scholars, only their skulls along with a coin depicting their dæmon are preserved and stacked in partitioned shelves.

Penrose and Palmer
Exeter College Chapel

The Hall

This is where the scholars dine. Three long tables with benches for seating are set parallel to one another, and at right angles to a dais on which the High Table is positioned. Cushioned chairs provide seating at the High Table for the College Master, his male guests and a few highly ranked scholars, and its place settings are of gold (in contrast to the silver used at the other three tables). A door at the same end of the room as the High Table leads to the Retiring Room.

The Library

Lit by anbaric lights, it has a white-painted lantern atop its tower. Lyra is more interested in its roof than its contents: when her "uncle" Lord Asriel asks during a visit to Jordan College if she used the Library, Lyra readily admits that she doesn't, and moves on to describe her recent discovery of a rook with a hurt foot on its roof.

Master's Lodging

Decorated with gloomy pictures and old silver objects, the Master's house opens into Yaxley Quad and backs up to Library Garden. Lyra first met Mrs Coulter here. It was here that she was summoned to his Lodgings and given the alethiometer by the Master.

Pilgrim's Tower

Located across from the Sheldon Building, Pilgrim's Tower displeases Lyra. The only way onto the Sheldon's roof would be by jumping up from the tower and over a gap, and the position of a skylight and her small stature are standing in her way of traveling all around Jordan College without touching ground.

Retiring Room

His Dark Materials' opening scene is set in this

Penrose and Palmer
Exeter College Quadrangle and Chapel

room. Here, Lyra warns Lord Asriel that she has seen the Master poison his wine; hears about Dust, severed children, and Stanislaus Grumman; and sees a photogram slide of a city behind the Aurora.

The Retiring Room is entered through the Hall where the Scholars dine; its door is on the same end of the room as the High Table. Another door connects it to the corridor between the Library and the Scholars' Common Room.

Furnished with green leather armchairs, an oval table, sideboard and a large oak wardrobe, it is lit by naphtha lamps and warmed by a fireplace. The Retiring Room is off-limits to all but Scholars and their guests, who enter only at the Master's request. Its accoutrements include pipes, decanters and glasses, a basket of poppy-heads, and a silver chafing dish in which the Master cooks the poppies over a small lamp flame. On the walls are portraits.

Females, even maids, are never permitted entrance to this room, making it all the more interesting to Lyra. In spite of Pan's urge for caution, Lyra sneaks into the Retiring Room before the Scholars begin dinner. But she has left her investigations of the room too close to the dinner bell, and finds herself seeking cover as the room is visited in turn by the Butler, the Master, then the Steward, and finally, Lord Asriel.

<u>Wine cellars</u>

These have stone arches and pillars "as thick as ten trees," a flagstone floor, and a huge store of wine. During one of their escapades, Lyra breaks open a bottle. A | 140
sick Roger can't believe anyone could enjoy drinking wine, but Lyra claims she does.

Role: Jordan College is Lyra's childhood home and the location Lord Asriel (her father) brought her to after withdrawing her from the priory where she had been sent by court order. When Lord Asriel placed her in the care of the Master of Jordan College, he stipulated that Lyra's mother, Mrs Coulter, not be allowed to see her. The scholars and servants of the College separately constitute the only family Lyra has ever known. Lord Asriel is a member of the College, and Stanislaus Grumman, scientist and shaman, once studied there. The gyptians too have connections with Jordan College; Lord John Faa receives reports from the pastry-cook, Bernie Johansen, who is half-gyptian, about Lyra's well-being, an interest stemming from their association with Lord Asriel.

Exeter College

Penrose and Palmer

The description of Jordan College is that it is so rich "you could walk from Oxford to Bristol in one direction and to London in the other, and never leave Jordan land." There is no question in Lyra's mind that Jordan is the | 141
superior college academically, as well: "she regarded visiting scholars and eminent professors from elsewhere with pitying scorn, because they didn't belong to Jordan." | 142

In Cittàgazze when Lyra learns that Will plans to go into Oxford, she is determined to go with him to consult Jordan College's experimental theologians about Dust "because Jordan had the best ones." Arriving at Broad and Cornmarket Streets in Will's Oxford, | 143
Lyra is shocked to find Balliol College, Broad Street, and Bodley's Library just where she left them, but no Jordan College. She feels very much alone, no longer "Lyra of Jordan" but just a "lost little girl in a strange world, belonging nowhere." | 144

As *His Dark Materials* closes, Lyra returns to the College; she tells the Master and Dame Hannah Relf, "I came back to Jordan because this used to be my home, and I didn't have anywhere else to go... I'm lost, really, now" to which the Master responds, "You will never be lost while this college is standing, Lyra. This is your home for as long as you need it."

"Lyra's Jordan" is the title of the third chapter of *Northern Lights* (*The Golden Compass*).

Update: In the **10th** anniversary editions of *Northern Lights/The golden compass* and *The Subtle Knife*, the Jordan College Library is revealed as the likely site of a window between Lyra's and our world. An appendix to the first volume presents papers of Lord Asriel's, with the Jordan College Library stamp, that belonged to a deceased academic in our world. And the appendix to *The Subtle Knife* includes notes and drawings by Stanislaus Grumman/John Parry, not bearing the Library's catalogue stamp, that were discovered in the Jordan College Library.

The first Lantern Slide in *Northern Lights/The Golden Compass* likens Jordan College to a "great clockwork mechanism."

Facts: *Like Jordan College in Lyra's world, Exeter College in Will's has a Palmer's Tower, dating from the Middle Ages and named for a rector or scholar from the 15th century. The Library's lantern: A* lantern *is a structure on top of a dome or tower that has openings for ventilation or lighting purposes. A common example of a lantern is the top of a lighthouse tower.*

Observation: *Hiding in its closet of the Retiring Room the night of Asriel's visit was a turning point in Lyra's life; Retiring Room is used subsequently in* Northern Lights/The Golden Compass *particularly as shorthand for all she learned there.*

Although it is not named, the Master's Lodgings is surely the site where, at the end of The Amber Spyglass, *Lyra meets with the Master and Dame Hannah Relf.*

Note: Chapel, Library *and* Hall *are capitalized in* Northern Lights. Chapel *and* library *are lowercased in* The Golden Compass, *as is* hall, *with two exceptions. In* Northern Lights *and* The Golden Compass, *Retiring Room is always uppercased, except for one instance in* The Golden Compass; *in both UK and US editions of* The Subtle Knife *it is always lowercased, but in both UK and US editions of* The Amber Spyglass, *it is always uppercased. Additionally, chapter 3 of* The Golden Compass *states that Jordan is one of twenty-four colleges in Oxford (35), but this passage does not appear in* Northern Lights, *and the map in* Lyra's Oxford *shows just twenty-three.*

NL/GC Hall, Retiring Room, servants 1; Master and scholars of, Asriel's presentation at, Master's political problems 2; history and description, status in experimental theology among other colleges, Lyra's childhood at, wine cellars, crypt, Oratory, Turl Street, Lodge, Kitchen, Lyra's room on Staircase Twelve, view from rooftop, Master's Lodgings 3; Lyra meets Coulter at, Master's summary of Lyra's situation in, Lyra receives alethiometer before dawn and then departs, beauty of compared to prettiness of Coulter's flat 4; quality of Lyra's education at, Lyra discusses with Boreal 5; Faa on Lyra's history at, gyptians' connections with, its Master's dilemmas 7; Santelia rages about Trelawney of and Lyra remembers what Trelawney said about Raknison 19; Asriel's prison on Svalbard reminds Lyra of, Lyra tells Asriel of receiving the alethiometer from its Master and her efforts since last she saw him at, Asriel reminds her of photograms he showed in its Retiring Room 21; [LS] Lantern Slides 1, 7, 8 (Kitchen)
> *brief mentions:* by Lyra of Roger and 6, to gyptian kids 8, to Coram about Librarian and photo-mill 9; of Mrs. Lonsdale, Master 10; of crypt 11 and its dæmon-coins 12; by Lyra to Scoresby about Grumman 13; and voices of its scholars and doctor at Bolvangar 14; of Roger, crypt 15; Bolvangar conference room and Retiring Room compared 16; Lyra and Coulter discuss Master of, Coram prepared to take Roger home to 17; of Palmerian Professor 18

SK Lyra expects to find in Will's Oxford, her surprise when she doesn't 3
> *brief mentions:* scholars, Master of 4; cats at 5; Pan's anxiety at Tower compared to same at crypt of 7; Retiring Room recalled by Lyra and Pan 13

AS Lyra's true story in world of the dead 23; Lyra meets with Master and Relf, is assured she always has a home at 38

> *brief mentions:* Lyra remembers playing with Roger 13, and being looked after by Mrs. Lonsdale 14; Coulter on rescuing Lyra from 16; amber spyglass and Asriel's photograms displayed at 17; Lyra acting polite as if being scrutinized at 19, pretending to be as fearless at abyss as she was on roofs of 26, recalling life since night in Retiring Room 33, wondering about her future 35

10TH: *NL* appendix

10TH: *SK* appendix

LIBRARY, JORDAN COLLEGE [*See* Jordan College]

LIBRARY GARDEN, JORDAN COLLEGE [*See* Jordan College]

LIMEFIELD HOUSE

World: Will's

Role: Sir Charles Latrom's Old Headington, Oxford, residence, "it spoke of wealth and power, the sort of informal settled superiority that some upper-class English people still took for granted."

SK first visit 7, second visit 9

147

LODGE [*See* Jordan College]

MAGDALEN BRIDGE, MAGDALEN COLLEGE

World: Will's

Role: Magdalen College is located across High Street from the Botanic Garden in Will's Oxford. Will and Lyra can hear the traffic on Magdalen Bridge as they part.

> [*See also* **Botanic Garden**]

AS 38 *[brief]*

Penrose and Palmer

Magdalen College

MAGDALEN COLLEGE [*See* Magdalen Bridge]

MASTER'S LODGING [*See* Jordan College]

MELROSE QUADRANGLE [*See* Jordan College]

Penrose and Palmer

Magdalen Bridge crosses the River Cherwell. Once over the bridge, heading into Oxford, Magdalen College and its impressive tower are on the right hand side of the High Street; the Botanic Garden is on the left.

NORHAM GARDENS

World: Will's

Role: Residential road, not far from Mary Malone's lab in the Physical Sciences Building, where Sir Charles Latrom stops his Rolls Royce, offers Lyra a ride, and steals her alethiometer.

Facts: *When Norham Gardens curves around the University Parks, it terminates at a fork. One prong merges into Parks Road, which heads into the University's science area, and the other into Banbury Road.*

In Lyra's Oxford, *one of the stray bits collected in the volume is a card posted by Mary Malone. Mary writes her friend that her apartment is just a little ways from a house in Norham Gardens pictured on the card.*

SK   7 [brief]

Philip Pullman on Exeter

"...there are few better places to wander about in than Oxford, as many novelists have discovered...I shall always be grateful to Exeter".... from "Exeter to Jordan," *Oxford Today.*

Oxford–the town ❖ ⚔ ✎

World: Lyra's, Will's

Role: Oxford is Lyra's hometown, in her world. In Will's world, Oxford is where he follows a cat through a window seemingly cut out of the air and into another world. Will's Oxford is where Lyra's alethiometer is stolen, leading to Will becoming the bearer of the subtle knife, and Lyra meets Dr Mary Malone. Will's Oxford is where Lyra and Will part, and Lyra's is where His Dark Materials ends.

The city's name provides the title of Part One of Northern Lights/The Golden Compass. Lyra's Oxford is a city of "spires and towers;" its "beauty" is "grand and stony and masculine." In Lyra's world, its children amuse themselves by forming alliances and waging "wars."

Will visits Oxford to consult his family's lawyer about his father's disappearance. The lawyer is not forthcoming. But he does find some answers at the public library and Oxford's Institute of Archaeology. Lyra heads for the University.

Lyra's Oxford has in no way prepared Lyra for the traffic or the "vast numbers of people swarming on every pavement." She finds his Oxford "disconcertingly different, with patches of poignant familiarity right next to the downright outlandish."

Will's Oxford combines elements familiar to Lyra, like old stone churches and some of the colleges, with others she has never encountered: department stores, teller machines, traffic lights, and cinemas. Although she readily adjusts to the idea that the beings she sees are humans—even though she can't see their dæmons—her experience of Will's Oxford is that "it was all much harder to read than the alethiometer."

When Lyra and Will venture into the exclusive Oxford neighborhood of Old Headington, she feels their walk through Oxford is harder than her journey to Bolvangar. In the Arctic she had the help of Iorek Byrnison and the gyptians, "and even if the tundra was full of danger, you knew the danger when you saw it. Here, in the city that was both hers and not hers, danger could look friendly, and treachery smiled and smelt sweet."

The disruption caused by Asriel's blast

Penrose and Palmer

High Street

Penrose and Palmer

View of Oxford from Magdalen Tower

has set the two Oxfords far apart, resulting in both Asriel's bridge and the Sunderland Avenue window leading to Cittàgazze. The angel Xaphania explains after the battle between the republic and kingdom of heaven has ended, when all the windows are closed, and the worlds are "restored to their proper relations with one another…Lyra's Oxford and Will's would lie over each other again, like transparent images on two sheets of film being moved closer and closer until

Their Oxfords' Colleges

There are 23 colleges in Lyra's world's Oxford University; in Will's, there are 39. Although only 7 colleges are named in *HIS DARK MATERIALS*, another 16 are found on the fold-out map in *LYRA'S OXFORD*, and the site of each of these 23 corresponds to a college in Will's.

Colleges in both Will and Lyra's Oxfords [based on the map key in *LYRA'S OXFORD*] (11)
[*mentioned in *HIS DARK MATERIALS*]

Balliol*
Brasenose
Hertford
Magdalen*
Merton
Oriel
Somerville
St Edmund Hall
St John's*
University
Worcester

Colleges in Lyra's Oxford and their spatial equivalents in Will's (12)
[*mentioned in *HIS DARK MATERIALS*]

Lyra's	*Will's*
Broadgates Hall	Pembroke
Cardinal's	Christ Church
Durham	Trinity
Foxe	Corpus Christi
Gabriel*	Wadham
Jordan*	Exeter
Queen Philippa's	Queen's
St Michael's*	Jesus
St Scholastica's	All Souls
St Sophia's*	Lady Margaret Hall
Wordsworth	St Hugh's
Wykeham	New College

Will's world's connections to names of Lyra's Oxford's colleges

Four of the colleges of *HIS DARK MATERIALS* with spatial counterparts bearing different names in Will's Oxford (Gabriel/Wadham, Jordan/Exeter, St Michael's/Jesus, and St Sophia's/Lady Margaret Hall) are exceptional among those on the map in *LYRA'S OXFORD* because their fictional names do not represent a historical aspect of their Will's world's history.

Michael and Gabriel are both archangels, and Sophia is the Gnostic god of wisdom. Pullman has noted that the Oxford district of Jericho inspired his choice of Jordan for Exeter College ("Dreaming of Spires," *Guardian*, July 27 2002).

Three colleges of Lyra's Oxford retain names they once bore in Will's world, and the circumstances surrounding two of these suggest that in her world, Henry VIII either did not reign or did not part company with the Catholic Church:

• **Durham/Trinity** – The site of Trinity College was once home to Durham College, which from 1286 to 1555 accommodated Benedictine monks from Durham Cathedral. When Henry VIII broke with the Roman Catholic Church and dissolved the monasteries, the institution was refounded as Trinity.

- **Cardinal's/Christ Church** – Cardinal Wolsey, founded Christ Church in 1524 to train future cardinals and other high ranking clergy, taking over the site of a centuries' old monastery. Henry VIII renamed it in 1546.
- **Broadgates Hall/Pembroke** – Before being granted its status as a college and named in honor of the Earl of Pembroke in 1624, this institution was known as Broadgates Hall.

Three other colleges in Lyra's world are named after their founders in Will's:
- **Wykeham/New College** – William of Wykeham founded New College in 1379.
- **Wordsworth/St Hugh's** – St Hugh's was founded in 1886 by Elizabeth Wordsworth, a great-niece of the poet William Wordsworth, who named the college in honor of Hugh of Avalon, a 12th century bishop of London.
- **Foxe/Corpus Christi** – The founder of Corpus Christi was Richard Foxe.

Finally,
- **Queen Philippa's/Queen's** – Queen's College was named after Queen Philippa of Hainault, wife of Edward III.
- **St Scholastica's/All Souls** – The cornerstone for All Souls was laid on St Scholastica's Day, February 10, in 1437 or 1438.

Colleges of Will's Oxford not found in Lyra's (16)

Green (1979)**
Harris Manchester (1889)
Keble (1870)
Kellogg (1990)**
Linacre (1962)**
Lincoln (1427)
Mansfield (1886)
Nuffield (1958)**
St Anne's (1878)
St Antony's (1953)**
St Catherine's (1963)
St Cross (1965)**
St Hilda's (1893)
St Peter's (1929)
Templeton (1995)**
Wolfson (1966)**

Penrose and Palmer

Cloister Quad of Magdalen College

Eight of these colleges are for graduate students only (indicated by double asterisks). Of the remaining eight, only one was founded before 1870: Lincoln College.

The exclusion of Lincoln College, founded in 1427, is of more interest. Lincoln is one of the three colleges sharing Turl Street; the other two are Exeter (Jordan) and Jesus (St Michael's). As may be expected, rivalries among the three are well established. However, Exeter's main rival is considered to be Jesus, not Lincoln. Lincoln in turn has a long history of mutual discontent with its neighbor, Brasenose. In Lyra's Oxford, there is no Lincoln College, and the site it occupies in Will's world belongs to Brasenose.

they merged; although they would never truly touch."

NL/GC children of, gyptians and, Gobblers arrive in 3; Lyra misses, talks to guests about Gobblers and 5

> *brief mentions:* other colleges in, masculine beauty of 4; gyptians and 6, 7; search for Lyra in 8; Bodley's Library in 9; Jordan College in 10, 13; Claybeds in 17; by Scoresby, Serafina 18; Jordan College in 19; by Roger 21

SK Will arrives in, Will and Lyra find there are two of 1; Will prepares Lyra not to stand out in his, Lyra enters and is hit by car, Will relinquishes his plan of staying behind and enters, Lyra's first views of Will's 3; Will seeks answers about his father in, Lyra disturbed by contrast of his and her Oxfords, Lyra seeks answers about Dust in 4; Lyra and Will go to movies in, return to Sunderland Avenue and leave through window 5; Lyra visits alone, runs through streets eluding officials, accepts ride and has alethiometer stolen in, returns with Will, their walk through to Headington for visit with Latrom 7; return from Headington to in Rolls Royce 7; Mary packs belongings at home in, finds destination on map of, enters tent and leaves through window in 12

> *brief mentions:* by Scoresby 2, by Will 11, 13

AS Lyra, Will, Serafina, and Mary enter north part of through window Will cuts, walk to Botanic Garden, Lyra finds in his same tree and bench as in hers, Lyra and Will part, Will and Mary go to her home in his, Lyra returns to Jordan College in hers 38

> *brief mentions:* by Will 2, in Lyra's dream between 6 & 7, of window in 7, of Will's sight of golden monkey in 11, window 18, in Lyra's tall tale 19, in Lyra's true story 23, of swimming in Cherwell 33

OXFORD – THE UNIVERSITY ⚲ [LS]

World: Will's

Role: When Lyra and Will meet in the world of Cittàgazze and both discover that neither belongs in that world, they find one thing in common: both need to do research in their Oxfords. But since Will's is the only one they know how to get into, that is where Lyra goes, fully confident she will soon be conferring with Jordan College's experimental theologians about Dust. Lyra assumes her scholar will be installed in a college, and is disappointed in the building she enters—its interior was "…not to the scholarship and splendour of Oxford."

The Institute of Archaeology is one of the University affiliates, as are Dr Mary Malone's Dark Matter Research Unit, the Pitt-Rivers Museum, the Bodleian Library, and

Will's world's Oxford University

Oxford University is the oldest English-speaking university, with its origins variously dated as early as 1096; it is certain that between 1249 and 1264 three of its colleges, University, Balliol (which Lyra recognizes from her world), and Merton, were established.

The University awards degrees to students of 39 colleges (as compared to 23 in Lyra's world), most of which are situated within about one square mile. While the colleges are responsible for selecting their undergraduate students, providing housing and meals and in general taking care of their physical and social needs, the University provides for shared facilities like museums and labs, oversees course content offered by the colleges, selects graduate students, conducts examinations, and ultimately grants degrees. Women were awarded degrees beginning in 1920, and all but one of the colleges (St Hilda's is for women only) are coed.

If it were in Will's Oxford, Jordan College would be part of Oxford University, but the term for the allied colleges doesn't occur in Lyra's world.

a number of other institutions.

SK   4 *[brief]*

AS   LS Lantern Slide 5

OXFORDSHIRE ❖

World: Lyra's

Role: Location of her father Lord Asriel's estate, where Lyra spent her earliest days under the care of gyptian Ma Costa.

NL/GC 7 *[brief]*

OXPENS ❖

World: Lyra's

Role: Where the Royal Mail zeppelins land.

NL/GC 3 *[brief]*

PALMER'S TOWER *[See Jordan College]*

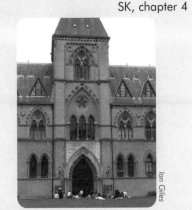

"...she found herself outside a grand building, a real Oxford-looking building that didn't exist in her world at all, though it wouldn't have looked out of place."

SK, chapter 4

The Oxford University Museum of Natural History

PHYSICS (SCIENCE) BUILDING, OXFORD UNIVERSITY ⚑

World: Will's

Role: Location of Dr Mary Malone's Dark Matter Research Unit in Oxford's science area. It is a "tall square building" across from a playing field near the Pitt-Rivers Museum. Although Lyra recognizes that the materials used in the building's fixtures are not cheap and shoddy, compared to what she is used to, its walls and hallways are "all flat and bare and plain in a way Lyra thought belonged to poverty."

Note: *These references are to the exterior and interior of the building (named casually only once as the* physics building *and once as the* science building*) housing Mary Malone's office and lab.*

SK   described, Lyra's first visit to 4; lacking porter's lodge 7, heightened security in 12

PILGRIM'S TOWER *[See Jordan College]*

PITT-RIVERS MUSEUM ⚑

World: Will's

Role: Located near the University Park and Science Area. The museum's collections are the source of the items loaned to Dr Mary Malone and her colleague for testing that reveal Shadow-Particles are attracted to objects from as far back as 30,000 to 40,000 years ago.

Wandering through Will's Oxford, Lyra is attracted to the museum because it looks grand, like the type of Oxford building she is used to, and unlike the steel and glass boxes she finds offensive. As she enters, Lyra is reminded of the Royal Geological Museum of her own world. A room in the rear turns out to be filled with artifacts from the Arctic, including, she is certain, a photo of the same Samoyed hunters who kidnapped her from the gyptians.

Lyra consults her alethiometer about an exhibit of trepanned skulls, and later tells Mary Malone that the museum's card saying they are Bronze Age specimens is wrong – the alethiometer reports that one belonged to a sorcerer who lived 33,254 years ago.

Pitt Rivers

Ian Giles

Here, Lyra meets Sir Charles Latrom, who recognizes her as the girl he met in his own world at Mrs Coulter's party. When Lyra accepts a ride from Latrom, he mentions that he heard that the Pitt-Rivers museum also has some Neanderthal skulls she might be interested in seeing.

Facts: *The Bronze Age is considered as beginning in roughly 3300 BC, when more complex societies began to emerge in the Near East, especially in Egypt and Mesopotamia. The name derives from the increasing use of bronze in the manufacture of tools and ornaments.*

The Neanderthal (Homo neanderthalensis), *precursor to modern* Homo sapiens, *was believed to have lived in Europe and Western Asia from about 230,000 to 29,000 years ago, or the early and middle Stone Age. Stanislaus Grumman, Mary Malone, the mulefa, and the alethiometer place the development of human consciousness at 30,000 to 35,000 years ago, in other words, when the Neanderthals gave way to the Cro-Magnon of the upper Stone Age.*

SK   Lyra visits, discusses with Mary 4; first use of name when Mary tells Oliver Payne about Lyra 12
   brief mentions: by Latrom in Rolls Royce, Lyra to Will 7; Latrom to Coulter 9

Port Meadow ✣ LS

World: Lyra's

Role: Open space along the River Isis in the Oxford district of Jericho, where the gyptians hold their annual Horse Fair and Lyra hears of Billy Costa's abduction.

Facts: *In the spring of 2005, Philip Pullman became involved in a struggle to save a boatyard in Jericho from destruction by real estate developers, after he was sought out by Port Meadow residents familiar with the importance of the canals and narrow boats to the gyptians of* His Dark Materials. *In the second Lantern Slide of* Northern Lights/The Golden Compass, *this same boatyard, Castle Mill, is identified as the site outside Oxford where the gyptians of Lyra's world docked.*

NL/GC *brief mentions:* by Lyra to Asriel, gyptians and 3; Lyra at cocktail party 5, LS Lantern Slide 2

Retiring Room   [*See* Jordan College]

Ring road ⚑

World: Will's

Role: Very busy east-west thoroughfare near Sunderland Avenue in Oxford where Lyra is hit by a car, toppled, but only slightly injured, when she first enters Will's Oxford through the window linking the English town to Cittàgazze.

Note: *Usually lowercased in both the UK and US editions.*

SK   *brief mentions:* roundabout, hornbeams, cat at 1; Lyra hit by car on 3; and window 5, 8

RIVER ISIS ❖

World: Lyra's

Role: The Thames River is known as the River Isis within Oxford, and although there are stretches where Lyra and Roger could swim, the Isis or Thames is also a means of transporting products to London, and so is "thronged with slow-moving brick-barges and asphalt-boats and corn-tankers."

159

[*See also* **Thames**]

NL/GC brief mentions: pathway to London 3, of swimming in 21

SHELDON BUILDING ❖

World: Lyra's

Role: This building with a pearl-green cupola, visible from Jordan College's Yaxley Quad is of interest to Lyra only as a problem in her efforts to leap from building to building in the vicinity of Jordan College.

Facts: *In Will's world's Oxford, the Sheldonian Theatre, designed by the most prominent architect of his day, Christopher Wren, and built in 1669, is now used largely for ceremonial purposes. Originally, the building was used as the University of Oxford's printing facility.*

NL/GC brief mentions: of its roof 3, cupola 4

The Sheldonian Theatre

Penrose and Palmer

SOUTH PARADE ⚔

World: Will's

Role: Suburban road in Summertown, Oxford within walking distance of the Sunderland Avenue Oxford/Cittàgazze window.

When she accepts a lift from him, Lyra has Sir Charles Latrom drop her off on South Parade. Then, when Will and Lyra (in Latrom's car) are driving out of Headington, seeing police on this road, Will directs the chauffeur to continue toward Sunderland Avenue. This decision may account for the police presence Mary Malone encounters when she wants to go into Cittàgazze.

SK   brief mentions: Latrom leaves Lyra at 7; Will directs Latrom's chauffeur from 8 [unnamed]

160

ST BARNABAS THE CHYMIST ❖

World: Lyra's

Role: When hearing of Billy Costa's disappearance from the Horse Fair in Port Meadow, Lyra and several dozen gyptian children scour the streets of Jericho, an area of Oxford that has as its most recognizable landmark the "great square-towered oratory" of this church.

Observation: *In* LYRA'S OXFORD, *a stray page from a guide to Jericho describes the Oratory of St Barnabas the Chymist, noting that it "towers over the back-streets of Jericho" and can be seen "from as far away as the woods of White Ham." The St Barnabas for which it was* *named, according to the guidebook, was a third century experimental theologian and chief perfumer to a Queen Zenobia.*

   In Will's world, St Barnabas is at the intersection of Canal and Cardigan Streets in Jericho.

NL/GC 3 [brief]

ST JOHN'S COLLEGE ⚱

World: Lyra's, Will's

Role: College in Lyra's and Will's Oxfords. In spite of so much else not seeming familiar or making any sense to her in Will's Oxford, Lyra immediately recognizes its gates (which look just

Penrose and Palmer

St John's College

those she once climbed with Roger in her world).

Remarks: *Jordan College dominates Lyra's Oxford. But in Will's Oxford, St John's tops the list:* "This college is so wealthy, it is said that one can travel from Oxford to Cambridge without setting foot off land owned by St John's. Whether or not this is true, St John's does own most of North Oxford and other property throughout the country." (The Scholar's Guide to Oxford)

St John's College

Penrose and Palmer

Penrose and Palmer

St John's College

SK   4 [brief]

ST MICHAEL'S CHAPEL ✤

World: Lyra's

Role: Part of St Michael's College, which is next to Jordan College. In the evenings Lyra can track the progress of the Royal Mail zeppelin as it rises above the chapel's spires on its nightly journey to London.

NL/GC 3 [brief]

ST MICHAEL'S COLLEGE ✤

World: Lyra's

Role: Next to Jordan College in Lyra's Oxford. Several of its kitchen-boys join forces with Lyra and Roger in the Claybeds battles against the gyptians' and brick-burners' kids.

Observation: *Although there isn't a college by this name in Will's Oxford, there is a St Michael's Street. It is a few blocks west of Turl Street near the intersection of Cornmarket and Broad, where Will and Lyra get off their bus, and from where she recognizes Balliol College and the Bodleian, but sees no sign of Jordan College. There is also St Michael-at-the-North Gate Church on Cornmarket Street, which is the present city church; the oldest building in Oxford is its early 11th-century tower. This may be the church Lyra recognizes when she and Will get off the Banbury Road bus in the Oxford city center.*

161

NL/GC kitchen-boys of, location next to Jordan, Hugh Lovat and, youthful smokers of 3; searched for

Lyra 8 *[brief]*

St Sophia's College ❖ ✎

World: Lyra's

Role: Women's college headed by Dame Hannah Relf, which Lyra will attend when she is old enough to do so. Until that time, she is likely to enroll at a boarding school associated with the College.

NL/GC brief mentions: Relf's introduction at Master's Lodging 3, Coulter member of "Dame Hannah's college" 4 [unnamed]

AS and Lyra's future 38

Staircase Twelve [*See* Jordan College]

Summertown ⚓

World: Will's

Role: Suburb ten minutes walk south of Sunderland Avenue.

SK brief mentions: location of teller machine 3, near window 7

Sunderland Avenue ⚓ ✎

World: Will's

Role: Site of the Oxford/Cittàgazze window. Will discovered it when he watched the curious disappearance of a cat as he rested and contemplated his options, the evening of his flight from Winchester.

He and Lyra later use this window to move between the two worlds, referring to the Avenue's hornbeam trees to remember the passage's location. Mary Malone, following instructions from the Shadow-particles, passes through the window, now tented and guarded—likely under Latrom's orders—on the first step of her journey to Will and Lyra.

Will closes it from the Cittàgazze side before opening one nearer the Botanic Garden the night he parts from Lyra.

Facts: *When he was writing* His Dark Materials, *Philip Pullman lived just a few blocks from Sunderland Avenue, where he worked in the now legendary backyard shed mentioned in many late 1990s and early 2000s interviews.*

SK Will sees cat disappear 1 and Lyra and Will enter his Oxford through window on 3 [unnamed]; Shadows instruct Mary, Mary arrives, enters tent 12
 brief mentions: Will sees cat from 5, Will recalls 13

AS brief mentions: Mary reminded of 7, Will closes window on 38 [unnamed]

Turl Street ❖

World: Lyra's

Role: Jordan College is on this Oxford street.

Facts: *A Turl Street is part of Oxford today. Just as in Lyra's world, in Will's world, three colleges share the street: Lincoln, Jesus, and Exeter.*

NL/GC 3 *[brief]*

UNIVERSITY LIBRARY [*See* Bodley's Library *and* Jordan College]

WATLINGTON ✧

World: Lyra's

Role: Site of the Sisters of Obedience priory in England where Lyra spent her first years, after the courts had removed her from her father's (Lord Asriel's) home. He soon moved her from the priory and placed her in the care of the Master of Jordan College.

NL/GC 7 [brief]

WHITE HAM ✧

World: Lyra's

Role: Wooded area to the west of Oxford that Lyra can see when she climbs out of her bedroom window and up to the roof of the building housing Staircase Twelve.

NL/GC 3 [brief]

WINE CELLARS [*See* Jordan College]

YARNTON ✧

World: Lyra's

Role: Town near Lyra's Oxford. On the road from Oxford to Yarnton, one would pass by the Anbaric Park, a power station of some sort.

NL/GC 2 [brief]

YAXLEY QUAD [*See* Jordan College]

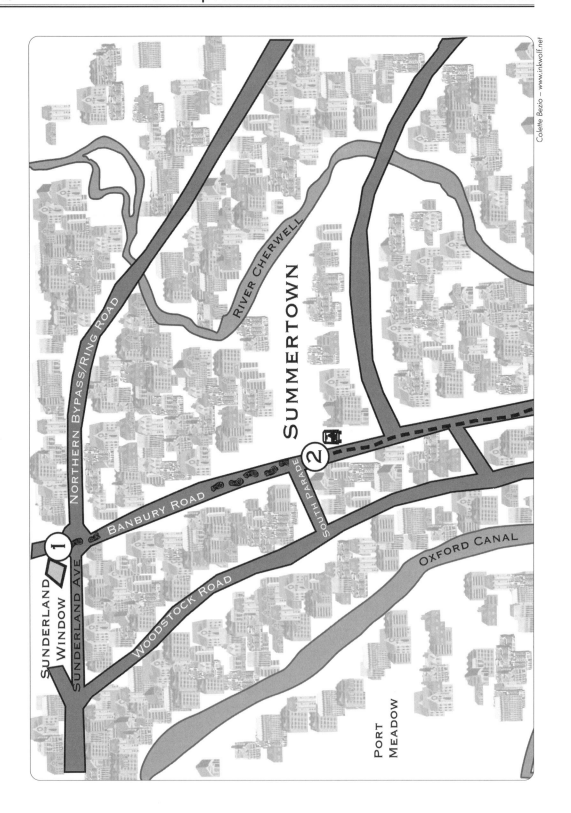

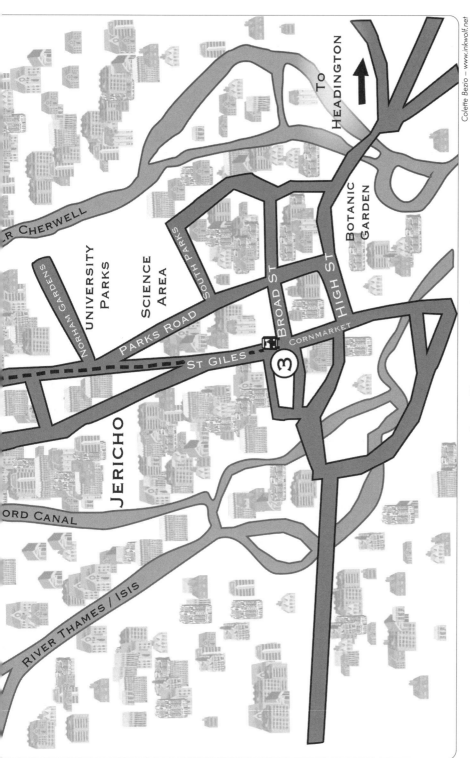

Colette Bezio – www.inkwolf.net

Lyra and Will Visit Oxford

1. Lyra and Will enter Oxford through the Sunderland Avenue window.
2. They walk down the Banbury Road into Summertown, stopping at an ATM. They then board a bus which takes them to the City Centre.
3. They disembark near an old church or roughly at the intersection of Broad and Cornmarket.

Will Alone in Oxford

1. After using a phone box, Will heads to a public library, likely the one at the Westgate Shopping Centre.
2. He then visits the Oxford University Institute of Archaeology.
3. Needing to think about what he learned there, he wanders into a museum on Beaumont Street, no doubt the Ashmolean.
4. He heads to the family solicitor Mr Perkins' office somewhere on the High.
5. He meets Lyra near the Bodleian Library.

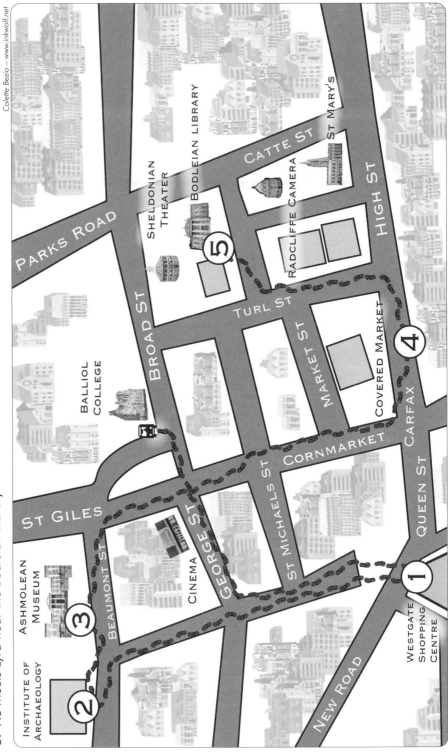

Colette Bezio – www.inkwolf.net

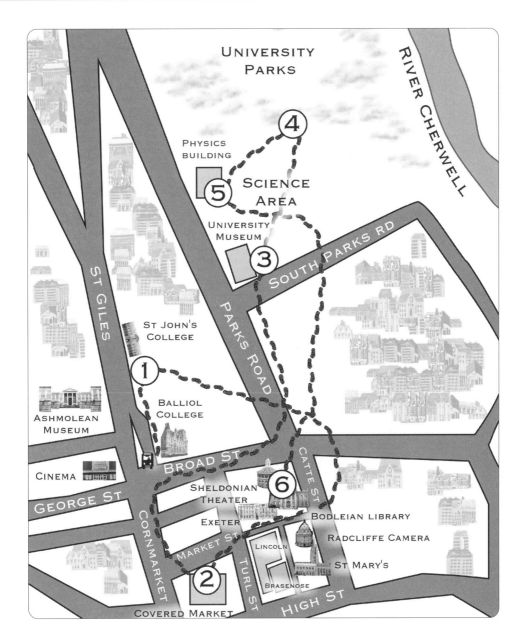

Lyra Alone in Oxford

1. Lyra walks past the gates of St. John's College and then over to Catte Street.
2. She visits the Covered Market and then heads to the University Parks.
3. She stops at the Pitt-Rivers Museum, entering through the University Museum.
4. Leaving the museum, Lyra goes into the Parks and sits under some trees across from the University Physics building.
5. The alethiometer sends her there.
6. She meets Will near the Bodleian Library.

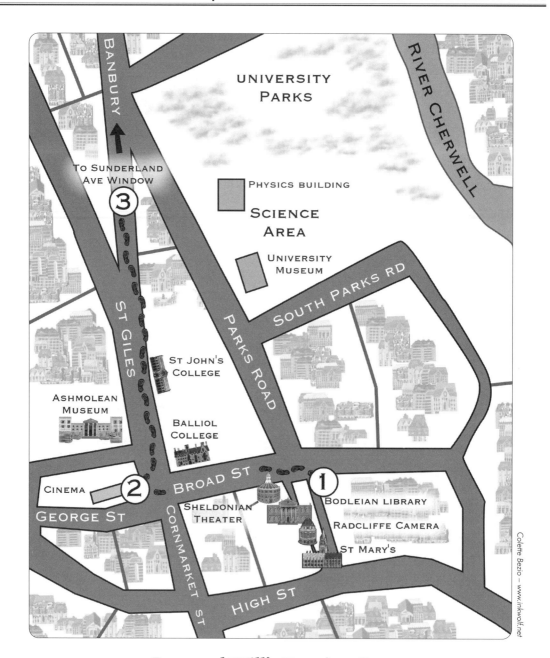

Lyra and Will's Evening Out

1. From a bench near the Bodleian, Lyra and Will walk toward what they see as a round building in a square. This would be the Radcliffe Camera, on Radcliffe Square.
2. They walk to the City Centre to go to the movies. After watching one movie, they decide to see a second, in a different theatre around the corner from the first.
3. Lyra and Will return to the Sunderland Avenue window, this time on foot, walking up the Banbury Road.

AFRICA, AFRICAN ✦ ⚲ ⚲ ⑩

World: Lyra's

Role: Mrs Coulter's activities in Africa included investigations into how *zombis* are made and procuring spy flies.

Ethnicity of King Ogunwe, one of Asriel's high commanders. African riflemen under the command of Ogunwe on the side of Asriel battle with the church's Swiss Guard for Lyra at Coulter's Himalayan hideout.

NL/GC brief mentions: source of spyflies 9, and zombi 21

SK   brief mentions: *zombi* of 2, in Will's Oxford 4

AS   brief mentions: referring to Ogunwe or troops 9, 12, 13, 14, 16, 29

10TH: *NL* appendix

AMERICANS ⚲

World: Will's

Role: The Americans and Russians see the Arctic as an ideal spot for radar installations.

SK   4 [brief]

DANES ⚲

World: Lyra's

Role: In the country of Texas, the child Lee Scoresby and his playmates re-enacted their battles with the French.

[*See also* **New Danes**]

SK   14 [brief]

ENGLISH/ENGLISHMAN

[*See* **England/English/Englishman** *in* **Cities, etc.**]

ESKIMO ✦ ⚲

World: Lyra's, Will's

Alaskan Eskimo Ivory Carver

Edward S. Curtis, Library of Congress, LC-USZ62-74131, 1929

162

Role: A term used in Lyra's world to denote an indigenous people of the Arctic, including Alaskan tribes whose legends tell of "a doorway into the spirit world." An example is Alaskan Matt Kigalick, who provides John Parry the coordinates for the anomaly he seeks near Lookout Ridge.

Lord Asriel, in a condescending attempt to placate Lyra when she asks to go north

163   with him on his next expedition, tells her that if she's a good girl, he'll bring her back a "tusk with some Eskimo carving on it."

[*See also* **Inuit**]

NL/GC 2 *[brief]*

SK   5 *[brief]*

EUROPEAN [*See* **Europe/European** *in* Cities, Countries, Regions, and Elements of Topography]

FRENCH ⚑

World: Lyra's

Role: Battled the Danes at the Alamo in the Country of Texas in New Denmark.

[*See also* **Europe/European, Texas** *in* Cities, Countries, Regions, and Elements of Topography]

SK   Scoresby recalls at Alamo Gulch 14 *[brief]*

GERMAN ⚑

World: Lyra's

Role: Stanislaus Grumman gave some people the impression he was German. In spite of his name, he is an Englishman, the former John Parry of Winchester.

SK   *brief mentions:* astronomer claims 6, and Grumman refutes, as his nationality 10

GREEK ✴ ⚑

World: Lyra's

Role: Limehouse Gobbler abductee Tony Makarios is part Greek, as his last name suggests.

NL/GC brief mentions: Tony Makarios 3, source of word *alethiometer* 7

GYPTIANS ✴ ⚑ ✎ LS

World: Lyra's

Role: The gyptians are good friends to Lyra and a force to reckon with. They shelter and protect Lyra from Mrs Coulter at considerable personal risk, and organize a successful rescue expedition to Lapland to find their children who've been abducted by the General Oblation Board. Even before the 170 men pledged leave England, their efforts to discover where the children had been taken cost several gyptian men their lives. When they learn Lyra again needs their help, the gyptians voyage to the world of the mulefa and bring Lyra, Will, and Mary Malone home to their worlds of origin.

Based in the fens of Eastern Anglia where "gyptians ruled" and "no

164   one else dared enter," for generations

Narrow-boats docked along the Oxford Canal

Ian Giles

these families have regularly traveled the rivers and canals from the marshlands of England's southeast counties into London and Oxford. Their Spring and Fall fairs find the gyptian families converging on Oxford, docking their canal-boats (also called narrow-boats) at Castle Mill boatyard along the River Isis in the suburbs of Jericho and Port Meadow.

Some of the men have gone much further afield. As a young man, Farder Coram, elder and advisor to John Faa, was injured in a Skraeling war, and John Faa has battled Tartars in Kazakhstan. Coram has also visited Africa, and is knowledgeable about the universities in Uppsala, Sveden, and Heidelberg. The gifts they bring their mulefa hosts include genniver, carved walrus tusks, Turkestan tapestries, silver from Sveden, and enamel from Corea.

The gyptians of Eastern Anglia are comprised of six extended families that form a self-governing unit with a leader, King John Faa, and a council on which each of the six families is represented. When needs arise, they convene at Byanropings (or Ropings) to debate strategies or discuss problems. Their society is "tight-knit" and within it "all children were precious and extravagantly loved" with all adults watching over any child.

Their pleasures include card games, fried eels, smokeleaf, and genniver. They value courtesy and acceptance. In the mulefa's world, Faa "was determined that these strangest of all people should receive nothing but grace and friendship" from the Lord of the western gyptians.

Treated as second-class citizens in their homeland ("we gyptians got little standing in the law"), they have formed an informal alliance with Serafina Pekkala's witch clan on the basis of favors given and received. They are loyal to Lord Asriel, who, though a landloper, has provided them significant personal and political help. They have, John Faa tells Lyra, "connections in all sorts of places you wouldn't imagine, including Jordan College."

When Lyra runs away from Mrs Coulter, they provide her safety and shelter and continue to hide her even though rumor has it that if they harbor the child it is at the risk of losing their "ancient privileges" of "free movement in and out the Fens." Victimized more than other

Watercourse Bill

Gyptian King John Faa cites this piece of anti-gyptian legislation that was finally defeated in Parliament (through Lord Asriel's efforts) as an example of the gyptians' debt to Asriel, and among the many reasons why none among them should turn his daughter Lyra over to the authorities for the bounty money, or to prevent harassment. Faa also cites Asriel's willingness to allow the gyptians to navigate through canals on his property. It is likely the Watercourse Bill also had to do with protecting transit routes used by the gyptians between the Fens and neighboring towns.

In Will's world, the gyptians of England are referred to as travellers. While most live in caravans or trailer campers, there are still some boat dwellers, and their battles with governmental regulations concerning use of waterways continue. An example of such legislation is a proposal for "continuous cruising licenses" which requires boat dwellers without permanent mooring to travel a minimum of 120 lock miles every 3 months. This would interfere with children's schooling and maintaining regular work. The alternative would be renting increasingly scarce and consequently expensive docking space.

populations by the Gobblers, they are convinced that the abductions are happening "with
171 the help of the landloper police and the clergy."

172 While Lyra longs to belong to the gyptians' world, Ma Costa, gyptian matriarch, tells
the girl her element is fire ("marsh-fire") while they are "water people all through."

Observation: Gyptian *seems to combine the words* Egyptian *and* gypsy; *in fact, gypsies came
to be known as such because they were once believed to have originated in Egypt.*

NL/GC Lyra's mischievous adventures and, Billy Costa taken during Horse Fair 3; rescue Lyra in
London while hunting Gobblers 6; life aboard narrow-boats, gathering of in Fens for Ropings,
social organization, low status with majority culture including law enforcement, wide-ranging
travels of, connection with Jordan College 7; debt to Asriel, experience as fighters, organization
of rescue party 8; death of spies in London, preparations for journey, travel to departure point
and sailing of ship 9; in Trollesund 10 where sledges are rented, supplies secured, card games
played, and Scoresby and Iorek hired 11; journey toward Bolvangar 12; reaction to Tony
Makarios, living conditions in wilderness 13; attacked by Samoyeds 14; Kaisa reports on safety
of, approach to Bolvangar 15; battle Tartar guards, liberate Bolvangar, reunited with their kids
and take all to safety 17; [LS] Lantern Slide 2

    brief mentions: by Lyra to Coulter 4; London's fashionable women compared with gyptian
mothers, Lyra says at cocktail party that they steal children 5; by Lyra to kids of rescue
party coming to Bolvangar 16; in Serafina's conversations with Scoresby, Lyra 18; at
Asriel's 21

SK   *brief mentions:* by Cardinal, tortured witch to Coulter and Scoresby to witches 2; in Lyra's
thoughts on walk to Latrom's 7; by Scoresby to Grumman 10

AS   in mulefa's world, their presents to mulefa, journey to Cittàgazze 38

    brief mentions: by Serafina to Iorek 3; by Lyra to Will comparing her journey with them to
going to world of dead 14, by Iorek to Lyra about Serafina going to see 15, in Lyra's story
in suburbs of world of dead 19, Lyra
to Roger's ghost 23, by Lyra to Will of
living with when she gets home 35, by
Serafina to dæmons 36 and Pan to
Lyra 37 of their approach to mulefa's
world

HOLLANDERS, HOLLANDS [*See* Holland, Hollanders, Hollands in Cities, etc.]

INUITS ⚕

World: Lyra's

Role: One of Lyra's world's words for native
people of the Arctic.

    The barman from the Samirsky Hotel
in Nova Zembla who reported that
Stanislaus Grumman was buried alive
under an avalanche in the Sakhalin region,
said the source of his information is an
Inuit who was with Grumman's expedition
when the accident occurred.

173 *SK* 6 *[brief]*

IRISH ✦

World: Lyra's

Inuit and Eskimo

Inuit began to replace *Eskimo* for
referring to all Arctic indigenous peoples
when it became widely known that some
linguists had translated *Eskimo* as
meaning "eaters of raw meat." *Inuit*, in
contrast, is inoffensive; it is the plural of
the Inuit word *inuk*, which means human
being. *Inuit* is also used to refer to the
language spoken by these people.

However, not all indigenous peoples
of the Arctic are Inuit-speaking. In
Alaska and Arctic Siberia, there are
groups who are not Inuit speakers; there,
the languages are Inupiaq and Yupik.
So, while Inuit works for the peoples of
the Canadian Arctic and Greenland,
Eskimo is still the only term that covers all
non-Inuit speaking Arctic peoples.

Lord Asriel uses *Eskimo* when telling
Lyra he'll bring her back a gift, which
may or may not be an accurate usage,
but when the Nova Zembla barman
speaks of the Inuits of Beringland, he
probably should use *Eskimo* instead.

Role: Part of Limehouse Gobbler victim Tony Makarios' ethnic heritage.

NL/GC 3 [brief]

ITALIAN

World: Will's

Role: Nationality of Mary Malone's lover, Alfredo Montale, whom she met at a scientific conference in Lisbon.

AS 33 [brief]

LASCAR ✧

World: Lyra's

Role: Tony Makarios' ancestry—Lascar, Skraeling, Irish, Chinese, and Greek—is a globally wide mix.

Facts: Lascar *derives from the Persian word* lashkar *meaning army or camp. It was once used in England to refer to oriental sailors, especially those from India.*

NL/GC 3 [brief]

LATVIAN [*See* Latvia/Latvian in Cities, etc.]

MUSCOVITE(S) [*See* Muscovy, Muscovite(s) in Cities, etc.]

NAVAJO ⚕

World: Lyra's

Role: Lee Scoresby is astounded when the shaman Stanislaus Grumman returns to him a

The Navajo

The Navajo people, one of the largest surviving Native American nations in the US, are renowned as silversmiths and often work with turquoise, a desert mineral. In Will's world, many reside in northwest New Mexico and northeast Arizona.

In Lyra's world, Lee Scoresby is from the "country of Texas" and spent some of his childhood in the vicinity of Will's world's San Antonio, Texas, site of the Alamo. Whether Scoresby's country of Texas extended to include what we know of as Arizona and New Mexico or if he had firsthand contact with the Navajo is not clear. As in Will's world, the popularity of their jewelry could well have exceeded any geographical boundaries.

Navajo Silversmith

Library of Congress, LC-USZ62-99580, 1915 William J. Carpenter,

174

ring Lee's mother owned, which Lee hasn't seen for decades. The ring is described as "silver and turquoise, a Navajo design."

SK   Scoresby receives his mother's ring 10; Scoresby places ring nearby as battle starts 14 *[brief]*

New Dane/New Danish/New Denmark ✤

World: Lyra's

Role: Aëronaut Lee Scoresby's nationality or, more likely, continent of origin across the ocean. Skraelings are among its populace and smokeleaf its exports. The New Danes have a tenuous relationship with the French, who also have territories on the same continent. The New Danes fought the French at the Alamo in the Country of Texas, a skirmish that captured the imagination of the child Lee Scoresby. [*See also* **Europe/European, Texas** *in* **Cities, Countries, Regions, and Elements of Topography**]

NL/GC brief mentions: Skraelings and 2; by Lyra to Coulter 5; Scoresby's background 10; and smokeleaf 14

Nipponese [*See* **Nippon, Nipponese** in **Cities, etc.**]

Northlanders ✤

World: Lyra's

Role: The witches designate as Northlanders the human inhabitants with whom they, usually peacefully, co-exist in the far North.

NL/GC 10 *[brief]*

Norwegian ⚑

World: Will's

Role: When John Parry and his Alaskan gold-miner friend finished exchanging stories about Eskimo tales of a window between worlds, they discussed other polar legends, like the one about a Norwegian ghost ship that's been drifting in the Arctic for more than half a century.

SK   5 *[brief]*

Pole (nationality) ⚑

World: Lyra's

Role: One of the nationalities represented among the scientists at the Imperial Muscovite Academy's Nova Zembla observatory.

SK   6 *[brief]*

Russian/Russians ⚑✎

World: Lyra's, Will's

Role: The Oxford University archaeologist who tells Will that a journalist had recently been asking about Will's father's expedition thinks that the angle of interest is the historical context of the mid-1980s, when both Americans and Russians were competing to install the most powerful radars in the Arctic.

In Lyra's world, Russian is the first language of the Imperial Guard of Muscovy and of the Siberian priest Otyets (Father) Semyon Borisovitch.

[*See also* **Soviets**]

Observation: *The archaeologist with whom Will talks seems to have forgotten that until late 1989, the chief adversaries in the Cold War were not the United States and Russia, but rather the United States and the Soviet Union.*

SK   by archaeologist 4, and John Parry 5 about Alaska and; by Hester as language of troops who attack Scoresby 14 *[brief]*

AS   Borisovitch's language 8

SAMOYEDS ◈ ⚲

World: Lyra's, Will's

Role: Ethnicity of the hunters (described as having wide faces and black eyes) who ambush the gyptians. The hunters injure John Faa and capture Lyra, whom they drag on a sledge through the wilderness to sell for a handful of silver at the General Oblation Board's Bolvangar Experiment Station. The sale seems routine and the hunters have an idea how much money a child should fetch, suggesting that they've run this racket before.

In Will's Oxford, Lyra sees photos and displays of Samoyed artifacts in the Pitt-Rivers Museum and is convinced that what she sees depicted in the exhibit – the hunters, their sledge, and even its ropes – are the same ones she had a long look at on her way to Bolvangar.

NL/GC abduct Lyra 14
     brief mentions: by Kaisa 15, doctors who capture Lyra 16, Lyra to Coulter 17

SK   Lyra's surprise at seeing photos depicting in museum in Will's Oxford 4

SIBERIAN/SIBIRSK

[*See* **Siberia/Siberian/Sibirsk** in Cities, etc.]

SIX FAMILIES, THE ◈

World: Lyra's

Role: This alliance of Eastern Anglia gyptian families is led by John Faa. The patriarchs of these families—

> # Samoyeds:
> # An Endangered People
>
> Like the Lapps, Samoyeds were traditionally reindeer herders in Northern Siberia and the Taymyr Peninsula. Of the estimated 16,500, some 4,000 live in the Kola Peninsula, which they share with the Lapps, 5,000 between the White Sea and the Yenisei River, and the remainder between the Yenisei and the Ob.
>
> *Samoyed* can also be used as a general description of a number of sub-ethnic groups, with the most populous being the Nenets (*Nenets* is now frequently used to mean *Samoyed*, much as *Sami* has replaced *Lapp*).
>
> Although they resisted 19th century efforts to convert them to Christianity and more settled ways, they were less able to defend themselves against 20th Soviet domination. Some were relocated to Nova Zembla to keep Norwegians from settling the island, and to the Kola Peninsula for similar reasons. Mineral and oil deposits in their traditional hunting and herding grounds spurred Soviet efforts to force the Samoyeds to assimilate, and nuclear testing on Nova Zembla has posed other dangers. Acid rain accumulates in the mosses eaten by reindeer, which are central to the Samoyeds' diet and their way of life.

Skraelings

Skraeling is the term found in Norse sagas to describe native North Americans, most likely Inuits. Around 1000 AD, Norse explorers reached Greenland; from there, expeditions were launched to Newfoundland and Labrador, which they called Vinland.

In the twelfth century Book of the Icelanders, Ari the Wise reported, "In both the eastern and western parts of the country they [settlers] found human dwellings, fragments of skin boats, and stone artifacts from which it appears that the same kind of person had passed that way as those who inhabited Vinland, whom the Greenlanders [i.e. Norse] call skraeling." Skraelings were described as "short people with threatening features and tangled hair on their heads… large eyes and broad cheeks."

Later that century, another writer noted in *Historia Norvegiae* (History of Norway): "On the other side of Greenland, toward the North, hunters have found some little people whom they call Skraeling… They have no iron at all; they use missiles made of walrus tusks and sharp stones for knives."

The word *Skraeling* may come from the Old Norse word for "to glide," but is usually considered a derogatory term, meaning "scared or scruffy one," or "small people."

Rokeby, Stefanski, van Poppel, Hartmann, de Ruyter, and Canzona—serve as council to the gyptian king. Faa assigns each family responsibility for a specific activity crucial to the expedition to Lapland, and each family contributes money to the endeavor.

NL/GC leaders appear at first Roping 7; receive assignments 8

Skraeling, Skraelings ✧ ⚘

World: Lyra's

Role: One of the less prominent, and perhaps less tolerated, ethnic groups of Lyra's world.

The first mention of Skraelings is when Lord Asriel shows Jordan College scholars what he claims is the head of the missing explorer and scientist Stanislaus Grumman. The head has been scalped in a manner similar to those of Tungusk and Siberian aboriginals. The Sub-rector then gratuitously remarks that the same patterns had been adopted by Skraelings, but New Denmark is trying to ban the practice.

Talk among doctors at the General Oblation Board's Experiment Station about the relative brutality of various techniques of intercision suggests that Skraelings tore dæmons from their enemies by hand for hundreds of years. They also use poison arrows in battle; when he was a young man gyptian Farder Coram was among their casualties. Grumman is rumored to have been involved in their wars in Beringland.

Gobbler victim Tony Makarios is part Skraeling, and the Magisterium's censor at the Nova Zembla observatory is known only as "the Skraeling."

Observation: *In Lyra's world, Skraelings and Europeans apparently had far more extensive and long-lasting contact than in ours, where conflicts with Skraelings likely contributed to the failure of Norse settlements in Vinland.*

NL/GC brief mentions: scalping and 2; ancestry of Tony Makarios 3, and Broken Arrow 4; armoured bears and 6; poison arrows of 10; technique of severing dæmons 16; 18, 19

SK referring to Magisterium's censor 6

The Tartars

In Will's world, the *Tartars* or *Tatars* are variously defined, most narrowly as a Turkic-speaking people of Russia's Ural Mountain region. Although the Tartars likely originated as a people in Siberia, their name is based on that of a 5th century Mongolian tribe, the Tata or Dada.

By the 13th century Tartar was broadly used to describe armies led by Mongols who invaded Europe; later it became a term used in Europe to refer to any Asian invaders. As the Russian and Ottoman empires gained strength in the late 15th century, the Tartars became less of a threat to Europe, although as late as 1572 they conducted a raid on Moscow. The Tartars, who had converted to Islam in the previous century, became more stable, raising crops in settled communities rather than primarily herding cattle and sheep as nomads, and establishing institutions for the study of Islam. Siberia and the Crimea were among their last strongholds; their influence on Russian culture was significant. When the USSR dissolved, many ethnic Tartars returned to the Crimea, and there is a movement to form an independent Tartarstan.

Walking around Will's Oxford, Lyra sees "a group of Tartars meekly following their leader, all neatly dressed and hung about with little black cases"—a description of camera-laden Asian tourists, perhaps.   176

Soviets/Soviet Union ⚕

World: Will's

Role: Sir Charles Latrom (the alias of Lord Boreal in Will's world) tells Coulter that the Soviet Union is equivalent to Muscovy in their world, and that in Will's world, the government intelligence agencies were "preoccupied for years with the Soviet Union." He states that he became a spy, but never told his bosses all he uncovered. Whether Latrom 177 spied for or against the Soviets or was a double agent is left to speculation, but Soviets have been in the Brooks Range of Alaska, seeking the opening to another world.

[*See also* **Muscovy, Russia**]

SK   brief mentions: by John Parry in letters about Alaska 5, Latrom 9

Tartars ✦ ⚕

World: Lyra's

Role: The Tartars are among the most feared fighting forces in Lyra's world, the subject of misconceptions and derogatory tales. Of all the societies he encounters in Lyra's world, the Tartars are the one which shaman and scientist Stanislaus Grumman (John Parry of Will's world) seems to appreciate most.

Tartars inhabit the region between the Ob and Yenisei rivers of Siberia, but as *Northern Lights/ The Golden Compass* opens, they have invaded Muscovy and their eventual domination of Europe is feared.

Alleged to scalp their victims and eat children, the Tartars are also said to half-kill their enemies by snapping apart their ribs and yanking out the lungs. The victim's dæmon then must apply continuous artificial respiration to keep its person alive. Other rumors regarding the Tartars are that they buy children taken by the Gobblers to use as slaves or to eat. After she flees Coulter and a full-scale campaign is mounted to find Lyra, the tale goes around that Lyra is an adult shrunken by their magic to act as a spy in advance of an invasion.

Tartars are strong fighters. Gyptian King John Faa says, "I never met fiercer," and as such they have attracted the attention of Mrs Coulter, who deploys them in her schemes. Her General Oblation Board hires Sibirsk Tartar riflemen equipped with flame throwers to guard the Bolvangar Experiment Station. That notwithstanding, Lyra's cunning allows the Bolvangar children to stand up against them.

Some Tartar tribes, or at least their prominent members, are polygamous, *e.g.* the village headman of the Yenisei Pakhtars. Their facial features—Asiatic, broad, dark eyes—are similar to the Samoyeds'. Lyra initially mistakes the hunters who abduct her from the gyptians for Tartars.

Siberian Tartars practice trepanation, not to terrorize enemies, as some assume, but as a means of honoring their own and in conjunction with their religious faith. Their holy men are shamans, who undergo a ritualized trepanation "so the gods can talk to them."

Notes: *John Faa recalls his slaying of "the Tartar champion on the steppes of Kazakhstan" in* Northern Lights — *but not in* The Golden Compass.

NL/GC scalping patterns discussed in Retiring Room 2; suspected in abduction of children 6; Scoresby on fighting in Tunguska campaign, trepanation and 13; guards prepare to attack Bolvangar escapees, children throw snow through helmets' eye slits, witches and Iorek attack followed by gyptians 17; troops arrive on Svalbard in Coulter's zeppelin, battle bears 22
  brief mentions: invasion of Muscovy 1, Lyra mistakes Samoyeds for 14, trepanation and 15, guards 16, Serafina on 18, in Lyra's fears for Iorek 19, alethiometer warns of 20

SK   and trepanation 4, rumors about Grumman and 6, Grumman's village 10

Texan [*See* Texas, country of; Texan in Cities, etc.]

Tungusk [*See* Tungusk/Tunguska in Cities, etc.]

Yenisei Pakhtars ✦ ⚑

World: Lyra's

Role: Tartar tribe into which the shaman Stanislaus Grumman was initiated. He stayed as an honored guest in one of their villages until he summoned aëronaut Lee Scoresby to take him to another world to find the bearer of the subtle knife.

NL/GC 13 [implied] *[brief]*

SK   *[brief];* their village 10

Yoruba ⚑

World: Lyra's

Role: One of the astronomers on Nova Zembla is described as a Yoruba.

Facts: Yoruba *is a term that can variously refer to one of the tribes or nationalities of Nigeria, the language spoken by this people, or a religion of West Africa.*

SK   6 *[brief]*

CREATURES, BEINGS, & EXTRAORDINARY HUMANS

Creatures, Beings, & Extraordinary Humans

Angels to *Zombi*

*When a group or species is mentioned simply in the place of a character's name (e.g. the bear instead of Iorek Byrnison) its chapter is not listed, unless the passage in question provides information about those creatures or beings in general. For information about a particular individual from any of these groups, see **Characters**.*

ANGELS ✤ ⚔ ✎ ⑩

World: All

Examples: Baruch, Balthamos, Xaphania, Metatron

Alliances: Not uniform – differs by individual

Physical characteristics: "All they are is light," says witch Ruta Skadi, who, like other mortals, is impressed with their appearance. Angels assume human form because that is what human eyes expect; if one could see "their true form, they would seem more like architecture than organism." The intensity of the light a viewer perceives varies with the status of the angel. Metatron's light renders Coulter "too dazzled to see," while Balthamos and Baruch, who are physically weaker than people and of a lowly angelic order, are barely visible in full daylight.

Metatron has feathered wings, as did the angel whom Will killed, slashing at his feathers with the subtle knife "until the air was filled with whirling flakes of white."

Will learned from Balthamos that angels are bewildered at humans' failure to fully enjoy the world and the pleasures of having bodies and senses. Mrs Coulter intuitively understands that those angels who were once human have a vulnerability she can exploit: "Lacking flesh, they coveted and longed for contact with it." The physical status of angels seems variable and quickly, inexplicably mutable. Mrs Coulter reaches for Metatron's hand as she leads him toward the abyss, but there is nothing for her to grasp, even though the angel seems to yearn for physical contact with a woman. Moments later, Metatron delivers skull crushing blows and experiences great pain when Coulter stabs her fingers into his eyes.

Angels can live thousands of years unless killed. Only the subtle knife can kill those of the highest orders; for the rest, assault with a far less potent weapon will work. Their manner of dying is like the dissipation of the ghosts who leave the world of the dead. Mortally wounded, Baruch

"Suprema," 1869

resists death, "straining and quivering to hold his wounded form together," but with a draft of air, "particles of the angel's form, loosened by the waning of his strength, swirled upwards into randomness, and vanished."

"*The Guardian of Paradise*" by Franz von Struck, 1889

Background: There are "uncountable billions" of angels. The realm of angels extends beyond the confines of the worlds of mortals; their "knowledge extend[s] over a million universes." Angels don't need windows to travel between worlds. The Shadow-particles, communicating through Mary Malone's computer, present themselves as angels, and confirm what Malone learned as a nun from St Augustine's teaching on angelic nature: "Angel is the name of their office, not of their nature . . . from what they are spirit; from what they do, angel." However, they substitute *matter* for *angel*, asserting, "…from what we do, matter. Matter and spirit are one."

Lord Asriel's manservant, Thorold, discusses the rebel angels with Serafina Pekkala. He says that according to the Church, some angels rebelled against the Authority "before the world was created, and got flung out of heaven and into hell." Thorold is skeptical but not entirely unconvinced that Asriel will achieve what these angels could not. Asriel's ally, King Ogunwe, undermines the foundations of Mrs Coulter's religious training when he says he has learned, presumably from the angel Xaphania, that the Authority did not create the angels but was simply the first angel to come into being. Malone's Shadow-particles, who identify themselves as angels, claim that they subsequently intervened in human evolution out of vengeance for being cast out of heaven when they challenged the Authority's legitimacy.

It is very rare for people to become angels when they die, but it can happen, and when it does, that person is spared from going to the world of the dead.

There are various names for angels. When Baruch and Balthamos first appear to Will, they identify themselves as "Watchers. *Bene elim.* In your language, angels." Watchers and lighted fliers are terms used among the people of Cittàgazze.

Behavior: Angels perceive all there is to know about a person, including "that aspect of [Will's] nature Lyra would have called his dæmon." Another aspect of this penetrating knowledge is experienced by Mrs Coulter in the presence of Metatron. Coulter felt that "every scrap of shelter and deceit was stripped away."

"*Angels' visits*," 1869

In some respects, the behavior of angels is not unlike humans'. They don't necessarily behave kindly, as Baruch's plea to Balthamos to show Will some compassion demonstrates. Balthamos and Baruch claim that angels tell the truth, although Balthamos' hesitancy in warning Will of the danger he faces from Metatron indicates that they are not compelled to tell all, and Metatron's susceptibility to Coulter's wiles suggests that self-deceit is possible. Moreover, the rebel angels say that the Authority is an angel whose claim to power is based on a lie. Their practical or worldly knowledge is not all-encompassing; it doesn't extend to all there is to know about human inventions, including the subtle knife.

Strong emotional attachments between angels, as Balthamos and Baruch clearly demonstrate, are obviously possible, but whether such partnerships are common is another question.

Role: In NORTHERN LIGHTS/THE GOLDEN COMPASS, angels are mentioned specifically only twice: as one of the thirty-six symbols on the alethiometer, and metaphorically in a description of the Aurora. It is not until midway through THE SUBTLE KNIFE that angels are first seen. Then they are in flight above Cittàgazze. Will is told that angels are behind his selection as bearer of the subtle knife, and that they will come to his aid. Not until THE AMBER SPYGLASS are individuals of this form of being named, yet with the exception of Metatron, they serve primarily as guides or helpers. Asriel's opponent, it turns out, is not the Authority, but his Regent, an angel.

An angel with upraised wings is the subject of the woodcut for chapter 6 of THE SUBTLE KNIFE, "Lighted Fliers." A falling angel is the subject of the woodcut for chapter 31, "Authority's End," in the **10TH** anniversary edition of THE AMBER SPYGLASS.

NL/GC brief mentions: 4, 10, 17

SK Joachim Lorenz on, Skadi joins 6; and Shadow-matter 12; watchers 13; Grumman on, bene elim 15
> *brief mentions:* battle in heaven 2, on alethiometer 4, carvings at Tower of Angels 7; on subtle knife's handle, Paradisi on 8

AS Will questions, appearance, origin, history of 2; watchers at basalt fortress 5; Ogunwe and Coulter discuss 16, Asriel on 28, in battle 29, of Clouded Mountain 30, their strength exemplified by Metatron 31, Will and Mary discuss 33, Balthamos vs. Gomez 35, and windows 37
> *brief mentions:* 3, knife's power to kill 6; Balthamos's age, angels' insights 8; 13, Lyra tells Tialys one commanded she go to dead 19, ghosts debate 23, and preparations for battle 24, Serafina on 36

ARMOURED BEARS ❖ ⚔ ✎

World: Lyra's, Asriel's republic, Cittàgazze (Iorek)

Examples: Iorek Byrnison, Iofur Raknison

Alliances: "The side that gave advantage to the bears," Lyra, witch Serafina Pekkala, Lee Scoresby, Asriel | 15

Physical characteristics: Standing ten feet tall, these bears have yellow-white fur and small black eyes. Like humans, they have opposable thumbs. All are left-handed, and their palms are "covered in horny skin an inch or more thick," with claws longer than Lyra's hands. In conversation, their voices are flat and deep. Their gait is characterized by | 16 moving both legs on the same side of their body simultaneously. Dogs in particular are extremely fearful of them.

Their strength, armour, and claws serve them well in hand-to-hand combat. When fighting witches, they wait for a witch to swoop down to fire her arrows and then reach out to grab her with their claws. With a single blow, armoured bears can crush a seal's skull or tear off a man's limb, but they are also capable of using these same claws with great delicacy and precision, as shown when Iorek Byrnison rejoins the pieces of the broken subtle knife. They also have a

Like the armoured bears of Lyra's world's Svalbard, male polar bears can reach over ten feet in height

fierce bite—in one-on-one combat Iorek kills Iofur Raknison not with his claws but by lunging at his throat. Bullets do not harm their armour, but they have one vulnerable spot where helmet and shoulder plates can't quite meet.

Background: Armoured bears generally are not social beings – they are fearsome warriors. As Iorek Byrnison tells Farder Coram and Lyra, "I am an armoured bear: war is the sea I swim in and the air I breathe." Traditionally they have lived in ice forts, forging their armour of sky-metal, and avoiding entanglements with humans. When they sleep, they pile snow over themselves for warmth, and they dress their wounds with bloodmoss.

Classical Greek Helmet

Raised by their mothers, they have little to do with their fathers, and in public gatherings the sexes sit apart. Some, for example Iofur Raknison, are polygamous; this may be correlated with status. Seal meat is their preferred food. Among their weapons are fire hurlers, for attacking at a distance.

The exile of bear-king Iorek Byrnison and the ascendancy of Prince Iofur Raknison have brought Svalbard's armoured bears to a crossroads. Raknison has rejected ice forts for a palace of marble, iron for gold, and independence for alliances with humans such as Coulter and the General Oblation Board, all in an effort to make his subjects live less like bears and more like humans. He and Byrnison represent opposing "kinds of beardom ... two futures, two destinies." When Byrnison vanquishes Raknison, the bears speedily eliminate all the human accoutrements Raknison forced upon his subjects.

Behavior: While they claim to have no dæmons, Iorek Byrnison says that a bear's armour, which he makes out of sky iron, is a bear's soul, the equivalent of a dæmon; Lyra is intrigued by idea that bears can "make their own souls." Byrnison notes too that although, like humans, they use language and tools, bears are not troubled by beliefs or by doubts. They have "no gods, no ghosts or dæmons. We live and die and that is that." What holds their society together is tradition: "Bear-nature is weak without custom, as bear-flesh is unprotected without armour."

Iorek tells Lyra that bears are never tricked by adversaries: "We see tricks and deceit as plain as arms and legs. We can see in a way humans have forgotten," a way comparable, he says, to Lyra's state of mind when she reads the alethiometer. When Lyra and Serafina Pekkala talk about how the bear king has been deceived by humans, Lyra thinks it is acting more like a human and less like a bear that gets one of them in trouble.

Their collective behavior reveals a pragmatic rationality. Faced with the climate change wrought by Asriel, several dozen bears choose to leave their ancestral kingdom of Svalbard. They head for the highest mountains on earth, but when they learn that they need the sea as much as they do the snow, they accept that the experiment has failed, and return home.

Although fights are common, murder is rare. When a fight to the death is undertaken deliberately, it is a public, ceremonial event. If the vanquishing of Iofur Raknison by Iorek Byrnison is typical, the victor finishes the fight by eating the heart of his slain opponent.

Armoured bears are viewed with both fear and respect. They are renowned for their skill in working with metals and notorious for their ruthless ways in battle. Having no dæmons of their own, they have no inhibitions about attacking a dæmon as well as its person. Iorek Byrnison slashes opens a Tartar guard's wolf dæmon at Bolvangar, killing its human at once. Gyptian Tony Costa tells Lyra that they've "been raiding the Skraelings for centuries" and are commonly employed as mercenaries because they are "vicious killers, absolutely pitiless. But they keep their word." [22]

Lee Scoresby affirms their trustworthiness, noting that he has never known any condition under which Iorek would break his word. He adds that the bears who accepted the General Oblation Board's job and agreed to keep Asriel imprisoned "will hold him on Svalbard until the last drop of blood drains from the body of the last bear alive." [23]

The bears' sense of duty and loyalty extends to their respect for their king. While they seem joyous at Iorek's defeat of Raknison, when Raknison was king, they went along with his various schemes. One, Søren Eisarson, is said to have "suffered" during Iofur's reign; still, he must have submitted since he is alive and not imprisoned.

Role: The first mention of armoured bears is in the opening scene of *HIS DARK MATERIALS* when Asriel shows the Jordan College scholars what he claims to be the scalped head of Stanislaus Grumman, found off the coast of Svalbard. While his colleagues refuse to consider that armoured bears might be scalping their victims, Professor Trelawney claims that, given the enthusiasm of the new bear-king Iofur Raknison for all things human, he wouldn't be so quick to dismiss the idea. Lord Asriel's investigations into the source of Dust eventually lead to his imprisonment in the armoured bears' kingdom of Svalbard.

When Farder Coram asks Witch-Consul Martin Lanselius what he would want to know, were he in the gyptian's place, the Witch-Consul replies that he'd ask where to hire an armoured bear.

The armoured bears are last seen fighting for Asriel's republic.

[*See also* **Panserbjørne**]

Bears without Armour

The Eskimos of Will's world claim that polar bears are left-handed, and scientists have recorded incidences of polar bears using tools. Like the armoured bears of Lyra's world, polar bears move both limbs of one side of the body simultaneously when they run, and stand between nine and ten feet tall.

In the 1960s, trappers and sportsmen were killing roughly 400 polar bears a year in Svalbard alone; at least another 900 were slaughtered in Canada, Greenland, and Alaska. Russia had outlawed hunting the bears in 1956, but it took until the mid-1970s for other Arctic nations to address the threat to the bears. Barry Lopez's *Arctic Dreams* provides a wealth of information about the natural history, peoples, and exploration of the Arctic, including its bears.

Polar bears are one of earth's largest surviving carnivores but weigh less than two pounds at birth

Note: *Much of what is said about armoured bears is specific to descriptions of Iorek. With the exception of one mention of a brown bear in the Himalayas and one of a polar bear by the Oxford University archaeologist Will visits (both animals),* bear *and* armoured bear *in* His Dark Materials *refer to the same creatures.*

NL/GC Trelawney on 2, Lanselius on 10; Kaisa on, lack of dæmons, armour and bear's soul 11; trustworthiness, gait 12; dexterity and strength of, social conventions, Iorek on why they can't be tricked 13; Scoresby and Serafina, Serafina and Lyra discuss 18; Lyra among Raknison's subjects on Svalbard, Santelia on, lefthandedness 19; polygamous, mortal combat tournament 20; treatment of political prisoners, including Asriel 21; battle witches and Tartars 22
> *brief mentions:* Asriel their prisoner 5, Tony Costa on 6; 7, gyptians oppose rescuing Asriel because of 8; 23

SK brief mentions: 1, 5, 8

AS and difficulty with environmental changes 3; Borisovitch on, hostility of villagers toward 8; Will among on journey to Himalayas 9, skill with metals exemplified in Iorek's mending of subtle knife 15, in battle on side of republic 31
> *brief mentions:* lack of gods, ghosts, dæmons 14; 16, 29, 32; Lyra wonders if she should go to live among 35, 38

Bears [*See* Armoured bears]

Bene elim [*See* Angels *and chapter on* Language]

Black Shuck ✵

World: Lyra's
Role: Lyra is intrigued by the gyptians' tales of this ghost dog of the Fens.
Facts: *English folklore includes stories of ghostly dogs, often black and headless, which in some places are referred to as "Shuck" (e.g. Dunstable) or "Old Shuck" (e.g. Norfolk). "Shuck" may be derived from a word meaning demon in Old English:* scucca.
NL/GC 6 [*brief*]

Breathless Ones ✵

World: Lyra's
Role: Gyptian Tony Costa claims that the Tartars torture their enemies by reaching into their chests and ruining their lungs, rendering them half-dead. These so-called Breathless Ones survive only as long as their dæmons can provide what amounts to artificial respiration—pressing air into them day and night without ceasing.
NL/GC 6 [*brief*]

Cliff-ghasts ✵ ⚔ ✎

World: Lyra's, Cittàgazze, and Asriel's
Alliances: None
Physical characteristics: Described as "half the size of a man, with leathery wings and hooked claws ... a flat head, with bulging eyes and a wide frog mouth." They smell awful and shriek or make a "yowk-yowk-yowk" noise.

Background: Found on the cliffs of Svalbard and in rural Cittàgazze, although witch Ruta Skadi claims the thousands she encounters flying out of her world and into that of Cittàgazze must be from a third world altogether. A cliff-ghast elder alleges to have been alive since before the advent of humans and to have witnessed the war between the Authority and the rebel angels.

Behavior: Enemy of humans, witches, and all other living beings. Cliff-ghasts find Arctic foxes tasty but hard to catch. Whereas the other creatures of the far North don't listen to these scavengers' gossip, knowing them to be liars, the cliff-ghasts listen to the foxes' tales, and then kill the little beasts. They travel in loosely organized gangs or flocks. Younger cliff-ghasts bring food scraps to the most ancient of their number, but make no effort to restrain their greediness with their peers. Regarding the coming war between Asriel's republic and the Authority's kingdom, they rejoice in the prospect of large numbers of casualties.

Role: Svalbard's cliff-ghasts attack Lee Scoresby's balloon, and in the ensuing chaos, Lyra tumbles out and becomes a prisoner of the armoured bears.

Ruta Skadi reports overhearing Grandfather cliff-ghast claim that Asriel cannot win since he lacks Æsahættr.

A cliff-ghast and his cronies attack the Authority's crystal litter, but before they can get it open, Will and Lyra chance upon them. When Will cuts off the head of one of them the others retreat.

NL/GC attack Scoresby's balloon 18
　　brief mentions: 13, 20

SK　2 *[brief]*, Ruta Skadi on Æsahættr and 13

AS　torment arctic fox 3; attack crystal litter 30; Will battles, Tialys dies after spurring 31
　　brief mentions: 2, 24, 29

DÆMONS ❖ ⚲ ✎ ⑩ LS

World: All

Examples: Pantalaimon, the golden monkey, Kaisa

Alliances: Their person

Physical characteristics: The visible dæmons of Lyra's world have two significant physical attributes: they appear as animals and their form can change while their person remains a child. At puberty, the form settles, never to change again. The dæmon is said to choose its "settled" form.

This settled form reflects the dæmon's person's character. Those who don't like the settled form of their dæmon are frustrated until they achieve self-acceptance. It is unusual but possible for a person's dæmon to be his/her own gender. Shaman Stanislaus Grumman, who (as John Parry) lacked a visible dæmon in his world of origin, finds that knowing his dæmon is female has heightened his understanding of the feminine aspect of his own nature.

Settled forms vary from insects (Father Gomez's beetle) to reptiles (Charles Latrom's/Lord Boreal's snake), to birds (the Master of Jordan College's raven) to mammals (Lord Asriel's snow leopard). One former Jordan College Master's dæmon took the form of a basilisk, and Pan turns briefly into a dragon and a gargoyle, but otherwise all animals mentioned as dæmon-forms are known in Will's world, as well as

Lyra's.

All witches, who spend much time aloft, have bird dæmons. Dogs are common among servants (*e.g.* Jordan College's), while soldiers' tend to be wolves (the Swiss Guards', the Tartar mercenaries' at Bolvangar), at least in the northern hemisphere. An African soldier fighting for Asriel has a wildcat dæmon, and Asriel's high commander in the field, warrior King Ogunwe, has a cheetah. Dæmons of very dull-witted children, like Tony Makarios', change infrequently, while those of the more quick thinking, like Lyra's Pan, can flash through a number of forms in rapid succession.

As with the angels of *HIS DARK MATERIALS*, the physical substantiality of dæmons is peculiar. They take the forms of animals, but not their physical development: they do not begin as newborns and mature, their life expectancies are not that of the animals whose form they suggest, they do not reproduce, nor do they eat – which is one explanation for the lack of the natural hostilities otherwise to be expected between such combinations as Will's cat and Mary Malone's bird dæmons.

And yet, their chosen forms limit some of their capacities. Bird dæmons can fly; cat dæmons can't. Watching Pan at play in the form of a dolphin, Lyra wonders what would happen if he settled as a sea creature. The able seaman, her friend on the gyptians' voyage, tells of a sailor who, because his dæmon was a dolphin, could never go ashore.

There are other indications that dæmons have some physicality. Those whose dæmons are mammals, for example, Lord Asriel and Farder Coram, stroke their feline dæmons' fur. The Bolvangar doctors measured a dæmon's weight separately from its person's. In the dæmon-cages, the severed beings making "faint cries of pain and misery" are described as "ghost-like" and "pale as smoke," but a dæmon with its person is as colorful as the animal its form suggests. The rich blend of colors in the coats of Farder Coram's and Will's cat dæmons is memorable, and the golden monkey is, of course, golden. Pan at play with the Gallivespians' dragonflies makes himself even more vibrantly colored and patterned than they are. As the Bolvangar Experiment Station burns and the fleeing children wait in freezing winds for the gyptians' rescue party, Pan admonishes the dæmons to make themselves large to provide warmth to their people.

And although it is taboo for a dæmon to touch a person not its own, they can physically intimidate; Stelmaria's snarl quells Lyra's disobedience. Lyra resists her impulse to smash the dæmon-cages at Bolvangar when Serafina Pekkala's dæmon Kaisa orders her to stop. She respects his age, strength, and status as a witch's dæmon. Although dæmons may attack dæmons but not others' humans, they have enough physical substantiality to attack a non-dæmon successfully. For example, when the spy flies sent by Mrs Coulter attack Pan on the gyptians' ship, the tillerman's cormorant dæmon is successful in snatching one in flight, which she drops onto the ship's deck. The Gallivespian spy captain Lord Roke is captured by a witch's dæmon.

Armoured bears have no dæmons, and thus don't respect the taboo against touching a person's; they are in turn attacked by dæmons. When Iorek Byrnison breaks into the Trollesund priest's house to retrieve his stolen armour, the sentry's dæmon, a husky, goes for the bear's throat, but Iorek brushes her off.

Angels are vulnerable to attack by dæmons. The Swiss Guard's wolf-dog dæmons threaten the angel Balthamos. He also suffers from the stings of Father Gomez's beetle dæmon. The golden monkey and Stelmaria are as instrumental in the defeat of Metatron as their people, Mrs Coulter and Lord Asriel, are.

When its person dies, a dæmon fades, "drifting away like the atoms of smoke." It seems that the person must die before the dæmon can dissipate; the dæmons trapped in jars at Bolvangar linger on, weak, frail and pathetic, as long as the mutilated children manage to survive, which generally is not long.

But it is possible for a dæmon to be directly annihilated, either before or simultaneously with its person. When Iorek's claws rip into a Tartar guard's wolf dæmon at Bolvangar, "bright fire spilled out of her as she fell to the snow, where she hissed and howled before vanishing" as the guard died simultaneously.

The physical perception of dæmons by humans not of Lyra's world is complicated. The working assumption is that these humans' dæmons are internalized, but Will and Mary Malone are eventually able to see their dæmons. They are thus not exclusively internal, or even invisible. Instead, the visibility of these dæmons requires faith or specialized sight. Seeing is believing is inverted, and believing is seeing, so it would seem.

John Parry sees his osprey dæmon as soon as he enters Lyra's world, but his later assumption of the role of shaman suggests a greater than normal capacity for heightened perception. His son, Will, in contrast, journeys through Lyra's world without seeing his own dæmon, although he sees those of all the people he meets. In spite of this evidence, Will doesn't fully accept that he too has a dæmon until he is wretched with despair at having to leave her behind to enter the world of the dead.

In the mulefa's world, Will finally meets his dæmon when she and Pan come out of hiding. Will quickly learns to tell Kirjava from Pan even while the dæmons are still changing. Interestingly, Will (with only his experience of Lyra's dæmon Pan) is the one to figure out from a quick glance at the serpent up his sleeve that Sir Charles Latrom/Lord Boreal, is of Lyra's world.

Mary Malone has no trouble seeing Pan and Kirjava in the mulefa's world. She suggests to Serafina that Will never saw his dæmon in Lyra's world because he didn't believe he had one. Still, Mary has to be taught to see her own dæmon. Serafina advises Mary that the way to see her dæmon is to achieve a state of mind comparable to that which Lyra uses to read her alethiometer but to couple this with ordinary perception. Interestingly, while

"Lady With an Ermine"
by Leonardo da Vinci, 1485

In a 2001 profile, Pullman told Catherine Andronik that his notion of the dæmon-human bond was strengthened by his response to this painting: "There's a real connection between the girl and the animal. That is her dæmon," and, he adds, the girl "if you made a few small alterations...could be Lyra," and that he now collects images that capture this bond. As the program for the National Theatre's 2003 season production of HIS DARK MATERIALS observes, "Philip Pullman considers that previously unrecognised dæmons have appeared in portraits throughout the ages." It is illustrated with six other such examples, including William Hogarth's *Self Portrait with his Dog Trump*, Tiepolo's *Young Woman with Macaw*, and a medieval woodcut of a boy and wolf.

Serafina can see Mary's in the mulefa's world, she couldn't see Will's in Cittàgazze, and Lyra couldn't see Will's in that world, or Mary's in the mulefa's world. Moreover, Serafina tells Mary that others in her world won't be able to see her dæmon or Will's unless they are taught to, but Will and Mary will be able to see their own and each other's.

Until a person sees his or her own dæmon, typically no ordinary human can either. Lyra can only imagine Will's dæmon. Sometimes she pretends his dæmon is a cat sleeping alongside him. Other times she seems simply frustrated, knowing that Will's dæmon "*must be here somewhere.*"

Witches are a special category of humans in Lyra's world, and one aspect of their difference is that witches' dæmons can be much further apart, miles even, from their people than can ordinary humans' dæmons. Witches achieve this power through an initiation ritual involving leaving their dæmons behind while they travel into a different realm. By journeying to the world of the dead, Lyra and Will inadvertently engage in a comparable task, and like witches, are subsequently able to be apart from their dæmons. Shaman Stanislaus Grumman also learned to be apart from his dæmon, but he doesn't elaborate on how he managed this. The morning Lyra awakens in the mulefa's world, she realizes on some level that she and Pan can now be separated without pain. He is not near her, but what she feels is not comparable to how she felt in the world of the dead.

Like their people, witches' dæmons don't feel cold, and they have unusual powers or skills; for example, as Lyra blows a bit of snow toward each cage, by just making a clicking noise, Kaisa can unlock the Bolvangar dæmon-cages. The powers of a shaman extend to his dæmon; for example, Sayan Kötör, Stanislaus Grumman's dæmon, marshals the force of flocks of numerous species of birds to act as one.

Background: Mary and Will find the concept of a soul to be the closest approximation, in their world, to the dæmon that in Lyra's world is seen as evidence of a being's humanity.

Mary Malone equates Will's speculations on the "three-part nature of human beings"—human ghosts, dæmons, and bodies—with Catholic theology's spirit, soul, and body. When Will and Lyra discuss visiting the world of the dead, they decide that a person has a body, a dæmon, and a third part that thinks about his or her body and dæmon, and continues after the body decays and the dæmon dissipates, which is the ghost or spirit.

The identification of soul and dæmon is part of Lyra's culture. For example, when the Skraeling censor dies on Nova Zembla, and his owl dæmon disappears, Lee Scoresby believes his soul has left his body. The dæmons of martyrs are depicted in religious paintings as being carried away by cherubs. Because only those with dæmons can be baptized, no amount of emulation of humans or devotion to the Magisterium will gain armoured bear Iofur Raknison the baptism he seeks to prove his status is as great as any man's.

The relationship between Dust and dæmons explains the curious behavior of Spectres. This is shown to be true when Lena Feldt, a witch with an externalized dæmon,

28

29

Philip Pullman on Dæmons:

From an interview on the UK website achuka.co…

"Dæmons came into my head suddenly and unexpectedly, but they do have a sort of provenance. One clear origin is Socrates' daimon. Another is the old idea of the guardian angel."

falls victim to the Spectres. Spectres consume the witch's dæmon, and she is forced to watch him "fluttering and shrieking as if he were in a glass chamber that was being emptied of air." 30

Serafina Pekkala tells Lyra that witches believe having dæmons is the way people differ from animals, and in the world of Cittàgazze, where people's dæmons are internal, when Serafina sees Spectres feasting, she believes they are making a meal of "some quality the man had, his soul, his dæmon." 31

In the Book of Genesis in Lyra's world, in addition to knowledge of good and evil, the serpent promises Eve that she will know her dæmon's "true form"; until then, even though they were adults, Adam's and Eve's dæmons' forms shifted. With their dæmons' fixed forms also came, according to Asriel, "sin and shame and death." Mrs Coulter 32 claims that dæmons are "infected with Dust," and she tells Lyra that at puberty, dæmons "bring all sort of troublesome thoughts and feelings, and that's what lets Dust in." 33

Another critical aspect of the relationship between dæmon and person, one that is exploited by Lord Asriel, is the tremendous amount of energy that exists in the bond. Lord Asriel's realization that the dæmon-bond is key to opening a passage to the world behind the Aurora and his long-term efforts to find the most efficient means to sever this bond are mentioned in the appendix notes to the **10ᴛʜ** anniversary edition of *Northern Lights/The Golden Compass*. When the dæmon-bond is severed, that energy is very briefly available, and Asriel harnesses the energy to blast through the Aurora to another world. The bond is also utilized to power and direct his war machine, the intention craft.

There is one final characteristic of dæmons which would have rendered futile Asriel's effort to build a republic of heaven in a neutral world, had he lived, and which proves emotionally devastating to Lyra and Will. Dæmons cannot thrive in any but their own worlds. Those who have divided their time between worlds, like Latrom/Boreal, know that they have to return to their world of origin regularly. Those who find themselves unable to, like John Parry, die young.

Behavior: The behavior of a dæmon ideally is based in its purpose, which, witch Serafina Pekkala reminds Pan and Kirjava, is to help their humans, especially in times of great sorrow and need.

The relationship between a person and dæmon should be mutually beneficial. Lyra tells Will that the cat he saved from a mob of Spectre-orphans and who came to Will's aid against the golden monkey, "done what a good dæmon would have done ... We rescued her and she rescued us." 34

A child's dæmon, like Pan, might try to talk its person out of taking unnecessary risks, like hiding in the Retiring Room, or into facing unpleasant truths, like Mrs Coulter's fundamental untrustworthiness, but an adult's dæmon behaves like a co-conspirator. The golden monkey, for example, supports Mrs Coulter in all her schemes, from seducing and murdering Charles Latrom/Lord Boreal to stealing the intention craft.

Children's dæmons skirmish to resolve differences between their people, but these battles are displays to establish dominance and no injury is inflicted. The dæmons of adults will act against other dæmons, even when their person is not at risk. Lyra's shock at this behavior, demonstrated by the dæmons of the doctors forcing her and Pan into the silver guillotine, suggests that such aggression is something that children's dæmons would never consider.

And while Lyra and Pan, Coulter and the golden monkey, or Scoresby and Hester may argue and sulk with one another, never would they cause the other intentional harm. For better or worse, dæmon and person act as a team. The Gallivespian spy captain Lord Roke understands this, explaining to Mrs Coulter that he always sends spies on missions in pairs so that humans with dæmons aren't at an advantage. A notable exception, however, is when Father MacPhail decides to martyr himself through intercision. His dæmon resists mightily, but to no avail. MacPhail kills them both. His dæmon's resistance may mean that on some level MacPhail is divided about his decision, or it may underscore the un-naturalness or perversity of his action.

Lyra is flummoxed when she meets Will because her usual skill at manipulating people and situations is dependent on reading the subtle signs their dæmons send. Not being able to see Will's dæmon restricts her understanding of the strange boy. Even though his wouldn't yet have a settled form, all dæmons provide by their reactions and postures clues for evaluating a person's behavior. A nervous person may strive to appear outwardly calm, but the dæmon's behavior will betray an inner agitation.

Although usually contentedly solitary, Will seeing Lyra with Pan is surprised how lonely he feels. Lyra pities what she perceives as loneliness in Iorek, which she supposes is worsened by having no dæmon. But unlike Will, the bear expresses no sense of deprivation; having never had a dæmon, he doesn't miss it. Will, of course, has one; he just doesn't yet know she is there for him.

Dæmons provide safe outlets for emotional expression. For example, children's dæmons enjoy play-fighting, and conflicts between children can be settled by one of their dæmons achieving dominance. This horseplay, common among children's dæmons, is useful when Lyra needs for Roger to pretend not to know her when they meet at Bolvangar; Pan attacks Roger's dæmon Salcilia setting up a diversion, and then tells the boy's dæmon what's up. The love-play of adults' dæmons, for instance of Stelmaria and the golden monkey as their two people debate going into another world, may be comparable to the play-fights of children's dæmons; it suggests an outward display of what in a world of internalized dæmons would be a possibly confusing subtext to a conversation.

Dæmons share alterations in their person's physiological state. For example, when Roger and Lyra get drunk in the wine cellars at Jordan College, their dæmons do too. Pan is as groggy as Lyra when she is awakened from many weeks of drugged sleep. Dæmons share their people's dreams, as well.

Having an external dæmon provides certain practical advantages. A dæmon can provide its person a second set of eyes and ears, so to speak, in scouting out lurking dangers or by serving as look-out while the person's attention is otherwise engaged. The animal attributes of a particular dæmon can also be useful to its person; the Tartar sledge driver Umaq relies on his Arctic fox dæmon's nose rather than a compass to navigate, and Lee Scoresby lowers his hare dæmon Hester to the ground to find their way through thick fog. Pan assumes the form of a bird to look in the windows of the Tower of Angels. For shamans and witches, this skill is enhanced by their dæmons' ability to be unusually far from their people.

The dæmons of Lyra's world communicate with their people by thinking to them, which suggests the way Stanislaus Grumman/John Parry describes the dæmons of humans in Will's world: "a silent voice in the mind and no more." But Lyra's world's dæmons also have a vocal presence in the world: they talk, a behavior that Will finds particularly astonishing.

Generally, dæmons speak with dæmons, but they can speak in place of their human

Of dæmons and demons:

When Lyra first meets Will, she immediately asks where his "dæmon" is. Will answers that he hasn't a "demon," and that in his world, demon means "devil, something evil." What is recapitulated in this brief exchange is a historical confusion and misreading by early Christian theologians of the Greek philosophers. [36]

In Greek classical usage, *daimonion* referred to usually helpful and positive spirits or lesser gods who mediated between humans and the more powerful gods, and thus were not unlike guardian angels. Socrates, for example, referred to an inspirational, divine voice that aided him in making ethical choices as his *daimon*.

But when Early Christian writers rejected pantheistic gods, the helpful spirits were dismissed along with the evil and destructive ones. Over time, the good were forgotten, but the malevolent became demons, and the chief demon was the devil, or, in other words, Satan and the fallen angels.

Later Christian writers, and in particular 19th century England's Cardinal Manning, on re-examining Xenophon, Cicero, and Plato, determined that the association of Socrates' daimon with an evil spirit was unjust, and to the contrary, Socrates' daimon was his conscience, which is divinely inspired.

in extreme circumstances, for example, when their human is dying (*e.g.* the gyptian spy Jacob Huismans) or deeply ashamed (*e.g.* Lyra when she feels she's given Will away to the police). Witches' dæmons speak in the absence of their person to humans and dæmons alike, and Pan, because Will lacks a visible dæmon, addresses the boy directly.

When people don't speak the same language, their dæmons can still communicate—the dæmons then relay messages telepathically to their people. Fortunately for Will, the angel Balthamos has learned many languages in his travels. When he is posing as Will's dæmon during their trek through Lyra's world, he can both attain needed information and not be immediately recognized as a fraud – although true dæmons don't trust him. Of course, Balthamos' transference of messages is not near-simultaneous as a true dæmon's would be (as he has to translate and then whisper them to Will).

The two most critical restrictions on the behavior of dæmons are the prohibition against touching another person's dæmon, and, with some exceptions, the necessity of dæmon and person being physically within a few yards of one another.

When even briefly separated more than usual (*e.g.* children testing just how far apart they and their dæmons can be), both feel intense psychological and physical pain. For example, Pan, knows they need to tell Iorek Byrnison where his armour is, yet Lyra fears approaching the massive bear alone, so he forces her to face the bear by moving away from her, toward Iorek. As he moves away from her, Lyra must follow, and, of course, finds that Pan would not have led her into danger. Any residual apprehension she feels about facing Iorek is nothing to the pain of being separated from Pan: she "would rather die than let them be parted and face that sadness again; it would send her mad with grief and terror." Although they can't see their own dæmons, Will and the Gallivespians feel [37] the same kind, if not degree, of agony as Lyra as they cross into the world of the dead. There, the ghosts they meet, even those from worlds like Will's where dæmons are internal, long for their dæmons with an unremitting sense of loss. The longer they are apart from their dæmons, the more fatigued and despondent Lyra and Will become.

This fear of the pain brought by being just a few feet or even inches too far apart is inestimably amplified when permanent severance is imagined. Lyra encounters firsthand the horror of being severed from one's dæmon when she meets Tony Makarios. She thinks: "A human being with no dæmon was like someone without a face, or with their ribs laid open and their heart torn out." The typically courageous Pantalaimon is perhaps even more frightened than Lyra when they approach the shed where the severed Gobbler victim clutches a frozen fish in place of his lost dæmon.

After his initial repulsion, Pan wants to comfort Tony but is inhibited by the taboo against a dæmon touching any but its own person. This makes Pan's willingness to break it for Will, without even asking Lyra's consent, all the more startlingly significant. Even those released from the Bolvangar dæmon-cages, starved for contact with their own person, don't violate the taboo by clinging to Lyra, although they come very near to doing so. They cluster around Lyra, much as the ghosts will do in the world of the dead.

When a person does grasp another's dæmon, as for example when the Bolvangar doctors catch Pan, it is not only the dæmon who is overcome with terror. Lyra felt "as if an alien hand had reached right inside where no hand had a right to be, and wrenched at something deep and precious." The exception is when the people touching each other's dæmons are loved ones. In the mulefa's world, when Will, resting alongside Lyra, and "knowing exactly what he was doing and exactly what it would mean ... stroked the red-gold fur of her dæmon," Lyra's "surprise was mixed with a pleasure," and she responds in kind. As people fall in love, so do their dæmons. Even before they are reconciled with Will and Lyra, Kirjava and Pan are in love with one another. Dæmons will engage in sensual touching in ways suiting their varied settled physical forms to mirror their people's love-play.

Role: Dæmons, the inner voice of a person externalized in the form of an animal, fixed in adults and shifting in children, are one of the most intriguing aspects of the world introduced in the first volume of His Dark Materials.

It soon becomes evident that these beings are of great significance to the trilogy. The culture of Lyra's society; the threat to the children and their dæmons posed by the General Oblation Board (Gobblers); Lyra's mother's crucial role in this activity; Lyra's desire to rescue her friend Roger; the revelation of the cruel and horrific practice of intercision performed at the Board's Bolvangar Experiment Station; the gradual clarification of the relationship between Dust and dæmons; and finally the harnessing of the energy held in the bond between body and dæmon to break open the sky and bridge Lyra's to the world of Cittàgazze: all of these actions and themes have at their center the dæmons of Lyra's world.

In the world of the dead, Gallivespian spy Tialys tells his colleague Salmakia that he believes that there is a relationship between Lyra's being a world in which one's dæmon is external and Lyra's world being the one that has produced a leader willing to challenge the Authority and to establish a republic of heaven.

An attack by marauding Tartars lands Lyra herself in Bolvangar, where she and her dæmon Pan are nearly severed by the silver guillotine. Severed dæmons trapped in jars languish in a shed; and the Bolvangar nurses, who seem strangely but not apparently defective in their reactions and attitudes, prove to be severed adults.

Finding herself in the usurper-king armoured bear Iofur Raknison's palace dungeon, Lyra talks herself out of the cells by telling Raknison that she herself is a dæmon, made by Bolvangar doctors after Iorek Byrnison volunteered for experiments in creating dæmons. She argues since humans' dæmons have animal forms, naturally animals' dæmons would have human forms.

In THE SUBTLE KNIFE, Lyra moves through two worlds in which dæmons are most conspicuous by their apparent absence. When she and Pan meet Will Parry in Cittàgazze, they are initially repulsed since the boy has no dæmon. Lyra concludes that his dæmon is internalized, as are, she soon learns, those in the world of Cittàgazze as well as in Will's own. Still, when she visits his Oxford, the alienation she feels at seeing so much that is at once familiar and bizarre is heightened by the strangeness of seeing people apart from their dæmons.

The nature of the human-dæmon bond is further explored in THE AMBER SPYGLASS. Pantalaimon does not want Lyra to go to the world of the dead; he has seen what happens to people and their dæmons when the person dies. But he knows he has to let Lyra go and shows his love by not condemning her for her choice.

Will's cutting a window and releasing the ghosts now means Pan will not be separated forever from Lyra at her death. When she leaves the world of the dead, she, like Pan, will dissolve and their molecules will mingle again in the universe of living things.

Will meets his dæmon, Kirjava, for the first time in the mulefa's world. While Will and Lyra struggled through the world of the dead, the dæmons visited a number of other worlds. Kirjava and Pan play hard-to-get, but as the children sleep, the two come to them, and touch their people "softly with nose, paw, whiskers, bathing in the life-giving warmth they gave off," and check that Will's hand is healing and Lyra is comfortable. [41]

When Will finally meets his dæmon, "he felt his heart tighten and release in a way he never forgot." He will have with him always the memory of his dæmon "being torn from his unsuspecting breast" when he crossed over to the world of the dead. But he will also remember "the sweet rightfulness of her coming back to him at the edge of the moonlit dunes" in the mulefa's world. [42]

Observation: *Pullman's concept of the nature of dæmons appears to have been refined as* NORTHERN LIGHTS *progressed. In* NORTHERN LIGHTS, *when Roger and Lyra examine the Masters' coffins in the Jordan College crypt, the images depicting the deceased dæmons include "a fair woman," but she has dropped out of the same passage in* THE GOLDEN [43] COMPASS. *A basilisk is also mentioned in this passage, and other than the times Pan becomes a dragon and a gargoyle, this is the only suggestion of a dæmon taking a mythical animal's form. Moreover, when the dæmon of the Jordan College Enquirer—an adult—is described, the passage reads: "His dæmon at the time was coiled around his neck in the form of a snake," which suggests that her form is variable.* [44]

Update: The second Lantern Slide in THE SUBTLE KNIFE explains why the cat Will rescues in Cittàgazze is unimpressed by Pantalaimon. A dæmon is "not an animal" but instead is a "person." Thus, when a cat encounters what a person would see to be a dæmon in cat form, the cat "would see a human being."

NL/GC challenging person's decisions, servants' 1; Dust, children, and 2; get drunk, old Masters' forms included fair woman and basilisk, Pan as dragon, forms assumed reflect child's imaginative powers, share person's emotions 3; Pan looks away when Lyra bathes 4; and person feel each other's physical pain 5; what happens when their person dies 6; effect of cedar on, sex of 7; Lyra and Pan experience flashes of understanding simultaneously 8; taboos surrounding touch, can speak for person 9; witches', significance of settled forms 10; sleep when person sleeps, compared to bears' armour, can speak to another one while person's attention is seemingly elsewhere, limited range of movement away from person of, sentry's willingness to physically challenge Iorek, comforting of injured and distressed person 11; mutilated condition of severed Tony Makarios 12; instinctive revulsion from severed, death and severance, Lyra equates armour-making to making soul 13; Bolvangar nurses', dullness of dull people's 14; Bolvangar doctors' tests 15; severed caged dæmons, severing techniques, feeling of violation when another person touches, share their person's dreams 16; Coulter on Dust and puberty and, can choose form to keep person warm, Iorek kills dæmons 17; Lyra and Serafina discuss 18; Raknison's desire for, baptism and, Lyra pretends to be Iorek's 19; Dust and, children's and, Adam and Eve and original sin and, zombis' lack of, energy linking body and 21; flirtatious behavior of Coulter's and Asriel's, a whole person is never truly alone 23

SK   Lyra's initial fear of Will's lack, Will's confusion of demon and dæmon, Lyra decides Will does have one 1; Lanselius on zombi, Magisterium, severance and 2 [brief]; Will's reactions to Pan, surprise when he speaks 3; strangeness to Lyra of not seeing dæmons in Will's world 4; tabby cat isn't fooled by Pan in cat form 5 [brief]; helps person with navigation, at person's death 6; Pan speaks for Lyra 7; Will realizes he has seen Latrom's, Pan tries to intimidate but wouldn't have been able to touch Tullio, Pan comforts Will 8; Coulter and Latrom consider zombis' lack of, Lyra on what good ones do 9; Grumman on meeting his 10; Will on children's and zombi's 11; Pan's empathy for animals, Will confides his fears to Pan 13; of shamans 14; Spectres consume 15; *LS* Lantern Slide 2

AS   can understand other languages, convey meaning to person telepathically 1; Will tells Balthamos he must pretend to be dæmon 2; tulku's shows person how to compile potion 4; susceptible to suggestion when asleep 5; severance of and energy release 6; angel aware of Will's although boy isn't, dæmons not fooled by Balthamos 8; sailors consider Will's like witch's 9 [brief]; grogginess of Lyra matched by Pan's 12 [brief]; attack angel, Lyra and Will consider as third part of people along with ghosts and bodies, Gallivespians uninhibited by taboo against touching 13; Iorek on 14; Lord Roke on, and intention craft 16; Lyra's musing about Will's, and the dead 18; Lyra's death claims closeness to her she says she shares with Pan 19; parting from Pan as Will, Gallivespians feel separation from their dæmons 21; ghosts' longing for, Gallivespians discuss Lyra's world's giving rise to Asriel and 22; released ghosts will vanish like their dæmons 23; MacPhail's resists intercision 25; Parry's warning 26; Metatron and 28; Lyra and Will grow progressively weaker the longer they are apart from theirs, sicken when Spectres approach Pan and Kirjava 29; "body and ghost and dæmon" 30; attack Metatron, Spectres and, Will and Lyra seize each other's 31; Will and Lyra feel no anguish and pain although physically apart from theirs in mulefa's world 32; Mary compares Will's idea of body-dæmon-ghost to body-spirit-soul 33; Will and Lyra discuss settling, Will's worry having one would be too revealing 35; Serafina tells Pan and Kirjava they will be like witches', lectures them on providing their people support and comfort in crisis 36; Will meets his, Parry's warning recalled, Dust and dæmons 37; Mary learns to see, Lyra learns Pan and Kirjava have secrets they've not yet shared with their people 38; *LS* Lantern Slide 3

10ᴛʜ: *NL/GC* appendix

10ᴛʜ: *SK* appendix

Death(s) ✎

World: Suburbs of the world of the dead

45   **Examples:** Lyra's, Magda's

Physical characteristics: Pale, shabbily dressed beings, "people-shaped things."

Background: A person's death is present with him or her from birth onwards, although people are not aware of their presence. Because they are not liked, they stay out of sight, according to the death accompanying Magda, the very old grandmother of the family Will and Lyra meet before crossing over to the world of the dead. Magda's death says that deaths hide themselves to be polite, staying just out of sight.

Lyra's death describes himself as knowing her better than she knows herself, but Lyra counters that Pan holds that honor, and although her death doesn't argue the point, Pantalaimon realizes that death and dæmons are not compatible, and that Lyra's death will accompany her when Pan has vanished.

Behavior: Polite, kindly, and boring, they don't interfere until it is time for a person to die.

46   Then "death taps you on the shoulder, or takes your hand, and says, come along o' me, it's time" and leads the way to the lake one crosses to the world of the dead. In the suburbs

of the world of the dead, Peter, Will and Lyra's host, explains that "your death comes into the world with you, and it's your death that takes you out." [47]

Role: Lyra and Will learn about people's deaths when they stay with a family who has inexplicably landed in the suburbs of the dead before it is their time to die. During the family's long wait for their own deaths to tell them it is time to cross over to the world of the dead, these deaths bide their time, staying close to one another and drawing no attention to themselves. The exception is the elderly grandmother's death, who stays very close to her – she is near death quite literally. This death tells Will and Lyra that their only way into the world of the dead is through welcoming their deaths.

To Lyra's query about how to summon her death, Magda's death answers that if she wishes to speak with him, he will come to her. Lyra's death agrees to show her the way to the land of the dead, but tells her he can offer no help with getting her back to the world of the living.

AS Lyra's 19, 21; ghost girl on confusing deaths and dæmons 22 *[brief]*

GALLIVESPIANS

World: Gallivespians' (origin), Lyra's, Asriel's, Desert world, Beach world, World of the dead, Mulefa's (burial)

Examples: Lord Roke, Chevalier Tialys, Lady Salmakia, Madame Oxentiel

Alliances: Asriel

Physical characteristics: The Gallivespians are so small that hailstorms are deadly to them because hailstones are bigger than two of their fists.
Even with a height equivalent to a human's hand span, they are accorded respect and caution, however, because on their heels are spurs that deliver an excruciating sting of paralyzing poison. Their lifespan is nine to ten years. If Tialys and Salmakia are representative of Gallivespians, they are stylish dressers. These beings possess great strength for their size; Lyra is surprised by the ease Tialys shows in hoisting his lodestone resonator, which she figures must be quite heavy for someone of his body weight

Male Flame Skimmer Dragonfly

and musculature. The spies are skillful at maneuvering their dragonfly steeds.

Background: These self-described outlaws in their own world have pledged their support to Lord Asriel in his campaign against the Authority's kingdom of heaven. The other conscious beings in their world are humans who follow the Authority and consider the Gallivespians an evil in need of extermination.

Their area of expertise is espionage, but their poisonous spurs make them effective warriors as well. Gallivespian spies always travel in pairs. High Commander Lord Roke compares these pairs to a human and her dæmon. However, as conscious beings they have dæmons as well – or so the anguish experienced by Tialys and Salmakia as they cross from the suburbs to the world of the dead suggests.

The venomous spurs of the Gallivespians paralyze their opponents, but their poison's potency deteriorates with each use. The generation of this poison must run in approximately 24-hour cycles since it is restored to full strength each day.

The Gallivespians travel on insects resembling dragonflies, or, in the case of the most prominent, diminutive hawks. The Gallivespian spy network has developed a lodestone resonator, a communications device based on the principles of quantum entanglement, which suggests a technologically sophisticated civilization.

Behavior: Because of their size, Gallivespians make good spies in spite of their haughty attitudes and opinionated touchiness. They have a strong sense of honor, and in fact do not allow their work as spies to compromise their trustworthiness, once they have made a promise. They are outspoken but not closed-minded; although Lyra and Will's relationship with Tialys and Salmakia is initially mutually hostile, both the human and Gallivespian pairs develop respect and affection for their counterparts.

Spur on boot

As Tialys' speech to the harpies (who can't be harmed by the Gallivespians' spurs) amply demonstrates, their capacity to command respect and argue effectively far exceeds what might be assumed possible in beings so much smaller than those they are trying to persuade.

As warriors, the Gallivespians are brave and self-sacrificing.

Role: These allies of Asriel's republic are initially charged with the task of infiltrating the Magisterium, with the aim of locating Lyra and Will before the Authority's forces get to the children and facilitating their removal to Asriel. The spies, Tialys and Salmakia, failing to get the children to Asriel, decide their duty is to continue to accompany them even as far as the world of the dead. There, the Gallivespians are the ones to negotiate the deal with the harpies that allows Lyra and Will to leave that world, and, most importantly, will henceforth permit the ghosts to exchange their life stories for passage to the window Will cuts. The liberation of the ghosts undermines the Authority's dominance over conscious beings more effectively than any military victory achieved by Asriel's forces.

Lord Roke and his successor, Madame Oxentiel, are the other two Gallivespians at work in *His Dark Materials*. Lord Roke's bravery in stealing the keys to Coulter's manacles at the Consistorial Court of Discipline's bomb site allows the woman to escape intercision and live to bring down Metatron. Mme Oxentiel's warriors join Iorek Byrnison's armoured bears at a critical moment to provide cover from the Authority's forces for Lyra and Will as they find their dæmons on the battleground by Asriel's fortress.

Note: *When* Gallivespian *appears simply in the place of a character's name (e.g. Tialys, Salmakia) it is not listed, unless the passage in question provides information about Gallivespians in general.*

AS size, personalities 5; life span 6; dragonflies 9; support for Asriel, poison 13; Coulter discusses with Ogunwe, Roke 16; their world's intolerance of, sense of honor 18; pain crossing to world of dead 21; conclude they must have dæmons after all 22; excited by Will and Lyra's plans, fearless with harpies 23; vulnerable to attack by dæmons 25; and dragonflies versus pilots and flying machines, clan colors 29; Will and Lyra protected by swarm of 31; Pan and Kirjava on visit to their world 36

GHOSTS ⚔

World: Lyra's

Role: What a dæmon-less person would be considered in Lyra's world.

Facts: *The Old English word* gasten, *from which* ghastly *derives, meant "to strike aghast" or* "to frighten."

Note: *Ghasts are not to be confused with cliff-ghasts. When cliff-ghast is shortened to ghast, it is clear from the context that the* ghasts *on these pages are the ones that plague Svalbard's cliffs. However, the relationship between ghast designating a dæmonless person and a night-ghast is likely quite close.*

SK   4 *[brief]*

Ghosts/Ghostlike ✧ ⚕ ✎

World: World of the dead, mulefa's

Examples: Roger's, John Parry's, Lee Scoresby's

Physical characteristics: The ghosts retain the physical features of the people they once were; Lyra has no trouble recognizing Roger's and Lee Scoresby's. But their bodies do not show damage. For example, one way Will realizes he has found the world of the dead is when he sees in a newly entered world the man he just saw dead in the bushes with his throat cut — only now his neck shows no sign of trauma. Always cold, their physical status is like fog or smoke's. When Lyra and Will try to touch them, their hands feel nothing. Ghosts can walk through the living, and they do so "to warm themselves at the flowing blood and the strong-beating hearts of the two travelers." Conversely, the living can pass through them: [48] when Lyra begins her tumble into the abyss, she finds herself "hurtling through them like a stone through mist." Their voices are faint and weak. Although an individual ghost is [49] barely audible, the combined whispers of a multitude of ghosts can drown out the shrieking harpies. Ghosts wear clothes. In the world of the dead, a child clutches his mother's skirt as the two ghosts circumvent the edge of the abyss. They cannot sleep, but if lucky, can occasionally escape into a relatively restful doze.

Background: All conscious beings with dæmons (external or internal) who are not changed to angels upon dying (*e.g.* humans, Gallivespians, mulefa, but not, for instance, armoured bears) become ghosts and then exist in the world of the dead.

Lyra and Will conclude that a ghost must be the part of a person that is neither body nor dæmon. The ghost is the part that thinks about the body and dæmon and eventually dwells in the land of the dead. The identification of ghost and spirit occurs in several situations. Mary Malone and Will discuss parallels between the trio of ghost, dæmon, and body, and the Catholic Church's teachings on the three-part nature of humans: spirit, soul, and body.

Behavior: Looking for the world of the dead, Lyra and Will encounter ghosts of the recently dead who are compelled to join with others of their kind. They move disinterestedly toward an unknown destination through a landscape that grows duller and greyer the further the dead move from their lives. As time passes, ghosts lose memory. While new ones may still know their own names, children who have been dead for millennia have forgotten all about the world except for the feel of sunshine and the wind.

Ghosts retain some capacity for pleasure, and are immensely grateful for Lyra's stories of her adventures with Roger. They also still experience fear, horror, and anxiety; even though the prospect of dying is no longer an issue, the opening of the abyss scares the ghosts as it does the living travelers. Even separated from their dæmons, ghosts retain more interest in their own fates than do the Spectres' victims.

The ghost of a shaman retains at least some of the powers the man had when alive;

Parry/Grumman's ghost knows when the Consistorial Court of Discipline's bomb will hit and where Lyra's and Will's dæmons are.

Without dæmons, the ghosts have nothing to fear from the Spectres, and in spite of their fog-like substance, are able to engage the equally insubstantial Spectres in a kind of hand-to-hand combat.

Role: As early as midway through Northern Lights/The Golden Compass, ghosts, the legendary beings of tales of the supernatural, begin to be granted the status of the other unusual but real beings. In the first two books, *ghostly* and *ghost-like* are used to create a sense of foreboding. As the gyptians trudge toward the General Oblation Board's Bolvangar Experiment Station, theirs is "a ghostly journey." When the alethiometer reports that a village in the area is troubled by a ghost, Lyra's suspicion it may be a severed child proves correct. The forms of the severed dæmons Lyra finds in a Bolvangar shed are described as "ghost-like." Later, as Lyra tries to reach Roger before Lord Asriel kills him, she struggles through the "ghostly-gleaming snow." Even in the ordinary landscape of an English neighborhood, Will moves through "ghostly grey pre-dawn light" on the morning he finds his father's letters and flees his home.

The plight of the ghosts in their unchanging, hopeless world, sometimes tormented by harpies but always aware that nothing ever again will happen, inspires Lyra and Will to use the subtle knife to allow the ghosts to return to where they want most to be – the world of the living.

Through the window Will has cut into the mulefa's world, Mary Malone watches ghosts emerging from the world of dead, "like refugees returning to their homeland": "They . . . looked around, their faces transformed with joy . . . and held out their arms as if they were embracing the whole universe; and then, as if they were made of mist or smoke, they simply drifted away, becoming part of the earth and the dew and the night breeze."

Observation: *When Lyra and Kaisa free the severed dæmons from their cages in the Bolvangar Experiment Station shed, the dæmons gather around Lyra's legs, wanting but not daring to touch her. She understands why, knowing intuitively that "they missed the heavy solid warmth of their humans' bodies . . . they longed to press themselves against a heartbeat." The severed dæmons' behavior resembles the ghosts' response, who, unrestrained by the taboo on touching a person other than their own, walk through the living Will and Lyra.*

NL/GC brief mentions: 3, 4, 7, 9, 11, alethiometer on Tony Makarios 12; 13; appearance of severed dæmons 15; 17, 23

SK brief mentions: 1, 2, 11

AS in Lyra's dreams between 1 & 2, 2 & 3, 3 & 4, 5 & 6; Baruch on 2; neither dæmon nor body 13; Iorek says bear have none 14; Lyra and Iorek discuss 15; Will and Lyra first encounter, follow to suburbs of dead 18; in world of the dead 22, 23, and emerge from world of dead 26; their release discussed at adamant tower 28; warrior ghosts fight Spectres 29; Asriel sees near abyss 30; Lyra and Will part from 31; Mary and mulefa view 32; Will and Mary discuss 33; gyptians view 38
brief mentions: 3, 11, 35, 37

HARPY/HARPIES ✐

World: World of the dead
Examples: No-name/Gracious Wings
Alliances: The Authority (initially), autonomous

Physical characteristics: Foul-smelling, vulture-sized birds with women's heads and breasts, their faces bear a belligerently cruel expression, repulsively runny eyes, tangled dirty black hair and lips coated in dried, vomited blood. Although not wrinkled, their faces look ancient all the same. Harpies have strong wings, scaled legs, and sharp claws. The Gallivespians' poisonous spurs do not affect them; they seem beyond physical harm, although they do avoid the subtle knife. Their cries are a torment, and their hideous laughter is vicious and spiteful.

Background: The harpies have been in the world of the dead ever since the first ghosts arrived. The Authority granted them the ability to "see the worst in everyone." To be immersed in unending ugliness is not pleasing to them, but since the reactions they elicit are always ones of fear and repulsion, hatefulness, says No-Name/Gracious Wings, is all the harpies have ever had to sustain them. [57]

What most angers the harpies about Will's plan to liberate the ghosts is that the harpies will become useless and have nothing at all, not even the hatred of the ghosts. Fortunately, they are amenable to reason and adaptable. They decide that the deal Tialys and Salmakia offer, stories of lives fully lived as payment for the work of guiding ghosts to the window out, beats the task assigned and compensation offered so long ago by the Authority.

Behavior: Although their dive at Lyra yields a hank of the girl's hair, Will soon figures out that this contact was accidental, and the harpies' actual aim is to scare and intimidate, not to cause physical damage. While refraining from physical abuse of their victims, these creatures are masters of psychological torment, homing in on a person's greatest vulnerability. They play on Will's guilt about leaving his mother on her own, and Lyra's need to believe she can always lie her way out of a jam. They focus their barbs on newcomers in particular because over the thousands of years of a ghost's existence, the harpies' repetitive spiel becomes boring and unaffecting. For the new arrivals, like Roger, the way "them bird-things" wait until he is dozing—ghosts can't escape into sleep—to start pouring into his ears streams of hateful taunts about mistakes he made when alive, is one of the worst things about being in the world of the dead.

After the harpies are satisfied that the ghosts will tell true stories about life in their worlds in exchange for guidance to the window leading out of the world of the dead, they become helpful and encouraging. The harpies are not intimidated by the abyss.

Role: The harpies, initially Lyra and Will's adversaries in the world of the dead, become their allies after the Gallivespians Tialys and Salmakia propose that in exchange for guidance out of the world of the dead, the ghosts will tell about their lives. The alliance means the harpies will aid rather than hinder the ghosts trying to escape that world and ensures Will and Lyra's own survival. It is their spokes-harpy, the erstwhile No-Name, later Gracious Wings, who saves Lyra from the abyss. Through her encounter with the harpies, Lyra also learns that the richness of her real life is greater than any she can imagine, and that truth is more compelling than lies.

"The Harpies" is the title of chapter 21 of THE AMBER SPYGLASS.

Observation: *The harpies' involvement in the release of the ghosts also, indirectly, brings to Mary Malone a renewed sense of purpose in her life, awakens in Lyra and Will the awareness of their deep love for one another, and returns sraf to the mulefa's world. When the ghost who stops on her way out of the world of the dead says to Mary, "Tell them stories," Mary believes the message is that she should tell Will and Lyra the story of her coming to choose the* *pleasures of the immediate world in which she lives over the promise of treasures in another world after death. This is a fortunate mistake since the* them *referred to by the ghost are not Will and Lyra but are instead the harpies. Mary could not know this, of course.*

[*See also* No-Name *in* Characters]

AS   described 21; Will realizes that they engage in psychological torture but don't pose physical threat 22; Roger on, their interest in Lyra's story, outrage at plan for releasing ghosts, history, the bargain 23; No-name fulfills bargain, guides Will to place he can cut window, unafraid of abyss 26, 37 [*brief*]

The Harpies of Legends

Classical sources for Pullman's harpies include Homer, Hesiod's *Theogony*, and, most extensively, Virgil's *The Aeneid*. The word *Harpy* derives from the Greek *harpazein*, which means to snatch or carry away. In Virgil's *The Aeneid*, the Harpies dwell among the living; in the underworld, the Harpies' counterparts are the Furies.

In *The Aeneid*, Jason and the Argonauts encounter the Harpies as they torment Phineus, a seer whose accuracy in predicting the future has angered the god Zeus, who resents a mortal sharing some of the knowledge the gods consider their own. Every time Phineus tries to eat, the Harpies dive at him, stealing or fouling his food. Zetes and Calais, the sons of Boreas, the god of the North Wind, fly to Phineus's aid, and drive the Harpies to an island.

Pullman's harpies share a number of physical characteristics with the creatures Virgil describes in *Book Three* of *The Aeneid*:

Harpy

> "Monsters more fierce offended Heav'n ne'er sent
> From hell's abyss, for human punishment:
> With virgin faces, but with wombs obscene,
> Foul paunches, and with ordure still unclean;
> With claws for hands, and looks for ever lean.
> When from the mountain-tops, with hideous cry,
> And clatt'ring wings, the hungry Harpies fly;
> They snatch the meat, defiling all they find,
> And, parting, leave a loathsome stench behind."
> (lines 280-4; 293-6)

A prose re-telling of the incident appears in Padraic Colum's *The Golden Fleece and the Heroes Who Lived before Achilles*: "They were things that had the wings and claws of birds and the heads of women. Black hair and gray feathers were mixed upon them; they had red eyes, and streaks of blood were upon their breasts and wings."

HORSE-PEOPLE

World: World of origin is unknown; encountered below Asriel's fortress

Physical characteristics: The riders of these horse-like beasts resemble their steeds, even down to the hair on their bodies.

Alliances: Kingdom of heaven

Role: These creatures are among those Lyra and Will encounter while searching for their dæmons during the war between Asriel's republic and the Authority's kingdom. They attack the Gallivespian forces, trapping the dragonfly-mounted warriors in their nets. When armoured bear Iorek Byrnison enters the fray, he is netted as well. Will is able to use the subtle knife to rescue him from the "steel-string cobweb." The strength of the enormous bears and the sting of the diminutive Gallivespians prove a potent combination against these beings.

AS   *brief mentions:* 30, 31

LIGHTED FLIERS   [*See* Angels]

MULEFA ✒ ⑩ LS

World: Mulefa's

Examples: Atal, Sattamax

Physical characteristics: These sharp-horned invertebrates look "like a cross between antelopes and motorcycles" with small elephant-like trunks. The mulefa's ears are usually not upright, but become so as an expression of interest. They smell of their seedpods combined with horse flesh. Mulefa torsos are shaped like diamonds with legs centered on each side front and back, on which they use seedpods as wheels. The limbs that bear the wheels have very tough hornlike claws set at right angles to the legs, and these claws slip neatly into holes in the center of the seedpod wheels. Their side legs are used to push-start themselves; once in motion, they steer by leaning one way or the other. Seated, the mulefa keep their legs folded under them with their wheels lying flat.

> ## Philip Pullman on his inspiration for the mulefa:
>
> *From an interview on Readerville.com...*
>
> "I remember a day with my younger son, who was then 15... in two or three hours we had invented the mulefa. At least, we'd got the creatures and the trees and the seedpods and the wheels. But on their own they would have meant little and added nothing to the story; so then the connection had to be made with Dust and the basic theme of the story, which of course is the difference between innocence and experience." 59

When Mary, Will, and Lyra ride on the mulefa, a saddle isn't needed because of the mulefa's diamond-shaped backs. The absence of a backbone makes sitting atop the mulefa more comfortable than riding a vertebrate. To transport seedpods, they wear a saddle of sorts to which the pods can be anchored.

Their flexible trunks end in two finger-like appendages, and are used both as if they were another arm and in communication as well, with various movements differentiating among several possible definitions of a word. Mary speculates that the position of their trunks—up, down, left, right—acts as varying inflections do in the Chinese language, but thinks that there must be more to it than this, since they can talk while their trunks are employed as hands. Still, in spite of the versatility of their trunks, two mulefa are required 60 to tie a single knot. The mulefa are fascinated by the dexterity of Mary's hands.

Background: "Mulefa" is the closest approximation Mary Malone can make to the sound that these beings repeat while pointing with their trunks to their chests in imitation of Mary's introduction of herself.

In spite of the mulefa's superficial resemblance to the grazers they raise for meat, "these were individuals, lively with intelligence and purpose. They were people." 61

The mulefa date their acquisition of consciousness to a turning point 33,000 years ago, when a snake told a female zalif (individual) that if she were to place her foot into a hole in a seedpod, she would gain wisdom, memory, and awareness. At this point they began to use names for one another and developed a mutually beneficial relationship to their world's seedpod-producing trees. The pods' "oil was the centre of their thinking and feeling." Just as in Lyra's world the dæmons of children attract less Dust, among the mulefa "young ones didn't have the wisdom of their elders because they couldn't use the wheels, and thus could absorb no oil through their claws."

Behavior: The mulefa live in small settlements of several dozen dwellings. Work is approached cooperatively and communally. The mulefa have created a system of roads that seem as integral to the landscape they traverse as would waterways, although Mary wonders if their roads were not so much built as co-evolved.

Artist's rendition of mulefa

Couples are monogamous, and childhood lasts at least ten years, during which children are dependent on their parents. Until they reach adolescence, mulefa are unable to handle seedpod wheels.

A special raised area with ramps is designated as a speaking ground for mulefa from neighboring villages to gather to address common concerns. Village elders are accorded respect and provide leadership.

Physical contact is encouraged, with grooming being a favorite means of offering support to one another. The mulefa are kindly and good-humored toward the stranger, Mary Malone, recognizing her as like themselves, despite her most unusual body, because she too attracts sraf.

Although the mulefa are pre-literate, perhaps a consequence of lacking hands, they have an effective oral tradition for passing along their myths and history. Their doorways are decorated with patterned wood, not carved, but chosen for its natural beauty. Dreams, for which they have many words, among them *night-pictures*, are accorded respect, and the messages thereby delivered are considered true. Mary notes that their epics are not about "wars and empires and so on but who first made a net and how he discovered the principle—elaborate dramas concerned with slow processes of discovery and elaboration" that are captivating and satisfying.

Mulefa are conscientious stewards of the environment. The mulefa, using their trunks, milk the grazers. They slaughter the beasts for meat and other uses, but try to use techniques causing the animals little pain and terror. Fish caught with nets also supply protein, as do nuts. Mollusks are a delicacy, plentiful but hard to gather since moving on sand is awkward for the mulefa. Cushions and rugs, perhaps made of grazer skins or furs, or perhaps of the same fiber as their nets, furnish their huts. What they consider worthy of giving as gifts to their gyptian guests are knot-wood, lacquered dishes and fishing nets "so strong and light that even the Fen-dwelling gyptians had never seen the like."

Role: The mulefa provide sanctuary to the battle-weary Lyra and Will. The mulefa's account of their origin suggests a way to re-interpret the story of Adam and Eve, one in which the emergence of consciousness, memory and wakefulness is celebrated. To them, Dust is sraf, a precious gold-dust, and not the equivalent of ash or the end product of decay. Among the mulefa, adulthood and experience — not childhood's innocence — are equated with grace and wisdom.

Observation: *These creatures also provide a counterpoint to the inhabitants of Cittàgazze. In their world, the mulefa live in an Edenic harmony with their environment, crafting what they need to enhance their lives in a communal society. In Cittàgazze, the elite have no higher ambition than ceaseless acquisition achieved by plundering other worlds, and the privileged classes thus ruin their world for all.*

Melissa Rogers

Update: According to the first Lantern Slide in *The Amber Spyglass,* although the mulefa "had forgotten nothing they'd ever known," their notion of what kind of events constitute a history was so different from what Mary M alone was used to, she didn't recognize their elaborate chronicles of storms 15,000 years in the past, the discovery of the cord-fibre plant, or the week-long trek on his one remaining wheel of the sole survivor of an earthquake south of their village as having anything in common with her world's accounts of wars and empires.

AS   Mary first views, makes contact 7; their language, culture, seedpods, threat posed by tualapi 10; sraf, myth of origin of consciousness, Sattamax's speech 17; anxiety at sraf's failure, practicality at devising means for Mary to make observations 20; among ghosts in world of dead 23 [brief]; Mary senses lost of sraf means consignment to oblivion 27; Lyra and Will meet, food, interest in dreams 32; houses and roads 33; and sraf 34; Gomez on 35; 36 [brief] ; with gyptians 38;   *LS* Lantern Slide 1

10th: *AS* appendix

Nälkäinens ❖

World: Lyra's

Locale: Far North

Role: These are child-size, headless ghosts, according to Gyptian Tony Costa, who tells Lyra that the Gobblers take their victims to forests haunted by them. When the Nälkäinens find a sleeping human, they tightly seize their victim and never let go.

NL/GC 6 *[brief]*

Night-ghasts ❖ ⚱

World: Lyra's, Cittàgazze

Role: Night-ghasts haunt Lyra's dreams after she visits Jordan College's crypt and flippantly swaps out dæmon-coins she finds among the skulls lining the catacomb's ledges. When Lyra and Pan meet Will Parry in Cittàgazze, they at first think he might be such a being since he lacks a visible dæmon.

NL/GC brief mentions: after playtime in crypts 3, dream recalled 9, compared to sight of Tony Makarios 15

SK   first reaction to dæmonless Will 1 *[brief]*

Panserbørne /Panserbørn ❖

World: Lyra's

Locale: Svalbard

Role: Term used by Scholars, clergy, gyptians, and Samoyeds to refer to armoured bears.

　　　[*See* **Armoured bears**]

Notes: Panserbørne [panserbørn] *is used in* Northern Lights; *the spelling is* panserbjørne [panserbjørn] *in* The Golden Compass. *Context suggests that the first* [panserbørne/panserbjørne] *is the plural form.*

SK   term used by *[brief mentions]:* Trelawney 2, bishop at cocktail party 5, Tony Costa 6, Coram 10, Trelawney recalled 13, Samoyed trader 14,

Philip Pullman on the word *panserbjørne:*

65
66
67
68

From a BBC radio4 webchat…

"It's another word I made up from the Nordic languages: the bjørne part is bear, and panser means armour. So putting the two bits together, it was easy to make the word I have now."

Trelawney recalled 19

SCAVENGERS [*See* Arctic Foxes *in* Natural Sciences: Animals]

SHAMAN ⚡✒ ⑩

The shaman is physically indistinguishable from his fellow ordinary human mortals, but his abilities are extraordinary. Also in contrast to the other entries in this section, this category has only one member: Stanislaus Grumman.

World: Lyra's

Physical characteristics: A distinguishing attribute of a Siberian Tartar shaman is his full-length, feather-trimmed cloak with a brass buckle fastener. In his trance-state, Grumman shakes a rattle or moves from one hand to the other a beaded and feathered object. Like witches, shamans and their dæmons can learn to be physically far apart without ill effect.

Behavior: In Lyra's world, the man who was John Parry in his world of origin becomes the shaman Jopari. A Tartar tribe initiates him into a skull cult, a ritual involving trepanation.

The headman of the village where Grumman lives tells Scoresby that he must treat the shaman with respect, and the villagers have ritually decorated Grumman's hut. When Grumman leaves, the people come to him and touch his hand, and he gives them his blessings.

Grumman tells Lee Scoresby that as a shaman he enters trances allowing him to "discover things in the spirit where I cannot go in the body." This was how he was able to learn about Cittàgazze and the

Siberian Shamanism

William Henry Jackson, Library of Congress, LC-USZC2-6391, 1895

Goldi Shaman Priest and Assistant

Siberian shamanism may have existed for 30,000 to 50,000 years, or since the Alpine Paleolithic era. Shamans are revered as healers and visionaries mediating between the spirit and physical worlds. In Siberian shamanism especially, becoming a shaman is not a voluntary choice. Instead, the spirits, including those of deceased shamans, choose the man or woman. If the person chosen resists, the result is weakness or illness, known as "shaman's sickness," which is eliminated once the new shaman accepts the role the spirits impose. Becoming a shaman, then, has some similarities with becoming the bearer of the subtle knife.

The shaman's cloak of animal skins and feathers, most often of reindeer or bear skins and eagles' feathers, is an outwardly manifestation of the powerful link between the shaman and animal spirits, or in some traditions, spirits who take the forms of animals. Siberian shamans' rhythmic drumming accompanies their trance states in which they summon the spirits' power. Stanislaus Grumman's use of a rattle rather than a drum is irregular for a Siberian shaman, but the rattle is the instrument of choice of North American Arctic shamans.

Siberian shamanism was suppressed under the Soviet regime but is experiencing a small revival in some emerging republics, including Tuva in Central Asia near Mongolia. The source of the Yenisei River is in Tuva's mountains.

subtle knife.

 In trance, Grumman's eyes are closed, and he sways rhythmically, moaning. The effort seems physical as well as mental; he sweats in spite of the cold of a balloon flight and is weakened and exhausted at its end.

 His special talents include the ability to direct winds and summon storms, compel a Spectre to attack an enemy, and see, to some extent, into the future. The ghost of the shaman retains at least some of the powers the man had when alive. Grumman/Parry's ghost knows when a bomb is about to hit Lyra in the world of the dead. His powers extend to his dæmon as well, who marshals the force of numerous flocks of birds to act as one and attack an enemy zeppelin.

 Scoresby has heard that a shaman can fly, and so asks Grumman why he didn't take himself into Cittàgazze. The shaman replies that he does, indeed, have "the gift of flight" after all: "I needed to fly ... so I summoned you, and here I am, flying."

Role: Parry/Grumman's powers as a shaman have several ramifications for Lyra and Will. He learns in shamanic trances of the subtle knife. His desire to find the bearer leads to his finding the son he'd left behind when he walked out of his own world. In turn, Will's far too brief reconciliation with his father makes the boy receptive to Lyra's idea that they use the knife to enter the world of the dead. There, his father's ghost saves Lyra and Will's lives; as a shaman he knows when the Consistorial Court of Discipline's bomb will hit and what Will must do, and his shamanic powers also are the means by which a weakening Will and Lyra are able to know in which world their dæmons are to be found.

Shaman's Cloak

Institute of Archaeology and Ethnography of the Siberian Division of the Russian Academy of Sciences

 The title of chapter 10 of *The Subtle Knife* is "The Shaman."

Observation: *On page 115 of the US edition of* The Amber Spyglass, *Will consults a map as he and Iorek Byrnison approach a Himalayan valley: "If he was right, the valley where Lyra was captive, according to the shaman, lay some way to the east and south." This is a mistake, of course, for it was the angel Baruch, not the shaman Stanislaus Grumman, who provided the information, and on page 121 of the UK edition,* angel *not* shaman *appears.*

Update: The appendix to the **10**TH anniversary edition of *Northern Lights/ The Golden Compass* includes notes by Lord Asriel on the apparent contradiction between the witches' lack of belief in spirit and their knowledge of what the shamans call "spirit-doorways." Grumman's papers in the appendix to the **10**TH anniversary edition of *The Subtle Knife* reveal that a Turukhansk shaman showed him how to make a bloodmoss ointment.

NL/GC appendix

SK Scoresby hears of 6; Grumman as 10; trances, power to summon winds and storms, able to direct Spectre to attack pilot 14; cloak described 15

AS *brief mentions:* 5, 26, similarities with witches 36

10TH: *NL* appendix

10TH: *SK* appendix

Spectres ⚜🗡

World: Cittàgazze, Asriel's

Physical characteristics: Spectres consume Dust and dæmons, growing in size and power as they do so. When they attack, their victims appear to be "enveloped in a transparent shimmer that moved busily, working and feeding in some invisible way." Although they hover in the air and congregate near bodies of water, Spectres cannot fly to the heights witches achieve.

Background: Cittàgazzean Joachim Lorenz tells witches Ruta Skadi and Serafina Pekkala that the "Spectres of Indifference" mysteriously began arriving in his world 300 years ago. Following a recent "great storm" that sounded "as if the whole world was breaking and cracking apart" and a prolonged fog, their numbers increased dramatically and catastrophically. He says some claim that the Guild of the Tower of Angels is to blame, while others believe God sent them as retribution for a horrific sin. Giacomo Paradisi, a former bearer of the subtle knife, attributes their appearance to the Guild's experiments into finding the most elementary constituents of matter. But none of these theorists has knowledge of the abyss.

In the mulefa's world, their dæmons and the angel Xaphania explain to Will and Lyra that Spectres are "like the children of the abyss" – every time a window is cut, part of the abyss enters the world as a Spectre. This explains their invasion of Cittàgazze, the crossroads of worlds, where so many windows have been left opened. Pan adds that they feed on Dust and adults' dæmons, which are closely related. The solution of closing all but the one window leading out of the world of the dead and to break the subtle knife, is agonizing. Xaphania tells Will and Lyra that angels will "take care of the Spectres" once all but one window has been closed.

Behavior: Harmful only to adults, whom they render like zombies. The Cittàgazze Spectre-orphan Angelica explains to Will and Lyra that the adults they attack are frantic at first, but then cease to care: "They still alive, but it's like they been eaten from the inside. You look in they eyes, you see the back of they heads. Ain nothing there." Their victims feel "nausea of the soul," and believe "the world was not made of energy and delight but of foulness, betrayal, and lassitude. Living was hateful, and death was no better, and from end to end of the universe this was the first and last and only truth."

Spectres remind Serafina and shaman Stanislaus Grumman/John Parry of vampire legends from each of their worlds of origin. Grumman says that while vampires feed on blood, Spectres feed on attention, that is, "a conscious and informed interest in the world."

Spectres are afraid of the subtle knife, and Grumman's shamanic powers keep them away from himself and Lee Scoresby. They pose no danger to dæmonless Zombis, angels, or ghosts. Strangely, they do not attack Mary Malone or Father Gomez.

Role: The rapid acceleration in the number of Spectres rendered travel between Cittàgazze and any of its adjacent worlds inconceivable. The Spectres will not threaten the bearer of the subtle knife. It is his desire for such invulnerability that prompts Sir Charles Latrom/Lord Boreal to steal Lyra's alethiometer; he wants to force Will or Lyra to bring him the knife to exchange. This leads to Will discovering his role as the next bearer of the subtle knife, and all that follows.

The relationship of the Spectres and the subtle knife is more complex than that of an enemy and weapon. The windows the knife cuts bring the Spectres into being, and the only way to prevent their devastation of the conscious beings in the worlds where windows have been left open is to close these openings and destroy the knife itself. And this in turn means Lyra and Will will be permanently separated.

SK   Angelica and Paolo on 3; witches watch attack of, and Lorenz discuss Spectres of Indifference 6;

Cittàgazzean children on 7; Latrom, Paradisi on 8; Latrom and Coulter discuss zombi and 9; Grumman tells Scoresby about 10; victims remind Will of his mother 11; Lyra and Will discuss 13; Grumman on Spectres of Indifference, resists Scoresby's desire to save threatened youth, directs attack of pilot by in trance 14; Coulter commands 15

   brief mentions: 5; Shadows tell Mary not to fear 12

AS   angels unaffected by 2; Malone unaffected 7; Gomez unaffected 10; Lyra and Will sense presence of on battlefield, threat to their dæmons 29; surround dæmons, attacked by ghosts 31; grow more powerful if they consume dæmons, windows and 37

   brief mentions: Lyra mistakes ghosts for 19; Scoresby's Parry's ghosts resolve to fight 26; 35

SPECTRES OF INDIFFERENCE [*See* Spectres] ⚲

VAMPYRES/VAMPIRES ⚲ ✎

World: Cittàgazze, Lyra's, Will's

Role: The Spectres of Cittàgazze bring to mind legends of vampires.

   When witch Serafina Pekkala first sees a victim of the Spectres, she recalls travelers' tales from her own world of vampyres, and she knows, even though dæmons are not visible in the world of Cittàgazze, that Spectres destroy the dæmon or soul of those they attack. Similarly, as they fly into Cittàgazze, shaman and scientist Stanislaus Grumman tries to explain Spectres to aëronaut Lee Scoresby by drawing an analogy to vampyres, and Mary Malone is horrified by the damage she witnesses in Cittàgazze caused by "those ethereal vampyres."

Note: *Spelling in the US edition is* vampire.

SK   *brief mentions:* 6, 14

AS   7 *[brief]*

78

WATCHERS [*See* Angels]

WEREWOLF ✤

World: Lyra's

Role: Lyra claims a werewolf howls at Godstow nunnery near the open fields of Port Meadows.

NL/GC 5 *[brief]*

WINDSUCKERS ✤

World: Lyra's

Role: These shimmering monsters of the North float along in clusters and can drain the strength of humans through a touch.

Observation: *These sound quite similar to the Spectres.*

NL/GC 6 *[brief]*

WITCHES ✤ ⚲ ✎ ⑩

World: Lyra's. Visit world of Cittàgazze, Asriel's republic. One witch-queen visits Will's and the mulefa's worlds.

Examples: Serafina Pekkala, Ruta Skadi, Lena Feldt

Alliances: Not uniform – varies by clan.

Physical characteristics: Always female, witches can live more than a thousand years, which gives them an opportunity to achieve more experience, and with it wisdom, than ordinary humans. Even when several hundred years old, they look like vibrant, sensual, and fit young women. They dress in what appears to be just strips of black silk; some wear wreaths of flowers atop their heads, like Serafina, while her counterpart Ruta Skadi wears gold earrings and a crown adorned with tigers' teeth. But none wears winter garb like coats, gloves, or hats, even when flying through the clouds above Svalbard. Witches do feel the cold, but knowing it will not harm them, prefer not to cut themselves off from "the bright tingle of the stars...the silky feeling of moonlight" on their bare limbs. Seen from a distance, their shapes appear as "elegant ragged black shadows;" their arrival is announced with the sound of the wind flapping their silk dresses and rustling the cloud pines.

As part of their initiation or coming-of-age ritual, witches enter an area in the northlands into which their dæmons cannot follow; witches thus learn to be further separated from their dæmons than is usual. While witches can't achieve "true invisibility," by using a kind of "mental magic," they can achieve a "fiercely-held modesty that could make the spell-worker not invisible but simply unnoticed." The practice, both risky and exhausting, is used sparingly.

Witches fly on cloud-pine branches—any branch they tear off a tree works—and are expert navigators and proficient archers. They are strong enough that just six are able to pull Lee Scoresby's balloon, loaded with the aëronaut, two children, and Iorek Byrnison with all his armour, against the wind toward Svalbard and away from Lapland. Their dæmons are birds.

Background: Witches bear the children of ordinary men. Their daughters become witches like their mothers, but their male children don't. Because witches live for hundreds of years, marriage is impractical, since a witch will stay youthful as her mate ages, weakens, and dies. Over the hundreds of years of their lifetimes, the repeated loss of lovers and sons means that witches' "hearts are continually racked with pain."

The witches of the North in Lyra's world are organized in clans (*e.g.* Taymyr, Lake Enara) under the leadership of a witch-queen. Among the papers of Col. John Parry/Stanislaus Grumman that appear in the appendix to the **10th** anniversary edition of *The Subtle Knife* is a map of Lapland designating the territories of a number of witch lands, with the notation that "The borders between witch-clan lands are definite but irregular, and they vary from season to season with the flowering of plants and the migration of animals and birds." The queens do not rule as autocrats but seek the counsel of their subjects; the final decision is, however, the queen's. A witch-queen must put the clan before herself. Even when he comes to Bolvangar to tell Lyra the gyptians are a day's march away, Kaisa is still unable to tell Lyra with any certainty whether Serafina will be joining them to rescue the children held captive. Clans can choose to join forces, as do Serafina's Lake Enara clan and Ruta Skadi's Latvian witches, but a single unified effort of all witch clans has never occurred.

The gods (or goddesses) of witches are different than humans', and the source of their wisdom and knowledge is the observation of Nature. Witches read pine marten entrails, perch's scales, and crocus-pollen, for example, for information with which to interpret their world. Witches cherish physical sensation and experience, but their theological speculations extend beyond what they can perceive. While believing that "we are all subject to the fates," Serafina says, "we must all act as if we are not… or die of despair." She tells Lyra, "There are powers who speak to us, and there are powers above them; and there are secrets even from the most high." The witches know of the existence of many thousands of other worlds.

Witches appear not to be subject to – or do not acknowledge – the authority of either church or state. The Magisterium is not unilaterally hostile to witches, and there are witch clans aligned with Mrs Coulter and the Consistorial Court of Discipline. Attitudes in the secular world vary, but witches have been reticent about revealing themselves too fully to ordinary humans.

Ruta Skadi tells Serafina that there are witches in other worlds, including one much like her (Lyra's) own. However, in that world, Ruta reports, the witches "live no longer than our short-lifes, and there are men among them too."

Behavior: With little interest in the affairs of ordinary mortals, witches live in forests or other wilderness areas. They do not deal with money; they have "no means of exchange apart from mutual aid." Their consuls dwell in towns to protect their interests. The consul keeps a branch of cloud-pine, which she has used in flight, for each witch he represents; using her particular spray, he can—somehow—request contact.

Serafina Pekkala, discussing fate and freedom with aëronaut Lee Scoresby, says that witches may have a different understanding of choice than do other humans because of their very long lives, rejection of individual ownership, and different ideas about values such as honor.

They take seriously their obligations of loyalty. Because he once saved her life (and she bore his child), gyptian Farder Coram does not doubt that Serafina will help his people locate their missing children, although he has not seen her for decades. They take their feuds seriously as well. Stanislaus Grumman's journal notes an "ancient enmity between Tikshozero and Miekojärvi clans" so severe that "Reina Miti and Katja Sirkka sworn to kill each other on sight."

Role: The first Lyra hears of a connection between herself and the witches is when gyptian Ma Costa tells her, "you got witch-oil in your soul." The witch consul in Trollesund, Dr Martin Lanselius, tells gyptian Farder Coram that he believes Lyra to be the child the witches for centuries have prophesized will appear. The witches' involvement in the story begins with the arrival of Serafina Pekkala's snow-goose dæmon, Kaisa, who comes to the gyptians docked in Trollesund the evening after Lyra and Farder Coram's visit with Lanselius.

When Serafina's Lake Enara clan learns what is going on at Bolvangar, they are appalled, and determine that if Lyra is those people's enemy, the witches are her friends. When Lyra decides her purpose is to help Will find his father in the world of Cittàgazze, a battalion of witches representing several clans tries to assist. Clans of witches rally for Asriel's republic, taking on angels.

Not all witches are friendly to Lyra or those that oppose the Magisterium. A witch provides Lord Asriel critical help, flying the wire into the Aurora to provide the electrical current needed to perform Roger's severing. Another assists Fr MacPhail as he launches the bomb intended for Lyra.

The role of the witches in *His Dark Materials* diminishes in the last volume, *The Amber Spyglass*. Their prophecy regarding Lyra is discussed more times than they are seen.

"The Witches" is the title of chapter seventeen of *Northern Lights/The Golden Compass*, and "Among the Witches" is the title of the second chapter of *The Subtle Knife*.

Observation: *The life expectancy of the witches of Lyra's world is comparable to that of humans in Will's pre-lapsarian (before Noah's Flood) world. For example, Adam lived to be 930 years; Jared, father of Enoch, lived 962 years; and Enoch's son Methuselah, 969 years. (Enoch's life span of 365 years was thus relatively short, but he was elevated to the status of an angel at the end of his earthly life.)*

Notes: *When "witch" appears simply in the place of a witch's name (e.g. Serafina Pekkala, Ruta Skadi), it is not listed, unless the passage in question also provides information about witches in general.*

NL/GC   Coram on, Lanselius on, prophecies of 10; Kaisa on clan obligations, knowledge of other worlds, interest in Asriel and Lyra 11; Iorek on 12; Coram considers Lyra and Iorek's sighting of 13; Kaisa comments on their politics at Bolvangar 15; and liberation of Bolvangar 17; Serafina discuss what it means to be a witch with Scoresby, Lyra 18; battle between clans reported 20; attack armoured bears 22
    brief mentions: 4, 7, 19, 21, 23

SK   most but not all turn against Coulter, prophecy regarding Lyra, goddess of death, council at Lake Enara 2; Umaq on, arrival of in world of Cittàgazze, means of navigation 6; rescue Lyra and Will at belvedere 11; spells, potions, interest in Asriel, those of other worlds compared, their prophecies considered in regards to Asriel, subtle knife, Lyra 13; shamans and witches compared 14; prophecy revealed to Coulter 15
    brief mentions: 5, 9, 10

AS   sight of Spectres' victims 2; changes in their homelands 3; prophecy recalled by Consistorial Court 6; Coulter on prophecy, church, Lyra's safety 16; Lyra tells Roger about 23; MacPhail helped by 25; battle angels 29; initiation, spells for entering dreams 36; technique for seeing dæmons, Will and Lyra's power to be apart from dæmons compared to 38
    brief mentions: 8, 9, 10, 14, 28, 31, 33, 35

10ᴛʜ: *NL* appendix

10ᴛʜ: *SK* appendix

Zombi ❖ ⚑ ✎ ⑩

World: Lyra's; Will's, Cittàgazze

Physical characteristics: Resemble corpses. In Lyra's world of externalized dæmons, it is apparent that they lack what matters most: dæmons. Even in the world of Cittàgazze, where dæmons are internalized, witch Lena Feldt can immediately tell that the soldiers guarding Coulter are dæmonless.

Background: These are people, primarily or perhaps exclusively men, who have undergone intercision.

Behavior: Unquestioning and absolutely obedient, "they have no fear and no imagination and no free will, and they'll fight till they're torn apart."

Role: According to Asriel, Mrs Coulter learned in Africa of a way to make a slave of a person to the extent that "it has no will of its own; it will work day and night without ever running away or complaining" but is still alive; this inspired Coulter's founding of the General Oblation Board for further studies of severing.

After Asriel breaks through to another world, the Magisterium, anticipating a war, sends troops comprised of *zombi* into the Far North.

Observation: *Presumably Coulter kept her zombi guards under cover in Will's Oxford; they don't seem to have been along for her night out with Sir Charles Latrom.*

Although they too have been severed, the nurses at Bolvangar are not referred to as zombies. *While the women are characterized as incurious and always obedient, unlike the* severed soldiers, they do not seem threatening. This may be because they can keep their ⁹¹ severed dæmons nearby as pets. There is no indication that the soldiers' dæmons remain at their sides. Moreover, the physical vitality and strength of the soldiers and nurses do not seem to have been compromised. In contrast, Tony Makarios, and the other severed wandering children the villagers describe to Iorek and Lyra, are sickly and cannot survive long.

Facts: *In Will's world, zombies are rumored to be dead people re-animated by a sorcerer or magician. While a zombie may initially appear to behave as a human does, he or she lacks free will, doing instead whatever its reanimator commands.*

Zombies are associated with voodoo in the Caribbean island nation of Haiti. Voodoo has its roots in Vodun, the national religion of Benin, a West African nation. Haitian voodoo incorporates elements of Roman Catholicism, the religion practiced by the French plantation owners who enslaved West Africans and transported them to the island.

Update: Notes from Lord Asriel's papers included in the appendix to the **10**TH anniversary edition of NORTHERN LIGHTS/ THE GOLDEN COMPASS record an interest in beings similar to *zombis* called *sepikwu* or *sempekwu* that he heard of in the Sunda Straits.

Notes: *Only Asriel and Lanselius use the term* zombi, *but the dæmonless soldiers and guards* ⁹²₉₃ *referred to in these chapters are clearly by definition* zombi. *Asriel uses the pronoun "it" when he refers to* zombi, *and Lanselius uses "they," so the word's status as a singular or plural noun is ambiguous.*

NL/GC 21 *[brief]*

SK brief mentions: in Trollesund 2; Latrom's interest in 9; Will's fears 11; Coulter's in Cittàgazze 15

AS 11 (implied: "strange and frightening men") *[brief]*

10TH: *NL* appendix

Some Unsettled Dæmon Forms
Not Including Those Represented in the List of Settled Forms

MAMMALS	BIRDS	INSECT
Cougar	Eagle	Dragonfly
Ermine	Goldfinch	
Lemur	Kestrel	
Leopard	Mockingbird	**OTHER**
Lion	Owl	Dragon
Mongoose	Stormy petrel	Gargoyle
Mouse		
Polecat		
Porcupine	**REPTILES**	
Porpoise	Rattlesnake	
Rat	Salamander	
Squirrel		
Stoat		
Tiger		
Wildcat		

Settled Dæmon Forms

MAMMALS

Arctic fox	Umaq
Baboon	Dr at Bolvangar, 3
Bat	Pagdzin tulku
Brown monkey	locomotive engineer
Cat	Coram, Docker, Will
Cheetah	Ogunwe
Dolphin	Sailor
Ferret	Huismans
Golden monkey	Coulter
Hare	Scoresby
Husky	Sentry, Trollesund
Lemming	Seal hunter
Lemur	Man in top hat
Marmoset	Relf
Marmot	Dr, Bolvangar, 1
Monkey	Jordan Master
Muskrat	man at meeting
Pine marten	Lyra
Pinscher	Thorold
Rabbit	Cooper, Louis Br
Red setter	Cawson
Retriever	Lonsdale
Snow leopard	Asriel
Terrier	Orderly, Sentry
Wolf-dog	Swiss Guardsman
Wolverine	Village Headman

BIRDS

Alpine chough	Malone
Bluethroat	Skadi
Cormorant	Tillerman
Crow	Borisovitch, Dada, Faa
Finch	zeppelin pilot
Hawk	Ma Costa, Tony Costa
Macaw	Sturrock
Nightingale	Basilides
Osprey	Grumman
Pelican	priest, Trollesund
Raven	Master, Witch flies wire
Robin	Kamainen
Seagull	Jerry, Steersman
Snow bunting	Feldt
Snow Goose	Pekkala
Snowy owl	Skraeling
Tern	Tortured witch

REPTILES

Frog	Pavel
Lizard	Heyst, Fr, MacPhail
Serpent/Snake	Boreal, Lanselius, Santelia, Jordan Master

INSECTS

Beetle	Gomez
Butterfly	Starminster
Moth	Dr, Bolvangar, 2

OTHERS

Basilisk	Jordan Master
Fair woman*	Jordan Master

* in NORTHERN LIGHTS only

THE ALETHIOMETER,
THE SUBTLE KNIFE,
THE AMBER SPYGLASS

The Alethiometer, The Subtle Knife,
The Amber Spyglass:

The Alethiometer

and associated entries

ALETHIOMETER ✦ ⚱ ✎ ⎣LS⎦

World: Lyra's (origin)

Background: Gyptian Farder Coram notes the Greek origins of the word: *alethia* or *truth*, and *meter* or *measure*, thus defining the instrument as "a truth-measure." When Lyra asks [1] what it does, the Master of Jordan College replies, "it tells you the truth." Fra Pavel, who [2] reads the alethiometer for the Magisterium, says that the alethiometer "does not *forecast*; it says, "*If* certain things come about, *then* the consequences will be..." According to Dr [3] Lanselius, it was invented in Prague by a seventeenth century scholar looking for a way to measure astrological influences of planets but hasn't been used seriously for 200 years.

The Master says that Asriel's, now Lyra's, is one of only six in the world; Coulter tells her it is one of two or three, and Fra Pavel claims his and Lyra's are the only two remaining in the world. But the whereabouts of at least four are known: Lyra's, Pavel's, Asriel's alethiometrist Teukros Basilides', and that belonging to the alethiometrist for the Society of the Work of the Holy Spirit. Moreover, it is reasonable to assume that the Head of St Sophia's College, Dame Hannah Relf, a scholar of the instrument, must at least have ready access to one. Farder Coram saw one used in Uppsala.

Appearance: The alethiometer is described as "something like a large watch or a small clock: a thick disc of brass [gold in THE GOLDEN COMPASS] and crystal." Its hands point to [4] pictures: "instead of the hours or the points of the compass, there were several little pictures, each of them painted with extraordinary precision, as if on ivory with the finest and slenderest sable brush" (in THE AMBER SPYGLASS, the pictures are said to be actually [5] "painted on ivory"). [6]

Operation/Usage: Three "winding wheels" control "three shorter hands" that can be arranged "to point at any of the pictures, and once they had clicked into position, pointing exactly at the center of each one, they would not move." The fourth, longer hand then swings "where it wanted to, like a compass needle, except that it didn't settle." [7]

Coram notes that each symbol has multiple meanings: an anchor can stand for hope, steadiness, a snag, the sea, and so on and on, and that to read it one must first know these many variants and then hold them in mind "without fretting at it or pushing for an answer, and just watch while the needle wanders." Lyra says that she "feel[s]" her way [8] through multiple meanings of symbols, and that reading it works when she makes her [9] mind "go clear and then it's sort of like looking down into water," the "clearness and [10] understanding going so deep you can't see the bottom." When Will is learning to use the [11] subtle knife, Lyra tells him about the state of mind she has to achieve to read the alethiometer.

When Lyra speculates that a "spirit" might control the hands, Pan suggests [12] "elementary particles." Lord Asriel concurs with Lyra that Dust communicates through the instrument. Lyra comes to see it as having "moods, like a person, and to know when it wanted to tell her more" but complains to scientist Dr Mary Malone that when it comes to Dust, "the alethiometer won't exactly tell me what I need to know." She tells Will that she has come to "sort of know when it's going to be cross or when there's things it doesn't want me to know." Lyra guesses too that it would stop working if she used it just to "spy on people." Handling the alethiometer, Lyra treats it "like a mother protecting her child."

Role: This truth-telling instrument guides Lyra on her journey through the worlds of *His Dark Materials*.

Its first mention occurs when the Master of Jordan College confides to the Librarian that the alethiometer "warns of appalling consequences if Lord Asriel pursues [his] research" and, moreover, Lyra has a major part to play in coming events but "must do it all without realizing what's she's doing." The Master gives an alethiometer to Lyra before she departs with Mrs Coulter, telling her that it is one of only six ever made, that Asriel had presented it to Jordan College, and that her possession of it is best kept a secret from Coulter. Lyra decides to trust gyptian king John Faa and Farder Coram and shows them her alethiometer, which they call in conversation the "symbol-reader." Lyra begins teaching herself to read the alethiometer when she is in hiding from Coulter aboard the gyptians' boats. Her first reading

The Alethiometer's Thirty-six Images

Only 29 of the alethiometer's 36 images are mentioned in *His Dark Materials*: alpha and omega, anchor, angel, ant, baby, beehive, bird, bull, camel, candle, chameleon, compasses, cornucopia, crucible, dolphin, elephant, garden, globe, griffin, helmet, horse, hourglass, loaf of bread, lute, Madonna, moon, puppet, serpent, and thunderbolt.

In three cases, what is likely the same image is referred to differently at different times: baby, child, and infant; chameleon and lizard; thunderbolt and lightening. The last two cases are simple enough. A chameleon is a kind of lizard and a thunderbolt is lightening. The first is a little trickier. A baby and infant are the same, but a child is something different. Unless, that is, you are a pre-adolescent reading an alethiometer and in its message you are represented by a symbol, and that symbol is the image of a baby. It is easy to imagine Lyra's reluctance at seeing herself as a baby, and telling Farder Coram that the child represents herself, even though the image she has just seen the needle indicate is clearly an infant.

The seven others, as determined by the illustrated pamphlet on the alethiometer's history by Philip Pullman included with the program materials for the Royal Theatre's production of *His Dark Materials* are: apple, crocodile (caiman), owl, sun, sword, tree, and wild man. The text and the pamphlet refer a bit differently to a few images, respectively, garden and walled garden, puppet and marionette, crucible and cauldron, and compasses and compass.

Readings that mention these images are those relating to:
- the fate of gyptian spies trying to enter the General Oblation Board's headquarters and the source of the spy flies sent after Lyra;
- in answering witch consul Dr Martin Lanselius' questions;
- suggesting the presence of a ghost child in the wilderness as the gyptians advance toward Bolvangar (i.e. Tony Makarios); and
- explaining how people in Will's world can talk with Shadows.

Images mentioned in the text of HDM
Chapter numbers are provided for the ***first mention only*** *of the image.*

1. alpha and omega (*SK* 4)
2. anchor (*NL/GC* 4)
3. angel (*NL/GC* 4)
4. ant (*NL/GC* 9)
5. baby (*NL/GC* 10)
   [*child* (*NL/GC* 9);
   infant (*NL/GC* 9)]
6. beehive (*NL/GC* 4)
7. bird (*NL/GC* 10)
8. bull (*NL/GC* 4)
9. camel (*NL/GC* 10)
10. candle (*NL/GC* 4)
11. chameleon (*NL/GC* 4)
    [*lizard* (*NL/GC* 9)]
12. compasses (*NL/GC* 4)
13. cornucopia (*NL/GC* 10)
14. crucible (*NL/GC* 9)
15. dolphin (*NL/GC* 4)
16. elephant (*NL/GC* 9)
17. garden (*SK* 4
18. globe (*NL/GC* 4)
19. griffin (*NL/GC* 12)
20. helmet (*NL/GC* 4)
21. horse (*NL/GC* 4)
22. hourglass (*NL/GC* 4)
23. loaf of bread (*AS* 2)
24. lute (*NL/GC* 4)
25. Madonna (*NL/GC* 9)
26. moon (*SK* 4)
27. puppet (*AS* 2)
28. serpent (*NL/GC* 9)
29. thunderbolt (*NL/GC* 4)
    [*lightning* (*SK* 4)]

Update: Images not mentioned in the text of HDM but included in The National Theatre program:

30. apple
31. crocodile (caiman)
32. owl
33. sun
34. sword
35. tree
36. wild man

reveals the death and capture of gyptian spies. Faa, concerned for Lyra's safety, had refused to let her join the rescue party, but finally must acknowledge that the alethiometer's guidance could prove useful and so lets her go on the journey North.

In Trollesund, her tool tells Lyra where exiled bear-king Iorek Byrnison's armour has been hidden, and for that information, Iorek in exchange gives the girl his loyalty forever. Along the way to find the children abducted by the Gobblers, the alethiometer directs Lyra to Tony Makarios, one of their victims, who has been severed from his dæmon. From Serafina Pekkala's dæmon and the witch consul Martin Lanselius, Lyra discovers that the witches are interested in her ability to understand the answers the instrument communicates. As a captive at Bolvangar, she turns to the alethiometer for reassurance that the gyptians survived the attack by Samoyed hunters and that they are on their way to the Station. There, Coulter tries to convince Lyra to give the alethiometer to her. Coulter thinks that the Master gave it to Lyra in order to get it in Asriel's hands, but Coulter says that this was a mistake on the Master's part since Asriel would use it to advance a wicked scheme of his.

After being taken prisoner by Svalbard's armoured bears, Lyra uses the alethiometer to gain her freedom and save the life of Iorek Byrnison, the rightful king.

She is still determined to take the alethiometer to her father. Lyra, however, has misunderstood what the alethiometer says about what she has that Lord Asriel wants. Lyra learns that Asriel neither wants nor needs her alethiometer after all—and that she has inadvertently and to her horror and sorrow brought him exactly what he needed most.

In THE SUBTLE KNIFE, another alethiometer and reader are at work. Attempting to rescue a witch held by the Consistorial Court of Discipline, Serafina Pekkala overhears Fra Pavel tell the assembled clerics, "if it were possible to disbelieve the alethiometer, I would do so" for he can not fathom Lyra being able to read hers, as it claims. He has been instructed to use the instrument to learn Lyra's significance in the coming war with Asriel.

When Lyra meets Will Parry in Cittàgazze, the alethiometer answers her question of whether Will is friend or enemy: *"He is a murderer."* This response she finds reassuring.

Looking for a place to ask the alethiometer where to find a Scholar in Will's Oxford who is an expert on Dust, Lyra wanders into the Pitt-Rivers Museum and is intrigued by the display of trepanned skulls. The dating the alethiometer provides conflicts with that on the museum's display, a discrepancy that will hold great interest for Dr Mary Malone. When Lyra does ask about a Scholar, it not only directs her to Mary Malone, but admonishes her not to lie and, unprompted, tells Lyra her task is to help Will find his father. As she did with Iofur Raknison, Lyra uses the alethiometer to answer a question of Malone's in order to gain her confidence.

When the alethiometer is stolen by Sir Charles Latrom (Lord Boreal of Lyra's world), Lyra's and Will's fates become entwined. Its theft leads Will to the moment he becomes the bearer of the subtle knife. Will retrieves the alethiometer for Lyra, but the guilt she feels at what Will suffered to do this makes her strangely reluctant to use her symbol-reader. Lyra does not consult the alethiometer to find out more about Will's father, although Pan encourages her to, or even to find out why Serafina Pekkala had to go abruptly to Lee Scoresby's aid, and as they journey through Cittàgazze, Lyra only "warily" asks it for directions. When Lyra vanishes, Will discovers that her alethiometer has been left behind in her rucksack.

Again, Will is the bearer, reuniting Lyra and the alethiometer in the Himalayas as he did in Headington, Oxford. His knife has been broken, however, and Iorek Byrnison sets as a condition for repairing it whether the alethiometer thinks he should. While its answer is affirmative, it is also complex, warning of the "delicate kind of balance" that can make the knife "harmful" or "good," both "the death of Dust" and "the only way to keep Dust alive." When the two discuss going to the world of the dead, they seek the answer from the alethiometer. It warns that while they should go to the world of the dead, they "might not survive," and the alethiometer surprises Lyra, advising her not to try to get rid of the Gallivespian spies dispatched by Asriel.

When she is separated from Pan in the world of the dead, Lyra finds reading the alethiometer to be difficult: "she had to do it laboriously, and her grip was failing."

Safely in the mulefa's world, the alethiometer assures Lyra that she and Will have nothing to fear from the mulefa and that Mary Malone is nearby. When Lyra realizes she has lost her ability to read it, the angel Xaphania tells Lyra that as a child she read the alethiometer "by grace" and can regain the ability "by work." Back home in Jordan College, Lyra considers the Master's advice that she make the alethiometer the "subject of [her] life's work," beginning with formal study at St Sophia's College with alethiometrist Dame Hannah Relf.

"The Alethiometer" is the title of Chapter 4 of NORTHERN LIGHTS and THE GOLDEN COMPASS.

Observation: *In the United States, the title of the first volume of* HIS DARK MATERIALS *was changed from* NORTHERN LIGHTS *to* THE GOLDEN COMPASS. *But unlike the phrases that provide the titles for the other two volumes,* THE SUBTLE KNIFE *and* THE AMBER SPYGLASS, *the phrase* golden compass *never appears in* HIS DARK MATERIALS.

Compass *appears ten times in reference to the alethiometer, and four of those are when the Master of Jordan College presents the instrument to Lyra.* Compass *is never used in* THE AMBER SPYGLASS *to refer to the alethiometer, although* golden instrument *is; this phrase is also used twice in* THE SUBTLE KNIFE, *but never in* NORTHERN LIGHTS/THE GOLDEN COMPASS. *Usually,* golden *precedes* monkey, *but the word is also used to describe Lyra's hair and Dust as it flows into the abyss.*

Moreover, twice in NORTHERN LIGHTS, *but not in* THE GOLDEN COMPASS, *it is referred to as made of brass: "thick disc of brass" and "the brass body exquisitely machined."*

In fact, the equation of the alethiometer to a golden compass is based on a mistake made by the first US editors of HIS DARK MATERIALS. *Pullman at first considered calling the trilogy* THE GOLDEN COMPASSES, *referring to the geometer's tool. But an editorial misreading transformed* compasses *to* compass *and* NORTHERN LIGHTS *became* THE GOLDEN COMPASS. *By the time Pullman discovered the error, too much advance publicity had begun to reclaim his original title.*

A compass is one of the alethiometer's 36 images, but not the navigator's type—rather, a geometer's compass is one of its symbols, based on the illustration in the Royal National Theatre's production of HIS DARK MATERIALS *program insert, "The Alethiometer," by Philip Pullman.*

NL/GC basis of Master's fears for Lyra 2; described, Lyra receives, Master's advice 4; first attempts by Lyra to read in London 5; discussed with Faa and Coram 7; Lyra's first readings on gyptian losses at Gobbler headquarters, spy flies 9; Lanselius on its history, tests Lyra's ability to read 10; Lyra trusts its evaluation of Iorek's character, consults for location of his armour 11; consulted about Bolvangar's defenses, alerts Lyra to lost boy 12; Lyra realizes retrospectively that it had revealed Tony Makarios lacked a dæmon, Iorek doubts adults can read it without books 13; Lyra prevents confiscation of by Bolvangar nurses 14; Coulter mistakes its case for spy flies', Lyra determined to take to Asriel 17; used to trick Raknison 19; Roger asks Lyra not to consult, Asriel confirms elementary particles move its dials, Asriel rejects Lyra's gift of hers 21
> *brief mentions:* Lyra protects, keeps private 6; practices with Pan 8; hides above ceiling tiles 16; Lyra tells Pekkala about wanting Asriel to have 18; reports Coulter on way to Svalbard 20; Lyra realizes it was Roger that Asriel needed 22; 23

SK Fra Pavel reads 2; sighted by Latrom, tells Lyra to help Will, directs Lyra to Malone, used by Lyra to establish credibility with Malone 4; stolen, Latrom refuses to return and sets knife as ransom for 7; Will retrieves from Latrom's 9; Lyra reluctant to use, Will gets her to ask about his mother 11; says to keep moving through Cittàgazze countryside, discussed by Serafina and Ruta Skadi 13
> *brief mentions:* says Will is a murderer 1, Will's first sighting of 3, Lyra uses to check on Will's mother 5, reading of compared to using subtle knife 8, Mary tells Payne about 12; left behind by Lyra's abductor 15

AS Balthamos questions Lyra's ability to read 2; Basilides told to seek Coulter's location 5; Pavel reports his readings to Court 6; returned to Lyra by Will 13; consulted about situation in Himalayas, reading of and operating lodestone resonator compared 14; consulted about repairing knife, going to world of the dead 15; warns Lyra not to ditch Gallivespian spies 18; tells what will happen to ghosts who leave world of dead 23; Basilides reports its news of Metatron's plan for dæmons 28; Lyra finds increasingly difficult to read, tells where Will should try to cut through from world of dead to find their dæmons 29; Lyra discovers she can no longer read, Xaphania on grace and work and 37; Relf and Master suggest studying 38; [LS] Lantern Slides 6, 9
> *brief mentions:* 9, 11, 16, 17, 22, 24, 26, 27, 32, 33

SYMBOL-READER ❖ ⚲ ✎

Role: This term is used conversationally by Lyra to certain audiences as a synonym for the alethiometer, and is particularly favored by gyptians John Faa and Farder Coram, armoured bear Iorek Byrnison, and witch Serafina Pekkala. The first time she shows it to Will, Lyra calls her instrument a symbol-reader, but afterwards they refer to it as the alethiometer.

NL/GC   term used by Coram, Faa 7; Lyra to Iorek 11; Faa, Lyra 12; Iorek 13; Serafina 17; Lyra, Iorek 20; Lyra to Roger 21

SK   term used by Lyra to Will 3

AS   term used by Serafina to Mary 36

VELVET CLOTH/BUNDLE ❖ ⚲ ✎

Role: When the Master of Jordan College gives Lyra the alethiometer, it is wrapped in a piece of black velvet cloth, and so it remains, from her world to Cittàgazze, Will's Oxford, the desert world, the suburbs of and world of the dead, and the mulefa's world.

Observation: *With one exception, the black velvet in which Lyra keeps the alethiometer is described as a piece of loose cloth that can be wrapped or folded. The exception refers to a "black velvet bag."*

NL/GC   brief mentions: 4, 5, 7, 9, 10, 12, 14, 17, 22

SK   brief mentions: 3, 4, 7, 11

AS   brief mentions: 2, 18, 37

The Subtle Knife
and associated entries

Abyss ✎

World: World of the dead

Role: The abyss was created by the Consistorial Court of Discipline's bomb launched with the intention of destroying Lyra. Due to a last second intervention by the ghost of John Parry, the bomb instead opens a huge chasm into which Dust "like a luminous misty rain" flowed from the worlds of conscious beings into "vast black emptiness." Because he can feel its edges have the same special, unforgettable quality as the edges he brings together when he closes windows cut by the subtle knife, Will knows that the abyss is like a giant window, but not one leading to another world.

On their journey through the world of the dead, the children and spies must creep along a narrow ledge, which is all that is between the cavern's walls and the abyss. Despite their efforts to keep their eyes forward and not to look into its darkness, "it pulled, it tempted, and they couldn't help glancing into it." Lyra, showing off to Roger, slips and falls into the abyss but is rescued by the harpy No-Name, and delivered into Will's arms.

Beneath his basalt fortress, through one of the many fissures created by the bomb, Asriel makes his way to the edge of the abyss and sees Dust for the first time, as will Mrs Coulter: "Everything, every surface, every cubic centimetre of air, was permeated by the falling Dust, which gave a soft clarity to every tiny detail." But this "nimbus of golden mist" is deceptive in its beauty, since each of the "billions of particles... was a little fragment of conscious thought."

Lured by Mrs Coulter to the edges of this chasm, Metatron is defeated when Coulter, Lord Asriel, and their dæmons attack. After a violent battle they force the angel into the abyss, but are compelled to fall with him, using their weight to keep Metatron's wings pressed against his sides.

Will's dæmon, Kirjava, tells him what the angel Xaphania told her: each time they opened a window, "the knife cut into the emptiness outside. The same emptiness there is down in the abyss." Dust slips out of the worlds and into the abyss—is lost—and brings into the worlds the Spectres: "Every time we open a window with the knife, it makes a Spectre. It's like a little bit of the abyss that floats out and enters the world."

The title of chapter 26 of *The Amber Spyglass* is "The Abyss." In the **10th** anniversary edition of *The Amber Spyglass*, the woodcut for this chapter is a solid black square.

Observation: *On her platform high in a wheel-oil tree in the mulefa's world, Mary Malone has what she thinks must be an out-of-the-body experience when the bomb hits. Mary felt Dust leaving the world in a massive rush and threatening to sweep her along with it over an "invisible edge" into an "abominable drop."*

The abyss is also referred to as the gulf *or* cavern, *which recalls the gulf between worlds that was bridged by Asriel. When attempting to rescue Roger, Lyra tries to cross an ice bridge that will not bear the weight of Iorek Byrnison. With each step Lyra takes, another bit of ice "fell off near her feet and tumbled into the abyss."*

AS   described, Lyra's fall into 26; Basilides on bomb and 28; Asriel at its edge, Dust streaming into 30; battle with Metatron 31; Serafina on what Xaphania told her 36; and cutting windows, loss of Dust, creation of Spectres 37

ÆSAHÆTTR ⚑

Role: The use by an ancient cliff-ghast of this term for the subtle knife suggests that legends of its powers preceded its existence.

After witch Ruta Skadi leaves Lord Asriel's basalt fortress, she takes refuge in a spot inhabited by the oldest of all cliff-ghasts. There she hears the beast cackle to his fellow cliff-ghasts that Asriel will fail in his war against the Authority because he lacks Æsahættr, and in fact doesn't even know it exists. Her presence becomes known to the creatures before she learns who or what Æsahættr is.

When Ruta tells her sister witch Serafina Pekkala about the cliff-ghasts' dialogue, Serafina suggests that the word might mean "god-destroyer," and wonders if it is Lyra who will play that role, while Ruta Skadi thinks the term may refer to witches.

When Mrs Coulter finally flatters Sir Charles Latrom/Lord Boreal into telling her what object he seeks in Cittàgazze, he mentions Æsahættr as another name for the subtle knife.

The title of Chapter 13 of *THE SUBTLE KNIFE* is "Æsahættr."

SK   witches on 13; Latrom uses when describing subtle knife to Coulter 15 *[brief]*

ANOMALY ⚑

Role: In his letters from Alaska home to his wife, Elaine, explorer John Parry refers to the passage into the spirit world of Eskimo legends as "the anomaly." He records his progress in securing directions to its location in the mountains of the Brooks Range.

SK   5

BEARER OF THE SUBTLE KNIFE ⚑🖋

Role: In *HIS DARK MATERIALS*, the *bearer* is the holder of the subtle knife, a responsibility passed by Cittàgazze's Giacomo Paradisi to his successor, Will Parry. According to Paradisi, "The knife knows when to leave one hand and settle in another," and only one bearer can teach another how to use it—and only the one who is to be the bearer can learn.

On a Cittàgazze mountaintop, before they realize their identities as father and son, Will tells the stranger he's encountered that he doesn't want the knife. Grumman retorts, "You haven't any choice: you're the bearer: it's picked you out." Paradisi sees the work of angels in the bearer's selection: even if Will doesn't understand what his task is, "the angels do who brought you here." Grumman also tells Will that "Someone will appear to guide you; the night is full of angels."

Paradisi doesn't choose Will, and only recognizes him as the next bearer since Will, during his struggle with Tullio, has been physically marked by the loss of the pinkie and ring fingers of his left hand, just as Paradisi himself had been when the knife chose him.

Traditionally, the bearer has served on behalf of the Guild of Torre degli Angeli, the creator of the subtle knife, and has been bound by its rules, but when Will takes possession of the knife, the Guild is in disarray if not disgrace, vanquished from Cittàgazze by the Spectres, and Will owes no allegiance to the Guild. He does, however, assume responsibility for the knife. When it shatters in Mrs Coulter's hide-out, in spite of a gun battle raging around him, Will gathers up the pieces—not only to insure his own return to his world but because "he was the knife bearer, and he had to gather it up safely." 51 No longer the bearer—it will never again be whole—Will again picks up its piece after deliberating shattering it at the entrance to the Botanic Garden.

SK   Paradisi declares Will his successor as, rules for the 8; Grumman persuades Scoresby to take him to find 10; 14 *[brief]*; Grumman's surprise 15

AS   *brief mentions:* by angels 2, 5; 7; Will's sense of responsibility as when knife breaks 12

Door/Doorway ⚜ ✎ ⑩ Ⓛⓢ

Role: These words, most often *doorway*, are used occasionally in His Dark Materials to refer to the windows into other worlds.

Cittàgazze's Joachim Lorenz tells the visiting witches Ruta Skadi and Serafina Pekkala that he believes the philosophers of the Tower of Angels cast spells that open such doors. Lord Boreal, in his guise of Sir Charles Latrom, also uses this term when commanding Will and Lyra to bring him the subtle knife and in conversation with Mrs Coulter.

The former John Parry of Will's world, who was looking for what he once termed the "anomaly" in his own world, refers to the passages by which he arrived in Cittàgazze and then in Lyra's world as *doorways* when, as shaman Stanislaus Grumman, he recounts his journey to Lee Scoresby.

When in rural Cittàgazze Mary Malone happens upon the "square patch of difference" that offers a way to the mulefa's world, she recalls that the I Ching and *The Book of Changes* had suggested to her that she pay attention to "*a bypath, little stones, doors and openings.*" 52

Update: Lord Asriel's papers in the **10**th anniversary edition of Northern Lights include a brief note that Stanislaus Grumman told him of what the shamans refer to as spirit-doorways in Alaska. He wonders how the witches' lack of belief in spirit can be reconciled with knowledge of these doorways.

The introduction to Lord Asriel's papers speculates on their appearance in this world, suggesting that between this world's and another's Oxford, two college libraries share a doorway or wormhole, allowing these bits to have been misplaced in our world.

SK   *term used by* Parry in letters to Elaine about Eskimo legends 5; Lorenz to witches 6; Latrom to Will and Lyra 7, 8 and Coulter 9; Grumman to Scoresby 10, 15; appendix; Ⓛⓢ Lantern Slide 6

AS   Mary finds in Cittàgazze 7 *[brief]*

10th: *NL* appendix

10th: *SK* appendix

GOD-DESTROYER ⚔️✒️

Role: Serafina Pekkala suggests that the word Æsahættr, which Ruta Skadi heard the cliff-ghasts discuss, might mean "god-destroyer."

Father MacPhail of the Consistorial Court of Discipline warns Mrs Coulter that cliff-ghasts call the subtle knife "god-destroyer," but doesn't reveal the source of his information.

[*See also Æsahættr.*]

SK Serafina and Ruta Skadi consider term 13 *[brief]*

AS MacPhail uses with Coulter 24 *[brief]*

"She approached the little patch of air with passionate curiosity...touching the edge, moving around to see how it became invisible from the other side, noting the absolute difference between this and that, and found her mind almost bursting with excitement that such things could be."

PATCH ⚔️✒️

Role: The word *patch* is the first term used to describe passageways into other worlds.

Will Parry chances to find in North Oxford what "looked as if someone had cut a patch out of the air...roughly square in shape and less than a metre across." It can be seen only straight on and only from one side, and the world into which it offers passage closely resembles Will's: "But Will knew without the slightest doubt that that patch of grass on the other side was in a different world. He couldn't possibly have said why. He knew it at once, as strongly as he knew that fire burned and kindness was good."

Mary Malone's thoughts on finding the Cittàgazze/mulefa's world window echo Will's.

SK in Sunderland Avenue 1 *[brief]*

AS Mary finds in Cittàgazze 7 *[brief]*

SUBTLE KNIFE, THE / THE KNIFE ⚔️✒️ ⑩ LS

World: Cittàgazze (origin)

Background: Will first encounters the knife when he is threatened with it in the Tower of Angels by the crazed Cittàgazze youth Tullio. Will responds immediately and effectively, not to gain the knife but to keep from being killed, losing two fingers in the struggle. Will doesn't want the knife—yet finds he has no choice—he must be its new bearer.

Will's predecessor as the bearer of the subtle knife, Giacomo Paradisi, feels too rushed to provide any but scant background to the impetus for the development of the knife. However, he claims the Torre degli Angeli's alchemists' and philosophers' efforts to penetrate the most elementary bonds holding matter together led to the creation of the knife.

Early in its history, the Guild of the Torre degli Angeli had set rules for the bearer. Paradisi briefly provides Will four instructions: close all windows opened, allow no one else to use it, keep his identity as its bearer private, and use it for honorable purposes.

Stanislaus Grumman/John Parry holds its creators in contempt, telling Will that its devisers succeeded in inventing "a device that could split open the very smallest particles of matter, and they used it to steal candy. They had no idea that they'd made the one weapon in all the universes that could defeat the tyrant. The Authority." 56

Appearance: The knife is described as initially appearing to be "an ordinary-looking dagger," with a double blade roughly eight inches long; a crosspiece of the same metal as the blade's separates it from a rosewood handle. 57

Closer examination proves that it is far from ordinary.

Its handle is intricately designed. Inlaid gold wires portray angels: on one side, an angel with wings folded, and on the other, an angel with raised wings, recalling the statues at the Tower of Angels' entrance.

The blade's metal seems to harbor a "swirl of cloudy colors" just below its surface. On one side of the knife its color reminds Lyra of the silver guillotine's; this side will cut through any material. The other edge, which seems so sharp as to be made of clear steel, is "more subtle still" and cuts windows to other worlds. 58

Armoured bear Iorek Byrnison, to whom "nothing made of iron or steel is a mystery" easily identifies the side that can cut through his armour but is baffled by the other and after hours of examining it in every way he can, tells Will that he has some impressions of what it might do, but he does not "understand what" as it is the "strangest thing" he's ever seen. 59

The knife's sheath, attached to a belt worn at the bearer's waist, is made of leather fortified with horn. Buckles restrict the knife's movement since otherwise it would cut through its own sheath.

Operation/Usage: The knife's greatest power is opening passages between worlds. But it also offers protection against the Spectres of Cittàgazze, a singular distinction, and the cliff-ghasts off the coast of Svalbard, as well as any mortal enemy. Even the harpies in the world of the dead don't risk contact with its blade.

Only a bearer can use the knife to cut windows to other worlds, and a bearer can learn only from his predecessor. And yet, the knife retains its ability to cut through any material when in the possession of one who is not the bearer, for example, when it slips from Tullio's grasp it plunges into lead like a table knife into butter. However, Tullio would never have been able to cut a window.

Sir Charles Latrom/Lord Boreal steals Lyra's alethiometer in a thwarted scheme to get the knife. But simply possessing the knife would have done him no good; Latrom/ Boreal knows much about the subtle knife, but fails to grasp this one fact. His presumption is shared by the Consistorial Court of Discipline's president Father MacPhail, who seems to think that if he takes the knife from Will he'll be able to benefit from its "extraordinary powers." The ancient Grandfather cliff-ghast of Svalbard's coast believes that if Asriel had the subtle knife, he could defeat the Authority. But again, unless Asriel has the allegiance of the bearer, the knife alone is limited in its powers. Only the angels Baruch and Balthamos, Stanislaus Grumman/John Parry, and the Gallivespian spy commander Lord Roke understand that the knife's power depends on the will of the bearer. 60

As he instructs Will, the former bearer Giacomo Paradisi stresses that it is not only the knife, but the bearer's mind, that cuts through to other worlds. Physical force is not relevant—it is, Paradisi says, "a subtle knife, not a heavy sword." Mental strength, the ability to relax and focus one's mind simultaneously, entering a state of concentration similar to that allowing Lyra to read the alethiometer, is essential. To find a window or to close it, the bearer must put his "soul" into his fingertips. The knife's point works by "search[ing] out the gaps inside the atoms."

Similarly, when the knife breaks, its repair depends as much on Will's concentration as on armoured bear Iorek Byrnison's metalcraft; even after all but one piece has been joined, Will still must bring to the task "his full consciousness" to hold it "together with all the others" else "the knife would simply fall apart as if Iorek had never begun."

Latrom believes "nothing, no one, matter, spirit, angel, air—nothing is invulnerable to the subtle knife," and Fra Pavel interprets the alethiometer's description of the subtle knife as saying that "there is nothing this knife cannot destroy." But there is something stronger even than the subtle knife—something that can destroy it—and that is selfless love. When Will's consciousness is split between the act of cutting and his love for his mother (and later for Lyra), love proves stronger.

Role: The first specific mention of the knife is when the man who has stolen Lyra's alethiometer, Sir Charles Latrom/Lord Boreal, claims he will return Lyra's property in exchange for Will and Lyra stealing a knife they'll find in the possession of an old man in Cittàgazze. The term *subtle knife* is not used until Giacomo Paradisi tells Lyra and Will that he is the bearer, that is, he holds "the subtle knife on behalf of the Guild" of the Tower of Angels.

However, the subtle knife is alluded to much earlier in the second book of *HIS DARK MATERIALS*. Lee Scoresby announces to the assembled witches of Serafina Pekkala's clan his intention of doing what he can to help Lyra, and his best idea is to find the shaman Stanislaus Grumman, whom he has heard knows how to find "some kind of object that gives protection to whoever holds it." He hopes to gain this magical device for Lyra. Arctic hunters and traders in Nova Zembla confirm his memory of hearing that Grumman knows the whereabouts of some special tool.

The subtle knife is the tool by which Will Parry and Lyra are able to enter the world of the dead and liberate its ghosts from the hopelessness of being forever conscious of their separation from all of life. It is the means by which Lyra regains her alethiometer, and Will is brought together for a few moments with his father. The subtle knife brings Will and Lyra to the mulefa's world where they bring back Dust to that world. Finally, the knife lets Will and Mary Malone return to their own world.

It is the knife—or rather John Parry's determination to convince the bearer to go to the aid of Lord Asriel's army—that has brought him out of Lyra's world. On a personal level, when Will is away from his world and the knife breaks, his fear is that his mother might believe he has abandoned her, too. He thinks that if the knife can't be mended, then it would have been "directly responsible for both their desertions. He *must* use it to return to her, or never forgive himself."

When Will and Lyra ask his help in repairing the knife, Iorek Byrnison is reluctant, recalling Will's ambivalence about being its bearer: "I have never known anything so dangerous...It would have been infinitely better if it had never been made," noting that the "knife has intentions, too," and because Will cannot see its sharpest edge, he can't know all it does. Will counters that he "must still use it, and do what I can to help good things come about. If I did nothing, I'd be worse than useless. I'd be guilty." Lyra agrees, noting that knowing the evil done at Bolvangar, not to use the weapon against such a force would be wrong.

70

71

Monroe S. Tarver

Artist's rendition of the subtle knife

Iorek decides to let the alethiometer decide the question. It says that the subtle knife can do good or evil, and because "the faintest thought or wish could tip it one way or the other," Will must be clear in his thoughts and wishes. Together Will and Iorek mend the knife, forging together the seven broken pieces and then joining them to the knife's hilt. Once he again can cut a window, Will realizes how much he has come to care for the knife.

When Will cuts a window into the world of the dead the surface seems smooth and the knife initially moves easily, but it then meets great resistance. Once they leave the suburbs of the world of the dead and cross the river, there is still one more barrier: a heavy door of rotting wood in a stone wall guarded by harpies. The subtle knife provides the means of opening the door. On their journey through the world of the dead, only Will's quick cutting of a window in which to place the lock of Lyra's hair guiding the Consistorial Court of Discipline's bomb saves their lives. Finally, he is able to find a place to cut a window to release the ghosts. The last time Lyra and Will leave that world, they must enter Asriel's world because that is where their dæmons are. With the subtle knife and an army of ghosts to protect them, Will and Lyra emerge into a battlefield dominated by Spectres. The knife allows their escape into the calm mulefa's world.

Will's dæmon Kirjava tells Lyra and Will that each time the knife was used to enter a different world, it "cut into the emptiness outside. The same emptiness there is down in the abyss," a consequence, Iorek would not be surprised to know, of not being able to see the knife's edges. What escapes is Dust. When a window is closed quickly, not much harm is done, but so many have been left opened and so much Dust lost that the worlds' conscious beings are threatened and vulnerable to the Spectres.

72

The last window Will cuts leaves him and Mary Malone in the Botanic Garden of their Oxford and Lyra under the care of Serafina Pekkala and the gyptians in Cittàgazze. That window closed, Will touches one of Lyra's tears still resting on his cheek as he uses his other hand to try to cut a window. The knife shatters. Perhaps because he is concerned that they do no harm or perhaps because he is the bearer still, Will carefully collects the pieces.

The woodcut for chapter 14, "Know What It Is" in the **10TH** anniversary edition of THE AMBER SPYGLASS depicts the pieces and hilt of the broken subtle knife.

Update: In the **10TH** anniversary edition of THE SUBTLE KNIFE, included among Col. John Parry/Stanislaus Grumman's papers is a drawing of the subtle knife made after his meeting with the previous bearer, Giacomo Paradisi. It shows the angel on one side of its hilt with the annotation that the handle is made of rosewood and the angel of inlaid golden wire. A note on the drawing records his complaint that the knife's power has been used to accomplish trivial purposes, and his desire that it be used in Asriel's campaign. Another jotting showing more hesitancy is on living with the knowledge that he could have asked Paradisi to cut a window to his world so he could return to his wife and son, but decided instead that his greater responsibility was to play his part in the great battle in the midst of which he has landed.

SK   Scoresby seeks Grumman to get Lyra under protection of special tool [unnamed] 2, 6; Latrom demands as ransom for alethiometer 7; fight for at the Tower of Angels, history, description, Will cuts first windows 8; Will uses to reclaim alethiometer 9; Grumman tells Scoresby about 10; Lyra and Will discuss Spectre-orphans' reaction to Tullio losing prior to mob attacking, used to keep mob away in fight at belvedere, Will realizes Spectres fear it 11; witches cast spell over to stop Will's bleeding, Will reconciled to being bearer because it keeps Spectres away, used to kill cliff-ghast 13; Grumman and Scoresby discuss 14 [brief]; Latrom and Coulter discuss, Grumman/Parry and then angels implore Will to use it to aid Asriel's rebellion 15; [LS] Lantern Slide 3

AS   angels try to persuade Will to take it to Asriel, Will practices cutting windows, discovers resonance, kills attacking angel, escapes from Metatron 2; Baruch tells Asriel about 5; Pavel testifies before Court about using to enter other worlds, its power to kill angels, MacPhail determined to secure 6; Will uses to defuse situation between villagers and armoured bears 8; Iorek studies on boat, Will shows him what it can do in Himalayas 9; Coulter suggests to Will he use it to keep her and Lyra safe 11; Will cuts through to get to Lyra in Coulter's cave, knife breaks 12; Will keeps break secret from Gallivespians, discusses with Lyra asking Iorek to fix 13; Iorek considers whether knife should be repaired 14; Iorek and Will repair 15; Roke reports on its breaking, its repair, and its effect on his spies' ability to force Will to obey their orders 16; Will uses to enter suburbs of world of dead 18; cuts through lock on door to entrance to world of dead 21; harpies avoid 22; difficulty finding world to cut into 23; Coulter and MacPhail discuss, Coulter claimed she caused it to break 24; used to cut remainder of lock from Lyra's head and to put hair into uninhabited world, cuts window to release ghosts 26; cuts window into battlefield in Asriel's republic 29; frees Iorek from nets of steel, cuts opening in crystal litter, opens window to world of mulefa 31; cutting windows and seeing daemons as functions of negative capability, Lyra and Will discuss his keeping the knife so they can visit each other 35; and the loss of Dust, creation of Spectres 37; cuts last window, shattered 38; [LS] Lantern Slide 4

   brief mentions: window between Cittàgazze and mulefa's world 7, Angelica and Gomez discuss 10; 27; not needed in world of mulefa 32, 33; 34

10TH: *SK* appendix

TELEUTAIA MAKHAIRA ⚔

73   **Role:** Another name for the subtle knife, which means "the last knife of all," or so says Lord Boreal.

   [*See also Æsahættr.*]

SK   Latrom uses with Coulter 15 *[brief]*

WINDOWS ⚔ ✎ ⑩ [LS]

Role: Will Parry introduces this term when he meets Lyra and explains that he too is a stranger in the world in which they both find themselves. *Window* is the most frequently used word to describe passageways into other worlds, likely favored over *door* or *doorway* since the size of the passages suggests an opening more likely stoopingly entered than strolled through—one that could be cut in four equally swift motions while standing. Larger ones can be cut, however, as Will does when he devises the passage to release the ghosts from the world of the dead.

   As the bearer of the subtle knife, Will Parry holds the tool for creating these windows; however, windows between worlds existed long before the subtle knife's manufacture 300 years previously by the Guild of the Torre degli Angeli, as the witches of the North in Lyra's world and the native shamans of the Arctic lands in Will's can attest. But several of the most significant windows in *HIS DARK MATERIALS* are cut by the knife: the one through which Will enters Cittàgazze that was deliberately left open by Giacomo Paradisi; the window from Cittàgazze to the mulefa's world used by Mary Malone and Fr Gomez, cut by the knife's bearer in the 1770s; and the window allowing ghosts to escape the world of the dead, cut by the knife's last bearer, Will Parry.

When Will at last feels safe enough to read his missing father's final letters home and discovers that John Parry searched in Alaska's wilderness for what his son found by chance in the city of Oxford, he feels a strong sense of connection: "His father was describing exactly what he himself had found under the hornbeam trees. He too had found a window—he even used the same word for it!" [74]

The senior Parry refers to this legendary passage as "the anomaly," explaining to his wife that according to Eskimo legends, a medicine man has to go through "a doorway into the spirit world" and return with a trophy as part of his initiation. From his Eskimo [75] informant Matt Kigalik, Parry gathered that it's "a gap in the air, a sort of window" apparently hard to see since what it opens onto resembles what is on the viewer's side; this [76] attribute of the windows in particular fascinates Mary Malone and the Gallivespians. Kigalik provides Parry coordinates for the Alaskan window: 69° 02'11[or12]''N, 157°12'19''W. But when Parry passes through it, a blizzard hits, and never again does he find a way back to his own world.

His son, however, gains the ability to open windows when he becomes the bearer of the subtle knife, learning by following the retiring bearer Giacomo Paradisi's instructions. Finding the equivalent of a surface in the air through which he can cut depends on the bearer "letting his mind flow along to the very tip of the blade ... until his consciousness nestled among the atoms themselves, and he felt every tiny snag and ripple in the air" or "delicately [77] searching out the gap between one stitch and the next with the point of a scalpel." The gaps [78] are "anywhere, but not everywhere, or any slash of the knife would open a window." [79]

To close them, the bearer finds the edges through their feel and pinches them together, and just as no one but the bearer can use the knife to cut a window, only the bearer can find the edges to close them. Will is, however, able to teach the angel Xaphania how to close windows.

When Will is in a world away from Cittàgazze's marauding youth and the authorities of his own home world, he practices cutting windows, anxious to make sure that once he sees to Lyra's safety he can return to his mother. He discovers that windows to different worlds feel different from one another, and that the presence of a sense of "resonance" means "that the ground in the world he'd opened was in the same place" as the one from which he is cutting. The gaps in the air which means he has found a place to cut a [80] window most easily come to his attention when the window is to his own world.

In the world of the dead, Will tells Lyra that he feels as if the abyss were an enormous window, one he wishes he could close. He senses too that whenever windows are left open, "things go wrong" and is certain that the enormity of the abyss-window will lead to disaster. [81]

Changes wrought by too many windows include physical or geographical displacement of worlds, but most seriously, it is through windows that Dust empties out of worlds into the abyss and Spectres enter. After their journey through the world of the dead and Will's creation of a window through which the ghosts can escape, Lyra and Will's happiness is short-circuited when their dæmons tell their people that all windows must be closed to keep Dust from leaking into the emptiness that the knife cuts into.

The angel Xaphania says one may remain, because what Dust is lost through it can be replenished by people living compassionate and constructive lives, and while Lyra and Will want it to be one between their worlds, they sacrifice their only means of being together so that the window out of the world of the dead can remain open. The angels plan to close even those windows not cut by the subtle knife; the explanation Xaphania supplies is that otherwise Lyra and Will could waste their lives attempting to find a window to the other's world. It is unclear why windows not cut by the knife will have to be closed in worlds other than these two, nor is there an explanation of how these windows came to be.

The last window Will cuts returns him and Mary Malone to their world, but when he closes it, he and Lyra are forever separated.

[*See also*: **Door/doorway, Patch, Subtle knife**]

82 **Observation:** *Malone considers a window "a square patch of difference," and on examining both sides of one, finds their dissimilarity to be "the absolute difference between* this *and*
83 that." *This definition is echoed much later in* THE AMBER SPYGLASS *when, explaining to Serafina how Will and Lyra's love returned the flow of Dust to the mulefa's world, Mary says: "If you wanted to divert a mighty river into a different course, and all you had was a single pebble, you could do it, as long as you put the pebble in the right place to send the first trickle of water* that *way instead of* this. *Something like that happened yesterday ... They saw each other differently ... And then the Dust was attracted to them, very powerfully, and it stopped*
84 *flowing the other way."*

Update: The **10**TH anniversary edition of NORTHERN LIGHTS/THE GOLDEN COMPASS appendix reveals that Grumman told Lord Asriel about the Alaska window, and according to Grumman's papers in **10**TH THE SUBTLE KNIFE, the former John Parry shared this information with Giacomo Paradisi, the bearer of the knife before Will, who repaid Grumman's confidence by demonstrating the use of the subtle knife.

According to the sixth Lantern Slide in *THE SUBTLE KNIFE*, although the Alaskan natives recognize the window through which John Parry left his world as "a doorway to the spirit world," this is unusual. Most windows in our world are ignored because "people don't like the uncanny, and rather than look fully at something disturbing, they'll avoid it altogether."

Note: *Included here are synonymous terms for window such as* opening, anomaly, *or* "invisible gateway" *and descriptions of the process of* "cutting through" *or* "opening up" *and closing windows.*

SK on Sunderland Avenue, Oxford 1, 3 and in Alaska 4; Ruta Skadi follows angels through to Asriel's republic 6; Sunderland Avenue's 7; Will learns to open and close 8; at Latrom's Headington house as means to locate, retrieve alethiometer 9; appendix; **LS** Lantern Slide 6
    brief mentions: 11, Mary enters Cittàgazze through 12; 13, Grumman and Scoresby enter Cittàgazze through 15

AS resonance and 2; Baruch tells Asriel about 5; Pavel's testimony about 6; Mary finds connecting Cittàgazze's and mulefa's worlds, description 7; Will's demonstration for Iorek 9; Headington windows, views of golden monkey through recalled at Coulter's cave 11; demonstration for Ama, cut in Coulter's cave to locate, rescue Lyra 12; Gallivespian spies examine, description 14; looking for the world of the dead, difficulty of cutting 18; poor results of finding ones leading to above-ground worlds 23; harpies begin trek toward place for Will to cut, compared to abyss, ghosts' way out 26; way out of world of dead discussed at basalt fortress 28; ghosts of Parry and Scoresby leave through 29; Mary sees ghosts coming through 32; speculation on entrance used by man Mary saw 35; windows and Spectres, necessity of closing all 37; at Sunderland Avenue closed, Will cuts his last, Will breaks knife while cutting and thinking of Lyra 38
    brief mentions: 13, 15, 19, 20, 27, 33, 34, 36

10TH: *NL* appendix

10TH: *SK* appendix

The Alethiometer, The Subtle Knife,
The Amber Spyglass:
The Amber Spyglass

AMBER SPYGLASS ✐ LS

World: Mulefa's

Background: Physicist Mary Malone is inspired to build a tool to see sraf after her friend Atal compares the appearance of sraf to light sparkling on water. Mary speculates that since "reflected light like the glare off the sea was polarized," what she calls Shadow-particles might share this property of light waves.

Appearance: The two lenses of the amber spyglass are each roughly the size of a half of a page from a common paperback, perhaps 3½ by 2 inches (9 by 5 cm) and 0.2 inches (5 mm) thick.

These lenses are almost certainly not perfect circles, since the only tool Mary had to work with was a Swiss Army Knife and cutting her original sheet was itself a difficult task. The lenses are held in place in a bamboo tube. The mulefa devised this solution to leave Mary with one hand free; how they joined the lenses to the tube isn't described. The device is small enough to fit in her pocket when Mary climbs the wheel-pod trees.

Operation/Usage: For the amber spyglass to function, two conditions have to be met. The lenses have to be a hand's width apart, and the lenses have to be coated with seedpod oil, that functions to some extent, perhaps, like the photographic emulsion that allows Asriel to see on developed film that which cannot be seen by the human eye alone: Dust. Unlike the alethiometer or subtle knife, no special state of mind is required to use this telescope-like instrument. The user simply looks through the two lenses.

Constructing the Amber Spyglass

Mary Malone's first step in constructing her amber spyglass is to devise a mirror made of the sap lacquer that the mulefa use as a varnish. The sap-lacquer's natural shade of transparent amber "had the same curious property as the mineral known as Iceland Spar. It split light rays in two, so that when you looked through it you saw double."

After applying several dozen coats to a piece of soft wood, polishing the surface, then painstakingly removing the wood, she decides to split the remaining lacquer sheet into two parts. Her experiments with moving the resulting two discs together and apart don't provide a means for seeing sraf; however, separated by a hand's width, the colors she sees are natural rather than amber-tinted and "brighter and more vivid." Mary then accidentally smears some wheel seedpod oil onto the lenses—and finds she can see sraf.

When the mulefa see how awkward it is for Mary to hold the lenses of amber lacquer just the right distance apart, they use a bamboo tube to create a spyglass that holds the discs in place.

85
86
87

Role: Mary Malone devises the amber spyglass so she can see sraf. Her efforts are facilitated but not rushed or dictated by her mulefa friends, even though they know that once she can see its beauty, Mary will accept the mulefa elder's challenge to help his people find a way to keep sraf from leaving their world.

Through her amber spyglass Mary witnesses the departure of sraf, which should be falling into the upturned flowers of the seedpod trees but instead moves away from the

land, changing from an apparently aimless drifting to an ever-escalating flow more comparable to a flood. Mary sees two opposing movements: the wind and the clouds are valiantly attempting to keep Dust in the worlds.

Several days after Will and Lyra arrive, Atal tells Mary she feels something good happening and asks Mary to use her spyglass and look into the sky. Mary sees that instead of streaming out of their world, the Dust or sraf was falling gently and steadily back into it to the awaiting trees' flowers. Then she sees Will and Lyra emerge from the grove. She starts to use the spyglass to watch them, but knows without doing so what she would see: "they would seem to be made of living gold. They would seem the true image of what human beings always could be."

Artist's rendition of the amber spyglass

Monroe S. Tarver

88

When Serafina Pekkala comes to the mulefa's world, Mary shares her tool with Serafina so that the witch too can see Dust; in turn, Serafina teaches Mary to see her dæmon.

AS   construction, description 17; first use of term, Mary begins observations with 20; Mary witnesses sraf's drift 27; ⊡ Lantern Slide 5
       brief mentions: 32, 33; Gomez sighting 34; return of sraf 35; Serafina uses 36

PHILOSOPHY, PSYCHOLOGY, AND THEOLOGY

Philosophy, Psychology, and Theology:
Multiple worlds, Prophecy, Stories

Barnard-Stokes business/heresy/hypothesis ❖ ✎

World: Lyra's

Role: According to the Jordan College Master, while the Holy Church claims there are only two worlds, one physical and the other "the spiritual world of heaven and hell," Barnard and Stokes, a couple of "renegade theologians," theorized that there are numerous physical worlds, "material and sinful...close by, but invisible and unreachable." The Master tells the Librarian that although the Church considers the hypothesis heresy, some mathematical arguments in its favor appear sound.

At the Consistorial Court of Discipline's headquarters, Dr Cooper, charged with designing a foolproof way to kill Lyra, hesitantly tells Fr MacPhail that the range of the bomb he has designed includes other worlds. MacPhail has learned already that Lyra is in a different world, and so treats very matter-of-factly Cooper's admission that his weapon "makes use" of the Barnard-Stokes "heresy." [*See also* **Other worlds** *in* **Places: The Worlds**]

NL/GC discussed at Jordan College 2; Santelia claims to have proven 19 *[brief]*

AS and Cooper's bomb 24 *[brief]*

Many-worlds hypothesis ⚷ ✎

World: Will's

Role: Sir Charles Latrom alludes to this hypothesis (which he attributes to work presented in 1957 by a scientist identified only as Everett), during his visit to the Dark Matter Research Unit, Oxford University. He implicitly connects this hypothesis to explorations of means of manipulating consciousness, and suggests that he can facilitate funding for Malone and Payne through Defense contracts—if he dictates the Unit's research towards subjects of his choosing. [*See also* **Barnard-Stokes heresy, Other worlds** *in* **Places: The Worlds**]

Facts: *The 1957 Princeton doctoral thesis of Hugh Everett is considered the original formulation of the many-worlds theory of quantum physics. Very, very basically, it is much the same as Lord Asriel's description to Lyra of possibility-collapses and worlds springing into being: the world splits into as many co-existing worlds, oblivious to one another's existence, as are required to accommodate all viable possibilities.*

SK Latrom on 12 *[brief]*

AS and Cooper's bomb 24 *[brief]*

Prophecy ❖ ⚷ ✎

World: Lyra's

Role: With the entry of the witches in *His Dark Materials* comes the suggestion that far more than the fates—or even the lives—of Lyra and her friend Roger are at stake in the story. As Lyra sleeps in a balloon heading to Svalbard, witch Serafina Pekkala tells aëronaut Lee Scoresby of a witches' prophecy about a child, whom she believes is Lyra, who "is destined to bring about the end of destiny," but will succeed only if she doesn't know "what she is doing, as if it were her nature and not her destiny to do it." If she fails, "death will sweep through all the worlds; it will be the triumph of despair, for ever. The universes will all become nothing more than interlocking machines, blind and empty of thought, feeling, life."

This prophecy is alluded to far earlier in the story. Dr Martin Lanselius tells the gyptian Farder Coram that the witches have heard the "immortal whispers" of "beings who pass between the worlds" regarding a child with a great destiny. That Lyra is the child the witches have been waiting for was determined by the test Lanselius set for Lyra. The church learns of the existence of a prophecy relating to Lyra, and known to the witches and the gyptians, before Mrs Coulter does. Her frustration that she knows nothing of the prophecy concerning her own child and her fury at a Cardinal's insinuations that she knows, but won't tell, culminate in Coulter's cruel torture of two witches. The first, a witch of the Taymyr clan, nearly reveals Lyra's "true name! The name of her destiny," adding that Lyra "is the one who came before, and you have hated and feared her ever since!" Lena Feldt, a witch from Serafina's clan, tells Coulter that Lyra's true name is Eve: "She will be the mother—she will be life—mother—she will disobey." Coulter's initial reaction is to destroy Lyra to prevent the reprise of Eve's fall, although she will later claim that Feldt's revelation prompted her to whisk Lyra out of Cittàgazze and into hiding from the church.

The church's alethiometrist Fra Pavel reports to the Consistorial Court of Discipline that Lyra "is in the position of Eve...the cause of all sin." The court decides that Lyra must die.

But prophecies are not explicit, and theirs seems ambiguous even to the witches. When Serafina and another witch queen discuss Lyra, they wonder if perhaps the child is what the cliff-ghasts call Æsahættr, "the final weapon in the war against the Authority." And in the mulefa's world, on hearing from Mary Malone that Lyra's and Will's celebration of their love returned Dust to this world, Serafina is clearly as surprised as Malone.

In the world of the dead, the Gallivespian spy Salmakia wonders to her counterpart if the choice alluded to in the prophecy was whether Lyra would leave Pan behind or forego her trip beyond the world of the living. This recalls one of the two other instances of the use of *prophecy* in His Dark Materials that doesn't directly refer to the witches' legends. When Lyra is forced to leave Pantalaimon behind in order to enter the world of the dead, "the prophecy that the Master of Jordan College had made to the Librarian, that Lyra would make a great betrayal and it would hurt her terribly, was fulfilled."

And Lord Asriel's alethiometrist interprets his instrument as saying that Lyra once heard it prophesized that death would end, and it was her determination to effect this revolution that brought her to the world of the dead. But Lyra remembers it was her father proclaiming, "*Death is going to die*," along with what she heard Lanselius tell Coram at Trollesund, and the gyptians' saying that she has witch-oil in her soul, that came together in her dreams of Roger and the ghosts, and inspired her to go to the world of the dead.

Note: *In some chapters the word* prophecy *does not appear but context and content strongly suggest that the topic of discussion is what I've described as the witches' prophecy regarding Lyra. These chapter numbers are italicized.*

NL/GC Lanselius and Coram discuss 10; Serafina and Scoresby discuss 18

SK   Coulter tortures witch for information about 2; Skadi and Serafina discuss in regards to Asriel, subtle knife, Lyra 13; Coulter tortures Feldt to learn of 15

AS   discussed by Court 6; Coulter claimed that when she came to know what it entailed she took Lyra to keep her safe 16; the Master's prophecy fulfilled 21; Lyra tells Roger's ghost she overheard Lanselius and Coram discussing 23; Serafina's reaction to Mary's account of return of sraf 36 [*brief*]

Stories ✤ ⚷ ✎ [LS]

Role: Stories are what bring Lyra and Will out of the world of the dead, persuade the harpies to become guides to the ghosts rather than tormentors, and return sraf to the mulefa's world.

To get the harpies to open the gate into the world of the dead, Lyra offers a story of where she and her companions have been and what they've seen, but then launches into one of her preposterous lies. It had worked the evening before when she tried it out on the family with whom the travelers stayed in the suburbs of the world of the dead, but here, the harpy, No-name, attacks her because of the lie. When Lyra finds Roger's ghost and describes all that has happened since he died, and then tells the other ghosts of when she and Roger were children together at Jordan College, the harpies do not launch an attack. Lyra has found what the harpies need: true stories. No-name consents to aid Will and Lyra. The harpy's willingness is founded on a deal brokered by the Gallivespian spies Tialys and Salmakia, that in the future, ghosts will tell the harpies stories about their lives in exchange for guidance to the window Will needs to cut.

The ghost of an old woman, emerging from the world of the dead into the world of the mulefa, stops before dissipating to instruct Mary Malone, "Tell them stories…You must tell them true stories, and everything will be well, everything." Mary follows the ghost's advice that evening. | 14

Lyra tells Will that in spite of their sadness at being separated, they will need to live lives worth talking about, and tell others they must do so as well, so that the harpies will lead their ghosts to the window out of the world of the dead.

While these are the most dramatic situations involving stories in *His Dark Materials*, there are a number of other direct and indirect references to storytelling. The mulefa's culture appears to be pre-literate; at least there are no mentions of books or papers when Mary observes their culture. However, their rich oral storytelling tradition is shown in the "make-like" Atal tells Mary about her kind's origins. Moreover, Atal implies that the mulefa have a history of the 33,000 years of their existence.

Lyra's process of story-making is described as like weaving a tapestry, or shaking episodes "into order as if she were settling a pack of cards ready for dealing," but for Lyra | 15
telling a story is primarily "something natural" "like running or singing." Lyra's gradual | 16
shift away from telling outlandish, improbable, silly stories begins when she is told the true story of her parentage and early infancy by gyptian John Faa. She is in the curious position of having to replace the fiction she had considered truth for twelve years with her own true story. Lyra begins to feel as if she is remembering the events of Ma Costa's anecdotes; Lyra "wove the details into a mental tapestry even clearer and sharper than the stories she made up." | 17

When Lyra finally returns to her Oxford, she tells Dame Hannah Relf that while she admits to having lied and made up stories throughout her childhood, she has changed.

The ways stories are used

Stories are used to speculate about or to try to make sense of what is known when not enough is certain. In Lyra's world, sightings of the Gobblers are followed by stories blending fact and fiction. Anecdotes about the shaman Stanislaus Grumman abound, some reporting his death, others his continuing adventures. Lord Asriel's manservant Thorold tries to piece together a story from what he knows to predict what Asriel will do after his master's escape from Svalbard. Will reads and rereads his father's letters home and the few brief news articles about his disappearance in an attempt to find, if not the man, then the reason others seek him.

Stories give comfort. Making the decision to go to the world of the dead, what worries Will most is abandoning his mother, and the memory that heightens that emotion is of stories; Will remembers that once when he was a little boy, sick and scared, his mother sat with him all night long, singing nursery rhymes or telling him stories, making him feel safe. This is something that Lyra never had. As she prepares to go to the world of the dead, she is inspired by Salmakia's voice to daydream about one day giving a child of her own what she has missed.

There are also times when a story is safer than the truth. The truth can be dangerous when the listener can't be trusted. For example, when Mrs Coulter discovers Lyra at Bolvangar, Lyra scrambles to invent a plausible tale to keep her friends, the gyptians, safe. Mary Malone and Will are looking at a great storytelling feat when they return to Oxford. As Mary tells Will, "We'll have to decide on a story and stick to it."

18

19   She needs their assurance that they will believe her because the story she wants to tell them about all she has seen since leaving Oxford with Mrs Coulter is "too important…to tell if you're only going to believe half of it."

20   Lyra's understanding of the alethiometer's pictorial language harkens back to witch consul Martin Lanselius's explanation of its history as a product of the seventeenth century when "symbols and emblems were everywhere. Buildings and pictures were designed to be read like books." Mary's reading of the I Ching blends the two languages; when she casts the yarrow sticks she creates hexagram patterns, a kind of pictograph or ideograph. But she relies on the words in the *Book of Changes* corresponding to the hexagram cast to interpret their meaning. The woodcut illustrations Pullman devised to head each chapter in the UK editions of Northern Lights and The Subtle Knife, and the epigraphs occupying the same spaces in The Amber Spyglass, also suggest that words and pictures are evocative in comparable ways.

However, the stories shared aloud to form emotional connections are the most vital use of language in the lives of the characters of His Dark Materials. They alone can assure that all will be well.

Update: The first Lantern Slide in The Subtle Knife speculates that a story about how Lee Scoresby's mother's turquoise ring ended up in Stanislaus Grumman's possession, and a story about Lee's life from childhood until the moment when he saw that ring in the shaman's hut, would "diverge, and move a very long way apart" before coming together again. The convergence of the ring's and Lee's stories ends with Lee's death, but the ring's story continues: "It must still be around, somewhere."

Note: *Unlike in other entries, this list of chapters where stories within the grand story of* HIS DARK MATERIALS *can be found is not intended as comprehensive.*

NL/GC about disappearances of children, Gobblers 3; Tony Costa on creatures of the North 6; Faa tells of Lyra's parents, infancy, early life 7; Lyra's outlandish lies about Asriel, Ma Costa's true stories 8; Lanselius on reading the world in 17th century 10; Lyra's and doctor's versions of how she came to be at Bolvangar 14; Lyra's story for Coulter about how she came to leave London and be at Bolvangar 17; Serafina tells Lyra about Iorek 18; Lyra tricks Raknison with one 19; of Adam and Eve 21

SK Will told himself about his father 1; Thorold's about Asriel 2; newspaper stories about John Parry, telling the truth to Malone, reading Cave 4; Lyra tells hers to Will, in Parry's letters home 5; anecdotes about Grumman, Lorenz's of Cittàgazze 6; poorly maintained books of Tower of Angels, Paradisi's account of Guild 8; Grumman/Parry tells of his life 10; LS Lantern Slide 1

AS Coulter's for Ama 1; childhood comfort of 14; Coulter's for Asriel's commanders 16; and mulefa 17; Lyra's for Peter's family in suburbs of world of dead 19; Lyra on nursery songs, No-Name's fury at Lyra's lies 21; Lyra's story for ghosts, harpies' bargain, ghosts on what they had been told about afterlife 23; Coulter on those about Authority's involvement with humanity 24; what the ghost told Mary 32; Mary's 33; Xaphania, Lyra, Will discuss harpies' bargain 37; Mary tells Will they need to work on one, Lyra's insistence to Relf and Master that they believe hers 38; LS Lantern Slide 1

The Written Word

Interestingly, for a novel in which stories play a central part, the importance of oral storytelling is far more apparent than telling stories in print. The Bible and *The Book of Changes* are the only two books mentioned specifically by name. Lord Asriel orders some books for his Svalbard lab while under house arrest; an unidentified book rests in Mrs Coulter's lap when Will approaches her at the Himalayan cave. Books of reference for interpreting the alethiometer are indispensable to all who read the instrument but Lyra. The priest Will meets in Siberia hauls out an atlas. Mary Malone's office is "crowded with tottering piles of papers and books," the Tower of Angels' walls are "lined with bookshelves containing badly preserved volumes," and, as might be expected, Sir Charles Latrom's study is filled with "bookshelves, pictures, hunting trophies." Lyra recognizes Will's Oxford's Bodleian Library as being the Old Bodley in hers, and Will makes his way to the public library to read about his father's disappearance.

Philosophy, Psychology, and Theology:
Dust, Rusakov particles, Shadows/Shadow-particles, Sraf

DUST ✦ ⚲ ✎ [LS]

World: Lyra's

Background: Experimental theologian Boris Mikhailovitch Rusakov of Muscovy discovered the elementary particle that came to bear his name, but is more popularly called Dust. Rusakov distinguished these particles as requiring a separate category because they do not interact with other particles, but are attracted to humans. Their tendency to concentrate around adult humans to a much greater extent than adolescents, and around those on the verge of puberty more so than children, seemed so peculiar and unlikely to the Magisterium's censors that it initially attempted to prove Rusakov either a charlatan or possessed by devils. Failing, in spite of Inquisitorial tactics, to discredit the man, the Magisterium declared the particles to be evidence of original sin.

In the Pitt-Rivers Museum of Will's Oxford, Lyra learns from the alethiometer that Dust surrounds human artifacts and skulls younger than 30-40,000 years old—especially those of trepanned sorcerers. Mary Malone makes the connection between the beginning of human consciousness and the presence of Dust, which she calls *Shadow-particles.*

According to the angel Balthamos, Dust is "only a name for what happens when matter begins to understand itself. Matter loves matter. It seeks to know more about itself, and Dust is formed." Angels, he tells Will, are composed of Dust, and the Authority is as well. The angel Xaphania emphasizes the role of a particular configuration of matter in Dust's genesis: "Conscious beings make Dust—they renew it all the time, by thinking and feeling and reflecting, by gaining wisdom and passing it on." According to Mrs Coulter and the Magisterium, it is "something bad, something wrong, something evil and wicked." When she learns of the attacks by Spectres on adults but not children in the world of Cittàgazze, Coulter sees this as evidence to bolster her claim that the mystery of Dust is linked to the settling of dæmons.

Serafina Pekkala tells Lyra that witches have never sought to analyze it, "but where there are priests, there is fear of Dust;" she later tells Mary Malone that witches first became concerned about Dust during the recent wars between Asriel's republic and the Authority's agents. And although Svalbard's armoured bears are disinterested in such matters, they are sensitive to "the air of mystery and spiritual peril surrounding anything that had to do with Dust."

The term Dust for these particles has its basis in a passage from Genesis, chapter three, in Lyra's world's Bible: *"for dust thou art, and unto dust shalt thou return."*

Appearance: Dust is not typically visible to humans without the aid of a filtering device like the amber spyglass. Lord Asriel manages to develop a special emulsion for developing photographs that captures Dust on film; it appears as streams of light that envelop human adult subjects but fail to illuminate objects.

As he inches along the edge of the abyss to which Mrs Coulter will lure Metatron, Asriel sees Dust directly. This is possible because the opening of the abyss has caused a concentrated outflow of Dust, giving everything in its path "a nimbus of golden mist." 30

Role: The mystery of Dust—its nature, cause, effects, and origins—is arguably the subject of *His Dark Materials*, determining the movement of its plots and defining its themes. In *The Subtle Knife*, the Dust of *Northern Lights/The Golden Compass* surfaces as Shadows; in *The Amber Spyglass*, as sraf.

Lyra's quest to learn about Dust begins when Lyra demands that Asriel tell her what Dust is. He dismisses her, saying Dust is not her concern, and Lyra retorts, without knowing how true her words will prove, "It *is* to do with me." The Master of Jordan 31 College considers discussing Dust with his young ward, but the Librarian dissuades him. However, Lyra never stops asking. Her conviction that Asriel must be stopped before he destroys Dust, her quest to save it from him, and her fear that Asriel will destroy its source compel her exodus out of her own world, to Cittàgazze's, and into Will's.

Dust drives others in her world too. Lyra's vague sense that somehow Dust might be behind the Gobblers' crimes is confirmed first at Mrs Coulter's cocktail party, and again when gyptians John Faa and Farder Coram make the connection. In Trollesund she learns that witches call the Gobblers *Dust-hunters*. Kaisa, Serafina Pekkala's dæmon, says that while there isn't agreement among the Dust-hunters about whether Dust has always been around or has newly fallen into this world, their reaction is uniform: fear. His impression is that the fear of Dust is behind their schemes in the Far North and the exile of Lord Asriel.

In Svalbard, Lyra once again asks Asriel to tell her about Dust, and this time he answers that the Magisterium decided Dust provides evidence of original sin, that is, the movement from innocence to experience of Adam and Eve in the Garden of Eden. The Church interprets it as a loss repeated, thereafter, in each individual's maturation. Asriel tells Lyra that he believes if he goes beyond the Aurora, he'll find "the origin of all the Dust, all the death, the sin, the misery, the destructiveness in the world. Human beings can't see anything without wanting to destroy it, Lyra. *That's* original sin. And I'm going to destroy it. Death is going to die." 32

When the Aurora appears to dim, even before Asriel opens a passage between his world and Cittàgazze, Lyra "sensed the presence of the Dust, for the air seemed to be full of dark

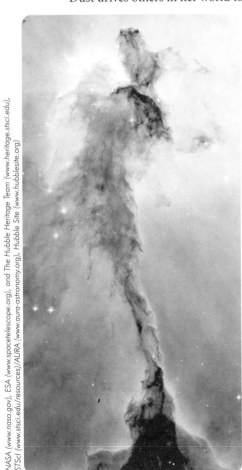

The Eagle Has Risen: Stellar Spire in the Eagle Nebula

intentions, like the forms of thoughts not yet born." As Lyra and Pan battle Stelmaria for Roger, she feels like she is also "fighting the forms in the turbid air, those dark intentions, that came thick and crowding down the streams of Dust."

When Coulter reaches Asriel as he prepares to cross over to Cittàgazze, she doesn't share his joy at the flow of Dust into their world. She believes that with it comes sin and death. Asriel then changes tack, and tries to persuade her to come with him to destroy the source of Dust. Only when near the end of their lives does Coulter realize that its destruction was never Asriel's intention, and that he lied because he wanted her with him.

> # Philip Pullman on Dust:
>
> *Philip Pullman in Readerville:*
> "Dust permeates everything in the universe, and existed before we individuals did and will continue after us. Dust enriches us and is nurtured in turn by us; it brings wisdom and it is kept alive by love and curiosity and diligent enquiry and kindness and patience and hope. The relationship we have with Dust is mutually beneficial. Instead of being the dependent children of an all-powerful king, we are partners and equals with Dust in the great project of keeping the universe alive."

As THE AMBER SPYGLASS opens, the Consistorial Court of Discipline has learned from its alethiometrist that Lyra is in the position of re-enacting Eve's role in the temptation in the Garden of Eden. She is likely to succumb as well, with the result that "Dust and sin will triumph." No longer is simply understanding Dust (the task of the erstwhile General Oblation Board) a worthy goal. The President of the Court proclaims that Dust must be destroyed, even if the Holy Church itself is demolished in the process.

The Court fails, but the threat to Dust remains. It will continue to pour from the huge window out of Asriel's world "into nothingness." As the Dust flows into emptiness, bits of that abysmal nothingness take the form of Spectres, and sneak into the worlds exposed by opened windows to feed on dæmons and Dust.

Xaphania tells Lyra and Will that even keeping one window open to release the ghosts from the world of the dead means they must teach others that "Dust is not a constant. There's not a fixed quantity that has always been the same." Instead, it is made when conscious beings "learn and understand about themselves and each other" and are "kind instead of cruel, and patient instead of hasty, and cheerful instead of surly, and above all… keep their minds open and free and curious."

Note: *Not included are mentions of ordinary, lowercased (household) dust.*

NL/GC Lyra first hears of, Asriel shows photograms of, Master and Librarian discuss 2; Coulter reacts when Lyra mentions, Rusakov's discovery of and Asriel's experiments with discussed at cocktail party 5; Lyra and Faa discuss 7; Lyra's speculations on Aurora and, Kaisa on 11; discussed at Bolvangar 14, 15, 16; Coulter on intercision and 17; Serafina on 18; Asriel on alethiometer and, Rusakov, original sin and, finding source of 21; Aurora and 22; Asriel and Coulter debate going into other worlds to find source of, Pan and Lyra resolve to beat Asriel to it 23; [LS] Lantern Slide 9
  brief mentions: 3, 13

SK Lyra asks Will about 1; alethiometer on trepanned skulls and, Lyra's description of for Mary Malone, Mary on evolution of consciousness and, Shadows and 4; Scoresby mentions at observatory 6; Coulter and Latrom discuss 9; Shadows on 12
  brief mentions: 3, 7, 13; Grumman on Oblation Board's, Spectres' interest in 14

AS Court on destroying 6; and I Ching 7; alethiometer on knife and 14; and sraf 17, 20, 27; Asriel admits to Coulter he lied about wanting to destroy 28; Asriel sees falling into abyss 30; Coulter sees at abyss 31; Mary, matter, and 34; begins fall into rather than flow out of mulefa's world 35; Serafina

sees through spyglass 36; and windows, Spectres and, Xaphania on 37; [LS] Lantern Slide 3
  brief mentions: 2; Coulter to Asriel's commanders on church and 16; Coulter claims no
  opinion of to MacPhail 24

RUSAKOV PARTICLES ✧ ⚑ [*See* Dust]

SHADOWS, SHADOW-PARTICLES ⚑ ✎

World: Will's
Background: Boris Mikhailovitch Rusakov discovered Dust in Lyra's world; in Will's world,
  Mary Malone is the first to identify an elementary particle responding to consciousness.
  Shadows communicate with Mary through her scientific equipment and by means of the
  I Ching, just as Dust provides Lyra with direction through the alethiometer. The Shadows
  are blunter to Mary in the few moments they have with her, wasting no time in clarifying
  that they are communicating with her because she has work to do.

  Her account (simplified for Lyra's benefit) of the technical details of this discovery,
  is vague, but it seems that she and a colleague configured a detector which employs an
  electromagnetic field to limit the elementary particles recognized to Shadow-particles.
  The detector then amplifies these particles' signals. The particles' attribute of
  consciousness is studied using a configuration linking an amplifier to heighten the
  particles' signals, an encephalograph device and electrode sensors to detect the
  investigator's brain waves, and a computer with specialized hardware and software that
  allows feedback between the investigator and the Shadow-particles.

  Strangely, the investigator has to be willing to believe communication is possible, and
  must approach the encounter with a particular state of mind or mental openness for it to
  occur.

Plato's Cave

The Greek philosopher Plato (427 BC to 347 BC) was a student of Socrates and a
teacher of Aristotle. Platonic philosophy is dualistic, dividing reality into two categories:
what is perceived through the senses and what is understood by the mind. Things that can
be apprehended through the senses are imperfect versions of those eternal and perfect
forms or ideas that are known through the intellect.

The Allegory of the Cave is found in Plato's *The Republic*, and is generally regarded as
illustrative of the difference between what we accept through ignorance as ordinary reality
but which is really a weak imitation of Truth. Imprisoned and immobilized all their lives,
those in the cave cannot even turn their heads. Behind them is a fire, and between their
backs and the fire is a walkway where men pass carrying various objects. All those bound
in the cave know of the world is the shadows these things project onto the wall straight
ahead of them; moreover, if a carrier on the walkway speaks, the cave's echo makes it
seem as if the words are coming from the shadows.

If one of the dwellers were ever freed, he wouldn't be able to see when he emerged
from the cave, but would be blinded by the sunlight. After his vision adjusts and he is able
to see all he has missed, if he were to re-enter the cave to rescue his fellows, he would likely
fail because the contrast between their darkness and the light he has grown accustomed to
would again render him blinded even to the shadows. Thus his claims that what he now
cannot see, but they still can, is not real would seem incredible and suspect.

Once Mary writes a program to communicate in language with the Shadows, she learns they are interested in human affairs. Identifying themselves as what humans call angels, the Shadows claim to have played a part in directing the course of human neuro-evolution, and explain the basis of their decision to "intervene" as "vengeance" for the presumption of the Authority to declare himself creator.

Appearance: Mary describes the Shadow-particles as a poet might. She tells Lyra that they "flock to your thinking like birds." A similar image is evoked by the display on her computer's monitor, one that recalls the Aurora as well, with "dancing lights" that "burst into showers of radiance that suddenly swerved this way or that like a flock of birds changing direction in the sky." Shadows react in the presence of evidence of conscious interest in an inanimate object, lingering long after the conscious being who once handled the object has died. Among museum artifacts tested, a plain piece of ivory evokes no reaction, a carved one does. Mary has noted that while a carving and a ruler, objects handled by humans, both attract Shadows, the degree of activity around a carving is greater than that around a mass-produced object. The response is registered as a display of light patterns on the monitor of Mary's computer, or Cave.

Gas Pillars in the Eagle Nebula (M16): Pillars of Creation in a Star-Forming Region

NASA (www.nasa.gov), ESA (www.spacetelescope.org), STScI (www.stsci.edu), J. Hester and P. Scowen (Arizona State University), Hubble Site (www.hubblesite.org)

Mary assumed that the Shadows simply respond to the attention she is giving them. She never guessed that they would, given the chance, communicate on a higher level. But when Lyra tests the Cave and imagines the screen to be the alethiometer, its light patterns settle to form the alethiometer's symbols in response to Lyra's questions.

Role: Shadows are Dust. Lyra's journey into Will's world brings into the story Dr Mary Malone, who will, upon the Shadows' command, leave this world, travel through Cittàgazze, and wait in the world of the mulefa for Lyra and Will. Thus, Shadows, like Dust, compel the characters' movements, and the presence of the mysterious Dust of Lyra's world as Shadows in Will's links their two worlds.

The Shadows convey instructions to Mary. They tell Mary where to find the window out of her world and to expect "a long journey…Your work here is finished." With no other reason than these words, Mary wrecks her lab and leaves her world. After arriving in the mulefa's world, she learns that there Shadows are called sraf.

Note: *There are inconsistencies within and between the UK and US editions in nomenclature.*

Both editions always capitalize Shadows. Lowercase is used for shadow particles in the US, but in the UK, Shadow-particles is used, with one exception: the first time Mary mentions them to Lyra. Moreover, in the US, shadow particles are always two words; in the UK, it is one, hyphenated.

Listed here are only those chapters in which Shadows [or shadow-particles, etc.] appear. There are, however, some interesting uses of the word shadow in reference to the ordinary type. For example, the subtle knife is said to be "shadow-coloured," and the angels Baruch, Balthamos, and Metatron are described as shadows, as are the Spectres.   43 44 45 46

SK   Mary and Lyra discuss 4; Mary receives her instructions from 12

AS   Mary recalls instructions of, tries asking for their guidance through I Ching 7; and sraf 17, 20, 27;   outflow of 32 *[brief]*; Mary tells Lyra she took her advice about using language to communicate in Cave with Shadows 33;   Mary, matter, and 34;   seeing dæmons compared to seeing 38

SRAF

World: Mulefa's

Background: The mulefa have two notions about the provenance of sraf. One is that it comes from the stars. The other is that their existence and the presence of sraf in their world are interdependent. When Mary asks her friend Atal how long there have been mulefa, she is startled by the answer—33,000 years—both because it corresponds to her own theories relating to the evolution of human consciousness, and because her friend seems so certain.   According to Atal, sraf entered their world when the mulefa began to use the seedpods as wheels. When they used these wheels, the beasts they once were became something else, the mulefa, and the mulefa made sraf. This is what Atal means when she answers Mary that sraf comes "From us, and from the oil."

Their myth of origin has similarities to the story of Adam and Eve in the bibles of Will's and Lyra's worlds. There is a female, a snake, a promise of wisdom, and a permanent change, but here the change is celebrated. The snake encourages the first mulefa to put her foot through the hole in the seedpod, the seedpod's oil saturates her foot, and this mulefa sees sraf for the first time. She shares this joyous experience with her mate, and together they discover that they are mulefa and

A Powerful Mistake

Interestingly, Mary Malone's conclusion that Christianity is "a very powerful and convincing mistake" could be made about the mulefa's world view.   The mulefa believe that their use of the wheelpods generates sraf, which fertilizes the trees, and so when the trees fail, they conclude that something is wrong with the sraf or the trees. They are obviously wrong.   They break the seedpods, enabling the trees to germinate, but the essence that fertilizes the seeds falls from the sky—and there is nothing wrong with the sraf itself. There is nothing wrong with the trees either. The problem is that gravity has failed, the sraf is somehow lured through windows that have never been closed, and this passive intrusion of nothingness has disrupted the dynamics of a delicately balanced system.

Although the mulefa were mistaken about Dust or sraf, their world view does metaphorically express what the angel Xaphania tells Lyra and Will, "Conscious beings make Dust—they renew it all the time, by thinking and feeling and reflecting, by gaining wisdom and passing it on."   49 50 51 not animals or grazers. When their children are old enough to use seedpods as wheels, they too generate sraf. Sraf in turn ensures the growth of the trees that provide the wheels. The mulefa cherish sraf, the essence that has given them "memory and wakefulness." Their name for it is much like their word for light.

Appearance: Sraf appears as "sparkles of light," broadcast throughout their environment. It is, however, "thicker and more full of movement" around adult conscious beings. Through the amber spyglass, sraf appears as a "swarm of golden sparkles."

Role: Sraf is Dust or Shadows. NORTHERN LIGHTS/THE GOLDEN COMPASS explores the link between Dust and dæmons. In THE SUBTLE KNIFE, the same essence is found not only to be a particle of consciousness but to actively take an interest in human affairs. The behavior of sraf in the mulefa's world in THE AMBER SPYGLASS offers another dimension of understanding about this particle: the delicate balance between its existence and the continuation of civilizations.

Despairing as she watches the flow of sraf out of the mulefa's world, Mary Malone realizes that all conscious beings will suffer at the departure from their worlds of these particles. Although most do not even know they are in trouble, Malone comprehends there is a "feedback system" between Dust and conscious beings that must remain intact. What stops this drain is Lyra's and Will's love. Even without looking, Mary guesses that Will and Lyra, having fully realized the depth of their feelings, will now be surrounded by the golden light of sraf, and "would seem the true image of what human beings always could be, once they had come into their inheritance."

Note: *Sraf is always italicized in the US edition of* THE AMBER SPYGLASS; *in the UK edition it is only italicized when it appears in a passage of mulefa/Mary dialogue, all of which is set in italics in both the UK and US books.*

AS and mulefa's myth of origin of consciousness, Sattamax requests Mary to investigate 17; cause of failure of 20; Mary senses loss of means consignment to oblivion 27; 32 *[brief]*; Matter tries to hold back flood of leaving mulefa's world 34; returns 35

Cosmic dust

The two photographs, "Gas Pillars in the Eagle Nebula (M16): Pillars of Creation in a Star-Forming Region" and "The Eagle Has Risen: Stellar Spire in the Eagle Nebula," were relayed to Earth by the Hubble telescope. Nebulae are made of gases and dust, and what are shown here are densely packed gaseous towers called EGGs, or evaporating gaseous globules. When the density of the gas becomes greatly compacted, the towers will collapse, and a new star will be born.
[See also Natural Sciences: Physical Sciences: Dark matter]

APPLIED METAPHYSICS

Applied Metaphysics
Book of Changes to Trepanning

BOOK OF CHANGES

World: Will's; brought to and used in Cittàgazze and mulefa's

Role: Dr Mary Malone packs *The Book of Changes,* a guide to interpreting the I Ching, into her rucksack to take into the new world.

> [*See also* **I Ching**]

AS consulted in world of Cittàgazze 7, and mulefa's 10

EXCOMMUNICATE

World: Lyra's

Role: The church excommunicated the first experimental theologians who wrote mathematical proofs that other worlds existed. When Asriel tries to persuade her to walk across the bridge in the sky from Svalbard to a new world, Mrs Coulter argues that the Church will excommunicate anyone who does so. This argument matters not at all to Lord Asriel, who responds that his act will destroy the Church.

NL/GC brief mentions: 21, 23

EXORCISM

World: Lyra's

Role: An exorcism of Rusakov's lab was performed because the Magisterium was so threatened by the findings of Boris Mikhailovitch Rusakov, the Muscovite who discovered the elementary particle commonly called Dust.

When an experimental theologian built a model to illustrate his theory that there were more than three spatial dimensions, the model was seized, exorcised, and burnt.

Facts: *In Will's world, the premise behind the exorcism of objects in the Roman Catholic Church is that fallen angels have retained their power to act on the physical world and its objects for their evil purposes. Exorcising an object is a means of asking God to use His supernatural powers to neutralize the evil influence.*

NL/GC of Rusakov's lab 21 *[brief]*

AS of heretical model of universe 30 *[brief]*

Excommunication

In Will's world, excommunication is the most severe punishment that the Roman Catholic Church can impose on its members. The assumption behind the practice is that since the Church is a society, and a society can include, exclude, and regulate its members, the Church can send into exile (not physically, but effectively) one who knowingly breaks its rules or repudiates its teachings. Excommunication is not considered a vindictive punishment since its intent is for the excommunicated to seek absolution and re-admittance to the community. Excommunication applies only to members of the society, *i.e.* baptized Christians, and means that the censured person cannot receive the sacraments or participate in public worship.

GUILLOTINE

[*See* **Silver guillotine**]

HERESY

[*See* **Censors** *in* Social Structures: Ecclesiastical]

I CHING ⚷✎

Worlds: Will's, Cittàgazze, mulefa's

Role: Lyra had noticed a poster in Dr Mary Malone's office showing some Chinese designs, but Malone, embarrassed, shrugs off this display of I Ching hexagrams as merely decorative. When Lyra asks Malone's Cave, or specially configured computer, how people in Will's world can communicate with Dust or Shadows, Lyra interprets its answer, given in the form of alethiometer symbols (camel: Asia, garden: sticks, moon: divination), to mean that this ancient Chinese ritual is, like the alethiometer, such a device or technique.

The poster is one of the few things Mary Malone takes from the lab, and at home, she packs *The Book of Changes*, a guide to interpreting the I Ching. Using yarrow sticks as her tool for casting the I Ching, and entering into a state of mind similar to Lyra's when reading the alethiometer, Mary seeks guidance on her trek through Cittàgazze. Mary interprets the commentary in *The Book of Changes* corresponding to the hexagrams resulting from her division of the sticks to mean she needs to be on the look-out for windows. Later, when she reaches the mulefa's world, the Shadows use the I Ching to tell her to stay put.

Eight trigrams and the symbol for yin/yang form the woodcut for chapter 12 of *THE SUBTLE KNIFE*, "Screen Language."

SK   Cave using alethiometer's symbols notes as way to contact Shadows 4; Mary takes poster showing 12 *[brief]*

AS   technique of consulting described 7; and Mary in mulefa's world of 10; 32 *[brief]*

What Is I-Ching?

The I Ching is an ancient (estimated as early as 2800 BCE) Chinese tool for divination. A question is asked; a technique (like dividing yarrow sticks) is followed, and the answer is suggested by one of 64 six-line figures, or hexagrams. The hexagrams are composed of two 3-line figures, or trigrams. The three trigram (or six hexagram) lines can be any combination of solid or divided lines. The top trigram indicates the outer influences surrounding the question, while the bottom is the inner aspect. Each hexagram is poetically interpreted in *The Book of Changes*.

The solid lines are Yang lines; the divided are Yin. Each line is also either stable (young) or changing (old), as yin and yang are in the process of becoming their opposites, and that too is taken into account with a reading. The numbers 6, 7, 8, and 9 are assigned to these states of old yin, young yang, young yin, and old yang.

INTERCISION / "THE OPERATION" ❀⚷✎

World: Lyra's

Role: This is the formal term for the severance of a person and his or her dæmon, and the focus of the General Oblation Board's activities at the Bolvangar Experiment Station.

Reading the I Ching

To read the I Ching using yarrow sticks, Mary would start with 50 dried stalks about a foot in length. Setting one aside, she'd then use prescribed motions to transfer the remaining 49 from hand to hand until she is left with 6, 7, 8, or 9 piles of 4 stalks, repeating this six times. This is the source of the hexagram that suggests an answer.

The hexagram that tells Mary to watch for a window linking the world of Cittàgazze to another, which proved to be the mulefa's, is hexagram 27: The Corners of the Mouth (Providing Nourishment), which is composed of solid, broken, broken, broken, broken, and solid lines. The top trigram (solid, broken, broken) is the mountain, keeping still and the bottom (broken, broken, and solid) is thunder, arousing. Together, they form hexagram 27, and *The Book of Changes'* commentary reads:

Michelle Heran

Turning to the summit
For provision of nourishment
Brings good fortune.
Spying about with sharp eyes
Like a tiger with insatiable craving.
No blame.

All but the last line is quoted in THE AMBER SPYGLASS. Later, when Mary asks whether she should stay among the mulefa, the answer the I Ching provides, "*Keeping still, so that restlessness dissolves; then, beyond the tumult, one can perceive the great laws.... As a mountain keeps still within itself, thus a wise man does not permit his will to stray beyond his situation,*" suggests that she drew hexagram 52: Keeping Still, Mountain or Bound, which is depicted as two Mountain trigrams (solid, broken, broken; solid, broken, broken). *The Book of Changes'* commentary for hexagram 52 is not quoted directly (as it is for hexagram 27), but reads:

Michelle Heran

Mountains standing close together:
The image of Keeping Still.
Thus the superior man
Does not permit his thoughts
To go beyond his situation.

Once achieved by physical tearing as an act of torture, the General Oblation Board has developed less gruesome means which it continues to perfect through experiments with kidnapped children; the Maystadt anbaric scalpel, and later the silver guillotine, marked two refinements in the procedure.

Her encounter with the *zombi* of Africa was the inspiration for Mrs Coulter's founding the General Oblation Board to explore what would happen to children who were severed before their dæmons settled. Mrs Coulter's bodyguards and the troops sent to occupy Lapland following Asriel's opening the passage to another world have undergone this process. They are *zombi*: men without dæmons and thus without fear, imagination, or free will.

The term is used in HIS DARK MATERIALS first by Dr Martin Lanselius, the Witch-

Consul for Lapland, but Lanselius won't elaborate on its meaning, probably since Lyra is present. Snatches of conversation at Coulter's cocktail party likely pertained to intercision; there are assurances that the children don't suffer and reports that experiments conducted in the North have shown there is a relationship between Dust and the dark principle.

Lyra witnesses its horror firsthand when she encounters Gobbler victim Tony Makarios after he has been severed from his dæmon, Ratter, and she nearly becomes a victim of the practice herself at Bolvangar. There she overhears the Station's "doctors" discuss with Mrs Coulter improvements in instruments and techniques, which reduced deaths due to shock and had the added advantage of making the practice less stressful to those who perform it routinely. Their current favorite, the silver guillotine, is considered an improvement over the Maystadt scalpel. The Maystadt process was highly traumatic. Survival rates improved when those subjected to severing by this means were placed under general anesthesia, but even so, the death rate from just the immediate shock of intercision was nearly five percent.

The silver guillotine, in contrast, allows experiments with severing conscious children. When, after Mrs Coulter leaves the meeting, they discover that Lyra has been eavesdropping on their conversation, the four men decide to take the girl straight to the silver guillotine since after intercision, the victim "won't remember who she is, what she saw, what she heard."

Mrs Coulter claims to Lyra that the purpose of intercision is to circumvent the infection with Dust that occurs when a person matures into an adult. Lyra, of course, having met the severed Tony Makarios and discovered the trapped dæmons in the station's storage shed, knows the despair and agony of those who've had the "little operation."

On Svalbard, Lyra asks her father about cutting. He compares the process to castration, but agrees with Lyra that as grisly as it may sound, castration is mild compared to intercision. He acknowledges Coulter's hypothesis that intercision might prevent the attraction of Dust, explaining that the Church equates Dust with original sin.

What seems of greater interest to Asriel, however, is the "phenomenal burst of energy" that is released at the moment of intercision, which he notes has never been of interest to the General Oblation Board. Lord Asriel harnesses that energy to blast through to the world beyond the Aurora, using a lightning strike to set off the reaction— much as the hydro-anbaric generating station in the Alps will be used with another intercision.

NL/GC mentioned by Lanselius 10 *[brief]*; mutilated condition of severed Tony Makarios 12; instinctive revulsion from severed, death and severance 13; Lyra questions Bolvangar doctor about, severed caged dæmon described 15; severing techniques, Coulter's ghoulish pleasure in watching 16; Coulter on its purpose 17; Lyra tells Raknison about 19; Asriel on 21

SK *brief mentions:* alluded to by Lanselius 2; Coulter's *zombi* and 9, 11

AS Cooper testifies to Court on Lyra's near miss, energy release 6; Coulter's near miss of, MacPhail's dæmon resists, silver guillotine effects 25
      brief mentions: Coulter on saving Lyra from 16, Cooper on energy release and 24

Maystadt anbaric scalpel [*See* Intercision]

MAYSTADT PROCESS [*See* Intercision]

PILGRIMAGE ⚔
Role: While the word *pilgrimage* is unknown to witches, Serafina Pekkala intuitively understands the concept immediately when she witnesses angels gathering in the presence of Lyra and Will as the children sleep during their journey through the world of Cittàgazze.
SK   13 *[brief]*

PRE-EMPTIVE ABSOLUTION [*See* Pre-emptive penance]

PRE-EMPTIVE PENANCE ✎
World: Lyra's
Role: This doctrine, along with pre-emptive absolution, was developed by the Consistorial Court of Discipline and is unknown to the church in general.

Pre-emptive penance consists of performing "intense and fervent penance accompanied by scourging and flagellation, so as to build up, as it were, a store of credit" … "for a sin not yet committed." Once "the penance had reached the appropriate level for a particular sin, the penitent was granted absolution in advance, though he might never be called on to commit the sin." It is therefore useful to potential assassins, like Father Gomez, particularly since the mortal sin he seeks to commit—murder—will occur in a world without an institution from which he could seek absolution. But this system will make Gomez's "murder of Lyra no murder at all."

The title of chapter 6 of *THE AMBER SPYGLASS* is "Pre-emptive Absolution." [*See also* **Consistorial Court of Discipline** *in* **Social Structures**]
AS   6; 9 *[brief]*

SILVER GUILLOTINE ✦⚔✎
World: Lyra's
Role: The pride of the General Oblation Board's Bolvangar Experiment Station, with this device intercision, the severing of a person and his or her dæmon, can be performed without general anesthesia.

Mrs Coulter speaks about the silver guillotine as if it were something "she herself had invented;" however, at Bolvangar, the doctors have to explain the structure and operation of the mechanism to her, suggesting that she is exaggerating where the credit should lie.

The silver guillotine's blade is made of an alloy of manganese and titanium that insulates a person and the dæmon, as is the mesh for the separate cages in which they are placed immediately prior to intercision. The silvery color of the blade is like that of the subtle knife's edge that cuts windows into other worlds. When the blade drops between

Isaac Cruikshank, Library of Congress, LC-DIG-ppmsca-05528, 1793

In Will's world, guillotines severed heads not dæmons, including that belonging to Louis XVI, King of France.

the cages, severance occurs.

The hum of the electronic devices in Mary Malone's lab reminds Lyra of the chamber in which the silver guillotine was housed at Bolvangar and where she was nearly severed from Pan.

The title of Chapter 16 of NORTHERN LIGHTS and THE GOLDEN COMPASS is "The Silver Guillotine."

Note: *The phrase "silver guillotine" is used only three times in* HIS DARK MATERIALS: *as a chapter title in* NORTHERN LIGHTS / THE GOLDEN COMPASS, *and one time each in* THE SUBTLE KNIFE *and* THE AMBER SPYGLASS. *Although the specific phrase is usually not found in the following pages, the silver guillotine is clearly what is being described or discussed.*

NL/GC operation described 16; 18 *[brief]*

SK brief mentions: sound recalled in Mary's lab 4, blade's color compared to subtle knife's 8

AS Coulter on saving Lyra from 16 *[brief]*; employed by Court in Alps 25

Guillotin's Machine

In Will's world, a guillotine was a machine used for executions. The guillotine was the official means of execution in France for 200 years until 1981, when capital punishment was abolished. It was extensively used during the French Revolution, particularly between 1793 and 1794, when thousands went under the blade. The device takes its name from Dr Joseph-Ignace Guillotin, who argued that it would be more humane than the alternatives, like hanging, burning at the stake, or beheading with an ax or sword.

The guillotine is a simple machine. The condemned is laid on a trestle, his head held still, in a vise. A heavy blade attached to a rope is raised high, and then the rope is released.

SPELL AGAINST BODILY CORRUPTION ☍

World: Cittàgazze

Role: As a courtesy to Iorek Byrnison, Serafina Pekkala puts a spell on Lee Scoresby's corpse "to preserve it from corruption," that is, against putrefaction or decay, until she can notify the bear and he can pay his last respects to his fallen friend.

AS 3

SPELL, ENCHANTER'S ☍

World: Lyra's

Role: Mrs Coulter tells Ama, the Himalayan child who brings her fresh food, that Lyra has been put under a sleeping spell by an enchanter. There is, of course, no spell and no enchanter.

AS 1, 4

SPELL FOR ENTERING DREAMS ☍

World: Mulefa's

Role: When Serafina Pekkala comes to the world of the mulefa to talk with Pan and Kirjava, she uses this spell to let Mary Malone know what is going on. It is night time, and she doesn't want to startle the sleeping woman, so she paces her breathing to Mary's, and her "half-vision" lets the witch see Mary's dreams, at which time "Serafina stepped in among them." In the dream, Serafina tells Mary it is time she wakes up, and when she does, |10 although she will find someone sitting beside her, she must not be alarmed.

AS 36

Spell, holding 🗡️✎

World: Cittàgazze

Role: When Serafina Pekkala sees the extent and nature of the injury to Will's hand she concludes that herbs alone won't be enough to heal it, and that a spell is required. As the herbs steep and the other witches clap and stamp a rhythmic beat, Serafina chants, first to the knife, and then to the wound. The spell is a holding spell rather than healing spell because what the chant asks of the body is that it form a wall to hold back the flow of blood.

Serafina Pekkala slices open first an alder branch and next a rabbit's belly to test the efficacy of her concoction and spell. Both heal to their unmarked state quickly. Concluding that the preparation is ready for Will, she applies the herbs and dresses his wound.

But the spell doesn't work. Serafina wonders if perhaps the herbs in the world of Cittàgazze aren't as potent as those in her own.

SK proposed 11, cast 13, failure of 15

AS *brief mentions:* 2, 9

Spell, invisibility 🗡️✎

Worlds: Lyra's, Cittàgazze

Role: To get to a witch undergoing torture, Serafina Pekkala does the closest thing possible to making herself invisible: "she brought all her concentration to bear on the matter of altering the way she held herself so as to deflect attention completely." Working this spell |11 is always exhausting and under these circumstances particularly so. For a moment Serafina loses her concentration and becomes visible, but no one notices. Finally, when she is ready to act, Serafina immediately becomes the center of everyone's attention.

So she can hear what Lord Boreal/Sir Charles Latrom and Mrs Coulter are discussing at their campsite, Lena Feldt makes herself invisible. Or at least Lena thinks she has—but Coulter turns on Lena, with the comment, "Well, witch...did you think I don't know how you make yourself invisible?" |12

In Cittàgazze, Ruta Skadi describes using the spell, first, to get past all the others wanting Lord Asriel's attention and make her way to his bedroom in the adamant tower, and later to eavesdrop on the cliff-ghasts discussing Æsahættr.

SK used successfully by Serafina 2, but not by Lena Feldt 15

AS Pavel recalls Serafina's 6 *[brief]*

Spells and herbs ❖

World: Lyra's

Role: When gyptian Farder Coram was shot with a poisoned arrow by Skraelings, witch Serafina Pekkala sent spells and herbs to speed his healing.

NL/GC 18 *[brief]*

SPELLS, OTHER ✧↓✎

Worlds: Lyra's, Cittàgazze

Role: There are several instances of speculation about the use of spells. Farder Coram thinks a spell might be involved in the mechanism of the spy-flies, and Joachim Lorenz says that some people think that the Guild of the Tower of Angels enter other worlds through the use of spells. Lee Scoresby considers shaman Stanislaus Grumman's manipulations of the weather as spells, and in preparing the waking potion for Ama to use on Lyra, the Pagdzin *tulku* doesn't just make a compound of herbs and powders but casts a spell on them as he works.

Finally, the one thought in common that Iorek Byrnison and the angel Balthamos share is that Mrs Coulter put a spell on Will when he visited her cave, since nothing else could account for his fascination with the woman. The mature Lyra sees that long ago, when she was so enchanted with Mrs Coulter, she acted as if under a spell.

NL/GC   and spy flies 9 *[brief]*

SK   *brief mentions:* and Guild 6, shaman's 14

AS   *brief mentions:* for mixing potions 4; Coulter and Will 11, Coulter and Lyra 38

TREPANNING / TREPANNED SKULLS ✧↓

Worlds: Lyra's, Will's

Role: Trepanning is a surgical procedure consisting of drilling a hole in the front, sides, or top of the skull. According to aëronaut Lee Scoresby, during initiation ceremonies, shamans are trepanned so "the gods can talk to them." Scoresby tells Lyra that Tartar tribesmen first cut a half-circle of skin on the subject's scalp, forming a flap that is lifted to expose the skull. A small circle is cut out of the bone with great care so that the brain is not compromised. Then the skin in is sewn back in place. Later Scoresby learns from a seal hunter who witnessed Grumman's trepanation that a bow drill is the main instrument involved.

Lord Asriel leads the Jordan College scholars to believe he found the scalped and trepanned head of missing scientist Stanislaus Grumman off the coast of Svalbard. Asriel draws attention to the skull's holes as evidence that the skull is Grumman's, which would suggest that the scholars knew Grumman had voluntarily undergone trepanation by the Tartars prior to being adopted into one of their tribes. The scalping patterns are consistent with those employed by the Tartars, but the scholars do not question why the Tartars would scalp one of their own people, getting distracted by Trelawney's speculation that perhaps the armoured bears of Svalbard are imitating the scalping practices of the Tartars.

Lyra, however, seems confusedly to equate trepanning and scalping, and is surprised to hear from Lee Scoresby that trepanning is voluntary and in fact "a great privilege," not a means of torturing enemies. Witch Serafina Pekkala knows that the practice has to do with the Tartar's beliefs about Dust, and this seems to be vaguely understood by some of the children

Trepanned skulls in the anthropology laboratory of the US National Museum

at the General Oblation Board's Bolvangar Experiment Station, one of whom suggests that perhaps they will be having their skulls drilled to let Dust in like the Tartars do.

When Lyra sees trepanned skulls at the Pitt-Rivers Museum in Will's Oxford, the alethiometer tells her that one of the skulls belonged to a "sorcerer, and that the hole had been made to let the gods into his head," adding that trepanned skulls attract more Dust than those damaged in battle. These skulls provide a conversational opener for Sir Charles Latrom (Lord Boreal), who has been watching Lyra's movements in the museum. Latrom mentions to Lyra that trepanning was among the devices used by hippies seeking a high better than the drugs they'd tried, and offers to introduce the girl to someone who has had the operation, an invitation Lyra declines.

When Lee Scoresby tracks Stanislaus Grumman down, the shaman confirms that he was "initiated into the skull cult," which likely means he did, as rumored, undergo trepanation.

The title of the fourth chapter of THE SUBTLE KNIFE is "Trepanning."

Opened Minds

While in Lyra's world trepanning may have been used to allow the shaman easy access to the spirit world, most researchers speculate that its early usages were therapeutic attempts to alleviate mental illness, epilepsy, severe headaches, deafness, demonic possession or some similar malady. The earliest known remains showing evidence of trepanation are Neolithic, estimated to be from between 5100 and 4900 BC. Trepanation using traditional techniques is still practiced by the Bantu people, and, furthermore, is advocated by some contemporary Europeans and North Americans. Trepanation is derived from the Greek word for borer or drill, trypanon. Thomas Wilson Parry(!) classified four different methods in the early twentieth century.

15

16

Note: *The term* trepanning *appears only in the second chapter of* NORTHERN LIGHTS/GOLDEN COMPASS *and the fourth of* THE SUBTLE KNIFE, *where it also serves as that chapter's title. However, trepanning is clearly alluded to, if not named, in the chapters listed below.*

NL/GC   discussed in Retiring Room 2; Scoresby on 13
          brief mentions: alluded to by Lyra 7; discussed at Bolvangar 14, 15; Serafina on 18

SK   of skulls in museum and Dust, Latrom on, Lyra and Malone discuss what alethiometer says about skulls 4; Scoresby discusses with seal hunter, Umaq 6; Grumman and "skull cult" 10; Malone tells Payne about 12

Applied Sciences and Technology

Clothing and Accessories
Anorak to **White Coats**

ANORAK / COAL-SILK ANORAKS ✤

World: Lyra's

Role: Essential outerwear for the frigid North. The superb protection offered by Lyra's reeking fur anorak is contrasted with the inadequacy of the new coal-silk anoraks supplied to the children at Bolvangar Experiment Station. [*See also* **coal-silk**]

Facts: *An anorak is a hooded jacket that goes over the head and thus has no zippers or buttons.*

> <u>Lyra's anorak</u>

NL/GC 12, 13, 14, 16, 18

> <u>Coal-silk anoraks</u>

NL/GC 13, 14, 16, 17

CASSOCK ✐

World: Lyra's

Role: Worn by Siberian priest Semyon Borisovitch.

Facts: *These long robes, sometimes tailored, are worn by clergy and choirs.*

AS 8

Cassock

CLOAK ⚑✐

World: Cittàgazze, Lyra's, Beach, Suburbs of the Dead

Role: Will takes up his father's cloak, trimmed with feathers and fastened with a single brass buckle. It provides him warmth and a small degree of comfort on his journey through the Siberia of Lyra's world. [*See also:* **Mantle** (*in* **Allusions**) *and* **Shaman** (*in* **Creatures**)]

SK Will takes from father's body 15

AS 2, 8, 18

COAL-SILK ✤

World: Lyra's

Role: This fabric is described as being acceptable for shower curtains and shopping bags, but inferior to fur for Arctic winter coats.

Facts: *Most likely equivalent to nylon or polyester.*

NL/GC 5, 13, 14, 16, 17

FURS ✤⚑⑩

World: Lyra's, Will's

Role: They are a means of survival in the Far North, offering far superior protection than can be provided by any man-made or natural fiber.

Observation: *Only Mrs Coulter and her circle in London wear fur garments as status symbols in* His Dark Materials.

Update: The appendix in the **10th** anniversary edition of *Northern Lights* includes a drawing by Lord Asriel of the subject of the photogram projected in the Jordan College Retiring Room: "a man in furs, his face hardly visible in the deep hood of his garment."

NL/GC 2, Coulter's fox-fur 3; 5, Coram buys Lyra gear made of various furs and skins 10; 12, 13, 14, 15, 16, 17, 18, 20, 22, 23

SK   2, 4, 10

10th: *NL* appendix

Money belt / Oilskin pouch ❖

World: Lyra's

Role: During the sea voyage, Lyra acquires a water-resistant oilskin pouch that she wears around her waist. Referred to by the Bolvangar nurses as a money belt, it keeps her alethiometer safe. While her money belt would not have been conspicuous under the layers of clothing required in the Far North, it probably would have been under the lightweight skirt she wears in Cittàgazze and Will's world. Instead, she puts the alethiometer into a rucksack.

> Oilskin pouch

NL/GC 10, 14, 17

> Waterproof bag

NL/GC 10

> Money belt

NL/GC 14

Rucksacks ❖ ⚑ ✎

World: Cittàgazze, Will's, Lyra's, Beach, Suburbs of and world of the Dead, Mulefa

Role: When Will and Lyra begin their journeys, each starts with nothing to hold the few things they've chosen to carry along except for disposable shopping bags (totes). Lyra's bag is from one of the trendy shops her mother frequents; Will's is described as "tattered." At some point (probably when Will takes Lyra to buy some clothes appropriate for his world), they both acquire rucksacks, although the first mention of Will's is of a "canvas pack" in the last scene of *The Subtle Knife*.

   In addition to its main compartment, Lyra's blue canvas rucksack has a small outside pocket where she keeps the alethiometer. Unfortunately, the rucksack is not as secure as her money belt.

   When Mrs Coulter takes Lyra out of Cittàgazze, she leaves behind Lyra's rucksack and alethiometer. Will must have stowed it inside his, because she has it for the trip to the world of the dead and in the world of the mulefa. One of the memories Will takes home to his world is that of Lyra with the blue rucksack she carried everywhere.

   Mary Malone, Father Gomez, and Mrs Coulter also use rucksacks, but Lee Scoresby's bag is described as a knapsack.

Observation: *Lyra's bag is a shopping bag in both* NORTHERN LIGHTS *and* THE GOLDEN COMPASS, *but Will's shopping bag in the UK edition of* THE SUBTLE KNIFE *becomes a shopping tote in the US edition. A rucksack is more commonly referred to as a knapsack in the US.*

<u>Lyra's shopping bag</u>

NL/GC 6, 10

<u>Lyra's rucksack</u>

SK   3; holds alethiometer during first Oxford visit 4; 5; Latrom steals alethiometer out of 7; 9, 11, Will sees abandoned 15

<u>Will's shopping (tote) bag</u>

SK   1, 3

<u>Will's rucksack</u>

SK   15 [canvas pack]

AS   2; holds knife in Siberia 8; 9, 11, 13, 14, 15, 18, 19, 21, 32

<u>Mary Malone's rucksack</u>

SK   12

AS   on travels 7, 10; 38

<u>Lee Scoresby's knapsack</u>

SK   14

<u>Fr Gomez's rucksack</u>

AS   10, 27

<u>Mrs Coulter's rucksack</u>

AS   1, 28

SKINS: GOAT, REINDEER, SEAL, SHEEP, WOLF, & YAK ❖ ⚑ ✒

World: Lyra's, Cittàgazze

Role: When Lyra runs away from Mrs Coulter's apartment, she is wearing a dark wolfskin coat, likely among the purchases of "furs and oilskins and waterproof boots" made when Coulter was presumably outfitting her for an expedition north.

Wolfskin, however, is not as good as reindeer skin for extreme cold, and when gyptian Farder Coram takes Lyra to be outfitted in Trollesund, Lapland, she gets "a parka made of reindeer skin, because reindeer hair is hollow and insulates well;" her hood is "lined with wolverine fur, because that sheds the ice that forms when you breathe." Completing her outfit are reindeer calf undergarments, reindeer skin mittens, and boots with sealskin soles. Her waterproof cape is made of "semitransparent seal intestine."

In the Cittàgazze countryside, Will and Lyra buy a couple of goatskin flasks for carrying water, but when the opportunity comes to take a lightweight canteen from the former campsite of Mrs Coulter and Sir Charles Latrom, Will abandons the flasks. Three days' walk from Coulter's hideout, he buys yak-leather boots and a sheepskin vest.

Facts: *In Will's world, yak roam the high plateaus and mountains of Central Asia north of the Himalayas. Wild male yak can weigh over 2000 pounds; the females are much smaller. Well-adapted for their climate and terrain, with thick coats and large lungs, they can survive temperatures down to 40 degrees below zero and climb about rocky ledges with surprising agility for animals of their bulk. Yak leather boots would be tough, longwearing and well insulated.*

NL/GC Lyra's wolfskin 5, 6, 7; Coram buys Lyra gear made of various furs and skins 10; 23

SK 13, 15
AS 2, 9, 25

WHITE COATS ✦ ⚑

World: Lyra's, Will's
Role: Standard garb for experimental theologians in Lyra's world and for scientists in Will's.

NL/GC 14, 15
SK 4, 12

What They Wore

Note: These page numbers are not linked to an individual word.
They are intended to provide a representative sample of passages in
which the character's garments and accessories are mentioned.

Lyra

As a child growing up among Scholars at Jordan College, Lyra's wardrobe mainly consisted of hand-me-downs. In spite of her exploits, she had always worn skirts or dresses, and she scoffs at Will when he suggests she wear jeans. When she had to look presentable, the Jordan College housekeeper would bully her into a more or less clean dress and patent leather shoes.

When Lyra moves to London, the first thing Mrs Coulter does is to take Lyra shopping, as much for the woman's own vanity as out of concern for the girl. It wouldn't do for the fashionable Mrs Coulter to be linked to a child whose clothes were all chosen for practicality and who sported a "shabby overcoat." One practical acquisition that will prove useful to Lyra when she runs away from Coulter is a wolfskin coat, bought for the journey to the North Coulter kept promising Lyra.

At first, Lyra is enchanted by the prettiness of her new things, and the simple luxury of clothes like a "flannel nightdress with printed flowers and a scalloped hem, and sheepskin slippers dyed soft blue," but the sweetness wears thin. Lyra's first clear insight into Mrs Coulter's character is superficially a fight about appearances. To keep the alethiometer within her sight, Lyra places it in a white shoulder bag she wears nearly all the time.

When she tries to wear it the night of the cocktail party, Mrs Coulter forbids it.

In Trollesund, gyptian Farder Coram takes Lyra shopping, and the emphasis is again on practicality—this time what Lyra will need to survive a trip on an open sledge to the interior of Lapland in winter. Coram buys her traditional garments constructed of furs and skins. These warm, natural garments will prove critically important during the crises to come in the Arctic winter.

The white shoulder bag had been replaced during the sea voyage with a water-resistant oilskin pouch Lyra wears around her waist, referred to by the Bolvangar nurses as a "money belt." It keeps the alethiometer safe through Lyra's struggles with Samoyeds, Tartars, Coulter, and armoured bears.

In Cittàgazze, Will outfits Lyra so she won't attract attention in his world. She refuses jeans but accepts a plaid skirt and green blouse to replace her "ragged dirty clothes." Lyra observes later that Will was right when he told her girls do wear jeans, noting that Mary Malone sported those "blue canvas trousers so many people wore." Lyra claims never to have washed her own hair, but she learned to do so at Mrs Coulter's apartment—or at least, Coulter tried to teach her.

When Lyra reaches the world of the mulefa, once again she arrives in a new world filthy and tattered. This time the mulefa take charge of cleaning her clothes, and Lyra makes do with a shirt of Mary Malone's and a piece of cloth provided by the mulefa, which she wears as a sarong. [*See also* **Anorak, Furs, Money belt, Skins**]

> *NL/GC* dressed by Lonsdale 3 and by Coulter 4; hair and cosmetics, shoulder bag dispute 5; 6, 7, 9; outfitted by Coram 10; 13, 14, 15, 17
>
> *SK* her dirtiness 1; dressed by Will 3; 4, 13
>
> *AS* 14; clean clothes in mulefa's world 33; 35, 37

Mrs Coulter

Prettiness is important to Mrs Coulter. Even in the most dire of circumstances, such as arriving at Lake Geneva to be intercised in the silver guillotine, her dæmon treats the woman in the same way a "fastidious courtier" would a fashion model. Mrs Coulter is first seen in an auburn fox-fur. The elegant breviary she holds seems to be a fashion accessory chosen more for how its jeweled front will complete her look than for its contents. She selects a coordinated outfit of khaki clothes, suitable for hunting or traveling, for commanding Spectres, murdering a lover, and abducting her daughter. Even Will notices that what would likely look utilitarian and dull on another woman, on Mrs Coulter "looked like the highest of high fashion." She wears a fur-lined coat over a skirt and blouse to meet Metatron and wrestle him into the abyss.

> *NL/GC* first view of 3
>
> *SK* 15
>
> *AS* at campsite 11; facing intercision 25; leaving adamant tower 28; at abyss 31

Will

To Will, the right clothes are the ones you don't notice. As he tells Lyra, "You got to look as if you fit in. You got to go about camouflaged." To this end, Will wears commonplace clothes—jeans and a tee-shirt—not trendy ones. His trainers (US: sneakers) are such poor quality they are on the verge of falling apart the day his journey out of his world begins.

After his bloody battle with Tullio in Cittàgazze, Will has to obtain a new set of clothes before he can go to Charles Latrom's house (even his shoes are blood-soaked). When he returns from Oxford, his struggle to claim the alethiometer and get out of his world again renders his clothing bloody. This time, Lyra finds jeans and a shirt for Will. Later, out in the country, Will uses one of Lyra's coins to buy a linen shirt to replace his tee-shirt, which was ruined by the siege at the belvedere and his continual bleeding. When he parts from his father's body, Will takes with him John Parry/Stanislaus Grumman's shaman's cloak.

Three days' walk from Coulter's hideout, Will buys yak-leather boots and a sheepskin vest. [*See also* **Cloak**]

> *SK* 1, 3, 7; after fight with Tullio 8; 11, 13, 15
>
> *AS* 9, 14, 35

Others

The only other figure as fashion-conscious as Mrs Coulter is the equally malevolent **Sir Charles Latrom/Lord Boreal**. His typical attire—"rich clothes," as Lyra puts it—is a "beautifully-tailored linen suit" with a "snowy handkerchief" in the coat pocket, a "snowy white shirt," and a panama hat. In contrast, **Dr Mary Malone's** wardrobe is plain and functional. At work, she wears a white lab coat over a plain green shirt and jeans. In the world of the mulefa, she wears a faded blue work shirt and likely, as an experienced camper would, rugged jeans suitable for roughing it.

Aëronaut **Lee Scoresby** has furs for cold climates and high altitudes, but keeps a canvas coat on hand for journeys to warmer parts. He wears one for the low-altitude flying over the treetops of the hot Cittàgazze countryside. When Scoresby met his passenger for the trip to Cittàgazze, **Dr Stanislaus Grumman**, the "shaman-academic," was "dressed in skins and furs"; Grumman packs the few things he needs on his last journey in a deerskin bag.

And among the **gyptians,** the young men favor leather jackets, kerchiefs, and silver rings before settling into their fathers' checked shirts and canvas jackets. Checkered patterns are also common on gyptians' blankets. [*See also* **Gallivespians, Witches**]

Sir Charles Latrom

 SK 4, 7, 12

Dr Mary Malone

 SK 4
 AS 32, 33

Lee Scoresby

 NL/GC 18
 SK canvas coat 14

Stanislaus Grumman

 SK 10, 15

Gyptians

 NL/GC young men's dress 7; old men's 13

Jewelry in *His Dark Materials*

Of the pieces of jewelry mentioned in *His Dark Materials,* the most significant are **the Magisterium's ring, Scoresby's mother's ring,** and **Mrs Coulter's locket.**

Magisterium's ring: The Magisterium's officers wear rings that identify them as having the authority to act on behalf of the church. Hester, aëronaut Lee Scoresby's dæmon, is thus able to identify the silent Skraeling at the Imperial Muscovite Observatory in Nova Zembla as one of the censors the Magisterium requires to be present at any research institution. When Scoresby kills the Skraeling in self defense, Hester encourages Scoresby to take the ring. Showing the ring allows Scoresby to retrieve his impounded balloon but also alerts the Imperial Guard to his whereabouts.

Scoresby's mother's ring: Lee Scoresby thinks that his interviews on Nova Zembla resulted in his success in locating Stanislaus Grumman. The shaman surprises his visitor by producing an object Scoresby hasn't seen for 40 years—his mother's Navajo turquoise and silver ring—saying that he used the ring to summon the aëronaut. No longer needing it, with no account of how it came into his possession, Grumman returns the ring.

Mrs Coulter's locket: At her Himalayan cave, Mrs Coulter wears a golden locket that opens to reveal a small chamber. When the herdsman's daughter, Ama, witnesses the woman cut a lock of Lyra's hair and place it in the charm, she believes that Coulter has some magic in mind requiring strands of its subject's hair. At the Consistorial Court of Discipline's headquarters in Geneva, Father MacPhail notices Mrs Coulter's nervous habit of fiddling with the locket, and orders a priest to bring him the necklace. Inside he finds exactly what he needs to guide a bomb to Lyra, a lock of her hair.

Several other mentions of jewelry in *His Dark Materials:*
- Young **gyptian** men wear several **silver rings** at once for social events.
- **Bears** trying to keep the approval of the usurper Iofur Raknison wear **gold chains, badges, sashes,** and **coronets** or **small crowns,** and the usurper king himself sports a particularly heavy gold **necklace** which is adorned with an oversized jewel. His claws are coated in gold leaf.
- Witch **Ruta Skadi** wears heavy **earrings** of gold and a **crown** of snow tigers' teeth.
- Among the **mulefa,** marriage partners give one another **rings,** shaped from copper collected from riverbeds, to adorn their horns.

> • **Father Gomez** wears a **crucifix** around his neck. **Mary Malone** did so
>   as well when she was a nun. To mark her rejection of her vows, she
>   tossed it into the Atlantic Ocean off the coast of Portugal.
> *NL/GC* gyptians' 7; Raknison's 19
> *SK*   Skadi's jewelry 2; Magisterium's ring 6; Scoresby's mother's ring 10; 14
> *AS*   locket 3; mulefa's rings 17; Gomez's crucifix 20; locket 24; Mary's crucifix 33

Imagine No Possessions

The main characters of *His Dark Materials* travel a lot and they travel light.

Lyra leaves Jordan College with a single "battered little suitcase," and she leaves [20]
Mrs Coulter's with even less—whatever warm clothes she can wear and a few others
she can stuff into a plastic shopping bag. Of course, both times, Lyra has her
alethiometer, which is the only thing she carries out of her world to Cittàgazze.
However, when Mrs Coulter takes her from Cittàgazze, she doesn't even have that.

Will has a little more time to plan. Thinking he will only be gone for a few days,
he stuffs a "tattered shopping bag" with his mother's wallet, a letter from the family's
lawyer (so he'll have the office phone number and address), a map of southern
England, some chocolate, toothpaste, socks and underwear, and what he wants to
keep safe for his mother—a green leather case holding his father's last letters home. [21]
Later, in Cittàgazze, Will and Lyra each acquire a canvas rucksack. For his journey to
Lyra's world, Will scavenges the Latrom/Coulter campsite, considering carefully what
will be of most use and still fit in a single rucksack.

Dr Mary Malone, an experienced camper, also has to leave home quickly and
with only as much as she can carry. Some of the things she chooses are a sleeping
bag, empty bottles for water, a Swiss army knife, as well as *The Book of Changes* and
yarrow sticks for casting the I Ching.

> Update: Mary Malone's papers in the appendix to the **10th** anniversary edition of *The Amber*
>   *Spyglass* reveal that she kept a journal of sorts during her travels, and what she
>   most regrets not carrying on the journey out of her world is a camera.

Lee Scoresby, upon having to leave his balloon in the Cittàgazze forest, takes his
aëronautical instruments (crammed into a knapsack) and a loaded rifle. [22]

Stanislaus Grumman/John Parry leaves Lyra's world with a deerskin pack
holding an oilskin, matches, a tin lantern, and a horn box filled with bloodmoss
ointment. When leaving the mountain where he found and lost his father, Will takes [23]
the matches, lantern and ointment, along with his father's cloak.

Sir Charles Latrom/Lord Boreal and **Mrs Coulter** were far better equipped for their
deliberate trip to Cittàgazze. At their abandoned campsite, Will finds a half-dozen
camouflage tents, a canvas chair, and supplies. Will selects those he thinks will be most
useful: matches, a magnifying glass, twine, fishing hooks and line, pocket notebook and
pencil, flashlight, binoculars, gold coins, first-aid kit, water purification tablets, instant
coffee, strips of dried meat, dried fruit, oatmeal cookies, and six Kendal Mint Cake candy
bars. He also exchanges the goatskin flask he bought in the Cittàgazze countryside for
a lightweight canteen and cup. Mrs Coulter had removed several items from the campsite [24]
for her use in the Himalayan cave hide-out: a sleeping bag, a rucksack with clothes,
washing soap, an insulated canvas case, various unspecified instruments, and a pistol. [25]

Smokes and Medicinals
Antiseptic cream to Waking potion

ANTISEPTIC CREAM ⚱

World: Cittàgazze's, Will's

Role: After the struggle with Tullio costs Will two fingers, Paradisi administers a "precious ointment" he says is "very difficult to obtain." Will notices that what Paradisi cherishes is just a "dusty, battered tube of ordinary antiseptic cream" available at any pharmacy he's ever visited.

SK   8 [brief]

BLOODMOSS ❖⚱🩹🗡 ⑩

World: Lyra's

Role: A type of lichen (rather than a moss) and requiring a cool climate to grow, this plant material is used to promote the healing of wounds. Considered essential by witches, armoured bear Iorek Byrnison, and shaman and scientist Stanislaus Grumman. However, if the reaction of a fur trader to Grumman's insistence that his wounded leg be treated with it is indicative of general opinion, the humans of Lyra's world generally

consider it just "stuff the bears use."

In his discussion with Lee Scoresby, John Parry suggests that discovering the process for compounding a bloodmoss-based ointment that works as well as the raw plant material is what he considers to be the most significant accomplishment of his alternate identity as Stanislaus Grumman.

Even though the word "bloodmoss" is not mentioned in the scene, Grumman apparently treated Will's badly wounded hand with his ointment. We know Grumman had prepared it as an ointment previously, and "Bloodmoss" is the title of the last chapter of THE SUBTLE KNIFE in which Will Parry and his father are so very briefly re-united.

Blood and Moss

Although there doesn't seem to be any real moss known among English speakers as bloodmoss, a number of mosses have been found to have useful applications when it comes to bloody wounds. They function as antiseptics and can be used to stem the flow of blood and perhaps even promote coagulation. Peat moss, *Sphagnum spp.*, an Arctic moss, is one that has antiseptic properties. Undoubtedly long known to indigenous peoples, this came to the attention of the scientific world when shortages of basic medical supplies became desperate during World War I in France. Patients whose wounds were staunched, in the absence of ordinary bandages, with *Sphagnum* suffered fewer infections than those receiving cloth bandages. The moss had been chosen to dress wounds because of its absorbent properties.

Will takes the ointment, one of the few things he has of his father's, with him as he leaves the world of Cittàgazze. Although it is the only way to staunch Will's bleeding, he uses it to soothe Lyra's feet when they are on the run in the Himalayas.

Update: The appendix to the **10TH** anniversary edition of *THE SUBTLE KNIFE* includes a drawing of the bloodmoss plant and instructions for preparing the ointment, which a Turukhansk shaman introduced to Grumman. The bloodmoss and a pinch of harp flower are boiled down, pressed, and steeped in alcohol for several days before being blended with goose grease and then sealed in a horn box.

NL/GC used on Iorek's wounds 14, 18, 20

SK Grumman's experiments with 6; Lyra wishes she had for Will's fingers 8; Grumman and Scoresby discuss 10; witches on failure to grow in Cittàgazze 13; Grumman/Parry treats Will 15; appendix

AS Will realizes it has worked 2; Will and Iorek discuss 9; Lyra applies to Will 13; Will treats Lyra's feet 14; and her head 22

10TH: *SK* appendix

Brazier herbs, Asriel's

World: Ariel's

Role: Lord Asriel twice throws handfuls of herbs on his brazier fire at the adamant tower, and breathing their smoke seems to calm mortally injured Baruch.

AS 5 *[brief]*

Chamomile infusion

World: Lyra's

Role: Mrs Coulter takes Lyra to her rooms, and gives her a warm drink with something in it, after finding her about to be severed from Pan at the General Oblation Board's Bolvangar Experiment Station. On that occasion, Pan assures Lyra it is just an infusion of chamomile.

Facts: *Chamomile is an herb that is meant to calm frazzled nerves and upset stomach. In the famous children's stories by Beatrix Potter, Peter Rabbit's mother sends him to bed with a cup of chamomile tea.*

NL/GC 17 *[brief]*

Cigar

World: Lyra's

Role: On the ground, aëronaut Lee Scoresby enjoys a good "ceegar," but when his hydrogen balloon is inflated, he must be content with chewing the end of an unlit cigar.

NL/GC brief mentions: 11, 17; 18 *[also ceegar]*

SK brief mentions: 7, 10, 14

Cigarette

World: Lyra's, Cittàgazze

Role: Lyra and her pals "ostentatiously" take deep draws on a stolen cigarette at the Horse

Fair in Jericho's Port Meadow.

A half-smoked cigarette remains in a Cittàgazze café ashtray, witness to the city's sudden emptying.

NL/GC 3 *[brief]*

SK   1 *[brief]*

CIGARILLO ❖

World: Lyra's

Role: Cigarillos are smoked during Mrs Coulter's cocktail party.

NL/GC 5 *[brief]*

HONEY ⚱

World: Cittàgazze

Role: Will applies honey to the torn ear of the cat he followed into the world of Cittàgazze after he rescues her from being beaten with sticks and stoned by the Spectre orphans. He tells Lyra that honey supposedly acts as an antiseptic.

Facts: *Will is right about honey preventing or clearing bacterial infection in wounds. Scientific studies have confirmed what traditional medicine has known for hundreds of years.*

SK   5 *[brief]*

JIMSON-WEED ⚱

World: Lyra's

Role: In the unnaturally warm arctic, Lee Scoresby tries to keep midges away with an ointment made from jimson-weed and a cloud of cigar smoke.

Observation: *While jimson-weed is a real plant, Scoresby's choice of a jimson-weed ointment as an insect repellent is unusual.*

SK   10 *[brief]*

POPPY-HEADS ❖

World: Lyra's

Role: Sautéed in butter, served after feasts at Jordan College, they "clarified the mind and stimulated the tongue." Preparing the delicacy is the prerogative of the College Master, one that he assumes during the opening scenes of *HIS DARK MATERIALS*.

Facts: *Opium is derived from unripened poppy-heads (Papaver somniferous). While opium is usually considered a sedative or hypnotic (and can be lethal), taken in very small amounts, it acts as a stimulant.*

NL/GC 1

28

A Human Repellent

Jimson weed (or jimsonweed), a common name for *Datura stramonium,* is found worldwide in warmer temperate and tropical regions. Related species can vary in size from weeds to small trees. Its seeds are held in a thorny pod and its leaves give off a nauseating scent; these properties account for two of its other common names: thornapple and stinkweed. A traditional medicinal use of the weed is for relieving asthmatic symptoms. Jimson weed contains a narcotic poison not unlike belladonna and historically has been used to incapacitate or kill. While all parts of the plant are considered poisonous if ingested, despite the weed's prevalence, it does not pose a danger to livestock because they will not go near it. One of jimson weed's other names, Jamestown weed, is based on an incident that occurred in 1676 in what would become the state of Virginia. Colonial rebels secretly added jimson weed to the salads of British soldiers. The soldiers spent the next several days hallucinating.

RAKNISON'S POTION

World: Lyra's

Role: Iofur Raknison, the prince who succeeded Byrnison, may have acquired a drug from Mrs Coulter. The young bear who challenged Iorek Byrnison, contrary to normal bear behavior, may have been acting under its influence.

NL/GC 5 brief mentions: Serafina on 18; bear counselor says supplied by Coulter 20

SAGE-LIKE LEAVES

World: Cittàgazze

Role: Witch Serafina Pekkala gives these bitter, astringent leaves to Will after he loses his fingers. In spite of the weakening he has experienced from blood loss and pain, chewing on the leaves renders him "more awake and less cold."

SK 13 *[brief]*

SALTWEED

World: Cittàgazze

Role: Saltweed is one of the ingredients in the potion Serafina Pekkala prepares to try to stop the blow flow from Will's mutilated hand.

Facts: *Saltweed or saltbrush is native to the American Southwest. Its medicinal uses are limited, but one species, Atriplex Canescens, was used by the Jemez, Navajo, and Zuni to treat ant bites, presumably to reduce swelling and pain. The Jemez also burned the leaves in order to restore a person weakened by an injury. Serafina*

Philip Pullman says:

From "Exeter to Jordan," a description of the transformation of our world's Oxford into Lyra's:

"Heaven forefend that the Rector of Exeter should feel obliged to serve opium after dinner, but this is an alternative universe, after all. I lifted that dainty detail from the diary of an English lady living in India before the Mutiny, which I'd come across ten years before, while I was looking for something else entirely."

Pekkala includes saltweed in the concoction she applies to Will's injury, but since the preparation is first boiled, Will likely would have inhaled the herb-scented steam as well.

SK   13 *[brief]*

SLEEPING PILLS ❖

World: Lyra's

Role: The Bolvangar doctors or nurses give Lyra a sleeping pill the night the Samoyed trappers sell her to the General Oblation Board's Experiment Station.

NL/GC 14 *[brief]*

SLEEPING POTION, COULTER'S ✐

World: Lyra's

Role: The compound Mrs Coulter administers to Lyra in their cave in the Himalayas keeps the girl in a deep, drugged sleep. It has to be made up and administered repeatedly. Herbs, powders, and a yellow oil, of such astringency they can be smelled at a distance, are added to water at boiling point, cooked while stirring for five minutes, and then left to settle or cool.

AS   preparation of 1; Ama sees administered 4
        brief mentions: 11, 12, 16

SLEEPING POTION, WITCHES' ⚲

World: Cittàgazze

Role: Serafina Pekkala gives Will a sleeping potion while the witches wait for the moonrise, at which time they can begin to cast a "holding spell" to heal Will's hand. The potion is sweetened with honey to cover the bitter taste.

SK   11 *[brief]*

SMOKELEAF/SMOKEWEED/SMOKING-LEAF ❖⚲✐

World: Lyra's

Role: This product of New Denmark is variously referred to as "smokeweed," "smoking-leaf," and "smoke-leaf" (or "smokeleaf"). Smokeweed is likely the uncut product. When aëronaut Lee Scoresby gives some, as a tribute, to shaman Stanislaus Grumman's Tartar village headman, it is referred to as a bundle. In contrast, smokeleaf is kept in tins. Lyra has armoured bear Iorek Byrnison fortify one of the empty tins into a case resembling the alethiometer's to be used as a prison for the spy-flies that attacked Pantalaimon.

Captured by Samoyed hunters, Lyra claims that she had been with traders selling New Danish smokeleaf and buying furs. [*See also* **Cigar, Cigarettes, Cigarillo**]

Observation: *If New Denmark is North America, smokeleaf is likely tobacco.*

NL/GC brief mentions: 2; smoking-leaf 5; 7; smoke-leaf 9, 13; 14, 18

SK   10 (smokeweed) *[brief]*

AS   5 (smoke-leaf) *[brief]*

WAKING POTION, AMA'S

World: Lyra's

Role: Ama, the Himalayan child, walked three hours to the monastery of a renowned healer for a remedy to Lyra's sleeping potion. As he prepares the waking potion, the herbs and powders he selects are shown to him by his bat dæmon. The healer, or Pagdzin *tulku,* also recites what seems to be a spell as he compounds the potion, and wraps it in a paper on which he writes certain characters.

Ama insists to Will that she will apply the powder herself as instructed by the *tulku,* who stressed brushing it lightly over the sleeper's nostrils, and Ama carries this procedure out in spite of a war going on just outside the cave.

AS   acquired 4; Ama tells Will about 11; administered 12; 14 *[brief]*

MH

Food and Drink

Apples to Wine

Foods by Worlds

Foods are listed by their world of origin only.

LYRA'S WORLD

Apples
Asparagus
Bacon
Bacon and eggs
Barley
Barley-cakes
Beefsteak pie
Beetroot soup
Berries
Bilberries
Biscuits
Black bread
Bourbon whiskey
Brandy
Brantwijn
Bread
Burgundy
Cabbage
Cake
Calves' liver
Canapés
Canary
Cheese
Chocolatl
Cocktails
Coffee
Corn
Corn flakes
Dried fish
Dried fruit
Dried meats
Eels

Asparagus

Some in Will's world insist that asparagus must be eaten without utensils in formal settings, but it is notoriously difficult to handle.

Biscuits

Same as cookies in the U.S. Iorek Byrnison used a biscuit tin to make an outercasing for the box holding the spy flies, and biscuit tins are used as a roofing material in the suburbs of the world of the dead.

Canapés

Canapés are bite-sized appetizers that resemble tiny open-faced sandwiches. Thin slices of bread, toast, or crackers are topped with cheese, meat, or meat-based spread, and often a garnish, like parsley.

Canapés

Chocolatl

The Aztecs of South America called their hot-chocolate drink *chocolatl*.

Coffee

In Lyra's world, there is nothing unusual about children drinking coffee, and in Cittàgazze, Will and Lyra both seem to be veteran coffee drinkers. Tea seems less prized in Lyra's England than might be expected, perhaps because continuing troubles with the Tartars have interfered with trade in the Far East.

Eggs
Fish
Fish and chips
Flour
Fruit
Gazelle
Genniver
Gingerbread
Goat
Ham sandwich
Hazelnuts
Honey
Honey-bread
Ice cream
Jam
Jenniver
Marchpane (marzipan)
Mashed potatoes
Milk
Oil
Pan-bread
Pickled fish
Plum-duff
Porridge
Potatoes
Reindeer
Rye bread
Seal
Sherbet dip
Smoked haddock
Smoked herring
Smoked mackerel
Soft drinks
Spice cakes
Spiced honey-cakes
Stew
Sticky rice
Swans
Sweet rice
Sweetbreads
Tea
Tinned peaches
Toast
Toffee-apple
Tokay
Vodka

Jack Daniel's

While Jack Daniel's is often referred to as a Bourbon, the whiskey Lee Scoresby looks forward to drinking during his retirement, Jack Daniel's, is a Tennessee whiskey from the U.S. Its basic ingredients of corn, rye, and barley malt are the same as those of Bourbon (named after Bourbon County, Kentucky, where it originated), but after distilling, the processes for producing a Tennessee whiskey and a Bourbon diverge. From the distillery's copper vats, Jack Daniel's is sent to be mellowed by slowly seeping through ten feet of charcoal in order to remove any impurities commonly found in grain alcohol.

Jenniver, jenniver-spirit

Jenniver may be a Fens spelling of the Dutch *jenever*, which means *juniper*. Juniper berries are used to flavor gin.

Kendal Mint Cake

Kendal Mint Cake is a candy made by George Romney, Ltd. of Kendal, Cumbria in northwest England. The basic mint cakes are brown or white, depending on the sugar used, and the only other ingredients are glucose syrup, water, and peppermint oil. Their consistency is firm but not hard, and the taste is very sweet and minty.

This candy was a favorite of British explorers. The wrappers include this note: "Romney's Kendal Mint Cake was carried to the summit of Mount Everest by Sir Edmund Hillary and Sirdar Tenzing on the 29th May, 1953. 'We sat on the snow and looked at the country far below us...we nibbled Kendal Mint Cake.'"

A candy bar is the subject of the woodcut for chapter 2, "Balthamos and Baruch" of *THE AMBER SPYGLASS* **10TH** anniversary edition.

Wine

WILL'S WORLD
- Apples
- Bacon
- Bacon and eggs
- Baked beans
- Birthday cake
- Bread
- Chewing gum
- Chocolatl
- Coffee
- Cola
- Corn flakes
- Dried fruit
- Dried meats
- Eggs
- Ginger biscuits
- Grilled sardines
- Hamburgers
- Hotdogs
- Jack Daniel's whiskey
- Kendal mint cakes
- Margaritas
- Marzipan
- Oatmeal biscuits
- Popcorn
- Tea
- Tokay
- Wine

WORLD OF CITTÀGAZZE
- Baked beans
- Berries
- Blueberries
- Bread
- Butter
- Casseroles
- Cheese
- Coffee
- Cola
- Condensed milk
- Corn
- Corn flakes

Margarita

An alcoholic beverage made with tequila, triple sec, and lime juice. The Margarita is said to have been invented in Tijuana, Mexico, just south of the border, and is particularly popular in the American Southwest.

Marzipan

Marzipan is made from finely ground almonds, generous amounts of sugar, egg whites, and a smidgen of lemon juice or vanilla. It is a favorite of cake decorators because it can be worked like dough, rolled out and cut into shapes, but hardens as it dries.

Marzipan-frosted cake

Plum-duff

Plum-duff is a steamed pudding, sometimes made with raisins or prunes rather than plums.

Polar bear liver

During lunch at the Royal Arctic Institute, Mrs Coulter told Lyra that seal liver is edible, but that eating polar bear liver will kill within minutes. Mrs Coulter is right—to some extent—about avoiding polar bear liver. The problem is the concentration of Vitamin A in their livers. Because a fairly small amount of polar bear liver can contain more than two years of the Vitamin A required by humans, Vitamin A poisoning is the consequence of eating the organ. For the same reason, polar bear liver is not fed to sledge dogs.

However, one is not likely to die within minutes of eating the liver. Some explorers have survived, and the symptoms of toxicity have ranged from mental confusion and fatigue to local or pervasive skin-peeling. The severity of the effects depended on the quantities consumed and the concentration of the vitamin in the bear's liver.

Dinner rolls
Eggs
Espresso
Fruit
Goat's cheese
Honey
Lemonade
Milk
Olives
Omelette
Plum brandy
Risotto
Roasted birds
Roasted rabbits

WORLD OF THE MULEFA

Bread (tortilla or chapatti-like)
Carrot-like roots
Cheese
Corn
Dried meats
Fish
Flour
Fruit
Grains
Grazer meat
Hazelnut-like nuts
Milk
Mint-like tea
Mollusks
Red fruits
Salad leaves
Sweet-roots

Carrot-like Roots

ASRIEL'S WORLD

Bread
Cheese
Coffee
Wine

HOLLAND-LIKE WORLD

Apples
Cheese
Rye bread

Red fruits (the fruit)

If Lyra is Eve, and Mary is the serpent, then the red fruits Mary gives Lyra and Will to eat in the world of the mulefa must be the equivalent of that forbidden in Eden.

Risotto

Many rice-based Italian dishes are called risotto; a true risotto begins with the rice being lightly fried in oil before water or broth is added.

Sherbet dip

British and American sherbets are not the same. In the US, sherbet refers to a fruit flavored ice cream. In Britain, sherbet is a powder with a bicarbonate of soda and tartaric acid base, to which sugar and flavors are added. When it gets wet, it fizzes, and thus is used to make bubbly drinks. Sherbet is also packaged with lollipops for dipping. If Lyra and Roger poured sherbet dip on their tongues, when it made contact with their saliva, they would indeed appear to be foaming at the mouth.

Laurie Frost

Sherbet Dip

Sweetbreads

Experiencing the taste of sweetbreads was one of the opportunities provided by Mrs Coulter for Lyra during the girl's stay in London. Sweetbreads are not sweet and are not breads. They are animal organs. What is known as stomach sweetbreads are an animal's pancreas, and neck sweetbreads are an animal's thymus gland.

Tea

In Siberia, the priest Semyon Borisovitch gives Will hot tea that has been brewed and served in a samovar. A traditional Russian samovar is a metal urn-shaped vessel with a spigot heated by coal and used to brew and serve tea.

WORLD OF THE GALLIVESPIANS
Honey
Oil

SUBURBS OF THE WORLD OF THE DEAD
Biscuits
Bread
Butter
Cheese
Jenniver
Potatoes
Stew
Tea

WORLD OF THE DEAD
blood

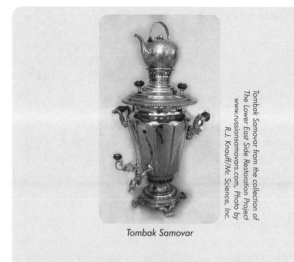

Tombak Samovar

Tokay ("the wine")

In the opening scene of *HIS DARK MATERIALS,* Lyra and Pan, hiding in Jordan College's Retiring Room, are astonished to see the College Master sprinkle poison into a decanter of Tokay. This wine is made from grapes grown in the Tokaj-Hegyalja region of Hungary's Carpathian Mountains. Its yellow-golden color comes from the vats it is stored in as it matures. First produced in the 1560s, Tokay was a favorite of Pope Pius IV, Louis XV, Voltaire and Frederick the Great.

Foods in Lyra's World by Locale

HIMALAYAS
Barley
Barley-cakes
Dried tea
Fruit
Gazelle
Goat
Honey-bread
Sticky rice
Sweet rice

LONDON
Asparagus
Calves' liver and bacon
Canapés
Cocktails
Sweetbreads

GYPTIANS
Bacon and eggs
Coffee
Eels
Genniver
Gingerbread
Milk
Pan-bread
Plum-duff
Porridge
Potatoes
Soup

BOLVANGAR
Bacon and eggs
Biscuits and milk
Cake
Coffee
Corn flakes
Ice cream
Mashed potatoes
Milk
Stew
Tinned peaches
Toast

SIBERIA
Beetroot soup
Bilberries
Black bread
Pickled fish
Vodka

Eel (Anguilla Rostrata)

Road Food

THE FOOD THEY CARRIED

Fruit, dried or preserved; bread, and cheese are the most easily acquired and carried foods for journeys within and among the worlds of *HIS DARK MATERIALS*.

Sir Charles Latrom brought these from Will's world to Cittàgazze's, and Will took them from his campsite to Lyra's world, the desert and beach worlds, and into the suburbs/world of the dead: **Dried fruit and meat strips, oatmeal biscuits, and Kendal Mint Cakes** (but the candy bars are finished before he reaches Lyra in the Himalayas).

Will buys **fruit and rye bread** in Lyra's world, which he shares with Lyra in the desert world; they leave coins for another **loaf, cheese,** and **apples** in the kitchen of the farmhouse in the Holland-like world on their way to the world of the dead.

In the Cittàgazze countryside, Mary Malone is given **goat's cheese** wrapped in vine leaves, and takes this along with **dried figs** to the world of the mulefa.

CAMPERS

Witches: Roasted birds and rabbits, blueberries.

Gyptians: Pan-bread, soup.

Coulter and Latrom: Dried fruit and meat strips, oatmeal biscuits, wine, and Kendal Mint Cakes.

CITTÀGAZZE CAFÉ AND APARTMENT

Risotto, dinner rolls, casserole, lemonade, espresso, eggs, condensed milk, corn flakes, milk, butter, cola, bread, baked beans, salt & pepper.

WILL'S OXFORD

On the first night of his journey, Will eats at a Burger King in Oxford.

During her visit to Will's Oxford, Lyra buys a chocolate bar and an apple in the Covered Market. That night, Will and Lyra dine on movie theatre popcorn, hot dogs, and Coca-cola, and they buy some burgers from a cart to eat as they walk back to the Sunderland Avenue window. Its cuisine—and the movies—are the only things in Will's Oxford that impress Lyra.

Applied Sciences and Technology:

Information Technology

Airmail paper to Typewriting machine

AIRMAIL PAPER / LETTERS

World: Will's

Role: The title of chapter five of *THE SUBTLE KNIFE* is "Airmail Paper."

Other than his mother's infrequent descriptions of his father, Will's two sources of information about John Parry are newspaper articles about the explorer's disappearance, and a few letters posted from Alaska shortly before he vanished.

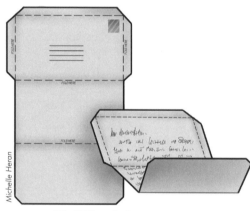

Michelle Heran

Facts: *Airmail paper is thin but sturdy postage-paid stationery that has pre-glued foldover flaps on three edges so that once folded the back of the letter becomes the envelope. Thus it affords more space and privacy than a postcard but without the additional weight of an envelope. No enclosures (including additional sheets of paper) are permitted. Also called aerogrammes, airmail paper is popular with letter writers in the UK, but never caught on firmly in the U.S., where it was first offered in 1947 and last issued in 1995.*

The cost of Elaine Parry's most prized possessions? Twenty pence (36 cents) a piece.

[*See also* **Green leather writing-case**]

SK   Will reads 5

    brief mentions: 1, 4, 7; Will tells Lyra she can read 9; 10, 11, 13

ANBAROGRAPHS

World: Lyra's

Role: Purchasing these items, as well as books, for Jordan College's library is among the institution's many expenses.

Observation: *While we haven't any additional clues about an equivalent item in our world, we can make a guess from the word's etymology. In Lyra's world, anbaro is used for what we would call electrical. English borrows graph from the Greek; it relates to drawing or writing (photograph, autograph, phonograph), and by extension recordings of these. So a good guess is that an anbarograph is a recording of some sort played on an anbaric (electrical) machine: something like a CD or tape, perhaps.*

NL/GC 3 *[brief]*

COMPUTERS ⚱️✏️

World: Will's

Role: Lyra's first impression of a computer is that it is a piece of "anbaric machinery" which hums in a manner unpleasantly reminiscent of the room in which the silver guillotine was kept at Bolvangar. This "engine" is fronted by a glass screen, and a scrambled alphabet is represented on "grimy little blocks in an ivory tray."

To Dr. Mary Malone, the computer she has configured with specialized hardware and software is at the center of her Cave, a complex apparatus that allows feedback between the investigator and Shadow-particles. A detector employs an electromagnetic field to limit the elementary particles recognized to Shadow-particles. It then amplifies these particles' signals. To investigate whether these particles are aware that they are being studied, the amplifier is linked to an encephalograph device and electrode sensors to detect the investigator's brain waves.

The Shadows tell Lyra to leave Mary's world, but first to destroy the equipment she is using.

Note: *The chapters listed here might not contain the word* computer *but may instead refer to one of the components of Mary's system.*

SK Cave described, used 4, 12

AS brief mentions: 7, 17, 27, 33, 38

GREEN LEATHER WRITING-CASE ⚱️

World: Will's

Role: Finding this small battered case is the last thing that Will has to do before leaving his Winchester home for Oxford in his quest for information about his father. Will finds the case in a compartment on his mother's treadle sewing machines.

This green case is Will's mother Elaine Parry's "most precious possession" because it holds the last letters her husband wrote before disappearing in Alaska. When Will goes with Lyra to Sir Charles Latrom's to retrieve the alethiometer, he asks Lyra to take charge of the case. He even tells her she can read the letters inside it, an indication of how he has come to trust the girl in a few days.

Observation: *Will tells Lyra that after leaving his mother with his old piano teacher, he "went back to the house to look for these letters, because I knew where she kept them, and I got them and the men came to look and broke into the house again." While this is obviously a much abbreviated version of events, it seems to suggest that Will knew just where the case was kept, which he did on a subconscious level, but it took sleep to bring*

Bain News Service, Library of Congress, LC-DIG-ggbain-38995

Treadle sewing machines were mounted to cabinets with narrow side drawers. Seamstresses operated these machines by placing both feet on a large treadle, with one foot slightly higher than the other, and alternating pressure in an even rhythm.

the memory to his conscious mind. The last we hear of the green leather writing-case it is nestled with Lyra's alethiometer in her rucksack.

SK   Will finds 1; Will leaves in Cittàgazze for safe-keeping 3, 4; Will reads contents of 5; Will gives to Lyra for safe-keeping 9, 11

LODESTONE RESONATOR ✐

World: Gallivespians (origin) / Asriel's, Lyra's (used)

Role: With this long-distance communication device, the Gallivespian spies, Tialys and Salmakia, can communicate their progress in Lyra's world to their controller, Lord Roke.

The lodestone resonator looks like "a short length of pencil made of dull grey-black stone, resting on a stand of wood" and is stored in a box resembling a violin-case but of Gallivespian scale, appearing to Lyra and Will as "no longer than a walnut." It is remarkably heavy, relative to the size of a Gallivespian.

To operate the "speaking-fiddle," as Lyra calls it, the message sender uses a bow to stroke the end of the resonator while pressing points along the stone's surface. Messages are received by wrapping a wire attached to headphones around pegs on opposite ends of the stone and adjusting the pegs until an ideal tension in the wire is achieved that allows the message to be heard. As Tialys explains the process to Lyra: "When I play on this one with my bow [its counterpart] reproduces the sounds exactly, and so we communicate."

According to Tialys, the lodestone resonator is a practical application of the concept of quantum entanglement. In the Gallivespians' world, "there is a way of taking a common lodestone and entangling all its particles, and then splitting it in two so that both parts resonate together." Lyra senses that playing the lodestone resonator requires the same state of mind as reading the alethiometer.

Tialys' lodestone resonator cannot make contact with any others when the spy is in the world of the dead.

Observation: *In Chapter 9, "a Gallivespian lodestone operator" accompanying Ogunwe allows the commander to stay in touch with Lord Asriel at the basalt fortress; on 125, Lord Roke is said to be with Ogunwe. Who then is at the basalt fortress?*

Note: *Mary and John Gribbin's* The Science of Phillip Pullman's His Dark Materials *(London: Hodder, 2003) considers this example of Gallivespian technology.*

AS   transmissions between Roke and Tialys 11; appearance and procedure described 14; Tialys bargains with Will to put in his possession in exchange for information 18
          brief mentions: Lord Roke and spies say in touch with 5, 6; communication with Roke by Ogunwe's Gallivespian operator and by spies in Court's zeppelin on 9, 12; case's size compared to walnut 13; 15, 19; useless in world of the dead 22

MICROFILM / MICROFILM READERS ⚲

World: Will's

Role: Will visits a public library, and uses *The Times* index, to find the dates of the issues with stories about his father. These documents are stored on microfilm, and Will uses a microfilm reader to view them.

Observation: *To be a 12-year-old fugitive in a library he'd never visited, in addition to everything else he's been through, and still to have found what he wanted on microfilm, is an early suggestion of the exceptional determination possessed by Will Parry.*

Facts: *Before information was stored digitally, Microfilm readers were used as a means to reduce the amount of space needed to store back issues of periodicals, especially newspapers. Every page of the newspaper was photographed on a little strip of film. The film would then have to be read through a magnifying lightbox.*

SK 4

PHOTOGRAM ❖ ♀ ✐ ⑩ LS

World: Lyra's

Role: Lyra's world term for a photographic image, used variously to refer to projected slides and prints.

Lord Asriel projects photograms onto a screen to illustrate his talk on his latest journey into the far North. They show Jordan College's Scholars what they've never seen before: Dust streaming down from the sky toward a man's upraised hand, and a city in the sky behind the Northern Lights.

A page of the 1985 Times viewed on a microfilm reader

Asriel had concocted a new emulsion for developing his film that filters out moonlight and auroral light. Asriel says the difference between ordinary and his special photograms is that the Dust "registered as light on the plate because particles of Dust affect this emulsion as photons affect silver nitrate emulsion."

A mural-sized photogram of a tropical beach covers one of the cafeteria walls at the

37

Data Storage, Circa 1995

Microfilm was very cumbersome. First, the user had to determine the issues in which the information wanted were to be found. This is what Will does when he consults *The Times* index. He needed a story about the departure of the expedition, its arrival in Alaska's interior, and its disappearance. If the middle one was published in June, 1985, and six weeks had passed since the first, that first one would have appeared in late April or early May. The last set was two months after the second, or August and September. So Will needed to find at least three different reels of film.

Microfilm reel and The Times' London index from 1985

To view these, he would use a microfilm reader. First he would have placed a reel on one spindle, threaded it through the viewer, and then either manually or with the aid of a motor, unwound the tape to the page sought—a process requiring guesswork to estimate where on the reel the particular photo frame would be found. Once located, the magnifier would be clamped in place, and then he would have to bring the page into focus on the screen. After he read the story, he would have to rewind and remove the tape reel, and start the process again for the next month's reel.

General Oblation Board's Bolvangar Experiment Station.

In Will's Oxford, Lyra is first astounded by the Pitt-Rivers Museum's photogram of the Samoyed hunters who kidnapped her from the gyptians during their journey to Bolvangar, and then again by the cinema. While she had seen projected photograms, movies ("the best thing I ever saw in my whole life") are not part of her world.

38

Update: 10TH anniversary edition of *NORTHERN LIGHTS:* The man in the photogram Asriel showed to the Jordan College Scholars was a Tungusk hunter.

NL/GC of Dust, city behind Aurora displayed in Retiring Room 2; Lyra and Boreal discuss Asriel's 5; of tropical beach in lunchroom at Bolvangar 14, 15 *[brief];* **LS** Lantern Slide 7

SK brief mentions: at museum of Samoyeds 4; Lyra compares to movies 5; Grumman's of rock formations 6

AS amber spyglass lubricated with oil compared to Asriel's special developing emulsion 17 *[brief]*

10TH: *NL* appendix

PROJECTING LANTERN/LANTERN SLIDE ✧ LS

World: Lyra's

Role: Used at the Consistorial Court of Discipline's headquarters.

Update: The 2007 US Omnibus and UK Collector's Editions of the three volumes of *HIS DARK MATERIALS* include what Philip Pullman introduces in each book as Lantern Slides, ideas or images about his novels that came to mind after they were finished. He explains that he thinks of these bits as Lantern Slides because they remind him of the pictures painted on glass that his grandfather collected and now and then used a magic lantern to project on a screen.

E & H T Anthony & Co's Illustrated Catalogue of Photographic Equipments and Materials for Amateurs, 1891

Anthony's Triplexicon Magic Lantern used kerosene oil and three wicks for heightened illumination.

NL/GC in Retiring Room 1, 2
        brief mentions: lantern slides recalled 3, Lyra tells Faa about Asriel's lantern slides 7

TYPEWRITING MACHINE ✐

World: Lyra's

Role: Father MacPhail assures Dr. Cooper that he will provide a typewriting machine or a stenographer—whatever the experimental theologian desires—as long as progress is made on developing a bomb that will follow Lyra to any world and kill her.

Observation: *This is an example of one of the ways in which certain technologies in Lyra's world seem a generation or two behind those of Will's; another peculiarity is the persistence of crank telephones, not only at the College of St. Jerome, but in the guard hut at Lord Asriel's basalt fortress as well.*

39

AS 6 *[brief]*

Marceau, Library of Congress, LC-USZ62-70770, 1918

Underwood Typewriter

Is Lord Asriel's Photogram Projector a Magic Lantern?

The closest approximate device in Will's world to that used by Lord Asriel to display his photograms in the Retiring Room may be the magic lantern or optical lantern, forerunners of twentieth century slide projectors. A reflector and lens focused light on a glass slide, and a lens tube magnified the slide's image. The light source was a lamp or lantern fueled by kerosene, vegetable oil or whale oil and housed in a metal box capable of withstanding high temperatures. The box was secured to a base that protected the surface of the table on which the magic lantern rested from transferred heat. A smokestack was essential to keep the image clear and the flame burning.

The slides used in magic lanterns were pieces of heavy glass placed in wooden or metal frames. Sizes and shapes varied; Asriel's slides project a black and white "circular photogram." He mentions that had he had more time he would have tinted his slides of the Aurora to show its crimson curtains of light. Hand-tinting was the means to add color to these slides.

The origin of the magic lantern is obscure, but one candidate for its inventor is Athanasius Kircher, a seventeenth century German monk and scientist, whose writings include a description of the physics of projection and a design for a *lanterna magica* (the Latin term for magic lantern favored in Europe).

Interestingly, Athanasius Kircher appears on the list of books advertised by Smith and Strange Ltd. on the map in LYRA'S OXFORD. He is the editor of *Polymathestatos: A Festschrift in Honour of Joscelyn Godwin* (festschrifts are books published in recognition of the achievements of a scholar featuring essays by fellow scholars). In Will's world, Joscelyn Godwin is a contemporary composer and the author of *Athanasius Kircher: A Renaissance Man and the Quest for Lost Knowledge*, among a number of other works on math and music, esoteric philosophy and theosophy, as well as a historical survey of some of the more fantastic notions about the North and South Poles.

40

Strohmeyer & Wyman, Library of Congress, LC-USZ62-112599, 1892

Crank phone

Philip Pullman says:

"I think it was my grandfather's magic lantern that Lord Asriel used in the second chapter of NORTHERN LIGHTS".

Applied Sciences and Technology:
Transportation
Aërodock to Zeppelin

Aërodock ✤

World: Lyra's

Role: Likely an airport for zeppelins or airships. One is mentioned in the context of having not yet sent word to Jordan College about the arrival in Oxford of Lord Asriel.

NL/GC 1 [brief]

Airships ✤

World: Lyra's

Role: *Airship* and *zeppelin* appear to be synonyms. Both words are used to describe the vehicle that transports Lyra and Mrs Coulter to London, and both are used again when Lyra and the other Bolvangar Experiment Station escapees watch Lee Scoresby fill his balloon with that vehicle's gas. [*See also* **Zeppelins**]

NL/GC brief mentions: Oxford to London 4; over the Fens 8; Scoresby takes fuel from 17

41 ### Anbaric locomotive ✎

World: Asriel's

Role: Beneath the basalt fortress, an anbaric locomotive pulls carriages softly lit by "glowing crystals, held on silver brackets against mirrored mahogany panels," riding a track to Lord Asriel's armoury.

AS 16 [brief]

Balloon ✤ ⚷ ✎ [LS]

World: Lyra's and Cittàgazze

Role: The balloon piloted by aëronaut Lee Scoresby (and hired by the gyptians seeking to rescue their children from the Bolvangar Experiment Station) brings Lyra and Roger to Svalbard and Stanislaus Grumman to Cittàgazze. In the first case, it inadvertently provides the opportunity for Iorek Byrnison to reclaim his throne and for Lord Asriel to open a passage to another world. In the second, also inadvertently, it provides the occasion that will reunite Will with his father—John Parry/Stanislaus Grumman, which in turn triggers several events crucial to the trilogy.

Scoresby's balloon is damaged when attacked by cliff-ghasts off the coast of Svalbard, but having repaired it, he uses it to travel to Nova Zembla, where he leaves it in storage when he goes to the Tartar village. Upon his return, Scoresby finds the balloon has been requisitioned by the military.

When Scoresby embarks on what will be his final voyage, he sights through his telescope

Michelle Heran

Balloon in Flight

another larger balloon, a Muscovite's, sharing the skies with him. He leaves behind forever his balloon and basket in Cittàgazze, but takes with him its instruments to fly again some day, if he survives the shoot-out at Alamo Gulch.

When he finally allows his ghost to dissipate, "the last little scrap of consciousness that had been the aëronaut Lee Scoresby floated upwards, just as his great balloon had done so many times." 42

Observation: *These references are limited to passenger balloons. Nelson, the physicist on the archaeological survey expedition in Alaska, from which John Parry and two others vanish, is presumed to be carrying weather balloons into the mountains, but when Parry looks in the crate, he finds instead radiation suits.* 43

Note: *The subject of the woodcut for "Fog and Ice," chapter 18 of* Northern Lights / Golden Compass, *is a balloon.*

NL/GC fueling and capacity described 13; Scoresby fuels from zeppelin at Bolvangar, witches hold steady while Roger and Lyra then Iorek board, mechanics of described, witches pull toward Svalbard 17; flight to Svalbard, temperature and altitude, flight mechanics described, attacked by cliff-ghasts 18; ⎡LS⎤ Lantern Slide 3

> *brief mentions:* Faa's excitement at hiring one 10; carried on two sledges 11; Scoresby travels with two, one small 14; Lyra's plans for Scoresby's 15; crash aftermath reported by alethiometer 19 and Roger 20; Lyra tells Asriel she'll get Scoresby to come for her 21; flight recalled 22

SK damage by cliffghasts repaired at Lake Enara 2; Lyra tells Will about 5 [brief]; Scoresby puts into storage at mouth of Yenisei River, retrieved with presentation of Magisterium's ring, departure for Cittàgazze under fire with one soldier clinging too long to rope 10; entering Cittàgazze, quick descent into forest, abandoned 14

AS *brief mentions:* recalled by Iorek, mocked by cliff-ghasts 3; recalled by Iorek to describe Scoresby to Will 9; Scoresby's dissipating ghost's movement upward compared to 31

Barges ❖

World: Lyra's

Role: Lyra once liked to watch the barges on the Thames from Mrs Coulter's apartment. The night she flees from the cocktail party, those same barges' "gallows-like cranes"

Lee Scoresby's Balloon

Lee Scoresby's is a hydrogen balloon. Scoresby's primary balloon can carry up to six people, and can handle, in addition to Scoresby, the weight of Iorek Byrnison and his armour, along with two children. He travels with a back-up, smaller balloon for emergencies or to use when flying without passengers, for example, to survey surrounding areas for the gyptians as they approach Bolvangar. Packed, the balloons can fit onto two dog sledges.

Scoresby can tell from the air if the ground below looks promising for fueling. He can secure hydrogen from ground-gas vents found near fire-mines, which is the most efficient means, or he can make gas from rock-oil or coal. Another option, although time-consuming, is to capture the gas released by pouring sulphuric acid over iron filings. At

Bolvangar, Scoresby inflates his balloon with the hydrogen of Coulter's zeppelin's gasbag.

Ropes criss-cross the balloon portion, and are secured to an iron ring protected by a sheath of leather; this is the balloon's suspension ring. Around the leather-edged rim of the balloon's basket is an instrumentation panel, including a compass and an altimeter. The basket's rim comes up level with Lyra's chin. Even when ground surface conditions are warm, the balloon flies at elevations where the air is always cold. Scoresby carries oxygen tanks and piles of furs to offer some protection from the extreme cold of high altitude (minus twenty at 10,000 feet en route to Svalbard), open-air flying in the Arctic. At times he employs a canvas sheet as a bivouac.

Buoyancy is controlled by a spring-levered gas-valve attached to a rope, which can be looped around a cleat in the suspension ring in order to hold the valve open. He can also choose to attach sandbags around the basket to use as ballast; releasing a bag's sand causes the balloon to rise.

To descend, Scoresby releases gas. Typically, ropes wrapped around bollards, or posts, would hold down a fully inflated balloon. When he has to make a quick landing, as in Cittàgazze, he can release the gas from a flap in the balloon's top.

One hazard is that a nearly empty balloon can catch the wind, acting as a sail. In an emergency, the aëronaut can cut its ropes and let it blow away on its own. Using a grapnel, which is like an anchor, the balloonist can snag onto a treetop, simultaneously slowing and ensuring his descent.

Once landed, to ascend from the ground, Scoresby would have to add gas; so he needs to be sure of a proximate source of fuel beforehand. When aloft, to gain altitude, he can drop ballast or increase the gas flow.

The use of a balloon depends on weather conditions. Just like with a zeppelin, lightning poses the risk of explosion, and fog renders navigation, at best, difficult. The speed and direction of the balloon depends on the prevailing winds. If witches are involved, they can drag against opposing directional winds and speed things up—as they do when getting Scoresby and his passengers to Svalbard. While his ability to navigate a strict course is limited, Scoresby can control his balloon with such finesse that, for example, he is able to approach what is likely the Tower of Angels in Cittàgazze head on, then calmly empty the sand of one ballast, and

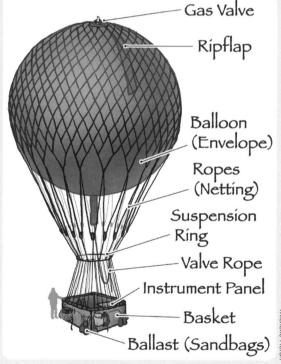

Gas Valve

Ripflap

Balloon (Envelope)

Ropes (Netting)

Suspension Ring

Valve Rope

Instrument Panel

Basket

Ballast (Sandbags)

Michelle Heron

Anatomy of a Balloon

without incident, pass over the tower with just six feet to spare.

Pursued by an armed zeppelin, a balloonist is helpless. That is what forces Scoresby, trying to evade the Imperial Army's zeppelins, to land in a forest in the hills of Cittàgazze.

become scary. ⁴⁴

NL/GC brief mentions: route down Isis 3; viewed from Coulter's 5; frightening at night 6; on River Cole 9

BICYCLE

World: Will's

Role: Will's experience with bike riding proves better preparation for riding the mulefa than Lyra's experience atop armoured bears. Lyra has never ridden a bicycle.

SK   in Will's Oxford 7 *[brief]*

AS   riding mulefa compared to 32 *[brief]*

BOAT, LEE'S RENTAL

World: Lyra's

Role: Lee Scoresby rents a small, possibly open, boat with a gas engine for the three-day journey from the mouth of the Yenisei River to a Siberian Tartar village, the last stretch of his journey to find shaman Stanislaus Grumman.

SK   10

BOAT, WORLD OF THE DEAD

World: world of the dead

Role: An "ancient rowing boat, battered, patched, rotting" rowed across a misty lake by an equally ancient boatman is the only way to get from the suburbs of the world of the dead to the island where the entrance to the world itself is to be found. When Lyra boards this boat, the boatman will not begin the trip until she accepts that Pantalaimon must stay behind on the slime-covered jetty.

AS   officials in suburbs tell travelers of 19; boarding, the journey 21; feeling during journey in recalled by Tialys 22 *[brief]*

BUS

World: Will's

Role: Will and Lyra take a bus from Summertown down the Banbury Road to Oxford's city centre.

SK   brief mentions: Will rode two day he left home 1; on Banbury Road 3; in Oxford's traffic 4; 11

Other Boats and Ships

Boats are mentioned throughout the trilogy: Sharing the Oxford canal with the gyptians' narrowboats are butty boats. ⁴⁵

The working boats on the Thames include brick-barges, asphalt-boats, and corn-tankers. ⁴⁶

After their zeppelin lands in Falkeshall Gardens, Lyra and Mrs Coulter take a boat across the Thames to her Embankment apartment. ⁴⁷ ⁴⁸

Approaching the fish house where she finds Tony Makarios, Lyra sees the villagers' boats, drawn in for the winter, at rest under mounds of snow. ⁴⁹

Lyra thinks perhaps a boat could take her to Svalbard, so she can rescue Lord Asriel. Boats aren't a part of that island's culture because there is no wood with which to build them. ⁵⁰ ⁵¹

Lyra's tall tale she tells her hosts in the suburbs of the dead features a gyptian narrow boat and a three-masted clipper. ⁵²

Lee Scoresby takes a boat from Nova Zembla to the port city at the mouth of the Yenesei. When he returns with shaman Stanislaus Grumman, he finds that all the ships in its ports have been requisitioned by the Magisterium. ⁵³ ⁵⁴

Facts: *Butty boats are unpowered working narrowboats originally towed by horses but now by motorboats.*

CANAL-BOATS/NARROW-BOATS ✦ ✎ [LS]

Ian Giles

World: Lyra's

Role: Canal-boats, or narrow-boats, are the foundation of the "tight-knit gyptian boat-world." Lyra briefly experiences this boat-world in its home surroundings when she is sheltered from the authorities in the Fens, as the gyptians discuss how to reclaim their children stolen by the Gobblers. There, so many families have gathered for byanropings, or meetings, that it is possible to walk for a mile without touching ground, moving from

Narrow-boat

boat deck to boat deck. Before she traveled and lived on one, Lyra thought that each "brightly painted" narrow-boat had a "bung," something like a bathtub plug that, were it removed, would cause the boat to sink immediately. As the term narrow-boat implies, they are long and narrow, and powered by petrol/gasoline engines. They are also low, to allow passage under bridges. The Costa family's boat has a sleeping cabin with narrow bunk beds, a kitchen cabin with an iron stove, and a cockpit. Daily chores include greasing the propeller shaft and cleaning out the weed trap over the propeller.

Herbert E. French, Library of Congress Prints and Photographs Division, LC-USZ62-131447

Lyra travels from the Fens to Colby on Farder Coram's narrow-boat.

Note: Narrow-boat *and* canal boat *seem to be interchangeable terms. Canal boat is always two words. Narrow-boat is two words in the UK version (hyphenated is the preferred spelling). The US version uses the single-word spelling.*

Often in these chapters, simply boat *(or* boats*) appears, but it is apparent that narrow-boats are the boat meant.*

Narrow-boat

Update: The second Lantern Slide in *NORTHERN LIGHTS/THE GOLDEN COMPASS* notes that the canal-boats belonging to a particular gyptian family were distinguished by the floral design painted on its exterior. The boats of the van Poppel family, for example, were decorated with a pattern composed of roses and lilies.

NL/GC docked in Jericho 3; aboard Costas' in London 6 and in Fens, gathering of for byanropings 7, 8; from Fens through Coleby prior to departure for North 9; [LS] Lantern Slide 2

> *brief mentions:* Lyra tells Coulter about at first meeting 4; Coram recalls bringing Serafina aboard his when he rescued her 10

> *AS brief mentions:* in Lyra's lie about her childhood 19; Lyra reminds Roger's ghost of Costas' 23

CANOES ✎

Edward S. Curtis, Library of Congress, LC-USZ62-47019, 1914

World: Lyra's

Role: As Will makes his way with the armoured bears through Siberia on their hired boat, he witnesses people canoeing through what were once their villages. They have come to salvage belongings from the floodwaters that were caused by the extreme cataclysmic climate upheaval.

AS   9 [brief]

CARS ✦⚔️✎

World: Lyra's, Will's

Role: When she meets up with Mrs Coulter at Bolvangar, Lyra claims to have been abducted by a man and a woman in a car. Upon entering Will's Oxford, Lyra inadvertently dashes in front of a car. Mary Malone leaves her car parked in a street near Sunderland Avenue when she leaves her world through the window to Cittàgazze.

> [*See also* **Rolls Royce**]

NL/GC 17 [brief]

SK   Lyra's encounter with on Sunderland Avenue 3; Mary Malone's 12
>   *brief mentions: in Winchester 1; on High Street 4; on Sunderland Avenue 5; Lyra dodges near Mary's lab 7*

AS   brief mentions: in Mary's memories 27; near Botanic Garden 38

CARTS ⚔️

World: Will's

Role: In Will's world, the milkman uses an electric cart to make his deliveries, and ice cream men use hand-wheeled carts in city centers. Lyra tells Will that in her world there are fewer carts and they don't speed by nearly so fast.

> [*See also* **Horse-drawn carts**]

Note: *There's an extra cart reference in the US edition; Will and Lyra buy hamburgers from a cart. In the UK edition, they buy them at a mobile stall.*

SK   brief mentions: milkman's 1; Lyra on 3; hamburger [US only] and ice cream 5

CHARIOT [*See* **Clouded Mountain**]

CHTHONIC RAILWAY ✦

World: Lyra's

Role: Coulter advises Lyra that underground transport in London is "not really intended for people of their class." Of course, Lyra would like to give it a try, but her first opportunity is the night she runs away from Coulter's apartment. She decides against it, thinking she has a better chance of not being caught if she remains out in the open.

Rendering of Underground Railway

Facts: *The London subway system is commonly known as the* Underground. Chthonic *comes from the Greek word* khthonios, *meaning in or under the earth; in modern usage,* chthonic *is frequently associated with things or places that are darkly evil.*

NL/GC 6 [brief]

57

CLOUDED MOUNTAIN, THE (ALSO KNOWN AS THE CHARIOT) ✎

World: Kingdom of Heaven

Role: Formerly known as the Chariot, the Clouded Mountain is the mobile citadel, or palace, of the Authority. For millennia no one has seen the peak of the citadel because of a steady thickening of surrounding clouds. The Authority stays deep within its center in a crystal chamber. From the ground, the Clouded Mountain appears to glow; the clouds swirl in a constant motion. The source of the light illuminating the citadel comes "from the substance of the mountain itself, which glowed and faded in a slow breath-like rhythm, with a mother-of-pearl radiance." A deep low tremor warns of its approach.

The injured Baruch implies he and Balthamos learned that Metatron is planning to turn the Clouded Mountain into "an engine of war" after having moved the Authority elsewhere. Using binoculars, Lord Asriel and King Ogunwe see gun emplacements on the Clouded Mountain.

Much later, from the roof of the adamant tower, King Ogunwe and Asriel see thousands of warrior angels emerging from the Chariot before swirling clouds again obscure it. Will and Lyra witness armed angels departing the Clouded Mountain to do battle with witches.

Mrs Coulter, approaching the Clouded Mountain in an intention craft, is reminded of "a certain abominable heresy" and a model of the same illustrating that there are more than three spatial dimensions. She considers the Authority's citadel to be "less like a rock than like a force-field, manipulating space itself to enfold and stretch and layer it into galleries and terraces, chambers and colonnades and watch-towers of air and light and vapour." "The Clouded Mountain" is the title of chapter 30 of THE AMBER SPYGLASS.

[*See also* **Kingdom of Heaven** *in* **The Worlds**]

AS   Metatron threatens Will and angels in 2; Baruch tells Asriel about 5; viewed from Adamant Tower 28; Will and Lyra see angels emerge from to attack witches 29; Mrs Coulter enters, described 30

CRYSTAL LITTER 🖉

Worlds: Kingdom of Heaven, Asriel's Republic of Heaven (battlefield)

Role: In a crystal-embellished enclosed sedan chair contraption borne by a small procession of angels, the Authority is removed from the Clouded Mountain to a presumably safe spot during the battle between the kingdom of heaven and Asriel's republic.

Mrs Coulter sees the crystal litter being carried out of the Clouded Mountain by a group of angels singing psalms. The litter is covered in crystals that catch the light emanating from the Mountain. Her impression is that the occupant is an angel of "terrifying decrepitude," and when it lets out a howl, the anguish it conveys forces her to cover her ears.

Will and Lyra chance upon the litter while searching for their dæmons. Lyra, taking pity on the figure trapped within, has Will cut through the litter's crystal. Its ancient angelic passenger seems relieved to be released, and dissolves into the air.

Facts: *A litter is an enclosed chair attached to two poles and carried by at least four men, two front and back. This means of transport was used by the wealthy in Egypt, Rome, China, India, Mesopotamia, and throughout the ancient world, and continues to be used for ceremonial purposes or to indicate status in modern times.*

AS   Coulter sees leaving Clouded Mountain, abandoned on battlefield, cliff-ghasts attack 30; Will cuts through crystal 31

FRIGATE ✤

World: Lyra's

Role: Captain Rokeby lets Lyra pull the steam-whistle to signal a Hollands frigate during the gyptians' voyage North.

NL/GC 10 *[brief]*

GYROPTERS

Helicopter

World: Lyra's

Role: Likely the equivalent of helicopters in Will's world, gyropters are used widely by Lord Asriel's republic. While being faster than zeppelins, on long distance flights across unpop-ulated regions, they must fly accompanied by a tanker zeppelin, which limits their speed.

The inhabitants of the far North of Lyra's world are less familiar with gyropters than zeppelins. Although armoured bear Iorek Byrnison can readily identify the sound and sight of distant airships, he has no experience with gyropters. Will tells him that what they hear are approaching helicopters.

The terrain in the Himalayas puts Asriel's forces at a disadvantage. While the zeppelin's soldiers can descend on ropes, the gyropters have to land to unload.

AS on way to Himalayas 9; Ogunwe prepares for battle, Will hears helicopters approaching cave, problems landing in Himalayan terrain, attacked by zeppelin fire 12; losses reported, used as decoys at basalt fortress during intention craft demo 16
brief mentions: Asriel readies squadron of 5; Tialys reports Court's information regarding 11; remains of following battle 14; Tialys expects Will and Lyra to board one on way from Asriel's 15; Coulter tells MacPhail she flew one to Geneva 24; in battle on the plain 29; compared to intention craft 30

HORSE-DRAWN CARTS

World: Cittàgazze

Role: Looking for Lyra, witches Serafina Pekkala and Ruta Skadi encounter evacuees from the world of Cittàgazze's cities, some traveling in horse-drawn carts, trying to escape the menacing Spectres.

SK 6 *[brief]*

KAYAKS

World: Lyra's

Role: Kayaks are used for seal hunting in the far North near the Siberian island of Nova Zembla.

SK 6 *[brief]*

LAUNCHES

World: Lyra's, mulefa

Role: The fog is so thick off the coast of Svalbard that a launch is sent for Mrs Coulter, who has come to attend the torture of a witch. Serafina Pekkala gets aboard the ship as well.

The gyptians who come to the world of the mulefa use a launch to get to the mulefa's land, since there is no harbor where they can dock a ship. A steam launch carries Gobbler victims from the Limehouse wharf to Captain Magnusson's ship.

Facts: *Launches are small boats intended for carrying people short distances, like from an anchored ship to the shore.* [*See also* **Ship, church's off Svalbard**]

NL/GC in Limehouse 3 *[brief]*

SK   off Svalbard 2 *[brief]*

AS   in mulefa's world 38 *[brief]*

LIFEBOATS ❖ ⚓

World: Lyra's

Role: Lyra considers hiding under a lifeboat as a means of getting to go North when John Faa initially refuses her permission to go with the gyptians. Serafina Pekkala hides in shadows cast by the lifeboats while getting her bearings on the ship where a witch is being tortured.

NL/GC 9 *[brief*

MOBILE STALL ❖

World: Will's

Role: Will and Lyra buy hamburgers from a mobile stall to eat as they walk up the Banbury Road to the Sunderland Avenue window after going to the movies in his Oxford.

Note: *This phrase appears only in the UK edition. In the US edition, they buy their burgers at a cart.*

SK   5 [UK only] *[brief]*

MOORING MAST ❖

World: Lyra's

Role: One method of securing an arriving zeppelin is at a stout mooring mast. Ground crew climb ladders up the mast pole to secure cables to the airship. A mooring mast is used at the Bolvangar Experiment Station. [*See also* **Zeppelins**]

NL/GC brief mentions: 15, 17

MOTORIZED SLEDGE ❖

World: Lyra's

Role: Mrs Coulter arrives on the grounds outside the Bolvangar Experiment Station's buildings in a motorized sledge with anbaric headlights.

NL/GC 17 *[brief]*

NARROW-BOATS [*See* Canal-boats]

PEDAL-BOATS ⚓

World: Cittàgazze

Role: These boats are available for visitors to Cittàgazze's beaches.

SK   brief mentions: 1, 7

Punt ❖

World: Lyra's

Role: Lyra considers herself an expert in maneuvering these small river pleasure boats after just three days.

Facts: *These boats are flat-bottomed with squared ends. They are propelled by one person standing at the punt's end with a long pole and pushing the boat along.*

NL/GC 8 [brief]

Rolls Royce ⚜

World: Will's

Ian Giles

When Lyra accepted a lift in Sir Charles Latrom's Rolls Royce, she asked to be let out on South Parade

Role: When Lyra accepts a ride from Sir Charles Latrom, his "large dark-blue" car seems "smooth and soft and powerful." When Will sees it parked outside Latrom's Headington residence, he knows that it is more than just a vehicle, it is a display of the "settled superiority that some upper-class English people still took for granted." 63 64

During Lyra's first ride in the Rolls, Sir Charles sits in the rear, strategically positioned so that she has to crawl past him to exit. The next time, Latrom sits up front with his butler/chauffeur, when he tells her and Will what they must do to get the alethiometer back. Lyra last views the Rolls the night she and Will return to Latrom's.

"The Rolls Royce" is the title of Chapter 7 of *The Subtle Knife*.

Facts: *Rolls-Royce began in 1904 when engineer Frederick Henry Royce produced his first car and several months later met Charles Stewart Rolls, an importer of motor cars and a balloon aeronaut. Together they formed the company that in 1906 produced the Silver Ghost, the car that made their reputation and established the Rolls-Royce as the world's best car. Throughout its history, every Rolls-Royce car engine has been completely hand-built. However, since 2003 when the trademark Rolls-Royce was licensed to BMW, only the Phantom is called a Rolls-Royce.*

SK Lyra's ride 7; Will and Lyra's ride 8; Coulter emerges from 9 [brief]

Rowing boats ⚜✎

World: Cittàgazze, Lyra's

Role: Will witnesses people using rowboats to navigate through what were once roads, trying to salvage belongings from the ice-melt floodwaters that claimed their villages.

Note: Rowboats *is used in the US editions in place of the* UK's rowing boats.

SK in Cittàgazze 1 [brief]

AS in Siberia 9 [brief]

Ship, church's off Svalbard ⚜✎

World: Lyra's

Role: Somewhere near Svalbard, Serafina Pekkala's help is sought by a witch's dæmon whose person is being tortured on a ship. When a launch

GW

A row boat

approaches, Serafina sees an opportunity to get aboard the ship by posing as a witch serving the church who has come to guide the launch through the fog.

There is a large structure in the middle of the ship, and ventilators between it and the ship's railings. Below the bridge (the place where the boat is driven), toward the front of the boat, is a saloon or lounge which has windows rather than portholes on three sides. This ship is the subject of the woodcut for chapter 2 of The Subtle Knife, "Among the Witches."

SK   Serafina boards, described, witch's torture on, Serafina shoots way off 2
> *brief mentions:* Serafina's invisibility on compared to Will making self inconspicuous 4; recalled by Serafina 13

AS   recalled by Pavel in Court testimony 6 *[brief]*

Ship, gyptians' to Norroway ✢

World: Lyra's

Role: The gyptians hire a ship to take them across the German Ocean, from Colby, England to Trollesund, Norroway, to find their children who have been abducted by the Gobblers. Gyptian Nicolas Rokeby is in charge of the ship. It has a high foc'sle or forecastle (the front of the ship), a funnel in the middle, a wheelhouse, and a crane, or derrick. On the foremast there's a crow's nest, but Lyra isn't allowed to climb to it. She does get to sound the ship's steam-whistle. Lyra soon learns that aboard ship she goes down the companionway (not stairs) to reach its saloon or common room. Also below deck are tiny cabins with scuttles (portholes). The boat has a wooden deck and is largely made of timber, and the gyptians use the ship's engine rather than its sails.

NL/GC Faa assigns responsibility for to Rokeby 8; 9 *[brief]*; described, boarded, sets sail 9; voyage of 10; docked in Trollesund, Kaisa visits 11

Ship, gyptians' to world of the mulefa ✐

World: Lyra's, Mulefa's, Cittàgazze

Role: Witch Serafina Pekkala guides a ship carrying John Faa, Farder Coram, and other gyptians to the world of the mulefa. They pick up Will, Lyra, and Mary Malone to sail to the world of Cittàgazze, from which Will can cut a window into his and Mary's Oxford. The ship then sails on to Lyra's world.

The harbor of Ragusa, a city on the Adriatic Sea that along with Venice served as a model for Cittàgazze

AS   arrival in mulefa's world, voyage, docked in Cittàgazze's harbor 38
> *brief mentions:* Serafina tells dæmons, Mary about 36; Pan, Xaphania tell Lyra and Will about 37

Ship, Iorek's chartered ✐

World: Lyra's

Role: The boat Iorek Byrnison hires to take himself and several dozen bears to the Himalayas, and on which Will catches a ride, is a rusty, coal-fueled steamer.

AS   plans for 3 *[brief]*; docked 8; journey 9

Ships, Trollesund ⚲

World: Lyra's

Role: When she comes to visit witch consul Martin Lanselius, Serafina Pekkala sees many ships docked or riding at anchor in the Trollesund harbor, including a large ship with an African registration. The increased activity at this small port village is connected with the army the Magisterium is assembling, but whether the African ship has anything to do with the regiment of zombis who are supposedly among the Magisterium's soldiers is unknown.

SK   2 [brief]

SLEDGES ❖ ✎ ⑩

World: Lyra's, Will's

Role: Sledges pulled by dog teams are the only mode of travel in the remote North of Lyra's world. After sailing from Colby, England, to Trollesund, Norroway, the gyptians secure sledges and dogs to begin their trek toward the General Oblation Board's Bolvangar Experiment Station. Over snow, the motion of the sledges is "swift and smooth." But the sledges offer no protection from the cold, wind, and snow. The gyptians devise some type of tent structure on the sledges for use when stopped, and heaps of furs are secured to the sledges with rope. On their fronts are hung lanterns.

    At the Pitt-Rivers Museum in Will's Oxford, Lyra sees a display which she is certain includes the same sledge she was tied to by the Samoyed hunters but she is convinced too that the traces are incorrectly tied.

    When he reaches the peak where he intends to break out of his world, Asriel turns his sledge over and uses it as a work platform to hold batteries, various scientific devices and a reel of wire.

    Iorek Byrnison's armoured bears haul a sledge loaded with a cauldron of burning coal to use in their fire-hurlers.

    Lee Scoresby hires a sledge and Tartar driver to take him from a port town on Nova Zembla to the Imperial Muscovite Observatory.

    Sledge tracks are the subject of the woodcut for chapter 22 of NORTHERN LIGHTS/ GOLDEN COMPASS, "Betrayal."

    [*See also* **Motorized sledge**]

Update: The appendix of the **10**TH anniversary edition of NORTHERN LIGHTS includes a drawing by Lord Asriel of his plans for an upended sledge laboratory.

Facts: *Traces are the harnesses, reins, ropes, and other gear that organize the pack of dogs*

65

Sledge and dog team

Library of Congress, LC-USZ62-34903, 1920

pulling a sledge.

NL/GC Gyptians rent, depart Trollesund on 11; speed and maneuverability of compared to Iorek's 12; at camp, furs, traces 13; Samoyeds' 14; Lord Asriel's described, Iorek and Lyra follow its tracks 22; Asriel's upended to serve as work station 23

> *brief mentions:* on Asriel's lantern slide 2; Northern Progress Company's 10, gyptians' at Bolvangar 17, bears use for fire-hurler 20, 21

SK   in museum exhibit 4 *[brief]*; on Nova Zembla 6

10ᴛʜ: *NL* appendix

STEAM TRAIN ✤

World: Lyra's

Role: Lord Asriel is to take a steam train from Oxford to London as soon as he finishes talking to the Scholars in the Retiring Room.

NL/GC 2 *[brief]*

STEAMER ✤ ✐

World: Lyra's

Role: Lee Scoresby had planned on taking a steamer home to his native Texas when his days as an aëronaut ended. In Siberia, Will hopes to find a steamer going south to take him closer to Lyra.

> [*See also* **Ship, Iorek's chartered**]

NL/GC 18 *[brief]*

AS   8 *[brief]*

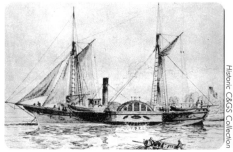

Coast Survey Steamer BIBB Sketched by Xanthus Smith, NOAA Photo Library-Historic C&GS Collection

Steamer. The gyptians' ship for the voyage to Norroway could well have been an early steamer like this one with a single funnel amidship, a foremast tall enough for a crow's nest, and a high forecastle.

TRACTORS ✤

World: Lyra's

Role: Iorek Byrnison is working on a gas powered tractor at the sledge depot in Trollesund when Lyra comes to tell him where his armour is hidden.

NL/GC 11 *[brief]*

TRAMCARS ✤

World: Lyra's

Role: Anbaric tramcars are part of the transportation system in Lyra's London.

NL/GC 6 *[brief]*

TRANSIT VAN ⚔

World: Will's

Role: Mary Malone immediately notices a white unmarked transit van with darkened windows when she arrives at Sunderland Avenue.

SK   12 *[brief]*

TRUCKS ✤ ⚷ ✎

World: Lyra's, Will's

Role: A child in Jericho tells Lyra, her friends, and the gyptians hunting for Billy Costa that in Banbury he saw a white truck drive away from the garden where a little boy was playing one minute and gone the next.

    The car that almost hits Lyra in Will's Oxford has to slam on its brakes, and in turn, is rear-ended by a van. The driver of the van is referred to as both a van driver and a truck driver.

NL/GC 3 *[brief]*

SK   brief mentions: at night on Sunderland Avenue 1, and the next day 3

AS   25 [brief]

TUG ✤

World: Lyra's

Role: Tugboats pull barges along the Thames in Lyra's Oxford.

NL/GC 5 *[brief]*

VANS ✤ ⚷

World: Lyra's, Will's

Role: Vans carry goods to the Covered Market in Lyra's Oxford. It was a van that Lyra said was used by Gobblers to abduct her when telling her tale to Mrs Coulter at Bolvangar.

    In Will's Oxford, Lyra dashes in front of a car that brakes quickly and is then rear-ended by a van.

NL/GC brief mentions: in Lyra's Oxford 3; 17

SK   3 [brief]

WAGONS ⚷

World: Cittàgazze

Role: Evacuees from the world of Cittàgazze's cities, some traveling in horse-drawn carts and wagons, try to escape the menacing Spectres.

SK   6 [brief]

ZEPPELINS ✤ ⚷ ✎

World: Lyra's

Role: In the Oxford of Lyra's world, the days are punctuated by the regular visits of the Royal Mail zeppelin, and Lyra leaves with Mrs Coulter for London in a passenger zeppelin. A mooring mast is on the grounds of the General Oblation Board's Bolvangar Experiment Station, and Mrs Coulter uses a zeppelin to get to this remote site, as she does to Svalbard.

    The Imperial Muscovite Army uses zeppelins to chase Lee Scoresby as he flies his

Zeppelin over water

balloon to Cittàgazze. The Consistorial Court of Discipline dispatches a squadron of eight zeppelins to the Himalayas to seize Mrs Coulter, Lyra, and Will. They will again use a zeppelin to transport its bomb, the silver guillotine, its prisoner Mrs Coulter, and assorted personnel to the hydro-anbaric power plant in the Alps.

[*See also* **Airships**]

66 **Observation:** *Lee Scoresby once uses the term* dirigible *rather than* zeppelin *or* airship.

NL/GC Coulter's arrival at Bolvangar in 15, 16; Scoresby uses fuel from for his balloon 17; Coulter, Tartars arrive in Svalbard on, gondola's machine gun, crashes after gas envelope hit by fire-hurler 22

> *brief mentions:* Royal Mail 3; Oxford to London 4; as transport to Svalbard 13; balloon compared to 18; on bears' mural 19; alethiometer warns of Coulter's approach to Svalbard on 20, and Lyra tells this to Asriel 21; Lyra passes beyond sight of wrecked 23

SK Skadi sees headed to Asriel's 6 *[brief]*; pursue Scoresby and Grumman to Cittàgazze, Grumman sends storms to bring down, Scoresby dreams of seeing pilot of attacked by Spectre, Sayan Kotor and massed birds bring down another, remaining one disgorges troops, Scoresby shoots out one engine and uses last bullet to shoot into its envelope and cause explosion 14

AS Court uses to transport troops to Himalayas 9; Court's approach Himalayas, spies exit through slit in envelope 11; troops exit down ropes 12; 13 [brief]; transports MacPhail and soldiers, Coulter, and bomb to launch site in Alps 25

> *brief mentions:* Iorek sees remains of in Cittàgazze 3; tanker used to fuel gyropters 5; floodlights 13; wreckage 14; losses of 16

Zeppelins of Lyra's World

These vehicles are used for passengers and for freight, and have civilian and military applications. They are made of oiled fabric, often silk, stretched over a rigid metal frame, and this "skin" is filled with hydrogen. Under this is a structure variously referred to as a cabin or a gondola, which can be large enough to carry thirty to forty men or heavy materials (such as a bomb) and on which machine guns can be mounted. Lights under the zeppelin's nose and along the cabin provide illumination. There are apparently at least two engines, one port and one aft, to power the airship. At the battle of Alamo Gulch, Lee Scoresby disables an Imperial Muscovite Army zeppelin's port engine with a single shot.

The airships can be parked at mooring masts, where ground crews mount ladders to attach stabilizing cables. During battle, if landing or docking is not possible, as in the Himalayas, the zeppelins try to stay steady while the troops descend on ropes and sharpshooters provide fire coverage from the airship.

Its gas engines, coupled with the "streamlined smoothness" of the zeppelin, make it faster and more controllable than a hydrogen balloon, but it is also much noisier. Its engine is described as "throbbing" with a "heavy thump." Even from a distance, a zeppelin's approach is audible, sounding like the drone of swarming mosquitoes. Although fairly dependable, its skin can be penetrated by a Gallivespian-sized knife or the edges of sulphur rock.

The zeppelin's biggest drawback is its vulnerability to lightning and, particularly in the case of battle zeppelins, fire from fire-hurlers or gunfire. An airship can very quickly be turned into a fireball and a heap of scrap metal.

67
68

Zeppelin of Will's World, the L II

Applied Sciences and Technology:

Weapons

Armour to Winchester rifle

ARMOUR (BEARS') ✤ ✐ ⑩

World: Lyra's

Role: Both as a group and as individuals, the armoured bears of Svalbard are defined by their armour. Iorek Byrnison tells Lyra that a "bear's armour is his soul, just as your dæmon is your soul." She is fascinated by the idea that bears can make their own souls. When Iorek expresses hesitation about repairing the subtle knife, Will counters by asking whether Iorek has considered that perhaps the first bear to make armour brought into the world a tool that caused harm as well as good. Iorek responds that nothing is known of the bears before there was armour, but with the armour came bear customs, and so, it seems, their culture, history, or identity.

A bear fashions his armour from sky metal. This is a metal far stronger than that used in the manufacture of the tractors on which Iorek works in the Trollesund sledge depot (which he can rip open with a single swipe). The weapons the bears possess—knife-sharp claws as long as Lyra's hands—demand strong armour. A bear when armoured weighs over two tons, but the strength of the bears is such that they are not slowed down or rendered awkward by the extra weight. The armour is impervious to attack by arrows or bullets and unaffected by high temperatures. In fact, in the forge Iorek devises to repair the subtle knife, his armour's backplate serves as his work surface. Iofur Raknison, the usurper-king of Svalbard, supplements his sheets of metal with enameled designs and a sark (similar to a long shirt or nightshirt) of chain-mail, but it is not well-suited to battle.

Bear armour consists of separate sheets of metal up to an inch thick, which are linked together using joiners that the bear twists open and closed with his claws. The helmet is pointed to accommodate the bear's muzzle, has slits for the eyes, and ends above the lower jaw so it doesn't impede the bear using his jaws to bite or seize his enemy. Iorek's helmet is as long as Will's arm, as thick as his thumb, and very heavy. The helmet does not join to the shoulder plates, leaving an area unprotected from a rear-attack if the bear must lower his head. That area provides a point where a bear can use a claw to strip his opponent of his helmet, as Iorek Byrnison does to Iofur Raknison during battle. Seal blubber is used to prevent or remove rust. The movements of an armoured bear are accompanied by the clang of metal. The armour does not cover a bear's underside.

An aspect of banishment as severe as a shunned bear's exile from Svalbard is the confiscation of his armour. When Iorek Byrnison was de-throned and exiled, he managed to make himself another suit of armour from sky metal secured on Nova Zembla. That armour was stolen from him in Trollesund, leaving him in near enslavement to the town's humans and to alcohol. When Lyra and gyptian Farder Coram ask for his help to rescue the children kidnapped by the Gobblers, Iorek's price is the return of his armour. He vows that if they meet that condition the gyptians can count on his help "either until I am dead or until you have victory."

69

Iorek's helmet is the subject of the woodcut for chapter 20 of *Northern Lights*, "À Outrance."

Observation: *Iorek links the armoured bears' historical origin to their armour in much the same way that Atal sees the emergence of the mulefa as inextricably linked to the adaptation of the seed-pod wheels.*

The usurper king Iofur Raknison's obsession with imitating human manners and ways of life is illustrated in the contrast between his bears' shiny armour, decorated with enameled designs and plumed helmets, and the banished Iorek's: utilitarian, dented and battle-scarred.

Update: Iorek's helmet, sliced into pieces by the subtle knife, is the theme of the woodcut for chapter 8 "Vodka," in the **10th** anniversary edition of *The Amber Spyglass*.

NL/GC Lyra tells Iorek where his is, made of sky-metal, compared to dæmon or soul, plates and helmet described, vulnerable place, oiled with seal blubber, thickness of 11; left behind during search for lost boy 12; loss of as punishment associated with exile, weight 13; Scoresby thinks Lyra's help in getting back reason for Iorek's attachment to her, Lyra and Serafina discuss 18; Iorek's and Raknison's soldiers' compared 19; Iorek's and Raknison's compared, contrast in performance of during battle 20; as protection against arrows and bullets 22
  brief mentions: Iorek sets return of his as price for helping gyptians 10; sound of 14; weight and balloon 17

AS Will slices Iorek's helmet 8; parts used as improvised forge 15; advantages of two-ton weight of in battle against kingdom's forces, poses difficulty for Lyra and Will as riders 31
  brief mentions: 9, 12, 13

Arrows ❖ ⚕ ✎ ⑩

World: Lyra's, Cittàgazze, republic of heaven

Role: Bows and arrows are most often associated with witches in *His Dark Materials*, although witches are not the only competent archers. Arrows need to be shot from fairly close range to have a likelihood of finding their target, and so the witches make a sudden dive, shoot, and ascend. In battle, the witches keep such a barrage of arrows coming down on their enemies that some are bound to hit, and all cause confusion.

Apparently, different witch clans can be identified by the color of their arrows' tail feathers. The arrows shot by Serafina Pekkala's clan at the Tartar guards have grey feathers; those used in the attack on the armoured bears in Svalbard have green.

In the Far North, for a witch to lay her bow and arrows on the ground in front of her before approaching a stranger, or one whom she may have accidentally wronged, is a sign of peaceful intent.

Gyptian Tony Costa rescues Lyra from Turk traders with a well-aimed arrow, but another gyptian is mortally wounded by an arrow that hits him when he is in London's Ministry of Theology. Samoyed hunters' arrows kill several gyptians before the men steal Lyra to sell her at the Bolvangar Experiment Station. The bow and arrow is also a weapon of choice for Skraelings; gyptian Farder Coram was crippled by a poisoned arrow that found him during battle. The Magisterium's Skraeling censor at the Muscovite observatory on Nova Zembla fires an arrow at Lee Scoresby, but the aëronaut's alert dæmon warns him in time to dive out of its path.

After Serafina witnesses Mrs Coulter torturing a witch, she selects her very best arrow in her quiver and reserves it for use on the woman. The night Serafina meets Mary Malone, she breaks that arrow. The title of chapter 36 of *The Amber Spyglass* is "The

Broken Arrow," and the woodcut for this chapter in the **10**ᴛʜ anniversary edition is a single broken arrow among a dozen or so unbroken.

Observation: *There is one peaceful use of an arrow. When Mary wishes to climb high into a seedpod tree, she attaches a rope to a arrow, turns a branch into a bow, and sends the arrow over as high a branch as she can. When it falls back to the ground, the length of rope is left in place to aid her climb.*

NL/GC witches use against Tartars, grey feathered ends of, witch shoots through Tartar's helmet's eye slits 17; witches use against armoured bears, green feathered ends of 22

  brief mentions: gyptians use against Turk kidnappers 6, gyptian spy shot with at Ministry of Theology 9, Coram once victim of Skraelings' 10, Samoyeds use against gyptians 14, Serafina recalls Coram's injury by 18

SK Serafina uses on church's boat, against cliff-ghasts, lays down bow before Thorold 2; Skraeling shoots at Scoresby, useless against Spectres, Serafina lays down bow before Lorenz, sound of angels' above Cittàgazze 6; witches shoot at belvedere's roof 11; Skadi kills cliff-ghast with 13; Feldt nearly shoots Coulter with, Grumman killed by 15

AS *brief mentions:* Serafina lays down bow before Iorek 3, Will recalls father's death by 13, Mary's arrow 20, Coulter dodges witch's 25, sound of during battle on plain 29, Serafina breaks one reserved for Coulter 36

Bomb ✐

World: Lyra's

Role: The Court's president, Fr. MacPhail, commands Dr Cooper, formerly of the General Oblation Board's Bolvangar Experiment Station (and now a "guest" of the Court), to develop a bomb that will track and kill Lyra should the Consistorial Court of Discipline's assassin fail.

 A tremendous amount of energy is needed to effect the process. The energy that is released as a by-product of intercision will be combined with that generated at a hydro-anbaric power station.

 When detonated, the bomb causes fissures beneath the basalt fortress in Asriel's world, through which he will eventually enter and await the arrival of Metatron and Coulter at the rim of the abyss. Like the windows cut by the subtle knife and the opening above Svalbard made by Asriel, the abyss created by the impact of the bomb will, Xaphania says, be closed by angels. [*See also* **Resonating chamber**]

Observation: *At the end of chapter 25, the bomb is listed in a series of things destroyed when a zeppelin set on fire by a shell from the intention craft falls out of the sky: "the blazing zeppelin fell slowly, slowly down on top of the whole scene, bomb, cable, soldiers, and all." However, by this time, the bomb already would have been launched.*

AS resonating chamber, guidance system 24; transport, preparations for and launch of 25; reverberations from strike in uninhabited world, and opening of abyss 26; Basilides' report of 28; Xaphania on closing 37 *[brief]*

Bow and arrow [*See* Arrows]

Cross-bows ✐

World: Lyra's

Role: The Swiss Guard is armed with cross-bows that can fire fifteen times a minute, virtually soundlessly and kill from a distance of 500 yards. The arrows don't have feathers; instead, horn fins shaped as spirals ensure precision.

AS   brief mentions: mechanics of, fins 12; poised to fire at Will 13

FIRE BOMBING

World: Lyra's

Role: The Imperial Navy invented a fire bombing technique ("naphtha blended with potash, which ignites when it touches water") that the Imperial Guard of Muscovy uses to force Lee Scoresby and Stanislaus Grumman out of the dense forest cover of Cittàgazze.

Observation: *Although Grumman had summoned storms the night before this attack, rain could not inhibit the effectiveness of the Imperial Navy's weapon. This suggests a chemical composition similar to that of napalm, which also cannot be extinguished with water. Although napalm is associated with modern warfare, especially the Vietnam War, the ancient world had its own version, "Greek fire," which water couldn't touch. This was probably a mixture of petroleum distillate and resins or sulfur, much like what Grumman describes to Scoresby before they flee their very wet hiding place.*

SK   14 [brief]

FIRE-HURLERS

World: Lyra's

Role: Fire-hurlers are one of few, if not the only, weapons armoured bears rely on beside their own physical attributes.

The hurlers resemble catapults, and consist of two main parts: a long arm at the end of which is a three-foot wide receptacle and an iron tank of fiery sulphur rock. The bears load the incendiary (sulphur rock) into the hurler and those holding the arm's end let go, sending the flaming material toward its target.

The fire-hurlers prove an effective defense against armed zeppelins. The sulphurous rock penetrates the airship's silk bag, and when the sulphur combines with the hydrogen, the zeppelin explodes. The bears take a fire-hurler with them on their voyage to the Himalayas. The kingdom of heaven's forces use a flame-thrower, and the Tartar guards at Bolvangar have a fire-thrower; how these compare to the armoured bears' weapon isn't clear.

NL/GC Raknison's bears' 19; Iorek's bears use against witches, Coulter's Tartars' zeppelin 22
       brief mentions: of Tartars' at Bolvangar 12, Iorek's bears' on way to Asriel 21

AS   bears use against hostile Siberians 8; of troops fighting for kingdom (flame-throwers) 29 *[brief]*

INTENTION CRAFT

World: Lyra's

Role: Mrs Coulter flies an intention craft she has stolen

Artist's rendition of an Intention Craft

Melissa Rogers

from Asriel's armoury to the headquarters of the Consistorial Court of Discipline in Geneva; Asriel uses another to rescue Coulter from its clutches; and Coulter takes one to reach Metatron's Clouded Mountain.

Its name is based on the source of its power: the pilot's intentions. Only humans with dæmons can operate the craft, because a dæmon must hold one end of a handle attached to a helmet worn by the human. The current flowing between them is amplified, and that powers the machine.

Lord Asriel pilots one to show his high commanders the intention craft's efficacy in destroying single-handedly a raiding party of fliers, including a gyrocopter, two planes, a huge bird with two armed crew members, and several angels.

Chapter 16 of THE AMBER SPYGLASS is titled "The Intention Craft."

AS described, demonstrated, stolen 16; Coulter flies to Geneva 24; Asriel flies to rescue Coulter in Alps 25; Coulter flies to Clouded Mountain 30
brief mentions: Asriel and Coulter return in to fortress 28, Lyra and Will see over battleground 29

MACHINE-GUNS/MACHINE-RIFLES ❖

World: Lyra's

Role: Variously referred to as machine-guns and machine-rifles, these weapons are mounted to the gondola of the zeppelin that transports Mrs Coulter and a squadron of Tartar troops to Svalbard.

NL/GC alethiometer warns of 20 [brief]; used against Iorek's bears 22

PISTOLS ❖ ⚕ ✎ ⑩

World: Lyra's, Cittàgazze

Role: The Trollesund officials rapidly abandon their pursuit of Iorek Byrnison when they find Lee Scoresby guarding the bear's armour with "the longest pistol Lyra had ever seen." Much later, on Nova Zembla, Lee uses this pistol in self-defense when the Magisterium's censor shoots arrows at him.

Mechanics and Operation of the Intention Craft

The intention craft stands on "six legs, each jointed and sprung at a different angle to the body," which appears to be "a mass of pipe work, cylinders, pistons, coiled cables, switchgear and valves and gauge"; a "glass canopy" covers the cabin. [72] While the cockpit seems designed for a single pilot, it is large enough to hold two people and a large dæmon, since Asriel and Stelmaria are able to fit Coulter inside when Asriel rescues her. Gyropter-type controls are in the cockpit "for the sake of familiarity," but theoretically wouldn't be needed by an experienced pilot. For others, [73] like Mrs Coulter, they are used to direct the craft to launch and move forward or, perhaps, to focus her attention (and intention) on the movement.

It apparently needs no period of gradual acceleration for take-off. When it leaves the ground, the craft hovers with "no sound of an engine, no hint of how it was held against gravity." Even when Lord Asriel and [74] Stelmaria dash out of it to rescue Mrs Coulter in the Alps, the unmanned craft stays level and it is also unaffected by air turbulence from other crafts, like the gyrocopter decoys, or thunderstorms. In addition to its silence, the warcraft also has the advantage of requiring no illumination (although it is equipped with landing lights) while firing multiple shells at as many targets in rapid succession or dropping tear-gas bombs. The craft can intercept and neutralize enemy fire, and is [75] unharmed by the ball of fire that was once the Consistorial Court of Discipline's zeppelin.

*Pistol, 44 Hopkins & Allen
pistol, 1873 model*

The nasty boy in the striped tee-shirt, leading a mob of rampaging kids after Lyra and Will in Cittàgazze, is armed with a pistol.

Sir Charles Latrom comes after Lyra and Will with a pistol the night that Will reclaims the alethiometer. It is next seen in the hands of his murderer, Mrs Coulter, aiming it at Will when the Gallivespians intervene. When Tialys stings her, Coulter drops the pistol; Will grabs it, and within minutes is forced to shoot a Swiss Guardsman who is about to fire on him with a crossbow.

76 In the adamant tower, just before Asriel hears that Lyra's and Will's dæmons have been seen, Mrs Coulter reaches for a pistol. Asriel is gone before she acts. Whether she had murder, suicide, or murder-suicide in mind will remain unknown.

Observation: *The gun with which Scoresby shoots the Skraeling is also referred to as a revolver.*

Update: A pistol is the subject of the woodcut for chapter 28, "Midnight," in the **10**ᴛʜ anniversary edition of The Amber Spyglass.

NL/GC Police's, Lee Scoresby's in Trollesund 11; Lee's used against cliff-ghast 18 *[brief]*

SK Lee uses in self-defense on Nova Zembla 6; Latrom pursues Will with 9; Spectre-orphans threaten Lyra and Will with 11

AS Coulter's in Himalayas 1; Coulter aims at Will 12, but drops when stung, Will retrieves, uses against Swiss Guard 13
      brief mentions: Siberian villagers' 8; Coulter's in Adamant Tower 28

RESONATING CHAMBER 🖉

World: Lyra's

Role: A critical component of the bomb intended for Lyra is its resonating chamber. This device analyses a sample of its target's "genetic particles"—in this case a lock of Lyra's hair— and encodes its unique signature "in a series of anbaric pulses." Those are then
77 relayed to the bomb's aiming device, which, in turn, directs the bomb to the intended victim. The process of encoding and directing the aiming device must, it seems, be accomplished just before or during detonation.

This mechanism was developed by Dr Cooper, formerly of the General Oblation Board's Bolvangar Experiment Station.

AS purpose, operation of 24; Roke and golden monkey attempt to retrieve hair from 25

RIFLES ✦♩🖉

World: Lyra's, Will's, Cittàgazze, Mulefa's

Role: Rifles are common among villagers throughout the North of Lyra's world, from the Trollesund townsmen to the Siberian Tartars with whom Stanislaus Grumman lives. They are also a common military weapon, used by the Imperial Muscovite troops, Tartar guards, and those in service of the Magisterium. The priest assassin Fr. Gomez's weapon of choice is a rifle.

Those armed with rifles will lay their weapon on the ground before approaching a stranger, as a sign of peaceful intent. [*See also* **Machine-guns, Winchester**]

Observation: *Surprisingly, Fr Gomez's rifle draws no notice in Will's world as he seeks the trail of Mary Malone.*

NL/GC Lyra and Iorek confront villagers armed with 12; in battle at Bolvangar 17
> *brief mentions:* Tartars', Trollesund police's 11; gyptians use against Samoyed attackers 14

SK *brief mentions:* fired at Serafina on boat near Svalbard, Thorold's 2; Lorenz's 6; Scoresby's, Magisterium's soldiers 10; Spectre-orphans' 11

AS Court's soldiers' at bomb launch 25; Gomez uses against tualapi 27; of soldiers fighting for kingdom, useless against Spectres 29; Gomez prepares to use against Lyra 35
> *brief mentions:* Siberian villagers' 8; of armies in Himalayas 12; Gomez's 20, 34, 36

A.F. Randall, Wilcox, A.T., Library of Congress, LC-USZ62-36613, c1886

Famous Indian Chief Geronimo with a rifle

SPEARS

World: Lyra's, kingdom of heaven (Clouded Mountain)
Role: Metatron hurls a spear at Will, but just before it reaches him, Will is able to close the window to the world where Baruch, Balthamos, and he have fled. When Mrs Coulter reaches the Clouded Mountain, she must talk her way past a Watcher armed with a spear.

Observation: *Spears are used metaphorically at critical moments in* HIS DARK MATERIALS, *but as weapons are used only by angels. When Lyra encounters Asriel in the Retiring Room, she "felt the force of his glance almost as if it had physical form, as if it were an arrow or a spear" and at Sir Charles Latrom's home, being* [78] *the target of the golden monkey's "concentrated malevolence" makes Will feel as if he has been struck by a spear. When Asriel* [79] *severs Roger from his dæmon and uses that energy to break through to the world of Cittàgazze "the vault of heaven, star-studded, profound, was suddenly pierced as if by a spear."* [80]

SK on Tower of Angel's walls 8 *[brief]*

Raphael Sanzio

"St. Michael Vanquishing Satan"

AS *brief mentions:* Metatron's 2, of angels fighting for kingdom 29, Metatron's guards' 30

SPY-FLIES

World: Lyra's
Role: The gyptians have nearly left England when two mechanical insects attack Pan, driving relentlessly and painfully into his seagull form. One fly is stunned by the tillerman's dæmon and captured, but the other escapes. They are presumed to have been sent by Mrs Coulter.

The six-legged spy-flies have claws, are "about as long as Lyra's thumb," and although they appear black are actually "dark green." Their movement is comparable to that of [81] "flying beetles, heavy and direct, and with a droning sound." Farder Coram tells Lyra that [82] these "Afric things" are "deadly dangerous" but not alive: "There's a clockwork running in there, and pinned to the spring of it, there's a bad spirit with a spell through its heart." Because of this evil spirit, its clockwork never runs down. Instead, "the more he struggles, the tighter it's wound." Moreover, Coram adds, the spy-fly can never be vanquished. Even if it were sealed in a container then dropped into the ocean, it would eventually get out and go after its prey.

Coram temporarily stores the captured spy-fly in a smokeleaf tin, and at Lyra's request, Iorek Byrnison seals the tin in another case, about the size and shape of the alethiometer's, thus muting its noise. Lyra has it in her coat pocket when she is taken to the General Oblation Board's Bolvangar Experiment Station. There, thinking she at last has the alethiometer, Coulter pries the spy-fly case apart, and is attacked by her own weapon.

Monroe S. Tarver

Artist's rendition of a Spy Fly

Facts: *In Will's world, researchers are presently developing robotic, micromechanical flying insects for surveillance and reconnaissance.*

NL/GC attack Pan, Coram on 9; Iorek constructs case for 13; Lyra hides case in boot 14; Coulter releases, attacked by 17

AS tin recalled 13 *[brief]*

Swords ✦ ⚕ ✎

Worlds: Lyra's, Cittàgazze, kingdom of heaven (Clouded Mountain)

Role: Swords only appear in the hands of angels guarding the Clouded Mountain, but Joachim Lorenz reports hearing the clanging of swords in the sky. Will thinks he hears a similar sound as he descends the mountain in Cittàgazze after his father's death. Lyra fantasizes a duel between her father and Edward Coulter involving swords, and, frustrated in her attempt to fence with Iorek Byrnison, wishes she had a sword instead of a stick. Will uses the subtle knife to cut two sword-sized pieces from the iron railings so Lyra and he can defend themselves against the raging mob of Spectre orphans at the belvedere.

NL/GC brief mentions: Asriel's in Lyra's daydream 8; Lyra uses a stick instead of in duel with Iorek 13

SK brief mentions: sound of angels' above Cittàgazze 6, on Tower of Angel's walls 8, Will and Lyra use belvedere's railing as 11, above Will in Cittàgazze 15 *[implied]*

AS of angels fighting for kingdom 29 *[brief]*

PT

Weapons, other ✦ ⚕ ✎

Worlds: Lyra's, Asriel's

Role: There are some other interesting weapons that get brief mentions:

The hostile villagers who won't sell coal to armoured bears aim a large gun that takes several men to manage at Iorek Byrnison's charter boat. Other large weapons called "poison-spraying" cannons are used by the kingdom's forces.

The people on horses who so closely resemble their steeds wield scimitars and tridents, as well as throwing nets of fibers as strong as steel. Lyra was saved from the throwing nets of Turk traders in the streets of London by Tony Costa.

The battle between the republic and kingdom of heaven is a confusion of bursting rockets, exploding shells, rapid gunfire and flares. The witches hurl flaming pitch-pine torches at the angelic forces of the kingdom.

Witches carry small knives in their belts. Serafina Pekkala uses hers to end a tortured witch's suffering. The witch working for Fr MacPhail attacks Mrs Coulter with a knife, and Juta Kamainen stabs herself after shooting an arrow into John Parry's heart.

An atomic bomb is never used in *His Dark Materials*, but Dr Cooper, who creates a bomb for the Consistorial Court of Discipline, is familiar with the mechanics of atomic explosions and atomic bomb design.

Facts: *Scimitars are swords with curved blades; tridents are spears with three prongs.*

NL/GC throwing nets 6
    brief mentions: Edward Coulter's gun 8, Tartars' cannons 12

SK Serafina's small knife 2, and Juta's 15

AS rockets, "poison-spraying" cannons, flying machines, witches' torches 29; scimitars, tridents, throwing nets, flares 31
    brief mentions: atomic explosion 6, villagers' large gun 8, atomic bomb 24, witch's knife 25

WINCHESTER RIFLE

Role: His loaded Winchester rifle is among the few things Lee Scoresby takes with him when he leaves his balloon for the last time. He uses it to defend his position in the Cittàgazze mountains and to take out a troop of Imperial Guards and their zeppelin.

Facts: *The Winchester rifle is an icon of the American West. Oliver Winchester of New England entered the firearms business in 1857. His gun mechanic, Benjamin Tyler Henry, invented a 15-cartridge magazine soon after which had a repeating action mechanism. Moving the trigger down then back to its original position extracted the spent cartridge, loaded a fresh shell, and cocked the hammer, making the gun ready for firing again. The 1873 Winchester rifle was the company's most successful; over 700,000 were sold from roughly 1873 -1913.*

Observation: *Scoresby's rifle is called a Winchester by name only once. However, clearly throughout the siege of Alamo Gulch, he is using just the one weapon.*

SK 14

H. R. Locke, Library of Congress, LC-US262-50004, c1895

"Calamity Jane," seated with rifle as General Crook's scout

85

Applied Sciences and Technology:
Other Crafted Goods and Materials
Cauchuc to Teflon

ALCHEMY [*See chapter on* **The Natural Sciences: Scientific Studies**]

ATOMCRAFT [*See chapter on* **The Natural Sciences: Scientific Studies**]

CAUCHUC-COVERED CABLE ✦
World: Lyra's
Role: Large spools of this cable await shipment on the London wharves where Lyra, looking for shelter, is nearly captured by Turk net throwers.
Facts: Cauchuc *is an obsolete Spanish word for rubber.*
NL/GC 6 [brief]

DÆMON-COIN ✦
World: Lyra's
Role: Lyra and Roger find what they name "dæmon-coins" while playing in the crypts at Jordan College. Placed at the base of the Scholars' skulls resting on shelves, each "little disc of bronze" features a "crudely engraved inscription" designating the deceased Scholar's dæmon. Although less elaborate, the coins are comparable to the plaques on the Masters' coffins that bear their dæmons' likenesses.

As a joke Lyra switches out the dæmon-coins of several skulls, but a midnight visit from night-ghasts sends her back to the crypts to straighten things out.

To honor the memory of Gobbler victim Tony Makarios' dæmon, Ratter, from whom the boy had been cruelly severed, Lyra makes a dæmon-coin out of an ordinary gold coin. She places this into Tony's corpse's mouth before he is carried to his funeral pyre.
NL/GC in the crypt 3; switching of recalled 12 [brief]; Lyra devises one for Tony 13

FIRE-MINES ✦
World: Lyra's
Role: These mines on the island of Svalbard are where the bearsmiths turn sheets of sky iron into armour. While the creation of armour seems to be skilled labor, the conditions in the mines must be undesirable. One of the murals adorning Iofur Raknison's palace depicts enslaved Tartars working the mines, possibly a bear-fantasy. Raknison, moreover, was said to want to bring human engineers to Svalbard to expand and modernize the kingdom's fire-mines.
NL/GC armoury for Svalbard's bears 13
   brief mentions: proposed as possible destination for Gobbler victims 6, Raknison's plans for 18, murals depicting 19; 20, 21

HADFIELD PROCESS ⑩

World: Lyra's

Role: This process is alluded to in Lord Asriel's papers in the appendix to the **10TH** anniversary edition of *NORTHERN LIGHTS*. Apparently, it was an attempt to make an alloy of manganese, silicon, and carbon at a smelting operation in Sheffield. Asriel's notes reveal he thinks that titanium and manganese might be a better choice for the two principal elements, and the alloy he eventually made that was employed in the silver guillotine suggests he was right.

Facts: *Hadfield in Will's world is a small town located between Manchester and Sheffield, England.*

10TH: *NL* appendix

LACQUER/SAP, SAP-LACQUER ✐ Ⓛⓢ

World: Mulefa's

Role: In the context of *HIS DARK MATERIALS*, what is deemed lacquer is a varnish prepared by the mulefa from a sap harvested from trees. It is boiled and dissolved in alcohol until it is light amber with the consistency of milk. The lacquer can be made opaque by introducing oxides, but when left in its natural state of transparency, it refracts light rays.

Hoping that this visual effect could help her somehow to see sraf, Mary Malone paints dozens of layers of lacquer onto a strip of thin wood until she makes a surface nearly a quarter-inch thick. The resulting sheets will form the basis of Mary's amber spyglass.

"Oil and Lacquer" is the title of chapter 17 of *THE AMBER SPYGLASS*.

AS role of, process of using to make lenses 17; as material for vials holding seeds 38 *[brief]*; Ⓛⓢ Lantern Slide 5

Sap-lacquer *brief mentions:* lenses 20, bushes 35

PHILOSOPHICAL APPARATUS/ PHILOSOPHICAL INSTRUMENTS ❖ ⑩

World: Lyra's

Role: The Concilium, the body overseeing the financial affairs of Jordan College, assigns a high priority to purchasing equipment of this type for use in the College's chapel, possibly by experimental theologians.

Lyra recognizes examples of these "aerials, wires, porcelain insulators" in the slides accompanying Lord Asriel's report on Dust to the Scholars. The witch's dæmon Kaisa uses the term to describe what has been amassed by the Dust-hunters at the General Oblation Board's Bolvangar Experiment Station.

Updates: The appendix of the **10TH** anniversary edition of *NORTHERN LIGHTS* includes a sketch plan of a sledge loaded with "philosophical instruments" that Asriel would use on Svalbard to sever Roger and break out of his world.

NL/GC brief mentions: in Asriel's photograms 2, at Jordan College 3, at Bolvangar 11

10TH: *NL* appendix

PHOTO-MILL ❖

World: Lyra's

"Then it became clear: a little thing like a weathervane, with four sails black on one side and white on the other, that began to whirl around as the light struck it. It illustrated a moral lesson, the Intercessor explained, for the black of ignorance fled from the light, whereas the wisdom of white rushed to embrace it."

Photo-mill aka Radiometer

Role: Lyra's world term for radiometer. At Gabriel College's Oratory, it is kept on the high altar, covered in black velvet, and is considered "a very holy object" which illustrates a "moral lesson." Pan and Lyra think that if elementary particles move its four sails, perhaps they also move the alethiometer's needles.

NL/GC brief mentions: described, Lyra and Pan discuss 9; Lyra recalls 18

89

Swiss Army Knife

World: Will's (and brought to the mulefa's)

Victorinox Swiss Army Knife

Role: One of the few things Mary Malone took when she left for worlds unknown was a Swiss Army knife. It proves especially valuable in the mulefa's world, and fascinating to her new friends since the mulefa use metal only to fashion simple jewelry.

Her knife is indispensable in Mary's construction of the amber spyglass. She uses it to cut the hardened layers of lacquer into lenses. The knife is useful as well for fashioning arrows.

Facts: *Swiss Army knives range from simple two-blade versions to ones featuring 29 different tools. The Swiss Army knife originally produced in 1897 had a blade, screwdriver, can opener, and punch. Unlike today's knives, the originals had wooden handles. Two companies in Switzerland are under contract to produce the knives for the Swiss Army, but most of them are exported for sale.*

AS used to make lenses 17; and arrows 20 *[brief]*

Teflon

World: Will's, Mulefa's

Role: Mary Malone compares the smoothness of the claws of her mulefa friend Atal (which fit perfectly into an equally smooth hole on the seedpods that form the mulefa's wheels) to the texture of this chemical coating used in her world.

AS 17 *[brief]*

> Teflon is the trademark name registered by the DuPont Company for polytetrafluoroethylene, a polymer discovered accidentally by Dr. Roy Plunkett in 1938 during attempts to synthesize different forms of another of DuPont's discoveries, Freon (used in refrigerators and air conditioners). Teflon is of the largest known molecules. Even in a solid state it resembles a lubricant, and it has a melting point of 327° C or about 620° F.
>
> Used in military and industrial applications as early as the 1940s, in the 1960s the introduction of Teflon-coated pots and pans revolutionized home cooking, and made Teflon a household word synonymous with non-stick.

THE NATURAL SCIENCES

Physical Sciences
Anbaric to Weather disturbances

ANBARIC ✧ ⚷ ✎

World: Lyra's

Role: When Lyra points at streetlights in an effort to define *anbaric*, Will replies, "we call them electric." Among the means of generating anbaric power are hydro-anbaric power plants like that of Saint-Jean-Les-Eaux in the Alps near Geneva. In remote spots, such as the General Oblation Board's Bolvangar Experiment Station, imported coal spirit is used. [1]

In Lyra's world, anbaric lights have largely replaced naphtha for illumination, but oil lamps are still used much more frequently in her world than in Will's. Examples of sites lit anbarically are Coulter's London house, Bolvangar's buildings and grounds, the Consistorial Court's basement interrogation chambers, zeppelins' floodlights and cabin lights, ship decks, and, feebly, the streets in the suburbs of the world of the dead. Handheld sources of this type of light are called *anbaric lanterns*, likely the flashlights of Will's world.

Anbaric power is also used by tramcars in Lyra's London, underground conveyances at the basalt fortress, the silver guillotine, the fence surrounding Bolvangar, and (for unstated purposes) in the basement interrogation rooms of the Consistorial Court of Discipline's headquarters. The natural anbaric power of the Aurora, in combination with the energy released through intercision, is used by Lord Asriel to tear open the sky and create a passage out of his world to the one he's glimpsed beyond the Aurora.

Anbaric is also used metaphorically to indicate shock or alarm—for example, the panic Lyra feels when forced into the silver guillotine's mesh cage and the power she senses in armoured bear Iorek Byrnison as he prepares to fight to the death his rival Iofur Raknison for the kingdom of the bears. When Will's perceptions are involved, *electric* is similarly used; he feels "electric" with fear watching Lyra fall into the abyss and as if he has had an electric shock when he realizes his potential for visiting any number of worlds as the bearer of the subtle knife. The air to Will seems charged with electricity by the intensity of Lyra's and Pan's emotions when she leaves him to enter the world of the dead.

Another metaphorical use of *electric* has to do with cellular biology; the whispers among the ghosts of Roger's name as they seek to help Lyra find her friend are compared to the "electric message" that one cell in the body passes on to the next. [2]

Observation: *The narrative voice of the US edition of* THE AMBER SPYGLASS *(e.g. 255, 265) seems to favor Lyra's world's vocabulary, choosing* anbaric, *rather than* electric, *to describe lighting along the streets in the suburbs of the world of the dead; however, in the UK edition (e.g. 270, 279), Will's world's* electric *appears in these passages. But both use* naphtha *rather than* oil *to describe the fuel illuminating the home where the travelers spend the night (AS e.g. 273/258). Also, the US edition describes Mary Malone's lab equipment as "anbaric" (SK*

90) in contrast to the "electronic" equipment of the UK edition (SK 94).
   [*See also* **Anbaric Park (Places)**]

Current, force, forge

NL/GC inside Bolvangar 15, 16
      brief mentions: Anbaric Park 2, tramcars 6, Bolvangar's fence 11, by Scoresby 18, of Aurora 23

AS *brief mentions:* 6; basalt fortress 15, 16; 21, 24, 25, 30

US only: *SK* 4 *[brief]*

Lights

NL/GC at Bolvangar 14, 15, 17
      brief mentions: uses at Jordan 1, Coulter's 4; 5, 6; in Trollesund and on ship's deck 11, Scoresby's lantern 18, at Asriel's 21

SK *brief mentions:* 2, Will calls electric 3

AS *brief mentions:* 13, 16, 21, 30

US only: *AS* suburbs of world of dead 18

In metaphors: Anbaric

Force: *NL/GC* Coulter's temper 5, Lyra's panic 16, Iorek's power 20

Light: *NL/GC* Aurora's 23

In metaphors: Electric

AS Will with knife 2, Pan and Lyra's separation 21, communication of ghosts 22, Will's panic 26

Anbaromagnetism/Anbaromagnetic charges ✤ ⚕

World: Lyra's

Role: A specialization within experimental theology in Lyra's world that Will equates with electromagnetism.

   Having learned a smattering of "experimental theology" at Jordan College, Lyra tries to persuade gyptian leader John Faa that she would be an asset on the voyage North because she could "take anbaromagnetic readings off the Aurora."

NL/GC brief mentions: 5, 8

SK 3 *[brief]*

Astronomy [*See* **Celestial geography**]

Atomcraft [*See* **Scientific Studies**]

Philip Pullman on Anbaric, Amber, and Electric

In an interview for Textualities, an on-line literary magazine, Pullman elaborates on one of the first conversations between Will and Lyra:

"Anbaric is actually from Arabic—the word 'anbar' is the root of our word 'amber.' In the beginning of THE SUBTLE KNIFE— which is set in 'our' world—when Lyra meets Will for the first time she refers to street lights as 'anbaric lights.' Will says, 'No, they are electric lights;' to Lyra 'electric' is the tawny stuff that you get out of trees, which he calls 'amber;' then the difference of terminology dawns on them, they realise that the connection between their worlds meshes here in the form of language. Incidentally, the word amber foreshadows its important role in the third book in the trilogy..."

AURORA ✤ ⚕ ⑩

World: Lyra's

Role: Brighter than moonlight, the shimmering light green and rosy curtains, arcs, and loops of the Aurora appear at once to descend from Heaven and end in streaks of red suggesting the flames of Hell. The lights are accompanied by the faint music of "a vast distant whispering swish," a music that witch Serafina Pekkala says she can feel. "Faint trails" of light remain as the display diminishes. In aëronaut Lee Scoresby's balloon, Lyra has the sensation she is surrounded by the Aurora's "cascades of luminescent glory" and that she and her companions are "nearly part of it."

Lord Asriel understands the physical factors that account for the phenomena and

Aurora Folklore

The Aurora has inspired a number of legends and myths of Arctic peoples. In one of the myths Ernest W. Hawkes includes in *The Labrador Eskimo* (1916), the earth is said to be covered by a dome with a hole at its top through which the spirits of those who have died voluntarily ascend to the heavens. When new arrivals make the passage, these spirits light torches to guide the way, and the dancing flames of these torches are seen below as the Aurora. Sounds that reportedly accompany the Aurora occur when these spirits deliver messages to the living. The Labrador Eskimos also believe that at the ends of the earth's lands and oceans lies a great abyss beyond which are the heavens. A narrow bridge links these regions to the land of the living. Newfoundland and Labrador is a province of Canada located on the country's northeastern coast; Newfoundland, an island, and Labrador, a mainland peninsula, are southwest of Greenland.

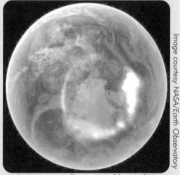

Image courtesy NASA/Earth Observatory

Aurora australis captured by NASA's IMAGE satellite and overlaid onto Blue Marble satellite photo, September 11, 2005

The Fox people, who lived in the region of Wisconsin, a northern state in the middle of the US, believed the Aurora brought warnings of war or destruction. The lights were thought to be the spirits of their enemies seeking vengeance.

East Greenland Eskimos, in contrast, saw in the Aurora's moving curtains of lights the spirits of their children who died at birth or in infancy, now dancing in the heavens.

The Eastern Canadian Salteaus people and the Kwakiutl and Tlingit of Southeastern Alaska also believed dancing human spirits created the Aurora's display, while Eskimos of the lower Yukon River region of western Canada saw the Aurora as a dance of animal spirits. A variation on the myth is that the Aurora is seen when the spirits play ball with an animal skull; Nunivak Island Eskimos, however, reversed the players, and one of their myths says that walrus spirits toss human skulls in play on nights when the Aurora is active.

In European Arctic regions, the mythologies associated with the Aurora are similarly varied. Danish folklore offers the whimsical account of the Aurora as occurring when swans that flew too far north and are trapped in an icy sky flap their wings, trying to get free. Scottish legends called the lights the "merry dancers," and legends from Norway and in the Viking era also associated the movement of the lights with a dance.

In contrast, other Nordic legends said that when the Aurora's lights resembled red flames, it was a sign the gods were angry. In medieval times the displays were feared as forecasting war and even causing other disasters.

explains it to his less informed colleagues at Jordan College: "It's composed of storms of charged particles and solar rays of intense and extraordinary strength—invisible in themselves, but causing this luminous radiation when they interact with the atmosphere." A theory Asriel doesn't propose to his fellow Jordan College Scholars is one he has heard from the witches, who believe that there is a relationship between heightened sunspot activity and the Aurora.

Serafina Pekkala's snow goose dæmon,

Aurora borealis in Alaska

NOAA Photo Library, Historic NWS Collection

Kaisa, who first appears flying across its fluttering curtains of light, says that these charged particles "have the property of making the matter of this world thin," thereby occasionally allowing us a glimpse of other worlds. Lyra seems to have some vague awareness of the physics behind the phenomena; she suggests, incredibly, that she'd be useful to the gyptians on the journey North because she'd be able to "take anbaromagnetic readings off the Aurora."

The Aurora is also associated with Dust and the alethiometer. Lyra speculates that the force that makes it glow could be the same as that which moves the hands of the alethiometer: Dust. Watching it for the first time, she falls into the same sort of trance she enters when reading her golden compass. The night Roger is severed on Svalbard, Lyra sees a fantastic display of the northern lights as "unseen billions and trillions of charged particles and possibly, she thought, of Dust, conjured a radiating glow out of the upper

Aurora Facts

An easily understood account of the Aurora is found at the Nordlys website developed by Professor Alv Egeland, University of Oslo, and Trond Abrahamsen, Andøya Rocket Range. This site also has an on-line movie that shows what is meant by references to the movement, so often likened to a dance, of the Aurora.

Basically, solar winds bring charged particles from the sun that are attracted to the earth's magnetic poles, where they are stopped by the earth's ionosphere (upper level of the atmosphere). When the solar particles collide with molecules of the different atmospheric gases, the collisions produce energy seen as light, and the lights' colors vary according to the gas the solar particles hit. High-altitude oxygen causes all-red Auroras, while lower level oxygen produces the yellow-greens (the most common color). Nitrogen accounts for the blues, but in a neutral state, nitrogen molecules colliding with solar particles glow red; together they produce the reddish-purple light often seen at the edges of the Aurora.

When solar winds reach the earth's magnetic field, tremendous amounts of electrical power are generated along with the Aurora's light display; these can interfere with radio and television signals, and satellite communications.

Daily forecasts of Auroral activity are provided by the University of Alaska-Fairbanks' Geophysical Institute (www.gi.alaska.edu/) where you can sign up for e-mail alerts that are posted when increased Auroral activity is predicted.

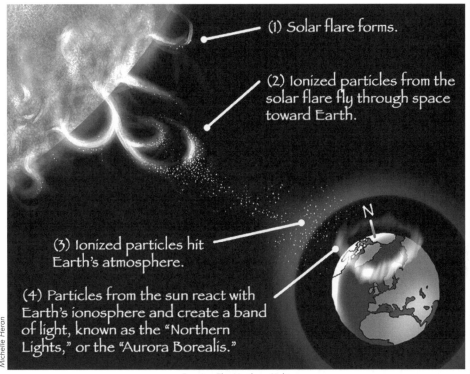

(1) Solar flare forms.

(2) Ionized particles from the solar flare fly through space toward Earth.

(3) Ionized particles hit Earth's atmosphere.

(4) Particles from the sun react with Earth's ionosphere and create a band of light, known as the "Northern Lights," or the "Aurora Borealis."

N

Michelle Heran

Forming The Northern Lights

atmosphere." Later in Will's Oxford, Lyra is reminded of the Aurora as she watches the swirling, recombining patterns of the Shadow-particles on Dr Mary Malone's computer monitor, which, like the alethiometer, proves a means of communicating with Dust. [11]

Asriel's notion of the relationship of the two is more literal; he believes that Dust comes from a city in another universe hidden behind the Aurora—through it to us. But what is most compelling to Lord Asriel and threatening to the Magisterium is what is visible beyond its streaming lights—another world. The first time she witnesses it, Lyra too thinks that beyond the Aurora she can see "the image of a city ... a whole universe away," the same city [12] that she heard Asriel describe at Jordan College in the opening scene of *HIS DARK MATERIALS* and where she will meet Will Parry: Cittàgazze. This idea, that beyond the lights is the source of Dust, provides another dimension to Kaisa's claim that what scares the Dust-hunters, or the Magisterium, is that Asriel intends to bridge his world and the one he has seen beyond the Aurora.

But Lord Asriel and Lyra are not the only ones drawn to the Aurora. The lights were the focus of the research conducted by the physicist accompanying the Oxford University Institute of Archaeology's survey in Alaska from which three men, including John Parry and the physicist, disappeared in 1985. In Parry's new life in Lyra's world as shaman and scientist Stanislaus Grumman, he engaged in his own investigations of the

NASA, Space Shuttle Discovery STS-39 mission (April, 1991)

Aurora Australis, Spiked and Sinuous Red and Green Airglow

13

phenomena, for which he was widely known to have had "a passion." Even Mrs Coulter claims to have spent time studying the Aurora in Greenland.

The photograms Lord Asriel shows the Jordan College Scholars in the first chapter of NORTHERN LIGHTS / THE GOLDEN COMPASS introduce several questions directing the movement of the story: what is the source of the Dust that gathers around a man but not a child? Has Asriel's photogram of the Aurora proven correct the Barnard-Stokes hypothesis that there are other worlds and does Asriel intend on his next expedition to try to enter one of these worlds? The Magisterium's fear that he will do just that leads to his imprisonment on Svalbard, an ideal location as it turns out for his endeavor, and Lyra's desire to rescue him leads her to bring Asriel the last element he needs: a child to sever.

> The auroras that occur in the southern hemisphere (south pole) are called *aurora australis*, or *southern lights*. Conversely, those in the northern hemisphere (north pole) are called *aurora borealis* or *northern lights*.

Observation: *There is no mention of the Aurora (or Northern Lights) in* THE AMBER SPYGLASS. [*See also* **Northern Lights**]

NL/GC discussed in Retiring Room 2; at Coulter's 4 [brief], with gyptians 7, 8 [brief]; Lyra's first view of 11, Kaisa on 12; in Lapland 13, 17; Serafina on 18, in Svalbard 20, Asriel on 21, night of Roger's intercision 22, 23

SK compared to Shadows' display, Nelson's interest in 4; Grumman's interest in 6 [brief]

10TH: *NL* appendix

BIG BANG ⚰

World: Will's

Role: Mary Malone suggests to her co-investigator at the Dark Matter Research Institute that Shadow-particles date back to the Big Bang but have been capable of being amplified

United States Air Force photo by Senior Airman Joshua Strong, Jan 2005

The Aurora Borealis, or Northern Lights, shines above Bear Lake, Eielson Air Force Base, Alaska

or detected by life forms for only the last thirty to forty thousand years, when human brains evolved consciousness.

SK   12   *[brief]*

BITUMEN

World: Lyra's

Role: Fighting for Asriel's side against the kingdom of heaven, clans of witches go into battle with torches made of pine branches dipped in bitumen with which they set fire to the wings of angels. Rain does not put out these torches' flames.

Facts: *Bitumen is a highly flammable, petroleum-based, tar-like substance.*

AS   29   *[brief]*

BYANPLATS

World: Lyra's

Role: Surrounded by miles of marshlands, these islands of ground above sea level in Eastern Anglia, England, are the only areas in the Fens suitable for building permanent structures, for example, the gyptians' *zaal* or meeting hall.

NL/GC 7 *[brief]*

CELESTIAL GEOGRAPHY

World: Lyra's

Role: Mrs Coulter says she will instruct Lyra in this subject to prepare the girl to serve as her personal assistant during an expedition north.

Observation: *Linked with mathematics and navigation as the third element in a series in this passage, it may be safe to assume that in our world* celestial geography *is astronomy.*

NL/GC 4 *[brief]*

COAL-SPIRIT

World: Lyra's

Role: Used as fuel; this natural resource's availability in the far North may be a cause of the Tartars and others' reputed incursions into Siberia.

Coal-spirit is apparently expensive to transport into the interior of Lapland; thus, witch Serafina Pekkala's dæmon, Kaisa, cites the use of imported coal-spirit at the Bolvangar Experiment Station as evidence of the Dust-hunters' wealth.

Lyra sees it stored in barrels and tanks for shipment from ports in Colby and London, respectively.

NL/GC brief mentions: 6, 9, 11, 13

COPPER

World: Mulefa's

Role: Unlike in Will's world, copper is not mined by the mulefa; rather it is gathered from their riverbanks' sand. Metals are not used by the mulefa for toolmaking but for jewelry, like copper wedding rings for their horns.

Facts: *Generally, copper is mined. However, in North America, early Native Americans collected copper in the streambeds of Lake Superior in the US states of Michigan and Wisconsin. Copper is a soft metal, and as such is easily worked into rings or beads.*

AS 17 *[brief]*

DARK MATTER ⚲

World: Will's

Role: When questioned by Lyra, Mary Malone explains her investigations into dark matter as looking not at the stars but for whatever causes universes "to hang together and not fly apart." She speculates it could be "some kind of elementary particle—something quite different from anything discovered so far," which she calls Shadow-particles and believes to be "particles of consciousness." Challenged by Lyra to use her specialized computer and its brain waves sensors to communicate with these Shadow-particles, Mary receives from them an affirmation to her query whether "dark matter is conscious."

[*See also* **Sraf, Dust (Philosophy, Psychology, Theology)**]

SK 4
    brief mentions: 7, 12

ELECTROMAGNETIC FIELDS/ELECTROMAGNETISM ⚲

World: Will's

Role: An original aspect of Dr Mary Malone's experimental design to investigate dark matter involves using electromagnetic fields to discriminate among elementary particles as a way to select those she wants to examine more carefully. More commonly, particle physicists place their detectors in underground laboratories as a means of screening out the noise, or unwanted particles, from those they seek.

In Lyra's world, the equivalent term is *anbaromagnetism*.

SK   brief mentions: 3, 4, 12

ELECTRONS ✦

World: Lyra's

Role: When Mrs Coulter tries to figure out what Lyra has learned from Jordan College's harried Scholars about the basic elements of experimental theology, Lyra pipes up that she knows all about these "negatively charged particles," which are "sort of like Dust." Coulter's tension during this exchange is readily apparent to Lyra, who learns that Dust is something she best not express interest in when Coulter is around.

Observation: *In Lyra's world, these are not to be confused with* electrum *[see below], which is amber.*

NL/GC brief mentions: 5, 21

ELECTRUM ⚲

World: Lyra's

Role: Amber, in Lyra's world. She is reminded of the word for this precious metal when she hears Will call those lights she says are *anbaric, electric.*

Facts: *The Greek word for amber,* electrum, *is the source of the English word* electron.

SK 3 *[brief]*

Dark Matter, Dark Energy, and Dust:
An Interview with Ray Villard

In her world, Mary Malone seeks invisible Shadow-particles in the lab of the Dark Matter Research Unit. In the mulefa's world, she sees them as sraf (Dust) in the sky. Her quest replicates what modern-day cosmologists and particle physicists both do in vastly different environments: study dark matter.

In our world, astronomers see a lot of cosmic dust in their observations of our Universe. In fact, a telescope isn't needed to see it on a clear night—just look at the dark patches in the Milky Way. But, is this dust a particle of consciousness? The simple answer is no. But when you consider that we are ourselves, in a way, stardust, the answer seems not so simple.

And now there are new questions about dark matter that Mary Malone could not have even been asking in the mid-1990's...

To begin to make sense of the differences between the dust, dark matter, and dark energy in our universe, in contrast to the Dust in the world of Philip Pullman, I consulted a master communicator.

Ray Villard, a frequent contributor to *Sky and Telescope* and *Astronomy* magazines, is news chief at the Space Science Telescope Institute in Baltimore, MD where data from the Hubble telescope is processed. Every 97 minutes, Hubble completes an earth orbit, and each week adds 120 gigabytes of data to our knowledge of this universe. I talked to Mr Villard in July 2006 about dark matter, dark energy, and dust.

Dark energy is not mentioned in *His Dark Materials*. That's because dark energy was discovered as the result of observations made by the Hubble in 1999, which Mr Villard says is the greatest contribution of the Hubble's ongoing explorations.

LF: What is the difference between dark matter and dark energy, and what do they tell us about the universe?

RV: Years ago astronomers thought that dark matter was a type of normal matter that just couldn't be seen. But now we believe it's a different form of matter. It surrounds us, but it is not made up of any subatomic particles we know about. It doesn't react chemically with normal matter. But it releases gravity, and that is how we know it is there.

Imagine that you've never seen the ocean and on your first visit you arrive on a pitch black night. Still, you can see the white sails of boats bobbing along. You can't see the water, but something has to be there to enable these crafts to float. Now, dark matter has matter. It provides gravity. Dark energy, in contrast, doesn't rely on matter.

The Hubble has revealed that the universe is expanding and accelerating, and these are processes requiring energy. Space is not passive; it has its own energy – dark energy. Dark energy can thus be considered a repulsive force or an anti-gravity.

LF: Are cosmologists looking across the universe for the same thing that particle physicists are seeking in underground accelerators?

RV: Fundamentally, yes. Both are looking for the underpinnings of matter and energy.

LF: Parallel universes are central to *His Dark Materials*; what do we know about them?

RV: There is one rather bizarre hypothesis, not the dominant view, but an intriguing one. Of the four fundamental forces, gravity is the weakest. It may be that the gravity, considered evidence of dark matter, is instead leaking into our universe from parallel universes.

LF: How may parallel universes are we talking about?

RV: Parallel universes could be infinite.

LF: Have experiments been proposed to prove their existence?

RV: There is always going to be a problem here. You can't construct an experiment that will show something belongs to another universe because by definition, if we can see this evidence, it is in our universe.

Image courtesy NASA

Supernova 1994D in Galaxy NGC 4526

Still, it is tough to imagine this universe is the only one. Our universe percolated up out of true vacuum, and if this could happen once, why not more than once?

LF: What are we seeing in the Hubble's images that looks like dust?

RV: Cosmic dust is normal matter. When the universe began, there was no dust, but over the course of the past 13.7 billion years, it has gotten dustier and dustier.

Stars are factories for making heavier elements, and dust is the byproduct of fusion events. In the first three minutes of the universe, there was hydrogen, helium, and dark matter. All the other elements have been cooked up in the first stars. So dust is all around you. All the molecules that comprise life forms, all of you: same as those of dust.

Dust is a byproduct of fusion—and the raw material for making planets. The universe recycles everything.

LF: So dust accumulates, forms a planet, and gives rise to life, which dies and returns to dust?

RV: Dust to dust: an ongoing cycle on a galactic scale of birth, growth, death, rebirth, in the poetic sense. The universe reinvents itself.

LF: Nothing is lost?

RV: Can't go anywhere…Consider the universe as a fixed account. It isn't making more matter or more energy, but instead is just shifting funds between accounts of matter and energy.

LF: Will we ever reach the point where we aren't describing but explaining what we see?

RV: Hard to say we'll never know – likely we will, some day. Consider this: we've been watching gravity for quite some time, we know how it behaves, but we still don't know what it is. Our questions about dark matter and dark energy will no doubt be lingering ones as well.

Ray Villard's latest book, illustrated by Lynette R. Cook, is *Infinite Worlds: An Illustrated Voyage to Planets beyond Our Sun* (Univ. of California, 2005).

ELEMENTARY PARTICLES ✦ ⚜

World: Lyra's, Will's

Role: What defines a particle as elementary, according to Lord Asriel, is that "there's nothing inside them but themselves." These include electrons, photons, and neutrinos— | 18 and the type discovered by Rusakov and known as Dust in Lyra's world, and as Shadow-particles in Mary Malone's and Will's.

When he explains other worlds to Lyra, Asriel uses the analogy of flipping a coin. When it is in the air, it is equally possible that it will be heads as tails, yet once it lands heads up, "the possibility of its coming down tails has collapsed… But on another world, it does come down tails. And when that happens, the two worlds split apart. …In fact, these possibility collapses happen at the level of elementary particles…in just the same way: one moment several things are possible, the next moment only one happens, and the rest don't exist. Except that other worlds have sprung into being, on which they *did* happen." | 19

Observation: *Asriel's explanation of the possibility of other worlds resembles Everett's many worlds hypothesis* [*See* **Many-worlds hypothesis** *in* **Philosophy, Psychology, and Theology**].

NL/GC Asriel on 21

    brief mentions: Lyra's knowledge of 5, 7; and photo-mill 9, 18

SK   3 *[brief];* and Shadows 4

ENERGY BINDING BODY AND DÆMON ✦ ✐

World: Lyra's

Role: Lord Asriel tells Lyra that the General Oblation Board's experimental theologians neglected to notice while performing intercisions that "the energy that links body and dæmon is immensely powerful. When the cut is made, all that energy dissipates in a fraction of a second." He further tells her he plans to harness that energy to break | 20 through to the world beyond the Aurora.

The enormous release of energy accompanying the severing of person and dæmon has also come to the attention of the Consistorial Court of Discipline's president Father MacPhail. Suspecting scientists at Bolvangar may have noticed such a thing, MacPhail charges Dr Cooper, formerly a lead investigator in intercision at the Oblation Board's Bolvangar Experiment Station, with devising a means of using this energy burst to launch a bomb into another world that will locate and kill Lyra.

NL/GC Asriel on 21; Roger's intercision and 22, 23

AS   Cooper on 6; bomb and 25

EVOLUTION ⚜ ✐

World: Lyra's

Role: Physicist Mary Malone sees evolution as the process that accounts for a cut-off point prior to which Shadows cannot be detected around human skulls. Based on Lyra's alethiometer reading and her own lab's dating techniques, she places this point at 30,000 to 40,000 years ago. Malone theorizes that while Shadows have always existed, it wasn't until then that, through evolutionary change, the human brain began to be able to receive and even amplify the traces of their presence.

When she is able to question Shadow-particles, her assumption is validated in the sense that the Shadows confirm a change took place. But the change wasn't the result of chance variation. Rather, the Shadows imply a more deliberate cause.

Identifying themselves as what humans call angels, the Shadows claim to have played a part in directing the course of human neuro-evolution, and explain the basis of their decision to "intervene" as "vengeance" for the presumption of the Authority to declare himself creator.

Her observations in the mulefa's world provide Mary with a sense of how such strangely configured beings as the mulefa could have evolved, by considering the circumstances of the mulefa's anatomy, the seed-pods' central holes, the oil the pods produce, and the geology of their world. As she gets to know these conscious beings, these people, and learns that they can see what they call sraf (her Shadows and Lyra's Dust), one of her first questions is how far back do the mulefa believe themselves to have existed. Her hypothesis about the amplification of Shadows by an evolutionary change in the human brain had to expand to include a parallel and simultaneous change in these beings' brains some 33,000 years ago.

SK   10

AS   *brief mentions:* 7, 17

FLOODS ⚜✏

World: Lyra's

Role: A consequence of the icemelt brought on by the heat entering the Far North of Lyra's world through the window into Cittàgazze is extensive flooding throughout the region of Siberia. Aëronaut Lee Scoresby estimates floodwaters to have run at least six feet high near the Yenisei River. Will learns that the floods and fog followed earthquakes in Kholodnoye and Siberia. Throughout his journey downriver to the Himalayas with the armoured bears who have evacuated the ice-melt in Svalbard, he sees ruined villages and displaced people attempting to salvage their possessions. From the sky, witch Serafina Pekkala sees that the lowland forests of Lapland are flooded.

Observation: *In the mulefa's world, Mary Malone witnesses a different, yet more devastating, flood as the ever-increasing flow of sraf from that world seems to her nothing less than "a great inexorable flood pouring…into some ultimate emptiness."*

[*See also* **Weather disturbances**]

SK   witches' sightings 6; in Siberia 10

AS   of Lapland's 3; in Siberia 8, 9

FOG ❖⚜✏

World: Lyra's, Cittàgazze world, Suburbs of the world of the dead, Island Landing for world of the dead, Asriel's

Role: From the first instance of fog rolling in from the Thames the night Lyra flees Mrs Coulter's, it is associated with times of strife and uncertainty. The gyptians are attacked and Lyra abducted by Samoyed hunters in heavy fog, and the cliff-ghasts on the coast of Svalbard take advantage of the near zero visibility from fog cover to attack Lee Scoresby's balloon, leading to Lyra's landing lost and alone in the armoured bears' kingdom.

When Lord Asriel blasts a hole in the sky over Svalbard, more fog rolls in, pierced intermittently by the otherworldly golden light of Cittàgazze. The fog adds to the navigation difficulties that follow the shifts in magnetism that the blast has also caused. The Far North of Lyra's world is affected, as is Cittàgazze world.

Fog coming off the river bordering the suburbs of the world of the dead adds to the gloom and uncertainty Will and Lyra feel the morning they leave for the world of the dead. And on the island where they must pass through the door leading to the world of the dead, their fear, as the harpies begin their assault, is compounded by the disorientation they experience in the island's thick fog.

Looking west from the basalt fortress, Lord Asriel and his ally General Ogunwe cannot figure out what threat lurks in the fog which surrounds the Authority's Clouded Mountain.

"Fog and Ice" is the title of chapter 18 of NORTHERN LIGHTS / THE GOLDEN COMPASS. [*See also* **Weather disturbances**]

NL/GC approaching Bolvangar 14; in Svalbard 18
    brief mentions: 6, 19, 20

SK   in Svalbard, Lapland 2, Nova Zembla and Cittagazze 6, Siberia 10
    brief mentions: by Lyra to Will 1, 3

AS   suburbs of world of dead 21
    brief mentions: 3, 8, 22, 24

FOUR FUNDAMENTAL FORCES/FUNDAMENTAL FORCES ❖ ⚲

World: Lyra's

Role: Subject of study in experimental theology. When Mrs Coulter quizzes the irregularly educated Lyra, she learns that the Jordan College Scholars have provided the girl with at least a passing familiarity with this concept.

Facts: *In Will's world, the four fundamental forces are gravity, electromagnetism, the strong force (binds protons and neutrons), and the weak force (allows radioactive decay).*

NL/GC 5 [*brief*]

SK   3 [*brief*]

GAMMA-RAY-PHOTONS ❖

World: Lyra's

Role: When Professor Jotham Santelia, a prisoner in armoured bear Iofur Raknison's dungeons, awakens to find a girl from Jordan College is his new cellmate, his first concern is whether his rival Trelawney, Jordan's Palmerian Professor, has already published a paper on gamma-ray-photons. His vehement claims that Prof Trelawney is a plagiarist and scoundrel suggest that Santelia is investigating this topic.

Facts: *In Will's world, a gamma ray is considered to be a very high energy burst of electromagnetic radiation; a photon is the smallest unit of light/electromagnetic energy.*

NL/GC 19 [*brief*]

GOLD (METAL) ❖ ⚲ ✎

World: Lyra's, Will's, Cittàgazze

Role: The metal, gold, is mined in Kamchatka, a region under the threat of attack by Tartars. Gold is also mined in the region of Alaska from which John Parry disappears. One of his informants about the anomaly, or window, he seeks is a gold miner.

Gold isn't mined on Svalbard. In fact, one of the symbols of the pretender king Iofur Raknison's rejection of traditional bear ways in favor of humans' is his ostentatious display of gold jewelry. Even Raknison's claws are covered in gold leaf. The return of the true king Iorek Byrnison means an end to valuing gold and a return to appreciation of iron. Other than Raknison, those fond of gold jewelry include witch Rudi Skadi and Mrs Coulter.

Accumulating gold and other riches also seemed a worthy use of the subtle knife to the Guild of the Tower of Angels, and some believe that the Guild was involved in alchemy—trying to turn lead into gold—when they opened the world of Cittàgazze to the Spectres. The rosewood handle of the subtle knife is inlaid with gold wires shaped into angels.

In *NORTHERN LIGHTS* (but not in *THE GOLDEN COMPASS*), when the alethiometer is given by the Master to Lyra, it is described as being made of brass. However, its gold-ness is what people notice first about the instrument.

Gold is significant in several other contexts in *HIS DARK MATERIALS*. There is the golden monkey, Tokay is a golden wine, Lyra's hair is golden, the currency of exchange in Lyra's world is gold coins, and, finally, Dust is golden.

[*See also:* **Golden light** and **Gold coins** (**Financial Structures**)]

Notes: *Also included below are uses of* golden.

NL/GC brief mentions: 1, Kamchatka mines 10, 19; at Raknison's 20

SK   brief mentions: 1, 2, 3, 4, Alaskan mines 5, Guild and 6, 7, 8, 9, 11, 12

AS   brief mentions: 13, 23, 24

US only: *GC* 4 *[brief]*

GOLDEN LIGHT ⚔️ ✒️

World: Lyra's, Cittàgazze, Mulefa's, world of the dead

Role: When Asriel blasted an opening between his world and that of Cittàgazze, warm sunlight streamed into the arctic of his world at the time of year when there should have been little light during the day at all. When the fog that ensued cleared, the strange and invasive golden light is felt by those in the region such as witch Serafina Pekkala. When Serafina visits the world of Cittàgazze, she sees the light in its appropriate context. Details are crisp by the gold-tinged light, even in the evening in Cittàgazze world.

But more is involved with the presence of a golden light than the contrast between the sunny Mediterranean-like world of Cittàgazze and the bleakness of Arctic from fall to spring. Dust is golden. Mary Malone discovers this in the mulefa's world when with her amber spyglass she sees the golden sparkles of sraf. In the world of the dead, Will and Lyra, not knowing what they see, watch Dust streaming into the abyss as a golden light that dies in its "black emptiness." The light over the savanna in the mulefa's world seems golden to Mary Malone, and to Will, the light emanating from Mrs Coulter's cave is golden.

Notes: *When Asriel and his dæmon Stelmaria descend into the cavern below the fortress to wait for Mrs Coulter and Metatron at the edge of the abyss, Asriel is surprised that there is any illumination at all. But there is, and its source would be the Dust falling into the abyss. It is not, however, in this passage characterized as* golden.

Not included are dawn or dusk descriptions of ordinary gold-hued sunrises or sunsets.

[*See also:* **Ice melt, Dust, Sraf**]

SK   brief mentions: 2, 6

AS   sraf and 17, and Dust at abyss 31
     brief mentions: 11, 20, 26, 35, 37

GRANITE ❖ ✎

World: Lyra's, world of the dead, mulefa's

Role: Granite can be found in many of the worlds. It is used in buildings in Colby, the last stop in England for the gyptians' rescue party. The throne of the armoured bear prince who exiled Iorek Byrnison and took over Svalbard is gilded granite. The window that Mary Malone finds connecting the world of Cittàgazze to that of the mulefa is next to a rock face on both sides: limestone, on Cittàgazze's, and granite in the mulefa's. The rock face on the edge of the abyss is granite.

NL/GC brief mentions: 9, 19

AS brief mentions: 7, 31

HYDROGEN ❖ ⚱

World: Lyra's

Role: This highly flammable gas is used in aëronaut Lee Scoresby's balloon and the zeppelins of Lyra's world. Two ways that Scoresby can make hydrogen when he needs to are by chemical reaction or by extracting it from ground gas, rock oil, or coal. At Bolvangar, he finds another means of fueling his balloon: taking the hydrogen out of Mrs Coulter's zeppelin. When the armoured bears' fire hurler delivers chunks of flaming sulfurous rock into the silk balloon of a hydrogen-filled zeppelin, it explodes.

NL/GC brief mentions: 13, 17 [implied], 18, 22

SK 14 [brief]

ICE MELT ❖ ⚱ ✎

World: Lyra's

Role: When Asriel blasts open a hole in the sky above Svalbard, golden light enters the Far North of Lyra's world, melting the arctic ice and permafrost. The first juxtaposition of the golden light and the melting ice comes at the end of *NORTHERN LIGHTS / THE GOLDEN COMPASS* as Lyra's hands cradling Roger's head appear golden, and Roger's cheeks glisten as the ice on the wolverine fur lining of his hood melts.

    The ice melt causes floods throughout the Far North, and decimates the snows of Svalbard, making hunting for the armoured bears, who rely on camouflage, a losing battle.

NL/GC 23 [brief]

SK brief mentions: 2, 6, 10

AS Svalbard 2; Siberia 9

ICELAND SPAR ✎

World: Will's

Role: In the mulefa's world, when Dr Mary Malone looks through the sap-lacquer used there as varnish, she can see double. This, she knows, means the sap splits light rays, just as Iceland spar, a mineral, does in her own world.

Facts: *Iceland spar is a type of calcite crystal* (CaCO3) *that*

Feldspar showing properties of Iceland spar. The doubled lines seen through this piece of Feldspar illustrate the property of birefringence or double refraction

possesses the quality of birefringence, or double refraction. This effect causes light to bend in two different directions—depending on the polarization of the light (refraction is when light bends as it passes, at an angle, from air or one transparent object into another transparent object made of a different material). In double refraction, one ray of light divides into two.

Much of the world's Iceland spar once did, in fact, come from Iceland, but its reserves have been depleted to the extent that Mexico is now the leading supplier. It is used to produce prisms for polarizing microscopes and other scientific devices.

AS   17 *[brief]*

Iron (raw metal) ✦ ⚷ ✎

World: Lyra's

Role: Iron is a foundation of traditional armoured bear culture. The return of the true king Iorek Byrnison means an end to pretender Iofur Raknison's valuing gold as a means to make bears more like humans and a return to appreciation of iron. While the bears use sky or meteoric iron for their armour, their facility with metallurgy extends to all forms of iron; their island kingdom of Svalbard features a "great grim iron-bound coast."

Aëronaut Lee Scoresby uses iron in his chemical process to make hydrogen when he needs it for his balloon. Iorek Byrnison starts fires by striking ironstones together. In his forge where he repairs the subtle knife, Iorek takes precautions against weakening of the steel by oxidation, or the "iron-eating air," by heating stones that give off a gas that wafts around the steel he works with, keeping oxygen away from the knife pieces as much as possible.

A curiosity: Will's despair at being separated from Lyra is characterized as "the ironbound coast of what had to be," recalling Iorek Byrnison's description of his kingdom. [*See also* **Sky or meteoric iron**]

Facts: *Metallurgists have long shared Iorek's concerns about "iron-eating air" weakening the items they forge. Iron oxides (Fe_2O_3) are so stable that they need reducing agents to draw the oxygen from the iron oxides in order to attain pure metallic iron (Fe). One way to do this is to burn carbon to produce carbon monoxide. The oxygen from Fe_2O_3 and that from carbon monoxide join, creating carbon dioxide gas (CO_2). What then remains from the Fe_2O_3 is Fe, or pure iron. Therefore, the stones that Iorek asks Lyra to gather would contain high quantities of carbon that when heated would produce the needed CO_2.*

Observation: *The description of Svalbard in Chapter 13 of* Northern Lights *is echoed in Chapter 37 of* The Amber Spyglass *as the dashing of Will's hopes when he learns he must live apart from Lyra is compared to a wave breaking on "the iron-bound coast of what had to be."*

NL/GC brief mentions: bears and 10; Svalbard's coast, and hydrogyn 13; Raknison's rejection of 20

SK   knife and 13 [brief]

AS   brief mentions: 9, 14, and Iorek's forge 15, in Asriel's armoury 16

Magnetic field(s), Magnetic Pole, Magnetic variations ✦ ⚷

World: Lyra's, Will's

Role: Following Asriel's blasting open a passage from his world to Cittàgazze world, Arctic peoples and animals were disoriented by unusually heavy fog, climate changes, and "magnetic variations." Migrating birds and other animals are particularly affected by changes in the earth's magnetic fields, as witch Serafina Pekkala witnesses when flying among "tight-knit skeins of geese disintegrated into a honking chaos" above Svalbard. |29

Aëronaut Lee Scoresby is impressed by the elderly Tartar sledge driver he employs on Nova Zembla, who relies on his Arctic fox dæmon to guide his way through the use of scent. Scoresby has found he can no longer rely on his compass to navigate effectively; in fact, much later, when he prepares his balloon for his last voyage, he notices that his compass's "needle was swinging around the dial quite uselessly." |30

At Nova Zembla's Imperial Muscovite Academy's Observatory, Scoresby learns of Grumman's interest in magnetic fields. Seemingly coming out of nowhere, with no prior standing, Grumman presented an impressive paper to the scientific community on terrestrial magnetic variations, theorizing that civilizations may have existed twenty or thirty thousand years ago but evidence of their existence has been lost, "buried under the ice," by extreme climatic shifts associated with magnetic variations. One of the observatory |31

Earth's Magnetic Field

The Earth has a magnetic field around it (similar to any bar magnet). Invisible lines of magnetic force surround the Earth—streaming between the North and South poles. Charged particles (ions and free electrons) become trapped on these field lines—forming the magnetosphere.

Michelle Heran

The impact of the solar wind (highly energetic particles) causes the lines facing sunward to compress, while the field lines facing away from the Sun stream back behind the Earth. The Earth's magnetosphere is about 45,000 miles on the side toward the Sun, but stretches out to 185,000 miles away from the Sun.

scientists claims Grumman was determined to find evidence of these civilizations lost to the ice, which recalls Lord Asriel's claim to the Jordan College Scholars that the German Academy had sent Grumman to the magnetic pole to make various observations.

While at Sir Charles Latrom's home, Will hears the man known as Lord Boreal in Lyra's world say that the scientists have detected recent extreme magnetic variations which they suspect may lend credence to theories about the existence of other worlds. They are seeking a man said to have been looking for a passage to another world when he disappeared twelve or so years ago. Finally, Will understands why the mysterious government men

Migration and Magnetism

Scientists have found that the brains of migrating species from birds to loggerhead turtles contain magnetite, and they theorize that this functions as a kind of internal compass. Some species' brains seem to have even more sophisticated mechanisms comparable to a GPS (global positioning system) that respond to the angle of magnetic field lines passing through the Earth. The Earth's magnetic field involves the liquid metal within its core and the Coriolis force, or the effect of the Earth's spinning on its liquid core. A change in the Earth's magnetic fields strong enough to confuse flocks of migratory birds would be accompanied by dramatic auroral displays. Earth's magnetotail, the result of solar winds interacting with magnetic field lines, is involved in the generation of auroras.

have been searching his home: the man in question is actually John Parry.

Magnetism is also used metaphorically. For example, Lyra's reading of the alethiometer is compared with an expert chess player's ability to focus on "lines of force and influence," filtering out other patterns on the board: "Lyra's eyes moved the same way, according to some similar magnetic field that she could see" but those watching her can't. In his dream of flying with Grumman's osprey dæmon, Scoresby feels like one of the flock "turning as one in the magnetic will of the eagle" to attack the enemy zeppelin.

Observation: _While we learn that the scientists in Will's world have noted disturbances in the earth's magnetic fields, it seems the associated climatic changes reported in Lyra's world have not been felt as far south as England. Of course, there are no observations of the Arctic in Will's world for that period, nor are there of England in Lyra's world, so it may be that his Arctic and her England are similarly affected and unaffected, respectively. However, when Lyra returns home, she learns that political upheavals occurred in her Oxford during her absence, but whether they were caused by environmental crises or the close association in her world of religion, science, and politics isn't clear._

NL/GC brief mentions: 2, 9

SK brief mentions: of bird navigation and 2; Grumman's interest in 6; Coulter on Asriel and, Latrom on Parry and 9

Manganese ❋ ⑩

World: Lyra's

Role: In his past, Asriel devised experiments showing that this element combined with titanium forms an alloy that insulates people's bodies from their dæmons. Although promoting their program was never Asriel's intention, the General Oblation Board uses this discovery to develop the silver guillotine's blade.

Facts: _Manganese is often used in alloys of steel and aluminum to improve strength and_ *resistance to wear.*

Updates: Lord Asriel's papers in the appendix to the **10TH** anniversary edition of NORTHERN LIGHTS include a note regarding his investigations into developing new alloys.

NL/GC 16 *[brief]*

10TH: *NL* appendix

MARBLE ❖

World: Lyra's

Role: Armoured bear usurper-king Iofur Raknison's rejection of traditional bear culture and its ice forts for a palace of imported marble ends with the reclaiming of the throne by the true king Iorek Byrnison, who orders the palace dismantled and its marble blocks hurled into the sea.

NL/GC brief mentions: Raknison and 2, 20

MARS ❖

World: Lyra's

Role: According to Dr Martin Lanselius, the Witch-Consul for Lapland, the alethiometer was invented coincidentally during a search for an astrological instrument that would respond to the movement of planets as a compass does to Earth's poles.

NL/GC 10 *[brief]*

MARSH-FIRE ❖ ⚱

World: Lyra's

Role: The gyptians, who categorize themselves as "water people," equate Lyra with this Fens phenomenon that they describe as "eerie." The gyptians consider Lyra a "fire person," or, as explained by gyptian matriarch Ma Costa: "What you're most like is marsh-fire, that's the place you have in the gyptian scheme; you got witch-oil in your soul. Deceptive, that's what you are, child." The church knows of this evaluation, and thinks that the gyptians' claim has something to do with the witches' prophecy regarding the child, attributing Lyra's success in liberating the General Oblation Board's Bolvangar Experiment Station to her association with the qualities of marsh-fire and witch-oil. [34]

NL/GC 7 *[brief]*

SK 2 *[brief]*

MATTER ❖ ⚱ ✎

World: Lyra's, Will's, Cittàgazze, mulefa's

Role: Spirit and matter are one, according to the Shadows (or Dust, or Dark Matter) that direct physicist Mary Malone to seek Lyra in another world.

According to the angel Balthamos, "Matter loves matter. It seeks to know more about itself, and Dust is formed," a conclusion reached separately in another world by the scientist [35] Mary Malone who interprets the movement of clouds, the moon, and wind as they struggle to keep Dust/sraf/Shadows from leaving the mulefa's world as proof that "Matter *loved* Dust." [36]

Earlier she felt this happening on a far more personal level. High in her observation tree, Mary had felt as if she were leaving her body and vulnerable to a fatal fall. Only by focusing on memories of physical, sensual experiences, in conjunction with the pressure of a benevolent force of Shadow-particles resisting the flow away from the mulefa's world, did she maintain her stability.

Witch Serafina Pekkala's dæmon Kaisa tells Lyra and her gyptian guardians that the "charged particles in the Aurora" make "the matter of this world thin," thereby allowing brief glances of worlds "interpenetrating" with their own.

In Lyra's world, experimental theologians research matter's most fundamental forms, elementary particles. Investigations into "the bonds that held the smallest particles of matter together" by the Guild of the Tower of Angels in Cittàgazze culminated in the invention of the subtle knife by Guild alchemists and philosophers, and all matter is vulnerable to division by its blade.

[*See also* **Dark matter**]

NL/GC 3 *[brief]*; Aurora and 11

SK   Mary on 4, knife and 8, and spirit 12, knife and 15

AS   Balthamos on 2, Mary on Shadow-matter 27, Dust and 34

METEORIC IRON ❖

World: Lyra's

Role: Gyptian Tony Costa tells Lyra that the *panserbjørne*, Svalbard's unusual bears, use meteoric iron to make their armour. The bears prefer to call the material *sky metal* or *sky iron*.

[*See* **Sky iron**]

NL/GC 6 *[brief]*

MILKY WAY ❖ ✑

World: Lyra's, Cittàgazze

Role: Observed in the same region in the sky in Cittàgazze as it is in Lyra's world. The Milky Way figures in the outlandish story Lyra tells her hosts in the suburbs of the world of the dead as the source of a cosmic gale force wind that blew the Gallivespians from the Moon, their home, to Earth.

Observation: *The constellation Ophiucus (see) is also in the same spot in the Cittàgazze world as in Lyra's. This is significant because it means that although HIS DARK MATERIALS describes multiple worlds with differing life forms, e.g. mulefa and Gallivespians, they all share the same location relative to the sun in the same universe. Notably, those from Lyra's and Will's worlds find what they need to survive in the mulefa's world, as do the Gallivespians in Lyra's. Moreover, the mulefa measure time in the same way as do those in Lyra's and Will's worlds; for three hundred years, they say, the wheel trees have been failing and three hundred years ago the alethiometer was invented in Lyra's and the subtle knife in the Cittàgazze world. This suggests that all these worlds are the same distance from the sun.*

Note: *Ophiucus is spelled differently—Ophiuchus—in the US edition.*

SK   6 *[brief]*

AS   19 *[brief]*

NAPHTHA ✦ ⚔ ✐

World: Lyra's

Role: An "older" form of illumination than anbaric power, it provides "softer" lighting, illuminating with a "warm creamy glow" in contrast to the "harsh white" of anbaric lights or, in the Arctic, the "smoky inconstant gleam of blubber-lamps." [41] [42]

While anbaric light is used in the Common Room and the Library of Jordan College, naphtha lamps are favored for the exclusive Retiring Room. Other examples of sites using these lamps include the Gobblers' warehouse or holding area in London, the gyptians' meeting place or Zaal, Asriel's "prison" on Svalbard, a Nova Zembla hotel bar, the ramparts of the basalt fort, Asriel's quarters in the adamant tower, Fr MacPhail's private rooms in Geneva, and Peter's house in the suburbs of the world of the dead.

Another use for naphtha is to fuel portable stoves, like the one Mrs Coulter uses in her Himalaya hide-away. And in Will's world, the naphtha or kerosene stench that Fr Gomez objects to is likely the exhaust of gas-powered combustible engines, or, in other words, traffic.

Mixed with potash it forms an explosive that ignites in contact with water—a fact aëronaut Lee Scoresby learns from his passenger to Cittàgazze world, shaman and scientist Stanislaus Grumman, who foresees its use by the Imperial Army to force the two out of a forest in which they're hiding, still wet from a night's rains. [*See also* **Anbaric**]

Facts: Naphtha *is short for* naphthalene, *a hydrocarbon discovered in 1819 by A. Garden in the "carbolic and heavy oil fractions of the coal-tar distillate."*

NL/GC brief mentions: at Jordan 1, Gobblers' warehouse 3, Zaal 7, 8, on Svalbard 21, 23

AS on Nova Zembla 6 *[brief];* as explosive 14

AS brief mentions: at Coulter's camp 1, at basalt fortress 5, in suburbs of world of dead 19, 21, in Geneva 24, fumes in Will's world 27, at adamant tower 28

NORTHERN LIGHTS ✦ ✐

World: Lyra's, Will's

Role: This term for the Aurora is used by Lyra; the Precentor of Jordan College; Serafina Pekkala's dæmon, Kaisa; balloonist Lee Scoresby; Scoresby's Tartar sledge driver, Umaq; and an archaeologist in Will's world's Oxford. In *HIS DARK MATERIALS,* the terms *Northern Lights* and *the Aurora* are used interchangeably.

Kaisa claims that although there are millions of other worlds "interpenetrating" with ours, "as close as a heartbeat," the only times they may be apprehended are in the Northern Lights. [43]

NORTHERN LIGHTS is the title chosen by Philip Pullman for the first volume of *HIS DARK MATERIALS;* however, the US edition is titled *THE GOLDEN COMPASS.*

Notes: *In the both the UK and US editions,* Northern Lights *and* Aurora *are always uppercased in the first book (NL/GC)—and always lowercased in the second book (SK). In spite of the title of the first volume of* HIS DARK MATERIALS, Aurora *is found far more frequently than is* Northern Lights. *The phrase* aurora borealis, *the Latinate version of northern (borealis) lights (aurora), is never used.*

NL/GC brief mentions: Retiring Room 2, by Kaisa 11, at Bolvangar 17

SK brief mentions: in Alaska 4, Umaq on 6, Scoresby and 10

PHOSPHOR 🖋

World: Asriel's

Role: In the armoury beneath Lord Asriel's basalt fortress, this element is combined with titanium to make a new alloy; however, Asriel's plans for it are not revealed.

Facts: Phosphor *is a shortened version of* phosphorous, *an element which has the property of phosphorescence or luminescence, that is, it emits light in the presence of radiation. Phosphor is used in a variety of products, ranging from fluorescent lamps and safety matches to fertilizers, pesticides and cleansers, and is used in manufacturing certain types of steels and china.*

AS   5   *[brief]*

PHOTONS ❖ 🖋

World: Lyra's

Role: Asriel can photograph Dust when he discovers how to make an emulsion that is affected by Dust in the same way that standard photographic silver nitrate emulsions are affected by light photons. Lyra and Pan, remembering that the Jordan College Librarian said photons are the power source that causes the weathervane within the Gabriel College photomill to spin, speculate that similarly elementary particles might move the hands of the alethiometer.

When Iorek leaves the Himalayas, Lyra cries. The description is that the light from the open fire is reflected off a snow bank and her tear-stained cheeks, which were in turn reflected in Will's eyes, "and so those photons wove the two together in a silent web."

[*See also* **Gamma-ray-photons**]

Facts: *Photons are elementary particles and are what makes up electromagnetic radiation, including visible light. They have no mass, are always moving at the speed of light, and can act both as particles and as waves.*

NL/GC brief mentions: in photography 2, and photo-mill 9, and Rusakov's research 21

AS   15   *[brief]*

POLAR STAR ❖

World: Lyra's

Role: Serafina Pekkala and her witches use this star to navigate toward Svalbard as they pull the aëronaut Lee Scoresby and his balloon's passengers, Lyra, Roger, and Iorek Byrnison, to the kingdom of the armoured bears and their prisoner-guest Lord Asriel.

NL/GC 17   *[brief]*

POLARIZED LIGHT 🖋

World: Lyra's

Role: Reasoning that if reflected light like the sparkles of ocean waves is polarized, and sraf looks like light sparkling on a wave, then sraf or shadow particles might share the same property of light, that is, capable of being polarized. Thus, Dr Mary Malone decides to make the amber spyglass.

AS   17   *[brief]*

Rainbow Facts

The cave valley rainbows are not the large after-rain arcs in the sky, but are experienced on their smaller scale. Nevertheless, they appear due to the same dynamics as the large ones: the dispersion of sunlight in water droplets. Light entering a water drop sphere is first refracted, then reflected off its back, and refracted again as it leaves the drop. Refraction happens when a light wave changes direction when it is no longer passing through air but is passing through water. All water droplets treat light the same way, and so seeing a rainbow depends on the position of the light refracted in the water drops relative to the viewer's eyes. Everyone sees a slightly different rainbow.

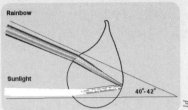

QUANTUM ENTANGLEMENT

Role: Quantum entanglement is mentioned in *His Dark Materials* by the Gallivespian spy, Chevalier Tialys, when he explains the operation of his communications device, the lodestone resonator. Tialys explains: "It means that two particles can exist that only have properties in common, so that whatever happens to one happens to the other at the same moment, no matter how far apart they are."

> [*See also* **Lodestone resonator.**]

AS 14 *[brief]*

RAINBOWS

World: Lyra's
Role: When she first sees the Aurora, Lyra is moved to tears that break "the light even further into prismatic rainbows."

The Himalayan cave where Mrs Coulter holds Lyra is in an area described as "the valley with the rainbows;" where "an odd effect of the light, and the ice, and the vapour enveloped the head of the valley in perpetual rainbows."

NL/GC 11 *[brief]*
AS *brief mentions:* 1, 2, 5, 9, 11, 14

ROCK-OIL

World: Lyra's
Role: Lee Scoresby can make hydrogen when he needs to by extracting it from rock oil.
Facts: *Rock-oil is another term for petroleum or crude oil.*

NL/GC 13 *[brief]*
SK 6 *[brief]*

Rainbow Legend

In Norse mythology, the rainbow is Bifröst, a bridge linking the realms of gods and humans.

In one retelling of the Greek legends of Hercules (Heracles), *The Hydra* by Bernard Evslin, the origin of the Northern Lights is associated with the mythology of the rainbow. Boreas, the God of the North winds, abducted the goddess of the rainbow, Iris. As he carried her off, Iris left behind her a shattered rainbow, which is the origin of the Aurora. Hercules later rescues her.

Sandstone ✐

World: Mulefa's

Role: Mary Malone used sandstone to rub a piece of bark to a smoothness suitable for making what will become the lens of her amber spyglass.

AS 17 *[brief]*

Sky iron/sky metal ✦

World: Lyra's

Role: Sky iron (or metal) is the term armoured bears or *panserbjørne* prefer for meteoric iron, the material they use for devising their armour. Sky metal is found on Nova Zembla as well as in the bears' island kingdom of Svalbard.

Facts: *While far northern Arctic regions may lack deposits of natural metals, meteors can supply an impressive amount of iron. In 1818, explorers discovered tools made of meteoric iron being used by Inuits in northwestern Greenland, but it wasn't until 1894 that the source was finally found. When a local guide took Robert E. Peary to Saviksoah Island, he found three huge meteorites. Two were relatively small (2.5 and .5 tons); the largest weighed 31 tons. It took three years to devise means of transporting the meteorites to New York City, where they are displayed at the Hayden Planetarium.*

NL/GC brief mentions: 11, 13, 18

Solar system ✦

World: Lyra's

Role: According to the science of Lyra's world, it consists of the earth and five other planets.

NL/GC 5 *[brief]*

Sulphur ✦ ✐

World: Asriel's

Role: Surrounding the basalt fortress is "a lake of molten sulphur...releasing its mephitic vapours in sudden gusts and belches." Fumes from this foul-smelling yellow mineral dominate the air of the armoury below the fortress.

Lee Scoresby can make hydrogen to fuel his balloon by pouring sulphuric acid over iron filings. The armoured bears use sulfurous rocks in their fire hurlers to bring down enemy zeppelins; sulphur introduced to hydrogen is hugely explosive. [*See also* **Armoury (Places)**]

NL/GC brief mentions: acid 13, and bears 22

AS brief mentions: basalt fortress 5, 16, 28

Thaw [*See* Ice melt]

Titanium ✦ ✐ ⑩

World: Lyra's, Asriel's, and Gallivespians'

Role: Asriel's experiments showed that "an alloy of manganese and titanium has the

property of insulating body from dæmon," unintentionally providing the material | 51
needed for the General Oblation Board to construct the silver guillotine used at its
Bolvangar Experiment Station.

In forges beneath Asriel's basalt fortress, it is combined, for unstated reasons, with
phosphor to make an alloy never used before.

The Gallivespians' stirrups are made of titanium.

Facts: *Titanium is found in meteorites, lunar rocks, and the earth's crust, where it is the ninth*
most abundant element. Titanium metal, which is not found as a free element, is derived
from igneous rocks and their sediments. Titanium is light, strong, able to withstand extreme
temperatures, and resistant to corrosion.

NL/GC 16 *[brief]*

AS   brief mentions: basalt fortress 5, spurs 11

10ᴛʜ: *NL* appendix

Venus ✧

Role: Dr Martin Lanselius, the Witch-Consul for Lapland, whom Lyra visits with gyptian
Farder Coram, refers to Venus when explaining to Lyra and Coram that the alethiometer
was invented coincidentally during a search for an astrological instrument that would
respond to planetary movement as a compass does to Earth's poles.

NL/GC 10 *[brief]*

Weather disturbances (climatic changes) ⚑✎

(No one word or phrase is consistently associated with this topic)

World: Lyra's, Will's, Cittàgazze

Role: In Lyra's world, after Asriel tears a gap in the sky, there is much fog, the air is "gold-
tinged," the sky is "turbulent with strange lights and shadows," and Arctic peoples and | 52
animals have been disturbed by the unseasonable warming.

The changes have far-reaching effects that reveal the delicate balance of elements in
that region. Iorek Byrnison, decides to lead his armoured bears south to the Himalayas
not because they cannot cope with rising temperatures but because when their habitat,
the bare black rocks of Svalbard, is no longer covered in snow and ice, they lose the
camouflage advantage they should have as hunters.

On Nova Zembla, Lee Scoresby's Tartar sledge chauffeur, Umaq, says similar
catastrophic changes have happened before, many thousands of generations back, when
a hole was opened between this and the spirit world ("Sky fall open"). At the mouth of | 53
the River Yenesei, down which Scoresby travels to Stanislaus Grumman's village, the rapid
thaw has brought with it uncommon species of fish, swift currents carry the corpses of
the drowned and other debris of the "milky-brown flood waters," and the permafrost | 54
thaws to a "swamp of churned mud." | 55

In the world of Cittàgazze, the heat rises with the land's elevation, which surprises Will
and Lyra. Will alludes to global warming in his world, noting that it may be caused by
technology. Lyra is quick to confirm that in her world such human intervention has
occurred—"And we're here in the middle of it"—but declines to mention how very | 56
abruptly and dramatically it happened or to speculate that what they are experiencing was

likely wrought by Asriel when he opened the passage between Cittàgazze's and her world.

When Siberian priest Borisovitch harangues Will, who is trying to make his way south in Lyra's world, the man claims that the odd weather is theologically significant, citing St. John: "The world is turned upside down."

As they climb the arid mountains in Cittàgazze, Will alludes to global warming in his world.

SK   in arctic 2, Nova Zembla 6, in Siberia 10, in Cittàgazze 15

AS   Iorek and 3, in Siberia 8; and bears, floods 9

The Real World Meltdown

In the real world, the effects of gradual climatic changes are far less dramatic than those in Lyra's, which is to be expected since the ones reported in THE SUBTLE KNIFE and THE AMBER SPYGLASS were sudden and catastrophic. Still, what is being documented in the polar regions of the real world is on a smaller scale comparable to what happened in Lyra's.

For example, villagers in Shishmaref, in a region of northern Alaska archaeologists believe to have been inhabited for 4000 years, have had to move further inland because as sea ice melts, storm surges along the coast worsen, and erosion along the coastline is accelerating due to thawing permafrost as well.

In Sachs Harbour, Northwest Territory, Canada, permafrost melting has weakened the villages' buildings' foundations. As the sea ice thins and moves away from the mainland, it becomes harder

According to the US Geological Survey, fewer than half of Alaskan polar bear cubs survive their first year

to hunt the polar bears and seals the community relies on for food, a situation that has been reported by many indigenous peoples in the Arctic regions. In the far north of Canada, the Ellesmere Island Ice Shelf, which covered about 5,530 square miles when Robert Peary explored Ellesmere Island in 1906, is now estimated to cover 559 square miles, a 90 percent reduction in size in less than 100 years.

Philip Pullman's report on his visit to a conference at the Environmental Change Institute at Oxford University in his September 2005 newsletter (philip-pullman.com) provides his personal account and an introduction to the complex issues of global warming.

When rising temperatures melt pack ice, hunting becomes difficult for polar bears, and this places the species at risk of starvation

The Natural Sciences:
Animals
Ants to Yak

Not included here are dæmon animal forms or metaphorical mentions of animal species (e.g. fly like a bird).

ANIMALS OF HDM

Ants
Arctic fox
Bats
Bears, brown
Bears, polar
Bees
Birds
Boar
Butterflies
Caribou
Carrion crows
Cats
Cattle
Cicadas, cicada-like insects
Coyotes
Crickets
Dogs
Dolphins
Doves
Dragonflies
Dragonflies (Gallivespian)
Eels
Elk
Fawn
Finches
Fish
Flies
Foxes
Frogs
Gannets
Gazelle
Geese

Lyra's world

England
Eels
Horses
Nightingales
Rooks
Swans

Martens
Perch
Pine Martens

Europe
Dogs

Siberia
Bees
Boars
Caribou
Elk
Foxes
Geese
Midges
Musk-ox
Snow tigers
Squid
Wolverines

German Ocean
Dolphins
Seals

Himalayas
Bats
Brown Bears
Doves
Gazelle
Glowflies
Goats
Sheep
Vultures
Yak

Svalbard
Arctic foxes
Flies
Gannets
Gulls
Narwhals
Seals
Skuas
Terns
Walrus

Lapland
Dogs
Geese
Gulls
Lemmings
Linnets

Texas, country of
Cattle

Glowflies
Goats
Grasshoppers
Grazers
Gulls, Seagulls
Hare
Hawk, Blue/Indigo
Heron-like bird
Horses
Hummingbirds
Insects
Lemmings
Linnets
Lizard
Lizard, blue
Magpies
Marten
Mice
Midges, midge-like insects
Monkeys
Moss-snakes
Moths
Musk-ox
Narwhals
Nightingales
Owls
Perch
Pine marten
Reindeer
Rooks
Shaggy blue fur beasts
Sheep
Skuas
Snakes
Snow-tigers
Sparrows
Spiders
Squid
Squirrels
Starlings, blue
Swans
Swifts
Terns
Toad
Tualapi
Vultures

Asriel's world

Rooks

Beach World

Insects

Desert World

Insects
Moths
Snakes

Gallivespians' world

Blue hawks
Dragonfly-like creatures
Spiders
Hummingbirds

Holland-like World

Flies
Horses

Will's world

Bees
Birds
Caribou
Cats
Dogs
Dragonflies
Horses
Insects
Mice
Polar Bears
Reindeer
Walrus
Wildebeest

Cittàgazze world

Birds
Boars
Carrion crows

Cats
Cicadas
Coyotes
Crickets
Fawn
Finches
Goats
Hare
Horses
Insects
Lizards
Magpies
Moss-snakes
Nightingales
Owls
Sparrows
Spiders
Squirrels
Swifts
Vultures
Woodpeckers
Wrens

Mulefa's world

Ants
Birds
Butterflies
Cicada-like insects
Crickets
Frogs
Grasshoppers
Grazers
Gulls
Heron-like birds
Insects
Lizards (blue)
Midge-like insects
Snakes
Tiny mud creatures
Tualapi

Rainforest World

Frogs
Insects
Monkeys

Walrus
Wildebeest
Wolverines
Woodpeckers
Wrens

BIRDS OF HDM

Blue (or Indigo) hawk
Carrion crows
Doves
Finches
Gannets
Geese
Gulls
Heron-like birds
Hummingbirds
Linnets
Magpies
Nightingales
Owls
Rooks
Skuas
Sparrows
Starlings
Swans
Swifts
Terns
Tualapi
Vultures
Woodpeckers
Wrens

Unknown world 1

Horses of horse-like
  people
Riders fighting for
  Authority

Unknown world 2

Shaggy blue fur beasts

Suburbs of the world of the dead

Flies
Moths
Spiders
Toads

Birds of Lyra's Oxford

At the heart of Lyra's Oxford is the story "Lyra and the Birds," in which the birds of Oxford try to warn Lyra she is in danger. But she doesn't understand, and finally only the swift action of a swan saves Lyra's life.

Five types of birds are mentioned: nightingales, pigeons, starlings, storks and swans. On the map alone 25 birds are drawn, including four tiny ones, and scores, if not hundreds, of birds are pictured throughout the book.

There are birds at rest and birds in flight over Oxford on the front cover's colored plate, and opposite the first page of "Lyra and the Birds," a huge flock that organizes itself in a pattern resembling one huge bird is depicted, reminiscent of the force that Sayan Kötör raised against a zeppelin pursuing Lee Scoresby and Stanislaus Grumman on what would prove to be the last night of these men's lives. An alert starling and a nightingale are featured against a daylight sky on the half title page, and on the last page of the story, these two again appear, this time against a night sky, and with the starling beginning to droop.

The very last picture in the book on the back flyleaf is of a nightingale alone.

GAZELLE

Observation: *In Will's world, these deer-like creatures, a type of antelope, are most commonly thought of in connection with African grasslands, but there are several varieties found in Central Asia and the Tibetan plateau of Mongolia north of the Himalayas.*

© David Blank

Female Goitered Gazelle Grazing

INSECTS

Observation: *As in every other terrestrial environment, there are more insects species and individuals than any other form of animal life in the Arctic, although their numbers in the Far North are smaller, compared to the variety of insect life in other habitats. Still an estimated 4000 species live above the tree line, in the tundra or taiga.*

The Natural Sciences:
Animals Exclusive to
His Dark Materials

Most of the animals of worlds other than Will's are either the same as those of our world or closely resemble them. Covered here are several noteworthy exceptions.

Gallivespians' world

DRAGONFLIES ✎ ⑩

While vastly different from the dragonflies of Will's world (they are as long as the boy's forearm), dragonflies are the closest approximation to the creatures that the diminutive Gallivespian spies and soldiers ride. These "steeds" are equipped with "spider-silk reins, stirrups of titanium, [and] a saddle of hummingbird-skin."

Different clans of Gallivespians can be identified by the colors of their dragonflies; for example, Chevalier Tialys' has red and yellow stripes, while the Lady Salmakia's is electric blue and glows in the dark. The dragonflies' markings remain bright and vibrant even as other colors drain away in the graying suburbs of the world of the dead, and Lady Salmakia's steed's luminous tail provides the only light in the world of the dead.

The spies carry the insect larvae with them on their missions and can prompt a new steed to hatch in 36 hours. Careful nurturing of the newborns promotes the mounts' attachment to their masters. The dragonflies eat moths, but in desperate circumstances, as in the world of the dead, they can feed on bits of human food or even the blood of the Gallivespians.

While brave and eager for battle (e.g. with the harpies), the dragonflies retreat if overpowered, but quickly regain their nerve. Their level of awareness seems higher than that of the beings they superficially resemble in Will's world. For example, when Will, Lyra, and the spies encounter the ghost of Dirk Jansen, the dragonflies try to get away, acting as if repulsed by the ghost.

"The Dragonflies" is the title of chapter 11 of *THE AMBER SPYGLASS*, and dragonflies are the subject of the woodcut for this chapter in the **10TH** anniversary edition.

Note: In the UK edition, the dragonflies strike Will as being "almost as long as his forearm" (169), but in the US edition, he thinks they are "as large as seagulls" (159).

AS 9 *[brief]*, hatching 11, described 12, Pan plays with 13; 14; fearful of ghosts, contrast of their colors to dullness of suburbs of world of dead 18; 19, conflict with harpies 21; 22, 23; Tialys's dead and Salmakia's dying 26; attack pilots 29, swarm on battlefield 31

10TH: *AS* chapter 11 woodcut

Hawk, Blue/Indigo ✎

This highly trained, obedient bird provides transportation for Gallivespian spy captain Lord Roke and his successor, Mme Oxentiel. The hawk is variously described as blue and indigo, and is equipped with stirrups, bridle, and saddle. During the battle on the plains in Asriel's world, it summons the dragonfly-mounted Gallivespians into battle with a mighty screech, thus clearing the way for Will and Lyra to follow Oxentiel and her steed to their dæmons.

AS   introduced as Roke's 5, 16, re-introduced as now Oxentiel's 28; described as indigo, in battle 31

Mulefa's world

Grazers ✎

The mulefa use these placid, four-legged, light-brown, deer-sized creatures for meat and milk. Like the mulefa, grazers' limbs are arranged in a diamond pattern, one forward, one back, and two at their sides.

When the mulefa cull the herds of grazers, they slaughter the animals selected by using their powerful trunks to break the beasts' necks. The mulefa make use of all parts they can of each animal killed, drying or salting the meat, tanning the hides, and so on.

AS   described, contrasted with mulefa 7; mulefa's uses of 10; contrasted with Mary 17

Tualapi ✎

These malevolent gigantic white birds are described as twice the height of Mary Malone and as long as rowboats, with six-foot long wings on the front and back of their bodies and legs on their sides. They can move as swiftly on water as in the sky. They are aggressive, with hook-shaped teeth in their beaks to supplement the power inherent in their huge, strong bodies.

The *tualapi* destroy the mulefa's villages, not only raiding their food supplies, but also vandalizing what they can't consume and spitefully wrecking the mulefa's stores of seedpods. In the three hundred years that the seedpod trees have been deteriorating, the number of *tualapi* and the threat they pose to the mulefa have grown.

Tualapi reasoning seems more sophisticated than would be expected of birds in Will's world. After watching a creature they had never seen before shoot and kill one of their flock, and understanding the implications of this power, they offer their services to Father Gomez.

AS   attack by 10, Sattamax on 17, encounter Gomez 27, not named but flight described 32; 33, and Gomez 34; 38 [implied]

Lyra's world

Arctic Foxes ✎ ⑩

These unusual foxes are the subjects of the title of chapter 3 of *The Amber Spyglass*, "Scavengers." They eat what remains of the walruses and seals killed by bears; moreover, they scavenge bits of conversations of witches and armoured bears. However, the foxes are considered unreliable witnesses because they are notorious liars and are capable only of understanding the present tense.

When a fox that once eavesdropped on witch Serafina Pekkala and armoured bear Iorek Byrnison is captured by the cliff-ghasts, it tries to buy time with news of troubled witches, bears moving south, and the death of aëronaut Lee Scoresby. It mangles Serafina's report of witch Ruta Skadi's description of angels' "crystalline clarity" and rich wisdom into "Flying things—angels—crystal treasure," which proves unlucky for the Authority, whose crystal litter on a remote section of the battlefield near Asriel's fortress attracts the attention of one of these cliff-ghasts.

The woodcut for chapter 3 of the **10**ᴛʜ anniversary edition of THE AMBER SPYGLASS depicts these foxes.

AS   3; cliff-ghast recalls 30 *[brief]*

10ᴛʜ: *AS* chapter 3 woodcut

The Natural Sciences:

Plants

Alder to Yew

PLANTS OF HDM

Alder
Anemones
Bamboo
Beans
Bog myrtle
Bougainvillea
Buttercup-like flowers
Cedar
Cinquefoil
Cloud-pine
Conifers
Corn
Cornflower-like flowers
Cornflowers
Crocus
Cypress
Dead tree
Dwarf rhododendrons
Ferns
Firs
Fruit trees
Gentians
Gold and silver grove
Harp-flower
Hawthorn bushes
Heather
Herbs
Holly
Hornbeams

Lyra's world

England
Fruit trees
Lyra and Will's tree
Oak
Pines
Willows

Europe
Plane trees
Spruce

Himalayas
Anemones
Cedar
Firs
Pines
Rhododendrons

Lapland
Cloud-pine
Crocus
Moss
Saxifrage

Siberia
Bog myrtle
Harp-flower
Heather
Larches
Lichens
Pines
Reeds

Will's world

Holly
Hornbeams
Hydrangea
Laurel
Lemon trees
Lyra and Will's tree
Moss
Passion flowers
Pines
Privet
Redwoods
Virginia creeper

Beach World

Marram grass
Tree-ferns

Holland-like world

Corn
Raspberry

Cittàgazze world

Alder
Bougainvillea
Cinquefoil
Conifers
Cornflowers
Dwarf rhododendrons
Gentians
Herbs
Lemon trees
Moss
Oak
Oleander
Olive trees

Hydrangea

Juniper-like shrubs

Knot-wood

Larches

Laurel

Lemon trees

Lichens

Lyra and Will's tree at
       Botanic Garden

Moss

Oak

Oleander

Olive trees

Palms

Passion flowers

Pines

Plane trees

Poppies

Poppy-like flowers

Privet

Raspberry

Redwoods

Reeds

Rhododendrons

Rosewood

Sage

Sap-lacquer bushes

Saxifrage

Seedpod trees

Shelter tree

Spruce

String-wood

Tree-ferns

Vegetables

Virginia creeper

Willows

Yew

Palms
Pines
Rosewood
Vegetables

Mulefa's world

Bamboo
Beans
Buttercup-like flowers
Cornflower-like
flowers
Ferns
Gold and silver grove
Juniper-like shrubs
Knot-wood
Moss
Oak
Pines
Poppy-like flowers
Reeds

Sap-lacquer bushes
Seedpods
Seedpod trees
Shelter tree
String-wood
Vegetables

World of the dead

Island of entry:
Cypress
Yew

Inside:
Dead tree

Asriel's world

Hawthorn

Bougainvilleas

Bougainvilleas are native to tropical forests of Brazil in South America. The plant grows as a rambling vine, and what most people take to be its flowers are actually modified leaves; the plants' tiny white flowers are hidden among its fuchsia petal-like bracts (or leaves).

Cypress trees

Cypress trees are often found planted in graveyards and are associated with mourning and death. Once cut back, a cypress will not grow again.

Hornbeam trees

These "strange childlike trees" along an Oxford boulevard attract Will Parry's attention, as does a cat hunting near the trees. This is where he sees the cat disappear through the window into another world. The trees provide a landmark for Will and Lyra to use when seeking the Oxford/Cittàgazze window to move between these worlds. When Mary Malone goes to Sunderland Avenue, she notices the hornbeam trees before the tent.

The title of chapter 1 of THE SUBTLE KNIFE is "The Cat and the Hornbeam Trees," and the trees are the subject of Philip Pullman's woodcut for this chapter.

Larches

Larches are an unusual type of tree. They are coniferous, that is, they bear cones, but they are deciduous, meaning they lose their leaves each fall (most conifers are evergreens). Larches are widely found in Siberia.

Oleander

Oleander shrubs are native to Mediterranean regions and are now popular in the southern US. Oleanders generally are 6 to 12 feet wide, but some can be trained to grow as small trees. The very fragrant flowers can be apricot, pink, red, purple, salmon, yellow, and white, or similar shades. All parts of oleander plants are poisonous to humans and animals if eaten, and some people can develop a rash through external exposure to the plant.

Redwoods

Mary Malone believes the wheelpod trees are about 50% taller than the tallest trees in her world. Redwoods can grow over 320 feet. This means the wheelpod trees are roughly 500 feet tall. *Sequoia semperviren*, among the oldest things living on earth, are found along the coast of California, from the vicinity of San Francisco up to the southwestern tip of Oregon. A tree felled in 1933 was an estimated 2200 years old.

Rosewood

Rosewood has nothing to do with the rose flower. Rather, rosewoods are a variety of tropical tree with the heartwood, or inner wood, having a purplish-black color (Brazilian and Honduras varieties) or purple-black with golden streaks (East Indian), or near-black (African). It is commonly used for piano casings, percussion instruments, and fine furniture.

Virginia creeper

Virginia creeper is an ornamental woody vine that can climb trees or walls, or trail along a path.

Will and Lyra's tree

A virtual tour of Oxford's Botanic Garden is available at chem.ox.ac.uk. If you follow the text of THE AMBER SPYGLASS and go through the main gates, past a fountain, past a wall with a doorway, then on to the very back of the garden, over a small bridge, and look around you, you will see the bench and the tree.

Yew

Yew trees are symbols of immortality, or rebirth and resurrection. Two of their characteristics account for this. They can live for hundreds (some are said to be over a 1000 years old) of years. Their branches are able to grow down into the ground and develop into new trunks that are separate but still linked to the original tree's, suggesting the cycle of new from the old, or death and rebirth. One of only a very few evergreen trees native to the British Isles, it played an important role in Druid legends and myths.

The Natural Sciences:

Trees exclusive to
His Dark Materials

Seedpod Trees in the Mulefa's World

In the mythology of the mulefa, a snake instructed a female mulefa to put her claw through the hole in the center of a seedpod, and she changed from one who could remember no past and anticipate no future to one who had consciousness of both. She then saw sraf (or Dust, Shadow-particles) for the first time, and ever since, the mulefa have believed that their distinction from other animals depends on their absorption of the seedpods' oil. These trees are thus essential to the mulefa's civilization. Moreover, the only way their pods can open (and new trees grow) is if the mulefa use them as wheels. Thus, the fates of the two species—the mulefa and these trees—are inextricably linked.

The Trees

Their diameter far exceeds five feet, and the circumference of their branches is comparable to that of the trunks of large trees in Will's world. The trees have a golden-red, ridged bark and leaves over a foot long. An amazed Mary Malone, new to the mulefa's world, is deeply impressed by the trees and estimates their height to be fifty percent greater than California's majestic redwoods.

In the past 300 years, the trees have declined. Mary Malone sees that the sraf comes from the sky, and while the trees' flowers have evolved to face upward and receive downward drifts, the sraf is now moving against the wind away from land and the trees, thus limiting the pollination of the flowers and production of the pods. This explains the mechanics behind the trees' failure.

As a parting gift, her mulefa friend Atal presents Mary Malone with a vial of wheel tree oil and seeds of the precious trees.

The Seedpods

The pods of the seedpod trees are initially the size of coins growing within the trees' off-white flowers. The seeds they hold are oval, lightly colored, and about as long as a pinkie fingernail. Mature, the seedpods are three feet across, a palm's width in thickness, and perfectly round. Covered with fibrous hairs that can be brushed in one direction only, they exude a slightly fragrant oil. They are attached to the trees at their centers, and it is at this spot that the oil within can be accessed.

When she applies the oil to her spyglass, Mary Malone is able to see sraf.

The mulefa maintain that their children lack the wisdom of adults because they cannot absorb the seedpod oils through their claws. The seedpods' oil is "the centre of their thinking and feeling," which means that failure of the seedpod trees signals a threat to the survival of these conscious beings.

Notes: Like the world in which they grow, there is not a single term used to describe the trees that produce the seedpods cherished by the mulefa. Included in these references are: seed-pod trees, wheel-trees, wheel-pod trees, climbing tree (and variations of the same), and sometimes just trees, if it is reasonably clear that what is being described is a tree that produces the seedpods of value.

Update: The fifth Lantern Slide in THE AMBER SPYGLASS reports that Mary gave three of the seedpod tree seeds, her parting gift from Atal, to a scientist at the Botanic Garden, Oxford. The seeds sprouted, and the young trees are doing well.

Seedpod Trees

AS described 7, co-dependence of trees and mulefa 10; in mulefa mythology, trees' failure 17; climbing tree platform 27; 32, 33, climbing tree falls 34; Will and Lyra in grove, return of sraf to 35; Serafina and dæmons among 36, Atal's gift 38, ⎣*LS*⎦ Lantern Slide 5

The Seedpods

AS as wheels 7; maintenance of by mulefa, destruction of by tualapi 10; and sraf 17, pollination of flowers 20

The Shelter tree

Outside Mary Malone's hut is a tree with "fragrant corkscrew leaves" and low hanging branches under which Will, and later Will and Lyra, nap and sleep, and in the night, Pan and Kirjava, who stay at a distance from their people during day, come to check on them tenderly. Its "curtain of all-concealing leaves" provides better security than Mary's hut when Fr Gomez searches the village for Lyra. He looks in the village's structures, but his "gaze swept past the tree."

AS *brief mentions:* 33, 34, 36

The Natural Sciences:
Scientific Studies
Alchemy to Quantum theory

ALCHEMY ⚱

Role: According to one of the children Will and Lyra meet in Cittàgazze, alchemy was among the pursuits of the Guild of the Torre degli Angeli (Tower of Angels). The former bearer, Giacomo Paradisi, mentions this study as well in connection with the subtle knife's inventors, when he passes the guardianship of the knife to Will.

Update: While alchemy is just mentioned in passing in HIS DARK MATERIALS, such is not the case in LYRA'S OXFORD. This novella ends with Lyra making a new friend, the sixty or so year old Sebastian Makepeace, an alchemist.

SK brief mentions: 7, 8

ANBAROLOGY ✧

World: Lyra's

Role: Under the haphazard tutelage of Jordan College Scholars, Lyra has acquired a smattering of knowledge in this subject of study, along with smidgens of geometry, Arabic, and history.

NL/GC 3 [brief]

ASTRONOMY

[*See* **Celestial geography**]

ATOMCRAFT ✧ ⚱

World: Lyra's

Role: In attempting to explain to Will what an experimental theologian is, Lyra defines these scholars' special interests as "elementary particles and fundamental forces ... stuff like that. Atomcraft."

Observation: *Atomcraft may refer to a field of study, the devices powered by uranium, or the crafting of atomic resources (such as nuclear power, or bomb research).*

NL/GC 3 [brief]

SK 3 [brief]

CELESTIAL GEOGRAPHY ✧

World: Lyra's

Role: A subject of study in which Mrs Coulter says she will instruct Lyra in order to prepare the girl to serve as her personal assistant during an expedition north.

Observation: *Since it is linked with mathematics and navigation as the third element in a series, it may be safe to assume, in our world,* celestial geography *is* astronomy.

NL/GC 4 [brief]

Saturn

Image courtesy NASA/PRC98-29, Space Telescope Science Institute, Hubble Heritage Team

EXPERIMENTAL THEOLOGIANS, EXPERIMENTAL THEOLOGY ❖ ⚔ ✎

World: Lyra's

Role: The areas of experimental theology include "atoms and elementary particles … anbaromagnetic charges and the four fundamental forces." In spite of Jordan College's prominence in the field, Lyra's knowledge of its tenets is slight. Other possible subjects of inquiry by experimental theologians are magic, astronomy, particle physics, or communicating with the dæmons of stars—according to Lyra. 67

Will equates experimental theology with physics in his world, as does Sir Charles Latrom. The Gallivespian spy Tialys would agree with Will and Latrom; he tells Lyra that the experimental theologians in her world would understand the principles of quantum entanglement that make possible the operation of his lodestone resonator.

Experimental theologians were among the personnel at the General Oblation Board's Bolvangar Experiment Station involved in severing children from their dæmons.

Observation: *In Will's world, the interest of theologians is religion. Boreal/Latrom, familiar with both worlds, equates experimental theologians in Lyra's with physicists in Will's. Occasionally, however, when theologians and theology are mentioned in Lyra's world, the term* experimental *does not appear. Whether there are two distinct categories—theologians (theology) and experimental theologians (experimental theology)—in Lyra's world is uncertain. Asriel and the Master of Jordan College both use* theologian *alone in discussing Barnard and Stokes, who offered mathematical proofs for the existence of other worlds and so are clearly experimental theologians. But whether the Ministry of Theology is a Ministry of Experimental Theology is a bit more ambiguous. References in the index entry include those to* theology *with and without* experimental.

NL/GC brief mentions: Jordan College and 2, 3, 5, by Asriel on 21

SK brief mentions: by Lyra to Will 3, by Latrom to Coulter 9, by Grumman to Scoresby 10

AS brief mentions: of Bolvangar's 6, by Tialys 14, Cooper as 24

LONG BASELINE NEUTRINO EXPERIMENT

[*See* **Particle Physics**]

MINOS PROJECT

[*See* **Particle Physics**]

PARTICLE PHYSICS ✐ ⑩

World: Will's

Role: Dr Mary Malone's area of expertise.

Facts: *Particle physicists study how elementary or subatomic particles (photons, electrons, atomic nuclei) interact.*

Update: In the appendix to the **10TH** anniversary edition of THE AMBER SPYGLASS, entries from Dr Mary Malone's journal suggest that she may have been considering an experiment to look for Shadow-particles comparable to those devised for the MINOS project (Main Injector Neutrino Oscillation Search) at the Fermilab designed to study neutrino oscillations.

AS   33 [brief]

10TH: *AS* appendix

QUANTUM THEORY ✐

World: Will's

Role: Mary Malone's familiarity with quantum physics, which accommodates the possibility of multiple worlds, is useful to her in thinking about her unusual journey through the world of Cittàgazze to the world of the mulefa.

Note: The Science of Philip Pullman's His Dark Materials *by Mary and John Gribbin (London: Hodder, 2003) discusses quantum theory in the context of Philip Pullman's world.*

AS   7 [brief]

MINOS & Dark Matter

Neutrinos are very hard to detect because they don't interact with other particles. Particle physicists are interested in establishing if they have mass; if so, they might account for some of the universe's dark matter. The theory of the MINOS experiment is, very generally, that it might be possible to detect neutrinos in a beam sent from the Fermilab, 40 miles west of Chicago, through thousands of tons of rock to a detector in an inactive iron mine in Minnesota. Mary seems to think that for her purposes shooting a beam roughly 7000 miles through the earth, rather than across 450 miles, might be necessary.

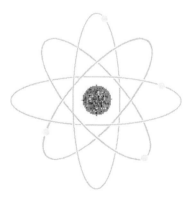

Atom—Nucleus with Electrons Orbiting

SOCIAL STRUCTURES
OF THE WORLDS

CATHOLIC, CATHOLIC CHURCH ⚑✎

World: Will's

Role: While no longer a nun or a Catholic, Mary Malone is still receptive to the notion that what she calls dark matter, and what Lyra calls Dust, could be what the Church calls angels. The three-part nature of humans that Will has observed—ghosts, dæmons, and the body—reminds Mary of Catholic teachings regarding "spirit and soul and body." [*See also* **Church**]

Observation: *While references to the* Church *in Will's world may be assumed to mean the Catholic Church, there is no indication that the same applies to the phrase's usage in Lyra's world. In the UK editions, unless the Catholic Church is specifically referenced, the phrase* the church *is lowercased. Interestingly, the US editions nearly always capitalize* the Church. *The word* Catholic *is only used twice in* HIS DARK MATERIALS, *and both times in relation to former nun Mary Malone of Will's world.*

SK 12 *[brief]*

AS 33 *[brief]*

CENSORS ✦⚑✎ ⑩

World: Lyra's

Alliances: Magisterium

Role: The chief occupation of the church of Lyra's world is to keep hold of its power. It has an adversarial relationship to the people whose lives it governs, and censors are the foot soldiers in the Magisterium's campaign to suppress any findings or speculations that contradict its teachings. More broadly, its censors aim, in Ruta Skadi's words, "to suppress and control every natural impulse." What it wants, John Parry argues, is for its subjects "to obey and be humble and submit."

Experimental theologians at philosophical research establishments are particularly at risk of being charged with heresy by the Magisterium. To this end, it requires the presence of a censor at any research institute to suppress findings it considers heretical. Even if a finding isn't deemed heretical, if it involves church doctrine in any way, then it can only be announced by the Magisterium. Censors or their counterparts also track the movements of explorers and other renegades. Those who fund investigations deemed heretical incur its wrath, and heretics are exiled, imprisoned, exorcised or executed.

The Magisterium is quick to censure the concept that there are worlds beside its own. Barnard and Stokes, the experimental theologians who proposed mathematical proofs for the existence of multiple worlds, were "silenced." Lord Asriel, exiled to Svalbard for his interest in other worlds, refused to abandon his "philosophical work" and would likely

5   have been executed.

The censor or inspector at the facility where Boris Mikhailovitch Rusakov made his discoveries reported back to the Magisterium that he considered Rusakov a victim of "diabolic possession." When the censor's exorcism of Rusakov and questioning of the man "under the rules of the Inquisition" failed to disprove what Rusakov had discovered, the Magisterium found a way to use the existence of Rusakov particles as a means to

6   strengthen its power. Not so lucky was the experimental theologian who suggested that there are more than three dimensions; he remains "languishing in the dungeons of the

7   Consistorial Court."

The Skraeling censor whom Lee Scoresby encounters at the Imperial Muscovite Observatory isn't content simply to report on Scoresby's activities to the Magisterium but decides to act as the aëronaut's executioner, a fatal mistake.

Fr Gomez equates evangelizing with censoring, entertaining the notion of forcing the

8   mulefa to give up their "abominable" "habit of riding on wheels." Abominable is a word frequently used by censors.

Even those in its employ try to act as self-censors, so great is the fear of the Magisterium. In Geneva, Dr Cooper assures the Consistorial Court of Discipline's Fr MacPhail that he didn't listen to the ideas proposed at Bolvangar about harnessing the energy released during intercision since he knew that "they might well be heretical." The

9   Court's alethiometrist Fra Pavel requires assurance that he won't be considered a heretic for reporting about Lyra's whereabouts and what his instrument has told him of her destiny.

Among the common people the sense of threat by censors is strong. Lord Asriel's manservant confesses to Serafina Pekkala his fear that his master would be executed if his goals were known by the church, and he adds that "I've never spoke of it before and I shan't again; I'd be afraid to speak it aloud to you if you weren't a witch and beyond the power of the church." [*See also* **Skraeling, the** *in* **Characters**]

10 **Facts:** *Deliberate, persistent contradiction of a doctrine of faith is heresy. It is the ecclesiastical equivalent of treason. Intolerance of subversive ideas or heretical views is not limited to any one faith or church.*

Update: Mary Malone's impressions of the world of the mulefa are characterized by the Magisterium as exemplary of the "wicked imaginings of heretics and the blasphemous" in its preface accompanying several pages of notes by Mary, now the property of the "Archive of the Magisterium," and presented as an appendix to the **10**TH anniversary edition of *The Amber Spyglass.*

Note: *Words indexed here also include* heretical, heretic, *and* censure, *and pages listed include those relating to the activities of censorship by the church.*

NL/GC brief mentions: by Master 2, at cocktail party 5, and Asriel's future 16, and Rusakov 21

SK   at Nova Zembla observatory 6
            brief mentions: by Thorold and Skadi 2, Parry 15

AS   *brief mentions:* Court and 6, 24, 28, 30, 35

10TH: *AS* appendix

Church/church/Holy Church, The ✦ ⚱ ✎ ⑩

World: Lyra's

Role: In *Northern Lights/The Golden Compass,* the Church (or church) seems little differentiated from the Magisterium, with a few notable exceptions. Examples of the terms being used interchangeably range from the conversation of the Master of Jordan College and his friend, the Librarian; to that of John Faa and Lyra; to witch Serafina Pekkala and Lyra; and to Lord Asriel and Lyra.

However, when the Master speaks of what has been taught over the ages, he chooses the phrase "the Holy Church," rather than "the Magisterium," and Asriel uses "the Church." Such teachings encompass the denial of the existence of other worlds besides the physical one, which we perceive through sensory experience, and the spiritual one of heaven and hell; and the assertion that sin came into the world when Adam and Eve transgressed and their dæmons ceased to change. Serafina says that witches, not liking to "fret and tear things apart to examine" them prefer to leave explanations of Dust to the Church, and Lyra considers "Church things" to be old and mostly kept "secret."

In THE SUBTLE KNIFE, the link between the Magisterium and the church is not quite as pronounced, but still occurs in more than half of the passages in which the church is mentioned. These include Lee Scoresby's conflict with the Skraeling censor at the Imperial Muscovite Observatory in Nova Zembla and witch Ruta Skadi's stance that if a war comes with the church/Church on one side, the witches must support the other— Asriel's: "I know whom we must fight. It is the Magisterium, the church."

Interestingly, Dr Martin Lanselius, the Witch-Consul for Lapland, does differentiate between the Magisterium and the church; he tells Serafina that the Magisterium is preparing for war but says that the church is "in complete confusion" following Asriel's opening of a passage to another world.

Lord Asriel, according to his manservant Thorold, does not plan to challenge either the church or Magisterium but has set his sights higher. Asriel plans to wage a war against the Authority. Thorold tells Serafina that Asriel, although fully aware that it is "death...to challenge the church," had considered raising a rebellion against it but decided that he didn't want to waste his efforts on such a weak adversary.

In THE AMBER SPYGLASS, there are relatively few mentions of the Magisterium; the emphasis has shifted to the church (UK) or Church (US). It is the church that Coulter hides from in the Himalayas. However, when Asriel introduces her as an erstwhile agent of the Church, her comments focus on knowing more about the Magisterium than anyone else. Father MacPhail argues that if all the Authority's agencies must be destroyed to eliminate Dust, then he is willing for that to happen, and speculates that perhaps "the Holy Church itself was brought into being to perform this very task and to perish in the doing of it. But better a world with no church and no Dust" than one in which sin exists.

During physicist Mary Malone's discussion of St. Paul's teachings with Will, she prefaces her remarks with "the church – the Catholic Church," and when she tells about renouncing her life as a nun, the Church refers to this body.

Upon Lyra's return to Jordan College, she learns that the Church (uppercased, both UK and US) had initially experienced a surge in power after Asriel's venture out of his world, but that this had diminished concurrently with instability in the Magisterium. [*See also* **Catholic**]

Observation: *The varying use of upper and lowercase, and the contrasts between the usage of church/Church in the UK and US, further complicate an understanding of the term in* HIS DARK MATERIALS. *With one exception, uppercase is used in* NORTHERN LIGHTS *and* THE GOLDEN COMPASS—*Professor Docker's explanation of the oblates. In* THE SUBTLE KNIFE, *the UK edition uses church and Church roughly the same number of times, but the US lowercases just twice.*

In THE AMBER SPYGLASS, *the UK edition has few references to the Church. Apart from*

Mary Malone's history and in the phrase "Holy Church," uppercasing is used only when Asriel introduces Coulter as "a former agent of the Church," and in the final update on its status in Lyra's world. In contrast, the US edition of THE AMBER SPYGLASS *always uppercases "Church," but when the plural is used, "churches" is lowercased.*

Update: The **10**ᴛʜ anniversary edition of THE SUBTLE KNIFE features an appendix that offers some journal entries by Col. John Parry/Dr Stanislaus Grumman. After meeting Lord Asriel, Parry notes that he can't imagine anyone better suited to challenge the church of Asriel's own if not other worlds.

Note: *When* church *denotes a physical structure, it is indexed in* **Places and Peoples.**

Uppercase [Church]

UK and US:

NL/GC Asriel on 21
        used by *[brief]:* Master 2, Faa 7, Serafina and Lyra 18, Asriel to Coulter, Pan to Lyra 23

UK:

SK used by *[brief]:* Coulter 2, Lyra 4, 5; regarding Skraeling censor 6; by Grumman 10

AS *[brief]* Asriel on 16; regarding Mary 34, changes in Lyra's world 38

US:

SK used by *[brief]:* Coulter, Serafina and Thorold, Skadi 2; Lyra 4, 5; regarding Skraeling censor and by Hester 6; Grumman 10

AS used *[brief]* regarding Coulter 1; by Will 2, Asriel 5, MacPhail 6; regarding Roke's spies 9; by Coulter 11, Coulter and Asriel 16, Mary and Will 33; regarding Mary 34, changes in Lyra's world 38

Lowercase [church]

UK and US:

NL/GC used by Docker 5 *[brief]*

UK:

SK used by *[brief]:* Serafina and Thorold, Skadi 2, Lyra 4, Skraeling censor, Hester 6

AS *[brief]* regarding Coulter 1; by Will 2, Asriel 5, MacPhail 6; regarding Roke's spies 9; by Coulter 11, Coulter and Asriel 16, Mary and Will 33

US:

SK used by *[brief]:* Skadi 2, Lyra 4

AS *[none]*

Lowercase [churches]

UK and US:

SK used by *[brief]:* Skadi 2

AS used by *[brief]:* Baruch 2, 5, Serafina 36

Holy Church

UK and US:

NL/GC used by *[brief]:* Master 2

AS used by *[brief]:* MacPhail 6, Borisovitch 8

Catholic Church

UK and US:

SK used by *[brief]:* Skad

CLERGY ✦

World: Lyra's

Alliances: Church

Role: According to gyptian leader John Faa, the clergy is on the side of the Gobblers. He tells his people that the police and clergy are aware of but not impeding the abductions of their children by the General Oblation Board (Gobblers).

NL/GC 7 [brief]

COLLEGE OF BISHOPS ✦ ✐

World: Lyra's

Alliances: Magisterium

Role: Part of the Magisterium and once its most powerful branch, the College of Bishops lost its prominence as the Consistorial Court of Discipline became more influential.

NL/GC 2 [brief]

AS   6 [brief]

CONSISTORIAL COURT OF DISCIPLINE ✦ ⚜ ✐

World: Lyra's

Alliances: Magisterium

Role: This branch of the Magisterium, devised by Pope John Calvin, was "the most active and the most feared of all the Church's bodies," securing "the Church's power over every aspect of life." Its twelve members, under the leadership of its president, Father Hugh MacPhail, convene at the College of St. Jerome in Geneva. The Court was in competition with the General Oblation Board for being "the most powerful and effective arm of the Holy Church," and this concerns the Master of Jordan College, who knows that Mrs Coulter is behind the Board. He fears Lyra could be caught in the middle of a power struggle between the two factions. Following the Board's debacle at the Bolvangar Experiment Station and Mrs Coulter's disappearance into the Himalayas with Lyra, the Court's chief rival within the Magisterium is the Society of the Work of the Holy Spirit.

The Court has secured its power through fear inspired by its ruthless treatment— including torture and assassination—of those it suspects of posing a threat to its absolute authority. Dr Cooper, once a prominent experimental theologian at the General Oblation Board's Bolvangar Experiment Station, was a witness before the Court in Geneva. His behavior, as well as the reaction of several of the Court's own members to the mention of their headquarters' cellar, suggests that the basement's "white-tiled rooms with points for anbaric current, sound-proofed and well-drained" were used for torture.

There are several references to the activities of the Consistorial Court of Discipline. It is known to have conducted an Inquisition-type interrogation and exorcism of Boris Mikhailovitch Rusakov following his discovery of the elementary particle that came to be known as Dust. Coulter tells the Bolvangar scientists that the Court is considering a death sentence for Asriel because of his refusal to abandon his inquiries into Dust, confirming Asriel's manservant Thorold's claim to witch Serafina Pekkala that Asriel would be executed if the Court learned of his plans. Even its own alethiometrist, Fra Pavel, is obviously terrified when required to testify at the Court's inquiry into Asriel's plans and the whereabouts of Lyra.

Covertly, and without the knowledge of the church at large, the Court has developed and applies doctrines of pre-emptive penance and absolution. Through practices such as self-flagellation, members perform penance for sins as yet uncommitted, which has proven useful, for instance, when it was "necessary to kill people," since "it was so much
28 less troubling for the assassin if he could do so in a state of grace." Father Gomez, the Court's eager volunteer for the task of assassinating Lyra, is a faithful practitioner of pre-emptive penance and is thus poised to receive absolution for the murder of Lyra even before he leaves Geneva.

According to President MacPhail, while the General Oblation Board sought to understand Dust, the Court "must destroy it altogether," even if doing so means
29 destroying the Holy Church and all its agencies.

The status of the Court is "confused and leaderless" following its failure to kill Lyra,
30 the defeat of Metatron, and the death of the Authority. [*See also* **Magisterium**]

NL/GC Master on 1; plans for Asriel 16; and Rusakov 21

SK Thorold on 2 *[brief]*

SK interrogations, MacPhail's decisions 6; Coulter on 16; Coulter in Geneva with MacPhail 24; bomb launch 25

brief mentions: in Roke's report 5, departure for Himalayas 9, and Gomez 10, plan for attack in Himalayas 11, approach to Himalayas 12, retreat 14, by Asriel 28, heresy and 30, its collapse 38

Dust-hunters

World: Lyra's

Alliances: General Oblation Board

Role: This is the term witches use to refer to those humans who set up Bolvangar and imprisoned Asriel (*i.e.*, the General Oblation Board or Gobblers), according to Serafina Pekkala's dæmon, Kaisa. The name refers to the compulsion the witches see within these people to find the source of Dust and destroy it. [*See also* **Child-cutters, General Oblation Board, Gobblers**]

NL/GC 11

General Oblation Board/Oblation Board

(**General Oblation Board** *and the* **Gobblers** *are one and the same, but passages that refer to them only by their street name,* **Gobblers**, *are not included in this entry.)*

World: Lyra's

Alliances: Magisterium

Role: The General Oblation Board's secret abduction of children to the Bolvangar Experiment Station, for the purpose of separating them from their dæmons, sets in motion the events of *His Dark Materials*. The end of Lyra's childhood begins when this Board, known through rumor as the Gobblers, chooses Lyra's best friend, Roger, as one of its victims.

According to the Master of Jordan College, the Board is a "semi-private initiative"
31 within the Magisterium not "entirely answerable to the Consistorial Court." A likely source for the General Oblation Board's name is the term used in the Middle Ages to refer

to children given by poor families to the church to become nuns and monks; these children were called *oblates*.

The agency has been in operation for at least a decade in the Ministry of Theology, White Hall, London. Among its prominent officials is the Council of State's Lord Boreal, seen in Will's Oxford operating as Sir Charles Latrom.

Witch Serafina Pekkala's dæmon, Kaisa, says the General Oblation Board's agents, whom the witches call Dust-hunters, have been in the remotest regions of Lapland for ten years. They have been setting up experimenting stations, including one the witches have named Bolvangar, meaning "fields of evil." Dr Martin Lanselius, the Witch-Consul for ⎸32 Lapland, tells Lyra and gyptian Farder Coram that the Board operates covertly in the region as the Northern Progress Exploration Company, under the pretense of exploring for minerals. The Board's powers extend to employing Tartar troops to guard Bolvangar and making deals with the armoured bears to ensure that Lord Asriel be indefinitely under house arrest on Svalbard.

The Board was founded and headed by Mrs Coulter. Lyra is shocked when she discovers that Mrs Coulter, the woman Lyra considered her patron and mentor, "*is the* ⎸33 Oblation Board"; this revelation sends Lyra on the run. Later, Lord Asriel refers to the Board in conversation with Lyra as "your mother's gang," adding that Mrs Coulter ⎸34 devised the Board to establish her own power base within the Magisterium. But when Coulter tries to justify her kidnapping of Lyra to Lord Asriel's high commanders, she downplays her role in the Board, arguing that she removed Lyra from Oxford to keep the child out of the Board's clutches. This truly may have been the Master of Jordan College's reason for breaking his promise to Lord Asriel not to let Coulter near Lyra and instead letting the woman have custody of the girl. He once told the college librarian that the Board is "run by someone who has no love of Asriel." Ironically, the safest place for Lyra ⎸35 is at the side of its founder.

The commonly held explanation for the origin of the Board is that it was set up to study Rusakov Particles. Asriel feels that the Board's foundation lies in "the Church's ⎸36 obsession with original sin." Shaman and scientist Stanislaus Grumman sees that the Board and the Spectres of Cittàgazze share a motive: both are obsessed by Dust.

The General Oblation Board is dissolved following the political upheavals in Lyra's world that occurred at the time of Asriel's rebellion against the Kingdom of Heaven. [*See also* **Gobblers, Dust-hunters, Child-cutters**]

NL/GC discussed in London 5; Faa on Coulter and 7; Lanselius on 10; Asriel on, their argument for intercision 21
   brief mentions: by Master 2, Kaisa 11; regardingTony 12, Bolvangar 15; by Pekkala 18, Santelia 19, Asriel to Coulter, Pan to Lyra 23

SK   Grumman 14 *[brief]*

AS   discussed by Court 6
   brief mentions: by Coulter 16, of its dissolution 38

GOBBLERS ✣ ✐

(General Oblation Board is one and the same as the Gobblers, but those passages that refer to it only by its formal name are not included in this entry.)
   World: Lyra's
   Alliances: Magisterium

Role: Followers or employees of the General Oblation Board who kidnap children off the streets acquired urban legend status and became known as "Gobblers." The name may originally have been a play on the agency's initials, but those affected by the unexplained disappearances think the word means that these abductors are "cannaboles" who gobble up the kids they steal.

The arrival of the Gobblers in Oxford marks the beginning of the end of Lyra's childhood. No longer will Lyra dare Roger to play "kids and Gobblers," a variation on hide-and-seek. Their victims include Limehouse urchin Tony Makarios, Lyra's best friend Roger Parslow, and her gyptian pal Billy Costa, as well as other children whose parents are not prominent enough for their complaints to gain much notice by the law.

The Gobblers are variously described as "enchanters" led by either a "beautiful lady," a "tall man with red eyes" or a "youth who laughed and sang," but Lyra reasons that the Gobblers must look like ordinary people since they operate in crowded places in broad daylight. Explanations for their stealing the children are similarly varied: take their prey to Hell or Fairyland, sell them as slaves, or imprison them on a farm where they will be fattened before being butchered for food to be sold to the Tartars. Gyptian Tony Costa, whose brother Billy is missing, initially speculated that the children were taken for use in medical experiments, but decided it was more likely that they were used in "some secret deal they're making up Siberia way" to placate Tartar chiefs, who "bake children and eat 'em."

The Gobblers' strategy of abduction is exemplified by the General Oblation Board's founder herself, the prima Gobbler Mrs Coulter, enticing a pathetic London street kid to be her guest for hot chocolatl. This child, Tony Makarios, a victim of intercision, is the first unforgettable example of the Gobblers' brutality Lyra encounters.

Tony Costa tells Lyra that they had captured Gobblers and forced them to talk – a strategy that has provided the gyptians with a general idea of where their children are being held. The leader of the Eastern Anglia gyptians, John Faa, believes that it is up to the gyptians themselves to organize a "band of fighters" to rescue the children since the Gobblers have the cooperation of "landloper police and the clergy. Every power on land is helping 'em." [*See also* **General Oblation Board, Dust-hunters, Child-cutters**]

NL/GC in London and Oxford 3; talk of in London, name explained 5; Faa and gyptians on 6, 7, 8; gyptians killed raiding their headquarters 9; and Tony's intercision 12, 13; Lyra's fear Samoyeds working for them 14; Lyra claims kidnap by 17; Asriel on 21

AS   brief mentions: Lyra to Will 13, last time Lyra had seen Faa and Coram 38

INQUISITION, OFFICE OF INQUISITION ❈ ✎

World: Lyra's

Alliances: Magisterium

Role: Boris Mikhailovitch Rusakov, the Muscovite who discovered the elementary particle commonly called Dust, was interrogated under "the rules of the Inquisition." Gyptian John Faa worries that, as the church's power continues to grow, the threat increases that the Office of Inquisition could be re-established.

Lord Asriel fears a victorious Metatron would institute "a permanent Inquisition, worse than anything the Consistorial Court of Discipline could dream up." [*See also* **Consistorial Court of Discipline**]

NL/GC 7, 21 *[brief]*

AS   28 *[brief]*

MAGISTERIUM ❖ ⚱ ✎ ⑩

World: Lyra's

Alliances: Church

Role: "A tangle of courts, colleges, and councils," the Magisterium arose after the Papacy was eliminated following the death of Pope John Calvin. Among its branches are the Consistorial Court of Discipline, General Oblation Board, Society of the Work of the Holy Spirit, and the College of Bishops. These divisions greedily guard their power and are often rivals.

Lord Asriel tells Lyra that the Magisterium encouraged Mrs Coulter's development of the General Oblation Board—but only unofficially, in order to retain deniability: "It suits the Magisterium to allow all kinds of different agencies to flourish. They can play them off against one another; if one succeeds, they can pretend to have been supporting it all along, and if it fails, they can pretend it was a renegade outfit which had never been properly licensed."

The Magisterium's authority encompasses Europe and some of Asia and apparently supersedes that of sovereign states to the extent that it has the power to send a nation's troops into battle. The Imperial Guard of Muscovy and the Swiss Guard are among the armed forces bound to defend it. Its interests extend to closely monitoring developments in experimental theology, and tracking the movements of explorers such as Stanislaus Grumman.

After Asriel blasts open a passage out of his world, the Magisterium takes measures to retain its control as it prepares for war. According to the General Oblation Board's Fra Pavel, the Magisterium has "acquired and destroyed" all alethiometers, except for the one he reads at the request of the Board, and the one in Lyra's hands, but he proves misinformed, possibly an instance of one branch of the Magisterium being led to believe it has privileges not afforded to the others. Dr Martin Lanselius, the Witch-Consul for Lapland, claims that the Magisterium is consolidating its forces into a massive army, and rumor has it that some of its troops deployed to the far North are *zombi*.

Asriel expected his bridge to other worlds to mean "the end of the Magisterium, the end of all those centuries of darkness." But while its power is diminished after his rebellion, the Magisterium hasn't been eliminated.

Update: The **10TH** anniversary edition of *THE AMBER SPYGLASS* features an appendix from the "Archive of the Magisterium," which has come into possession of some "Papers of Mary

THE Inquisition

In Will's world, the Inquisition was conducted by the Roman Catholic Church. Early in its history, the Church considered excommunication sufficient punishment for heresy, which under the Judaic system could be punishable by death. But in the Middle Ages, the popes appointed special, permanently installed judges to rule on matters of doctrine. The medieval Inquisition operated chiefly in Italy, southern France, and Germany, but never met in Scandinavia, and ventured into England only during the trial of the Templars. By 1542, during the Reformation, the Inquisition had been replaced by the establishment in Rome of the Holy Office, which was the body that tried Galileo for heresy. However, the Spanish Inquisition, begun in 1478 under the reign of King Ferdinand and Queen Isabella, was not abolished until 1820.

Malone" recording her observations on the world of the mulefa. The Magisterium's preface to Malone's jottings offers them as evidence that there is "no end to the wicked imaginings of heretics and the blasphemous."

NL/GC Master on 2; Asriel on, and Oblation Board 21
  brief mentions: by Serafina to Lyra 18, Lyra to Raknison 19; 23

SK   censors, search for Grumman 6; military power 10
  brief mentions: by Pavel, Lanselius, Skadi 2

AS   Coulter on 16
  brief mentions: by Roke 5, Court 6; 38

10ᴛʜ: *AS* appendix

Northern Progress Exploration Company ❖

World: Lyra's

Alliances: General Oblation Board

Role: The General Oblation Board uses this alias to cover its operations in Lapland, namely the Bolvangar Experiment Station. Their "company" has a branch office in Trollesund. While it claims its business is mineral exploration, according to Iorek Byrnison, most townspeople know otherwise—yet pretend not to, welcoming the money they spend.

NL/GC 10 *[brief]*

Oblation Board

[*See* **General Oblation Board, Gobblers**]

Office of Inquisition [*See* Inquisition]

Order of St. Philomel ✐

World: Lyra's

Alliances: Consistorial Court of Discipline

Role: Two members of this order of nuns serve as stenographers for the Consistorial Court of Discipline in Geneva during the testimony of alethiometrist Fra Pavel about Lyra. Since this order requires a vow of silence, its members make ideal stenographers for secret meetings.

Facts: *There is no St. Philomel in Will's world; however, in Greek mythology, the story of Philomel tells of a woman who was raped by her brother-in-law, Tereus, who then cut out her tongue so she could not tell of his crime. But she wove a tapestry that pictorially revealed her story. Her sister Procne took revenge on Tereus by killing their son and cooking him for her husband's dinner. Enraged to discover he'd eaten his own son, Tereus tried to kill the sisters, but all three were turned into birds before he could reach them. Philomel became the nightingale.*

AS   6 *[brief]*

Ring, Church's / Magisterium's

[*See* **Jewelry in His Dark Materials** *in* Applied Sciences and Technology: Clothing and Accessories]

SISTERS OF OBEDIENCE ❖

World: Lyra's

Alliances: Church

Role: A religious order. The courts placed the infant Lyra with them after removing her from Lord Asriel's home following his killing of Edward Coulter. Their priory is in Watlington, Oxfordshire.

NL/GC 7 *[brief]*

SOCIETY OF THE WORK OF THE HOLY SPIRIT ✎

World: Lyra's

Alliances: Magisterium

Role: This branch of the Magisterium, according to reports of the Gallivespian spy Lady Salmakia, considers Lyra the "most important child who has ever lived." The Society has a better alethiometer reader than the Consistorial Court of Discipline's Fra Pavel. The Court and the Society, normally rivals, pool resources to search for Lyra.

Observation: *Unknown alethiometrist—although mentioned several times, Fra Pavel's counterpart in the Society of the Work of the Holy Spirit is never identified.*

AS brief mentions: in Roke's reports 5, as rivals turned allies of Court 6, its superior alethiometrist 9

VATICAN COUNCIL ❖

World: Lyra's

Alliances: Magisterium

Role: A branch of the Magisterium. Mrs Coulter tells her cohorts at the Bolvangar Experiment Station that the Council may order the execution of Lord Asriel for defying the conditions of his exile and imprisonment on Svalbard by continuing to investigate matters about which the Church has forbidden inquiry.

Observation: *In the UK edition,* Vatican Council *does not appear. In its place is the* Consistorial Court of Discipline.

US: GC 16 *[brief]*

Social Structures of the Worlds:

Educational

Berlin Academy to Scientists

(Specific educational institutions and facilities
are indexed in **Places: Structures** *and* **Places: The Oxfords**)

BERLIN ACADEMY ✧ ⚑ ⑩

World: Lyra's

Role: Very likely the same as the "Academy in Berlin" and "German Academy" which Lord Asriel claimed to be the sponsor of Stanislaus Grumman's last trip North, and the Imperial German Academy.

Grumman confirms his visitor's surmise that he is Dr. Stanislaus Grumman of the Berlin Academy when Lee Scoresby finally meets the man he has been seeking. As he tells the aëronaut his life story, Grumman mentions his journey to Berlin and presentation to the Academy, where he had "no difficulty in gaining membership."

During the course of Scoresby's inquiries on Nova Zembla, the Imperial Muscovite Academy's Observatory's Director agrees with his deputy's report that Grumman was a member of the Imperial German Academy, but as he does so, the Director refers to the institute as the Berlin Academy.

NL/CG 2 [German Academy] *[brief]*

AS brief mentions: in discussion at observatory 6, between Grumman and Scoresby 10

10TH: *SK* appendix

CASSINGTON SCHOLARSHIP ✧

World: Lyra's

Alliances: Jordan College

Role: Jordan College's Cassington Scholar (otherwise unidentified) told Lyra that the story of the Garden of Eden was a "fairy tale." Asriel isn't surprised, noting that the scholarship is given to freethinkers who will question the assumptions of their colleagues.

NL/GC 21 *[brief]*

CONCILIUM ✧

World: Lyra's

Alliances: Jordan College

Role: The governing body of Jordan College, the Concilium oversees the institution's expenditures and investments, including the College's "farms and estates ... dye works and brick kilns, forests and atomcraft works."

NL/GC 3 *[brief]*

HIGH TABLE ✧

World: Lyra's

Role: High table is a physical place in the Jordan College dining hall; it is a shorter table on a dais set perpendicular to three rows of much longer tables. But its significance is its role in the hierarchical structure of the College. Its place settings are gold, the other tables', silver. Its seating is mahogany cushioned chairs; the others', benches.

There are fourteen seats at the high table. The Master presides, and his guests sit there as well with the more senior Scholars. Because women are not allowed a place at the high table, when the Master has distinguished women guests like Dame Hannah Relf and Mrs Coulter, dinner is instead served in his personal quarters.

NL/GC 1, 8 [brief]

MASTERS ✧

World: Lyra's

Role: The current Master (unnamed) of Jordan College is Lyra's guardian. The Master is a Scholar and the College head. Portraits of former Masters line the walls of the College Hall in honor of those who have presided over it. Certain privileges are afforded to the Master alone, for example, inviting guests into the Retiring Room and cooking the poppy heads after a feast. In the crypt of Jordan College, only former Masters are interred intact in coffins. The Master's Lodge (or Lodging) within the College walls includes a handsomely furnished house and a manservant.

Observation: *Dame Hannah Relf, who likely holds the position equivalent to the Master of Jordan College's at St. Sophia's College, is referred to as its* Head, *not its* Master *(or* Mistress). | 56 57

NL/GC brief mentions: of portraits 1, preparing poppy-heads 2, burial 3

SCHOLARS/SCHOLARSHIP ✧ LS

World: Lyra's

Role: At Jordan College, all the Scholars are men, and many (if not most) seem old to ancient, to the twelve-year-old girl. Lyra's makeshift family is composed of two sets of people, the Scholars and the servants of Jordan College.

There are Under-Scholars, who might be at the same professional level as the Junior Scholars—the relatively agile members of the campus community given the unenviable task of trying to run Lyra down and restrain her long enough to teach her bits of something. But although Lyra regards Jordan College's Scholars to be unsurpassed by any other institutions', to her the Scholars are "robed, bearded and gloomy," "suspicious and cranky" characters who speak in "precise and pedantic and lazily arrogant" voices. | 58 59 60
Communicating with them is a challenge to Lyra due to "how roundabout scholars could be. It was difficult to tell them the truth when a lie would have been so much easier for them to understand." | 61

In the Jordan College crypt, Lyra finds that although the Masters' bodies are interred intact, there are a number of skulls on shelves. She figures that so many Scholars have passed through Jordan College that they wouldn't all fit if buried in coffins. Cutting off their heads seems to Lyra a sensible solution to the shortage of space since their heads are the "most important part of 'em anyway." | 62

Particularly noxious to Lyra are female Scholars, who "could never be taken more
seriously than animals dressed up and acting a play." These "dowdy" women smell of
"cabbage and mothballs," and their College is no better than a "dingy brick-built
boarding-house" in North Oxford. When Lyra enters Will's Oxford and finds that the
Scholar the alethiometer has directed her to as an expert on Dust is a woman, she takes
this as even more evidence that Will's is a very "strange world."

Most of Lyra's experience with Scholars involves those who reside in Oxford most or
all of the time. But her father, Lord Asriel, is also in some sense a Scholar, although, in
witch consul Martin Lanselius's words, "scholarship is not his ruling passion." Asriel can
petition the Jordan College fellows to sponsor his expeditions, for example, and even
though the Master and Librarian speculate that they could invoke the College's residence
requirement that a Scholar spend thirty out of fifty-two weeks in Oxford to deny Asriel
funds, that clause is apparently routinely ignored. The shaman, scientist, and explorer Dr
Stanislaus Grumman was also at one point a Jordan College Scholar. Mrs Coulter belongs
to St. Sophia's College, and gyptian John Faa designates her as a Scholar, but Coulter is
quite willing to disassociate herself from the label Scholar when she first meets Lyra at
Jordan College.

Alethiometrist Fra Pavel, dumbfounded by Lyra's ability to read the alethiometer,
describes her as "like no human scholar I can imagine," and considering the girl's
impressions of scholars, Pavel's judgment would most likely be welcomed by Lyra.

While Lyra often finds Scholars tiresome, scholarship is something different. The
great pride she takes in Jordan College's reputation is for the "splendour and fame of its
scholarship." When she leaves her world and Will tells her of the window to his world's
Oxford, Lyra seeks out a Scholar to answer her questions about Dust. Other than the
description of Fra Pavel as "a scholarly-looking priest," it is not until the closing chapter
of *The Amber Spyglass* that Scholars (or scholarship) are again mentioned briefly when
Lyra returns to Jordan College.

Observation: Scholar *is sometimes capitalized and sometimes not in both the UK and US
editions of* His Dark Materials. *The UK editions favor* Scholar *more frequently than
scholar, but there is no consistency within or between the two sets of books.*

NL/GC at Jordan 1-4
> *brief mentions:* recalled in Coulter's London 5, in talks with Faa 7, those in crypt 9; the
> inventor of alethiometer as 10; 11, 13; compared to Bolvangar doctor 14; Santelia as 19;
> Asriel on Jordan's 21, [LS] Lantern Slide 1

SK Mary Malone 4, 12
> *brief mentions:* by Lyra to Will 1; Pavel compares Lyra to, Lanselius on Asriel as, Scoresby on
> Jordan's 2; of Jordan's 3; by Lyra, Will 5, 7; by Scoresby 10

AS 38

Scientists ♟✎

World: Will's, Lyra's

Role: Will tries to convince a skeptical Lyra that when they visit his world's Oxford, she
needs to look for scientists—not theologians, experimental or otherwise. By the time she
reaches the world of the mulefa, Lyra has adopted this term and uses *scientist* to refer to
Dr Mary Malone. The Gallivespian spy, Tialys, seems to prefer Will's world's term,
scientist, but knows that Lyra would understand him better if he called those who study

quantum entanglement "experimental theologians." His boss, Lord Roke, uses *scientist* in conversation with Mrs Coulter. Moreover, the designer of the bomb built in the basement of the Consistorial Court of Discipline's headquarters is the scientist, Dr Cooper, formerly an experimental theologian at Bolvangar.

The scientific persona of Dr Mary Malone cannot believe that she is communicating questions to and receiving answers from Shadow-particles. That may be why the Shadows present themselves as angels, appealing to the former nun in her instead. Until he learns of her past, Will assumes that as a scientist, Mary would not have been receptive to the notion that Shadow-particles are angels. Other things Mary considers as inappropriate for a scientist to do, but which she does anyway, are consulting the I Ching, paying attention to the content of her dreams, and thinking about what is good and what is evil.

SK   Mary on 4, 12
   brief mentions: Will corrects Lyra 3, at Mary's building 7, by Latrom to Coulter 9

AS   Mary's thoughts on 17, Will and Mary discuss 33
   brief mentions: by Tialys 2; Cooper identified as 24; Mary's dreams 32

AUTHORITIES, THE 🗡️ ✒️ ⑩

World: Will's

Role: To Will Parry, the authorities are teachers and social workers who pose a threat to his fragile world. Avoiding the notice of the authorities is essential to Will. That results in his taking on many of the adult responsibilities of running a household during the periods when his mother's mental illness makes it impossible for her to do so. It also prompts Will to offer no defense and feign remorse when teachers punish him for fighting boys who taunt Mrs Parry. He cannot go to the authorities for help when the mysterious men seeking his father break into his house, because to ask for help would expose the entirety of his precarious situation. When he returns to his world, Will is resigned his long absence will mean that the involvement of the Social Services is now unavoidable.

Sir Charles Latrom tells Mary Malone and Oliver Payne that should Lyra return to their lab, to alert him privately, and he'll tell the "proper authorities" who will deal with the situation neatly and discretely.

Update: Among Mary Malone's papers in the appendix to the **10**TH anniversary edition of *THE AMBER SPYGLASS* is a fragment from a letter or a journal entry noting Will's worry that in his absence his mother has been institutionalized. Mary doesn't intend for the same to happen to Will: "He'll need a place to live, a legal guardian or something – And I'll need him. I could help. I could do that."

SK 1

brief mentions: by Latrom 12, Will to Lyra 13

AS 38

BOY SCOUTS 🗡️ ⑩

World: Will's

Role: Long ago in another world, John Parry learned to "be prepared" in the Boy Scouts. At their camp in the forests of Cittàgazze, shaman and scientist Parry/Grumman replies to aëronaut Lee Scoresby's curiosity about how he got a fire started by telling the balloonist that dry matches, not magic, are the secret to lighting a fire in a thunderstorm.

Update: Among Mary Malone's papers in the appendix to the **10**TH anniversary edition of *THE AMBER SPYGLASS* is a fragment from a letter. Mary writes that after leaving the convent, only her work in particle physics really got her attention. She says she "Tried sex, rather dutifully. Like going for badges in the Guides."

Facts: *In the US, the Guides are the Girl Scouts.*

SK 14 *[brief]*

Cabinet Council ❖

World: Lyra's

Role: A council of advisors to the Prime Minister. Lord Asriel and the Master of Jordan College belong to this Cabinet.

　　　　Like the Council of State, it too meets in White Hall Palace.

Observation: *The Cabinet Council is possibly an informal term for the Council of State.*

NL/GC 1 *[brief]*

Council of State ❖ ⚔

World: Lyra's

Role: Lord Boreal belonged to the Council of State in Lyra's world. That experience proves useful for his identity as Sir Charles Latrom in Will's world in that it allows him to quickly grasp how to work this other world's political situation to his advantage.

NL/GC 3 *[brief]*

SK 　9 *[brief]*

Grumman expedition ❖

World: Lyra's

Role: The Grumman expedition, sponsored by the German Academy in Berlin, may have shifted from making "various celestial observations" to investigating the Aurora and what lay behind it (*i.e.* another world), shortly before Grumman and his associates vanished. Lord Asriel offers as evidence of Grumman's fate what he claims to be the scientist's scalped head, found preserved in the ice near Svalbard. 71

NL/GC 2

Guild/Guild of Torre degli Angeli ⚔ ⚒

World: Cittàgazze's

Role: The Guild are philosophers or alchemists who once occupied the Torre degli Angeli/Tower of the Angels, and three hundred years ago invented the subtle knife.

　　　　The people of Cittàgazze, who believe the Guild found a way to enter other worlds using a key, a spell, or alchemy, blame the Guild for ruining their world by letting in the Spectres. The last bearer of the subtle knife before Will, Giacomo Paradisi, confirms the people's accusation. He admits that the Spectres were let in when the Guild split the "bonds that held the smallest particles of matter together," but isn't sure where the 72 Spectres came from.

　　　　Paradisi implies that at the time of the knife's creation, the Guild conducted itself with dignity, devising strict rules for the use of the knife. Shaman Stanislaus Grumman says that when the Guild made the subtle knife, they "created a tool for their own 73 undoing." Cittàgazze ceased to produce anything. Instead, "that Guild of thieves," as 74 Cittàgazzean Joachim Lorenzo calls them, simply took what they wanted out of the other worlds the knife allowed them to visit.

　　　　What the Guild never realized, according to Grumman, was that the knife could have been used to challenge the Authority: "they invented a device that could split open the very smallest particles of matter, and they used it to steal candy."

SK   Lorenz on 6, Latrom on 7, Paradisi on 8
  brief mentions: Will to Lyra 11, Grumman/Parry to Will 15

AS   *brief mentions:* 26, 34, 37

IMPERIAL GUARD OF MUSCOVY ⚔️ ✎

World: Lyra's

Alliances: Magisterium

Role: "Most ferociously trained and lavishly equipped army in the world," it serves the Magisterium. To retrieve his balloon, commandeered by the Guard while he was away searching for shaman Stanislaus Grumman, aëronaut Lee Scoresby shows the Magisterium's ring, saying its "authority…trumps the Guard." It works, but showing the ring taken from the corpse of one of the Magisterium's censors unfortunately also alerts the Imperial Guard to the whereabouts of Scoresby and his passenger, Dr Stanislaus Grumman.

Several dozen blue-uniformed Muscovite troops in four zeppelins pursue Scoresby and Grumman to Cittàgazze. Scoresby stands up to them single-handed, but eventually dies of wounds inflicted by the Guard.

When Iorek Byrnison goes into the Cittàgazze mountains to pay his last respects to his friend Scoresby, he passes the wreckage of the Guard's zeppelins and walks over their bones—all that the scavenging animals have left behind of the Imperial Guard troops.

Note: *The dæmons of the Imperial Guard are wolves.*

SK   in Siberia 10, in Cittàgazze 14

AS   3 *[implied]*

IMPERIAL NAVY [*See* **Fire bombing (Imperial Navy)** *in* **Applied Sciences and Technology: Weapons**]

INTELLIGENCE SERVICES ⚔️

World: Lyra's

Role: One of the multi-faceted lies Sir Charles Latrom tells Dr Mary Malone and Oliver Payne is that the intelligence services are looking for Lyra because she has "an unusual piece of equipment, an antique scientific instrument, certainly stolen, which should be in safer hands than hers."

SK   12 *[brief]*

NUNIATAK DIG ⚔️

World: Will's

Role: Strictly speaking, the Nuniatak dig wasn't a dig at all but a preliminary survey. There were four archaeologists, a physicist interested in studying the Aurora and high-level atmospheric particles, and a former Royal marine and now professional explorer, Col.

John Parry. The archaeologist who answers Will's questions about an Oxford University Institute of Archaeology expedition that vanished in 1985 from Alaska uses this informal term for the project, otherwise unnamed.

Observation: *Only the archaeologist Will questions in Chapter 4 of* THE SUBTLE KNIFE *uses the phrase "Nuniatak dig." Here it is used, as the archaeologist employed it, to refer to the expedition during which John Parry left his world.*

SK 4, reports in Parry's letters 5, Latrom tells Coulter about 9, Grumman tells Scoresby about 10

OFFICIAL SECRETS ACT ⚔

World: Will's

Role: Sir Charles Latrom refers to this policy as an excuse to avoid questions from Oxford physicists Mary Malone and Oliver Payne about why he is so interested in Lyra's visits to their laboratory and their research into dark matter.

SK 12 *[brief]*

PARLIAMENT ❖

World: Lyra's

Role: Legislative body mentioned by John Faa as he reminds the assembled East Anglia gyptian families of incidences in which Lord Asriel has proven a friend. This includes leading the defeat of the Watercourse Bill, which, apparently, would have been detrimental to their way of life had it been passed by Parliament.

NL/GC 8 *[brief]*

ROYAL MARINES ⚔

World: Will's

Role: John Parry served in this branch of the British military before becoming a professional explorer.

SK 4 *[brief]*

ROYAL SOCIETY ✎

World: Will's

Role: Mary Malone is intrigued that the mulefa's seed-pod trees began to fail 300 years previously. In the world of Cittàgazze, that was when the subtle knife was invented, and in Lyra's world when the alethiometer was devised. During that same period in Mary's own world, the Royal Society was formed and Sir Isaac Newton "was making his discoveries about optics and gravitation."

Note: *The "Royal Society" is a casual way to refer to what is more properly designated The Royal Society of London for the Improving of Natural Knowledge, founded in 1662.*

AS 27 *[brief]*

SECURITY SERVICES ⚮

World: Will's

Role: This agency is trying to find Col. John Parry, who vanished from the Far North twelve years previously. They believe that recent anomalies in the earth's magnetic field and the man's disappearance both have to do with the existence of other worlds.

Latrom claims, in conversation with Mrs Coulter, that in Will's world he acted as a spy during the period when "the security services in this world were preoccupied with the Soviet Union" (known to her as Muscovy).

SK   9 *[brief]*

SOCIAL SERVICES [*See* **Authorities, the**]

SOLDIERS ⚮ ✎

World: Lyra's

Role: During the course of *THE AMBER SPYGLASS*, two worlds prepare and then engage in war. On the republic of heaven's side are armies of "lizards and apes, great birds with poison spurs, creatures too outlandish to have a name," Gallivespians, ghosts, and armoured bears. Among those fighting for the kingdom of heaven are horsepeople, the Imperial Guard of Muscovy, the Swiss Guard, and others not so easily named. These include soldiers supporting the Consistorial Court of Discipline's bomb launch by preparing the site and various apparatuses required or by guarding Coulter and the site.

The kingdom's side includes ground forces of riflemen and those manning flamethrowers, assisted by various flying machines whose pilots prove vulnerable to being spurred by a Gallivespian delivered on a dragonfly steed. Gallivespians fighting for the republic battle kingdom forces wearing light grey armour, helmets, and masks, accompanied by grey wolf dæmons. Angelic forces and witches are among the fighters on both sides. [*See also* **Angels, Armoured bears, Gallivespians, Ghosts, Horsepeople, Imperial Guard of Muscovy, Swiss Guard,** *and* **Witches**]

SK   Lanselius on zombi among 2; shoot at Scoresby and Grumman in Siberia 10; pursuit of Scoresby and Grumman 14
        brief mentions: by Skadi of those gathering at Asriel's 13

AS   in Himalayas 12, 13; their corpses 14, at bomb launch 25, in battle of republic and kingdom 29, 31

SPECIAL BRANCH ⚮

World: Will's

Role: According to Mary Malone's colleague, Oliver Payne, this term refers to the unit specializing in "Terrorism, subversion, intelligence... all that." When she tells him about the visit to their laboratory by Inspector Walters of the Special Branch, Payne clarifies her vague notion that Walters is a policeman.

SK   12 *[brief]*

Swiss Guard ✐

World: Lyra's

Alliances: Consistorial Court of Discipline

Role: Armed with crossbows as deadly as rifles but with the advantage of silence, the Swiss Guard attacks Lyra and Will as the children flee from Coulter's cave. Two of the Guard's zeppelins and seventeen men are lost in this battle, including one killed by Will.

Note: *The dæmons of the Swiss Guard are wolf-dogs.*

AS   brief mentions: leaving Geneva 9, at Coulter's cave 12, Will shoots one 13, losses tallied 16

Tartar guards ✤

World: Lyra's

Alliances: General Oblation Board and Mrs Coulter

Role: Mrs Coulter uses troops of Northern Tartars as guards at the General Oblation Board's Bolvangar Experiment Station, and she has drafted another regiment to fly with her to Svalbard to overthrow armoured bear king Iofur Raknison.

When Lyra starts a fire at Bolvangar to get the kids outside in anticipation of the arrival of the gyptian rescue party, she is initially intimidated by the ferocity of the Tartars' wolf dæmons. The Tartars, who wear padded mail and helmets with visors that cover their faces except for eye slits, are prepared to fire on the fleeing children.

Even knowing they are facing certain death and defeat, the Tartars perform as in a planned drill, with groups of four bending to one knee to fire their rifles as Iorek comes hurtling toward them, ready and able to slash open their throats.

Before she knew of Iofur Raknison's defeat on Svalbard by the returned king Iorek Byrnison, Mrs Coulter had planned to use Tartar troops to overthrow the government and take charge of the kingdom. As Iorek and Lyra try to get to Asriel before he can hurt Roger, the troop of bears with them are attacked first by witches on Coulter's side, and then by a zeppelin carrying Tartars and a machine gun.

Note: *The dæmons of the Tartar guards are grey wolves with yellow eyes.*

NL/GC battle at Bolvangar 17, battle with bears on Svalbard 22
        brief mentions: Kaisa on 11, alethiometer on 12, seen at Bolvangar 16; 20

Tunguska campaign ✤

World: Lyra's

Role: Upon Lyra's asking if his balloon could carry the armoured bear to Svalbard, Lee Scoresby recalls the time he rescued Iorek from the Tartars during this otherwise unidentified battle.

NL/GC brief mentions: Scoresby vouches for Iorek during first talk with Lyra 11; 13

Westminster ✤

World: Lyra's

Role: Informal reference to a political body, the counterpart to the parties at White Hall; on their zeppelin flight to London, Mrs Coulter entertains Lyra with insider stories about their conflicts with White Hall.

Facts: *In Will's world's London, the City of Westminster, itself part of the City of London, is where Parliament meets and the royal family lives; thus, "Westminster" has come to be a one-word means of referring to the constitutional democratic monarchy of Great Britain. Compare with* White Hall.

NL/GC 4 [brief]

White Hall ❖

World: Lyra's

Role: Location of the king's palace and the Ministry of Theology; also an informal reference to the political body governing England.

Westminister Palace with the River Thames in foreground

Facts: *In Will's world's London, the number of agencies and offices connected with the British Civil Service on Whitehall (one word) Road has led to "Whitehall" becoming a short way to refer to that complex of governmental branches. Compare with* Westminster.

NL/GC 2, 3, 4, 9 [brief]

Juvenile Alliances

Brick-burners' children to Townies

BRICK-BURNERS' [CLAY-BURNERS'] CHILDREN ◈ ✎

World: Lyra's

Role: In the children's wars of Oxford, the brick-burners' children (considered "slow and dull, with clay in their brains") were such a despised enemy of the townies and the colleges that these two warring factions would occasionally unite forces. They would attack the brick-burners' children on their own territory, the Claybeds, where there were unlimited supplies of mud to sling in battle.

    Remembering these battles inspires Lyra to urge the Bolvangar children to escape the Tartar guards by hurling snow into the eye slits of their enemy's helmets. Much later, she tells another group of children about these battles—the ghosts in the world of the dead.

Observation: *Lyra uses* brick-burners *when she describes her exploits in the suburbs of the world of the dead, and* clay-burners *when she later tells the ghosts about life in Oxford.*

NL/GC 3, 17 *[brief]*

AS 19, 23 *[brief]*

COLLEGERS ◈

World: Lyra's

Role: The collegers are the children of the staff of the Oxford colleges, plus Lyra, of course. While there are internal rivalries between the children whose parents work at different colleges, the collegers will team up to fight against townies, the brick-burners' children, or gyptians; moreover, townies and collegers might come together to wage war on brick-burners' children or gyptians.

NL/GC 3, 6 *[brief]*

SPECTRE-ORPHANS ⚑

World: Cittàgazze's

Role: The morning after Will and Lyra meet, they encounter two children, who tell them others will be coming soon, but no grown-ups. Many of those children are likely orphans. The city has been besieged by Spectres, which children do not see and which cause them no harm but are deadly to adults.

    Soon the city fills with unsupervised children. Later, when Lyra realizes the importance of the city's Tower of Angels and the subtle knife within it, she believes that the children returned from the hills to get under the protection of the knife because with it, "they could do anything, they could even grow up without being afraid of Spectres."

In the meantime, the orphans do as unsupervised children might be expected to do. Their propensity for destructive and violent behavior is strong and likely reflects the instability and decadence of their society.

Will and Lyra's first encounter with Spectre-orphan mob violence is when they come across the kids stoning the cat who Will followed into this world from Oxford. The next episode follows when Will has become the bearer of the subtle knife. Their sticks and stones are supplemented with pistols and rifles, and only the fortuitous arrival of the witches saves Will and Lyra.

The title of the third chapter of THE SUBTLE KNIFE is "A Children's World."

[*See also* **Angelica, Boy in Tee-shirt,** *and* **Paolo** *in* **Characters**]

Note: *Seldom does the term Spectre-orphan accompany the accounts of the children it denotes.*

SK   Will and Lyra's first encounter with 3; attack cat 5; evacuation of, Lorenz on 6; discussion of Guild, at play 7; rampage at belvedere 11
      brief mentions: 8, 9; by Will and Lyra 13, Grumman and Scoresby 14

TOWNIES ❖ ✐

World: Lyra's

Role: The townies are the children of those who live or work in the local area around Oxford, but not at the colleges. On special occasions, townies team up with collegers to fight the brickburners' children or gyptians.

NL/GC 3, 17 *[brief]*

AS   23 *[brief]*

Social Structures of the Worlds:
Financial/Commerce
From Automatic Teller to Wells Fargo Bank

AUTOMATIC TELLER ⚲

World: Will's

Role: Lyra is astounded when Will goes up to an automatic teller machine in his Oxford, inserts a card, punches in some numbers, and gets money in return.

SK 3 *[brief]*

COLCROFT'S ⑩

World: Lyra's

Role: Lord Asriel was planning to get more information about Colcroft's from Smith and Strange.

Update: The back of the map in *LYRA'S OXFORD* has an advertisement for a selection of catalogues available on request from Smith and Strange, Ltd., an Oxford publishing house. One of those catalogues is that of Theophrastus Colcroft and Sons'. They deal in various scientific and related equipment including microscopes, photogram supplies, and tools for navigation: from sextants to compasses to slide rules. [*See* **Smith and Strange**]

10TH: *NL* appendix

CORONA ⚲

World: Cittàgazze

Role: Currency of Cittàgazze

Facts: *In Will's world,* corona *is the Spanish word for the currency of the nations of Slovakia, Estonia, Iceland, Denmark, Norway, and Sweden. The Spanish word* corona *is translated in English as* crown.

SK 1 *[brief]*

British "dollar" (half-crown)

GOLD [COINS, DOLLAR, MONEY] ❖ ⚲ ✎ ⓁⓈ

World: Lyra's, Will's, Cittàgazze

Role: It was Lord Asriel's habit on his visits to Lyra at Jordan College to signal the completion of their interview by giving her a handful of coins—for example, "five gold dollars."

Lyra uses a gold coin to fashion a dæmon-coin for Tony Makarios.

Will is astounded when Lyra pulls out her gold coins in his world, and

U.S. silver dollar

tells her to put them out of sight. Later, a roll of gold coins is one of the things he takes from the deceased Sir Charles Latrom's campsite for use in his trip through Lyra's world. [*See also* **Sovereigns** *(below)*]

Observation: *John Faa uses gold figuratively to mean money, wealth, or resources, and literally when he talks about the response to his proposal that the gyptian families commit to an expedition to rescue their children in terms of the weight of the money which the heads of the families have presented him.*

In Will's world, dollar *is a British slang term for a half-crown coin, but the reason for this use of* dollar *was because of the coin's resemblance to an American* silver *dollar. There were a number of gold coins in circulation in England, notably sovereigns* [See below], *but they wouldn't have been called dollars, and dollars wouldn't have been gold.*

NL/GC gyptians' 7, 8
> *brief mentions:* Asriel gives Lyra gold dollars 3; Coram offers Iorek 10, daemon-coin 13, Scoresby's 18, Asriel's bribes for Raknison 21, ⓁⓈ Lantern Slide 3

AS *brief mentions:* Lyra shows Will 3, Scoresby and 10, used in Cittàgazze 13

AS *brief mentions:* Will takes Latrom's 2, bears' 9, Will leaves as payment for food in Holland-like world 18, boatman on 21

Economic systems of the worlds of *His Dark Materials*

The economic systems of the worlds of *His Dark Materials* vary. They run the full gamut from completely structured to very loosely structured—with extremes represented by the rigid class hierarchies of Lyra's England and the communal, money-less arrangements of the mulefa society. Only in the world of the dead is the acquisition and retention of any form of wealth or control of resources entirely irrelevant.

In Lyra's England, class structures are rigid and disparities in wealth significant. Yet limited movement may be possible. Mrs Coulter, we learn, was not "so well-born" as Lord Asriel, but was smart and married well. Asriel had been "richer than a king" but lost all his properties and lands in a court decision. However, he was still able to raise the capital to outfit expeditions North, and continued to serve as an advisor to the Prime Minister. Noble birth is of greater importance, then, than wealth. Even penniless Lyra believes herself inherently gifted not only with the power to lead and command respect, but to read the alethiometer without training ("So each image had several meanings, did it?

Why shouldn't she work them out? Wasn't she Lord Asriel's daughter?").

Her friend Roger, in contrast, would harbor no such illusions. Five generations of Parslows had worked as craftsmen and servants at Jordan College, and there is no reason to think that Roger's generation won't be the sixth. Already, at age 12 or so, he is a kitchen boy. There is no indication that public schooling exists in *Lyra's Oxford*.

In London, the world of Coulter's fashionable friends contrasts with that of the street urchin Tony Makarios and the other Gobbler victims. The Gobblers prey on poor children because protection under the law does not extend, it seems, to those who lack the wealth to demand it.

Co-existing with the mainstream society of Lyra's world are various counter cultures, including those of the gyptians, witches, and armoured bears. The gyptians live in England, but apart from it. They participate in local economies such as the Horse Fair trading days in Oxford, and are not impoverished. However, they are under no delusions that they command enough wealth

EXCELSIOR ⑩

World: Lyra's

Role: Lord Asriel was planning to get more information about Excelsior products from Smith and Strange.

Update: The back of the map in *LYRA'S OXFORD* has an advertisement for a selection of catalogues available on request from Smith and Strange, Ltd., an Oxford publishing house. One on offer is The "Excelsior" Cold Weather Clothing Company's General Catalogue. It features "the celebrated 'Blizzard-Proof' range, endorsed by the Royal Arctic Society's Equipment Committee." [*See* **Smith and Strange**]

10TH: *NL* appendix

POUND ⚖

World: Cittàgazze, Will's

Role: Pound Sterling is the currency of England in Will's world. Will pays for his lemonade in Cittàgazze with a one-pound coin; he gives Lyra one of the twenty-pound notes he withdraws from his mother's bank.

Facts: *For centuries, a pound sterling was worth 240 pence, written as 240d. The "d" stands*

to induce action from the authorities when their children go missing. Instead, they come together, and raise the money and manpower needed to launch a united campaign to rescue their children. Their voluntary self-taxation appears to be an equitable means of providing sufficient resources to respond to an emergency.

If the impression Martin Lanselius gives of the witches' tolerance of the Northern Progress Exploration Company is typical of their arrangements, the witches maintain minimal contact with the mainstream society of the Far North by retaining male consuls to keep relationships "cordial" and through deliberate non-interference in one another's affairs. Kaisa (Serafina Pekkala's dæmon) is more forthcoming, revealing that the witch clans had accepted payment in return for letting the company set up its sinister experiment stations. But once the nature of the Company's operations is discovered, Serafina's clan evicts these tenants forcibly.

The armoured bears are another culture that has limited involvement with the dominant economies of its world. Under the leadership of Iofur Raknison, they have accepted monetary bribes from groups, like the General Oblation Board, to imprison political enemies (e.g. Lord Asriel). The bears are wise about human affairs, however, and treat these prisoners well, knowing that political power in human society is transient. Raknison rejects the natural resources of Svalbard—its iron—in favor of those which must be imported—the human symbols of prestige and status: gold and marble. This means he needs more and more money, and to raise it he risks yielding his sovereignty over his own kingdom. When Iorek Byrnison is restored to power, he returns the nation to its reliance on its own natural resources but retains enough gold for emergencies, like hiring a ship to travel into the Himalayas.

Will's world's England isn't as rigidly hierarchical as Lyra's. It has a middle class, to which Elaine and Will Parry belong; while they haven't much to spare, they aren't really impoverished, like Tony Makarios and his mother, and Will's future career wasn't determined at his birth, as Roger's was. Still, the rich are different. Will knows without doubt that Sir Charles Latrom's wealth and status insure that his story about owning the alethiometer will be believed unquestioningly. And while the laboratories of Will's world don't have to put up with the presence of

88

censors, they are reliant on funding, which, as Latrom's proposal to the Dark Matter Research Institute suggests, may be contingent on compromising the direction or integrity of their research. In Will's world, as in Lyra's, there is a collective social acceptance that money is power. Some middle class individuals, like Mary and Will, feel contempt, not admiration, for the rich. Will's distrust of the rich is accompanied by respect for those who work at making a living and pay their own way; he won't, for example, take advantage of the absence of clerks and landlords in Cittàgazze.

The once-prosperous urban centers of the world of Cittàgazze have self-destructed as a consequence of greed. With the invention of the subtle knife, merchants, fishermen, craftsmen, and so on abandoned their trades since it seemed that all they required could more easily be attained by theft—taking from other worlds and giving nothing in return—than by work. Outside the cities, modest rural economies survived in areas where people continued to farm.

Finally, there are the mulefa, who have no currency and share their world's resources equitably—keeping what they value most, seedpods, in a common storehouse. Labor (maintaining the seedpod trees, vegetable gardens and grazer herds, building and repairing their thatched huts, and everyday tasks of cooking and childcare) gets done, but how it is determined who does what when is not explained. Their needs are satisfied easily enough that they have leisure to pursue some artistic endeavors, adorning their huts, for instance, and the products they make for practical purposes, like nets and ropes, show the degree of careful craftsmanship that the gyptians associate with articles of luxury in Lyra's world.

The economic system of the mulefa's world, then, has as little in common with that of Lyra's world as does the anatomy of the conscious beings of these two worlds. History, environment, biology—all could have contributed to the definition and distribution of wealth in the various worlds of *His Dark Materials*, but in each case, its commerce reflects that world's values and priorities.

for denarii, which was a unit of currency in ancient Rome. In 1971, British currency was changed to a decimal-based system, and the pound sterling was redefined as equivalent to 100p (new pence).

SK   1, 3, 4 *[brief]*

Quarter–Day ❖

World: Lyra's

Role: Every quarter the Jordan College Bursar collects rents from the properties it holds throughout Brytain, delivers a report to the Concilium, and prepares for a celebratory feast.

Facts: *Quarter-Days in the England of Will's world are March 25 (Lady Day), June 24 (Midsummer Day), September 29 (Michaelmas), and December 25 (Christmas).*

NL/GC 3 *[brief]*

Royal Mail ❖

World: Lyra's

Role: A Royal Mail zeppelin, bound for London, leaves Oxford in the evenings.

NL/GC 3 *[brief]*

SHILLING

World: Lyra's

Role: Two shillings buys a cup of coffee and a ham sandwich from a street vendor in Lyra's London.

Facts: *Under Britain's old currency system, shillings were coins worth one-twentieth of a pound, or 12d (old pence). After 1971, one-twentieth of a pound became 5p (new pence). Shillings were last issued in 1966.*

NL/GC 3, 6 [brief]

SMITH AND STRANGE ⑩

World: Lyra's

Role: Lord Asriel uses this business to secure items needed for his expeditions.

Update: Smith and Strange, Ltd., are the publishers of the Globetrotter series of maps and a variety of travel books. One of their Globetrotter maps is used in *LYRA'S OXFORD*. According to the advertisements on the back of that map, they also distribute other merchants' catalogues with items of interest to explorers. The offices of Smith and Strange, Ltd. are at Globetrotter House on Beaumont Street, Oxford, the same street where the Ashmolean Museum is located in both Lyra's and Will's Oxfords, and where the Oxford Institute of Archaeology is in Will's.

10ᴛʜ: *NL appendix*

SOVEREIGNS

World: Lyra's

Role: The currency of Lyra's world is sovereigns, very likely gold coins.

Lyra's disappearance from Mrs Coulter's apartment prompts an unidentified source to offer a reward of 1000 sovereigns for her capture, and when the gyptian family leaders present the money they've collected for the journey North, they give bags of gold.

[*See also* **Gold** *(above)*]

Facts: *In Will's world's Britain, sovereigns are gold coins. First issued in 1489, their worth was one pound sterling. In 1604, production ceased in favor of a coin known as the* unite. *That was followed briefly by the* laurel, *and then by the* guinea *in 1688, which reigned until 1816, when the invention of steam-powered minting led to the appearance of a new gold sovereign. But after a hundred years, the sovereign lost out in 1917 to the demand for gold bullion to pay for Britain's involvement in World War I. But for a brief run in 1925, the gold sovereign was no longer issued except as a collector's item to commemorate rare state events (e.g. the accession to the throne of Queen Elizabeth in 1953). Small numbers were produced from 1957 to 1968, while from 1979 onwards sovereigns have been minted annually for sale to collectors, but not for use as general currency in place of paper currency. A 2005 gold sovereign can cost approximately £75 ($140) to £130 ($250) for a grade of "uncirculated" or "proof" (rarest).*

NL/GC 5, 7 [brief]

TRUST FUND ⚔✒

World: Lyra's, Will's

Role: The Master tells Lyra that Lord Asriel left her a trust fund and named him executor, which isn't true, but the Master plans to take care of the girl's needs himself.

Four times a year, Will and his mother receive money from his father, John Parry, which is paid out of a family trust.

Observation: *Lyra's world's economic system may seem at first glance to belong to a world we've left behind, but these shared mechanisms of commerce—trust funds and executors—suggest otherwise.*

SK   4 *[brief]*

AS   38 *[brief]*

WELLS FARGO BANK ✦

World: Lyra's

Role: The ever-practical Lee Scoresby sends a deposit to his retirement account after every job so that when he is ready to give up piloting his balloons he can purchase a small ranch in his native country of Texas.

Facts: *Henry Wells and William G. Fargo established the Wells Fargo Bank of Will's world in 1852 during the California Gold Rush in the United States. It is still in operation today. The first Wells Fargo banks opened in San Francisco and Sacramento, California.*

Wells Fargo is best remembered as a stagecoach express for transporting gold, mail, and other valuables west from Nebraska to California, and north from Utah into Montana and Idaho, and California into Oregon—thousands of miles of undeveloped Western territories. Its logo today features a stagecoach drawn by six-horses, although it ran its own stageline for just three years, from 1866 to 1869. Wells Fargo continued using other companies' stagecoaches, as well as the Pony Express, trains, ships, and finally trucks to make deliveries through 1918, when it left the express business and focused on banking.

The Wells Fargo stagecoaches moving gold through the open, often lawless Wild West captured the American imagination both during their hey day and for long after the last coach ran. Wells Fargo's ongoing battles with stage robbers in Tombstone and Bisbee; lawman Wyatt Earp and Wells Fargo's shootout at the OK Corral in 1881 with the Clanton gang, and dozens of other true stories provided ready-made plots for Western movies, comics, pulp novels, and so on.

NL/GC 18 *[brief]*

John C.H. Grabill, Library of Congress, LC-DIG-ppmsc-02600, 1889

Deadwood coach, South Dakota, 1890

LANGUAGES AND DICTION

Languages and Diction

*Languages, Words from Languages Other than English
or Words with Uses Exclusive to* HIS DARK MATERIALS

Dialects

GYPTIAN	ENGLISH	CHAPTER
Byanroping	gathering of families	*NL/GC* 7
Landlopers	non-gyptians	*NL/GC* 7, 8
Roping[1]	short for byanroping	*NL/GC* 6, 7, 8, 9
Zaal[2]	meeting hall	[*See* **Places: Structures**]

Observation: [1]*Roping is capitalized consistently in* NORTHERN LIGHTS. *It is usually lowercased
in* THE GOLDEN COMPASS, *with the exceptions occurring on pages 113-14.*
[2]*Zaal is a Dutch word for lounge, parlor, or sitting room.*

WITCH	ENGLISH	CHAPTER
Short-life/short-lived[1]	ordinary humans	*SK* 2, 6, 13, 15
Child-cutters	Gobblers/General Oblation Board	*NL/GC* 10, 20; *SK* 2
Northlanders	short-lived of Far North	*NL/GC* 10
Vampyre	vampire	[*See* **Other Beings**]

Observation: [1]*Witches can live for a thousand years.*

CITTÀGAZZE	ENGLISH	CHAPTER
Mandarone	likely a mandolin	*SK* 6
Spectre-orphans[1]	Spectre victims' children	*SK* 6, 14
Tabaco	likely tobacco	*SK* 6

Observation: [1]*Stanislaus Grumman also includes among this group children left alone when the
adults in a city flee. Spectre-orphans roam the country; some hire themselves out to adults to
procure supplies from the cities, while others simply scavenge.*

Mulefa Language

MULEFA	ENGLISH	CHAPTER
Anku[1]	thank-you	AS 10
Chuh[2]		
(trunk sweep left-right)	water	AS 10
(trunk curled at top)	rain	AS 10
(trunk curled under)	sadness	AS 10
(trunk flick left)	young shoots of grass	AS 10
Make-like	metaphor	AS 17, 32
Night-picture[3]	dreams	AS 32
Sraf	Dust, Shadow particles, Rusakov particles	[*See* Philosophy]
Wise one	leader	AS 32
Zalif[4]	a single mulefa	AS 10, 17, 20, 38

Observation: [1]*Anku is actually how mulefa imitate Mary's "thank-you."*
[2]*The same word-sound can have different meanings depending on an accompanying movement of the trunk.*
[3]*Night-picture is only one of the mulefa's many words for dreams, which they take very seriously.*
[4]*The mulefa differentiate between gender. Mary can hear but not duplicate the difference in the sound between the word for male and female zalifs.*

Ordinary Words with Uses Exclusive to *His Dark Materials*

WORD	MEANING	CHAPTER
Cutting	intercision	NL/GC 19, 21; SK 2; AS 25
Entire child	unsevered child	NL/GC 2, 5
Sever, severance, severed child, severing[1]	pertaining to the process of intercision	NL/GC 2, 3, 12, 14, 15, 16 AS 6, 24, 25, 36

Observation: [1]*There are four instances of* severed *in* THE SUBTLE KNIFE *which do not pertain to intercision; these occur in the phrase "severed head" during discussion of Grumman's head, which Asriel claimed to have found and displayed in the Retiring Room of Jordan College, but which in fact is firmly attached to the shaman's neck.*

Other Unusual Words or Word Usages

WORD	MEANING	See [or CHAPTER]
Aërodock	airport	Applied Sciences: Transportation
Anbaric	electric	Natural Sciences: Physical Sciences
Anbarograph	recording	Applied Sciences: Information Tech.
Atomcraft	powered by uranium	The Natural Sciences: Scientific Studies
Chocolatl	chocolate	Applied Sciences: Food
Cliff-ghast	(no equivalent)	Other Beings
Coal-silk	polyester	Applied Sciences: Clothing
Coal-spirit	type of fuel	Natural Sciences: Physical Sciences
Dæmon	soul	Other Beings
Fire-mines	mines of Svalbard	Applied Sciences: Other
Genniver	juniper ·	Applied Sciences: Food
Ghast	dæmon-less person	Other Beings
Ground gas	type of fuel	Applied Sciences: Transportation [balloon]
Gyropter	helicopter	Applied Sciences: Transportation
Jenniver	juniper	Applied Sciences: Food
Nälkäinens	headless ghosts	Other Beings
Night-ghast	nightmare figures	Other Beings
Panserbjørne	armour + bear	Other Beings
Philosophical apparatus	scientific instrument	Applied Sciences: Other
Photogram	photograph	Applied Sciences: Information Tech.
Photo-mill	radiometer	Applied Sciences: Other
Projecting lantern	slide projector	Applied Sciences: Information Tech.
Roarer[1]	how Lyra recalls the word *aurora*	*NL/GC* 7
Rock-oil	coal?	Applied Sciences: Transportation [balloon]
Sky metal	meteoric iron	Natural Sciences: Physical Sciences
Smokeleaf	tobacco	Applied Sciences: Smokes & Medicinals
Spectres	(no equivalent)	Other Beings

Observation: [1]*Trying to describe to gyptian John Faa what she heard when Lord Asriel addressed the Jordan College Scholars, Lyra mentions the* Roarer; *while Faa is perplexed, the confusion is cleared up by Farder Coram, who understands she means* Aurora.

Foreign Words and Phrases

WORD	SOURCE/ENGLISH	CHAPTER
À outrance[1]	French/mortal combat	*NL* 20 (only)
Aletheia	Greek/ truth	*NL/GC 7. SK 7*
Adonai	Hebrew/God	Allusions
Bene elim	Hebrew/angels	Allusions
Brantwijn	Middle Dutch/brandy	*NL/GC* 2, 3, 4
Cauchuc	Spanish/rubber	Applied Sciences: Other
Château-Vert	French/green castle	Places: Oxfords
Chthonic	Greek/underground	Applied Sciences: Transportation
El	Hebrew/God	Allusions
Fra	Italian/Father	Characters (Pavel)
Otyets	Russian/Father	Characters (Borisovitch)
Requiescant in pace[2]	Latin/Rest in peace	Allusions
Torre degli angeli	Italian/Tower of Angels	Places: Structures
Tulku	Tibetan/reincarnated lama	Characters (Pagdzin *tulku*)
Yahweh	Hebrew/God	Allusions
Yambe-akka	Saami/Goddess of dead	Allusions

Observation: [1]*Not spoken, but used as the title for chapter 20 of* NORTHERN LIGHTS. *The English equivalent of this fencing phrase is used in* THE GOLDEN COMPASS: *"Mortal Combat."*
[2]*Lyra notices this phrase, commonly abbreviated as R.I.P., carved on the stone vaults in the Jordan college crypt. When she sees the hand-scrawled notice, "R.I.P. DIRECTOR: LAZARUS" added to the Dark Matter Research Institute's sign, Lyra doesn't connect this comment with the inscriptions on the tombs in her Oxford.*

References to Languages*

LANGUAGE	CONTEXT	CHAPTER
Arabic[1]	Taught at Jordan College	*NL/GC 3*
Chinese	Mary Malone compares its tonal inflections to mulefa's trunk positions	**10**TH: AS appendix
Fen-Dutch	Source of words in Gyptian dialect	*NL/GC 7*
Roman[2]	Lyra guesses as language of "Requiescant in pace"	*NL/GC 3*

*Either English is widely spoken in Lyra's world's Lapland and Siberia or dæmons spend much time translating. The dæmon-less armoured bears also speak English, however.

Observation: [1]*Lyra's mish-mash of an education at Jordan College included smatterings of Arabic.*
[2]*Used in reference to the Latin phrase "Requiescant in pace"; Latin might universally be called Roman in Lyra's world—or not. In* LYRA'S OXFORD, *Lyra uses her* Latin *homework as an excuse to turn down an invitation.*

ALLUSIONS

Religious – Biblical and Otherwise

Observations in this section presume that the Bible of Lyra's world is roughly comparable to that of Will's, although they are obviously unlike in some respects—as we know from the mention of dæmons in the Genesis of the Bible that Asriel reads to Lyra.

The Bible is divided into books, chapters, and verses. Thus, a reference to Genesis 1:22 would be to the twenty-second verse of the first chapter of the Book of Genesis.

Some books are divided into parts, for example, 1 Kings ("first Kings," often written I Kings) and 2 Kings ("Second kings", or II Kings). The King James Version is used here.

ADAM AND EVE ✦ ⚷ ✐

Role: In order to answer her question about the nature of Dust, Lord Asriel reads Lyra the story of the temptation of Adam and Eve. He recounts his world's version of Genesis, Chapter Three, of their temptation by the serpent, and subsequent banishment from the garden of Eden. When Lyra counters that she'd been told the story was "just a kind of fairy-tale," Asriel encourages her to "think of Adam and Eve like an imaginary number, like the square root of minus one: you can never see any concrete proof that it exists, but if you include it in your equations, you can calculate all manner of things that couldn't be imagined without it."

The serpent promises Eve that if she eats the fruit of the one tree forbidden to her and Adam, that their dæmons will "assume their true forms" and they'll be "as gods, knowing good and evil." Eve eats, and offers the fruit to Adam, who eats as well. Then they "knew their own dæmons" as promised, but also no longer felt "at one with all the creatures of the earth and air" or as if there were "no difference between them," but instead felt shame. When God discovers their disobedience, his punishment is that they will now have to work to survive and will die, or "return unto the ground…for dust thou art, and unto dust shalt thou return." Asriel's summary is that "the moment their dæmons became fixed" was when "sin and shame and death" began.

In Will's world, when the Shadow-particles identify themselves as angels who have tinkered with the course of human evolution for vengeance, Mary Malone immediately makes the connection between

> ## Philip Pullman on the Fall:
>
> "I try to present the idea that the Fall, like any myth, is not something that has happened once…but happens again and again in all our lives… For me it's all bound up with consciousness, and the coming of understanding of things—and making the beginning of intellectual inquiry, which happens typically in one's adolescence… With consciousness comes self-consciousness, comes shame, comes embarrassment, comes all these things, which are very difficult to deal with."
>
> *From:* "Question of faith: Philip Pullman debates religion with the Archbishop of Canterbury, Dr Rowan Williams."

the rebel angels and the expulsion of Adam and Eve from Eden. Mary concludes too that the sraf/Dust/Shadows' being far more attracted to adults than to children has "to do with the great change in human history symbolized in the story of Adam and Eve; with the Temptation, the Fall, Original Sin."

Facts: *The fall of Adam and Eve is the central topic of John Milton's* Paradise Lost. *In Will's world, the complete biblical account of the lives of Adam and Eve can be found in Genesis 1:26 to Genesis 5:5*

> *Biblical scholars have proposed several alternatives for the location of the Garden of Eden. Some favor the Persian Gulf; others a location in Asia Minor. The Biblical account mentions four rivers flowing from it: the Tigris, Euphrates, Pishon and Gihon.*

Note: *Generally,* Garden *either alone or in the phrase* Garden of Eden *is capitalized in the US edition, but lowercased in the UK.*

NL/GC Asriel on 21

SK   brief mentions: by Shadows 12, Coulter 15

AS   discussion by Court 6, mulefa's parallel version 17
      brief mentions: Coulter at fortress 16, Coulter to MacPhail 24, at adamant tower 28, in Metatron's ancestry 30

Why Milk and Honey?

The oft-repeated high praise for a land that it "flows with milk and honey" is a Biblical allusion. When Yahweh appeared to Moses, he promised to deliver the Israelites from slavery in Egypt to "a land flowing with milk and honey," the Promised Land (*Exodus 3:8;* see also *Numbers 16:13*). The phrase is also one of the first Biblical expressions to appear in a form of English; Aelfric, a monk of the Old Monastery of Winchester, translated the relevant passage in the Book of Numbers into Anglo-Saxon some time around the year 1000.

ADONAI [*See* God]

ALMIGHTY/ALMIGHTY FATHER [*See* God]

ANCIENT OF DAYS ✐

Role: This phrase (uppercased) is first used by Mrs Coulter in her argument with Father MacPhail to refer to the Authority. She feels he has become more remote from his creation, and theorizes that if he still exists, by now he must be "decrepit and demented." When Lyra and Will release the Authority from the crystal litter, the phrase is again used, this time lowercased, to emphasize the frailty of the being that emerges.

Observation: *Mrs Coulter says that even in the days of the prophet Daniel, the Authority was aged, and, in fact, her use of the phrase* Ancient of Days *alludes to the Old Testament Book of Daniel: "I beheld till the thrones were cast down, and the Ancient of Days did sit, whose garment was white as snow, and the hair of his head like the pure wool: his throne was like the fiery flame, and his wheels as burning fire" (Daniel 7:9). Other examples in the same chapter of the Book of Daniel are 7:13 and 7:22.*

Facts: Ancient of Days *is also the title of a painting by William Blake that shows a white-bearded figure reaching out of golden clouds; the fingers of his right hand seem to form a golden compass, this one the geometer's tool.*

AS   brief mentions: 24 [uppercased], 31 [lowercased]

APOCALYPSE OF ST JOHN ✎

Role: Siberian priest Otyets Semyon Borisovitch tells Will that the Apocalypse of St John predicted the climatic changes and redirection of rivers' flows that he has witnessed recently in his village.

Facts: *Also known as the Book of Revelation, this book, the last of the New Testament, concerns visions and signs that will precede the end of the world.*

AS   8   *[brief]*

ASSYRIANS ✎

Role: When Father MacPhail, President of the Consistorial Court of Discipline, accepts Father Gomez's plea to be the assassin designated to eliminate Lyra, MacPhail compares the eager young priest to the "invisible," "silent" "angel that blasted the Assyrians."

Facts: *MacPhail is likely referring to the thwarted plans recorded in 2 Kings 19:35 of the King of Assyria from 705 to 681 BC, Sennacherib, to conquer Jerusalem, a city in Judah, after laying waste to its countryside and imprisoning its king, Hezekiah. But Hezekiah, refusing to surrender, petitioned God for help, and in the night one angel killed 185,000 Assyrian troops. Sennacherib gave up on Jerusalem.*

AS   6   *[brief]*

CALVIN ✎

Role: Arguing her case before Lord Asriel's high commanders, Mrs Coulter defends her decision to hide Lyra away in a Himalayan cave by saying that once the church learns of the witches' prophecy, her daughter is as good as dead. As an example of the church's ruthlessness she alludes to Calvin, who authorized the killing of children.

Observation: *It is not clear whether this Calvin and Pope John Calvin (see below) are one and the same.*

Facts: *In Will's world, John Calvin (1509-1564) was a Protestant reformer who was once exiled from Geneva because it was feared he sought to establish a new papacy. Later when his supporters gained political power, he returned, but no Protestant papacy followed.*

This Calvin, like the one feared by Coulter, once ordered that a child who struck his mother be executed by beheading.

AS   16   *[brief]*

CALVIN, POPE JOHN ✤

Role: Pope John Calvin appears to have been the last pope in the church of Lyra's world; the papacy was abolished after his death and replaced by the Magisterium.

Under his leadership, the papacy was moved to Geneva. There he set up the Consistorial Court of Discipline, still headquartered in Geneva, and through this agency secured "the Church's power over every aspect of life."

NL/GC   2   [brief]

CREATOR ⚔✎

Role: This synonym for the Authority is in fact a misnomer, according to the angel

Balthamos, since although the Authority was the first angel, he is not different in kind, nor did he create, the ones who followed. Mrs Coulter is stunned when Asriel's high commander King Ogunwe shares this angelic wisdom with her at Asriel's fortress.

Note: *Generally, when* Creator *is used as another name by which the Authority is known, it is capitalized, but when "the creator" refers to an unknown force or one who is not the Authority, it is lowercased.*

SK Skadi on 13 [lowercased UK; uppercased US] *[brief]*

AS *brief mentions:* by Balthamos 2, Ogunwe 16

DANIEL 🖉

Role: Coulter alludes to this Biblical figure when challenging Father MacPhail, President of the Consistorial Court of Discipline, to explain what she perceives as God's withdrawal from man's affairs. She notes that long ago during the days of the prophet Daniel, the Authority was already called the "Ancient of Days."

Facts: *The physicist Isaac Newton wrote extensive commentaries on the Apocalypse of St John and another prophetic book, the Old Testament's Book of Daniel.*

SK 24 *[brief]*

EDEN, GARDEN OF [*See* Adam and Eve]

EL [*See* God]

ENOCH/METATRON [*See* Metatron/Enoch's Family Tree, Characters]

ENOSH [*See* Metatron/Enoch's Family Tree]

EVE ✦♀🖉

Role: A prophecy of the witches of the North is confirmed by the alethiometer. Lyra's "true name," according to the witches, is "Eve!...Mother Eve," and the Court's alethiometrist Fra Pavel reports that Lyra "is in the position of Eve, the wife of Adam, the mother of us all, and the cause of all sin" and that if tempted, she is likely to succumb.

Mrs Coulter tells Asriel's high commanders that after she learned the witches' name for her daughter, she knew she had to keep Lyra safe from the Consistorial Court of Discipline because they would kill her rather than take the risk of the prophecy being fulfilled. She believes that if it could, the church would go back to the garden of Eden and kill Eve. Mrs Coulter doesn't mention that after attaining her information by torturing a witch, she proclaimed her intention to "destroy" her daughter: "Lyra is Eve. And this time she will not fall. I'll see to that. There will be no Fall."

Facts: *In the Book of Genesis in Will's world's Bible, Eve is named by Adam after their fall from God's favor, and the name* Eve *means "mother of all the living" (Gen. 1:22).*

[*See also* Adam and Eve, *above, and* Prophecy in Philosophy]

NL/GC Asriel on 21

SK Feldt's confession 15

AS   discussion by Court 6, Coulter at Asriel's 16 [brief], Mary's thoughts 17, Coulter to MacPhail 24

FALL (OF MAN)   [*See* Adam and Eve]

A Comparison Between the Book of Genesis of Will's World and Lyra's World

The differences between the Books of Genesis in Lyra's world and Will's world are indicated by a change in font in the passages below. Note that Lord Asriel's edition closely resembles in wording the King James Version of Will's world, so-called because it was at the request of England's King James I, that the first English translation of both the Old and New Testaments was accomplished. This Bible was finished in 1611 and has been used by English-speaking Protestants ever since.

We do not know if the verses in Asriel's Bible are numbered in the same way as the Bible in Will's world, as Asriel did not read the numbers out loud to Lyra.

Will's 3:5:   For God doth know that in the day ye eat thereof, then your eyes shall be opened, and ye shall be as gods, knowing good and evil.

Lyra's: *For God doth know that in the day ye eat thereof, then your eyes shall be opened, and your dæmons shall assume their true forms, and ye shall be as gods, knowing good and evil.*

Will's 3:6:   And when the woman saw that the tree was good for food, and that it was pleasant to the eyes, and a tree to be desired to make one wise, she took of the fruit thereof, and did eat, and gave also unto her husband with her; and he did eat.

Lyra's: *And when the woman saw that the tree was good for food, and that it was pleasant to the eyes, and a tree to be desired to reveal the true form of one's dæmon, she took of the fruit thereof, and did eat, and gave also unto her husband with her; and he did eat.*

Will's 3:7:   And the eyes of them both were opened, and they knew that they were naked; and they sewed fig leaves together, and made themselves aprons.

Lyra's: *And the eyes of them both were opened, and they saw the true form of their dæmons, and spoke with them.*
But when the man and the woman knew their own dæmons, they knew that a great change had come upon them, for until that moment it had seemed that they were as one with all the creatures of the earth and air, and there was no difference between them.
And they saw the difference, and they knew good and evil; and they were ashamed, and they sewed fig leaves together to cover their nakedness.

The passage Lord Asriel indicates to Lyra as God's curse upon Adam for eating the fruit and the source of the term Dust for Rusakov Particles is exactly the same in his Bible as in Will's world's Genesis 3:19: *"In the sweat of thy face shalt thou eat bread, till thou return unto the ground; for out of it wast thou taken: for dust thou art, and unto dust shalt thou return."*

12

FATHER (GOD THE) [*See* God]

GARDEN [*See* Adam and Eve]

GOD, GOD OF THE CHURCH/CHURCH ◈ ⚲ ✎

Role: Although in Lyra's world *the Authority* and *God* are often used interchangeably, when the Bible is discussed and in common interjections, invocations, and praise, *God* is preferred by speakers ranging from Lord Asriel's manservant Thorold to Stanislaus Grumman, and Father MacPhail to the angel Balthamos.

The first discussion of God occurs near the end of NORTHERN LIGHTS / THE GOLDEN COMPASS when Lord Asriel and Lyra discuss Adam and Eve or, as Lyra puts it, the story about why "God threw them out of the garden." Lord Asriel tells Lyra it was God's curse to Adam, "*for dust thou art, and unto dust shalt thou return*" that led to Rusakov Particles being known as Dust.

In THE SUBTLE KNIFE, there are only five occurrences of *God*. Two of these refer to the Authority. The only new information about God is the claim of a Cittàgazze Spectre-orphan that God sent Spectres to their world as punishment "because people were bad."

In THE AMBER SPYGLASS, *God* appears in the interview between the Consistorial Court of Discipline's Father MacPhail and Mrs Coulter, and in the musings of the court's assassin Father Gomez, who judges the mulefa's wheels as "contrary to the will of God." But the most extensive consideration of God in HIS DARK MATERIALS is provided by Mary Malone in the last chapters of the novel.

MacPhail reasons that Asriel is not among those who believe God is dead since Asriel is intent on killing Him. Coulter believes that if God is "still alive, at some inconceivable age, decrepit and demented," then the "truest proof of our love for God" would be to kill him. Her doubt of his continued existence as a formidable force is based on his withdrawal from his creation since the time of Adam and Eve and his description "Ancient of Days" over two millennia ago.

When Will, Lyra, and Mary Malone talk

By their fruits shall ye know them...

When Lee Scoresby has to shoot a Magisterium's censor, he asks the dying man why he shot at him. The Skraeling's answer is that by asking about the scientist-shaman Stanislaus Grumman and knowing about Dust, Scoresby identified himself as "an enemy of the church." He then adds, "By their fruits shall ye know them. By their questions shall ye see the serpent gnawing at their heart."

The metaphorical parting comment of the Skraeling is a partial allusion to Matthew 7:16, which occurs in the third section of Christ's Sermon on the Mount. The first sentence the Skraeling quotes is accurate, based on Will's world's Bible, but the second appears nowhere. The rest of the passage develops the metaphor:

7:16 By their fruits you shall know them. Do men gather grapes of thorns, or figs of thistles?

7:17 Even so every good tree bringeth forth good fruit, and the evil tree bringeth forth evil fruit.

about their lives when they are together in the mulefa's world, Mary describes her movement from being as certain of her holiness as she was her cleverness to being uncertain of what she believed. When she remembered what it felt like to fall in love, she realized that by choosing to be a nun, she was giving up her one chance at life's pleasures—and no one would be any better off for her sacrifice. She isn't sure if now she believes that there is no God, but rejecting her faith meant that she did not have to answer to anyone—she was "free and lonely" and "didn't know whether I was happy or unhappy, but something very strange had happened." When Will asks if she misses God, Mary [25] replies, "what I miss most is the sense of being connected to the whole of the universe" [26] through the connection to God. She also explains that when she stopped believing in God, she continued to believe in good and evil, but began to consider them as means of describing people's actions, not the people themselves

[*See also* **Authority** in **Characters**]

Facts: *When Will asks Balthamos if the Authority is God, the angel replies: "The Authority, God, the Creator, the Lord, Yahweh, El, Adonai , the King, the Father, the Almighty—those were all names he gave himself."* [27]

The four-letter name, YHWH (Yahweh), first used in the Book of Genesis and considered the most important name for God in Judaism, is also referred to as the Tetragrammaton. One source cited for the name Yahweh *is the story of Moses and the burning bush. Moses is instructed to tell his people that* my Lord *has appeared to him, and* my Lord *is the source of another name that Balthamos lists as the Authority's,* Adonai. *Roman Catholic Church historians maintain that* El, *possibly defined as strength or power, was the first Hebrew name of God.*

Note: *Not included here are references to the Authority, unless* Authority *and* God *are both used in the passage, or to god, goddesses or gods (lc). Italicized pages are those in which* God *is not discussed but mentioned in passing, usually in a plea for help or of thanksgiving.*

Discussed:

NL/GC by Asriel and Lyra 21

SK   by Thorold and Serafina 2, Spectre-orphans 7 *[brief]*, Grumman/Parry 15

AS   by Balthamos 2, Gomez as "arrow of" 6 *[brief]*, by Borisovitch 8 *[brief]*, Coulter and MacPhail 24

Is the Authority God?

One of the charges leveled against HIS DARK MATERIALS by some factions is that it dramatizes the death of God. Even though this occurs in another world, it is felt that the Biblical allusions to the *God* of the Old Testament imply that the *Authority* of Lyra's world's is meant to be *God in* Will's world—and that the terms the *Authority* and *God* are used as synonyms. But being called God isn't much proof of divinity, nor does it necessarily follow that a being who calls himself God, or is called God by those living in the present, is the same as the one the Old Testament writers described.

In Will's world it is generally agreed that three characteristics define God: omnipotent (all-powerful), omniscient (all-knowing), and omnipresent (transcends the limits of time and space; also immutable). The Authority cannot release himself from a conveyance and is thus far from all-powerful; hasn't a clue what his Regent Metatron, a human elevated to an angel (no son of the Authority is ever mentioned) has in store for him, or what Coulter and Asriel have in mind for his Regent, and so is obviously not omniscient. Finally, he ages and dies as do beings that exist within time, and so fails to possess omnipresence.

Mentioned in passing, usually as invocation or in plea:

NL/GC 5, 6, 7, 8, 9, 10, 13, 14, 16, 17, 18, 19

SK　12

AS　7, 18

GOD/GODS/GODDESSES ❖ ⚱ ✎

Note: *This entry is for only those mentions that are lowercased. For references to the* Authority *and* God *see those individual entries.*

Role: Not all cultures in Lyra's world accept the Authority as their sole god. Some tribes of Tartars worship tiger-gods or practice trepanation to communicate with their gods. Witches worship different gods than do ordinary humans (perhaps goddesses would be more likely since men play peripheral roles in their culture). Yambe-Akka is their goddess of death. Armoured bears worship no god or gods at all.

　　When Lyra and Will, pursued by the gang of Spectre-orphans, take refuge in the belvedere, they pass through a room housing sculptures of goddesses (gods are not mentioned). Whether their presence is merely decorative is not known.

NL/GC brief mentions: of Tartars' 13, witches' 18, in Lyra's flattery to Raknison 19, serpent's promises 21

SK　*brief mentions:* of witches' and Tartars' 2, Tartars' 4, of Cittàgazze 11, by Skadi 13

AS　*brief mentions:* by Iorek 14, Coulter 24

HEAVEN ❖ ⚱ ✎

Role: In *NORTHERN LIGHTS / THE GOLDEN COMPASS* most references to *heaven*, *Heaven* or *heavens* are to space. An exception is when the Master makes a comment about the Barnard-Stokes heresy to the Librarian and reminds him that the Holy Church claims there are only two worlds, one physical and the other "the spiritual world of heaven and hell." Also, when Lord Asriel severs Roger and his dæmon, the energy released and directed toward the Aurora seems to defeat this majesty: "the vault of heaven… was suddenly pierced as if by a spear."

　　Most of the instances of *heaven* or *heavens* in *THE SUBTLE KNIFE* appear as speculation about Asriel's plans.

　　THE AMBER SPYGLASS is the only volume that includes the phrases *the kingdom of heaven* (US: *Kingdom of Heaven*) and *republic of heaven* (US: *Republic of Heaven*). King Ogunwe tells Mrs Coulter that Asriel doesn't intend to go on the offensive against the kingdom of heaven—but is prepared to defend his republic from invasion. The battles against the two take place in Asriel's world, which suggests that the kingdom launched the first assault.

　　In the world of the dead, two ghosts debate the veracity of what they learned during their lives about heaven and hell. One, a martyr when alive, says that she expected that devoting her life to prayer, rather than to enjoying all life had to offer, would mean she'd spend eternity in heaven, but another argues, unconvincingly, that "*This* is heaven, truly!"

　　[*See also* **Kingdom of heaven, Republic of heaven** *in* **Places and Peoples: The Worlds**]

NL/GC brief mentions: by Master 2, and aurora 11 [Heaven], sky 17, 23 [heavens]

SK　*brief mentions:* 2, 5; and angels 6; war in 9, 12, 15 *[implied]*

AS　ghosts' dispute 23; kingdom of 35, 36; republic of 37; kingdom, republic of 38
　　　brief mentions: by Balthamos 2; kingdom, republic of 16, 26; of sons of heaven 31; Mary on 33

Battle in Heaven

The story of the temptation of Eve and the fall of man is relatively clearly laid out in Genesis in the Bibles of both Lyra's and Will's worlds. In Will's Bible, at least, the story of the rebellion of the angels has to be pieced together from brief comments throughout the Bible, and the most extensive description appears in the last book, Revelations or the Apocalypse of St John: "And there was a great battle in heaven, Michael and his angels fought with the dragon, and the dragon fought and his angels: and they prevailed not, neither was their place found any more in heaven. And that great dragon was cast out, that old serpent, who is called the devil and Satan, who seduceth the whole world; and he was cast unto the earth, and his angels were thrown down with him" (Apocalypse 12:7-9). Other sources of the story are Jude 1:6 and II Peter 2:4.

The Old Testament also mentions what has come to be understood as the rebellion of Satan and his renegade angels. Among these is Isaiah 14:12-15: "How art thou fallen from heaven, O Lucifer, who didst rise in the morning? How art thou fallen to the earth, that didst wound the nations? And thou said in thy heart: I will ascend into heaven, I will exalt my throne above the stars of God, and I will sit in the mountain of the covenant, in the sides of the north. I will ascend above the height of the clouds, I will be like the most High. But yet thou shall be brought down to hell, into the depth of the pit."

John Milton's *Paradise Lost* greatly extends the story of the angels' failed rebellion; it opens with a defeated Satan rousing his troops to fight again. Rather than launch another hopeless attack, they decide instead that Satan alone will enter God's newest creation, this world, formed of the dark materials of the abyss, and tempt Adam and Eve to rebel against God. The angel Raphael relates the story of Satan's rebellion to Adam in Books V and VI of Milton's epic.

HELL/HELL ❖ ⚱ ✎

Role: The Holy Church of Lyra's world claims there are only two worlds, one physical and the other "the spiritual world of heaven and hell," and the popular culture of Lyra's world presents hell as a fiery place underground. For example, when children start disappearing without reason or trace, rumor has it that the Gobblers take the missing to Hell, and when she first sees the Aurora, its crimson streaks remind Lyra of Hell's fires. [31]

The witches of Lyra's world seem to be unaware of a hell to fear; Lord Asriel's manservant Thorold has to explain to Serafina Pekkala about angels, the rebellion in heaven, and the banishment of the renegades to hell.

When Lyra and Will first cut through to the entrance to the world of the dead, they encounter Dirk Jansen. This man fears he is headed to hell, and Lyra tells him "Hush…we'll go together," suggesting she believes the world of the dead is not the hell of [32] whatever stories brought its fires to mind when she watched the Aurora.

They find the world of the dead is not the hell commonly feared. However, the harpies, angered by Lyra's plan to liberate the ghosts, initially threaten to change the world of the dead from a wasteland into a hell by increasing their torment of those ghosts who haven't yet found their passage out.

Finally, *hell* is occasionally used as a mild curse, more on the level of an interjection. Users include Lord Asriel, Mary Malone, John Parry, and most frequently, Texan aëronaut Lee Scoresby.

NL/GC brief mentions: by Master 2, Gobblers and 3, Aurora and 11

SK   brief mention by Thorold 2 *[brief]*

AS   brief mention by Dirk Jansen 18 *[brief]*; harpies' threat, ghosts' dispute 23

In curses:

NL/GC by Asriel 1; Scoresby 11, 13

SK   by Malone 4, Parry 5; Scoresby 6, 14, 15

AS   by Asriel 5

HINDUS ❖

Role: As a deception, gyptian Farder Coram says that without Lyra having access to the books explaining its symbols, reading her alethiometer is akin to seeing the future in pots of ink, a feat reserved for Hindu mystics.

Observation: *This Eastern means of divination is described in Wilkie Collins'* The Moonstone *(1868), a classic mystery novel in Will's world.*

NL/GC brief mention 10 *[brief]*

JARED [*See* **Metatron/Enoch's Family Tree**]

JESUS ✎

Role: Mary Malone's desire to place her life "in front of Jesus to do as he liked with" led her to become a nun.

Observation: *Lyra's mention of Christian baptism is the only occasion in* HIS DARK MATERIALS *where the Christian religion is alluded to in Lyra's world. The words* Christ *and* Jesus *are never uttered in Lyra's world.*

AS   33 *[brief]*

KENAN [*See* **Metatron/Enoch's Family Tree**]

KING, THE [*See* God]

LAZARUS ⚕

Role: Along with R.I.P., Lazarus has been scrawled on the door of the Dark Matter Research Unit following the title "Director."

Facts: *There are two Lazaruses in the New Testament. The better known is "Lazarus of the Miracle," who Jesus raised from the dead.*

SK   brief mention 4 *[brief]*

LORD, THE [*See* God]

MAHALEL [*See* **Metatron/Enoch's Family Tree**]

MANTLE ⚕

Role: Elaine Parry has provided her son only a sketchy outline of his father, John Parry, who disappeared before Will was a year old. But she has told him often that one day he will "be a great man too. You'll take up his mantle." Lyra is the first person Will shares this with, and he reveals that while he isn't certain what his mother meant, he thinks it might mean that his father has been doing something important, and that as his son, he must carry on with this work.

Observation: *When Will decides to take with him from the Cittàgazze mountaintop his father's shaman's cloak, in a literal sense he is effectively taking up his mantle; a mantle is like a cape, but is hooded and has arm slits. But the expression that Elaine uses is likely a Biblical allusion to the story in 2 Kings:2 about the prophet Elias, who to show that God had told him to choose as his successor Eliseus, draped his mantle over Eliseus's shoulders. The mantle allowed Eliseus to cross the River Jordan; when he touched it to the river's waters, the river divided, and provided a means for him to cross on dry land. This miracle convinced the prophets of Jericho that he was Elias's true successor.*

SK brief mentions: 1, 13, 15

MARTYR'S PALM ⚔

Role: Attacked by the Magisterium's Skraeling censor, Lee Scoresby fires his pistol in self-defense, and the dying man refuses help, angry that Scoresby might deny him a martyr's death. The Skraeling mentions the "martyr's palm," which reminds Scoresby of a painting of the death of a saint showing his dæmon "borne upwards by cherubs and offered a spray of palm, the badge of a martyr."

Facts: *Early Christians adopted the palm, an ancient symbol of victory, as their own, and it came to be associated with martyrdom, the ultimate victory of faith over its enemies. A familiar example is Palm Sunday, the beginning of Easter week, when palms are used to commemorate the entry of Jesus into Jerusalem.*

SK   6 [brief]

J. & R. Lamb Studios, Library of Congress Prints and Photographs Division

Design drawing for stained glass window of St Lucy with palm leaf and sword.

METATRON/ENOCH'S FAMILY TREE ✎

Role: Metatron tells Mrs Coulter that when he was the man, Enoch, he loved many beautiful women. To give her a sense of how long ago this was, he provides his genealogy. He belongs, by his reckoning, to the seventh generation of man:

• Adam and Eve were Enoch's great-great-great-great grandparents.
• Enosh, a grandson of Adam and the son of Seth, was Enoch/Metatron's great-great grandfather.
• His great-grandfather was Kenan, whose son was Mahalel.
• Jared, the son of Mahalel, was the father of Enoch (later the angel Metatron).

Facts: *The genealogy of Enoch is found in Genesis 5:15-20. Seth, the third son of Adam and Eve, was born after their first son, Cain, killed his brother Abel. Seth lived to the age of 807 years and had a son, Enosh, when he was 105 (Genesis 4:25-26 and 5:6-8). The great-grandson of Enoch was Noah, who built an ark.*

[*See also* **Enoch, Metatron** *in* **Characters**]

AS   brief mentions: 5, 28, 30

MOSES

Role: Coulter alludes to this Biblical figure when discussing what she perceives as God's withdrawal from man's affairs. She noted that, as early as the time of Moses, the Authority was already forbidding anyone to look at his face.

Observation: *The allusion here may be to Exodus 33:20. When Moses asks to see God's glory, he is told: "...Thou canst not see my face: for there shall no man see me and live."*

SK 24 *[brief]*

MOTHER EARTH

Role: Witch Serafina Pekkala invokes the authority of mother earth in her incantation intended to stop the continuing and debilitating bleeding Will suffers (from the stumps of the two fingers he lost becoming the bearer of the subtle knife).

Note: Mother Earth *(but not the subsequent reference to* mother*) is capitalized in the US* Subtle Knife *but not in the UK edition.*

SK 13 *[brief]*

MOTHER OF ALL/ MOTHER OF US ALL [*See* Eve]

MUSTARD SEED

Role: Mrs Coulter says goodbye to Lord Asriel and worries that Metatron may have seen through her lies because of the love she now feels for Lyra: "All I could hope was that my crimes were so monstrous that the love was no bigger than a mustard seed in the shadow of them. ... But the mustard seed had taken root and was growing, and...was splitting my heart wide open, and I was so afraid he'd see."

Observation: *This is an allusion to the Parable of the Mustard Seed in the New Testament. Jesus often used parables, extended metaphors or allegories, in his sermons. In this parable, the growth of the kingdom of heaven is compared to a mustard seed's. This seed is tiny, but the plant it produces is a strong, vigorous, spreading bush (Matthew 13:31-32, Mark 4:30-32, or Luke 13:18-19).*

Mustard Seed

AS 31 *[brief]*

ORIGINAL SIN [*See* Adam and Eve]

SATAN, SATANIC

Role: Using her computer (or "Cave"), Mary Malone asks the Shadow particles if the story of "Satan and the garden of Eden" is true. The Shadows neither deny nor confirm this, but tell Mary to get on with

The Temptation

finding Will and Lyra because she must "play the serpent."

The only other instance of *Satan* or *Satanic* is when Father Gomez, Lyra's would-be assassin, musing on the necessity that the mulefa be converted, decides that "their habit of riding on wheels was abominable and Satanic, and contrary to the will of God."

Observation: *Mary's remembrance of the story of the garden of Eden seems to include Satan. The Shadows don't quibble, but their use of* serpent *rather than* Satan *in response is not arbitrary. Satan is never mentioned in Genesis. The biblical reason for equating Satan and the serpent is found in one of the passages from which the story of the battle in heaven is based, Apocalypse of St John (or Revelation) 12:9: "And the great dragon was cast out, that old serpent, called the Devil, and Satan, which deceiveth the whole world: he was cast out into the earth, and his angels were cast out with him."*

SK 12 [brief]

AS 35 [brief]

Keep behind me, Metatron

There are several obvious Biblical allusions (mustard seed, thief in the night) in Mrs Coulter's final appearance in HIS DARK MATERIALS. As she lures Metatron along the edge of the abyss, she encourages him with the words "Keep behind me, Metatron." This is highly reminiscent of Christ's "Keep behind me, Satan," a phrase used twice in the New Testament. One occurrence (Luke 4:1-13; Matthew 4:10) is when Jesus goes into the wilderness for forty days to plan his ministry and is taunted by Satan. The second is when one of his disciples, Peter, responding to Jesus' prediction of his coming crucifixion, cries out that such will not ever happen. One interpretation is that Jesus rebukes Peter because Peter's refusal to accept what lies ahead, when he should be offering support and understanding, is a satanic attempt to deflect Jesus from his mission (Matthew 16:23).

37

38

SERPENT/SNAKE, THE

Role: In the third chapter of Genesis in the Bible of Lyra's world, the serpent tells Eve that if she eats the forbidden fruit, "*your eyes shall be opened, and your dæmons shall assume their true forms, and ye shall be as gods, knowing good and evil.*"

39

Philip Pullman on the temptation of Lyra and Will:

"...in the mulefa world growing up was never seen as a loss, but a gain: their story of the snake and the wheel shows that. Mary is told to play the serpent, and in that world, that means bring wisdom."

Source: Philip Pullman in Readerville.

Although the word *snake* is used in place of serpent in the *make-like* (story) that Atal tells Mary Malone about the origin of the mulefa, the snake's role is the same—but the interpretation of the consequences for the first male and female mulefa to take its advice is different. A talking snake encourages the first mulefa to put her foot through the hole in a seedpod so that she will gain wisdom. When she does so, the seedpod's oil saturates her foot, and this mulefa sees sraf for the first time. Before they followed the snake's advice, these creatures had no memories or hopes for the future. Afterwards, "they knew who they were."

40

More Temptations

The primary temptation in HIS DARK MATERIALS is an allusion to the story of Eve being tempted by the serpent in the Garden of Eden.

There are a few other instances of *temptation* in HIS DARK MATERIALS that are of interest.

- John Faa warns that any gyptian "tempted by those thousand sovereigns" offered as a bounty for the capture of Lyra when she is on the run from Mrs Coulter "had better find a place neither on land nor on water."
- Giacomo Paradisi tried "to tempt" Sir Charles Latrom into entering Cittàgazze by leaving open the Sunderland Avenue window in Oxford.
- Lyra is "very nearly tempted" to leave the Pitt-Rivers Museum with Latrom, who offers to introduce her to someone who has been trepanned.
- Will finds it "pleasant and tempting," after his first visit to her hide-out, to think about Mrs Coulter's beauty and sensuality.
- King Ogunwe thinks Mrs Coulter doesn't belong at a meeting of the high command at the basalt fortress, and he warns Lord Asriel that if "she tempted" him, he "would not resist." The king is correct.
- Will must fight a "powerful temptation" to cut a way home to his own world when he is preparing to cut into the world of the dead; he is "tempted" against his better judgment to talk back to Iorek when the bear shoves him for not being honest. Both Will and Lyra find themselves "tempted" by the abyss to look down into its depths as they creep along its narrow edge.
- When Mary Malone, still a nun, is considering acting on her attraction to a colleague at a conference, she considers leaving the party, returning to her room to pray "and confess to the priest and promise never to fall into temptation again."

41
42
43
44
45
46
47

There are a few other instances of *serpent* in HIS DARK MATERIALS. At least three characters have serpent dæmons: witch consul Dr Martin Lanselius; scoundrel (in two worlds) Lord Boreal/Sir Charles Latrom; and the imprisoned mad scientist Joachim Santelia. A serpent is among the symbols on the alethiometer — its most immediate meaning is *cunning*.

[*See also* **Tempter/Temptation**]

U.S. Fish and Wildlife Service, Jan 2002

Serpent (Copperhead)

NL/GC in Eden 21
    brief mentions: Boreal's dæmon 3, poison 8, on alethiometer 9, Lanselius's dæmon 10, Santelia's dæmon 19

SK Shadows on 12
    brief mentions: Lanselius's dæmon 2, Skraeling censor on 6, Latrom's dæmon 15

AS Mary as 7, snake in mulefa's tale 17, harpies' hair 21 *[brief]*, tempter 24

SETH [*See* **Metatron/Enoch's Family Tree**]

St Augustine 🗡

Role: As a former nun, Mary Malone is well versed in the teachings of this Roman Catholic theologian. Malone remembers his speculations: "Angel is the name of their office, not of their nature. If you seek the name of their nature, it is spirit; if you seek the name of their office, it is angel; from what they are, spirit, from what they do, angel." When Mary Malone contacts the Shadows the first time they identify themselves as angels, suggesting he was right—with one change: "from what we do, matter. Matter and spirit are one."

Facts: *St Augustine (354-430), one of the Fathers (early teachers) of the Catholic faith, is credited with developing a number of ideas that have had a great impact on church doctrine, as well as bringing to Christian theology elements of classical philosophy, particularly Neo-Platonism. His writings focused on belief and authority, knowledge and illumination, the importance of free will, and a host of other complex and fundamental issues.*

> *The quotation that Mary Malone attributes to him is taken directly from the* Catechism of the Catholic Church: 329.

SK 12 *[brief]*

St Paul 🗡

Role: Mary Malone equates Will's description of human ghosts, dæmons, and bodies with St Paul's discussion of the three-part nature of human beings: "spirit *and* soul *and* body."

Observation: *Mary is here referring to the writings of St Paul in 1 Thessalonians 5:23 where he prays to God: "Your whole spirit and soul and body be preserved blameless." What body means is self-evident; the difference between soul and spirit, in contrast, is much debated.*

One interpretation is that the soul is the eternal essence of a person including intellect, will, and emotion, while the spirit includes conscience and intuition, allowing a person to connect with the spiritual realm through prayer or meditation.

AS 33 *[brief]*

Sin [*See* Adam and Eve, Preemptive Penance *in* Applied Metaphysics]

Tree of the Forbidden Fruit [*See* Adam and Eve]

Yahweh [*See* God]

Yambe-Akka ✦ 🗡

Role: The witches' goddess of the dead, "older than the tundra," comes "smiling and kindly" when it is time for a witch to die. The witch tortured by Coulter and the clerics calls out to Yambe-Akka to end her anguish, and Serafina

Thief in the night

Another allusion Mrs Coulter uses in her last scene is embedded in her description of the way her growing love for Lyra snuck up on her. It came, she says, "like a thief in the night." The phrase "thief in the night" is used metaphorically several times in the New Testament to describe the lack of warning which will precede the second coming of Christ. One example of such an exhortation to preparedness is 2 Peter 3:10: "But the day of the Lord will come like a thief, and then the heavens will pass away with a mighty roar and the elements will be dissolved by fire, and the earth and everything done on it will be found out." The phrase "thief in the night" is similarly used in Matthew 24:43; 1 Thessalonians 5:2; and Revelations 3:3.

Pekkala comes out of the shadows, kisses the witch, and ends her suffering.

Facts: *In Finnish mythology, Yambe-Akka, or the old woman of the dead, rules the underworld.*

NL/GC 18 *[brief]*

SK   *brief mentions:* 2, 13

51 ZOROASTRIAN HERESY ✦

Role: The phrase "Zoroastrian heresy" is among those Lyra hears at Coulter's cocktail party. The context of the phrase suggests it has something to do with the relationship of Dust to "the dark principle."

Facts: *In Will's world, Zoroastrianism is a religion based on the teachings of the prophet Zoroaster or Zarathustra, who could have lived as early as 1700 BC or as late as 600 BC. The religion emerged in Persia (now Iran) and is monotheistic, like Judaism, Christianity, and Islam.*

NL/GC 5 *[brief]*

EPIGRAPHS

Epigraphs:
Book Epigraphs

The US and UK editions of THE AMBER SPYGLASS *have two epigraphs in common. One is from the "Third Duino Elegy" by Rainer Marie Rilke; the other, "The Ecclesiast" by John Ashbery.*

The UK edition has a few lines from a hymn by Robert Grant.

The US edition has sixteen lines (the whole of one of the original engraved pages) of William Blake's America, a Prophecy.

Northern Lights / The Golden Compass

PARADISE LOST

Lines 911-19 from Book II of the epic poem *Paradise Lost* by John Milton provide the epigraph found in NORTHERN LIGHTS and THE GOLDEN COMPASS, and the source of the trilogy's name, HIS DARK MATERIALS.

Paradise Lost is also the source of epigraphs for five chapters of THE AMBER SPYGLASS (chapters 5, 6, 7, 16, 30 [see]) and is cited by Philip Pullman in his acknowledgments following the last pages of THE AMBER SPYGLASS as one of the three greatest influences on the development of HIS DARK MATERIALS.

Significance: The scene described in Book II, lines 911-19, finds Satan pausing on his way to seek revenge on God for casting him and his fellow rebels into hell. Satan plans to corrupt God's newest creations, Adam and Eve, in the Garden of Eden. The fallen angel looks into the abyss at "his dark materials," the raw forms from which God fashions earth, air, water, and fire into new worlds.

Facts: *Poet John Milton (1608-1674) was a Puritan who worked on behalf of Oliver Cromwell during the English Revolution and was lucky to escape imprisonment or execution following the restoration of the monarchy. Blind and discouraged at the failure of the English revolution, he wrote—or largely dictated—*Paradise Lost, *which was published in 1674.*

The Amber Spyglass

"O WORSHIP THE KING"

The second stanza of Sir Robert Grant's hymn "O Worship the King", from *Hymns Ancient and Modern,* appears as the first of three of the epigraphs for the UK (but not the US) edition of THE AMBER SPYGLASS.

Significance: The comparison of God's "chariots of wrath" to dark rain clouds is recalled in the description of the storms through which Mrs Coulter flies on her approach to the

Clouded Mountain. Storms also hamper Lyra and Will on the battleground where they find the abandoned crystal litter and its passenger, the Authority.

Facts: *Sir Robert Grant (1779-1838), a barrister, published several literary works including* A Sketch of the History of East India Company to 1733. *Grant became Governor of Bombay in 1834 and remained in office until his death four years later. Many of his religious poems were first published posthumously in 1839.*

"THIRD DUINO ELEGY"

Lines from the "Third Duino Elegy" by Rainer Marie Rilke comprise one of the epigraphs in both the UK and US editions of THE AMBER SPYGLASS.

Significance: The speaker sees the source of a lover's desire in the stars; "her pure features" have their counterpart in the "pure constellations." These images evoke the promises that Will and Lyra will make to one another the night their dæmons settle. They know that they will soon have to part forever, but promise that when they die and leave the world of the dead that the atoms of their dissipated ghosts will seek one another through all time and space—just as Lee Scoresby, when he "allowed [his] atoms to relax and drift apart...passed through the heavy clouds and came out under the brilliant stars, where the atoms of his beloved dæmon Hester were waiting for him."

Facts: *Rainer Marie Rilke (1875-1926) is regarded as one of the most influential twentieth century German poets. His poems are variously described as intensely personal, visionary, mystical, and superbly crafted. The* Duino Elegies *were named by Rilke after the Duino Castle, near Trieste, Italy, where he wrote the series of ten poems.*

> # Philip Pullman says:
>
> The passage from Rilke he chose for an epigraph to THE AMBER SPYGLASS "where he's addressing the stars and wondering if the lover's feelings for his loved one come from 'the pure constellations'...struck me with great force as soon as I read it."
>
> ("Darkness Visible: An Interview with Philip Pullman, Part 2" by Kerry Fried for amazon.com.)

"ECCLESIAST, THE"

Lines from "The Ecclesiast" by John Ashbery provide an epigraph for THE AMBER SPYGLASS.

Significance: The epigraph looks back to the ending of THE SUBTLE KNIFE, and forward to the conclusion of THE AMBER SPYGLASS. Stanislaus Grumman/John Parry's assurance to his son that "the night is full of angels" is recalled by the epigraph's line, "The night is cold and delicate and full of angels," and Ashbery's summation in "The Ecclesiast": "We are together at last, though far apart" is suggestive of the circumstances of Lyra and Will's relationship at the end of HIS DARK MATERIALS.

Facts: *John Ashbery (b. 1927) is an American poet much admired by other writers for his sophisticated, evocative, and innovative use of language and imagery. "The Ecclesiast" is from* Rivers and Mountains *(New York: Holt, Rinehart & Winston, 1966).*

AMERICA: A PROPHECY

The sixteen lines from object 8 of this poem by William Blake provide the prefacing epigraph for the US edition of THE AMBER SPYGLASS. The first line, lines 14-15, and line 16 appear as epigraphs for Chapters 32, 26, and 31, respectively, in the UK editions (see these entries).

Significance: In *America, A Prophecy*, Blake imagines a new republic free of the tyranny and oppression of the European empires in general and of England in particular. In the passage providing the epigraph, the victory of the parties committed to freedom and equality is described in terms alluding to the resurrection of Christ ("The grave is burst, the spices shed, the linen wrapped up"), only here it is not a literal death that is being overcome, but the death-in-life of those suffering under oppressive regimes.

These lines suggest several themes in THE AMBER SPYGLASS. The reaction of the liberated slaves in *America, A Prophecy* has much in common with the joyous relief of the ghosts emerging from the world of the dead. The people in Blake's poem have escaped "the oppressor's scourge," and the death of the Authority and failure of Metatron's schemes mean that at least temporarily, those most threatened by the Magisterium are safe. Finally, the personal liberation Lyra and Will feel when they have survived the journey to the world of the dead and found their way with their dæmons to a pleasant and peaceful world recalls two of the ending lines of this passage: "The Sun has left his blackness & has found a fresher morning,/ And the fair Moon rejoices in the clear & cloudless night."

Facts: William Blake *(1757-1827) was a visionary poet, engraver, and painter whose works expressed his personal mythology.* Blake's *works include* Songs of Innocence and Songs of Experience, America: A Prophecy, Jerusalem, *and* The Marriage of Heaven and Hell.

Philip Pullman says:

In an interview with Amazon.com, Phillip Pullman remembers his decision to use a few lines from John Ashbery's "The Ecclesiast" as an epigraph for THE AMBER SPYGLASS. The first time he looked into Ashbery's *Selected Poems*, the book opened at "The Ecclesiast," and "there was this wonderful stanza at the end … I just adore it. It's a little summary of what was going to happen at the very end of the book, and I thought, *I must have that*."

("Darkness Visible: An Interview with Philip Pullman, Part 2" by Kerry Fried for amazon.com.)

"On the Marionette Theatre"

In his Acknowledgments, Philip Pullman names three influences on HIS DARK MATERIALS: *Paradise Lost*, the works of Blake, and Heinrich von Kleist's "The Marionette Theatre." The first two are widely regarded and massive in scope; the last is short, simple, and scarcely read outside Germany (at least before Pullman's endorsement, that is).

Kleist, a poet and playwright, is associated with the German Romantic literary movement. Born in 1777, he was a younger contemporary of William Blake (1757-1837). Kleist took his own life in 1811, a year after the publication of his essay "On the Marionette Theatre," which takes the form of a conversation between a dancing master and his friend.

The essay describes three incidents. In one, an adolescent boy loses his gracefulness the moment he becomes conscious of it. The second is a duel between an experienced swordsman and a bear. The human loses his focus because his mind is more on the fight's outcome and how he must appear to his audience than on the fight itself. The bear, in contrast, isn't aware that he is being tested or playing a part, and can simply focus on the duel. The final example is the marionettes, who are the only ones who perform perfectly. This is partly because their construction provides "proportion, flexibility, lightness" and "a more natural arrangement of the centres of gravity." However, their greatest advantage is that their dance will never be flawed by "affectation," which is defined as an exclusively human condition that comes when "the soul, or moving force, appears at some point other than the centre of gravity of the movement."

The contest between Iorek Byrnison and Lyra in "Fencing" in NORTHERN LIGHTS/THE GOLDEN COMPASS is a tribute to Kleist. Lyra is frustrated by her inability to trick the bear, but Iorek explains that he has an advantage she can not overcome: he isn't human. Iorek then intuitively makes the connection between Lyra's status as a child and her ability to read the alethiometer without the use of reference books, something adults cannot do. Lyra wonders if that means she won't be able to understand her symbol-reader when she grows up. Much later, in the world of the mulefa, Iorek is proven correct. But the desperation Lyra feels at that loss is not the first time her grace has failed her.

The child Lyra was a superior climber, making her way around Jordan College on its rooftops. However, as she moves out of childhood, her physical agility is compromised because she has become self-conscious about how others see her. On the edge of the abyss in the world of the dead, Lyra loses her focus, becoming instead "more conscious of Roger, and a little flicker of vanity blazed up for a moment in her heart... She was Roger's Lyra, full of grace and daring; she didn't need to creep along like an insect." The next moment she loses her footing and falls into the abyss.

Kleist concludes his essay with an allusion to chapter three of Genesis, the story of Adam and Eve's fall from grace and the subject of *Paradise Lost*. The dancing master tells his friend that "the final chapter in the history of the world" will come when we "eat again of the tree of knowledge in order to return to the state of innocence."

At a Balliol College, Oxford University, English Society forum on November 6, 2002, Philip Pullman addressed a question about the role of work and craftsmanship in HIS DARK MATERIALS by offering an interpretation of the conclusion of "On the Marionette Theatre." Kleist's "message," Pullman said, "was that, although the Eden of perfect innocence is currently lost to the human race, it is not lost forever - it can be regained, if the human race is willing to spend its life trying. But the innocence it will find is a more mature one, in a way: in perfect innocence, one merely accepts that a fact is so, whereas, in the innocence of perfect wisdom, one accepts that a fact is so because one already knows why it is so. Working toward that end should be a joyful action."

Chapter Epigraphs

One of the most significant differences between the early US and UK editions of HIS DARK MATERIALS *is that the US publisher deleted the epigraphs chosen by Philip Pullman to head all but the final chapter of* THE AMBER SPYGLASS.

Another departure is that the UK editions of the trilogy have always included woodcut illustrations, created by Pullman, at the beginning of each chapter of NORTHERN LIGHTS *and* THE SUBTLE KNIFE. *Again, until 2002, these were not to be found in US editions. Originally, the epigraphs were presented as if they too were woodcuts, featuring words instead of pictures. For the tenth anniversary edition of* THE AMBER SPYGLASS, *Pullman added illustrative woodcuts to accompany the chapters, and the epigraphs were typeset as text.*

Philip Pullman used the spellings and mechanics of the original sources, all of which are in the public domain, and these are retained here as well. Bible verses are from the King James Version.

CHAPTER 1
Title: "The Enchanted Sleeper"
Epigraph: *While the beasts of prey*
　　　　　Come from caverns deep
　　　　　Viewed the maid asleep
Author: William Blake (1757-1827)
Source: "The Little Girl Lost" from *Songs of Innocence and Experience*
Significance: The epigraphs for Chapters 1 and 13 are both from "The Little Girl Lost" in William Blake's *Songs of Innocence and Experience.* The verse is about the child, Lyca, who falls asleep in the wilderness. Lions and other large carnivores come to her side, and gently remove the sleeping child to a cavern. Lyca has been wandering alone for some time before stopping to rest, and wonders:

> Lost in desart wild
> Is your little child.
> How can Lyca sleep
> If her mother weep?
> If her heart does ake
> Then let Lyca wake;
> If my mother sleep,
> Lyca shall not weep.

Lyca, apparently unmourned, sleeps soundly.

Chapter 1 of THE AMBER SPYGLASS opens with Lyra in a drugged sleep induced by her mother Mrs Coulter.

Observation: *In Will's Oxford, as she and Will approach Sir Charles Latrom's to ask him to give back her alethiometer, Lyra reflects that she felt safer in the Arctic wilderness than in this*

4

city, where "treachery smiled and smelt sweet," and that without "her only guide...she was...just a little girl, lost," a phrase recalling another lyric in Blake's Songs, *"A Little Girl Lost." Its opening stanza could be describing the fear the Magisterium has of Lyra's approaching maturity:*

> Children of the future Age,
> Reading this indignant page;
> Know that in a former time,
> Love! sweet Love! was thought a crime.

CHAPTER 2

Title: "Balthamos and Baruch"

Epigraph: *Then a Spirit passed before my face; the hair of my flesh stood up*

Source: Job 4:15 (Bible)

Significance: The source of the epigraph for the second chapter of THE AMBER SPYGLASS, "Balthamos and Baruch," is from the episode in the Book of Job known as the vision of Eliphaz. To test his faith, Job, once a prosperous, lucky man, has been made to suffer terribly. Eliphaz is one of his so-called friends who come to offer comfort. His insight is that Job's misfortunes mean that Job has displeased God and so deserves his troubles. Job later regains what he has lost, and God chastises his friends for their comments. The spirit that visited Eliphaz and asked, "Shall mortal man be more just than God? Shall a man be more pure than his maker?" (4:17) is thus not considered to have been an angel in God's service.

In "Balthamos and Baruch," a suffering Will Parry, mourning his father and scared for Lyra, receives the advice of two angels and is attacked by two others.

William Blake published an illustrated *Book of Job*, which includes a painting of the vision of Eliphaz, as well as one of God titled "The Ancient of Days."

CHAPTER 3

Title: "Scavengers"

Epigraph: *The Knight's bones are dust,*
> *And his good sword rust;—*
> *His soul is with the saints, I trust.*

Author: Samuel Taylor Coleridge (1772-1834)

Source: "The Knight's Tomb"

Significance: Coleridge was a leading figure in the early 19ᵗʰ century English poetry movement known as Romanticism, along with two other poets quoted in these epigraphs: John Keats and George Gordon, Lord Byron.

A few lines from his poem, "The Knight's Tomb," serve as the epigraph for the third chapter of THE AMBER SPYGLASS, in which Iorek Byrnison journeys to the world of Cittàgazze to view (and then eat) the corpse of his fallen comrade-in-arms, Lee Scoresby.

CHAPTER 4

Title: "Ama and the Bats"

Epigraph: *She lay as if at play*

> *Her life had leaped away-*
> *Intending to return-*
> *But not so soon-*

Author: Emily Dickinson (1830-1886)

Source: "She lay as if at play"

Significance: The epigraph for this chapter looks forward to Ama's discovery of Mrs Coulter's deceit. Ama brings a cure for the spell that has cast Lyra into a sleep from which she can not awake, only to find that Mrs Coulter is, in fact, drugging the girl. Dickinson's poem ends "Devising, I am sure-/To force her sleep-/So light-so deep-."

CHAPTER 5

Title: "The Adamant Tower"

Epigraph: *...with ambitious aim*
> *Against the throne and monarchy of God*
> *Rais'd impious war in heav'n and battel proud.*

Author: John Milton (1608-1674)

Source: *Paradise Lost*, Book I, lines 41-43

Significance: Chapter 5 features Lord Asriel's basalt fortress and adamant tower, the center of his republic of heaven, from which he will launch an assault on the Authority's kingdom, or, at least, defend his world against threats from the kingdom.

Paradise Lost opens with Satan and his fellow rebel angels defeated and cast out of heaven. The lines before those of the epigraph make clear that Satan expected success:
> ... with all his Host
> Of Rebel Angels, by whose aid aspiring
> To set himself in Glory above his Peers,
> He trusted to have equal'd the most High,
> If he oppos'd; (37-41).

Three words—"With vain attempt" (44)—immediately follow those lines quoted in the epigraph, and bring Milton's passage to an abrupt end.

In the course of THE AMBER SPYGLASS, Asriel's defense of his republic proves to be a "vain attempt" as well, not because he is defeated, but because people can only enjoy full lives in the worlds of their birth.

CHAPTER 6

Title: "Pre-emptive Absolution"

Epigraph: *...Reliques, Beads,*
> *Indulgences, Dispenses, Pardons, Bulls,*
> *The sport of Winds*

Author: John Milton (1608-1674)

Source: *Paradise Lost*, Book III, lines 491-93

Significance: On his way to the gates of heaven, disguised as a lesser angel, Satan learns of the location of the world inhabited by Adam and Eve. He passes an empty region that in the future will be the crowded Paradise of Fools or Limbo of Vanities. Among those the Puritan Milton consigns to this limbo are clergy in the Roman Catholic church. *Reliques* are relics of saints; *beads,* the rosary; *bulls,* papal decrees. One of the factors behind the Protestant movement was corruption among some clergy, who would sell *pardons* and *indulgences, i.e.* special dispensations, which are exceptions to usual Church laws.

Chapter 12 includes descriptions of two perversions of Church teachings devised by the Consistorial Court of Discipline for use among its inner circle: pre-emptive penance and pre-emptive absolution.

CHAPTER 7

Title: "Mary, Alone"
Epigraph: *...Last*
               Rose as in Dance the stately Trees, and spred
               Thir branches hung with copious Fruit
Author: John Milton (1608-1674)
Source: *Paradise Lost,* Book VII, lines 324-26
Significance: The passage from *Paradise Lost* that provides this epigraph describes Earth before the creation of Adam and Eve.

In Chapter 7, Mary Malone enters the world of the mulefa, and as the first human to do so, finds a similarly unsullied world.

CHAPTER 8

Title: "Vodka"
Epigraph: *I have been a stranger in a strange land.*
Source: Exodus, 2:21 (Bible)
Significance: The source of the epigraph for Chapter 8 is biblical. The second chapter of Exodus tells of Moses fleeing Egypt and finding refuge in Midian, an area now included in Saudi Arabia. There, Moses married, and named his son Gershom. *Ger* is Hebrew for a *refugee,* and Moses considered himself a "stranger in a strange land."

Science fiction writer Robert Heinlein's novel about the visit to our world of an alien, superficially indistinguishable from human beings, is entitled *Stranger in a Strange Land.*

In Chapter 8 of THE AMBER SPYGLASS, Will begins his journey through a strange land, Siberia, in a strange world, Lyra's.

CHAPTER 9

Title: "Up-River"
Epigraph: *A shade upon the mind there passes*
               As when on Noon
               A Cloud the mighty Sun encloses
Author: Emily Dickinson (1830-1886)
Source: "A Shade upon the mind there passes"
Significance: Chapter 9, "Up-River," is about passages as Iorek Byrnison's bears arrive in the Himalayas, and Asriel's and the Magisterium's forces head toward Lyra. Iorek's examinations of the subtle knife leave him uneasy.

The poem's ending, "Oh God/Why give if Thou must take away/The Loved?", foreshadows Will's lament when he learns that after finally finding love he will lose it.

Chapter 10

Title: "Wheels"

Epigraph: *There ariseth a little cloud out of the sea, like a man's hand.*

Source: Kings I 18:44 (Bible)

Significance: In Chapter 10, "Wheels," Mary Malone, not knowing what she is seeing, warns the mulefa of a flock of *tualapi* approaching from the sea.

   The source of the epigraph for this chapter is biblical. The prophet Elijah was ordered by God to go to Ahab and tell the ruler of God's displeasure with his wicked ways. Elijah convinces Ahab of God's might by first bringing down fires from the heavens to slay the prophets of other gods, and then ends a drought by praying that rains come. The entire verse reads: "And it came to pass at the seventh time, that he said, 'Behold, there ariseth a little cloud out of the sea, like a man's hand.' And he said, 'Go up, say unto Ahab, Prepare thy chariot, and get thee down that the rain stop thee not.'"

Chapter 11

Title: "Dragonflies"

Epigraph: *A truth that's told with bad intent*
    Beats all the lies you can invent.

Author: William Blake (1757-1827)

Source: "Auguries of Innocence," lines 53-54

Significance: Auguries are prophecies or omens. In "Dragonflies," both Will and Lyra lie with good intent to the Gallivespian spies Tialys and Salmakia. Will acts as if he and Lyra are still under the protection of the subtle knife, reaching at times for its hilt, although the blade is in pieces. To do so is the only way to prevent the spies from stinging them into unconsciousness and arranging for their transport to Asriel's fortress. Lyra's lie is more blatant and opportunistic. When the Gallivespians ask the children their plans, Will truthfully says that they intend to go back into Lyra's world and see Iorek Byrnison. When Lady Salmakia accepts this, but adds that afterwards they must go to Asriel, Lyra agrees with her plans.

   Some of Blake's most widely quoted lines are from this poem, "To see a world in a grain of sand/ And a heaven in a wild flower,/ Hold infinity in the palm of your hand/ And eternity in an hour." And, "Some are born to sweet delight,/ Some are born to endless night."

Chapter 12

Title: "The Break"

Epigraph: *Still as he fled, his eye was backward cast,*
    As if his fear still followed him behind.

Author: Edmund Spenser (1552-1599)

Source: *The Faerie Queen*, Book I, Canto 9, lines 185-86

Significance: Spenser's allegorical epic poem *The Faerie Queen* supplies the epigraph for

Chapter 12, "The Break," in which Will's concentration falters and the subtle knife breaks, and the angel Balthamos is found to be cowering in fear in Mrs Coulter's cave, just when Will needs him most to rescue Lyra.

Spenser conceived his epic *The Faerie Queen* as an exploration of Christian virtues. In the first book, the Redcrosse Knight, representing Holiness, is sent to rescue Una, or Truth. He succeeds, but as they journey to save her parents from a dragon, Redcrosse is distracted by meeting a terrified knight who claims to be trying to escape from Despair, who has caused his friend to kill himself. Redcrosse decides to fight this evil-doer, but Despair turns out be nothing more than a weary old man, seemingly harmless. But when he argues with Redcrosse that death is not to be feared but welcomed as an end to sin, the young man finds himself tempted to do as the other knight did and commit suicide. However, Una arrives in time to lead him from Despair.

CHAPTER 13

Title: "Tialys and Salmakia"
Epigraph: *Frowning, frowning night,*
   O'er this desart bright,
   Let thy moon arise,
   While I close my eyes.
Author: William Blake (1757-1827)
Source: "The Little Girl Lost" from *Songs of Innocence and Experience*
Significance: Chapter 13's epigraph, like that of Chapter 1, is from "The Little Girl Lost" in William Blake's *Songs of Innocence and Experience*. While the poem is about the child Lyca, who wandering alone and unmissed is carried asleep to safety by wild beasts, the stanza providing the epigraph for Chapter 13 describes a brightly moonlit desert. It is similar to the landscape of the world to which Lyra, Will, and the Gallivespian spies flee and find a night's rest, following their escape from Mrs Coulter's cave.

CHAPTER 14

Title: "Know What It Is"
Epigraph: *Labour without joy is base. Labour without sorrow is base. Sorrow without labour is base. Joy without labour is base.*
Author: John Ruskin (1819-1900)
Source: *Time and Tide: Twenty-five Letters to a Working Man of Sunderland on the Laws of Work* (1867).
Significance: The source of the epigraph for Chapter 14 is a series of letters by John Ruskin. Ruskin first achieved prominence as a critic and historian of architecture and painting; his emphasis on the value of craftsmanship extended to social activism promoting better housing, educational opportunities, and greater respect for the working classes of Victorian England.

In "Know What It Is," Will and Lyra ask gifted metallurgist, armoured bear Iorek Byrnison, for his help in repairing the subtle knife.

CHAPTER 15

Title: "The Forge"

Epigraph: *As I was walking among the fires of hell, delighted with the enjoyments of Genius*

Author: William Blake (1757-1827)

Source: *The Marriage of Heaven and Hell*

Significance: Blake's *The Marriage of Heaven and Hell* reverses the conventional ideas of good and evil that deny sensual pleasures and favor rational restraint (and confuse hypocritical religiosity with spirituality) not to reject one for the other, but to argue that "Without Contraries is no progression." On a tour of hell, the narrator is fascinated by the industry of the fallen angels.

In Chapter 15, Iorek's genius is on display in his repair of the subtle knife in a make-shift forge—a process requiring not just physical skill but mental clarity and concentration as well.

CHAPTER 16

Title: "The Intention Craft"

Epigraph: *...From the archèd roof*
Pendant by suttle Magic many a row
Of Starry Lamps and blazing Cressets
Fed With Naphtha and Asphaltus
yeilded light

Author: John Milton (1608-1674)

Source: *Paradise Lost*, Book I, lines 726-29

Significance: The disconsolate fallen angels, having been inspired by Satan to plan another battle against heaven, create their own kingdom, Pandemonium; its arching roof and many lights may be an attempt to imitate the heaven they have lost.

In Chapter 16, Lord Asriel takes his high commanders and Mrs Coulter on a tour of his impressive armoury, with its cavernous vaults lit by torches or crystals in pillars or wall sconces.

Asphaltus is a solid fuel, and so would be burned in cressets, which are hanging iron baskets or bowls placed atop long poles, while naphtha is the oil form of the same fuel, and would be used in lamps. The word *asphalt* derives from *asphaltus*, and although most asphalt is today a by-product of petroleum

Paradise Lost

Of the three specific sources of inspiration Pullman names, the influence of John Milton's *Paradise Lost* is the most easily seen. The title, HIS DARK MATERIALS, alludes to a passage in Book II of *Paradise Lost* that serves as the trilogy's epigraph; the epic provides a number of the chapter epigraphs for THE AMBER SPYGLASS; and Lord Asriel's battle with the Authority's forces recalls in some ways the story of Satan's rebellion against God.

Published in 1667, Milton's epic poem is his attempt "to justify the ways of God to men" (I, 26) by telling the story "Of man's first disobedience, and the fruit/ Of that forbidden tree, whose mortal taste/ Brought death into the world" (I, 1-3). The poem is based not only on stories from the Bible, but draws on sources ranging from classical literature and mythology to scientific speculations.

In 2005, Oxford University Press issued an edition of *Paradise Lost* featuring a general introductory essay and brief comments on each of the poem's twelve books by Philip Pullman. Three aspects of *Paradise Lost* that Pullman celebrates are its poetry, plot, and imagery. Typically, editions of *Paradise Lost* have extensive footnotes. This one has none. Pullman recalls that the language of *Paradise Lost* is what first intrigued him, and while later on readers may want to consult annotated editions of the work, footnotes are distracting. There's little pleasure to be had from repeated interruptions: stop for the note, restart the poem, stop a few lines later for more notes, restart the poem—this is not the way _Paradise Lost_ was meant to be read.

William Blake said that Milton writes better when he is describing Satan's schemes than when he is describing God's judgments, and Pullman notes that Milton's decision to begin _Paradise Lost_ with Satan's arguments to rally his troops after their expulsion from heaven immediately places Satan at the center of the story.

William Blake's claim that Milton was of Satan's party without knowing it is one of Blake's most widely quoted literary opinions. Pullman has on several occasions claimed that in his own case, he is on the side of the fallen angels, and well aware of it. But if our sympathies incline toward the character we first meet, Pullman is of Eve's party—if Lyra stands, as the witches speculate, in the position toward the Authority that Eve once held toward the Old Testament's God.

There are obvious parallels between Asriel's rebellion and Satan's, and the fantastic construction of the basalt fortress and the building of Pandemonium, where the fallen angels dwell, but more is at stake in _Paradise Lost_ than who will be the victor and who the vanquished.

In Milton's epic, even before God creates our world from the dark materials of the abyss, he knows that Satan will tempt Eve, she will fail the test and Adam will follow her, and the two will be evicted from Eden. Furthermore, he has already accepted his Son's offer to go to earth in the form of a man to redeem humankind. Both the Father and Son know too that this will be seen as a great sacrifice that will prove God's goodness.

But if all this is known, even before the creation of the world, then is it pre-destined to occur? Did Eve truly have free will? If God is all knowing and all powerful, why not fix the problem before it occurs? God could have chosen to eliminate free will from his creation, or not created the tree of knowledge, or simply not issued an arbitrary rule not to eat the fruit of one particular tree. From such a perspective, Adam and Eve (and even Satan) seem like playthings, marionettes who believe they are acting of their own volition, while all the time their next move is scripted.

And yet, as characters, they seem far from wooden. Although we know they are deluded about their chance to succeed—one thing the serpent promises Eve is that she'll be able to fly—and perhaps are not even free to make their own mistakes, they still seem more real than their creator.

There are those, like Blake, who see the poem as taking on a life of its own, so to speak, arguing against the case Milton set out to defend. The opposing interpretation is that Milton knew exactly what he was up to, and by creating in his audience sympathy for Adam and Eve, he is showing readers they share in the original sin of the first man and woman.

How does this relate to _His Dark Materials_? First, the Authority of Pullman's novels is not all-powerful, all-knowing, and immortal, and thus not the God of _Paradise Lost_. But even if we exclude the Authority or God from our reckoning, as the witches do, the question of destiny persists.

In _Paradise Lost,_ Eve acts as if she has free will, but the status of her ability to act freely is ambiguous. In _His Dark Materials,_ the witches prophesize that Lyra has a destiny to fulfill, but can succeed only if she is unaware of the role she is playing. Lee Scoresby and Serafina Pekkala offer contrasting viewpoints on fate and freedom. Will revisits this question at the end of the trilogy when he asks the angel Xaphania to elaborate about the work she says he has to do, but then stops her from answering, knowing that if he is told what he ought to do, he will either do it and be resentful at feeling he must, or he won't and will feel guilty instead. He wants to act as if the work he chooses is his choice.

Paradise Lost ends with Adam and Eve leaving behind forever the security and predictability of the Garden of Eden. There is no turning back for them; the way is barred. In the Garden of Eden, nothing died and nothing changed, which may be someone's notion of Paradise, but sounds much like what the ghosts despair of most. Unchanging, predictable, and enclosed spaces—Jordan College's quadrangle, Mary Malone's convent, the world of the dead—are rejected in *His Dark Materials*. It isn't just the movement of the residents of such places that is restricted—their thoughts are, as well.

In all creation, one movement is disallowed by time if not by God. Just as Adam and Eve may never return to their pre-fall not-knowingness, re-entering a state of pre-conscious innocence is impossible. Once one grasps that there is innocence and there is experience, the first is gone—for good. Adam and Eve may lose Paradise, but

> The world was all before them, where to choose
> Their place of rest, and providence their guide:
> They hand in hand with wandering steps and slow,
> Through Eden took their solitary way. (XII, 646-69)

processing, asphaltus is also naturally occurring in a few lakes and in the Dead Sea.

Chapter 17

Title: "Oil and Lacquer"

Epigraph: *Now the serpent was more subtil than any beast of the field which the Lord God had made.*

Source: Genesis 3:1 (Bible)

Significance: The third book of Genesis tells of the serpent's temptation of Eve; the verse which provides the epigraph continues, "And he said unto the woman, 'Yea, hath God said, Ye shall not eat of every tree of the garden?'" Eve replies that on the contrary, she and Adam may eat of every tree—but one.

In Chapter 17 of *The Amber Spyglass*, the mulefa Atal tells Mary Malone about the role of a snake in the emergence of consciousness among her people. The snake doesn't tempt the mulefa to disobey—the mulefa's myth has no creator and no restrictions. The snake suggests that the female follow its example, putting her foot where its body had lately been, knowing when she does so that she will gain self-awareness.

Chapter 18

Title: "The Suburbs of the Dead"

Epigraph: *O that it were possible we might*
> *But hold some two days' conference with the dead*

Author: John Webster (1580?-?1625)

Source: *The Duchess of Malfi.* Act IV, sc. ii, 27-28

Significance: In John Webster's revenge tragedy, the widowed Duchess of Malfi outrages her brother and other noblemen by her remarriage; they respond by imprisoning and psychologically torturing the Duchess. In the scene that provides the epigraph for Chapter 18, she speaks to her lady-in-waiting Cariola. Knowing that it is just a matter of time before her brother has both women killed, the Duchess wonders if she and Cariola will know each other in the world of the dead; the Duchess adds that she believes there is much only the dead will ever know, and regrettably never be able to share with the living.

In "The Suburbs of the Dead," Lyra and Will begin their journey toward their conference with the ghosts of Roger and John Parry.

CHAPTER 19

Title: "Lyra and her Death"
Epigraph: *I was angry with my friend:*
             I told my wrath, my wrath did end.
Author: William Blake (1757-1827)
Source: "A Poison Tree" in *Songs of Innocence and Experience*
Significance: In Chapter 19, Lyra and the Gallivespian spy Tialys put aside all attempts at civility, and both express their anger at one another, Tialys at what he calls Lyra's thoughtlessness, and she at his heartlessness. But Tialys relents, seeing Lyra's fundamentally unselfish bravery and the intensity of her commitment to seeking Roger's forgiveness in the world of the dead. Lyra accepts his apology graciously, and makes of him an ally.

The epigraph is the first two lines of "A Poison Tree"; the next two, "I was angry with my foe: I told it not, my wrath did grow," introduce the subject of the poem, which is about the nurturing of grudges, and not, as the epigraph suggests, conciliation.

CHAPTER 20

Title: "Climbing"
Epigraph: *I gained it so—*
             By Climbing slow—
             By Catching at the Twigs that grow
             Between the Bliss—and me—
Author: Emily Dickinson (1830-1886)
Source: "I gained it so—"
Significance: While the opening lines of the poem providing the epigraph for Chapter 20, "Climbing" suggest that the bliss the speaker seeks may be attainable, the poem concludes on a different note: now fearful of losing what she has attained, the climber realizes that she was happier striving toward her goal than reaching it. In THE AMBER SPYGLASS, the elation Mary Malone feels at navigating her way to the seed-pod trees' canopy is lost when she realizes that the sraf that should be falling into the trees' flowers is moving past them and out to sea.

CHAPTER 21

Title: "The Harpies"
Epigraph: *I hate things all fiction...There should always be some foundation of fact*
Author: George Gordon, Lord Byron (1788-1824)
Source: Letter to John Murray, 2 April 1817
Significance: The epigraph for Chapter 21, "The Harpies" is a comment in a letter from Byron to his publisher John Murray: "I hate things all fiction... There should always be some foundation of fact for the most airy fabric—and pure invention is but the talent of a liar." The second half of Byron's remark, "pure invention is but the talent of a liar," sums

up No-Name the harpy's screeched criticism of Lyra: "Liar! Liar! Liar!" Later, when Lyra revises her tale of her past to include a "foundation of fact," the harpies are appeased.

In Venice, Byron visited sites serving as settings for the seventeenth century dramatist Thomas Otway's *Venice Preserved*, Fredrich von Schiller's novel *The Ghost-Seer*, and Shakespeare's *Othello* and *The Merchant of Venice*. He claimed that Otway's play, based on a real-life political conspiracy, had more of an impact on him than did *Othello* and *The Merchant of Venice*.

CHAPTER 22

Title: "The Whisperers"
Epigraph: *Thick as Autumnal Leaves that strow the Brooks*
   In Vallombrosa, where th' Etrurian shades
   High overarch't imbowr
Author: John Milton (1608-1674)
Source: *Paradise Lost,* Book I, lines 302-04
Significance: In Chapter 22, Will and Lyra travel among the ghosts, through the world of the dead, in search of Roger. The epigraph for this chapter is from the opening of *Paradise Lost*, which finds Satan and his followers cast out of heaven, defeated and despairing, before being rallied by their leader. The comparison of the fallen angels to autumn leaves and the use of the word *shades* to refer to the trees that have dropped their leaves make these lines suggestive of what is to come in "The Whisperers" since fallen leaves are dead ones, and ghosts are called shades. Two works that influenced Milton's epic use similar imagery in depicting the underworld or afterlife: Virgil's *Aeneid* and Dante's *Inferno*.

Vallombrosa is a heavily wooded area near Florence, Italy. Etrurian is the same as Etruscan; the kingdom of Etruria was in the region of today's Tuscany, Italy.

CHAPTER 23

Title: "No Way Out"
Epigraph: *And ye shall know the truth, and the truth shall make you free*
Source: John 8:32 (Bible)
Significance: In the world of the dead, after Lyra truthfully and vividly tells the ghosts about her life in Oxford, the harpies are persuaded to become allies of the ghosts who seek release, in exchange for the nourishment of the dead's life stories. They also agree to guide Will, Lyra and the Gallivespians to a place where Will can cut a window through to freedom.

In the biblical context for the epigraph, Jesus tells the Jews that those who become his disciples, "shall know the truth, and the truth shall make you free." Asked from whom or what they shall be free, Jesus replies that no longer will they be a "slave to sin" (8:34) or "see death" (8:51).

CHAPTER 24

Title: "Mrs Coulter in Geneva"
Epigraph: *As is the mother, so is her daughter.*

Source: Ezekiel 16:44 (Bible)

Significance: This epigraph's source is the narrative recounting the admonishments of the prophet Ezekiel to the people of Jerusalem (the daughter), whom he condemns for following the ways of their heathen ancestors (the mother).

In Chapter 24, "Mrs Coulter in Geneva," Father MacPhail decides that her mother is as much a threat to his church as is Lyra, and so decides to execute Mrs Coulter by intercision; and, with the energy released, launch the bomb that will kill her daughter.

CHAPTER 25

Title: "Saint-Jean-les-Eaux"

Epigraph: *A bracelet of bright hair about the bone*

Author: John Donne (1572-1631)

Source: "The Relique"

Significance: In this chapter, first the Gallivespian spy, Tialys, and then the golden monkey attempt to retrieve the lock of Lyra's hair from the resonating chamber of the bomb which will guide the Consistorial Court of Discipline's weapon to its target.

In the context of Donne's poem, the line refers to the speaker's hope that when he is buried, a bracelet made of locks of his lover's hair will be placed around his wrist so that even when all that remains of him is a skeleton, those who come across his bones will know of his love. His wish is that his bones will be left in peace, but if a misguided person removes the bracelet of golden hair and it comes to be declared a relic for adoration, he wants all to know that miracles need not be supernatural or otherworldly but as simple, corporeal and precious as the love and devotion of a man and his mate.

Locks of hair were common tokens of affection among seventeenth century lovers, but the practice of making jewelry from hair peaked in 19th century England when Queen Victoria began wearing such pieces during her prolonged mourning for her husband, Prince Albert.

John Donne, a dean of St. Paul's Cathedral, London, was the first of the seventeenth century Metaphysical poets; two others, George Herbert and Andrew Marvell, also contribute epigraphs to THE AMBER SPYGLASS.

CHAPTER 26

Title: "The Abyss"

Epigraph: *The Sun has left his blackness & has found a fresher morning,*
And the fair Moon rejoices in the clear & cloudless night

Author: William Blake (1757-1827)

Source: *America, a Prophecy*, Plate 6, lines 13-14

Significance: Much of Chapter 26 is bleak as Lyra and Will creep tentatively along the edges of the abyss. However, at its end, Will cuts a window to a world of the living, at rest under a starry sky. There he and Lyra will find temporary sanctuary, and the ghosts eternal freedom.

In *America, a Prophecy*, Blake imagines a new republic free of the tyranny and oppression of the European empires (in general) and England (in particular). These lines record the reaction of stunned mill workers released from their dreary factories into a clean and pleasant land. Their song continues: "For Empire is no more, and now the Lion & Wolf shall cease," which is the epigraph for Chapter 31, "Authority's End."

All of the text on Plate 6 of *America, a Prophecy* is included as an epigraph in the US edition of THE AMBER SPYGLASS, which lacks the chapter epigraphs. It does not appear in its totality in the UK edition.

CHAPTER 27

Title: "The Platform"

Epigraph: *My Soul into the boughs does glide:*
There like a Bird it sits, and sings,
Then whets, and combs its silver wings

Author: Andrew Marvell (1621-1678)

Source: "The Garden," lines 52-54

Significance: Metaphysical poet Andrew Marvell provides the epigraph for Chapter 27 in which Mary Malone initially experiences a sensation of bliss when she rests atop a seedpod tree on the platform the mulefa have constructed for her observations of sraf. But her contentment vanishes when she feels she is leaving her body and headed for an abyss, just like the Shadow-particles that are leaving the mulefa's world.

The speaker of "The Garden" cannot hold onto the sense of his soul belonging in nature as the bird does in the tree; of all humanity, only Adam, while he still lived alone in his garden, could share the uncomplicated joys of a preening bird on its bough.

Mary Malone is likened to a bird by the mulefa elder Sattamax, and her dæmon is an alpine chough.

Andrew Marvell was a younger contemporary of John Donne and George Herbert, Metaphysical poets who are also represented in THE AMBER SPYGLASS'S epigraphs. [*see also* Chapters 25 *and* 33]

CHAPTER 28

Title: "Midnight"

Epigraph: *For many a time I have been half in love with easeful Death*

Author: John Keats (1795-1821)

Source: "Ode to a Nightingale," lines 51-52

Significance: In "Ode to a Nightingale," a sleepless speaker addresses the nightingale singing in his garden, comparing his despairing self-awareness to the contentment expressed in the bird's song. The speaker considers seeking the certain oblivion of death, but realizes if he abandons life, he will leave forever not only his troubles but the pleasures of his senses, the scent of his garden and the sound of the nightingale singing, as well.

In Chapter 28, Lord Asriel decides that Lyra must live, even at the cost of his own life. When he tells Mrs Coulter his decision, she reaches in her rucksack for a pistol, but before she can use it, he leaves, alerted that Lyra and Will's dæmons are near his fortress. During their conversation, Mrs Coulter had revealed that she fears the oblivion of death more than any pain in life.

William Blake

In the Acknowledgments following the conclusion of *HIS DARK MATERIALS*, Philip Pullman identifies three particular influences: "On the Marionette Theater," an essay by Heinrich von Kleist; John Milton's epic poem *Paradise Lost*; and William Blake.

William Blake (1757-1827)

Blake's influence on *HIS DARK MATERIALS* is more subtle than *Paradise Lost's*, and might be overlooked were it not for the number of chapter epigraphs in *THE AMBER SPYGLASS* drawn from Blake's works. The works used include "Auguries of Innocence," *Songs of Innocence and Songs of Experience*, *The Marriage of Heaven and Hell; America, a Prophecy; Europe, a Prophecy;* and *Jerusalem.*

Pictures and Poetry

Blake is a poet and a painter—not at different times—but in the same works (unfortunately, when his poems are included in anthologies or textbooks, the paintings that accompanied his poems are left out). He included some full page illustrations in his books, but usually the poems and pictures share a page. Words may appear within drawings, or parts of letters take on the shapes of trailing vines and connect to the borders. It is as if Blake wants his audience to read his pictures as well as his words.

Pullman is also interested in visual images, both those made of words, and those that are drawn or painted. In the UK, each chapter of *NORTHERN LIGHTS* and *THE SUBTLE KNIFE* begins with a picture, a woodcut devised by Pullman himself. In *THE AMBER SPYGLASS,* instead of pictures there are epigraphs, lines of poetry that Pullman values, and these appear in boxes that are the same size and in the same position on the page as the woodcuts in the other two books. Pullman's inspiration for using pictures and poems in such similar ways could be this aspect of Blake's genius.

Lyra is a reader of images. While it is easy to imagine Lyra scurrying across the Library roof, it is much harder to picture the girl quietly reading in the stacks. She loves hearing and telling stories, but reading doesn't seem to be one of her pastimes or passions. Lyra is, however, a masterful *reader* of the alethiometer's 36 *images.*

Craftsmanship

Blake did not just write and illustrate his books, he *made* them. He did not turn them over to publishers, typesetters, and printers. He engraved the plates and printed the books, and those that have colored pictures were hand-tinted by the author himself. Craftsmanship is respected in *HIS DARK MATERIALS* as well, notably in the way Iorek Byrnison repairs the subtle knife and Mary Malone builds the amber spyglass.

Politics

Long before industrial pollution was widespread, Blake the visionary feared the griminess of England's factories would destroy the natural beauty of the country and the health of its people.

He had no patience with those who claimed to practice Christianity but lacked charity and compassion for the poor. He had no use for those who think that being religious means not enjoying the pleasures of this world and who force others to give up those things as well.

America won its independence from Britain when Blake was a young man, and he believed that this new democracy would be the first of many. He hoped the French Revolution would establish a new order in France, and prophesized that republics would rise as Europe's kingdoms fell.

His Dark Materials' depiction of the Magisterium, and the idea of establishing a republic of heaven in the world in which we live, are examples of ways in which the spirit of Pullman's books is similar to that of Blake's.

On Milton

Finally, Blake' interpretation of Milton's *Paradise Lost* interests Pullman. In *The Marriage of Heaven and Hell*, Blake argued that "The reason Milton wrote in fetters when he wrote of Angels & God, and at liberty when of Devils & Hell, is because he was a true Poet, and of the Devil's party without knowing it." In other words, Milton is at his best writing about Satan and Eve because he was attracted to the disobedient and rebellious. Blake finds Milton's poetry less impressive when Milton writes of the authoritarian God, and Blake's conclusion is that Milton found the Old Testament God an unsympathetic character.

CHAPTER 29

Title: "The Battle on the Plain"

Epigraph: *Each Man is in his Spectre's power*
Until the arrival of that hour,
When his Humanity awake

Author: William Blake (1757-1827)

Source: Jerusalem, plate 41, lines 33-35

Significance: On Plate 41 of Blake's epic poem *Jerusalem*, the epigraph for Chapter 29 appears in reverse writing as if seen in a mirror. The words comprise a message to Albion, who is tormented by self-loathing and despair, concluding, "And cast his Spectre/into the Lake."

   As Chapter 29 ends, Will and Lyra are desperate and scared sick, knowing that their dæmons are being pursued by Spectres.

CHAPTER 30

Title: "The Clouded Mountain"

Epigraph: *Farr off th'Empyreal Heav'n, extended wide*
In circuit, undetermind square or round,
With opal Towrs and Battlements adorn'd
Of living Saphire

Author: John Milton (1608-1674)

Source: *Paradise Lost,* Book II, lines 1047-50

Significance: In Chapter 30, Mrs Coulter journeys to the Clouded Mountain where she entices Metatron to go with her to the edge of the abyss, presumably to capture Lyra's dæmon. As she approaches the Authority's citadel, she is awed by its shape, which seems to have a fluid dimensionality far exceeding the usual three.

   The epigraph for this chapter is found at the end of Book II of *Paradise Lost*. Seeking vengeance for being cast out of heaven, Satan has connived his way out of hell and is on his way to Earth, where he plans to destroy the Creator's newest additions to the universe, Adam and Eve. Along the way he views heaven in the distance. Its width is so great to render its shape impossible for Satan to determine.

CHAPTER 31

Title: "Authority's End"

Epigraph: *For Empire is no more,*
And now the Lion & Wolf shall cease.

Author: William Blake (1757-1827)

Source: "A Song of Liberty" (l. 20) in *The Marriage of Heaven and Hell* or *America, a Prophecy* Plate 6, lines 13-14

Significance: With the disintegration of the Authority, the descent into the abyss of his regent Metatron, and the safe reunion of Lyra and Will with their dæmons, the kingdom of heaven is seriously crippled.

There are two sources for the epigraph for this chapter. These are the last lines of "A Song of Liberty," which concludes Blake's *The Marriage of Heaven and Hell*. This satiric, visionary poem imagines a restorative apocalypse, when repressive fragmentation yields not to traditional notions of either good or evil, heaven or hell, but to an accommodation of the tension sustaining contraries. The reference to the lion and wolf is an allusion to the prophecy of Isaiah of the promise of "new heavens and a new earth" where the "wolf and the lamb will feed together."

The second source is *America, a Prophecy*, where the line follows the two that provide the epigraph for Chapter 26, "The Abyss."

CHAPTER 32

Title: "Morning"

Epigraph: *The morning comes, the night decays*

Author: William Blake (1757-1827)

Source: *America, a Prophecy*, Plate 6, line 1

Significance: This is the third of the chapter epigraphs that can be found on the sixth engraved plate of *America, a Prophecy* [*see also* Chapters 26 *and* 31]; the whole text on plate 6 also appears as an epigraph in the US edition of THE AMBER SPYGLASS. These phrases are the first that the revolutionary figure, Orc, speaks to the angel of Albion (England) describing the emergence of the American republic in terms evoking the resurrection of Christ.

In Chapter 32, Will and Lyra awaken in the world of the mulefa, finally no longer on the run, and Mary Malone witnesses the procession of ghosts emerging from their spirits' graves.

CHAPTER 33

Title: "Marzipan"

Epigraph: *Sweet spring, full of sweet days and roses,*
A box where sweets compacted lie

Author: George Herbert (1593-1633)

Source: "Virtue" (from *The Temple*, 1633)

Significance: The metaphor of spring as a box of sweets seems appropriate for a chapter titled "Marzipan," and out of context, the two lines suggest the feeling of hopeful romantic excitement that Mary Malone's tale evokes in Lyra. But the stanza which begins so sweetly ends, "And all must die"; the poem's last stanza says only a virtuous soul endures.

George Herbert's fellow Metaphysical poets John Donne and Andrew Marvell are also among those quoted in THE AMBER SPYGLASS'S epigraphs. [*see also* Chapters 25, 27, *and* 36, *respectively*]

CHAPTER 34

Title: "There Is Now"

Epigraph: *...Shew you all alive*
The world, where every particle of dust breathes forth its joy.

Author: William Blake (1757-1827)

Source: *Europe: A Prophecy,* plate 3, lines 18-19

Significance: In the prologue of *Europe: A Prophecy*, the narrator describes asking a fairy he finds in a field, "What is the material world, and is it dead?" The fairy offers, in exchange for "love-thoughts" and "poetic fancies", to "Shew you all alive/ The world, where every particle of dust breathes forth its joy." The narrator takes the creature home, and the fairy then dictates this prophecy.

In Chapter 34, Mary Malone discovers that all of Matter cherishes Dust.

CHAPTER 35

Title: "Over the Hills and Far Away"

Epigraph: *...the birthday of my life*
Is come, my love is come to me.

Author: Christina Rossetti (1830-1894)

Source: "A Birthday"

Significance: The last two lines of Rossetti's lyric poem serve as the epigraph for Chapter 35, in which Lyra and Will briefly experience an uncomplicated pleasure in their love.

CHAPTER 36

Title: "The Broken Arrow"

Epigraph: *But Fate does iron wedges drive,*
And alwaies crouds itself betwixt.

Author: Andrew Marvell (1621-1678)

Source: "The Definition of Love," lines 11-12

Significance: Although the title of this chapter refers to the moment when Serafina Pekkala breaks the arrow she had reserved for killing Mrs Coulter, Serafina's purpose in visiting the world of the mulefa was to encourage Kirjava and Pantalaimon to be brave and helpful when Will and Lyra learn that they will never have a future together.

In "The Definition of Love," the poem's speaker curses the fates that keep him from his lover, characterizing their love as parallel lines that "Though infinite, can never meet" (l. 28), and concluding,

Therefore the love which us doth bind,
But Fate so enviously debars,
Is the conjunction of the mind,
And opposition of the stars (ll. 29-32).

CHAPTER 37

Title: "The Dunes"
Epigraph: *My soul, do not seek eternal life, but exhaust the realm of the possible.*
Author: Pindar (522 BC – 443 BC)
Source: *Pythian Odes*
Significance: Lines from Pindar's *Pythian Odes* provide the epigraph for Chapter 37, "The Dunes," in which Lyra and Will learn that their realms of the possible are the worlds into which they were born. There, they must live fully and encourage others to do likewise, because only in so doing will they later find release from the world of the dead.

CHAPTER 38

Title: "The Botanic Garden"
    There is no epigraph for the last chapter of THE AMBER SPYGLASS. The woodcut depicts entwined roses.

REFERENCE

Works by Philip Pullman

UK Editions of *His Dark Materials*

Northern Lights. London: Scholastic 1995, 1999; Point Ed. 1996, 1998; Adult Ed. 2001; 10th Anniv. Ed. 2005; Classic Ed., Collector's Ed., Junior Ed. 2007.

Northern Lights/The Golden Compass. Film Tie-in Edition. London: Scholastic 2007.

The Subtle Knife. London: Scholastic 1997, 1998; Point Ed. 1998; Adult Ed. 2001; 10th Anniv. Ed. 2005; Classic Ed., Collector's Ed., Junior Ed. 2007.

The Amber Spyglass. London: Scholastic/David Fickling Books 2000, 2001; Point Ed. 2001. Adult Ed. 2001; 10th Anniv. Ed. 2005; Classic Ed., Collector's Ed., Junior Ed. 2007.

His Dark Materials Gift Set: Northern Lights, The Subtle Knife, The Amber Spyglass. Slipcase ed. London: Scholastic Point 2001.

His Dark Materials: Northern Lights, The Subtle Knife, The Amber Spyglass. One volume. London: Scholastic 2002.

Audio Recordings

All of the following were published by BBC Audiobooks in London.

Northern Lights/The Subtle Knife/The Amber Spyglass Complete & Unabridged. Read by Philip Pullman and cast. 2002, 2007.

BBC Radio 4 Full-cast Dramatisation. 2 CDs or 2 cass. per book. 2003, 2007.

His Dark Materials Box Set. Complete & Unabridged. 29 CDs. Read by Philip Pullman and cast. 2002.

His Dark Materials Trilogy: BBC Radio 4 Full-cast Dramatisation. 6 CDs. 2003; Box Set. 7 CDs. 2003.

Note: Chivers Audio, an imprint of BBC Audiobooks, in 1999 produced *Northern Lights*, in three parts: "Oxford," "Bolvangar," and "Svalbard."

US Editions of *His Dark Materials*

The Golden Compass. New York: Knopf 1996, 1998; Ballantine-Random House 1997; First Pbk. Ed. 1998; Yearling-Random House 2001; Rev. Pbk. Ed. 2002; Laurel Leaf-Random House 2003; Deluxe 10th Anniv. Ed. 2006; Yearling 2007.

Subtle Knife. New York: Knopf 1997, Deluxe Ed. 2007; Del Rey-Random House 1998; First Pbk. Ed. 1999; Yearling-Random House 2001; Laurel Leaf-Random House Books 2003.

Amber Spyglass. New York: Knopf 2000, Deluxe Ed. 2007; Del Rey-Random House Books 2001; Yearling-Random House 2003; Laurel Leaf-Random House Books 2003.

His Dark Materials Boxed Set: The Golden Compass, The Subtle Knife, and The Amber Spyglass. Slipcase Ed. New York: Knopf 2002, 2007; Laurel Leaf-Random House 2003.

His Dark Materials Omnibus. New York: Knopf 2007.

Audiobooks

All of the following were published by Random House's Listening Library.

The Golden Compass/Subtle Knife/Amber Spyglass. Read by Philip Pullman. Unabridged. 1999-2001. Read by Philip Pullman and full cast. Unabridged. 2004.

Note: e-book editions are also available for each book.

OTHER BOOKS

Ancient Civilizations [Pullman, P.], illus. Gary Long. Exeter: Wheaton, 1981.

Aladdin and the Enchanted Lamp retold by Philip Pullman, illus. Sophy Williams. London: Scholastic, 2004; New York: Arthur A. Levine Books, 2005, 2007.

The Broken Bridge. London: Macmillan, 1990, 1998, 2001; London: Pan-Macmillan, 1992; Walton-on-Thames: Nelson, 1993; London: Young Picador, 2004; New York: Knopf-Random House, 1992; Dell Laurel-Leaf, 1994.

The Butterfly Tattoo. London: Macmillan, 2001. Originally *The White Mercedes* (London: Macmillan, 1992); New York: Knopf-Random House, 1993; Dell Laurel-Leaf, 1997.

Clockwork, or All Wound Up, illus. Peter Bailey. London: Doubleday 1996; London: Yearling, 1997; illus. Leonid Gore. New York: Arthur A. Levine Books, 1998; Scholastic, 1998, 1999, 2005.

Count Karlstein. London: Chatto & Windus, 1982; *Count Karlstein: the novel,* illus. Diana Bryan. London: Doubleday, 2002; *Count Karlstein, or The Ride of the Demon Huntsman,* illus. Patrice Aggs. London: Doubleday, 1991; Yearling, 1992; New York: Knopf-Random House, 1998, 2000.

The Firework-Maker's Daughter. London: Doubleday, 1995. *The Firework-Maker's Daughter,* illus. Nick Harris. London: Corgi Yearling, 1996; illus. S. Saelig Gallagher. New York: Arthur A. Levine Books, 1999; Scholastic, 1995, 2001, 2006.

Galatea. London: Gollancz, 1978; New York: Dutton, 1978, 1979.

The Gas-Fitter's Ball. London: Viking-Penguin, 1995. *The Gas-Fitter's Ball,* illus. Mark Thomas. London: Puffin, 1998.

The Haunted Storm [Pullman, Philip N.] London: New English Library, 1972, 1973.

How to Be Cool. London: Heinemann, 1987.

I Was a Rat!,or The Scarlet Slippers, illus. Peter Bailey. London: Doubleday, 1999; illus. Kevin Hawkes. New York: Knopf-Random House, 2000; Dell Yearling, 2002.

Lyra's Oxford, engravings John Lawrence. Oxford: David Fickling Books, 2003; New York: David Fickling-Knopf/Random House, 2003.

Mossycoat, retold by Philip Pullman, illus. Peter Bailey. London: Scholastic, 1998.

The New Cut Gang: Thunderbolt's Waxworks, illus. by Mark Thomas. London: Viking, 1994. *Thunderbolt's Waxworks,* illus. by Mark Thomas. London: Puffin, 1996.

Puss in Boots: The Adventures of That Most Enterprising Feline, illus. Ian Beck. London: Doubleday, 2000; New York: Knopf-Random House, 2000.

The Ruby in the Smoke. Oxford: Oxford University Press, 1985. Rev. ed. London: Puffin in association with Oxford University Press, 1987. London: Scholastic, 1999, 2004, new ed. 2007; New York: Knopf-Random House, 1987, 1994, 1997; Dell Laurel-Leaf, 1988, 2000.

The Scarecrow and His Servant, illus. Peter Bailey. London: Doubleday, 2004; Corgi-Yearling, 2005; New York: Knopf-Random House, 2005; Yearling, 2007.

The Shadow in the North. London: Penguin in association with Oxford University Press, 1988. London: Puffin in association with Oxford University Press, 1993. London: Scholastic Point, 2004, new ed. 2007; New York: Knopf-Random House, 1988, 1997; Dell Laurel-Leaf, 1989.

The Shadow in the Plate. Oxford: Oxford University Press, 1986.

Sherlock Holmes and the Limehouse Horror. Walton-on-Thames: Nelson, 1992.

Spring-Heeled Jack: A Story of Bravery and Evil, illus. by David Mostyn. London: Doubleday, 1989; Corgi-Yearling, 1998; New York: Knopf-Random House, 1991, 2002.

The Tiger in the Well. London: Viking, 1991; Penguin, 1992; Scholastic Point, 2004, new ed. 2007; New York: Knopf-Random House, 1990; Dell Laurel-Leaf, 1992.

The Tin Princess. London: Penguin, 1994; Scholastic Point, 2000, new ed. 2007; New York: Knopf-Random House, 1994; Dell Laurel-Leaf, 1996.

Using the Oxford Illustrated Junior Dictionary, Adapted ed. Oxford: Oxford University Press, 1995.

Using the Oxford Illustrated Junior Dictionary: A Book of Exercises and Games, illus. David Mostyn. New ed. Oxford: Oxford University Press, 1999.

Using the Oxford Junior Dictionary: A Book of Exercises and Games, illus. David Mostyn. Oxford: Oxford University Press, 1995. New ed. Oxford: Oxford University Press, 1998.

Using the Oxford Junior Dictionary: A Book of Exercises and Games, illus. Ivan Ripley. Oxford: Oxford University Press, 1979.

The White Mercedes. London: Pan-Macmillan, 1992.

The Wonderful Story of Aladdin and the Enchanted Lamp, as told by Philip Pullman, illus. David Wyatt. London: Scholastic, 1993, 1995.

BOOKS EDITED OR ADAPTED BY PULLMAN AND FOREWORDS OR OTHER CONTRIBUTIONS:

"A Word or Two About Myths" in *The Myths Boxset: A Short History of Myth, The Penelopiad, Weight*. London: Canongate Books Ltd., 2005.

Adaptation. *Frankenstein* (adapted from Mary Shelley's novel). Oxford: Oxford University Press, 1990, 2003.

Editor. *Detective Stories: Chosen by Philip Pullman,* illus. Nick Hardcastle. London: Kingfisher, 1998, 2004; New York: Kingfisher, 1998; Kingfisher—Houghton-Mifflin, 2003.

Editor; Introduction by. *Whodunit?: Utterly Baffling Detective Stories.* London and New York: Kingfisher—Houghton-Mifflin, 2007.

Foreword. *Alice's Adventures in Wonderland* by Lewis Carroll. London: Macmillan Children's Books, 2005.

Foreword. *Carmen* by Prosper Merimee. London: Hesperus Press Ltd, 2004.

Foreword. *Through The Looking-Glass: And What Alice Found There* by Lewis Carroll. London: Macmillan Children's Books, 2006.

Foreword. *The Raven and Other Poems and Stories* by Edgar Allan Poe. London: Franklin Watts, 2006.

Introduction. *Life and Death: A Collection of Classic Poetry and Prose.* Kate Agnew, ed. Cambridge: Wizard—Icon, 2004; New York: Totem Books, 2007.

Introduction. *The Magic Pudding* by David Lindsay. New York: New York Review Children's Collection, 2004.

Introduction. *Oliver Twist* by Charles Dickens. New York: Modern Library—Random House, 2001.

Introduction. *Paradise Lost* by John Milton. Oxford: Oxford UP, 2005.

HDM References

Primary Sources

Blake, William. *Collected Works.* The William Blake Archive
An amazing on-line resource that provides the opportunity to read Blake's work as he intended
www.blakearchive.org

von Kleist, Heinrich. "On the Marionette Theatre." Translated by Idris Parry. Available at Southern Cross Review (**www.southerncrossreview.org**), Issue 9, Nov. 16, 2005.

Milton, John. *Paradise Lost.* An illustrated edition with an introduction by Philip Pullman. Oxford: Oxford UP, 2005. (Not annotated)

Milton, John. *Paradise Lost.* Ed. Alistair Fowler. London: Longman, 1971. (Thoroughly annotated).

Pullman, Philip. *His Dark Materials.* [*See* **Philip Pullman Bibliography**]

Pullman, Philip. *Lyra's Oxford.* New York: Knopf, 2003.

Selected Essays & Lectures by Philip Pullman

"Art of Reading in Colour." *Index on Censorship.* Vol. 33, No. 4, Oct. 2004. pp. 156-163.

"Eric Rohmann." *Horn Book Magazine.* Vol. 79, No. 4, Jul./Aug. 2003. pp. 401-05.

"From Exeter to Jordan." *Oxford Today,* Volume 14 Number 3, Trinity 2002. (**www.oxfordtoday.ox.ac.uk**) (Search for "From Exeter to Jordan.")

"Gotterdammerung or Bust." *Horn Book Magazine.* Vol. 75, No. 1, Jan./Feb. 1999. pp. 31-34.

"Identity Crisis" in *Free Expression Is No Offence.* Lisa Appignanesi, ed. London: PEN/Penguin, 2005.

"Introduction." *Paradise Lost* by John Milton. Oxford: Oxford UP, 2005.

"Lecture at the Swedish House of Parliament." May 26, 2005. Website for the Astrid Lindgren Memorial Award. (**www.alma.se**) (Click on "Prize winners" and then on "2005.")

"Let's Write It in Red: The Patrick Hardy Lecture." Delivered at the English-Speaking Union, London, November 3, 1997. Published in *Signal* 85, Jan. 1998.

"Medtner." *Granta 76: Music* Jan. 2002.

"Once Upon a Time and What Happened Next." Philip Pullman at the Oxford Women's Luncheon Club, Feb. 8, 2005. *Oxonian Review of Books.* Vol. 4, No. 2, 2005. pp. 10-11.

"Philip Pullman: His Wonderful Materials" by Catherine Andronik. *Book Report.* Vol. 20, No. 3, Nov./Dec. 2001. pp. 40-45.

"Prize winning Lecture at the Swedish Royal Library." May 26, 2005. Website for the Astrid Lindgren Memorial Award. www.alma.se/page.php?pid=2072

"The Republic of Heaven." *Horn Book Magazine.* Nov./Dec. 2001, Vol. 77, No. 6, pp. 655-78.

Philip Pullman's official website has four main divisions: *About the Books, About the Writing, About the Worlds,* and *About the Author* in addition to the home page. Notes on links of interest are indicated here.

Home page: Philip Pullman's newsletters and an archive of recent news stories.

About the Books: links to pages showing the woodcuts in the UK editions of *Northern Lights* and *The Subtle Knife.*

About the Writing: commonly asked questions and answers.

About the Worlds: lectures, essays, and articles.

About the Author: autobiographical and other essays; links to interviews.

"Writing Fantasy Realistically." Presented to the *Sea of Faith Network* 2002 UK national conference. (**www.sofn.org.uk**) (Click on "Conferences" and then scroll down to the article.)

Selected Interviews with Philip Pullman

"Achuka Interview: Philip Pullman." *Features: ACHUKA Interviews.*

Archived. (**www.achuka.co.uk/archive/main.php**). (Search for "Pullman," click "ACHUKA - Children's Books UK - Philip Pullman," then click on the "Interview" button.)

"Heat and Dust, an interview with Philip Pullman." Interviewer: Huw Spanner. *Way Past* (Interviews) on *Third Way* (**www.thirdway.org.uk**). (Click on "Way Past" and then on the word "Interviews.")

"The *Dark Materials* debate: life, God, the universe..." Philip Pullman debates religion with the Archbishop of Canterbury, Dr Rowan Williams. Moderator: Robert Butler. *Telegrah.co.uk*. March 17, 2004. **weather.telegraph.co.uk/arts/main.jhtml?xml=/arts/2004/03/17/bodark17.xml&sSheet=/ arts/2004/03/18/ixartright.html#con** (Advanced search for "Robert Butler" and limit search to the date of the interview.)
Note: The *Telegraph's* transcript is an edited version of a Platform performance at the National Theatre. Transcripts of the *His Dark Materials* theatrical production Platforms are no longer on line at the National Theatre's website, but they are available in the book *Darkness Illuminated,* published by the National Theatre/Oberon Books.

"Darkness Visible: An Interview with Philip Pullman." Interviewer: Kerry Fried. **www.amazon.com/exec/obidos/tg/feature/-/94590/002-6573485-2891212**

"Philip Pullman answers your questions." 2003. Responses to readers' questions. *Gloucester Gets Fresh* on *Where I live: Gloucester* from the BBC. **www.bbc.co.uk/gloucestershire/getfresh/2003/10/philip_pullman_qa.shtml**

"Philip Pullman in Readerville 02/05/01-02/09/01." *Readerville Events.* Discussion Areas, Readerville.com (**www.readerville.com**). (Click on "All Discussions.")

"Philip Pullman Interview." Interviewer: Jennie Renton. *Writing* at *Textualities,* an online literary magazine (**www.textualities.net**) 2005. (**www.textualities.net**) (Search for "Pullman.")

"Philip Pullman Interview." *Teenreads.com*. December 11, 2001. **www.teenreads.com** (Search for "Philip Pullman.")

"Philip Pullman Reaches the Garden." Interviewer: Dave Weich. *Powells.com*. Aug. 31, 2000. (**www.powells.com**) (Scroll down to "From the Authors," click on "Interviews," then look on the left sidebar for "Philip Pullman (2000).")

"Philip Pullman: Some Rarely Asked Questions." Abridged transcript by Thea Logie of a question and answer session. Balliol College English Society. November 6, 2002. **http://urchin.earth.li/cgi-bin/twic/wiki/view.pl?page=PullmeisterRAQ**

"Philip Pullman, Tamora Pierce, and Christopher Paolini Talk Fantasy Fiction." Interviewer: Dave Weich. *Powells.com*. July 31, 2003. (**www.powells.com**) (Scroll down to "From the Authors," click on "Interviews," then look on the left sidebar for "Philip Pullman (2003).")

"Some enchanted author." Interviewer: John Cornwell. *The Sunday Times Magazine.* October 24, 2004. (**www.timesonline.co.uk/article/0,,2099-1311328_1,00.html**)

"Talking with Philip Pullman." Interviewers: Wendy Parsons and Nicholson Catriona. *The Lion and the Unicorn.* Vol. 23, No. 1, 1999. pp. 116-34.

Webchat on the website for the Radio 4 dramatisation of Philip Pullman's Trilogy, *His Dark Materials.* Radio 4 on BBC. **www.bbc.co.uk** (Go to the UK version of the website. Click on "Entertainment" and then search for "His Dark Materials.")

Books About Pullman

Butler, Robert. *The Art of Darkness: Staging the Philip Pullman Trilogy.* London: National Theatre/Oberon Books, 2003.

Colbert, David. *The Magical Worlds of Philip Pullman: A Treasury of Fascinating Facts.* New York: Berkley Books, 2006.

Gribbin, Mary and John. *The Science of Philip Pullman's His Dark Materials.* Introduction by Philip Pullman. London: Hodder Children's Books, 2004. New York: Knopf, 2005; Laurel Leaf, 2007.

Haill, Lyn, ed. *Darkness Illuminated: Discussions on Philip Pullman's His Dark Materials.* London: National Theatre/Oberon Books, 2004.

Haill, Lyn and Dinah Wood. *Philip Pullman's His Dark Materials Programme.* National Theatre, London. Winter 2003.

Lenz, Millicent and Carole Scott, eds. *His Dark Materials Illuminated: Critical Essays on Philip Pullman's Trilogy.* Detroit: Wayne State UP, 2005.

Parkin, Lance and Mark Jones. *Dark Matters: An Unofficial and Unauthorized Guide to Philip Pullman's Internationally Bestselling His Dark Materials Trilogy.* London: Virgin, 2005.

Squires, Claire. *Philip Pullman's His Dark Materials Trilogy: A Reader's Guide.* (Continuum Contemporaries). New York: Continuum International Publishing Group, 2003.

Tucker, Nicholas. *Darkness Visible: Inside the World of Philip Pullman.* Duxford, Cambridge: Wizard Books, 2003.

Watkins, Tony. *Dark Matter: A Thinking Fan's Guide to Philip Pullman* (republished 2006 by InterVarsity as *Dark Matter: Shedding Light on Philip Pullman's Trilogy, His Dark Materials*). Southampton, Hampshire, UK: Damaris, 2004.

Wright, Nicholas, adapt. *His Dark Materials.* By Philip Pullman. London: Nick Hern Books, 2004.

Wright, Nicholas, adapt. *His Dark Materials: New Edition.* By Philip Pullman. London: Nick Hern Books, 2005.

Yeffeth, Glenn, ed. *Navigating the Golden Compass: Religion, Science & Dæmonology in Philip Pullman's His Dark Materials.* Dallas: BenBella, 2005.

Yuan, Margaret Speaker. *Philip Pullman* (Who Wrote That?). New York: Chelsea House, 2005.

About *His Dark Materials:* Reviews, Critiques, Book Chapters

Bird, Anne-Marie. "Without Contraries is no Progression": Dust as an All-Inclusive, Multifunctional Metaphor in Philip Pullman's *His Dark Materials.*" *Children's Literature in Education.* Vol. 32, No. 2, Jun. 2001. pp. 111-123.

Brown, Tanya. "Philip Pullman: Storming Heaven." *Locus: The Newspaper of the Science Fiction Field.* Vol. 45, No. 6, 2000. pp. 8, 80-82.

Carter, James. "An Introduction to Philip Pullman" in *Talking Books: Children's Authors Talk About the Craft, Creativity and Process of Writing.* London, New York: Routledge, 1999. pp. 178-95.

Chabon, Michael. "Dust & Daemons." *New York Review of Books.* Vol. 51, No. 5, March 25, 2004.

Cornwell, John. "Some enchanted author." *Sunday Times.* Oct. 24, 2004.
www.timesonline.co.uk/newspaper/0,,176-1311328_1,00.html

Lenz, Millicent. "Philip Pullman" in *Alternative Worlds in Fantasy Fiction.* Peter Hunt and Millicent

Lenz, eds. pp. 122-69. London: Continuum International Publishing Group, 2003.

Lenz, Millicent. "Story as a Bridge to Transformation: The Way Beyond Death in Philip Pullman's *The Amber Spyglass.*" *Children's Literature in Education.* Vol. 34, No. 1, Mar. 2003, pp. 47-55.

Lyall, Sarah. "The Man Who Dared Make Religion the Villain." *New York Times.* November 7, 2000.

Mackey, Margaret. "The Survival of Engaged Reading in the Internet Age: New Media, Old Media, and the Book." *Children's Literature in Education.* Vol. 32, No. 3, Sep. 2001. pp. 167-189.

Miller, Laura. "Far from Narnia: Philip Pullman's Secular Fantasy for Children." *The New Yorker.* Dec. 26 2005/Jan. 6, 2006.

Moruzi, Kristine. "Missed Opportunities: The Subordination of Children in Philip Pullman's His Dark Materials." *Children's Literature in Education.* Vol. 36, No. 1, March 2005. pp. 55-68.

Odean, Kathleen. "The Story Master." *SLJ.com* (a service of the *School Library Journal*). Oct.1, 2000. www.schoollibraryjournal.com (Search for the title of the article.)

"Philip Pullman and the Republic of Heaven." **www.richardpoole.net** (Click on "Criticism" and then scroll down to find the article.)

Townsend, John Rowe. "Paradise Reshaped." *Horn Book Magazine.* Vol. 78, No. 4, Jul/Aug. 2002. pp. 415-21.

Vulliamy, Ed. "Author puts Bible Belt to the test." *Observer.* August 26, 2001. **www.observer.guardian.co.uk** (Search for the title of the article.)

Walsh, C. "From `capping' to intercision: metaphors/metonyms of mind control in the young adult fiction of John Christopher and Philip Pullman." *Language and Literature.* Vol. 12, No. 3, 2003. pp. 233-51.

Wood, Naomi. "Paradise Lost and Found: Obedience, Disobedience, and Storytelling in C. S. Lewis and Philip Pullman." *Children's Literature in Education.* Vol. 32, No. 4, Dec. 2001. pp. 237-259.

Selected Websites about Philip Pullman

BBC

The website for the Radio 4 dramatisation of Philip Pullman's Trilogy, *His Dark Materials* features a dictionary, quizzes, messageboards, and a webchat with Philip Pullman. **www.bbc.co.uk/radio4/arts/hisdarkmaterials**

The Guardian/Observer

The *Guardian/Observer* online maintains a huge section of archived material about and by Philip Pullman. The gateway page is located here: **http://books.guardian.co.uk**. Click on *Authors,* and then on *Authors M-Q* to find the Philip Pullman page. To find hundreds more, go to the *Guardian's* homepage (**www.guardian.co.uk**) and search "Philip Pullman."

Selections from *The Guardian/Observer.com:*

By Philip Pullman:

"The war on words." Nov. 6, 2004. Extract from "Art of Reading in Colour." *Index on Censorship.* Vol. 33, No. 4, Oct. 2004. pp. 156-163.

"Philip Pullman on Adapting Aladdin." Nov. 27, 2005.

"Let's pretend." Nov. 24, 2004.

"The science of fiction." Aug. 26, 2004.

"Theatre: The true key stage." March 30, 2004.

"Dreaming of spires." July 27, 2002.

Interviews:

"There has to be a lot of ignorance in me when I start a story." February 18, 2002. Responses to readers' questions.

"A wizard with worlds." Interviewer: Kate Kellaway. October 22, 2000.

"Driven by daemons." Interviewer: Sally Vincent. November 10, 2001.

News, Reviews, Critiques:

"How three writers adapted Pullman." Nov. 24, 2004.

"Epic children's book takes Whitbread." Jan. 23, 2002.

McCrum, Robert. "Not for children." Oct. 22, 2000.

National Theatre, London

Archival material primarily about the National Theatre's 2005 two-part adaptation of *His Dark Materials* adapted by Nicholas Wright and directed by Nicholas Hytner, the site also includes an edited transcript of the debate between the Archbishop of Canterbury Rowan Williams and Philip Pullman, as well as other resources about the novels. **http://website-archive2.nt-online.org** (Click on "His Dark Materials.")

Publishers' Sites

UK: Scholastic

http://www.scholastic.co.uk/zone/book_philip-pullman-hdm.htm

US: Random House

http://www.randomhouse.com/features/pullman/books/books.html

Selected Fansites

Hisdarkmaterials.org

This dynamic, regularly updated site is a virtual republic of heaven (the webname of its founder is, appropriately enough, Lord Asriel). Two sections, Columns and especially Essays, provide a place for users to present extended critical analysis. Galleries of fan art and movie, videogame, and stageplay promotional materials are among the visual resources divided into ten albums in Photograms. The site's vigorous message board, Cittàgazze, is huge and well organized. For entertainment, there's a downloadable alethiometer, dæmon name generator (Dæmonator), and role-playing game, and for reference, there's the Srafopedia. Of particular interest are interactive maps of Lyra's world in the trilogy and of her Oxford (search for Maps), and an interview with Philip Pullman conducted by one of the page's community members at the June 2005 Gothenburg Book Fair in Sweden (search for Gothenburg).

Bridgetothestars.net

This is one of the best HDM fan sites on the web. It is updated regularly and includes an encyclopedia, "photograms," interviews with Pullman, archived and current news stories, reviews of books about Pullman, information on the plays and forthcoming films, essays and commentaries, a message board, extensive links to Pullman resources, and cover art for over 130 different editions of *His Dark Materials*.

Works Cited and Information Sources

Following are the sources of the information that appears in Facts, Sidebars *and* Philip Pullman's *comments. All sites were accessed successfully in July 2006.*

I. CHARACTERS

Authority

"Philip Pullman in Readerville 02.05.01-02.09.01." Search: Pullman in Readerville Events, www.readerville.com

Byrnison

"Philip Pullman, Tamora Pierce, and Christopher Paolini Talk Fantasy Fiction" by Dave Weich on www.Powells.com. Search: Pullman under Authors.

Coram

"Pandemic Influenza [1957 Asian Flu Pandemic]." Homeland Security on www.globalsecurity.org

Enoch

"The Enoch Literature" by James C. VanderKam in "Thematic Guest Lectures Online" in *Old Testament Pseudepigrapha*, School of Divinity, St. Andrews College). Search by title.

"Henoch" (Greek Enoch) in *The Catholic Encyclopedia* at www.newadvent.org

Faa

"Kennedy" in The Moores, Kennedys & Related Families of Pitt & Beaufort Counties, NC at www.moore.greystar.org

Golden monkey

"Philip Pullman in Readerville 02.05.01-02.09.01" See **Authority,** above.

Koopman

"Norfolk Gale Disaster." Coastal Concern Action Group at www.happisburgh.org.uk

Scoresby

"Darkness Visible: An Interview with Philip Pullman" in two parts by Kerry Fried at amazon.com

"William Scoresby" in Attractions at Whitby-UK on www.whitby-uk.com

"Scoresby, William" and "Parry, Sir William Edward." *The Columbia Encyclopedia* at www.bartleby.com

Will

"Philip Pullman in Readerville 02.05.01-02.09.01" See **Authority,** above.

[1] *AS* 105/101	[12] *SK* 47/45	[23] *AS* 426/405	[34] *AS* 419/399
[2] *SK* 160/153	[13] *SK* 48/46	[24] *AS* 397/378	[35] *AS* 63/61
[3] *SK* 45/44	[14] *SK* 281/271	[25] *AS* 399/379	[36] *AS* 34/32
[4] *SK* 102-03/97-99	[15] *NL* 122; *GC* 122	[26] *AS* 416/396	[37] *AS* 28/26
[5] *NL* 6; *GC* 6	[16] *SK* 44/43	[27] *AS* 431/410	[38] *AS* 12/11
[6] *NL* 13; *GC* 13	[17] *SK* 49/47	[28] *AS* 432/310	[39] *AS* 24/22
[7] *NL* 11; *GC* 11	[18] *NL* 379; *GC* 379	[29] *AS* 222/210	[40] *AS* 27/25
[8] *NL* 6; *GC* 6	[19] *NL* 362; *GC* 362	[30] *AS* 33/31	[41] *AS* 27/26
[9] *NL* 124; *GC* 123	[20] *NL* 362; *GC* 362	[31] *AS* 33-34/32	[42] *AS* 25/23
[10] *NL* 274; *GC* 273	[21] *NL* 391; *GC* 391	[32] *AS* 35/33	[43] *AS* 98/93
[11] *NL* 187; *GC* 189	[22] *NL* 133; *GC* 132	[33] *AS* 331/316	[44] *AS* 98/93

45 *AS* 98/93
46 *AS* 98/94
47 *AS* 34/32
48 *AS* 34/32
49 *AS* 28/26
50 *AS* 37/35
51 *AS* 28/26
52 *NL* 167; *GC*167
53 *NL* 247; *GC* 245
54 *NL* 96; *GC* 95
55 *AS* 294, 295/280
56 *NL* 147; *GC* 146
57 *AS* 101/97
58 *AS* 106/101
59 *AS* 106/102
60 *AS* 106-7/102
61 *AS* 105/100
62 *AS* 105/101
63 *AS* 141/134
64 *AS* 40/38
65 *NL* 224; *GC* 223
66 *NL* 181; *GC* 181
67 *NL* 189; *GC* 190
68 *NL* 190; *GC* 191
69 *NL* 345; *GC* 345
70 *NL* 179; *GC* 180
71 *NL* 209; *GC* 209
72 *AS* 206/195
73 *NL* 218; *GC* 216-17
74 *AS* 201-02/191
75 *SK* 235/225
76 *AS* 44/42
77 *AS* 119/113
78 *NL* 372; *GC* 372
79 *SK* 21/20
80 *SK* 22/21
81 *AS* 76/72
82 *NL* 277; *GC* 276
83 *NL* 273; *GC* 272
84 *NL* 277; *GC* 276
85 *AS* 76/72
86 *NL* 278; *GC* 277
87 *SK* 236/226
88 *NL* 119; *GC* 118
89 *NL* 144; *GC* 145
90 *NL* 119; *GC* 118
91 *NL* 120; *GC* 119
92 *NL* 121
93 *GC* 120
94 *AS* 530
95 *AS* 532/503
96 *NL* 300
97 *NL* 300

98 *NL* 54; *GC* 54
99 *NL* 105; *GC* 104
100 *NL* 56
101 *NL* 106
102 *GC* 104-05
103 *NL* (10th Anniv. Ed.) 104
104 *NL* 42; *GC* 41
105 *NL* 66; *GC* 65
106 *NL* 271; *GC* 270
107 *SK* 207/198
108 *NL* 42; *GC* 41
109 *SK* 213/204
110 *NL* 88; *GC* 87
111 *NL* 92; *GC* 91
112 *NL* 76; *GC* 75
113 *NL* 374; *GC* 374
114 *NL* 124; *GC* 123
115 *NL* 395; *GC* 395
116 *NL* 44; *GC* 43
117 *NL* 96 ; *GC* 95
118 *NL* 268; *GC* 267
119 *NL* 69; *GC* 68
120 *NL* 77; *GC* 76
121 *NL* 133; *GC* 130
122 *NL* 275; *GC* 274
123 *SK* 327/313
124 *SK* 236/225
125 *AS* 164/156
126 *AS* 345/328
127 *AS* 3/3
128 *AS* 218/206
129 *AS* 150/142
130 *AS* 218/206
131 *AS* 419/398
132 *AS* 418/398
133 *AS* 427/405
134 *NL* 66; *GC* 65
135 *AS* 542/512
136 *AS* 268/253
137 *NL* 90; *GC* 89
138 *NL* 357; *GC* 357
139 *NL* 361/ *GC* 361
140 *AS* 393/373
141 *AS* 65/63
142 *AS* 419-20/399
143 *NL* 115; *GC* 114
144 *NL* 118; *GC* 117
145 *NL* 120; *GC* 119
146 *AS* 531/501
147 *AS* 532/502
148 *AS* 455/432
149 *NL* 42; *GC* 41

150 *AS* 145/138
151 *AS* 340/324
152 *AS* 145/138
153 *SK* 325/310
154 *SK* 213/203
155 *NL* 42; *GC* 42
156 *AS* 53/51
157 *NL* 87; *GC* 86
158 *SK* 213/203
159 *NL* 395; *GC* 395
160 *AS* 428/407
161 *AS* 389/370
162 *AS* 490/464
163 *AS* 290/276
164 *AS* 127/121
165 *SK* 284/272
166 *SK* 121/116
167 *SK* 219/210
168 *SK* 336/321
169 *SK* 333/318
170 *SK* 224/214
171 *SK* 133/128
172 *SK* 224/214
173 *SK* 224/214
174 *SK* 121/116
175 *SK* 293/280
176 *SK* 334/320
177 *NL* (10th Anniv. Ed.) appendix
178 *AS* 545/515
179 *SK* 314/301
180 *SK* 131/125
181 *SK* 308/295
182 *SK* 316/303
183 *SK* 132/127
184 *NL* 52; *GC* 51
185 *NL* 184; *GC* 185
186 *SK* 242/232
187 *NL* 185; *GC* 186
188 *NL* 184; *GC* 185
189 *NL* 263; *GC* 263
190 *SK* 30/29
191 *SK* 242/232
192 *SK* 338/323
193 *SK* 330/316
194 *SK* 330/316
195 *SK* 119/114
196 *AS* 527/498
197 *SK* 29/27
198 *AS* 500/473
199 *AS* 510/482
200 *AS* 528/499
201 *NL* 169; *GC* 169

202 *NL* 175; *GC* 175
203 *AS* 308-09
204 *AS* 323
205 *SK* 171/164
206 UK *AS* 13
207 *SK* 253/241
208 US *AS* 12
209 *SK* 81/78
210 *AS* 13/12
211 *SK* 80/77
212 *SK* 80/77
213 *SK* 80/77
214 *SK* 209/200
215 *AS* 17/16
216 *SK* 82/79
217 *SK* 82/79
218 *SK* 208/198
219 *NL* 32; *GC* 31
220 *NL* 33; *GC* 31
221 *NL* 65; *GC* 65
222 *SK* 138/132
223 *SK* 144/138
224 *SK* 144/138
225 *AS* 341/325
226 *SK* 25/24
227 *AS* 514/544
228 *NL* 35; *GC* 34
229 *NL* 37; *GC* 36
230 *NL* 35; *GC* 34
231 *NL* 175; *GC* 176
232 *NL* 310; *GC* 310
233 *NL* 113; *GC* 112
234 *NL* 249; *GC* 247
235 *NL* 70; *GC* 69
236 *AS* 169/160
237 *NL* 209; *GC* 209
238 *NL* 352; *GC* 352
239 *NL* 282; *GC* 281
240 *AS* 180/170
241 *NL* 209; *GC* 208
242 *SK* 322/308
243 *AS* 492/466
244 *AS* 546/516
245 *NL* 63; *GC* 62
246 *NL* 69; *GC* 68
247 *NL* 74; *GC* 73
248 *NL* 86; *GC* 85
249 *NL* 90; *GC* 89
250 *SK* 83/80
251 *AS* 280/266
252 *AS* 298/283
253 *AS* 544/514
254 *AS* 74/71

255 *AS* 365/347
256 *AS* 273/259
257 *AS* 279/264
258 *AS* 278/264
259 *AS* 279/264
260 *AS* 273/259
261 *NL* 215; *GC* 214
262 *NL* 216; *GC*15
263 *AS* 73/69
264 *SK* 87/84
265 *AS* 450/427
266 *AS* 465/441-42
267 *SK* 99/95
268 *SK* 100/96
269 *SK* 92/88
270 *AS* 246-47/234
271 *AS* 247/234
272 *AS* 386/368
273 *AS* 470/446
274 *AS* 508/480
275 *AS* 450/427
276 *AS* (10th Anniv. Ed.) appendix
277 *NL* 139
278 *NL* 246; *GC* 244
279 *AS* 336/320
280 *NL* 69; *GC* 68
281 *NL* 6 ; *GC* 6
282 *NL* 71; *GC* 70
283 *NL* 66; *GC* 65
284 *NL* 129; *GC* 128
285 *AS* 544/514
286 *NL* 253; *GC* 252
287 *NL* 252; *GC* 251
288 *AS* 485/460
289 *AS* 418/398-99
290 *AS* 418/398
291 *AS* 428/406
292 *AS* 429/408
293 *AS* 63/60
294 *AS* 420/400
295 *AS* 417/397
296 *AS* 65/63
297 *AS* 419-20/399
298 *AS* 425/404
299 *AS* 63/61
300 *AS* 63/61
301 *AS* 393/373-74
302 *SK* (10th Anniv. Ed.) appendix
303 *AS* 336/320
304 *AS* 336/320
305 *AS* 336/320
306 *AS* 336/320-21

307 *AS* 466/442
308 *AS* 466/443
309 *SK* 291/279
310 *SK* 291/279
311 *SK* 293/280
312 *SK* 293/280-81
313 *SK* 116/111
314 *SK* 118/114
315 *AS* 331/316
316 *AS* 334
317 *AS* 213/202
318 *AS* 222/210
319 *AS* 215/204
320 *AS* 60/62
321 *AS* 527/498
322 *NL* 3; *GC* 3
323 *NL* 8; *GC* 8
324 *NL* 9; *GC* 9
325 *NL* 73; *GC* 72
326 *SK* 155/147
327 *NL* 232; *GC* 230
328 *NL* 71; *GC* 70
329 *NL* 281 ; *GC* 280
330 *AS* 298/284
331 *AS* 299/284
332 *NL* 134; *GC* 133
333 *SK* 288/276
334 *SK* 62/60
335 *SK* 2/2, 336/321
336 *SK* 2/2
337 *SK* 224/214
338 *SK* 13/12
339 *SK* 11/10, 275/263, 321/307
340 *SK* 9/8
341 *SK* 11/10
342 *SK* 11/11
343 *AS* 149/141
344 *AS* 162/153
345 *AS* 191/182
346 *SK* 10/10
347 *AS* 371/353
348 *SK* 116/112
349 *SK* 119/11
350 *SK* 118/114
351 *AS* 440/418
352 *SK* (10th Anniv. Ed.) appendix
353 *NL* 35
354 *SK* 36/34
355 *AS* 214/203
356 *AS* 69/66
357 *SK* 37/35
358 *AS* 72/69, 127/117

359 *SK* 248/237
360 *SK* 245/234
361 *NL* 314-15
362 *GC* 314-15
363 *NL* 314-15
364 *GC* 314-15
365 *SK* 334/320
366 *AS* 440/418
367 *AS* 271/257
368 *NL* 336; *GC* 336
369 *NL* 27; *GC* 26
370 *NL* 333; *GC* 332
371 *NL* 316; *GC* 316
372 *NL* 341; *GC* 341
373 *NL* 43; *GC* 42
374 *AS* 541/511
375 *NL/GC* 34
376 *NL/GC* 35
377 *AS* 382/401
378 *GC* 398
379 *AS* 60/57
380 *AS* 60/58
381 *AS* 60/57
382 *AS* 358/341
383 *AS* 218/206
384 *AS* 358/341-42
385 *AS* 176/167
386 *AS* 292/277
387 *AS* 292/278
388 *AS* 317/302
389 *AS* 251/237
390 *AS* 334/318
391 *NL* 331; *GC* 331
392 *NL* 330/330
393 *AS* 245/232
394 *AS* 243/232
395 *AS* 246/234
396 *SK* 223/214
397 *SK* 53/51
398 *NL* 192; *GC* 193
399 *NL* 309; *GC* 309
400 *SK* 231/221
401 *SK* 217/207
402 *SK* 299/287
403 *SK* 293/280-81
404 *SK* 316/303
405 *SK* 318/304-05
406 *SK* 307/294
407 *AS* 71/67
408 *NL* 240/238
409 *SK* (10th Anniv. Ed.) appendix
410 *SK* 51/49

411 *SK* 281/270
412 *SK* 51/49
413 *AS* 61/58
414 *NL* 143; *GC* 142
415 *AS* 527/498
416 *NL* 377; *GC* 377
417 *NL* 198; *GC* 198
418 *SK* 46/44
419 *SK* 46/45
420 *SK* 47/46
421 *NL* (10th Anniv. Ed.) appendix
422 *AS* 176/167
423 *AS* 178/168
424 *AS* 317/302
425 *AS* 333/317
426 *AS* 470/446
427 *AS* 467/443
428 *SK* 39/37
429 *NL* (10th Anniv. Ed.) appendix
430 *NL* 329; *GC* 329
431 *SK* 178/169
432 *SK* 179/170
433 *SK* 237/227
434 *SK* 126/121
435 *SK* 127/121
436 *SK* 156/149
437 *SK* 224/214
438 *SK* 2/2
439 *SK* 336/321
440 *AS* 533/504
441 *AS* 510/482
442 *SK* 9/9
443 *SK* 10/9
444 *AS* 483/458
445 *SK* 321-22/307-08
446 *SK* 11/10
447 *SK* 338/ 323
448 *SK* 16/16
449 *SK* 182-183/174
450 *AS* 171/162
451 *AS* 525/496
452 *SK* 77/74
453 *AS* 113/108
454 *SK* 337/322
455 *SK* 337/322
456 *SK* 287/275
457 *SK* 4/4
458 *AS* 203/193
459 *AS* 206/196
460 *AS* 191/182
461 *AS* 522/493
462 *AS* 538/505

[463] *SK* 322/306-07   [465] *AS* 219/208   [467] *AS* 519/491
[464] *AS* 440/418   [466] *AS* 519/490   [468] *AS* 34/32

II. Places and Peoples

2 . The Worlds

Cittàgazze, world of [captions]

Interview with Brian Aldiss by Nick Gevers. *Science Fiction Weekly.* Vol. 10, No. 33, Issue 382. August 16, 2004. (www.scifi.com/sfw/issue382/)

"There has to be a lot of ignorance in me when I start a story." Philip Pullman responds to readers' questions. *Guardian Unlimited.* February 18, 2002. (http://books.guardian.co.uk)

Kingdom of heaven

"The republic of heaven" by Philip Pullman. *The Horn Book Magazine.* Vol. 77, Issue 6, Nov. 1, 2001. pp. 655 (13).

"Heat and Dust, an interview with Philip Pullman" by Huw Spanner in *Way Past* (Interviews) on *Third Way* (www.thirdway.org.uk)

Suburbs of the World of the Dead (town)

Search term: "Top hat metal sign" in *Household Goods* in *Odds and Ends* at *Grateful Dead Official Store* via Grateful Dead Official Site (www.dead.net)

3 . Cities, Countries, Regions, Continents and Elements of Topography

Arctic *For more information on the Arctic, see:*

Arctic Studies Center, National Museum of Natural History, Smithsonian Institution (www.mnh.si.edu/arctic)

Arctic Institute of North America at the University of Calgary, Canada (www.arctic.ucalgary.ca)

Canada's Polar Life (www.polarlife.ca)

Inuit Tapiriit Kanatami (www.itk.ca)

National Oceanic & Atmospheric Administration's Arctic theme page (www.arctic.noaa.gov)

Polar Bears International (www.polarbearsinternational.org)

Scott Polar Research Institute, University of Cambridge (www.spri.cam.ac.uk)

Taiga Net (www.taiga.net)

University of Alaska Fairbanks' Centers & Institutes (www.uaf.edu/uaf/research/centers.html)

East Anglia Sidebar

"East Anglia," "Fens," "Anglo-Saxon England," and "England" at en.wikipedia.org

Falkeshall

"Vauxhall, Kennington and the Oval" at vauxhallandkennington.org.uk

Fens

"Philip Pullman Interview" by Jennie Renton in Writing at *Textualities*, an online literary magazine, 2005. (www.textualities.net)

German ocean

"On the History of Naming the North Sea" Article 3 on East Sea Forum by Shin Kim, Kyunghee Univ., Korea, www.eastsea.org.

Lena

"Lena River" at en.wikipedia.org.

Search term: "Lena River Delta" at Wild World at www.nationalgeographic.com/wildworld)

Mortlake

"Dr. John Dee." Channel 4: *Masters of Darkness* [History microsites]

Tunguska

"Tunguska Event" at en.wikipedia.org.

"Tunguska Event" and "Tungsuka Update" on Earth Impact at www.s-d-g.freeserve.co.uk.

"'The Sky Has Split Apart!': The Cosmic Mystery of the Century" by Roy A. Gallant in *Tunguska Documents* at www.galisteo.com/tunguska.

Umiat

"Umiat" in *Communities* on prudhoebay.com

4. Structures and Streets

Basalt sidebar

"Basalt" at en.wikipedia.org.

"Devil's Postpile" at National Park Service (www.nps.gov)

"Giants Causeway Official Guide" hosted by Ireland Unveiled (www.irelandunveiled.com)

Belvedere

"The Subtle Knife Illustrations" in *About the Books* on philip-pullman.com

5. The Oxfords

Covered market

"Virtual tour of the Oxford City Covered Market" in the *Virtual Tour of Oxford* by Karl Harrison (www.chem.ox.ac.uk/oxfordtour)

Jericho

"From Exeter to Jordan" by Philip Pullman. *Oxford Today,* Vol. 14, No. 3, Trinity, 2002 (www.oxfordtoday.ox.ac.uk)

Jordan

"From Exeter to Jordan" by Philip Pullman. *See* **Jericho**, above

Exeter College, University of Oxford (www.exeter.ox.ac.uk/college)

Oxford

"From Exeter to Jordan" by Philip Pullman. *See* **Jericho**, above

Oxford University

"The University and the Colleges" and "A Brief History of the University" in *About Oxford University* (www.ox.ac.uk)

Pilgrim's tower

"From Exeter to Jordan" by Philip Pullman. *See* **Jericho**, above

Pitt Rivers

"Pitt Rivers Museum" at www.prm.ox.ac.uk

"Neanderthal" at en.wikipedia.org

Port Meadow

"Boatyard Statement: My statement to the planning inquiry, 8 March 2005" by Philip Pullman *About the Author: Essays and Articles*, philip_pullman.com

St. John's

"Oxford Colleges" in *The Scholar's Guide to Oxford* at www.oxford-info.com

6. Peoples

Gyptians

Friends, Families and Travellers (FFT), a registered charity at www.gypsy-traveller.org

Inuit

"Inuit" in the *American Heritage® Dictionary* in Reference on Yahoo! Education
(http://education.yahoo.com)

Samoyed

"Samoyedes" in *The Columbia Encyclopedia* at www.bartleby.com.

"Nenets" in *The Red Book of the Peoples of the Russian Empire*, Institute of the Estonian Language
(www.eki.ee)

Skraelings

"Greenland," "Markland and Helluland", and "Vinland" in *History: Vikings: The North Atlantic Saga*,
National Museum of Natural History, Smithsonian Institution (www.si.edu)

Tartars

"Tatars" in *The Columbia Encyclopedia* at www.bartleby.com

"Baraba Tatars," "Chulym Tatars," "Crimean Tatars," and "Lithuanian Tatars" in *The Red Book of the
Peoples of the Russian Empire*, Institute of the Estonian Language (www.eki.ee)

Chapter 2 Notes

1 *AS* 82/79
2 *AS* 22/20
3 *AS* 82/79
4 *SK* 138/132
5 *AS* 35/33
6 *AS* 331/316
7 *AS* 280/266
8 *AS* 326/310
9 *AS* 220/209
10 *AS* 501/474
11 *AS* 548/518
12 *AS* 382/363
13 *AS* 506-7/479
14 *SK* 223/213
15 *AS* 86/83
16 *AS* 86/83
17 *AS* 133/127
18 *AS* 139/132
19 *NL* 187; *GC* 188
20 *NL* 187; *GC* 189
21 *NL* 188; *GC* 189
22 *NL* 188; *GC* 189
23 *NL* 187; *GC* 188
24 *NL* 376; *GC*376
25 *NL* 187; *GC* 189
26 *NL* 376; *GC* 376
27 *SK* 78/74

28 *AS* 18/17
29 *SK* 79/76
30 *SK* 282/270-71
31 *NL* 377; *GC* 377
32 *NL* 187; *GC* 188
33 *NL* 376; *GC* 376
34 *NL* 377; *GC* 377
35 *SK* 116/112
36 *AS* 273/259
37 *AS* 296/282
38 *AS* 524/495
39 *AS* 483/458
40 *SK* 16/16
41 *AS* 508/480
42 *SK* 311/298
43 *AS* 103/99
44 *NL* (10th Anniv. Ed.)
appendix
45 *SK* 140/134
46 *NL* 183; *GC* 184
47 *SK* 16/15
48 *SK* 66/64
49 *SK* 196/187
50 *SK* 141/135
51 *SK* 142/135
52 *SK* 142/136
53 *SK* 16/15
54 *NL* 34; *GC* 33

55 *NL* 160; *GC* 158
56 *NL* 112; *GC* 111
57 *AS* 2/2
58 *AS* 29/27
59 *AS* 65/62
60 *AS* 2/2
61 *NL* 139
62 *NL* 75; *GC* 74
63 *NL* 100; *GC* 99
64 *NL* 102; *GC* 101
65 *SK* (10th Anniv. Ed.)
appendix
66 *NL* 170; *GC* 170
67 *NL* 160; *GC* 159
68 *NL* 360; *GC* 360
69 *NL* 32; *GC* 31
70 *NL* 374; *GC* 374
71 *NL* 116; *GC* 115
72 *NL* 86; *GC* 85
[north]
73 *GC* 107,119
74 *NL* 134; *GC* 133
75 *AS* 105/100
76 *AS* 103/99
77 *NL* 309; *GC* 309
78 *AS* 122/117
79 *NL* 225; *GC* 224
80 *NL* 361; *GC* 360

81 *NL* 225; *GC* 224
82 *NL* 390; *GC* 390
83 *NL* 357 ; *GC* 357
84 *AS* 39/37
85 *AS* 206/196
86 *NL* 40, 365
87 *GC* 40, 365
88 *SK* 126/121
89 *SK* 53/51
90 *AS* 531/502
91 *AS* 222/211
92 *AS* 225/213
93 *AS* 225/213
94 *AS* 225/213
95 *AS* 225/214
96 *SK* 149/143
97 *AS* 58/56
98 *AS* /122-23
99 *SK* 128/122
100 *NL* 21; *GC* 19-20
101 *NL* 25; *GC* 24
102 *NL* 186; *GC* 187
103 *NL* 186; *GC* 187
104 *NL* 170; *GC* 170
105 *NL* 181; *GC*182
106 *NL* 239 ; *GC* 237
107 *NL* 259; *GC* 257

108 *NL 278; GC 277*
109 *NL 303; GC 301-02*
110 *NL 188; GC 188-89*
111 *SK 27/26, 58/56*
112 *NL 387-88*
113 *GC 387-88*
114 *AS 44/42*
115 *NL 76; GC 75*
116 *NL 178; GC 179*
117 *NL 212; GC 212*
118 *NL 336; GC 336*
119 *NL 354; GC*
120 *AS 341/325*
121 *NL 197; GC 198*
122 *AS 127/121*
123 *AS 534/504*
124 *SK 66/64*
125 *SK 104/99*
126 *SK 72/70*

127 *SK 105/101*
128 *SK 107/103*
129 *AS 537/507*
130 *AS 548/518*
131 *SK 87/83*
132 *AS 464/440*
133 *SK 87/83*
134 *SK 165/158*
135 *SK 158*
136 *NL 58; GC 57*
137 *NL 48; GC 48*
138 *NL 34; GC 33*
139 *NL 73; GC 72*
140 *NL 47; GC 46*
141 *NL 34; GC 33*
142 *NL 35; GC 34*
143 *SK 59/57*
144 *SK 72-3/70*
145 *AS 544/514*

146 *GC 377*
147 *SK 167/160*
148 *NL 62; GC 62*
149 *NL 76; GC 75*
150 *SK 78/75*
151 *SK 77/74*
152 *SK 77/74*
153 *SK 167/160*
154 *AS 532-3/503*
155 *SK 86/83*
156 *SK 83/80*
157 *SK 86/83*
158 *SK 155/148*
159 *SK 256/245*
160 *NL40; GC 40*
161 *NL 58; GC 57*
162 *SK 72/70*
163 *SK 116/112*
164 *NL 29; GC 28*

165 *NL 113; GC 112*
166 *NL 56; GC 55*
167 *AS 529/500*
168 *NL 124; GC 123*
169 *NL 124; GC 123*
170 *NL 136; GC 135*
171 *NL 116; GC 115*
172 *NL 113; GC 112*
173 *NL 29; GC 28*
174 *SK 221/212*
175 *SK 128-32/123-7*
176 *SK 78/75*
177 *SK 209/200*
178 *NL 205; GC 205*
179 *NL 230; GC 228*
180 *NL 139*

III. Creatures, Beings and Extraordinary Humans

Black Shuck

"Tale of Black Shuck" in *My Norfolk: Spooky Norfolk* (www.new.edp24.co.uk)

"Shuckland" at www.shuckland.co.uk

Dæmon

"Demon" in *The Catholic Encyclopedia* at www.newadvent.org

"Achuka Interview: Philip Pullman" in *Archive: Features: Interviews* at www.achuka.com

Andronik, Catherine. "Philip Pullman: His Wonderful Materials." *Book Report.* Vol. 20, No. 3, Nov./Dec. 2001. pp. 40-45. *See* Children Author's Information, Instructional Resource Center, Ashland University Library (www.ashland.edu)

Haill, Lyn and Dinah Wood. *Philip Pullman's His Dark Materials Programme.* National Theatre, London. Winter 2003

Harpies

"Chapter VII: King Phineus" in *Part I. The Voyage to Colchis* of *The Golden Fleece* by Padraic Colum at www.bartleby.com

"The Third Book of the Æneis" by Vergil in *Harvard Classics*, Vol. 13 at www.bartleby.com

Mulefa

"Philip Pullman in Readerville 02.05.01-02.09.01." See **Characters: Authority,** above.

Panserbjørne

"Philip Pullman Webchat" . Radio 4 dramatisation of Philip Pullman's Trilogy, *His Dark Materials* on Arts and Drama, Radio 4, BBC (www.bbc.co.uk/radio4)

Shaman

"Articles Related to Shamanism." Foundation for Shamanic Studies (www.shamanism.org)

"Healing interactions between shamans and clients (Kyzyl, Republic of Tuva)" by Konstantinos Zorbas in *Research: Research Projects of the Polar Social Science and Humanities Group,* Scott Polar

Research Institute, University of Cambridge (www.spri.cam.ac.uk)

"Tuva: The Treasure in the Centre of Asia" by Zora Freová (www.zorafresova.sk)

Zombi

"Vodou" and "Zombie" at en.wikipedia.org

Chapter 3 Notes

1 *SK* 289/277	25 *NL* 261; *GC* 259	49 *AS* 378/360	72 *SK* 142/136
2 *SK* 147/141	26 *NL* 105; *GC* 104	50 *NL* 222; *GC* 222	73 *AS* 514-15/486
3 *AS* 494/468	27 *NL* 292; *GC* 290	51 *NL* 261; *GC* 259	74 *AS* 522/494
4 *AS* 30/29	28 *AS* 249/236	52 *NL* 391; *GC* 391	75 *SK* 62/60
5 *AS* 420/399	29 *AS* 462/439	53 *SK* 6/6	76 *SK* 329/315
6 *AS* 66/63	30 *SK* 327/313	54 *AS* 456/433	77 *SK* 292/280
7 *SK* 260/249	31 *SK* 136/130	55 *AS* 455/432	78 *AS* 82/79
8 *AS* 425/404	32 *NL* 372; *GC* 372	56 *NL* 262; *GC* 260-1	79 *NL* 313; *GC* 313
9 *SK* 260/249	33 *NL* 285; *GC* 283-4	57 *AS* 331/316	80 *NL* 299; *GC* 298
10 *SK* 48-9/47	34 *SK* 215/205-6	58 *AS* 434/413	81 *SK* 34/33
11 *AS* 18/17	35 *SK* 223/213	59 *AS* 445-6/423	82 *NL* 314; *GC* 314
12 *SK* 339/324	36 *SK* 22/21	60 *AS* appendix	83 *SK* (10th Anniv. Ed.) appendix
13 *AS* 99/95	37 *NL* 195; *GC* 196	61 *AS* 446/425	84 *NL* 310; *GC* 310
14 *AS* 418/398	38 *NL* 215; *GC* 214	62 *AS* 135/129	85 *NL* 313; *GC* 313
15 *AS* 117/112	39 *NL* 276; *GC* 275	63 *AS* (10th Anniv. Ed.) appendix	86 *SK* 282/271
16 *NL* 226; *GC* 225	40 *AS* 527/498	64 *AS* 531/502	87 *NL* 309; *GC* 308-9
17 *NL* 181; *GC*182	41 *AS* 498/471	65 *NL* 27; *GC* 26-7	88 *SK* (10th Anniv. Ed.) appendix
18 *NL* 225; *GC* 224	42 *AS* 510/482	66 *NL* 97; *GC* 95	89 *NL* 113; *GC* 112
19 *AS* 192/182	43 *NL* 49	67 *NL* 109, 180; *GC* 108-9, 180	90 *SK* 209/199
20 *AS* 202/192	44 *NL* 22; *GC* 21	68 *NL* 236; *GC* 234	91 *NL* 375; *GC* 375
21 *NL* 227; *GC* 226	45 *AS* 270/256	69 *SK* 224/215	92 *NL* 375; *GC* 375
22 *NL* 110; *GC* 109	46 *AS* 275/261	70 *SK* 293/281	93 *SK* 44/42
23 *NL* 189; *GC* 190	47 *AS* 275/260	71 *SK* 135/130	
24 *SK* 45/43	48 *AS* 311/296		

IV. The Alethiometer, the Subtle Knife, and the Amber Spyglass

1. Alethiometer

Andronik, Catherine. "Philip Pullman: His Wonderful Materials." *See* **Dæmon**, above

Chapter 4 Notes

1 *NL* 126; *GC* 125	12 *NL* 148; *GC* 147	23 *SK* 29/28	34 *NL* 74
2 *NL* 74; *GC* 73	13 *NL* 149; *GC* 148	24 *SK* 269/258	35 *NL* 79
3 *AS* 71/68	14 *SK* 83/80	25 *AS* 192/182	36 *NL* 204; *GC* 204
4 *NL* 74; *GC* 73	15 *SK* 101/96-97	26 *AS* 192/182	37 *AS* 373/355
5 *NL* 79; *GC* 78	16 *SK* 109/105	27 *AS* 193/183	38 *AS* 375/356
6 *AS* 19/17	17 *SK* 109/105	28 *AS* 193/183	39 *AS* 422/401
7 *NL* 80; *GC* 79	18 *SK* 100/96	29 *AS* 403/384	40 *AS* 425/404
8 *NL* 127; *GC* 126	19 *NL* 153; *GC* 151	30 *AS* 520/491	41 *AS* 421/401
9 *NL* 152; *GC* 151	20 *NL* 30; *GC* 29	31 *AS* 545/515	42 *AS* 512/483
10 *NL* 173-74; *GC* 174	21 *NL* 32; *GC* 31	32 *AS* 173/163, 335/319	43 *AS* 515/486
11 *AS* 174/165	22 *SK* 37/35	33 *SK* 35/34, 108/104	44 *AS* 385-86/367

45 *NL 387-88/ GC 387*
46 *SK 286/274*
47 *SK 189/180*
48 *SK 334/320*
49 *SK 197/188*
50 *SK 336/ 321*
51 *AS 163/155*
52 *AS 85/81*
53 *AS 85-86/82*
54 *SK 15/15*
55 *SK 15-16/5*

56 *SK 334/319*
57 *SK 189/181*
58 *SK 189/181*
59 *AS 119/113*
60 *AS 74/70*
61 *SK 192/183*
62 *SK 194/185*
63 *AS 199/189*
64 *AS 200/190*
65 *SK 326/312*
66 *AS 70/67*

67 *SK 181/173*
68 *SK 53/51*
69 *AS 191/182*
70 *AS 190-91/180-181*
71 *AS 192/182*
72 *AS 512/483*
73 *SK 326/312*
74 *SK 119/114*
75 *SK 116/112*
76 *SK 119/114*
77 *AS 19/18*

78 *SK 193/184*
79 *SK 203/194*
80 *AS 21/20*
81 *AS 376/358*
82 *AS 85/82*
83 *AS 86/82*
84 *AS 506/478*
85 *AS 237/225*
86 *AS 238/226*
87 *AS 241/229*
88 *AS 497/470*

V. PHILOSOPHY, PSYCHOLOGY, AND THEOLOGY

Many-worlds hypothesis

"Physics' Best Kept Secret" by Tim Folger in *Discover*. Vol. 22, No. 09, Sept. 2001(www.discover.com)

"A Many-Worlds Product Paradigm for Quantum Inertia and Quantum Gravity" by William D. Eshleman on William D. Eshleman's website hosted by www.tripod.lycos.com

Philip Pullman on Dust

"Philip Pullman in Readerville 02.05.01-02.09.01." *See* **Characters: Authority,** above.

Chapter 5 Notes

1 *NL 31; GC 30*
2 *NL 32; GC 30*
3 *AS 350/334*
4 *NL 377; GC 377*
5 *NL 310; GC 310*
6 *SK 40 /38*
7 *SK 40/39*
8 *SK 328/314*
9 *AS 71/67*
10 *SK 287/275*
11 *AS 299/285*
12 *NL 310; GC 310*
13 *AS 325/309*
14 *AS 455/432*

15 *NL 108; GC 107*
16 *AS 403/384*
17 *NL 133; GC 132*
18 *AS 540/511*
19 *AS 542/513-14*
20 *NL173; GC 173*
21 *SK 87/83*
22 *SK 179/171*
23 *SK 169/162*
24 *AS 33/31-2*
25 *AS 520/491*
26 *NL 284; GC 282*
27 *NL 318; GC 318*
28 *NL 362; GC 362*

29 *NL 373; GC 373*
30 *AS 425/404*
31 *NL 29; GC 27*
32 *NL 377; GC 377*
33 *NL 390; GC 390*
34 *NL 392; GC 392*
35 *AS 71/68*
36 *AS 512/484*
37 *AS 520/491*
38 *AS 520/492*
39 *SK 261/248-9*
40 *SK 93/89*
41 *SK 97/92-3*
42 *SK 261-2/250-51*

43 *SK 190/181*
44 *AS 12/11*
45 *AS 424/403*
46 *AS 437/416*
47 *AS 426/405*
48 *AS 243/231*
49 *AS 464/441*
50 *AS 235/224*
51 *AS 520/491*
52 *AS 236/224*
53 *AS 243/231*
54 *AS 242/230*
55 *AS 476/451*
56 *AS 497/470*

VI. APPLIED METAPHYSICS

Excommunicate

"Excommunication" in *The Catholic Encyclopedia* at www.newadvent.org

Exorcism

"Exorcism" in *The Catholic Encyclopedia* at www.newadvent.org

I Ching

"Hexagram 52: Kên - Keeping Still, Mountain" in *Texts and Scriptures: I Ching Hexagrams* at Panlatrevo, an internet resource for texts and scriptures of Taoism (www.panlatrevo.com)

"27: The Corners of the Mouth (Providing Nourishment)" in *I Ching: The Hexagrams* in *Projects* on www.littlestcat.com.

"I Ching" and "I Ching divination" at en.wikipedia.org

Silver Guillotine

"Guillotine" at en.wikipedia.org

Trepanation

www.trepan.com, the website for ITAG™, the International Trepanation Advocacy Group

Chapter 6 Notes

[1] *AS* 84/81	[5] *AS* 79/76	[9] *AS* 41/39	[13] *NL* 230; *GC* 228
[2] *AS* 131/124	[6] *AS* 362/345	[10] *AS* 503/476	[14] *NL* 230; *GC* 228
[3] *NL* 277; *GC* 276	[7] *SK* 95/91	[11] *SK* 34/33	[15] *SK* 81/77
[4] *AS* 75/72	[8] *AS* 362/344	[12] *SK* 327/312	[16] *SK* 224/214

VII. APPLIED SCIENCES AND TECHNOLOGY

2. Medicinals

Bloodmoss

"Mosses—Division Bryophyta" in *Canada's Polar Life: Organisms.* eds. Hebert & Wearing-Wilde, University of Guelph (www.polarlife.ca)

Honey

"Honey as a topical antibacterial agent for treatment of infected wounds" in *World Wide Wounds* (www.worldwidewounds.com)

Jimson-weed

"Thornapple" in *A Modern Herbal* at www.botanical.com

"The Biogeography of Jimson Weed (*Datura stramonium*)" *by* Karissa Anderson, student in Geography 316 Spring 2005 (ed. Barbara Holzman, PhD), College of Behavioral and Social Sciences, San Francisco State University (http://bss.sfsu.edu)

Poppy-heads

"Poppy, White" in *A Modern Herbal* at www.botanical.com

"From Exeter to Jordan" by Philip Pullman *See* **Places: Jericho**, above

3. Food and Drink

Jack Daniel's

www.jackdaniels.com

Kendal Mint Cake

www.kendal.mintcake.co.uk

Polar Bear Liver

"Polar Bears in Depth" at Polar Bears International (www.polarbearsinternational.org)

"Ringed Seal" and "Polar Bear" in Wildlife, Inuit Tapiriit Kanatami (www.itk.ca)

Tokay

"Wine of the Kings" in *Hungarian Wine* in *Culture: Hungarian Cuisine* pwww.fsz.bme.hu/hungary/homepage.

4. Information technology

Photogram

"A History of the Magic Lantern" compiled by George Auckland for the Magic Lantern Society (www.magiclantern.org.uk)

"Magic lantern" in Laura Hayes and John Howard Wileman's Exhibit of Optical Toys. North Carolina School of Science and Mathematics Gallery (http://courses.ncssm.edu/gallery)

5. Transportation

Balloon

Search term: "Tissandier" at the Prints & Photographs Online Catalog, Library of Congress (www.loc.gov/index.html)

"Anatomy of a Gas Balloon" at www.gasballooning.net

Rolls Royce

"The Hon. Charles Stewart Rolls" in *Pioneers at Hargrave Aviation and Aeromodelling,* researched and created by Dr Russell Naughton and Prof John Bird, Monash University, Australia (www.ctie.monash.edu.au)

"Rolls-Royce_Limited" at en.wikipedia.org

6. Weapons

Fire Bombing

"Greek fire" in *Armies: Second Period: 400 CE - 1000 CE* in *Old World Contacts,* a multimedia history tutorial, Applied History Research Group, University of Calgary, Alberta, Canada (www.ucalgary.ca)

Spy-flies

"How Spy Flies Will Work." Science Division: Military Channel, www.howstuffworks.com

"Robotic Fly Gets Its Buzz." News release June 2002. University of California at Berkeley (www.berkeley.edu)

Winchester

"The Winchester Rifle" at Spartacus Educational, www.schoolnet.co.uk

7. Other crafted goods and materials

Swiss Army Knife

"Does the Swiss army really use the Swiss army knife?" A Straight Dope Classic. Jan. 27, 1995 (www.straightdope.com/classics)

Teflon

DuPont ™ company's Teflon site, www.teflon.com

Chapter 7 Notes

1 *NL* 21; *GC* 20
2 *SK* 7, 29/7, 27
3 *SK* 338/324
4 *NL* 81; *GC* 81
5 *NL* 177/ *GC* 177-8
6 *NL* 177/ *GC* 177-8
7 *NL* 79/ *GC* 78
8 *SK* 65/63
9 *SK* 21/20
10 *NL* 78; *GC* 78
11 *SK* 87/84
12 *AS* 357/340
13 *AS* 122/116
14 *SK* 163/155
15 *SK* 80/77
16 *SK* 171/164
17 *AS* 144/137
18 *SK* 64/61
19 *SK* 219/210
20 *NL* 75; *GC* 74
21 *SK* 8/8
22 *SK* 309/296
23 *SK* 338/324
24 *AS* 17/16
25 *AS* 5/6
26 *SK* 187/178
27 *SK* 121/116
28 *NL* 19; *GC* 18
29 *SK* 87/83
30 *SK* 13/12
31 *SK* 275-76/264
32 *AS* 184/175
33 *AS* 176/172
34 *AS* 253/239
35 *AS* 185/175
36 *AS* 185/175

[37] *NL* 22; *GC* 21
[38] *SK* 110-11/106
[39] *AS* 59, 341/57,325
[40] *NL* 21
[41] *AS* 223/211
[42] *AS* 440/418
[43] *SK* 116-18/111-14
[44] *NL* 102; *GC* 101
[45] *NL* 54; *GC* 53
[46] *NL* 40; *GC* 40
[47] *AS* 294/280
[48] *NL* 75; *GC* 75
[49] *NL* 211; *GC* 211
[50] *NL* 224; *GC* 223

[51] *NL* 226; *GC* 225
[52] *AS* 277/262-63
[53] *SK* 133/128
[54] *SK* 228/218
[55] *NL* 56; *GC* 55
[56] *NL* 36; *GC* 36
[57] *NL* 102; *GC* 100
[58] *AS* 416/395
[59] *AS* 63/61
[60] *AS* 415/395
[61] *AS* 420/400
[62] *AS* 416/396
[63] *SK* 160/153
[64] *SK* 167/160

[65] *NL* 202; *GC* 203
[66] *NL* 228; *GC* 227
[67] *NL* 264; *GC* 263
[68] *NL* 296/ *GC* 296
[69] *NL* 196; *GC* 196
[70] *NL* 181; *GC* 182
[71] *SK* 309/296
[72] *AS* 226/214
[73] *AS* 228/218
[74] *AS* 227/215
[75] *NL* 200; *GC* 201
[76] *SK* 131/125
[77] *AS* 350/333
[78] *NL* 16-17; *GC* 16

[79] *SK* 213/203
[80] *NL* 393; *GC* 393
[81] *NL* 156; *GC* 154
[82] *NL* 154; *GC* 153
[83] *NL* 156; *GC* 155
[84] *NL* 157; *GC* 156
[85] *AS* 407/388
[86] *NL* 50; *GC* 49
[87] *NL* 21/ *GC* 20
[88] *NL* 149; *GC* 148
[89] *NL* 149 ; *GC* 148

VIII. Natural Sciences

1. Physical Sciences

Anbaric

"Philip Pullman Interview" by Jennie Renton in *Textualities*. *See* **Places: Fens,** above.

Aurora

Nordlys by Alv Egeland, Univ. of Oslo and Trond Abrahamsen, Andøya Rocket Range (www.northern-lights.no)

"Aurora Borealis: The Northern Lights" by Joe Brady at *Virtual Finland*. (www.virtual.finland.fi)

"Overview of the Aurora." NASA's *Athena Curriculum: Space and Astronomy* (www.vathena.arc.nasa.gov)

Auroral Forecast and *Asahi Aurora Classroom*. Space Physics and Aeronomy Group, Geophysical Institute, Univ. of Alaska, Fairbanks (www.gi.alaska.edu)

The Science of Philip Pullman's His Dark Materials by Mary and John Gribbin (London: Hodder, 2003)

Dark Matter

Ray Villard. Telephone interview. July 26, 2006

Four fundamental forces

"The Four Forces of Nature." *Imagine the Universe!: Ask an Astrophysicist*

NASA's Goddard Space Flight Center

(www.imagine.gsfc.nasa.gov)

Iceland spar

"Double Refraction," an interactive Java tutorial provided at Molecular Expressions' *Science, Optics and You,* by the Optical Microscopy Division of the National High Magnetic Field Laboratory, a joint venture of The Florida State University, the University of Florida, and the Los Alamos National Laboratory. (www.micro.magnet.fsu.edu)

Iron (raw metal)

"How Iron and Steel Work." Science Division: Engineering Channel, www.howstuffworks.com

"How Sword-making Works." People Division: Culture Channel www.howstuffworks.com

"Bloomeries" by Roger Smith in *Ancient Roman Technology* (an electronic handbook. George W.

Houston, ed.). Univ. of North Carolina at Chapel Hill (www.unc.edu)

Naphtha

"Naphtha." LoveToKnow online encyclopedia based on the 1911 *Encyclopedia Britannica* (www.1911encyclopedia.org)

Photons

"Photons" at en.wikipedia.org

Pole

"Magnetic Storm." *Nova*. PBS. (www.pbs.org/wgbh/nova)

The Science of Philip Pullman's His Dark Materials by Mary and John Gribbin (London: Hodder, 2003)

Rainbow

Evslin, Bernard. *The Hydra.* (Monsters of Mythology) New York: Chelsea, 1989

Sky iron

"Cape York Meteorite." *Encyclopedia of Astrobiology, Astronomy, and Spaceflight*, part of the *Worlds of David Darling* (www.daviddarling.info)

Weather disturbances (climatic changes)

Philip Pullman. September 2005 newsletter at www.philip-pullman.com

"Human and Economic Indicators – Shishmaref," NOAA: *Arctic Change* (www.arctic.noaa.gov)

"Early Warning Signs: Arctic and Antarctic Warming" in *Global Warming* by the Union of Concerned Scientists (www.ucsusa.org)

2. Animals

Insects

Search "Insects" on *Taiga Net* (www.taiga.net)

3. Plants

Bougainvillea

"Bougainvillea glabra" on www.plantfacts.com.

Larches

"Larch." Archives [L]. Wisconsin Master Gardener program. Horticulture, University of Wisconsin (www.horticulture.wisc.edu)

Lyra and Will's tree

"Botanic Garden" in the *Virtual Tour of Oxford*. *See* **The Oxfords: Covered Market,** above.

Oleander

"Oleander." *Plant Care Guides.* National Gardening Association (www.garden.org/home)

Redwoods

"Sequoia" at en.wikipedia.org

Yew

"Yew-Ioho." OBOD Tree Lore in *Sacred Tree and Grove Planting Programme* by Order of Bards, Ovates and Druids (www.druidry.org)

Chapter 8 Notes

1 *SK* 60/57
2 *AS* 319/304
3 *NL* 141; *GC* 139
4 *NL* 183; *GC* 184

5 *NL* 216; *GC* 215
6 *NL* 302; *GC* 300
7 *NL* 23; *GC* 22
8 *NL* (10th Anniv. Ed.)

9 *NL* 187; *GC* 188
10 *NL* 141; *GC* 139
11 *NL* 382; *GC* 382
12 *NL* 183-84; *GC* 184

13 *SK* 125/119
14 *SK* 90/86
15 *SK* 91/88
16 *SK* 92/88

[17] *SK 259/248*
[18] *NL 370 ; GC 371*
[19] *NL 377; GC 377*
[20] *NL 375; GC 375*
[21] *SK 261/248-49*
[22] *AS 475/450*
[23] *AS 373/355*
[24] *AS 421-22/400-01*
[25] *NL 225; GC 224*
[26] *AS199/189*
[27] *AS 522/493*
[28] *AS 522/493*
[29] *SK 45/43*

[30] *SK 229-230/220*
[31] *SK 129/123*
[32] *NL 152; GC 151*
[33] *SK 307/294*
[34] *NL 113; GC 112*
[35] *AS 33/31-2*
[36] *AS 476/452*
[37] *NL 187; GC 188*
[38] *SK 196/187*
[39] *AS 384/365*
[40] *AS 384/366*
[41] *NL 10; GC 10*
[42] *NL 363; GC 363*

[43] *NL 187; GC 188*
[44] *AS 207/197*
[45] *AS 185/175*
[46] *AS 185/175*
[47] *NL 183; GC 184*
[48] *AS 122/117*
[49] *AS 2/2*
[50] *AS 57/55*
[51] *NL 274; GC 273*
[52] *SK 30/29*
[53] *SK 126/121*
[54] *SK 217/208*
[55] *SK 216/207*

[56] *SK 323/308*
[57] *AS 103/99*
[58] *AS 154/146*
[59] *AS 41/39*
[60] *AS 46/43*
[61] *SK 263/252*
[62] *AS 129/135*
[63] *AS 498/471*
[64] *AS 504/478*
[65] *AS 478/454*
[66] *SK 59/57*
[67] *NL 83; GC 82*

IX. Social Groups and Institutions

1. Ecclesiastical

A superior source of information about ecclesiastical matters is the encyclopedia at www.newadvent.com.

Inquisition
   "Inquisition" at en.wikipedia.org
   "Inquisition" in *The Catholic Encyclopedia* at www.newadvent.org

5. Financial/Commerce

Sovereigns
   "Sovereign" and "Unite" [search terms] in *Coins and Medals* in Museum Images at the British Museum
      (www.bmimages.com)

Wells Fargo
   "Overland via Stagecoach." *The Adventure of Wells Fargo: The Wells Fargo Stagecoach.* History,
      Museums, and Store on www.wellsfargo.com

Chapter 9 Notes

[1] *AS 462/439*
[2] *SK 52/50*
[3] *SK 335/320*
[4] *NL 32; GC 30*
[5] *NL 274; GC 273*
[6] *NL 371; GC 371*
[7] *AS 415/395*
[8] *AS 490/464*
[9] *AS 77/74*
[10] *SK 48/46*
[11] *NL 31/ GC 30*
[12] *NL 128; GC 127*
[13] *NL 318/ GC 318*
[14] *NL 373/ GC 373*
[15] *NL 31-32/ GC 30*

[16] *NL 373; GC 373*
[17] *NL 318/ GC 318*
[18] *SK 52/50*
[19] *SK 44/42*
[20] *SK 47/45*
[21] *AS 74/71*
[22] *AS 462/439*
[23] *UK AS 215*
[24] *UK AS 541*
[25] *NL 31; GC 30*
[26] *AS 73/70*
[27] *AS 74/71*
[28] *AS 75/72*
[29] *AS 74/71*
[30] *AS 541/512*

[31] *NL 31; GC 29*
[32] *NL 186; GC 187*
[33] *NL 89; GC 8*
[34] *NL 373; GC 373*
[35] *NL 31/ GC 29-30*
[36] *NL 375; GC 375*
[37] *NL 56; GC 56*
[38] *NL 46; GC 45*
[39] *NL 45; GC 45*
[40] *NL 108; GC 107*
[41] *NL 116; GC 115*
[42] *NL 371; GC 371*
[43] *AS 393/37*
[44] *NL 31; GC 30*
[45] *NL 373-4; GC 373*

[46] *SK 37/35*
[47] *NL 394; GC 394*
[48] *AS 61/59*
[49] *AS 72/69, 127/117*
[50] *NL 21; GC 19-20*
[51] *NL 25; GC 24*
[52] *SK 128/122*
[53] *SK 223/214*
[54] *NL 372; GC 372*
[55] *NL 34; GC 33*
[56] *NL 66; GC 65*
[57] *AS 541/511*
[58] *NL 4; GC 4*
[59] *NL 330; GC 330*
[60] *NL 225; GC 224*

[61] *SK* 88-89/85	[68] *NL* 71 ; *GC* 70	[75] *SK* 334/319	[82] *SK* 249/239
[62] *NL* 50; *GC* 50	[69] *AS* 69/66	[76] *SK* 227/218	[83] *AS* 330/315
[63] *NL* 67; *GC* 66	[70] *SK* 254/243	[77] *SK* 228-29	[84] *SK* 234/224
[64] *NL* 71; *GC* 70	[71] *NL* 25; *GC* 23	[78] *SK* 254/242	[85] *NL* 133; *GC* 132
[65] *SK* 87/83	[72] *SK* 197/187	[79] *AS* 384/366	[86] *NL* 123/ *GC* 121
[66] *SK* 44/43	[73] *SK* 224/215	[80] *SK* 209/200	[87] *NL* 124; *GC* 123
[67] *SK* 37/35	[74] *SK* 142/135	[81] *SK* 282/270-71	[88] *NL* 170; *GC* 170

X. Languages and Diction

Chapter 10 Notes

[1] *SK* 53/51, 57/55, 112/107, 220/211

XI. Allusions

1. Beliefs: Biblical, Religious, and Otherwise

Adam

"Descendants of Adam in Genesis." *Diagrams* at www.threetwoone.org

Adonai

"Names of God in Judaism" at en.wikipedia.org

Ancient of Days

"Glossary entry for Ancient of Days." *Glossary of Terms and References* by Michael Hayward. Van Morrison website hosted by Simon Fraser University's Harbour Centre campus, Vancouver, Canada (www.harbour.sfu.ca)

Apocalypse

"Observations on Daniel and the Apocalypse of St John" by Sir Isaac Newton at www. historicist.com

Calvin

Lord, John. Beacon Lights of History, Volume 3, Part 2.

www.fullbooks.com/Beacon-Lights-of-History-Volume-3-Part4.html

Daniel

"Observations on Daniel and the Apocalypse of St John" by Sir Isaac Newton at www.historicist.com

El

"El (god)" at en.wikipedia.org

Fall

"The Dark Materials debate: life, God, the universe..." [Philip Pullman debates religion with the Archbishop of Canterbury, Dr Rowan Williams; moderator Robert Butler]. 17/03/2004 www.telegrah.co.uk.

Mantle

"Eliseus" in *The Catholic Encyclopedia* at www.newadvent.org

Martyr's Palm

"Palm in Christian Symbolism" in *The Catholic Encyclopedia* at www.newadvent.org

Seth

"Seth" at en.wikipedia.org

St. Augustine

"Teaching of St. Augustine of Hippo" in *The Catholic Encyclopedia* at www.newadvent.org www.newadvent.org/cathen/02091a.htm.

Temptation

"Philip Pullman in Readerville 02.05.01-02.09.01." *See* **Characters: Authority,** above.

Yahweh

"Names of God in Judaism" at en.wikipedia.org

Yambe

"The Gods and Goddess of Finnish-Ugrian Places" in *Seanachaidh's Grove* (www.seanachaidh.com)

Chapter 11 Notes

[1] *NL* 372-3; *GC* 372-3	[14] *SK* 334/320	[27] *NL* 31; *GC* 30	[40] *AS* 237/224
[2] *NL* 372; *GC* 372	[15] *AS* 344/328	[28] *NL* 31; *GC* 30	[41] *NL* 116; *GC* 115
[3] *NL* 372; *GC* 372	[16] *AS* 33/31	[29] *NL* 393; *GC* 393	[42] *SK* 196/187
[4] *NL* 373; *GC* 373	[17] *NL* 371; *GC* 371	[30] *AS* 336/320-21	[43] *SK* 83/79
[5] *NL* 372; *GC* 372	[18] *NL* 373; *GC* 373	[31] *NL* 31; *GC* 30	[44] *AS* 151/143
[6] *AS* 235/223	[19] *SK* 47/45; 334/320	[32] *AS* 260/246	[45] *AS* 215/204
[7] *AS* 344/328	[20] *SK* 152/145	[33] *AS* 465/441	[46] *AS* 256/243
[8] *AS* 75/72	[21] *SK* 131/236	[34] *SK* 11/10	[47] *AS* 468-69/445
[9] *NL* 31; *GC* 30	[22] *AS* 490/464	[35] *SK* 132/126	[48] *SK* 260/249
[10] *SK* 328/314	[23] *AS* 344/328	[36] *AS* 427/405	[49] *AS* 463/439
[11] *SK* 328/314	[24] *AS* 345/328	[37] *SK* 261/250	[50] *NL* 314; *GC* 314
[12] *NL* 373; *GC* 373	[25] *AS* 469/445	[38] **AS 490/464**	[51] *NL* 97; *GC* 96
[13] *SK* 47/45	[26] *AS* 471/447	[39] *NL* 372; *GC* 372	

XII. Epigraphs

Introduction

"Darkness Visible: An Interview with Philip Pullman, Part 2" by Kerry Fried for amazon.com.

Chapter Epigraphs

Chapter 21

The full text of Byron's letter is available at Project Gutenberg in *The Life of Lord Byron, Vol. III, With His Letters and Journals* by Thomas Moore (www.gutenberg.net)

Book Epigraphs

Rilke

"Darkness Visible: An Interview with Philip Pullman, Part 2" by Kerry Fried for amazon.com

Blake

Blake, William. *Collected Works.* (www.blakearchive.org)

The Magical Worlds of Philip Pullman: A Treasury of Fascinating Facts by David Colbert (New York: Berkley Books, 2006) features a chapter on Blake and reproduces several illustrations from *America, a Prophecy*

Milton

Milton, John. *Paradise Lost.* An illustrated edition with an introduction by Philip Pullman. Oxford: Oxford UP, 2005

Milton, John. *Paradise Lost.* Ed. Alistair Fowler. London: Longman, 1971

David Colbert's *The Magical Worlds of Philip Pullman* begins with a discussion of *Paradise Lost* and *His Dark Materials*

"On the Marionette Theatre"

Heinrich von Kleist's "On the Marionette Theatre." Translated by Idris Parry. Southern Cross Review. Issue 9, Nov. 16, 2005 (www.southerncrossreview.org)

"Philip Pullman: Some Rarely Asked Questions." Abridged transcript by Thea Logie of a question and answer session. Balliol College English Society. November 6, 2002

Chapter 12 Notes

[1] *AS* 440/418   [2] *SK* 336/321   [3] *AS* 378/359   [4] *SK* 167/160

Acknowledgments

I began this book in the fall of 2001. My family—my husband Mark and my children Max and Iris—have been admirably patient with me, and I am grateful.

I want to thank my parents, Joe and Molly Adams, who years and years ago made it possible for me to take advantage of an opportunity to attend a study program housed at University College, Oxford. I lived for six weeks on the High, and from my window could see the spire of St Mary the Virgin, or University Church. Behind it is Radcliffe Square and the Bodleian, and west of the Bodleian is Exeter (Jordan) College. I had no idea then how useful this experience would prove, or why.

But it wasn't just Oxford that felt familiar when I entered HIS DARK MATERIALS. Dæmons did too. And for that I wish I could thank my cat Spike, who spent many hours of the last two of her twenty years purring on my lap as I read and reread these books.

One of the pleasures of writing about Philip Pullman has been coming into contact with a number of wonderful people who share my enthusiasm for his work: the webmasters at hdm.co.il and cittagazze.com, Israeli and French affiliates of bridgetothestars.net, and at The Daemon Page (daemons.envy.nu/). I've found the administrators and community at hisdarkmaterials.org particularly charming and visiting that site consistently invigorating. Special thanks are due to Ann Giles (http://bookwitch.wordpress.com/), a Pullman fan and writer who has extended to me her friendship and support in a number of ways, including going with her son Ian to Oxford to take pictures of some of the locales mentioned in this book (you can see a few of these in Places and Peoples: The Oxfords).

You would not be reading these words were it not for the creative vision of Catherine Buckley and her team at The Fell Press. Thanks are due to her team—illustrators Michele Hearn and Monroe S. Tavers; photographer Phil Thistlethwaite; Colette Bezio, who did a fantastic job on maps of our Oxford and Lyra's world; Lisa Krell, who kept track of all the bits, imposed order, and left nothing to chance; Dan Nolte, layout and design (dannolte.com), whose industry is matched only by his monumental patience; and especially to Lydia Ondrusek.

Lydia has worked on every aspect of this project; her contributions can't be spoken of in terms of weeks or months of work but years. She asked great questions that would lead me back to take another look at passages I thought I knew well. If I departed from the texts or slipped in an unverifiable assumption, Lydia caught me. Most importantly of all, Lydia was unfailingly optimistic, encouraging, comforting, and amusing. I'm grateful, Lydia, I truly am.

A generation or so from now someone will write a history of children and young adult publishers, and will discover what I already know: Catherine Buckley single-handedly changed this business. Her insight was a very simple one: people of all ages who love to read books enjoy reading books about the books they love. What could make more sense? But before her group's guides to the Harry Potter series, there were very, very few books published about the novels children or young adult readers cherish. Oh yes, there were books about novels these readers were assigned to read. And the same publishing houses that doubted they could ever sell this group a book about a book covered the shelves in retail outlets with volumes on cartoon characters and trading cards. But books about books? Too risky.

And like Lydia, Catherine has been great fun to work with. She has endless dynamic energy, great good humor, quick intelligence, far-reaching knowledge, and an aggressive creative spirit. What more could an author want? It has been a pleasure, and I thank you.

Finally, I owe so much to Philip Pullman, and not just for the self-evident reason that without HIS DARK MATERIALS there would be no PHILIP PULLMAN'S HIS DARK MATERIALS – THE DEFINITIVE GUIDE. He knows why.

LAURIE FROST